Levant Trade in the Later Middle Ages

Eliyahu Ashtor

PRINCETON UNIVERSITY PRESS
PRINCETON, NEW JERSEY

Published by Princeton University Press, 41 William Street,
Princeton, New Jersey 08540
In the United Kingdom: Princeton University Press, Guildford, Surrey

Library of Congress Cataloging in Publication Data will be found on the last printed page of this book

ISBN 0-691-05386-3

Publication of this book has been aided by The Paul Mellon Fund of Princeton University Press

This book has been composed in Linotron Aldus
Clothbound editions of Princeton University Press books are printed on acid-free paper, and binding materials are chosen for strength and durability

Printed in the United States of America by Princeton University Press, Princeton, New Jersey

To the memory of
my unforgettable friend

FEDERIGO MELIS

who introduced me to
the archives of Fr. Datini

Table of Contents

Tables

Preface

About a hundred years ago the German scholar W. Heyd published his *History of the Levant Trade in the Middle Ages*, which to this very day is the standard work in this field of historical research. In fact Heyd's work appeared in three editions. First he published in 1858-1864 a series of articles about the Italian merchant colonies in the *Tübinger Zeitschrift für die gesamten Staatswissenschaften*. Then there appeared in 1879 an enlarged edition of these papers as a book and finally F. Raynaud published in 1885-1886 a French translation of the work, which meanwhile had been considerably augmented by the author. The *Histoire du commerce du Levant au Moyen Age* of W. Heyd was in his day a great scholary achievement and it will remain a basic work forever. With great assiduity the author had collected any piece of information about his subject that he could find in travelogues, commercial treaties, privileges, and in many other sources. He also examined the data with great acumen, so that many of his conclusions can be considered as absolutely valid. But Heyd did not work in the rich archives of the Mediterranean trading towns, which held a foremost place in the Levant trade of the Middle Ages. The Bavarian scholar G. M. Thomas placed at his disposal notes and manuscripts of his own works, such as the *Diplomatarium Veneto-Levantinum*, but such basic sources as the registers of the Venetian Senate remained unknown to him. Another great failing in Heyd's work in the eyes of the modern economic historian is the neglect of various economic aspects of the mediaeval Levant trade, such as the volume of trade. This was partly due to the fact that the author had no access to the archives of Italy and Spain. Nevertheless, Heyd's work is a masterpiece of historiography, so that it is unnecessary to repeat his quotations from the sources he knew and the conclusions he drew from them. They are almost always correct and sound.

Since the publication of Heyd's work some excellent economic historians have dealt thoroughly with the international trade of the South European nations in the later Middle Ages. The works of Frederic Lane about the trade of Venice, the books and papers of Roberto S. Lopez about the economic expansion of Genoa in the Middle Ages, the *Histoire du commerce de Marseille* by Baratier, Reynaud, and others, the work of Mario Del Treppo about Catalan trade in the fifteenth century, and the painstaking publications of the Ragusan acts by Bariša Krekić are chefs d'oeuvre of solid research and shed bright light on many aspects of the commercial exchanges between Western and Southern Europe, on the one hand, and the Moslem Levant, on the other, in the period of the Crusades and in that which followed it. They provide us with a basis in attempting to draw now an overall portrait of this chapter of mediaeval history.

This is indeed the purpose of the present book. The development of the Levantine trade of the nations of Southern Europe will be sketched here as a phenomenon both of the economic history of these European nations and of the Moslem Near East. For any attempt to deal with the Levant trade without explaining the European expansion as a consequence of the economic decline of the Near Eastern countries would be inadequate. I have dealt with this phenomenon in some books and papers and can refer to them without repeating what has been amply elaborated there. Great stress will be laid in this book on the volume of the Levantine trade of the various South European nations, insofar as the sources known to us make it possible to deal with this problem. The changes which took place in the course of time in the categories of commodities exported to the Levant will be thoroughly examined. Further, an attempt will be made to sum up the results of the research done by some scholars about the development of the commercial methods and of transport in the later Middle Ages.

My research is based on a variety of sources.

The Arabic sources—in the first instance, the detailed chronicles of the Mamluk period, both printed works and manuscripts—have been carefully searched for relevant data. But as far as the relations with the Western Christian nations are concerned, they offer us rather ambiguous information about "Franks" who attacked the Moslem ports or the ships of the Near Eastern merchants. Only seldom do the Arabic chroniclers clearly say who these Franks were. However, the accounts which are to be found in the Arabic sources of the European aggression will be systematically analyzed and attention will be paid to the interdependence of the various traditions quoted by the Arabic historians.

The official documents of the South European states, on the other hand, are basic and reliable sources for our research. The various series of the registers of the Venetian Senate, the Misti, Senato Mar, and Secreta are certainly most valuable and contain firsthand information about the mediaeval Levant trade. The Misti reflect clearly the trends of the commercial policy of the Serenissima, the registers of the Secreta shed light upon the activities of the Venetian diplomacy, and the series Senato Mar contains many details about the life of the Venetian colonies overseas. Since the administration of the Venetian colonies was closely watched by the central legislative and executive bodies of the republic, often even trifling matters were dealt with by the latter.

The accounts of the results of the galley auctions in Venice, to be found in the Senato Mar and the Senato Incanti, give us a clue for sketching the upward and downward trends of the Levantine trade of the Venetians. But Gino Luzzatto has already warned against overestimating the value of these accounts (see his *Storia economica di Venezia,* Venice 1961, p. 138 f.). The conclusions which one can draw from them should be considered *cum grano salis.* Checking them against the data provided by Morosini (and other Venetian chroniclers) concerning the investments of the Venetian Levant traders and the value of the cargoes of the ships returning from the Levant, one becomes aware that they do not always correspond very well. In some years in which the auctions yielded relatively small amounts, the investments were very great and vice versa. Consequently, one will conclude that the latter data are more relevant for our research, although careful consideration should be given to those referring to the galley auctions.

The same is true for the customs registers, which have come down to us in the archives of Venice (Terminazioni of the *Giudici di petiziòn*), Genoa (Drictus Alexandriae 1367, the registers published by John Day, the Caratorum Veterum of the middle of the fifteenth century), and Barcelona (the Real Patrimonio). Even these registers are of the greatest value for our research. In the customs offices of Venice and Genoa and elsewhere, the merchandise was weighed, and in the registers both the weight declared in the Levantine ports, from whence it came, and that established after the arrival in the metropolis were noted. So these registers contain long columns of Oriental and European weights which provide us with a solid basis for the knowledge of the weight units and the standard parcels used by the merchant in the Levant.

Many data which are very useful for the study of the history of the Levant trade are to be found in the registers of the *Giudici di petiziòn,* a Venetian tribunal before which litigations between merchants (and merchants versus ship patrons) were brought. The various series of its registers, of which some hundred volumes have been preserved from the fourteenth and the fifteenth centuries, contain data about conflicts between merchants in Venice and their agents in the Levant and claims against patrons, who are made responsible for the loss of merchandise. The proceedings comprise accounts of shipments, data about prices, etc. However, in many of the proceedings of these litigations, which are contained in the series Sentenze a giustizia, there are no exact dates of the transactions dealt with. In this case one cannot be sure even approximately as to the date on which the transaction was made. In fact often the litigations were brought before the tribunal many years later. A transaction made in 1412 was judged in 1424 (see G. P., Sent. 36, f. 56a ff.), another made in 1415 was dealt with in 1438 (see same series 78, f. 96b ff.). A case which happened in 1421 was the subject of a litigation in the year 1431 (see Sentenze 56, f. 38a ff.). Sometimes thirty years and more passed before a matter was judged by the tribunal; a lawsuit in 1432 refers to a case which occurred in 1402 (see G. P., Sent. 61, f. 96b), and another in 1477 to a case in 1440 (see same series 165, f. 40b ff.). The series Terminazioni—that is, permits given to deliver merchandise retained in the customs offices—is particularly valuable, because many documents, contracts, and accounts are quoted in extenso (in addition to freight inventories mentioned above).

The acts of the notaries who specialized in drawing up contracts for the maritime trade contain much valuable material for the history of the Levant trade, such as data about the export goods, the investments of single merchants, the conditions agreed upon between lenders and borrowers who departed for the Levant, etc. In these acts one finds also much data concerning the ships which left for the Levantine ports. The collections of notarial acts which have come down to us represent only a fraction of the contracts which were made by notaries, while many agreements were not drawn up by notaries at all. Furthermore, for various reasons one often styled a contract in very ambiguous terms. Consequently some scholars have expressed doubts as to the conclusions one can draw from the notarial acts (see P. Earle, "The Commercial Development of Ancona, 1479-1551," *Ec. Hist. Rev.*, 2nd series, 22, 1969, p. 30). But for many years the collections of several notaries working in the same town have been preserved, so that the margin of error and the doubts as to how far they convey to us a truly representative portrait of the commercial activities in their town are reduced. This is true for some towns which ranked as second-class South European trading nations, such as Palermo, Messina, and Ancona. But even a study of the notarial acts drawn up in Barcelona is very fruitful for our subject, although these acts have been used by such excellent historians as Cl. Carrère and M. Del Treppo. The acts of the Barcelonan notaries of the end of the fourteenth century and of the fifteenth century are very numerous and make it possible to put into relief some phenomena of the Catalan trade with the Levant and to elaborate its structure in detail.

A very important source of information for the history of the mediaeval Levant trade can be found in the acts of the Italian notaries who exercised their profession in the Levantine emporia. To the acts drawn up in Creta and in Cyprus by Venetian and Genoese notaries a great number of deeds which were written in Egypt and in Syria should be added. The number of acts drafted by Genoese notaries in the Moslem Levant and known to us is unfortunalely very small, but those of the Venetian notaries of Alexandria and Damascus are very numerous. The chaplains of the Venetian consuls fulfilled the role of notaries for all the European merchants who resided or sojourned in these emporia. There have come down to us (known to the present writer) the acts of Antonello de Vataciis who worked in Alexandria from October 1399 until October 1401 and again from July 1404 until September 1406.[1] His successor as Venetian chaplain in Alexandria, Leonardo de Valle, left us notarial acts dating from November 1401 to April 1404. From the time he held the post of chaplain (and chancellor of the consulate) the proceedings of the Council of the colony have been preserved (as they were drawn up by him). The Venetian notary Cristoforo Rizzo, who practiced also in Tana, left us acts drawn up in Alexandria from November 1414 until October 1416. Giacomo della Torre, another wandering notary, held the office of chaplain and chancellor of the Venetians in Damascus from the end of 1411, leaving acts dating from December of that year until October 1413. Much more numerous are the acts drawn up in Damascus and Beirut by Niccolò Venier. They date from October 1417 until May 1419. Then the notary returned to Venice, but in the fall of 1420 he began to exercise his profession in Alexandria, and a copious collection of his acts drawn up in the Egyptian emporium has come down to us dating from October 1420 to December 1422. One of his successors in Alexandria was Cristoforo del Fiore from whom acts dated July 1425 to May 1426 have been preserved. In the middle of the fifteenth century he was notary in Damascus. The acts which he drew up in the Syrian capital and which have come down to us date from October 1454 to October 1457[2] and September 1460 to October 1463. A very rich collection of notarial acts drawn up in Alexandria is that of Niccolò Turiano. They date from October 1426 to November 1428, May 1434 to November 1435 and August to October 1436. Meanwhile the notary had been in Rhodes and had practiced there.

To these notaries who left us a great number of acts there should be added others from whom only few deeds have come down to us. These were notaries who never held the post of chaplain or who had given it up; they were true free lancers. But all of these notaries had in common great experience in the Levant and a thorough knowledge of the commercial methods. So their acts are a mainstay of our information about the Levant trade in that period. They also make it possible to estimate the numbers of the merchants who came from various countries to the Moslem Levant and lived there for a certain time. Certainly one will not believe that the names of all European merchants who lived in the Levantine trading towns in certain years figure in the deeds of the chaplains of the Venetian consul, who served all of them as notary. However, the difference between the

[1] A few acts date of Damascus, a. 1434-1437.

[2] One act is dated 29 Oct. 1457, Beirut, obviously drawn up by the notary when he was on his way back to Venice. The next act is already written on the galley and has the date 12 November 1457.

number of those who lived there and that of those whose names appear in the notarial acts must not have been great, and, adding up the numbers of merchants of the various trading nations who appear in those acts, one may suppose that the figures give us at least a reliable assessment of these different groups. The supposition that in the course of a certain year almost all the merchants residing in a Levantine trading town applied to a notary or were called to be witnesses is borne out by a comparison of the number of the Venetians mentioned in the acts of the Venetian notaries who worked in Alexandria in the year 1401, and the number of those who took part, according to the registers of the colony (see above), in a general assembly of the Venetian colony held in that year. In the notarial acts one finds 24, in the latter source 26. Another reason for the importance of the notarial acts is that the notaries drew up many acts which did not refer to the commercial activities of the European traders but to other matters which shed light on the social life of the merchant colonies. Wills of merchants and of their servants, contracts of sale of slaves and of slave girls, obligations of pilgrims and captives written and received by the merchants, reveal to us the conditions of life of the merchants overseas, which otherwise would have remained obscure for us.

Not less important than the notarial acts are the remnants of the archives of Levant traders, which have come into the possession of public archives. When the property of Venetian families passed to the endowment of S. Marco, the records and files of letters were also handed over to the *procuratori* of the fund. So the archives of many enterprising Levant traders and of family firms have been preserved and finally passed to the Venetian State archives. These archives comprise accounts, often whole ledgers, letters of agents in Egypt and in Syria, price lists compiled in Alexandria and in Damascus, freight inventories, reports about the total purchases made by the European trading nations in the Levant, etc. The archives of Biegio Dolfin, who from 1408 to 1410 and again from 1418 to 1420 held the post of Venetian consul in Alexandria, also contain lists of payments made to the consulate and others of its records. Unique among these archives of firms which engaged in international trade are those of Francesco Datini, the famous merchant of Prato. He was not a Levant trader *stricto sensu*, but chairman of commercial companies in Florence, Pisa, Genoa, Avignon, and Barcelona, the latter with branches in Majorca and Valencia, all of which engaged mainly in the trade of wool and cloth. But, like so many mediaeval merchants, he was active in other sectors of business, among which the spice trade was not the least important. Francesco Datini, like other men of genius, had the gift of finding collaborators, employees, and agents who distinguished themselves by their great capacity. In Damascus for a certain time Bertrando Mignanelli, a native of Siena, was a correspondent of his. Living many years in the Levant, Mignanelli had acquired a thorough knowledge of the Arabic language, so that in later years he could serve as interpreter at the council of Florence, where representatives of the Coptic Church appeared. He also became a friend of Sultan Barḳūḳ and wrote in Latin a biography of this Mamluk ruler (*Ascensus Barcoch*), as well as a book on the invasion of Syria by Tīmūr Lang (*Ruina Damasci*).

The agents and business friends of the Datini firm were required to supply its branches continuously with current information about the commercial movement, and the 125,000 of their letters which have been preserved in the Datini archives in Prato (in the Archivio di Stato of that town),[3] and have been put into order by the late Federigo Melis, are a true treasure house for all those interested in the economic history of the late fourteenth and the beginning of the fifteenth century. It is no exaggeration to maintain that this truly enormous collection of letters (the so-called *carteggio*), which comprises so many thousands of pieces, can be considered as the first series of the modern commercial bulletins which in fact gave birth to our newspapers. The letters contain news about ship departures and arrivals to and from the Levantine ports (and other Mediterranean ports); cargo inventories, apparently obtained from the secretaries of the ships or from customs officers; forecasts of the development of prices; and also political news, which of course influenced the commercial movement. The writers of the letters attached to them (or included in them) freight inventories of the ships of the various trading nations sailing from the Levantine ports to Venice, Genoa, Aigues-Mortes, and Barcelona and also price lists of the major emporia of the Levant, Southern and Western Europe. The Datini archives contain accounts of the transactions of the firm which also traded in spices and other Oriental commodities. In great commercial centers Francesco Datini had several business friends and agents, who regularly provided his firm with current information. So one can find in his archives letters written in Venice by two of such agents on the same day. Furthermore, they wrote frequently and it could happen that they wrote twice a day, or addressed on the same day letters to the Datini firms in two towns, e.g., in Pisa and Barcelona (see, for instance, Dat 712 and 927, letters of Zanobi di Taddeo Gaddi, and Dat 927, letters of the Commessaria of Zanobi di Taddeo Gaddi). The most diligent of Datini's correspondents was indeed this Zanobi di Taddeo Gaddi, from whom a very great number of letters has come down to us. The last of his letters (to the Datini firm in Pisa) shows the date of 10 July 1400, and the first of his successors (Commessaria) bears that of 6 October 1400. The whole of the Datini records (the letters

[3] F. Melis, *Aspetti della vita economica medievale*, p. 14, and see there, p. 18 ff., a table of the towns where the letters were written and their destinations.

written to this firm) extends from the 1370's to the year 1411. Box 930 contains letters of the year 1411 written by Tommaso di Giacomo & Cie in Venice, and others also written in Venice by Perluccio del Maestro Paolo, Paolo di Giovanni, Taddeo, son of Zanobi, Lorenzo di Francesco & Cie., and Giovanni di Domenico Ciampelli & Cie. In fact few letters written in the Levantine trading towns themselves have been preserved in the Datini archives, but they are so often quoted that the quotations alone make it possible to compile price lists of the Levantine markets.

For our subject the letters written in Venice and the correspondence of the Datini firm of Barcelona are the most important documents. The letters which the Venetian friends of Datini addressed to his companies, in Pisa, Florence, and Barcelona, contain many quotations from letters received from Alexandria and Damascus, news about the fluctuations of the prices of the Levantine articles in the South European emporia, and, last but not least, data about the shipments of cotton which were brought twice a year from Syria to Venice by the cog convoys of spring and fall. As these data are often found in letters of several friends of Datini, we can check them and rely upon their authenticity.[4] Many of the statements concerning the cotton trade of Venice are, however, prognostics, i.e., resumés of what the friends of Datini had heard from various acquaintances, who themselves relied frequently upon hearsay. The correspondents of Datini and other commercial agents indeed collected news from all sources—from customs officers, secretaries of ships, merchants, and *fattori*. Of course, the information concerning the shipments of cotton due to arrive have much less value than data about the freight of ships actually arrived. Furthermore, the writers of these letters often say in a very general way that a certain quantity of cotton will be in Venice at the next fair. So one cannot always be sure that only Syrian cotton is indicated (and not cotton of the Greek countries). But, despite these shortcomings, the data one finds in the Datini letters from Venice concerning the cotton shipments that were unknown to Heyd and other economic historians are of great importance for the history of the Levant trade in the later Middle Ages. They will lead us to a new evaluation of the commercial exchanges between Southern and Western Europe, on the one hand, and the Moslem Levant, on the other. The letters written to the Datini firm in Barcelona from various ports and trading towns of the Western basin of the Mediterranean shed bright light upon the Levantine trade of these emporia, which otherwise would have been shrouded in darkness. The letters from Genoa, on the other hand, have much less value for the study of the history of the Levant trade. They deal mainly with the wool trade in the countries around the Tyrrhenian Sea.

[4] See *op.cit.*, p. 30.

Whereas one finds in many letters accounts of the cargoes carried to the ports of Southern Europe by Italian, French, and Catalan ships, a whole batch (now Dat 1171) comprises only such inventories and in addition price lists. Other boxes contain collections of insurance acts. Even they comprise very valuable data for our subject.

In addition to official documents, notarial acts, and the archives of merchants, some literary works written by authors with a sound knowledge of the Levant trade and reliable firsthand information, contain most valuable data for our research.

The *Secreta fidelium crucis* of Marino Sanuto Torsello, who wrote in the first decade of the fourteenth century, has often been quoted as an authentic source. But in fact this treatise, which was destined to stir up anti-Moslem feelings and to induce the pope and the Christian princes of Europe to undertake a new Crusade against Egypt, should be used with great caution. For the author, in order to reach his goal, greatly exaggerated in describing the intense trade between Egypt and Europe and the great revenue that the sultan of Cairo had from it.

Of great value is the treatise of Emmanuel Piloti. Although it was written for the same purpose as that of Marino Sanuto—and a work should not be blindly relied upon—it distinguishes itself as a most original and authentic source for various reasons. Emmanuel Piloti, a Cretan merchant, lived for a very long time in Egypt, apparently from 1396 until 1438, though he went several times to other countries (Dopp's introduction to Piloti, p. xxv). He travelled much in Syria, Cyprus, and Greece, but had his head office in Egypt. Like most foreign merchants he lived in Alexandria, but he also had an office in Cairo (p. xix) and had contact with the court of the sultan. In 1404 he appeared before the sultan, together with the Venetian consul of Alexandria, and in 1408 he fulfilled a mission for the sultan (p. xx f.). As a Cretan, and so a Venetian subject, Piloti was not an objective, neutral author, but sided with Venice (see Piloti, p. 198 about the battle of Modon) and scoffed at the failures of the Genoese (see p. 197 of his account of the attitude of the Genoese during the attack of Marshal Boucicault on Beirut). As his book is not written on the basis of documents and was destined to substantiate his proposal (for a new Crusade against Egypt by the account of events which he remembered), it contains many errors (see p. 37, the end of Sultan Faradj in 1411; p. 54, the sultan buys every year 2,000 mamluks; p. 174, attack of the Cypriots on Alexandria in the days of Sultan Faradj, and Barsbāy; p. 175, the conquest of Cyprus in 1427, should be 1426, and see further pp. 228, 229 about the battle of Nicopolis, p. 103 the tomb of Mohammed, and see also p. 197, note c) and contradictions (see p. 205 and p. 209 talks with the duke of Naxos). But Piloti's errors are outweighed by the great merits of his book as a treatise summing up the experience and knowledge of a merchant who had carried on trade in Egypt during a lifetime and had distinguished himself by deep insight in economic matters. For he began to write his book in 1420 and did not finish it before 1440 (see pp. xxv, xxvi), writing first in Venetian or even in a vulgar French (some kind of lingua franca of the Mediterranean) and later translating it into Latin (p. xxxiv).

Among the Venetian chronicles (cf. Fr. Thiriet, "Les chroniques vénitiennes de la Marcienne et leur importance pour l'histoire de la Romanie gréco-vénitienne," *Mélanges d'histoire de l'Ecole française de Rome* LXVI, 1954, p. 241 ff.), that of Antonio Morosini is for our subject undoubtedly the most important. Son of a brother of the doge, Michele Morosini, he had access to official sources and could use the documents of the chancery of the ducal government and other records of the authorities of the republic. He had a great interest also in the economic life (rightly stated by G. Luzzatto, *Storia economica di Venezia*, p. 147) and inserted in his chronicle data which one seldom finds in other sources. His data about Venetian shipping have already been elaborated by F. C. Lane, but the economic historian is truly delighted when finding in this chronicle many data about the yearly investments of the Venetian traders, including the amounts of cash and the value of the merchandise shipped every year to the Levant. The chronicler who obtained his information apparently from official sources (the declarations made by the merchants before the *straordinarii*, see Morosini, c. 604) provides us with a solid basis for estimates of the volume of Venice's trade with the Moslem Levant in the period subsequent to the time of the Datini records. The chronicle of Morosini served as a source for that of Zorzi Dolfin for the period beginning in the year 1404 and this latter was a source for the *Vite de' duchi* of Marino Sanuto (see Morosini, *Chronique*, I, pp. 2, 15, 25, 122, 161; IV, pp. 178 ff., 253 ff.).

It goes without saying that the Merchant Guides are primary sources for our research. Certainly one has the right to suppose that the comparison of measures and weights which were used in various trading towns, a major topic of these works, points to the existence of commercial exchanges between them. But these books also supply us with data about the export of commodities to the Levant in periods for which one has no other information or almost none, e.g., the beginning of the fourteenth century. The data found in Merchant Guides of this period, as the Anonymous in the Marucelliana Library (cf. Bautier, "Les relations," p. 311 ff.), the Venetian *Zibaldone da Canal*, and the *Tarifa*, this too a Venetian treatise, are most valuable for our subject. The number of the Merchant Guides which were known to Heyd was very small, but nowadays many more have been found and some of them have been printed. The late A. Sapori discovered in the libraries and archives of Tuscany alone about a hundred (see his *Studi*[3] I,

p. 493). All of these works have two features in common: they are in fact collective works and the materials were assembled over a long period. For these Guides are essentially reference works for the merchant and had to be brought up to date time and again. When customs were increased or new imposts established, the old data were of no more use to the merchant, who actively engaged in international trade. Consequently the data to be found in such books refer most often both to the period in which the author (that means the last compiler) wrote and also to earlier periods. The most famous of these Merchant Guides, the *Pratica della mercatura* of Pegolotti, was apparently written in the years 1336-1340 (cf. Evans, introduction to the *Pratica*, p. xiv), but it also contains a chapter about conditions of trade in Acre at the time when the town was still under the rule of the Christians, that is, half a century earlier. Giovanni da Uzzano's book has the imprint 1440, but he apparently still distinguishes between the ducat and the gold coin of the Mamluks (see Uzzano, pp. 112-114), although since 1425 the dinar had been made equivalent to the ducat. The *Libro di mercatantie*, a Merchant Guide widely spread in the second half of the fifteenth century, was probably compiled in Ragusa in the middle of that century (see *Libro*, ed. Borlandi, p. xlv). But even this book was a collective work (see there, p. xxxvi f.) and contains many statements taken over from the *Tarifa*, Pegolotti, and Uzzano (see there, p. xxxix, xl). Consequently, all these books must be used with the greatest caution when drawing conclusions as to the period to which their data refer. Anyhow they contain many particulars which enable us to outline the history of the Levant trade in the later Middle Ages. The Merchant Guide of Bartolomeo Pasi is a particularly valuable source, insofar as it contains many data about weights and measures which are missing in other similar treatises. A striking feature of this work of the late fifteenth century is the habit of its author to compare the same weight with many others, much more than the authors of other Merchant Guides did, so that the checking of his data is very easy. The Anonymous Merchant Guide in the Marciana Library (It. VII 384) has the date 1493, but on f. 77b one finds the date 1469 and on f. 65b the tariff of imposts in Alexandria in 1486. So even this treatise was compiled over a long period. This Merchant Guide is particularly detailed as far as the payments to be made in the Levantine emporia are concerned. So it is a typical sample of the Venetian Merchant Guides (see U. Tucci, "Tariffe veneziane e libri toscani di mercatura," *Studi Veneziani* X, 1968, p. 89, 90 f.).

The conclusions drawn from all these sources should be considered as rather tentative. This book does not claim to be a definitive history of the Levant trade in the later Middle Ages. The author will be happy if the reader recognizes that it traces a certain progress and corrects the portrait one had so far of these commercial exchanges. It should show that the Levant trade of that period was a great export trade. The role of the export of various European commodities, both agricultural and industrial, into the Moslem Levant is put into relief. The study of the judicial acts (of the *Giudici di petiziòn*, for instance) and of the archives of Levant traders makes it possible to go much more into detail in studying this aspect of mediaeval Levant trade than one could before. A major result of the present research is the conclusion that the cotton trade was in the later Middle Ages not much less important in the commercial exchanges between Southern Europe and the Near East than the spice trade, at least for a long time. Great stress has been laid on the calculation of the total of the European investments in the trade with the Levant. But certainly one cannot pretend that the conclusions are sure. The data one finds in the chronicles concerning the cash carried by the merchants on the galleys and the round ships to the Levant are not beyond doubt. The Venetian chronicler Girolamo Priuli emphasizes (*I diarii*, I, pp. 30, 94) that one should beware of relying on them, because the merchants cheated the shipowners and customs officers, declaring less then they actually had. But if a step forward has been taken in this and in other respects in this book, despite all these handicaps, the author has achieved his aim. For according to an ancient Hebrew saying, "It is not incumbent upon me to finish the work."

May I finally express my sincerest thanks to the authorities of the Hebrew University of Jerusalem who have rendered possible my research by granting me a long leave and covering many of my expenses, and to the Deutsche Forchungsgemeinschaft for a generous grant which enabled me to spend a long time working in the archives of Italy. I am very thankful to Countess M. Fr. Tiepolo, now director of the Venetian State Archives, who encouraged me and accompanied with great helpfulness my first steps in the archives of Venice. Further, I am obliged to Professor R. Mueller, formerly of Tucson, Arizona, and now of Venice, and to Dr. Erwin Fenster of Augsburg, who drew my attention to various important manuscripts in the archives and libraries of Venice. For similar help I am also indebted to Dr. Giangiacomo Musso of Genoa, Dr. Alessandro Mordenti of Ancona, and Professor Marco Tangheroni of Pisa. Professor H.-E. Mayer was specially kind in making important suggestions to me, and Sta Angel Masiá de Ros was very helpful during my sojourn in Barcelona.

Jerusalem
Hebrew University
January 1981

E. Ashtor

Levant Trade in the Later Middle Ages

I
The Crisis of Levant Trade (1291-1344)

A. The Fall of Acre (1291)

The conquest of Acre by the Mamluks in 1291 was surely a heavy blow to Western Christianity. It was understood that it meant the end of that great undertaking, the Crusades, but its reverberations were strongly felt in other areas that had nothing to do with religious feelings. The economic interests of various groups in the nations of Southern Europe were at stake. In fact, for the Westerners, Acre had been the gate to the Moslem Levant and a cornerstone of the trade with the Near Eastern countries, in which they were more interested then than at any time before, as the economic development of Southern and Western Europe had reached a level at which trade with the Moslem Levant supplied articles much in demand and was an outlet for their own products. So suspension of the Levantine trade would have hit the economically most advanced countries of Europe very hard.

Just at the end of the thirteenth century, a long period of demographic growth in Western and Southern Europe was approaching its climax. The population of most European countries had grown almost continuously from the tenth century onward. The population of France had risen to 13.4 millions (based on the territory of 1328, but if that of 1794 is taken as the base, the figure is 17.6 millions). In the twelfth century it had been perhaps six millions. The number of inhabitants of England had grown from 1.1 million in 1086 to 3.7 millions (all the British Isles had 5.25 million inhabitants). In the late thirteenth century, Italy had perhaps 8.4 million inhabitants. An equally striking phenomenon of the demographic development of Western and Southern Europe in the period of the Crusades was the growth of the towns. Studying the medieval chronicles that recount the history of that period, time and again one finds accounts of the addition of new quarters to the walled towns. In many towns the area within the walls was enlarged twice. These texts are clear evidence of population growth. Certainly many towns, or even most of them, were still very small, compared with our own times, but some had become truly big towns. In 1338 Florence had about 75,000 inhabitants, Venice 100,000. Paris must have had about 90,000 inhabitants before the middle of the fourteenth century.[1]

The growth of the town population meant a considerable increase in the demand for such Oriental articles as spices and luxurious textiles, the use of which had formerly been the prerogative of the nobility and high clergy. Whereas in earlier periods rather small stocks, occasionally imported from Levantine ports, had been sufficient, the numerous new towns, which had come into being all over Western and Central Europe, were a great market for the Oriental articles, whose supply was the very profitable business of many merchants engaged in maritime and land trade. They offered not only spices but also silken stuffs in whose production the Oriental craftsmen still excelled. Interruption of the Levant trade would have brought disaster to all those who made a living from this trade, either directly or indirectly. At the end of the thirteenth century the Italian traders, encouraged by the king, also began to carry on regular trade with England. From 1278, at least, Genoese galleys visited England.[2] At the beginning of the fourteenth century these travels became more and more frequent.[3] Then, in 1319, Venice established a state line of galleys to Flanders,[4] while Catalan ships sailed to Southampton and other parts of England.[5] Certainly the main purpose of the travels to Flanders and England was to acquire English wool, so highly appreciated as raw material for the flourishing textile industry of Italy and Catalonia. But the Mediterranean traders also brought Oriental spices and drugs into the countries of Northern Europe, thus providing themselves with a large part of the funds needed for the purchase of the English wool.[6]

The trade with the Levant also opened markets for European industries. The manufacturers of various textiles, mainly woolen stuffs and linen, were

[1] J. C. Russell, *Late ancient and medieval populations* (Philadelphia, 1958) (Transactions of the American Philosophical Society, N.S. 48), pp. 105, 106 f., 110; K. J. Beloch, *Bevölkerungsgeschichte Italiens* (Berlin, 1937-1961) I, p. 129; II, pp. 3, 339.

[2] R. Doehaerd, *Les relations commerciales* III, no. 1356 ff.; idem, "Les galères génoises dans la Manche et la mer du Nord à la fin du XIIIe et au début du XIVe s.," *Bulletin de l'Institut historique belge de Rome* 19 (1938), p. 10 f., where a document referring to a travel by sea to Flanders in 1277 is quoted.

[3] A. Ruddock, *Italian merchants and shipping in Southampton, 1270-1600* (Southampton, 1951), p. 20 f.

[4] A. Schaube, "Die Anfänge der venezianischen Galeenfahrten nach dem Norden," *HZ* 101 (1908), p. 37.

[5] Ruddock, *op.cit.*, p. 22.

[6] *Op.cit.*, p. 79.

badly in need of new markets. For in many provinces of Central, Western, and Southern Europe the textile industries had reached a high level of technical skill and the volume of the output was substantial. The great development of these industries was mainly the consequence of two important innovations: the use of the treadle loom and the introduction of the water-driven mill for fulling. These innovations made it possible to produce more and better textiles. The woolen stuffs of Flemish and Florentine manufacturers were exported into the Near East from the end of the twelfth century and the beginning of the thirteenth century,[7] and the same is true for the linen of Champagne and of some districts in Southern Germany. As early as the beginning of the thirteenth century French, Flemish and German linen was exported to Egypt through the Genoese.[8] In a treaty between the Mamluk sultan and Genoa drawn up in 1290, just on the eve of the fall of Acre, the merchandise referred to for import into Egypt was woolen stuffs of various colors, linen of Reims and others.[9] Likewise, a flourishing fustian industry had developed in Southern France, Lombardy, Tuscany, and other regions of Western and Southern Europe. This industry, too, was oriented toward export of its products to other countries, including the Moslem Levant. The same can be said of the new Italian silk industry. From time immemorial the Near East had been famous for its costly silk products. How many churches and abbeys in Western Europe were proud of having garments made of the Oriental silk! But in the thirteenth century the Italian traders were already exporting the products of their own country's silk industry to Egypt and Syria.[10] The upswing of the Italian silk industry was also the outcome of a great technological innovation. Once more it was the use of water power. Francesco Borghesano began to use it in Bologna for the throwing of silk in 1272, and this innovation, while requiring fewer workers, made it possible to produce much more and much better silk. For this period we have reliable data for the volume of the production of the woolen industry of Florence, one of the major centers of the industry. They show that production reached a peak in the years immediately subsequent to the fall of Acre. According to the Florentine chronicler Giovanni Villani, at the beginning of the fourteenth century the output was 100,000 pieces a year with a value of 600,000 fl. This statement may have been exaggerated, but it testifies to the growth of the Florentine woolen industry. The Florentines also fashioned and dyed

[7] H. Laurent, *Un grand commerce d'exportation au Moyen Age, la draperie des Pays-Bas, en France et dans les pays méditerranéens (XII*[e]*-XV*[e] *siècles)* (Paris 1935), p. 66; E. Ashtor, "Les lainages," p. 673; Doehaerd, *Les relations commerciales* II, nos. 275, 429.

[8] Doehaerd, *op.cit.* II, nos. 271, 275, 371.

[9] Silvestre de Sacy, "Pièces diplomatiques tirées des archives de la république de Gênes," *Notices et extraits* XI (1827), p. 36.

[10] *Ibidem; Deliberazioni del Maggior Consiglio* III, p. 32.

cloth imported from Flanders and a large part of these textiles was even shipped to the Near East.[11] All these industries were closely linked to the Levant trade for another reason: they used Levantine flax, cotton, and raw silk and various Oriental dyes as well as alum for fixing the colors.

The export of European textiles became possible because the Near Eastern textile industries had begun to decline. The production centers in Lower Egypt, which had been famous for their fine linen and other textiles, decayed from the end of the twelfth century onward.[12] Some important centers of this industry discontinued production. This phenomenon, followed by the decay of other industries, is the background against which the commercial expansion of the European nations should be seen. Indeed, their expansion was possible only because of the industrial decay of the Near East, although this was a slow, progressive development.

The growth of the Levantine trade of the South European nations in the late thirteenth century and the development of their exchanges with Northwestern Europe would probably not have been so conspicuous if the techniques had not changed so considerably. Just in that period the commercial methods in Italy and in Southern France had advanced very greatly. In the first half of the thirteenth century, the merchants of these countries had begun to transfer funds by bills of exchange. This is first mentioned in documents of the 1220's and in the middle of the thirteenth century was frequently used in Southern France, judging from the acts of notaries of Marseilles. This system of combining the exchange of money with its transfer by a letter of credit, instead of actually transporting cash, rendered the activities of the merchants who needed money overseas much easier.[13]

It is also true that the nautical skills of the South European mariners had greatly increased in the thirteenth century. Some important innovations brought about a great change in navigation in the Mediterranean, and this change had substantial economic importance. The progress in nautical methods was particularly notable in the last third of the century, just when the last strongholds of the Crusaders fell. One of the innovations was a new kind of nautical chart, which distinguished itself by great accuracy and on which the windrose was included. The oldest of these charts that has come down to us, the Carta Pisana, dates from 1270-1275. Another

[11] *Chronicle of Giovanni Villani* XI, 94; A. Doren, *Die Florentiner Wollentuchindustrie vom vierzehnten bis zum sechzehnten Jahrhundert* (Stuttgart, 1901), pp. 122, 399; G. Luzzatto, *Storia economica d'Italia, il medioevo* (Florence, 1963), pp. 198, 202; M. F. Mazzaoui, "The cotton industry of Northern Italy in the later Middle Ages," *JEH* 32 (1972), pp. 263, 267, 268.

[12] See my *Social and economic history*, p. 246.

[13] A. Schaube, "Studien zur Geschichte und Natur des ältesten Cambium," *Jahrbücher für Nationalökonomie und Statistik* 45 (1895), p. 160 ff.; as to its South European origin see E. Ashtor," Banking instruments between the Muslim East and the Christian West," *JEEH* I (1972), pp. 553 ff., 562 f., 566.

new expedient was the navigation table arranged in columns, which the mariners of those days called *tavola de marteloio*. The use of these new charts and sailing directories would have been impossible if sailors had been unable to measure time exactly. So there is strong evidence for the assumption that by the end of the thirteenth century European seamen used the sandglass, which remained their timekeeper until the chronometer came into general use in the late eighteenth century. The first authentic reference to the use of the sandglass dates to 1345-1346.[14] Even more important was the general use of the compass. Many scholars still believe that the compass as we know it was invented in Amalfi; others differ with this view. The differences in opinion arise from the fact that the compass is the result of a long development. In any case, it is very probable that at the end of the thirteenth century the magnetic needle was amalgamated with the windrose, that is, attached to a compass card, so that they moved together and turned when the ship changed direction. The Chinese sailors, who had used the magnetic needle a long time before the Europeans, remained faithful to the floating compass until the sixteenth century, when the pivoting needle was introduced into the Far East. However, the question of who invented the compass or who introduced it into Europe is much less important than the evaluation of the practical consequences of its use, which clearly emerges form documents of the end of the thirteenth century. The importance of the compass to sailing in the Mediterranean was particularly great, because it made possible the crossing of the sea in winter, when the skies are clouded. As east winds can be expected in the eastern basin of the Mediterranean only in October and November, the merchantmen could sail in these months and no longer had to return from the Levant in a period when they did not enjoy favorable winds. So the Mediterranean became open the whole of the year and two trips could be made to the Levantine ports in twelve months. The schedules established by the authorities of the merchant republics in the late thirteenth century and at the beginning of the fourteenth century for the convoys to the Levant show the great change resulting from the use of the compass.[15]

So there were a number of reasons for which the fall of the last Crusader towns was a particularly heavy blow. These towns had been the destination of many ships that connected the Near East with South European ports.

[14] N. H. Nicolas, *A history of the Royal navy* (London, 1847), II, p. 476; Lynn White, *Medieval technology and social change* (Oxford, 1962), p. 166.

[15] K. Kretschmer, *Die italienischen Portolanen des Mittelalters* (Berlin, 1909), pp. 31, 70, 74, 80 f.; Bachisio R. Motzo (ed.), *Il compasso da navigare* (Cagliari, 1947) (Annali della Facoltà di lettere e filosofia della Università di Cagliari VIII), p. LXXXIX; E.G.R. Taylor, *The haven-finding art* (London, 1956), p. 109 f., 119; F. C. Lane, "The economic meaning of the invention of the compass," in his *Venice and history*, pp. 335 ff., 344; cf. J. Needham, *Science and civilization in China* IV, part 1 (Cambridge, 1962), pp. 279, 334.

The cargoes they transported seem to us very small, and indeed the volume of the Levant trade was rather limited, as compared with the total of the agricultural and industrial production and the trade of the countries of Southern and Western Europe, but the activities of the Levant traders infused blood into the veins of the fast-developing European economy. They made possible an increase in the output of industries and a rise in the standard of living in the towns.

It would be very one-sided, however, to overlook the fact that the Moslems of the Near East also had a great interest in these commercial exchanges. The European traders provided them with several articles in which they were very much interested. It is sufficient to have a look at the commercial treaties that the sultans of Cairo concluded at the end of the thirteenth century with European trading nations to understand this point.

The Near Easterners had always had a great liking for furs, and even in the days of the Abbasid caliphate the import of various furs, such as ermine and marten, from countries of Eastern and Northern Europe, had been a lively trade. The Mamluks, most of whom stemmed form regions north of the Caucasus, liked furs even more. The commercial treaty concluded between the Mamluk sultan and Genoa in 1290 contained a paragraph in which the import of furs was made duty-free.[16]

There were other articles that were even more in demand. The Moslems had a great need of timber and iron. At the end of the thirteenth century the rulers of the Near East were still engaged in the construction of warships. But they also needed timber and iron for weapons, such as rams and other siege engines to batter the walls of towns. These materials, lacking or very scarce in most of the Near Eastern countries, could easily be supplied by the South European merchants, and the latter were not reluctant to sell them to the Moslems, despite the prohibition of this trade by the Church. The kings of Europe and the governments of the merchant republics were not ashamed to oblige themselves by official agreements to deliver these war materials to the enemies of Christianity. In the treaty mentioned above, the Genoese agreed to pay 10 percent customs for the import of these commodities,[17] and they were certainly not the only European traders who supplied the Mamluks with war material to be used against the Christians. In the same year, King Alfonso III of Aragon made a treaty with the sultan of Cairo in which he undertook to allow his subjects and other Christian traders to export timber, iron, weapons, and similar articles to the Moslems Levant.[18]

[16] *Notices et extraits* XI, p. 35.

[17] *Ibidem*, p. 36.

[18] M. Amari, *La guerra del vespro siciliano* (Florence, 1876) II, p. 342. The text has been printed before, by Silvestre de Sacy (in the) *Magasin encyclopédique* (of Millin) VII (1801),

These facts were put forward by the champions of a new Crusade and were expounded in many treatises written by them. What was often overlooked was the fact that the supply of war material to the Moslems was associated with technical help. The famous Arab scholar Ibn Khaldūn (d. 1406), probably the first sociologist, when writing in the late fourteenth century about the decay of Moslem civilization, says that the Moslems are no longer skilled in building good ships and equipping war fleets, so that they need the assistance of European Christians.[19] This statement is fully borne out by papal bulls. In some of those, which forbid the supply of war material to the Moslems, one finds some vague references to the collaboration and help given them.[20] Others are more specific and dwell on the fact that Christians sell the Moslems ships, serve them as helmsmen on their ships, and take part in their naval expeditions against other Christians.[21]

The Moslem spice merchants certainly had the greatest interest in continuing the profitable trade in commodities so eagerly demanded by the South European traders. Even the Mamluk government was interested in it. The revenue the Royal Exchequer of the sultan received from the customs which were collected from the European merchants cannot be overlooked. Although the amount cannot have been too great if compared with the total of the sultan's tax revenues—the land tax in 1298 yielded about five million dinars—it should not be forgotten that the great majority of the rural estates was allotted as fiefs to the military (in 1298, 80 percent of the cultivated area), so that even some ten thousand dinars were appreciated as an additional source of income for the treasury.

As both the European traders and industrialists and the Moslems were so much interested in their commercial exchanges, they were carried on throughout the second half of the thirteenth century despite the ruthless war waged by the Mamluks against the remnants of the Crusader principalities.

Venetian trade with Egypt must have been intense, for in some years

part II, p. 145 ff., and Fr. Wilken, *Geschichte der Kreuzzüge* (Leipzig, 1807-1832) VII, p. 17 ff. and then by Amari, *Bibl. Arabo-Sicula* (Turin 1880-1881) I, p. 552 ff. This was certainly not a simple commercial treaty, as Wilken p. 713 says. It had far-reaching political implications; cf. Cerone in *Arch. Stor. Prov. Nap.* 27 (1902), p. 35. But Amari doubted if the Aragonese king ratified the treaty, since he changed his policy, see *La guerra del vespro* I, p. CXIII, 422.

19 *The Muaddimah*, transl. Rosenthal II, p. 46.

20 M. Fernandez de Navarrete, *Disertación histórica*, p. 179 f.; Reg. Clément V (Paris, 1886), no. 5090.

21 A. Germain, *Histoire du commerce de Montpellier* (Montpellier, 1861), piéces justificatives, no. 46 (a. 1272, "naves aut galeas vendere seu curam gubernationis in Sarracenorum piraticis navibus exercere vel in machinis aut quibuslibet aliis aliquod eis impendere consilium vel auxilium"); Reg. Boniface VIII (Paris, 1885-1939), no. 3421 ("aut in piraticis Sarracenorum navibus curam gubernationis exercent").

the merchants considered a single convoy of galleys to be insufficient. However, in 1278, the Maggior Consiglio ruled that there should be only one a year.[22] The regulation of the traffic was rigidly enforced. The convoys (then called *caravane*) for Acre and Alexandria left Venice in August for the yearly fall spice fair. It was ruled that merchants arriving earlier should not sell certain European commodities[23] and, on the other hand, no one should depart (for Venice) before the middle of September.[24] So the merchants travelling on the galleys did not have to fear competition. The Venetian authorities also took other measures to safeguard their interests. The Venetian galley service was known to be very regular and reliable, and consequently many non-Venetians shipped their merchandise on them from Alexandria. In 1286 an inquiry was made into the matter, which was considered to be a transgression of Venetian law.[25] The Venetians exported to Alexandria costly silken goods,[26] metals,[27] and many other commodities. They also supplied the Mamluks with timber[28] and iron.[29] The Venetian consulate was always filled by an appointee,[30] and, when it was considered necessary, as in 1288, the Venice government sent an embassy to the sultan and a new agreement was made.[31]

However, it is almost beyond doubt that in the second half of the thirteenth century supremacy in European trade with the Moslem Levant was in the hands of the Genoese. Genoa's foreign trade as a whole reached its peak at the end of this century.[32] In the history of Genoa this was in general a period of great economic expansion, but there were special reasons for its supremacy in the trade with the Levant. Since the army of the first Mamluk sultans, the so-called Baḥrites, consisted mainly of former slaves

[22] *Deliberazioni del Maggior Consiglio* II, p. 68; a decree of February 1291, forbidding anyone to sail to Alexandria without a special permission of the doge, *op.cit.* III, p. 291, was probably connected with the rumors about the forthcoming assault on Acre.

[23] *Op.cit.* III, p. 103 f.

[24] *Op.cit.* II, p. 135.

[25] *Op.cit.* III, p. 144.

[26] *Op.cit.* III, p. 32.

[27] *Op.cit.* III, p. 103 f.

[28] *Op.cit.* II, p. 72.

[29] *Op.cit.* III, p. 111.

[30] *Op.cit.* II, p. 358; III, p. 152.

[31] *Regesta regni Hierosolymitani*, ed. Röhricht, no. 1481; cf. P. Sambin, "La politica mediterranea di Venezia alla fine della guerra del vespro," *Atti del R. Istituto Veneto di scienze, lettere ed arti* 104 (1944-1945), part 2, p. 995. Probably it was the ambassador Niccolò Quirino who concluded the treaty in 1289 with the government of the sultan Ḳalā'ūn. The text quoted by Sambin apparently refers also to another embassy sent to al-Malik an-Nāṣir Muḥammad during his first reign (1293-1294) or at the beginning of his second reign (1299-1309).

[32] See the figures in the farming contracts of the commercial tax: H. Sieveking, "Aus Genueser Rechnungs- und Steuerbüchern," *Sitzungsberichte der phil.-hist. Klasse der Kais. Akademie der Wiss.* 162 (Vienna, 1909), p. 52; R. S. Lopez, "Market expansion: the case of Genoa," in his *Su e giù*, p. 50 f.

from Southern Russia, and Genoa was allied to the Palaeologi, its merchants enjoyed a privileged status in Constantinople and in the Black Sea area, so that the shipping of the recruits to Egypt was essentially their business. The Mamluk sultans concluded several treaties with the emperors of Constantinople to make sure that the traffic would go on regularly and be unhampered.[33] The position the Genoese had in European trade with Egypt and Syria was strengthened by a new treaty made by an embassy that went to Cairo in 1275.[34] So it came about that the Genoese ship line connecting Caffa, the great emporium on the shores of Crimea, with Egypt and Syria became a major axis of international trade. Notarial acts drawn up in Caffa witness this fact.[35] The Genoese exported grain from the Crimea to Syria, as to other Mediterranean countries.[36] The intensity of the commercial exchanges along this maritime trade route is also borne out by the relatively large number of Syrians, some of them rich merchants, who lived in Caffa, at the end of the thirteenth century.[37] Both Genoa and the Mamluks were interested in remaining on good terms with one another, and the dependence of the sultans of Cairo on the supply of the military slaves was so great that the Genoese could hold their position in Alexandria despite the expeditions of their war fleets, which supported the Crusaders against the sultan. When the Genoese admiral and diplomat Benedetto Zaccaria made a treaty in 1288 with the king of Cyprus, which was directed against the sultan of Cairo, the government in Genoa did not agree to this step and did not ratify it.[38] Then, in 1289, Benedetto Zaccaria seized a Moslem ship and, according to a reliable Arabic source, the sultan abstained from retaliating by the confiscation of the merchandise of the Genoese in Alexandria.[39] R. Lopez was certainly right in concluding that the position of the Genoese in Egypt was even stronger after the peace that had been made

[33] M. Canard, "Un traité entre Byzance et l'Egypte au XIIIe siècle et les relations diplomatiques de Michel Paléologue avec les sultans mamlouks Baibars et Qalā'ūn," *Mélanges Gaudefroy-Demombynes* (Cairo, 1935-1945), p. 219; *Ṣubḥ al-a'shā* 14, p. 72 ff., translated by Canard, "Le traité de 1281 entre Michel Paléologue et le sultan Qalā'ūn," *Byzantion* X (1930), p. 669 ff.; Fr. Dölger, *Der Vertrag des Sultans Qalā'ūn von Ägypten mit dem Kaiser Michael Palaiologos*, Serta Monacensia (Leiden, 1952), p. 60 ff. and cf. E. Ashtor, *Les métaux précieux*, p. 90.

[34] *Sulūk* I, p. 621, trad. Quatremère, *Hist. des sultans mamlouks* I, 2, p. 127; Ibn al-Furāt VII, p. 44.

[35] G. I. Brătianu, *Actes des notaires de Péra et de Caffa de la fin du treizième siècle (1281-1290)* (Bucarest, 1927) (Académie Roumaine, Etudes et recherches II), no. CLXVIII.

[36] *Les actes de Caffa du notaire Lamberto di Sambuceto, 1289-1290*, ed. M. Balard (Paris 1973), no. 886.

[37] *Op.cit.*, nos. 223, 252, 310, 335, 389, 410, 571, 595, 741, 771 (see index p. 414), 875-77; merchants: 140, 510, 518, 795, 882.

[38] *Chronicle of Jacopo Doria*, MGH SS 18, p. 322; R. S. Lopez, *Genova marinara nel Duecento: Benedetto Zaccaria* (Messina, 1933), p. 143; idem, *Storia delle colonie genovesi*, p. 234.

[39] M. Amari, "Nuovi ricordi arabi su la storia di Genova," *ASLSP* V (1867), p. 606 f.

between them and the sultan in 1290 than before.[40] This was indeed a great success of Genoese diplomacy, all the more remarkable since Genoa at the same time entered into close relations with the great enemy of the sultan of Cairo, the Īlkhān, ruler of Iraq and Persia. The attempt the Genoese made in the days of Arghūn (1284-1291) to help the Īlkhān in cutting Egypt's trade with India was only one of the services rendered him. Even in the Black Sea they supported the Īlkhāns. The Venetians, on the other hand, apparently even before the fall of Acre, began to pursue a policy that aimed at establishing a de facto alliance with the Mamluks and their friends, the Tatar rulers of Kiptchak in Southern Russia.[41] The account the French bishop Guillaume Adam gives of the construction of galleys by the Genoese in Iraq, aimed at interrupting Egyptian traffic in the Indian Ocean, is corroborated by a reliable contemporary author. Barhebraeus in his Syriac chronicle writes that 900 Western Christians came to Iraq and that 700 passed the whole of the winter of 1290 in Baghdad, building the galleys that were to be put into the sea in Basra.[42] A chapter in the Latin chronicle of a third contemporary writer also appears to testify to the trustworthiness of Guillaume Adam's account.[43]

The Genoese and the Venetians had established regular trade with Egypt a long time before, but the Catalans began to play the role of a major partner in the Levant trade only in the second half of the thirteenth century. At the beginning of Mamluk rule in Egypt, when Catalan trade with this country began to be more regular, Jaime I, king of Aragon and Catalonia, decided to establish a consulate in Alexandria. In 1262 he instructed Raimondo de Conchas, a merchant of Montpellier (then under Aragon's rule), to go to Egypt and to ask the sultan for permission to found a consulate in Alexandria. The envoy succeeded in his mission, and from then on there were a Catalan fondaco and a consulate in the Egyptian port.[44] In March 1264 Ramon Ricart, a merchant of Barcelona, was ordered by the king to organize the Catalan colony in Alexandria. But shortly afterward the king

[40] *Genova marinara*, p. 153.

[41] Brătianu, *Recherches*, p. 257.

[42] *Chronicon Syriacum*, ed. transl. P. J. Bruns-G. B. Kirsch (Leipzig, 1789), p. 620.

[43] *Chronicle of Johannes of Winterhur*, MGH SS N. S. III, p. 58; cf. J. Richard, "Les navigations des Occidentaux sur l'Océan Indien et la mer Caspienne," *Sociétés et compagnies de commerce en Orient*, p. 359; the chronicler recounts that there were many Christians in Baghdad, "a town on the sea," and that one of them committed a sacrilege in a mosque. It is true that this account is inserted in the chronicle between some texts referring to happenings at the beginning of the fourteenth century, but it was written in Switzerland by a monk who collected his materials from hearsay and since the Īlkhāns Ghāzān (1295-1304) and Öldjeytü (1304-1317) were already Moslems, it is rather unlikely that under their rule a Western Christian merchant had the courage to offend the Moslems in this way. Further, there is no evidence of the presence of European merchants in Baghdad in that period. It is also much more probable that a worker or a sailor behaved so aggressively toward the Moslems.

[44] López de Meneses, "Los consulados," p. 85 and appendix I.

appointed Guillem de Moncada of Barcelona as consul in Alexandria for two years.[45] The various decrees which have come down to us from the chancery of Jaime I show that there were difficulties and that consequently the king had to change his decisions several times. From a decree of King Jaime I, we see indeed that his subjects in Alexandria had not obeyed his orders. Two months after the appointment of Guillem de Moncada in June 1264, he again sent Raimondo de Conchas as ambassador to the sultan and entrusted him with the appointment of a consul in Alexandria. He was also to deal with the property left by a Catalan merchant who had travelled to Egypt on a ship of Narbonne and apparently had died in Alexandria. The king also ordered him to retaliate by the seizure of Egyptian ships, if the sultan would not comply with his requests.[46] However, soon the king returned to his former decision and confirmed the appointment of Guillem de Moncada.[47] Then, in 1266, he conferred upon the town council of Barcelona the right to appoint consuls in the Moslem Levant (*ultramar*) and two years later he authorized the council to appoint consuls everywhere.[48] At the beginning of 1268, however, he entrusted two citizens of Montpellier, Bernard de Molins and Bernard de Plan, with the direction of the Catalan colony in Alexandria.[49] This must have been an extraordinary measure, due to peculiar circumstances,[50] for henceforth the town council of Barcelona appointed the consul in Alexandria.[51] In any case, all these appointments and royal orders testify to the development of Catalan trade with Egypt. However, in 1274, King Jaime I, under the pressure of the Church, promulgated a decree that forbade any commercial exchanges with the dominions of the Mamluks.[52] But this prohibition was not serious. In

[45] *Art. cit.*, l.c. and appendix II.

[46] Pr. Bofarull Mascaro, *Selección de documentos inéditos del archivo de la Corona de Aragón* (Barcelona, 1847-1910) VI, p. 166 f.; Germain, *Histoire du commerce de Montpellier*, pièces justificatives, no. 38 (of December 27, 1264); A. López de Meneses, *art. cit.*, pp. 85, 86 ff.; the consul should, however, be the leader of the commercial expedition (and not a resident consul); about Raimondo de Conchas, see Heyd II, p. 421 (was he the same man who in 1223 was already consul of the town, see *op.cit.* I, p. 364, or perhaps the latter's son?).

[47] López de Meneses, *art. cit.*, p. 87 and appendix III.

[48] Capmany, *Memorias* 2.1, nos. 19, 23, pp. 35-36, 39; A. Gimenez Soler, "El commercio en tierra de infieles durante la edad media," *Bol. Acad. de buenas letras de Barcelona* V (1909), p. 182.

[49] Capmany, 2.1, no. 20, pp. 36-37. Since this appointment seemingly contradicts the permission granted to the Council of Barcelona, Capmany, 1, p. 811, has concluded that it meant the establishment of a consulate of Montpellier, but since in the documents of that period such a consulate is not mentioned, Heyd I, p. 421, was apparently right in interpreting it as an appointment to the direction of the colony.

[50] Cf. the document published by Germain and quoted by Heyd l.c.

[51] Capmany, 2.1, no. 25, pp. 40-41.

[52] Capmany, 2.1, no. 26, pp. 41-42. Heyd II, p. 423 interprets the document as referring to the export of war material only, but this interpretation is not in keeping with the text, and cf. Capmany, 1, pp. 241-42.

fact, the royal government considered only the sale of timber and iron to the Moslems as forbidden, and this embargo was not strictly enforced.

Even the successor of Jaime I, King Pedro III (1276-1285), was eager to establish friendly relations with the Mamluks, who were a very strong power in the Mediterranean world. Like his rival, King Charles I of Anjou, he tried to have the sultan on his side, even before the great contest over Sicily had begun and in 1279 sent an embassy to Cairo.[53] On the other hand, so as not to stir up the Church, in 1281 he reissued the prohibition of the export of war material into the Moslem countries. A request of the town council of Barcelona to revoke the decree was turned down.[54] The trade of other articles between Catalonia and Egypt continued unhampered.[55]

We have much less information about the commercial activities of the other trading nations, which one could call the "minor trading powers." But there can be no doubt that in the second half of the thirteenth century even these nations were engaged in a lively trade with the dominions of the Mamluks. Notarial acts of Marseilles refer to trade with Egypt in the 1270's and in the 1280's.[56] Among the commodities exported from Marseilles into the Near East in that period iron is mentioned. The traders of Southern France also traded with the provinces of Syria which were under Moslem rule. In 1262 a merchant of Montpellier, for instance, sold the king of Aragon "alum of Aleppo."[57]

Among the Italian "minor trading nations" the Pisans should be mentioned as one of those very active in the trade with Egypt during the period preceding the fall of Acre. According to a Genoese chronicle, a Pisan ship returning from Alexandria was captured, in 1282, in the Tyrrhenian Sea.[58] On the other hand, a chronicler of Cyprus suspected Pisans and Venetians familiar with the sultan of Cairo of having incited him against the Genoese in the late 1280's.[59] A Merchants Guide, compiled in 1278 in Pisa, contains much data on the Alexandrian trade, including the European commodities marketed there.[60] Traders of Pisa, Florence, and San Gimignano in fact travelled from Acre to Damietta and Alexandria in (about) 1270, and all of

[53] S. H. Wieruszowski, "Conjuraciones y alianzas politicas del rey Pedro de Aragon contra Carlos de Anjou antes de las Visperas Sicilianas," *BAH* 107 (1935), p. 600 f.

[54] Capmany, 2.1, no. 30, pp. 45-46. The decree refers to the Moslem countries in general, but in 1274 the sale of these articles to all Moslems had already been forbidden.

[55] Capmany, 2.1, nos. 68-69, pp. 100-101.

[56] L. Blancard, *Documents inédits sur le commerce de Marseille au moyen-âge* (Marseilles, 1884-85) II, pp. 415, 436.

[57] Germain, *Histoire du commerce de Montpellier*, Pièces justificatives no. 36.

[58] *Chronicle of Jacopo Doria*, MGH SS 18, p. 297.

[59] *Les Gestes des Chiprois*, ed. G. Raynaud (Geneva, 1887), pp. 234, 235 and cf. G. Caro, *Genua und die Mächte am Mittelmeer 1257-1321* (Halle a. S. 1895-1899) II, p. 127.

[60] Davidsohn, *Geschichte von Florenz* IV, p. 291.

them claimed to be citizens of Pisa, a trading nation that had a privileged status in Egypt then. They sold saffron and other articles in Alexandria in the fondaco of the Pisans.[61]

Even the coast towns of Apulia had commercial relations with Egypt and Syria in that period. The yearly Saint Nicolas fair in Trani, in the second half of the thirteenth century, was a great market for Oriental spices, sugar, cotton, silk, and other products of the Levant. King Charles I of Anjou himself, through his commercial agents, was engaged in the trade with the Levant. Not only Venetian, Genoese, and other Italian merchants but Orientals and the local traders offered these articles there.[62] Through the second part of the thirteenth century, there were always great stocks of pepper, sugar, and cotton in the royal castle of Trani, and both in this town and in Barletta there was a lively trade in these articles, even before and after the fair.[63] From that period the so-called *Consuetudines of Bari* have come down to us. These customs, compiled under the rule of Charles I of Anjou by Andrea di Sparano of Bari, also contain rules concerning merchant travels to Syria and Alexandria.[64] Arabic historians, on the other hand, recount that in 1268 Charles I of Anjou, through an embassy to Sultan Baybars, applied for the same rights and privileges for his subjects that the merchants of Naples and Sicily had had in his dominions in bygone times.[65] The sultan received the embassy well and sent an ambassador of his own, an emir called Badr ad-dīn, together with King Charles' returning envoys. From the registers of the Anjou kings of Naples, one learns that the Egyptian embassy sailed in the same year from Alexandria on a Genoese ship to Genoa and later travelled to Apulia. The Egyptian ambassador returned to Egypt only in 1271; during this time he visited other countries. One document indicates that the Egyptian embassy visited Marseilles. Upon the return of this embassy, King Charles sent another of his. In the documents referring to this second embassy of King Charles I, Guglielmo di Faronvilla, a high-ranking prelate and vice-chancellor of Sicily, Fra Berengario, the king's chaplain, and Pietro de Beana are mentioned as his ambassadors. At

[61] Idem, *Forschungen zur älteren Geschichte von Florenz* (Berlin, 1896-1908) II, part 2, no. 2310 (p. 299 ff.).

[62] Vincenzo d'Avino, *Cenni storici sulle chiese arcivescovili, vescovili e prelatizie (nullius) del regno delle due Sicilie* (Naples, 1848), p. 676.

[63] See the document of 1281 published by Domenico Forges Davanzati, *Dissertazione sulla seconda moglie del Re Manfredi e su loro figliuoli* (Naples 1791), no. LXXXIV (p. LXXVIII).

[64] G. Petroni, *Della storia di Bari dagli antichi tempi sino all'anno 1856 libri tre*, II (Naples, 1858), p. 537.

[65] M. Michaud, *Bibliothèque des croisades* IV (Paris 1829), p. 515 f.; cf. 483, 530 f. The source is the chronicle of Ibn al-Furāt, VI, f. 150a f., where the account of the coming of the embassy is to be found among the happenings of the year 667 of the hidjra. The year 667 of the hidjra began on September 10, 1268 and since the first royal letter referring to the Egyptian embassy which returned with it, see Del Giudice (according to next note) III, no. IX, dates to February 1269, it must have made the journey to Egypt in 1268.

least forty persons accompanied them, as they embarked in Brindisi on the ship of an Amalfitan, Remedio di Costa.[66]

The commercial exchanges between Sicily and both the Crusader towns on the Syro-Palestinian coast and Egypt evidently were quite lively in that period. The merchants of Messina were surely the most active in this trade. A notarial act dated 1279 refers to the death of Petronio di Puteo in Acre. He had travelled there on a merchantman of which he was part owner. The three executors testify that they were in Acre when the man died, and they acknowledge that one of them had received there goods belonging to him from two other citizens of Messina.[67] From this document one would conclude that the traders of Messina carried on a very lively trade with Acre. In fact, in the second half of the thirteenth century, Sicily exported great quantities of grains, and the Crusader towns were among the customers. The chapter in Pegolotti's work that compares the weights used in Acre with those used in other ports during the period of Christian rule points clearly to the export of spices to Messina and Palermo and to the import of Sicilian grains.[68] Accounts in Sicilian sources confirm this. But they also show that Catalans and Pisans took part in these exchanges too. In 1282 Syracuse is visited by Pisan ships and citizens of Messina who are returning from Acre. In the same year a group of Catalan traders obtains from the king permission to export grains, from his own stocks, *ad partes ultramaris*, and to bring back merchandise for the royal court. In January 1283 a trader of Messina, Bonagiunta di Scarlata, exports 300 salme to Acre on a Pisan ship. In the same year two ships, which had loaded cheese and

[66] D. Forges Davanzati, *Dissertazione sulla seconda moglie di Manfredi*, monumenti no. XVIII; C. Minieri Riccio, *Il regno di Carlo I, di Angiò negli anni 1271 e 1272* (Naples 1875), pp. 13, 15, 75; G. del Giudice, *Codice diplomatico del regno di Carlo I° e II° d'Angiò* (Naples, 1863-1902) I, p. 222 f., III, no IX. In the documents quoted by Minieri Riccio, Guglielmo de Faronvilla is not mentioned and, on the other hand, Messina is indicated as the port from which the ambassadors departed. The various documents complete each other, that is, that one may conclude that Fra Berengario and Pietro de Beana travelled to Messina and embarked there. But it may also be that the king changed his mind or that for some other reason Guglielmo de Faronvilla did not fulfill the task given him. About the second embassy of Charles I of Anjou as king of Southern Italy to the sultan (he had previously in 1264, sent him a letter and a present from France, see Ibn al-Furāt VI, f. 46b, *Sulūk* I, p. 513 cf. Quatremère, *Histoire* I, part 1, p. 239 and al-ʿAynī in *Rec. Hist. Crois.*, Hist. Or. II, part 1, p. 219) which came to Egypt in 1271 see Ibn al-Furāt VI, f. 203 b; *Sulūk* I, p. 601 and cf. Quatremère I, 2, p. 102 (the Arabic author says: ambassadors of Roger, i.e., the king of Sicily!). By his embassies to the Mamluk sultans, King Charles obviously continued the policy of the Hohenstaufen and especially that of Manfred, who did his best to maintain friendly relations with the court of Cairo and to safeguard the interests of his subjects. About the exchange of embassies between Manfred and Baybars, see al-Makrīzī trad. Quatremère I, 1, p. 174 f.; I, 2, pp. 16, 18, and cf. Fr. Gabrieli, "Le ambascerie di Baibars e Manfredi," in his *Saggi orientali* (Caltanisetta-Roma 1960), p. 97 ff.

[67] M. Alibrandi, "Messinesi in Levante nel medioevo," *Archivio Storico Siciliano*, series III, 21/22 (1972), p. 100 ff.

[68] *Pratica*, p. 65 ff.

wine, return to Syracuse from Acre. At the same time the royal authorities grant a permit to a Genoese to load his ship "Sant' Antonio," bound for Alexandria, with cheese, wool, honey, and other "permitted" commodities. Several other documents bear witness to the Sicilian trade with the Levant in that period.[69]

All these data show convincingly how eager the trading nations of Southern Europe must have been to foster their trade with the Moslem Levant and especially to establish good relations with the sultan of Cairo, the strongest Moslem king in the Mediterranean and the ruler of the country where the spices were easily obtained. But they also show forcefully that Acre was then the most important port in the Levant, the focus of the trade between Southern Europe and the Near East. The role of Acre in the complex relationship is clearly indicated by those chapters in the Merchant Guides compiled forty years and more after its fall, in which there are still comparisons of its weights and measures with those of several towns in Southern Europe.[70] These chapters show that the great Crusader port had been the gate to the Near East for the traders of Southern Europe.

B. Papal Prohibition of Trade (1291-1323)

After the conquest of Acre by the Mamluks, the popes issued a series of bulls forbidding trade with the Moslems, in order to hit them economically and primarily to interrupt their supply of war material. However, the bulls of Boniface VIII and Benedict XI forbid the trade with the Moslem Levant mostly in a general way. They could have been interpreted as forbidding only the supply of war material.[71] The trading nations under the pressure of the Church had to promulgate such decrees of their own, and they did it immediately. Genoa issued a general prohibition, acting as if it would be enforced strictly.[72] Venice forbade only the export of war material to the Moslem Levant. In 1292 the government also promulgated a decree forbidding the sale of slaves to the Egyptians.[73] How hypocritical the policy of the merchant republics was can be seen from the fact that in the same year, in which Tripoli fell, 1289, the government of Venice had concluded a new treaty with the sultan of Cairo. The attitude of the various governments, that is, their sincerity and willingness to implement the papal em-

[69] Giunta, *Aragonesi* I, p. 65 f. where the sources are given, and see also p. 68.

[70] *Zibaldone da Canal*, pp. 64, 67, 109; Pegolotti, p. 63 ff.

[71] Reg. Boniface VIII, nos. 1654 (a. 1296), 2338 (a. 1297), 3421 (a. 1299), 4420 (a. 1301), 5020 (a. 1302), 5346 (a. 1303); *Libr. Com.* I, lib. 1, nos. 161, 162, 169 (a. 1304). Some of these bulls also include the prohibition of the sale of victuals to the Moslems.

[72] For Genoa, see Jacopo Doria, p. 338; Reg. Clément V, no. 752; for Venice, see below.

[73] *Deliberazioni del Maggior Consiglio* III, p. 318; Thiriet, *Délibérations des assemblées*, I, p. 66.

bargo on trade with the Mamluk dominions, depended very much on their frequently changing relations with the Holy See. When the king of Aragon had made peace with the pope in 1302, he forbade any trade with Egypt and gave orders that his decree should be made known in all the major towns of the kingdom.[74] Venice withstood the pressure of the Church and enacted such a law only in 1317.[75] There were several reasons for the long delay. One was perhaps the conflict between the Serenissima and the Holy See, which had aroused her intervention in the struggle over Ferrara.[76] About the same time that Venice enacted this general prohibition of trade, Genoa once again forbade the selling of weapons and slaves to the Moslems. This was not an overall embargo on trade with the dominions of the Mamluks, as the first had been and as was required by the Church.[77]

The efficiency of the prohibition of trade with the Moslem Levant was also diminished by the way it was carried out by the Church itself. In fact the Holy See began to grant absolutions to those guilty of having sold war material to the Moslems. The absolution had to be obtained by payment of a considerable sum, such as the equivalent of the merchant's investment in the forbidden commercial activities.[78] In 1297 Boniface VIII authorized the bishops of Barcelona and Tortosa to grant such absolutions for the payment of a fifth or a fourth of the profit.[79] Sometimes the ecclesiastical authorities decided that the fine should be used for the equipment of new expeditions against the Moslem rulers of the Holy Land.[80] Anyhow, the absolution from excommunication became a source of income for the Church and for other authorities involved in the inquiries connected with the transgression of the papal bulls. A merchant who had good relations with high-ranking prelates could reasonably suppose that for the payment of a certain sum of money he would not be punished by excommunication. Before long, embassies of the merchant republics began to offer the Holy

[74] Fernandez de Navarrete, p. 180 ff.

[75] *Libr. Com.* I, lib. 2, nos. 64, 65 (a.1317); *Misti,* ed. Cessi, I, p. 169. It is true that this decree was issued on a later date, but it may be assumed that it was enacted under the pressure of the Church. That the sultan sent a present in the same year to the Serenissima (see below) may, however, hint to a conflict between him and Venice. Also, the fact that the prohibition referred only to Syria makes the impression that it was meant as a reprisal to acts of hostility committed there. Heyd II, p. 41 concluded that the prohibition was intended to warn the Venetian merchants against becoming involved in the contest between the Tatars and the Mamluks. But in that period the Tatars did not invade Syria. So the prohibition of trade with Syria, which was enacted by the Serenissima, could have served two purposes: to put pressure on the sultan and to make a concession to the Church.

[76] *Libr. Com.* I, lib. 1, nos. 426, 450, 466, 471.

[77] Monumenta Historiae Patriae II, c. 371 ff. (1316), cf. M. G. Canale, *Nuova storia della repubblica di Genova* (Florence, 1858-1864) II, p. 499 f.

[78] Reg. Clément V, no. 2994.

[79] Reg. Boniface VIII, no. 2338.

[80] Reg. Clément V, no. 5090; Fernandez de Navarrete, p. 179 f.

See considerable sums in advance for allowing them to trade with the Moslems.[81]

Clement V, however, changed the policy of the Holy See and initiated a more rigid policy. In 1308 he issued a general prohibition of trade with the dominions of the Mamluks, according to which transgressors would lose all civil rights, such as that of inheriting bequests, and should even be slaves of those who capture them. The archbishops of Genoa and Pisa, the doge of Venice, and the bishop and the town council of Ancona were ordered to make the bull known to all.[82] At the council of Vienne in 1311-1312, the pope took an additional step: apparently he authorized the Knights Hospitallers to capture the ships of Christian merchants, who carried on trade with the dominions of the Mamluks, off the coasts of Egypt and Syria and to sequester their freights.[83]

But how did the trading nations react? To what degree did they enforce the prohibition? Venice, whose merchants were not as involved in the slave trade with Egypt as were the Genoese, consequently distinguished between merchandise that it was permissible to export to Egypt and Syria and that which should not be supplied to the Moslems.[84] It seems that merchants travelling to Egypt or Syria had to give a warranty that they would not sell the Moslems forbidden articles.[85] Otherwise the goods of the merchants coming back from the dominions of the sultan were confiscated.[86] The records of the legislative bodies and the judicial authorities that have come down to us from that period, however, show a clear inclination to leniency towards transgression.[87] The Venetian government also strongly opposed the establishment of an inquisition against transgressors.[88]

Genoa opposed the measures taken by the Holy See in various ways. On one hand, for instance, in 1304, the government applied to the pope with the request that those who had exported timber, iron, and weapons to Egypt and could not afford to go to Rome should be granted absolution from excommunication in their own towns. This request referred to seamen only, however.[89] Another measure taken by the government of Genoa was the payment of restitution to those who had suffered losses by Genoese claiming to act on behalf of the Church. The so-called *Officium robarie*

[81] See Heyd II, p. 42.

[82] Reg. Clément V, no. 2994 (12 October 1308), 3088; *Libr. Com.* I, lib. 1, no. 381; lib. 2, no. 17.

[83] Lopez, *Storia delle colonie genovesi*, p. 271 f.

[84] *Libr. Com.* I, lib. 1, no. 166 (a. 1304); *Misti*, ed. Cessi, I, p. 109 (a. 1304), 137 (a. 1312).

[85] *Cassiere della bolla ducale, Grazie-Novus liber (1299-1305)*, ed. E. Favaro (Venice, 1962), no. 438 (a. 1303).

[86] *Op.cit.*, no. 138 (a. 1300).

[87] *Op.cit.*, no. 521 (a. 1304); ASV, Maggior Consiglio, Capricornus f. 23a (a. 1306).

[88] Heyd II, p. 42 f.

[89] Reg. Benoît XI (Paris, 1405), no 819.

was originally set up in order to indemnify merchants who had been victims of piracy committed by Genoese. But since pirates could always pretend to be authorized by the Holy See and the republic was interested in avoiding acts of reprisal, and, on the other hand, those who indeed had exported war material to the Moslems could claim that they had been attacked by true pirates, it turned out that in fact this office counteracted the papal prohibition of trade with the Moslems. The protests of churchmen were in vain.[90]

The contradictory measures that the Aragonese king Jaime II took in connection with the trade with the Moslem Levant reflected, on one hand, the vicissitudes of his contest with the house of Anjou, supported by the pope, and, on the other hand, the exploitation of the commercial exchanges by his own treasury. In 1292 Jaime II sent an embassy consisting of Ronteo de Marimon and Raymondo Alemany to the court of the sultan of Cairo, proposing a true political alliance directed against any aggressor and, as expressly stated in the documents which bear on the negotiations, also against those who would undertake a new Crusade. The king of Aragon obliged himself *expressis verbis* not to side with the pope in such a case and to fight against him and other Christians. In making this offer, the king of Aragon had acted in the names of the kings of Castile and Portugal as well. It goes without saying that the treaty thus concluded with Sultan al-Malik al-Ashraf Khalīl also dealt with commercial exchanges. It refers to the Catalan merchants who visit Alexandria and Damietta and to Moslem traders coming to the countries under the rule of the king of Aragon, then including Sicily, and contains the renouncement of both governments of any claim upon the bequests of merchants who were subjects of the other and had died in their territories and also upon the *ius naufragii*. Further, there was a paragraph concerning the delivery of war material. The king of Aragon obliged himself, as his brother Alfonso III had done before him, to allow his subjects to supply to the Moslems timber, iron, and weapons.[91] In the instructions given to the ambassadors, the king of Aragon had ordered them to ask the sultan for financial aid.[92] But after he had concluded peace with the House of Anjou and the pope had appointed him "vexillarius, capitaneus et amiratus ecclesie" in 1297, he entered into contacts with the

[90] L. de Mas-Latrie, "L'officium robarie," *Bibl. Ec. des chart.* 53 (1892), p. 264 ff.

[91] The instructions, dated August 10, 1292, were printed by Capmany, 2.1, no. 53, pp. 78-80; the treaty itself, concluded on January 29, 1293, by Amari, "Trattato stipolato da Giacomo II di Aragona col sultano d'Egitto il 29 gennaio 1293," *Atti della R. Accademia dei Lincei* XI (1883), p. 423 ff. (the Arabic text from Ṣubḥ al-aʿshā 14, p. 423 ff.); and then by Alarcón, no. 145 (from a copy in the archives of Barcelona); cf. Giunta, *Aragonesi* II, p. 81. The translation of Alarcón is wrong: bayāḍ does not signify "cloth," but, as stated by Amari, weapons. The Catalan text has been printed by Masiá de Ros, no. 3.

[92] Giunta, *Aragonesi* II, p. 80 believes that this was the primary aim of the king.

Īlkhān of Persia, the greatest enemy of the sultan of Cairo. In 1293 he had already sent an ambassador to Īlkhān Gaykhātū, and then in 1300 he sent another to Ghāzān to offer him his help against the Mamluks.[93] In the years subsequent to the conclusion of peace with the Holy See and the Anjou, the kingdom of Aragon indeed pursued a policy of both political and economic expansion. The various activities of King Jaime II fitted in the framework of a great conception.[94] In view of the changes in the policy of the king of Aragon, his conflicting orders concerning the trade with the Moslems in the Near East are not surprising. But, whatever he decreed, his aim was to have a share in the profits of the merchants. Even the papal prohibition of trade with the Mamluk dominions was a source of income for him. Since after his agreement with the pope the king had forbidden in 1302 any trade with the dominions of the sultan,[95] his magistrates inquired into the forbidden exchanges, and in 1308 his treasurer reported to him that they had taken from the transgressors what had been possible to extort from them. Thereupon the magistrates signed about 200 letters of absolution. As one reads in a document referring to these proceedings that without the export of grains (carried on by the transgressors) Alexandria would have remained uninhabited, the inquiry probably concerned shipping in 1296, when Egypt suffered from a serious dearth of grain;[96] in other words, the reference is to commercial activities before the enactment of the royal prohibition. The treasurer also reports that the decision as to how to proceed was made when the king set out for Sicily "pro gran cuyta que haviets de diners." According to the reports of the magistrates, some of the merchants who had exported war material to Egypt and had been imprisoned claimed to have permits and demanded to be brought before the king himself. Another document of the same year, 1308, refers to the imprisonment of the crew of a ship coming back from Alexandria. The captain claimed that he had loaded merchandise of foreigners, but the magistrates maintained that without any doubt it was the merchandise of Catalans and that consequently large fines could be levied on the merchants.[97] The documents quoted here illustrate the consequences of the prohibition of trade. In fact, King Jaime II had appropriated to himself the fines that were imposed by virtue of the ecclesiastical laws and that were due the Church. In 1306 the king had obtained from the pope that the abbots of San Cugat and Santa Creus could absolve those who had engaged

[93] Capmany, 2.1, no. 60, pp. 92-93.

[94] V. Salavert y Roca, "El tratado de Anagni y la expansión mediterranea de la Corona de Aragón," *EEMCA* V (1952), p. 209 ff.

[95] Masiá de Ros, no. 4.

[96] See my *Histoire des prix et des salaires*, p. 295.

[97] Finke, *Acta Aragonensia* II, no. 587; see also Masiá de Ros, nos. 15, 16 (about physical punishment of transgressors).

in the forbidden trade. But in 1309 Pope Clement V actually assigned the fines to the king so that he could prepare a new Crusade. In 1319 the pope repeated this grant.[98] For the export of commodities, which under ecclesiastical law could be sold to the Moslems before the prohibition made in 1308 (according to the more liberal interpretation of the earlier bulls), the king had imposed a fine of 10 percent of their value.[99] In 1311 the fines were increased, and in 1321 the king even authorized the judges to confiscate the goods of transgressors.[100]

The merchants who tried to continue the commercial exchanges with Egypt and Syria had to adapt themselves to a new situation. They had to take into consideration new risks and new expenses. However, in the last decennium of the thirteenth century, in the years immediately following the fall of Acre, the question of the continuation of the Levant trade was less urgent. War raged in the Mediterranean, and commercial exchanges with the Levant were often impossible. The war between Aragon and the House of Anjou necessarily brought the Levant trade of Marseilles to a stop. Its naval forces had to serve the aims of the king of Anjou and, on the other hand, Messina was in the hands of the enemy, so that the passage of the straits was blocked. From 1293 to 1299, Genoa was at war with Venice, so that the resources of the two great merchant republics were expended on other purposes, and the sea routes in the Mediterranean were not safe. Many documents show that even after the peace of Milan the fleets of both powers engaged in roving the sea against the merchantmen of the other, [101] but the traffic between the great ports of Italy, France, and Catalonia, on one hand, and the ports of Egypt and Syria was renewed. The continuation of trade with the Moslem Levant, despite the strictures by the Church and the interference by kings and public bodies, raises two questions: What was the character of the trade at the beginning of the fourteenth century? Were these commercial exchanges like those in the period of the Crusades or were they similar to those in the later Middle Ages? In addition, it would be interesting to know what the volume of Levant trade was, under the double pressure of the Church and secular authorities. Data from various sources and several documents make it pos-

[98] Masiá de Ros, nos. 5, 7, 11-14; Reg. Clément V, no. 5090 (the permission to grant absolution must have been valid for transgressions in the past, but there can be no doubt that one applied it also to future transgressions).

[99] Masiá de Ros, no. 6, cf. Giunta, *Aragonesi* II, p. 118. The document dates of December 18, 1303, but in fact the fine was levied at this rate two years before.

[100] Masiá de Ros, nos. 20, 98. But in 1328 Alfonso IV ordered the baile general of Catalonia to revoke this measure taken against a burgher of Manresa.

[101] *Libr. Com.* I, lib. 1, nos. 108, 111, 147, 149, 413, 557, 559, 560, 633; lib. 2, nos. 258, 266, 296, 324.

sible to answer the first question, and they give us some hints as to answer to the second.

Some European writers of that period thundered against the supply of timber and iron, weapons and whole ships, by Christian traders to the Moslems, and several documents that have been quoted before are in keeping with their charges. This export trade, however, was not a new phenomenon. The Italian traders had supplied war material to the rulers of Egypt throughout the period of the Crusades.[102] But Marino Sanuto the Elder, who wrote his book, or at least the draft of it, in 1306-1309, also dwells on the large amounts of imports of olive oil, honey, almonds, and hazelnuts into Egypt and Syria.[103] This statement is supported by other records, such as the Genoese-Mamluk treaty of 1290 and Merchant Guides of the first half of the fourteenth century.[104] This continuously growing import of victuals into the Near East points to the decay of agriculture in the Levantine countries. It shows that the production of olive oil in Syria, where it had been an important branch of agriculture from time immemorial, had already greatly decreased. Judging from data in different sources one would assume that the European traders also imported into the Moslem Levant at the beginning of the fourteenth century sizeable shipments of cloth, woolen stuffs, linen, and silken ware. In an anonymous Merchant Guide, which dates from the first decennium of the fourteenth century, one reads that the Italian merchants market linen in Damascus, Tripoli, and Cairo. In Damascus they sold, according to this source, much European cloth and in the Egyptian capital also scarlets. Copper and tin had a good market in both Syria and Egypt.[105] In addition they imported another industrial product into all the countries of the Levant—soap.[106]

That the Levant trade in that period was in a stage of transition, no longer like the commercial exchanges between the Near East and Southern Europe in the eleventh and twelfth centuries and not yet comparable to late medieval trade, emerges even more clearly from numerous accounts of the commodities purchased by the Westerners. Surely, the spices, aromatics, and dyes still held first place. The Near Eastern countries still produced much sugar and precious textiles, which were eagerly bought by the European traders. According to the said Merchant Guide one bought in Damascus much Persian silk and silken stuff which came from Baghdad

[102] Amari, *I diplomi arabi*, pp. 243, 258, and cf. pp. 264, 281.

[103] Marino Sanuto, *Secreta fidelium crucis*, p. 24.

[104] *Notices et extraits* XI, p. 39; *Zibaldone da Canal*, pp. 66, 67 f.; Pegolotti, pp. 74, 90 f., 101 f.

[105] Pegolotti, pp. 72, 101 f.; MS. Marucelliana (Florence) C 226, quoted by Bautier, "Les relations," p. 318 f.; about the date of the work see p. 313.

[106] *Zibaldone da Canal*, pp. 61 f., 70; Pegolotti, pp. 59, 70, 77.

and Tebriz.[107] The superiority of Levantine sugar at the beginning of the fourteenth century is attested to by the orders given by the Venetian government in 1308 to the captain of the galleys going to Alexandria: he was to acquire as much caffetino sugar as possible for the use of the doctor in the new hospital for sailors in Venice.[108] The industries of Egypt and Syria were not yet ruined. However, the most striking feature of the Levant trade in that period is the continuous growth of the cotton export from Syria and from Egypt. The conquest of the Crusader towns on the Syro-Palestinian coast, their subsequent destruction, and the exodus of the Christian inhabitants meant the loss of a great market for their grains to the peasants of the neighboring provinces. Marino Sanuto rightly dwells on this phenomenon.[109] Consequently, many went over to cotton growing. The growth of the cotton plantations in some regions of Palestine must have been spectacular. Certainly cotton had been grown in the district of Acre before the town was conquered by the Mamluks,[110] but after its fall the plantations were considerably increased. The comparison of the chapters which refer to this part of Palestine in geographical treatises (*Descriptions of the Holy Land*) and travelogues of the period preceding and subsequent to it point clearly to this change.[111] Rules fixed by the Venetian authorities in 1293 for cotton export from the Levant refer to Egypt and Little Armenia, but not to the Palestinian coast.[112] Characteristically, even in the hundreds of notarial acts of Lamberto di Sambuceto, drawn up in Famagusta in 1300 and 1301, there is no mention of cotton export from Acre. The increase of the cotton plantations, however, was also a consequence of the general depopulation in the Near East. In Northern Mesopotamia and in Iraq the cotton plantations were also very greatly increased.[113] The cotton production of Syria and Palestine was mainly directed to export to Europe. A part of the crops served the local industry, but probably the largest amount was bought by the Italian merchants, mainly by the Venetians.[114] Even in Egypt the cotton plantations were increased during this period, to supply the demand of the foreign traders. The shipments of cotton arriving in the Italian ports from the Levant at the beginning of the fourteenth century

[107] *Secreta fidelium crucis*, p. 24; Davidsohn, *Geschichte von Florenz* IV, part 2, p. 73; Bautier l.c.

[108] G. Giomo, *Lettere di collegio*, no. 35 (I have corrected "cafecchi" to caffettino) and cf. no. 36; see my paper "Levantine sugar industry," p. 233 f.

[109] *Secreta fidelium crucis*, p. 26.

[110] *Zibaldone da Canal*, p. 63 f.

[111] See my "The Venetian cotton trade in Syria," p. 680 f.; "Le Proche Orient au bas Moyen Age, une région sous-développée," *Atti della X settimana di studi, Istituto Fr. Datini* (Florence, 1983), p. 395 f.

[112] *Deliberazioni del Maggior Consiglio* III, p. 337 f.

[113] See "Le Proche Orient une région sous-développée," l.c.

[114] See *Zibaldone da Canal*, p. 67; *Misti*, ed. Cessi, I, p. 130.

must already have been sizeable. In 1308 a Genoese galley captured ships of the Venetian firms Sanudo and Soranzo which were transporting more than 500 sacks of cotton.[115] The demand for cotton, the raw material for the flourishing fustian industry of Upper Italy, was undoubtedly very great. In 1295 the Venetian authorities were already taking measures to foster the importation of cotton from various Levantine countries.[116] Both Egypt and Syria also exported alkali needed for the soap and glass industries of Southern Europe. The Maggior Consiglio of Venice issued several decrees to foster this import trade.[117] However, the economy of the Near Eastern countries had not yet reached the stage of actual underdevelopment; the export of raw materials to European industries in the first half of the fourteenth century was still a minor branch of their foreign trade. Syria had certainly become much poorer after the downfall of the Crusader principalities, but Egypt's economy was still vigorous and its balance of trade and payments resulted in a surplus. The Mamluks ruling over Egypt were a class of rich feudals who could afford to buy luxury goods. The European merchants sold them precious stones.[118]

In the first years of the fourteenth century, Venetian trade with Egypt and Syria was rather lively. The Venetian merchants were engaged in all the branches of the Levant trade; they exported to Egypt victuals, such as honey[119] and several kinds of textiles. Information about the export of Venetian textiles and others of its products to Egypt and Syria can be found in the lists of presents sent by the sultan of Cairo to the kings of Spain when embassies were exchanged among these rulers. The present sent by al-Malik an-Nāṣir Muḥammad in 1300 to Fernando II of Castile comprised Venetian cloth;[120] that sent to King Jaime II of Aragon in 1306 consisted, among other articles, of "Venetian linen," perhaps linen of Reims or of Southern Germany bought from Venetians,[121] and the present an Egyptian ambassador brought to the king of Aragon in 1315 apparently comprised Murano glass.[122] Among the Oriental commodities exported by the Venetians, spices certainly ranked first, in terms of investment. But they also exported considerable quantities of flax from Egypt and cotton from Syria

[115] Giomo, *Lettere di collegio*, no. 44 (the provenance of the cotton is not clear from the text).

[116] *Deliberazioni del Maggior Consiglio* III, p. 389 and cf. p. 435 (of 1298).

[117] *Deliberazioni del Maggior Consiglio* III, pp. 398, 401; *Misti*, ed. Cessi, I, p. 129 (a. 1308); the records of the early fourteenth century mention mainly Egyptian alkali.

[118] *Sulūk* II, p. 103 f.

[119] *Cassiere della bolla ducale*, no. 400 (a. 1303).

[120] Alarcón, p. 344 ff.

[121] Atiya, *Egypt and Aragon*, p. 29 ff.

[122] Alarcón, p. 361, transl. p. 364 f. (The place of "bunduḳ" in the inventory, namely, after billawr kabīr thalātha, points to a glass product, whereas Alarcón believed that linen is meant.)

and Palestine.[123] The purpose of the embassy sent to the governor of Galilee in 1304 undoubtedly was to obtain better conditions for the cotton export from his province, where the cotton production had very much increased.[124] But the Venetians also exported other cheap commodities, like great shipments of Syrian and Egyptian alkali[125] and Egyptian salt.[126]

That the commercial exchanges between Venice and the dominions of the sultan in the period immediately following the fall of Acre were by no means insignificant is clearly shown by the numerous decrees of the Maggior Consiglio and the Senate that dated from those years. They point to the fact that it was a regular and continuous trade. Not only the professional merchants but also people belonging to other classes engaged in this trade and travelled to Egypt.[127] How great the value of the cargoes of the Venetian Alexandria galleys was, and consequently the importance the government of Venice attributed to the maintenance of regular trade with Egypt, is indicated in an order given in 1308 that warships should escort the galleys because of the danger of attacks by the Genoese. The number of the galleys, which went every year to Alexandria, was not insignificant either. In 1312 they numbered five.[128] Apparently it was in those years that certain rules concerning the service of the State galleys were finally fixed and others changed.[129] The main purpose of these rules was to keep a fixed schedule for the galleys, which every year at the end of summer sailed to Alexandria to ship home spices. Further, the Venetian authorities insisted that they should travel together.[130] There was also a galley traffic between Venice and Syria, but it was certainly much less regular. It was also ruled that the cogs should not load precious articles, neither gold, nor silver, nor foreign cloth.[131] In Egypt too the cogs were allowed to load only cheap commodities, such as flax, dates, and alkali.[132] The Syrian cotton was transported by cogs, which sailed to the Levant in February. They went to the so-called spring *mudda* (fair) held in March. Exceptionally it was extended to April or even to the first half of May.[133] Sometimes measures had to be taken for the transport of cotton which could not be loaded on the cogs

[123] ASV, Mag. Cons., Clericus Civicus, f. 29a (a. 1316); *Dipl. Ven.-Lev.* I, p. 8.

[124] *Dipl. Ven.-Lev.* I, no. 17.

[125] *Misti*, ed. Cessi, I, p. 104.

[126] *Cassiere della bolla ducale*, no. 217 (a. 1301); ASV, Mag. Cons., Capricornus, f. 5a (a. 1306), 34b (a. 1307).

[127] ASV, Mag. Cons., Clericus Civicus, f. 28b.

[128] Giomo, *Lettere di collegio*, nos. 43, 50; *Domenico, prete di S. Maurizio, notaio in Venezia (1309-1316)*, ed. Maria Fr. Tiepolo (Venice, 1970), p. 154 (act of 3 June 1312); see also below.

[129] *Misti*, ed. Cessi, I, p. 104 (a. 1303); ASV, Mag. Cons., Magnus, f. 68b (a. 1304), 95b (a. 1305).

[130] *Misti*, ed. Cessi, I, pp. 115, 116 (a. 1305), 122.

[131] *Op.cit.*, pp. 159, 264, 266, 285.

[132] *Op.cit.*, p. 129 (a. 1308).

[133] *Op.cit.*, pp. 106 (a. 1303), 122 (a. 1307).

because of lack of space.[134] The Venetians carried on trade with Egypt not only in Alexandria, but also in Damietta and Tinnīs.[135] In Syria, they visited the ports of Beirut and Latakia, and in the interior of the country, Damascus, Ḥamā, and Ramla.[136] The consulate in Alexandria, however, was vacant at the turn of the century; but from the time of the successful negotiations of the Venetian embassy with the sultan in 1302, there was a consul there,[137] and any time it was considered opportune an ambassador was sent to Cairo. In 1302 the ambassador Guido da Canal obtained an agreement from the sultan that the Venetians should have another fondaco, and that they should not pay any customs for gold, silver, and furs.[138] Another embassy went to the sultan in 1304,[139] while in 1317 the sultan sent presents to the doge and informed him that he had liberated Venetians imprisoned in Alexandria. Evidently there had been a conflict between the Venetians and the Mamluk authorities.[140] It goes without saying that from time to time there were such conflicts. In May 1309 the Venetian traders in Alexandria were ordered by the government of the metropolis to leave and to embark on two galleys despatched for this purpose.[141]

Meanwhile, the pressure brought upon the Venetian government by the Holy See was steadily increasing. It was urged that the trade with the dominions of the sultan be suspended altogether. In 1304 the government of Venice sent an embassy to the pope, asking him not to oppose the export of articles that were not war material and also to permit the purchase of the Oriental commodities.[142] Then, in 1317, the Venetians approached the papal legate, making it clear that the trade with the Moslem Levant was a vital interest of the republic. Two years later another embassy went to the

[134] *Op.cit.*, p. 130 (a. 1308).

[135] *Op.cit.*, p. 129 and cf. Pegolotti, p. 89 ff.

[136] Pegolotti, p. 90 f., 101 f.; *Misti*, ed. Cessi, I, p. 55.

[137] *Misti*, ed. Cessi, I, pp. 47 (1301), 111 (a. 1304); ASV, Mag. Cons., Magnus, f. 89b (a. 1305), Presbiter, f. 67a (a. 1312, but refers to an earlier period).

[138] See Heyd II, p. 38 and also *Misti*, ed. Cessi I, pp. 47, 53, 54 f., 58; *Dipl. Ven.-Lev.* I, no. 4 (Heyd believed that the text of this treaty had been lost); one of the paragraphs establishes that the Venetians should not pay "cuff and arss." These customs were certainly much higher than those paid by the Venetians; for many articles they amounted to almost 20 percent, see Cl. Cahen, "Douanes et commerce dans les ports méditerranéens de l'Egypte médiévale d'aprés le Minhādj d'al-Makhzūmī," *JESHO* VII (1964), p. 245. As to gold and silver, see Marino Sanuto, *Secreta fidelium crucis*, p. 24, according to whom the Europeans paid 3 1/2-4 1/2 percent. Further, the sultan offered a reward to the Venetians for the import of commodities whose sale to the Moslems was forbidden by the Church: they could invest the price in the purchase of any article and export it without paying customs. The request to have another fondaco refers apparently to a second one, as one learns from a document of the middle of the fourteenth century that the Venetians had two fondachi in Alexandria.

[139] See Heyd II, p. 39.

[140] *Libr. Com.* I, lib. 2, no. 75.

[141] Giomo, *Lettere di collegio*, no. 207.

[142] *Misti*, ed. Cessi, I, p. 109. In fact the Venetians sold to the Mamluks weapons, see *Dipl. Ven.-Lev.* I, nos. 9, 10 (of a. 1304).

pope to ask him to legalize the trade with Egypt and Syria, and especially to get permission for the export of precious metals, such as gold.[143]

In the first years of the fourteenth century, the volume of Venetian trade with Egypt and Syria must have been relatively great. In a decree of the Senate, dated 1306, convoys of three or more galleys to Alexandria are dealt with.[144] But certainly the galleys were then much smaller than those despatched to the Levant in the second half of the fourteenth and in the fifteenth centuries. A decree of the Senate, which dates to August 1308, establishes a maximal load of 225 sportas, each of 750 (light) Venetian pounds.[145] This was not much more than 50 t. The upkeep of the commercial exchanges with the dominions of the sultan was itself a great success. The pressure by the pope did not result in the abolition of the galley service. Even in the second decade of the fourteenth century, the Serenissima organized convoys of State galleys to Egypt and Syria.[146] New rules for the customs to be paid for the import of commodities bought in Egypt into Crete and Venice testify to the continuation of the commercial exchanges with this country even after 1308.[147]

Genoa's trade with the dominions of the Mamluks was different from that of the other trading nations, insofar as it was carried on along two major routes, one that connected the metropolis with Alexandria and the other connecting the Egyptian harbor and the Syrian ports with Constantinople and the emporia on the Black Sea, whence the slaves destined for the army of the sultan were brought. Several documents, such as some records of the inquiries made by the Catalan Treasury as to the trade with Egypt, refer to the activities carried on in that period on the latter route.[148] At the beginning of the fourteenth century the Genoese were still very much engaged in the supply of slaves to the sultan. An important Genoese trader, Segurano Salvaygo, was accused by an ecclesiastical writer of that period of having sold the Mamluks 10,000 slaves.[149] This is perhaps an exaggeration, but the same author's statement that the Genoese are the most active in this trade[150] was probably true. In fact they aroused not

[143] *Libr. Com.* I, lib. 2, nos. 64, 65; *Misti*, ed. Cessi, I, p. 200.

[144] *Misti*, ed. Cessi, I, p. 119.

[145] *Op.cit.*, p. 131 (it is not said there that the Alexandria galleys are meant, but there can be no doubt about it).

[146] *Op.cit.*, pp. 135, 138.

[147] ASV, Mag. Cons., Presbiter, f. 26a (a. 1310).

[148] Finke, *Acta Aragonensia*, no. 587, 2. Cf. A. Ehrenkreutz, "Strategic implications of the slave trade between Genoa and Mamluk Egypt in the second half of the thirteenth century," in *The Islamic Middle East, 700-1900, Studies in economic and social history*, ed. A. L. Udovitch (Princeton, 1981), p. 342.

[149] Guillaume Adam, *De modo Sarracenos extirpandi*, RHC Documents arméniens II, p. 525, 526.

[150] *Op.cit.*, p. 525.

only the anger of the Church, but also that of the Tatar rulers of the Golden Horde.[151] So the Venetians, whose position in the Black Sea area was much weaker and who could not compete with the Genoese, made a show of observing the papal prohibition of supplying slaves to the sultan of Cairo and sequestrated slave recruits transported by Genoese traders from Constantinople to Alexandria.[152] The Venetian government also congratulated the Knights of Rhodes upon their activities against the Christian merchants who supplied war material to the Moslems.[153] On the other hand, owing to their supremacy in the Levant trade and their good relations with the sultan, the Genoese, probably in that period, obtained the right to establish a consulate in Jerusalem for the protection of Christian pilgrims.[154] It goes without saying that Genoese traders also exported war material, iron, and weapons to the dominions of the sultan. In 1303 the pope authorized the archbishop of Genoa to grant absolution to twenty-two Genoese merchants who had been engaged in this trade.[155]

But the Genoese also imported cloth into Egypt and Syria in the first half of the fourteenth century. The same Segurano Salvaygo had first come to Egypt as an importer of cloth.[156] In the year 1312 Niccolò de Fossatello, a cloth merchant, left Genoa for Syria with scarlets of Brussels and cloth of Brussels and Malines.[157] In 1313 another merchant in Genoa received a commenda consisting of cloth of Châlons-sur-Marne to be sold in Syria.[158] A notarial act drawn up in Genoa in the same year refers to French (or Flemish) cloth, which Jacob de Nerona had received from Gabriel Spinola and which according to him had been confiscated by the Knights Hospitaliers in Rhodes.[159] In 1314 a certain Barnaba Bennus in Genoa received a commenda consisting of French cloth, worth perhaps 954 ducats, which he took with him to Syria.[160] A similar commenda, dating to the same year and received by Petronio, son of Januynus de Santo Lorenzo, consisted of a much smaller quantity.[161]

The spices were the most precious commodities the Genoese shipped

[151] See the text of an-Nuwayrī translated by M. d'Ohsson, *Histoire des Mongols* (The Hague, 1834-1835) IV, p. 757; on the Genoese slave trade see also *Libr. Com.* I, lib. 1, nos. 176, 183, 184, 187, 216, 217, 221.

[152] See Heyd II, p. 38 ff.

[153] Giomo, *Lettere di collegio*, no. 555 (a. 1310).

[154] W. Heyd, "Les consulats établis en Terre Sainte au Moyen Age," *AOL* II, p. 355 ff.

[155] Reg. Bénoit XI, no. 86.

[156] B. Z. Kedar, "Segurano-Šakrān Salvaygo: un mercante genovese al servizio dei sultani mamalucchi," in *Fatti e idee, Studi dedicati a Franco Borlandi* (Bologna, 1977), p. 79.

[157] Doehaerd, *Relations commerciales* III, no. 1753.

[158] *Op.cit.* III, no. 1809.

[159] *Op.cit.* III, no. 1813.

[160] *Op.cit.* III, no. 1820; for the value of the Genoese pound, see C. M. Cipolla, *I movimenti dei cambi in Italia dal secolo XIII al XV* (Pavia, 1948), p. 65.

[161] Doehaerd, *op.cit.* III, no. 1847.

from Egypt and Syria; they were certainly very active in this trade. A notarial act drawn up in Famagusta in 1300 refers to the spices Philippono de Nigro, a Genoese trader, had in Syria.[162] The same merchant exported, together with Baldo Spinola, galingale, Brazil-wood, frankincense, and sugar from Egypt.[163] But the Genoese also exported from the Moslem Levant cheap commodities, such as alkali from Syria.[164]

At the beginning of the fourteenth century, it was not only the leading commercial powers who carried on a regular trade with Egypt and Syria, but the smaller trading nations of Southern Europe did so, as well.

Although Venice did its best to exclude other towns of the Adriatic from the Levant trade, her success was never complete. The Serenissima claimed that having pacified the Adriatic (*nostro golfo*), she had the right to enjoy hegemony over it and to control its traffic. Ancona had to oblige herself, in a treaty concluded with Venice in 1264, that henceforth her ships would not carry the merchandise of foreigners to regions outside the Adriatic, or vice versa. This treaty was to prevent Ancona from becoming the port of Florence and an outlet for the industrial towns of Lombardy. It was a heavy blow to the thriving small town on the Adriatic coast. Ancona applied to the pope, her protector, but the lawyers appointed as arbitrators overruled her objections.[165] However, the Anconitans continued their activities in the Levantine ports, and, despite Venetian pressure, Ancona was always a market where spices and other Oriental commodities were offered. In that period, the merchants of Ancona visited the emporia of Egypt and Syria very often. A Catalan document of 1307 refers to the sale of a ship by a Catalan trader, Pere Broyl, to an Anconitan in Alexandria.[166] Merchant Guides dating to that time testify to the commercial relations between Alexandria and Ancona and to the fact that the latter town was well supplied with Oriental wares.[167]

Even the coastal towns of Apulia maintained relations with the Moslem Levant. The comparison made in the Merchant Guides of the weights employed in a Levantine port, such as Alexandria, with those of a town in Southern Italy certainly show that trade was carried on between them. In an anonymous Merchant Guide, undoubtedly compiled in Florence at the beginning of the fourteenth century, one finds a text of this kind. It points to the export of grain, olive oil, and cheese from Apulia to Egypt. Pegolotti compares the weights of Alexandria with those of Barletta.[168] It is true that

[162] Desimoni, *ROL* I, no. 255 and cf. no. 442 about his galley which is then in Syria.
[163] *Op.cit.*, no. 256.
[164] *Op.cit.*, no. 470 (a. 1300).
[165] R. Cessi, *La Repubblica di Venezia e il problema adriatico* (Naples, 1953), p. 67 ff.
[166] Masiá de Ros, no. 89.
[167] *Zibaldone da Canal*, p. 57; Pegolotti, pp. 74, 158; *Tarifa*, p. 39.
[168] Ms. Tordi 139, f. 7b; p. 73.

the supremacy the Venetians enjoyed in the economic life, and especially in the foreign trade, of Apulia became really crushing under the rule of the first Anjou. The French kings, who dreamed of conquering Constantinople with the help of the Venetian fleet, showered privileges upon the Venetians.[169] But the data in the work of Pegolotti leave no doubt that the direct trade between Apulia and the Moslem Levant was still lively.

The enterprising traders of Ragusa, on the other side of the Adriatic, did not lag behind those of the March of Ancona and Apulia. At the beginning of the fourteenth century even they were engaged in trade with the Moslem Levant. Ragusan merchants visited the ports of Egypt and Syria despite the papal prohibition. In 1304 the Holy See granted absolution to three Ragusan merchants who had engaged in trade in Alexandria. The stipulation that a sailor had included in a contract with a shipowner in 1342, namely, that he would not sail to Alexandria, points to the fact that seaborne traffic between Ragusa and Alexandria was not discontinued through the first half of the fourteenth century. But Ragusa was dependent on the good will of Venice and her activities had to be adapted to the schemes of the Serenissima. Part of the spices they brought from the Near East was destined for Venice or belonged to Venetian traders. Often the merchandise was loaded on Venetian ships when it arrived in Istria.[170]

Contradictory views have been expressed about the role that Naples and Sicily played in that period in the trade between Southern Europe and the realm of the sultan of Cairo. Some historians concluded that these parts of Italy at the end of the thirteenth century and in the first half of the fourteenth century became underdeveloped regions supplying grains, olive oil, and other agricultural products to the industrialized provinces of Northern Italy. According to these historians Naples and Sicily had altogether lost their share in the trade with the Levant and served only as ports of transshipment. A characteristic feature of the economic life of these regions was indeed the fact that the foreign trade was mainly in the hands of foreigners.[171] But this picture is distorted. Messina, Palermo, Naples, and other towns of Southern Italy were great emporia in that period, where spices and other Oriental commodities were continuously discharged or shipped to Northern Italy and Catalonia. A notarial act drawn up in Palermo

[169] G. Yver, *Le commerce et les marchands dans l'Italie méridionale au XIIIe et au XIVe siècles* (Paris, 1903), p. 248 ff.

[170] Krekić, no. 74, 206 and cf. introduction, p. 115 f.; ASV, Mag. Cons., Clericus Civicus, f. 36b (a. 1316); cf. Heyd II, p. 50, note 3.

[171] O. Caggese, *Roberto d'Angiò e i suoi tempi* (Florence, 1922-1930) I, p. 537; L. Gennardi, "Commercio e diritto marittimo in Napoli nei secoli XIII, XIV e XV," in *Studi di storia napoletana in onore di Michelangelo Schipa* (Naples 1926), p. 114 f. See, on the other hand, A. Petino, "Aspetti del commercio marittimo della Sicilia nell'età aragonese," *Bollettino Storico Catanese* 1/12 (1946-1947), pp. 64 ff., 74.

in 1299 refers to chartering a ship for the transport of spices to Pisa;[172] a similar contract made in Palermo in 1309 for the transport of various articles from Trapani and Palermo to Majorca and Barcelona contains the rates of freight to be paid for pepper, ginger, cinnamon, and sugar.[173] There are other data that point clearly to the commercial exchanges between Sicily and the Moslem Levant in that period. In a notarial act drawn up in Palermo in 1328, one finds the name of Percivallo de Alexandria.[174] So the comparison of the weights of Alexandria with those of Messina, Naples, and Salerno, which is found in the work of Pegolotti, served practical purposes.[175] To judge from the data given by the Florentine author, both Messina and Naples, at the beginning of the fourteenth century, were great markets for Oriental spices, drugs, and dyes and, on the other hand, exchanges for the precious kinds of cloth of France and Flanders, which were exported to the Levant to be bartered for the spices.[176] It is however beyond any doubt that the greatest part of the trade between these regions and the Moslem Levant was then in the hands of foreigners. Ever since the Anjou had lost Sicily to the Aragonese, the Catalans and other foreigners had the greatest share of the island's international trade, whereas the Florentines and, even more so, the Provençals dominated the foreign trade of Naples. But the Genoese and Pisans also took an active part in the trade between Naples and the Moslem Levant.[177]

The merchants of Marseilles enjoyed the privileged status of subjects of the House of Anjou, which ruled over Southern Italy. When the war between the Anjou and the king of Aragon came to its end, they once again took up their activities in the Eastern Mediterranean and traded with Egypt. A notarial act dating to 1303 relates to the travels some years earlier of two merchants of Marseilles to Alexandria.[178] Naples, where they had a flourishing colony, served the traders of Marseilles for their Mediterranean trade as a mainstay, an emporium where they supplied themselves with many commodities to be marketed in the Near East.[179]

The Levantine trade of the Catalans was apparently lively in that period. Both official and other documents contain valuable information about these

[172] R. Zeno, *Documenti per la storia del diritto marittimo nei secoli XIII e XIV*, no. XLIX.

[173] *Op.cit.*, no CLII.

[174] ASPal, Notai, 77, Giacomo di Citella, f. 27b. Also, the mention of Greeks who lived in the towns of Sicily points to the fact that seaborne trade of Sicily with the Levant was still lively in that period; see in the acts of the same notary f. 28a, 99a; ASPal, Notai 79, Enrico di Citella, f. 170b.

[175] Pp. 72 f., 74. Pegolotti also compares the weights of Naples with those of Damietta, see p. 188.

[176] Pp. 109, 110, 111, 179, 180.

[177] G. Yver, *op.cit.*, p. 146 ff.

[178] Baratier, p. 209.

[179] *Libr. Com.* I, lib. 1, no. 221.

commercial exchanges, showing that through this period they were never discontinued altogether. Letters of the town council of Barcelona in 1301-1302 to the Moslem authorities of Alexandria and to the Catalan consul in the Egyptian port refer to the activities carried on there fifteen years before by Guillem de Banyoles. Another letter of the town council, of the same year, is addressed to the Count of Ampurias which had sequestered the goods of a merchant coming from the Levant.[180] A royal decree of 1315 deals with certain dues imposed upon ships arriving from overseas; those coming from the Near East had to pay the highest rate.[181] Much more interesting than the documents we have quoted so far are the records of the royal magistrates who had to collect the fines from the traders for having travelled to Egypt and Syria when trade with these countries had been forbidden. They contain many data about Catalan trade with the Moslem Levant at the beginning of the fourteenth century. The magistrates also made inquiries into the activities of merchants who had already died, such as the Jewish merchant Isaac Vives, who had given several commenda for travels to Alexandria and had been very rich. The judicial authorities made a very thorough inquiry in this case. Records of 1308 refer to traders who had exported cuirasses and weapons to the dominions of the sultan and to a citizen of Barcelona who had shipped meat from Sicily to Alexandria.[182] Some responsa (juridical decisions) of Solomon b. Adereth, rabbi in Barcelona (d. 1310), have a bearing on travels of Jewish merchants to regions "overseas." This was the term usually used in Catalonia for the Levant, and certainly it can be assumed that in these responsa such travels were meant, at least for the most part.[183] The Catalans also engaged in trade between Egypt and other countries of North Africa and were already transporting Moslem traders and their merchandise in this period. From the requests made by King Jaime II to the Ḥafṣid ruler of Tunisia and Libya in 1307, we learn that the ship of Bernat Marquet, citizen of Barcelona, had been robbed in Tripoli of its cargo belonging to Christian and Moslem merchants.[184]

Several embassies sent by King Jaime II to the sultan of Cairo and the negotiations that resulted from them had essentially other purposes than commercial exchanges. The king of Aragon, continuing the policy of the Swabian dynasty, assumed the role of the protector of Christianity in the Moslem Levant and fulfilled this task by means of peaceful interventions at the court of the sultan. His ambassadors intervened on behalf of the

[180] Capmany, 2.1, nos. 66-68, pp. 98-100.
[181] *Op.cit.*, no. 97, p.140.
[182] Finke, *Acta Aragonensia*, no. 587.
[183] See *Responsa* I, no. 924, 930.
[184] Capmany 1, p. 744; 2.1, no. 79, pp. 112-114. In the text there is no date of the incident, contrary to what Capmany says.

Christian subjects of the sultan, asking they be granted freedom of worship, requesting the sultan to allow pilgrims to visit Jerusalem and other holy places, that the custody and administration of the Church of the Holy Sepulchre in Jerusalem be left in the hands of the Catholic clergy, and finally that European Christians, knights, and others, who were prisoners of the Mamluks, be liberated. But sometimes the problems connected with commercial exchanges were raised. The letter despatched in April 1300 by al-Malik an-Nāṣir Muḥammad to King Jaime II contains the promise that the Catalan merchants would enjoy security in the dominions of the sultan.[185] In 1303 King Jaime II sent Eymerich Dusay as ambassador to Cairo and, among other requests, he was to demand the restitution, by the custom authorities of Alexandria, of 12,000 dinars due to merchants of Barcelona.[186] When Eymerich Dusay went a second time as ambassador to Cairo in 1305, he was not to deal with questions of the Catalan trade.[187] However, in a letter he wrote from Sicily, where he had remained fearing to return to Catalonia, he mentioned that in the negotiations in Cairo the sultan had demanded that the king of Aragon should not forbid Christian merchants to export timber and iron to his dominions.[188] Neither did the Catalan ambassadors who visited the sultan in 1315, 1318 and 1323 deal with the commercial exchanges. But when in 1327 the Catalan ambassador Pere de Mijavilla came to Cairo and laid before the sultan the usual requests of his king, the Mamluk ruler found it necessary to raise the question of the trade between the two states. In his reply to King Jaime II the sultan said that he would be ready to comply with the King's requests, such as sending him the bones of Saint-Barbara, if he would order ships with "plenty of merchandise" to sail to Egypt.[189]

All these embassies were linked to commercial activities. Usually before sending an embassy, the king of Aragon applied to the pope, with the request that merchants with their merchandise be permitted to sail together

[185] Atiya, *Egypt and Aragon*, p. 17 ff.

[186] *Op.cit.*, p. 20 ff.

[187] Atiya, *op.cit.*, p. 28 says that the sultan's answer to the requests of the king included the promise that henceforth the governor of Alexandria would have orders to see to the security of the Catalan merchants and the subjects of the Crown of Aragon, but the Arabic original has *zuwwār*, which means pilgrims, see Alarcón, p. 356. Even Atiya's interpretation of al-Maḳrīzī's account of the measures taken by the sultan, when Dusay had expelled the Egyptian ambassador from the ship sailing to Catalonia, is not accurate. Atiya says, p. 33, that thereupon the Catalan subjects in Alexandria were arrested and their goods sequestrated. But, according to al-Maḳrīzī, orders were given only to arrest all the Catalans who would arrive in the future; see *Sulūk* I, p. 950 f. and transl. Quatremère, *Histoire* II, part 2, p. 229 f., and cf. Giunta, *Aragonesi* II, p. 108.

[188] Finke, *Acta Aragonensia* II, no. 461. Atiya, p. 27, says that this demand belonged to the draft of a treaty proposed by the sultan, but this is not said in the letter of Dusay.

[189] Alarcón, p. 368 ff. (where the translation is wrong).

with the ambassadors.[190] In the year 1322 the king asked the pope to allow him to despatch two ships with his embassy, claiming that he was sending the sultan many gifts and that it would also be dangerous to let the embassy travel on one ship.[191] The owners of the ships on which the ambassadors embarked and the ambassadors themselves were merchants. Others had to pay the king for the right to travel on an ambassadorial ship. So the embassies were not only diplomatic missions; they were also commercial and it was not only merchants who took part in the trade with the Moslems that was carried on upon arrival in Egypt. When in 1305 Eymerich Dusay departed on his ship for Alexandria, the king made an agreement with nineteen merchants who actually called on it and with others who only loaded merchandise. For permission to travel on the ship or to load merchandise they paid his treasurer Pedro Boyl 11,000 shillings, which were probably worth 600 fl.[192] But the king did not content himself with this relatively small sum. He himself invested money in the expeditions for the purchase of spices to be sold later.[193] He did not forget his worldly interests. The documents concerning the embassy in 1327 are particularly illustrative of the true character of these embassies. The Catalan ambassador Pere de Mijavilla was himself a merchant, engaged in trade with the Moslem Levant.[194] He travelled to Aigues-Mortes and there joined Guillaume de Bonnesmains, who set out to Cairo as ambassador of the king of France. The French ambassador, himself interested in trade with the Moslems, had already obtained papal permission to take merchandise with him. Then he and Pere de Mijavilla made a contract with a Catalan shipowner and merchant, Francisco Bastide, who undertook to sail to Alexandria. He was a veteran Levant trader and in 1307 had obtained absolution from the king for trade carried on in Egypt together with his brothers.[195] The king of Aragon allowed him, his two brothers, and the ambassador to load merchandise for a modest payment of 3,000 shillings, claiming that it was destined for two monasteries.[196] The Catalan and the French ambassadors, the latter accompanied by other French merchants, had silver ingots with

[190] Finke, *Acta Aragonensia* II, no. 468; Fernandez de Navarrete, p. 184 f. (a. 1317). In 1321 the pope, however, insisted that the merchants should take an oath before the bishop of the town where they loaded their merchandise, to make sure that it was not war material, see *op.cit.*, p. 185 f.

[191] Capmany, 2.1, no. 114, pp. 172-73.

[192] Fernandez de Navarrete, p. 182 ff. where the names of the merchants are given; cf. on the exchange rate of the pound of Barcelona Ch. E. Dufourcq, *L'Espagne catalane et le Maghreb aux XIIIe et XIVe siècles* (Paris, 1966), p. 530; see also Giunta, *Aragonesi* I, p. 116 (who counts twenty-three merchants).

[193] Masiá de Ros, no. 109 (unfortunately without date, and cf. Giunta, *op.cit.* I, p. 122).

[194] See below.

[195] Masiá de Ros, no. 85, 86; cf. Giunta, *op.cit.* I, pl. 116.

[196] Fernandez de Navarrete, p. 186 ff.

them, and a large number of falcons which they wanted to sell to the sultan and to other high ranking persons. They also took slaves with them despite the Church prohibition against selling slaves to the Moslems.[197]

The Catalan merchantmen sailed to Alexandria from Palermo, Candia, and other ports. Catalan trade with the dominions of the sultan was carried on not only along the Barcelona-Alexandria axis (with supplementary lines, such as Majorca-Alexandria), but also between the Greek territories and Egypt, as did, for instance, Berenguer de Moya, whose ship was seized on its return from Alexandria by the emperor of Constantinople in (about) 1308. In the formerly Byzantine territories and in Constantinople the Catalans carried on a lively trade, which served them to a certain extent as an alternative to the trade with the Moslem Levant.[198] But the commercial exchanges which they carried on with the Moslem Levant were still intense. Even the sailors bought spices and sold them in Barcelona.[199]

The accounts of the fines received by the royal treasury from merchants, who had been engaged in trade with the dominions of the sultan, are another interesting source, which sheds light on the volume of these exchanges. But these can be considered as referring to a small part of the Catalan-Mamluk trade only. What they show are its fluctuations. From the documents published by Masiá de Ros, the Sicilian historian F. Giunta has summed up the following data:[200]

Table I Catalan trade with the Mamluk dominions at the beginning of the XIVth century

1305	1653 fl.	1311	105 fl.	1321	1838 fl.
1306	833 "	1312	1278 "	1322	653 "
1307	1322 "	1313 - 1316	-	1323	22 "
1308	161 "	1317	447 "	1324 - 1325	-
1309	555 "	1318	461 "	1326	122 "
1310	-	1319 - 1320	-	1327	312 "

These figures clearly point to the fact that Catalan trade with Egypt and Syria was very irregular in that period. If the royal exchequer in some

[197] See the documents referring to the litigation between the two ambassadors and its sequel in the paper of H. Lot, "Essai d' intervention de Charles le Bel en faveur des Chrétiens d'Orient," *Bibl. Ecole des chart.* 36 (1875), p. 588 ff.

[198] Rubió i Lluch, *Diplomatari*, no. 410; AHPB, Pere de Torre V, 2, f. 106a, 108b, 109b, 110b (a. 1316).

[199] *Libros de tesoreria de la Casa real de Aragón*, ed. E. Gonzalez Hurtebise, I: *Reinado de Jaime II* (Barcelona, 1911), nos. 411, 413.

[200] Masiá de Ros, 133 ff. docs. 75-100; *Aragonesi* II, p. 119, where the figures are given in pounds of Barcelona. Here they are converted into florins.

years did not collect any fines, this cannot have been only the result of its inefficiency and of the cunning of the merchants. In any case, the volume of the commercial exchanges between Catalonia and the dominions of the sultan at the beginning of the fourteenth century cannot have been very small. In 1317 three ships sailed from Barcelona to the Levant, in 1321 five, in 1322 four, in 1329 only two, and in 1333 three. In some records of the royal administration, dating to 1305-1327, the names of not less than 163 merchants who visited Egypt and Syria are mentioned. One of them had travelled there three times, and eight had done so twice. Most of them went to the dominions of the sultan via Sicily and Cyprus. But some came to Alexandria from Naples, Marseilles, or Aigues-Mortes. Others arrived in Egypt from the Greek islands. Not all of them came to Egypt on Catalan ships; some had embarked on Genoese ships.[201]

In addition to Catalonia's Levant trade, there must also have been commercial exchanges between Castile and Egypt, although they certainly were rather casual. As has already been mentioned, the treaty of 1292 between the king of Aragon and the sultan was also made on behalf of the king of Castile. Then in 1300 Sultan al-Malik an-Nāṣir Muḥammad sent two ambassadors to the king of Castile Fernando IV, promising the king's merchants freedom of trade in his dominions. Among the gifts he sent to the Spanish king was Venetian cloth.[202]

As to the commodities the Catalan (and other Spanish) merchants exported to the Near East, some conclusions can be drawn from the presents that the ambassadors of the king of Aragon brought to the sultan. Certainly these were the articles the Catalans could offer and that were most in demand and most appreciated in the Near East. In 1314 the Catalan embassy brought the sultan, among various other things, colored cloth of Châlons-sur-Marne and Reims linen.[203] The embassy that went to Cairo in 1322 offered the sultan cloth of Douai, Ypres, and Châlons-sur-Marne and again linen of Reims.[204] This is convincing evidence that the inhabitants of Egypt and Syria, at least those belonging to the higher strata of society, were then already much interested in having textiles of Flanders and France. It is likely that the Catalan traders had been regularly exporting them to Egypt and Syria.

Although numerous documents show that at the beginning of the fourteenth century the commercial activities of the South European traders in Egypt and Syria were not discontinued, there cannot be the slightest doubt that their volume diminished, because of the strong opposition of the pa-

[201] See Masiá de Ros, p. 130 f.; Giunta, *op.cit.* I, p. 120.

[202] Alarcónino. 146. Of course one cannot be sure that it was not cloth bought from the Venetians.

[203] A. Capmany, *Antiguos tratados de paces y alianzas* (Madrid, 1786), p. 32 f.; cf. *Memorias* 2.1, no. 90, pp. 132-33.

[204] Capmany, *Antiguos tratados*, p. 34 f.

pacy. A document of 1335 indicates that for a long while the sultan had been paying every shipowner who obtained a papal license and went to Egypt 3,000 dinars.[205] One must not accept this assertion as absolutely reliable, but it shows that the sultan rendered him the sum he had spent and even more for obtaining the license. Surely many devout Christian merchants abstained from visiting the ports of Egypt and Syria or from investing money in trade with these countries.[206] On the other hand, Oriental commodities were much in demand in the Western world, so that the merchants had to find alternative channels for obtaining them. Consequently the major towns of Crete, Cyprus, and the Armenian kingdom of Cilicia, the Christian outposts in the Eastern Mediterranean, became flourishing emporia where all the Oriental articles could be obtained without visiting the dominions of the sultan. These towns were indeed always in close touch with Egypt and Syria, and the more so when many inhabitants of the former Crusader towns in Syria and in Palestine had settled there.[207] What was more natural, then, that they engaged in trade with the country from which they came and which they knew very well?

Even before the fall of Acre, Candia served as a port of transshipment for Oriental spices and for industrial and other products of European countries exported to the Levant. At the beginning of the fourteenth century this traffic increased very significantly. So the role of Crete as a base of European trade with the Moslem Levant should not be underestimated. Notarial acts drawn up in Candia at the beginning of the fourteenth century refer to the founding of companies for trade with Egypt,[208] and numerous commenda contracts were made for the export of various articles to Egypt without mentioning the final destination by name.[209] However, in some cases there could be no doubt about where the traffic was going.[210] How intense the traffic between Crete and Egypt was can be learned from some contracts made in Candia dated the end of August and the first half of September 1301: not less than two galleys and a cog sailing to Alexandria and other ports of the Moslem Levant are mentioned.[211] At the beginning of the fourteenth century Crete was already a great spice market. Payments

[205] Lot, "Essai d'intervention," *Bibl. Ec. des chart.* 36, p. 596.

[206] See *Benvenuto de Brixano*, no. 437 (a. 1301).

[207] On people of Acre in Famagusta, see Desimoni nos. 224, 255, 265, 292, 295, 298, 308 etc., and cf. D. Jacoby, "L'expansion occidentale dans le Levant: les Vénitiens à Acre dans la seconde moitié du treizième siècle," *Journal of Medieval History* III (1977), pp. 240 f., 243 f., 249; former inhabitants of Tripoli: Desimoni no. 335; of Beirut: nos. 211, 316, 384; of Tortosa (Anṭarṭūs): nos. 254, 298, 349, 374; of Tyre: nos. 295, 340; of Sidon: nos. 254, 264, 374; of Gibelet (Djubayl): nos. 400, 430; of Antioch: no. 410.

[208] *Benvenuto de Brixano*, no. 306 (a. 1301).

[209] *Op.cit.*, nos. 110, 189, 194, 209, 374, 462, 463, 476, 481, 520, 555.

[210] *Op.cit.*, no. 353.

[211] *Op.cit.*, nos. 307, 352, 354.

were made in pepper,[212] and great quantities of spices were shipped to Venice.[213] Not only Venetian merchants but Genoese[214] and Anconitans lived in the main towns of Crete and were engaged in the export of olive oil and other agricultural products of the island as well as in the slave trade.[215] There were also Catalans who marketed the agricultural and industrial products of their country.[216] Whereas the merchants of Cyprus traded mainly with Syria, those of Crete were in close touch with Alexandria and other ports of Egypt.[217]

In addition to Crete, Cyprus also played a great role in the trade with the Moslem Levant. Even in this period it was a very important base of the European Levant traders. The number of Western traders who lived in Famagusta or visited the town periodically must have been very great. In addition to Genoese, Venetians, Florentines, and Pisans,[218] there were many Anconitans who sent cotton to their home town in their own ships,[219] and there was also a great number of Sicilians, from Messina,[220] Syracuse,[221] Palermo,[222] and Trapani.[223] The traffic between Cyprus and the ports of Sicily was certainly intense.[224] There were also Amalfitan merchants[225] and even ships of Naples anchored in the ports of Cyprus.[226] The number of merchants of Narbonne must have been substantial, since the will of one of them drawn up in Famagusta in 1300 bears the names of thirteen witnesses who were natives of his town. Famagusta was also visited by traders and ships of Marseilles.[227] The firm Scotti and Borrini of Piacenza carried on trade between Famagusta, Lajazzo, and Marseilles.[228] The Catalans were represented by merchants of Barcelona, Tarrega, and Majorca.[229] On the other hand, one learns from an Arabic source that Cypriots lived in Beirut,

212 *Op.cit.*, nos. 233, 382.
213 *Op.cit.*, no. 131.
214 The Genoese also had a consulate in Candia; see *Libr. Com.* I, lib. 1, no. 183.
215 *Benvenuto de Brixano*, nos. 215, 280, 329; Pegolotti, p. 105. Pizolo, no. 594.
216 Capmany, 1, pp. 260-61.
217 *Libr. Com.* I, lib. 1, no. 22L. Pizolo, nos. 25, 73.
218 See Desimoni, no. 302, about the firm Agliati.
219 *Op.cit.*, no. 274; an Anconitan ship see also nos. 376, 377. On the cotton trade of the Anconitans in Famagusta see also no. 372.
220 *Op.cit.*, nos. 238, 253, 257, 266, 283, 284, 318, 324 (a ship of Messina), 374.
221 *Op.cit.*, nos. 241, 378 (*Saragossa* does not refer to the capital of Aragon, as Heyd believes II, p. 8, but to Syracuse).
222 *Op.cit.*, nos. 394, 395.
223 *Op.cit.*, no. 170.
224 See *op.cit.*, no. 338: a shipowner of Syracuse leases his ship to a trader of Messina.
225 *Op.cit.*, nos. 208, 209, 243, 332, 338, 384.
226 *Op.cit.*, no. 242.
227 *Op.cit.*, nos. 73, 457.
228 See Heyd II, p. 8, note 1; Desimoni, no. 429; Baratier, p. 212, and cf. C. Desimoni, "Documents relatifs aux Plaisançais," *AOL* II (1884), p. 208 ff., on the activities of the merchants of this town in the Crusader principalities.
229 See Heyd I, *l.c.* (I believe that his mention of traders of Saragossa is a misinterpretation.)

had there their storehouses, and transported merchandise on their ships to Cyprus.[230]

The long chapter in Pegolotti's work which deals with the trade of Cyprus convinces us most persuasively that the island served as a reloading point for many shipments of Southern and Western European products, various kinds of cloth being the most important. Certainly the great variety of Flemish, French, Catalan, and Italian cloth, to which many notarial documents of Famagusta refer, could not be absorbed by Cyprus alone, so that undoubtedly a large part of it was shipped to Syria and Egypt. The products of Cyprus itself had a great market in many European countries. Its sugar was exported to Genoa,[231] its cotton and salt to Venice[232] and Ancona,[233] its wheat to Little Armenia[234] and elsewhere, and its camlets had a great market both in the Near Eastern and Western countries. But, in addition, the European merchants shipped from Cyprus to the West the spices of the Far East, the cotton of Syria, and many other commodities that otherwise could not have been obtained without visiting the dominions of the sultan. Several notarial acts that have come down to us from that period show how Cyprus had become a great center for the distribution of Eastern goods and how intense the traffic was between it and the ports of Syria. A Venetian judicial act refers to the purchase of pepper in Famagusta in the 1330's.[235] Many of the Italian, French, and Catalan ships coming to Cyprus continued their travels to the ports of Syria; Syrian boats came over to Cyprus, and ships of Cypriots commuted between the island and the Syrian coast. So there is good reason to believe that much of the sugar and cotton exported from Cyprus had in fact been brought there from Syria or Egypt. There are quite a few documents that bear out this assumption, and others explicitly refer to trade between Cyprus and Syria.

The acts of Lamberto di Sambuceto, notary of Famagusta, which have come down to us from the years 1299 to 1301, comprise five commendas given on October 7, 1300, by Syrian Christians, consisting of spun cotton and amounting to 2,920 dinars. The merchandise was to be sold either in Apulia or in Venice. The merchants who gave them were of Latakia and Beirut.[236] The same Syrian Christians also export cotton to Ancona, giving commendas to Anconitan merchants.[237] So Syrian Christians came over to Cyprus and exported the cotton of their country from there. Sometimes,

[230] Ṣāliḥ b. Yaḥyā, *Ta'rīkh Bayrūt*, p. 39.
[231] Desimoni, nos. 41, 42, 60, 99, 101, 462.
[232] ASV, Mag. Cons., Magnus, f. 13a, 21a; Capricornus, f. 34b; Clericus Civicus, f. 135b.
[233] Desimoni, no. 376.
[234] *Op.cit.*, nos. 62, 106, 155, 206, 410, 414, 424, 440, 455.
[235] G. P., *Sent. Int.* V, f. 60b.
[236] *Op.cit.*, nos. 340-344.
[237] *Op.cit.*, nos. 349, 362, 366.

in years of scarcity, the Italian merchants exported grains to Syria. In April 1300 a Catalan shipowner leased his ship "San Salvator" in Famagusta to the agents of the Bardi Company and to those of another Florentine firm, the Bartoli, to transport wheat from Apulia to Cyprus and from there to Little Armenia or Syria, to Tripoli or Anṭarṭūs.[238] Because of the prohibition of trade with the Moslem Levant, many contracts were purposely styled in an ambiguous way. In June 1300 two Catalans received in Famagusta a sea loan for travel on their ship "to Candelor or to Syria." The document reads as follows: "in aliqua parte sive loca qui tenentur per cristianos." But the two merchants who received the loan were also allowed to travel to Tripoli in North Africa or to Cagliari.[239] As the Christians no longer held any ports in Syria, this contract meant making a mockery of the papal prohibition on trade with the dominions of the Mamluks. A commenda given in Famagusta in November 1300 by a Genoese trader is destined for trade in Armenia and Syria "excepto si esset inhibita" (except in the case of a general prohibition of trade).[240] In other contracts, there is no such limitation. A Venetian receives a loan to be repaid after his arrival in Tyre.[241] Genoese merchants travel to Syrian ports, like Anṭarṭūs, and from there export alkali.[242] This latter town (called Tortosa by the Christians) and the island of Arwad, opposite it, however, were in the possession of the Templars from 1300 to 1302.[243] But there can be little doubt that contracts made in this elusive style were not meant to restrict the receivers of the commendas to those ports temporarily held by the Christians. Several commenda contracts simply indicate "Syria" as the destination of the voyage.[244] However, there remain many contracts of commenda and other transactions where the goal of the journey is not indicated at all. Certainly more than a few of them were made for trade with the dominions of the sultan. The true goal of many ships had to be concealed, because the merchandise consisted of weapons and war material. Even in the years

[238] *Op.cit.*, no. 109.

[239] *Op.cit.*, no. 143.

[240] *Op.cit.*, no. 391.

[241] *Op.cit.*, no. 158.

[242] *Op.cit.*, no. 470. Other commendas given to Genoese and Ligurians for trade in Anṭarṭūs, see nos. 474, 479, 487 (Anṭarṭūs is mentioned in only one of these contracts, but since all of them are given by the same merchant it is clear that this Syrian port was the goal of the travels).

[243] A. Trudon des Ornes, "Liste des maisons du Temple . . . en Syrie, en Chypre et en France," *ROL* V (1897), p. 426 ff. Arwad was much longer held, and it was often confounded by the Europeans with the coastal town opposite to it.

[244] Desimoni, no. 485. A contract made on 25 February 1300, by the shipowner Pietro Rubeo and the Templar Pietro de Vares, *op.cit.*, no. 74, had apparently no commercial purpose. The shipowner undertakes to sail to Anṭarṭūs, Tripoli, Tyre, and Acre, to load and to unload "ad voluntatem tuam seu dicti domus (the order of the Templars) . . . equos et omnia onusta in dicta nave." This may have been a contract for the equipment of military activities.

immediately subsequent to the fall of Acre, trade with Syria continued and former inhabitants of Acre were not the last in exporting these commodities to Syria and Egypt. In 1301 the pope gave orders to the ecclesiastical authorities of Cyprus to grant absolution to Vivian de Gennibaldi, a former inhabitant of Acre, who had been engaged in the export of weapons to Egypt.[245] At any rate, the numerous commercial contracts drawn up in Famagusta leave no doubt as to the intensity of trade between Cyprus and Syria.

According to reports of the Arabic historians the coastal towns of Syria and Palestine had been destroyed after the conquest by the Mamluks in 1291: Acre, Tyre, Sidon, Beirut, and Djubail would have been razed altogether.[246] The documents quoted above prove that the destruction cannot have been total, and this is supported by some travelogues of the first half of the fourteenth century. William of Boldensele, who visited the Syro-Palestinian coast in 1332-1333, says that both Tyre and Acre were destroyed and that the port of the latter town was partly choked up by the remnants of the fallen buildings. Giacomo of Verona, who visited Palestine and Southern Syria in 1335, reported that Tyre was uninhabited, whereas Acre was ruined and only few Moslems lived there. But in Beirut he found a ship on which he embarked for Italy, so this town served as a terminus for the European ships. Ludolf of Suchem, who travelled in the Near East in 1336-1341, recounted that many poor lived in the ruined and destroyed houses of Acre. Further, according to him, there were some Jews and a garrison in the town. An anonymous Englishman, who came to Palestine in 1345, said that he found Acre in ruins. Niccolò da Poggibonsi, a Franciscan who made the pilgrimage to the Holy Places and sojourned in Palestine in 1346-1350, narrated that Acre had only a few inhabitants and that the Moslems had filled up the port, so that it could no longer be used.[247] These accounts are one-sided reports of Western travellers who bewailed the vanished splendor of the Crusader principalities. But even they show clearly that the former Christian ports were not altogether uninhabited. The fact that in addition to the account of the trade of Acre in the period of Christian rule that Pegolotti includes in his book a chapter on conditions of trade in the town after its conquest by the Moslems shows that at the beginning of the fourteenth century it continued to have some commercial traffic. Undoubtedly, some years after the fall of this last stronghold of the Chris-

[245] J. Richard, "Isol le Pisan," *Central Asiatic Journal* 14 (1970), p. 191 ff.

[246] G.Weil IV, p. 181.

[247] Travelogue of William of Boldensele in *Zeitschrift des historischen Vereins für Niedersachsen* 1852, pp. 242, 243; *Liber peregrinationis di Jacopo da Verona*, ed. U. Monneret de Villard (Rome, 1950), pp. 142, 143, 144; Ludolf de Suchem, *De itinere Terrae Sanctae*, in *AOL* II, p. 340; E. Hoade, *Western pilgrims* (Jerusalem, 1952), p. 62; Niccolò da Poggibonsi, *Libro d'oltramare*, ed. Bagatti (Jerusalem, 1945), p. 80.

tians in Syria and Palestine the ships of the South European trading nations again began to visit it and also to anchor in the ports of other towns on the Syro-Palestinian coast. In the first decades of the fourteenth century Acre was already an important port for the export of cotton.[248] At that time Anṭarṭūs was a point of support for the Mamluk fleet, and a former church had become a large storehouse.[249]

However, the Europeans must have felt insecure in Syria. A clear proof of the change is the modification of the commenda contracts. Studying the commendas in the acts of Leonardo Marcello, notary in Candia in the late 70's and the beginning of the 80's of the thirteenth century, one sees that the travelling merchant's share in the profit was a third or even a half.[250] The commenda contracts drawn up by Lamberto de Sambuceto in 1300 and in 1301 in Famagusta allowed the travelling merchant only a quarter of the profit. So the investors had become more apprehensive.

The role of the kingdom of Little Armenia as intermediary in the commercial exchanges between the Moslem Levant and Southern Europe in that period was even greater than that of Crete and of Cyprus. Lajazzo, where most of the kingdom's international trade was concentrated, had become the terminal of a very important trade route connecting it via Sivas and Erzindjan with Tebriz, from whence spices and other products of Persia and the Far East arrived.[251] On the other hand, Syrians and merchants of other Near Eastern countries offered spices, sugar, cotton, and many other commodities there.[252] The export of cotton from Lajazzo was certainly an extensive trade. It was exported to Venice,[253] by merchants of Narbonne to Southern France,[254] and by Florentines to various provinces of Italy.[255] Most of the cotton was certainly Syrian.[256] According to Venetian records, a merchant complained before the authorities of the Republic that in 1298 he had loaded cotton of Aleppo and ginger in Lajazzo to ship these commodities to Famagusta and that they were robbed by Genoese.[257] A con-

[248] Pegolotti, p. 69.

[249] E. G. Rey, "Les périples des côtes de Syrie et de la Petite Arménie," *AOL* II, p. 337.

[250] *Leonardo Marcello, notaio in Candia, 1278-1281*, ed. M. Chiaudano-A. Lombardi (Venice 1960), 1/3: nos. 37, 47, 57, 128, 145, 170, 171, 236, 535, 556; 1/2: nos. 55, 97, 129, 228, 241, 274, 355, 398, 495.

[251] See Heyd II, p. 113 ff.; E. Friedmann, *Der mittelalterliche Welthandel von Florenz in seiner geographischen Ausdehnung* (Abhdl. der K. K. Geogr. Gesellschaft in Wien X, no. 1, Vienna 1912), p. 38 ff. and see Pegolotti, p. 63; *Zibaldone da Canal*, p. 110: comparison of weights of Lajazzo and Sivas.

[252] *Felice de Merlis, prete e notaio in Venezia ed Ayas*, ed. A. Bondi Sabellico (Venice, 1973), no. 1316 (a. 1317): a merchant of Tripoli in Lajazzo.

[253] Pegolotti, p. 61; *Felice de Merlis*, no. 83 (a. 1317).

[254] Desimoni, no. 314.

[255] Davidsohn, *Geschichte von Florenz* IV, part 2, p. 263.

[256] Desimoni, no. 401.

[257] *Libr. Com.* I, lib. 1, no. 298.

siderable part of the great quantities of cloth imported into Little Armenia by Italian and other traders from Lombardy, France, and Flanders was certainly re-exported to Syria and other Levantine countries.[258] So there can be little doubt that the trade route of the Italian merchant republics with Little Armenia was a major artery of international trade in the Mediterranean at the beginning of the fourteenth century. The Venetian State line of galleys to Cyprus and Little Armenia then consisted of six ships a year on the average.[259] In 1301 the value of the merchandise the galleys transported to Lajazzo amounted to 90,000 ducats. But in addition other Venetian galleys and cogs visited Lajazzo every year.[260] The Venetian colony in Lajazzo was headed by a bailo, but it was not rare for the interests of the Venetian merchants to be represented by embassies to the king of Armenia. In 1306 an Armenian ambassador came to Venice.[261] The exchange of embassies resulted in concessions by the king. In 1307 and in 1310 the Venetians received new privileges, and in 1317 another embassy of Venice visited the king.[262] The Venetians held the lead in the trade between Southern Europe and Little Armenia, whereas the Genoese ranked first among the trading nations in Cyprus.[263]

c. Strict Embargo (1323-1344)

In the third decennium of the fourteenth century, the policy of the papacy in matters of trade with the Moslem Levant entered a new phase. The attitude of the Holy See had been stiffening continuously, and shortly after 1320 the pope categorically demanded that trading nations discontinue trade with the dominions of the sultan of Cairo altogether. The pressure brought upon them was so strong that they had to yield and promulgate decrees in the sense demanded by the Holy See.

In January 1323 the government of Venice issued a general prohibition of trade with the dominions of the sultan. Even travels to Egypt and Syria were forbidden. The prohibition was to become operative immediately upon promulgation. Transgressors were to pay a fine amounting to half the value of their merchandise.[264] Such a decree was issued in the same year by the duke of Crete also.[265] In July 1324 the prohibition was extended to Jewish

[258] Desimoni, no. 403.

[259] G. Giomo, "Regeste di alcuni deliberazioni del Senato Misti ecc.," *Archivio Veneto* 30, p. 156.

[260] *Art. cit.*, p. 155; *Felice de Merlis*, nos. 1,294, 1,295, 1,298, 1,300, 1,302.

[261] *Misti*, ed. Cessi, I, p. 119.

[262] *Libr. Com.* I, lib. 1, no. 319; ASV, Mag. Cons., Presbiter, f. 17b; *Misti*, ed. Cessi, I, p. 179.

[263] Lopez, *Storia delle colonie genovesi*, pp. 277, 278.

[264] *Misti*, ed. Cessi, I, p. 265.

[265] *Duca di Candia, Bandi (1313-1329)*, ed. P. Ratti Vidulich (Venice, 1965), no. 342.

merchants.[266] When Venetian merchants arrived in Crete with merchandise shipped from Egypt and claimed that it had been theirs for a long time (bought before the prohibition), it was sequestered by the authorities, who applied to the government in Venice for instructions.[267] Since many other merchants also claimed that they had merchandise belonging to them in Egypt and Syria, the Venetian authorities allowed them to go there in November 1323 and to ship it to Christian ports until the end of April 1324; however, they were to employ non-Venetian ships. Further, the merchants had to register the commodities and take an oath that they were really their property before the prohibition of trade. Those who shipped other merchandise, it was ruled, would be punished by its being confiscated. Again, it was decreed that all Venetians and subjects of the Republic—that is, inhabitants of the Venetian colonies who were entitled to the protection of Venice (*fideles*)—should leave the territories of the sultan before the end of April 1324; failing this, they would have to pay a heavy fine.[268]

To what extent were these decrees implemented? The Irish monk Symon Semeonis, who went on a pilgrimage to Jerusalem in 1323, narrated that when he came to Alexandria in October of that year he found fondachi of the Venetians, the Genoese, the merchants of Marseilles, the Catalans, and others. In another passage of his travelogue, he said that on his return from the Holy Land he dined in Alexandria at the table of the Venetian consul.[269] This account is apparently at variance with the decrees of the Venetian authorities insofar as it shows that there were still Venetians in Alexandria. But it could be assumed that only the consul was left in the great Egyptian port, in order to supervise the exodus of the merchants and to wind up all the unfinished business. It was indeed a very short time after the general prohibition of trade with the dominions of the sultan. In fact, some time later the Venetian consulate in Alexandria was suspended. The service of the Venetian galley line to Alexandria was suspended too, nor did the Venetian cogs sail to the ports of Egypt. In 1345 the sultan included in the text of a commercial treaty with Venice the statement that for twenty-three years no Venetian ship had anchored in the ports of his countries.[270] But the trading nations could not acquiesce in the discontinuation of the trade with Egypt and Syria. Genoa applied in 1324 to the Holy See with the request to carry on trade in Latakia. Owing to a conflict with her colony in Pera, Genoa had lost the connection with the Persian

[266] *Op.cit.*, no. 371.
[267] *Op.cit.*, no. 382.
[268] *Misti*, ed. Cessi, I, p. 275; *Duca di Candia*, no. 383.
[269] *Itinerarium Symonis Semeonis ab Hybernia ad Terram Sanctam* (Dublin, 1960), p. 74, 98.
[270] *Dipl. Ven.-Lev.* I, p. 291. The twenty-three years are the Moslem years 723-745, corresponding to 1323-1344/5.

markets and was looking for another route there. In 1328 the government of Venice intervened with the papal legate and then the Serenissima sent an embassy to the Holy See, to ask the pope to again permit commercial exchanges with the Moslem Levant.[271] But the request of the Republic was denied.

The other trading nations also complied with the orders of the Church and issued new decrees concerning trade with the Moslem Levant or took other measures to show their faithfulness to the Holy See. But they did not go as far as Venice did, or were not sincere. Certainly in this way they were sure of taking care of the interests of their subjects.

The king of Aragon imposed fines on those who visited the dominions of the sultan of Cairo. In 1326, for instance, Jacob Dolvan, a merchant of Barcelona, had to pay 140 fl. for having travelled there from Cyprus. He must have been a very enterprising merchant and the volume of his trade considerable, for he had sent his merchandise to the Levant on several ships.[272] So the fine he had to pay for the travel only (which was not considered as atonement for his commercial activities) was rather small. Although the prohibition to travel to Egypt and Syria was officially upheld by the king of Aragon, those guilty of transgression were often not punished at all. In 1335 King Alfonso IV absolved Jacob Olivella, captain of a cog, and his crew, who had sailed to Beirut with merchandise loaded in Famagusta. The pretext for the absolution was their assertion that they feared the Genoese would attack them.[273] A year before, in 1334, King Pedro IV sent three ambassadors, Bernardo de Boxadon, Pedro Castilleri, and Fernando Gruny, to the Holy See, asking that his subjects who had carried on trade in the dominions of the sultan be forgiven and that a prelate be entrusted with their absolution from excommunication. On the other hand, the king gave orders to the royal fleet and to the captains of Catalan ships not to attack the subjects of the sultan of Cairo.[274] Four years later, his successor gave orders to stop action against merchants who had travelled to the Moslem East or who shipped merchandise there.[275] Some time later, still in the same year, the king decreed that henceforth no one should be sued for these transgressions by his magistrates. The town council of Bar-

[271] Lopez, *Storia delle colonie genovesi*, p. 293; *Misti*, ed. Cessi, I, pp. 361, 370.

[272] de Mas Latrie, *Histoire* III, p. 720 ff.

[273] *Op.cit.* III, p.732 ff.

[274] Capmany, 1, p. 812; 2.1, no. 135, p. 204 and cf. Heyd II, p. 468.

[275] *Op.cit.*, 2.1, no. 140, pp. 212-13. Contrary to the interpretation given by Sáez Pomés, *EEMCA* V, p. 365, the decree also refers to future transgressions. It reads: "et etiam in quibusvis aliis inquisicionibus racione predicta contra quosvis alios cives vel habitatores Barchinone inchoatis vel inchoandis omnino supersederi velimus . . . usque quo a nobis super eo aliud receperitis mandamentum." Even Capmany has the decree interpreted in this sense.

celona paid him a substantial sum for this decree.[276] But a short time later the king again collected fines from merchants who had travelled to Egypt and Syria.

In 1317 Genoa had enacted a new decree forbidding the sale of war material of any kind to Moslems of North Africa, Spain, or any other country. The supply of military slaves was especially mentioned among the forbidden activities.[277] In 1341 another decree was issued: it again forbade the transport of war material to the Moslem countries.[278]

In the 20's and 30's of the fourteenth century, the Holy See, at least officially, was adamant on the question of the general prohibition of trade with the dominions of the Mamluks. The pope refused to renounce the embargo. In 1326 Pope John XXII decreed that henceforth all those who maintained that it was lawful to sell the Moslems commodities that were not war material and whose sale to them had not been forbidden by his predecessor Boniface VIII and before him by other popes and councils should be considered as heretics and be excommunicated.[279] On the other hand, the Holy See could not estrange the trading nations from itself completely, for their war fleets were indispensable for the execution of a new Crusade and expeditions against the Turks. Perhaps another consideration was no less weighty in inducing the Holy See to make some concessions. A total discontinuation of the Levant trade meant lowering the level of the standard of living of the upper strata of European society, contrary to the tendency prevailing in most of the Western nations. So again the Church began to grant permission, for a fee, which became a source of income for it. The grant of these licenses apparently began in about 1330, but actually it was the outcome of a long development. It seems that the first stage was the granting of absolution to single merchants, as early as the end of the thirteenth century.[280] At the beginning of the fourteenth century, the Holy See was rather liberal in this respect, of course, in return for certain payments. A bull of John XXII, of 1322, authorized the papal "collectors" to absolve the Venetian merchants who had engaged in the trade of "forbidden articles" (war material, etc.) with the Moslems and ordered them to issue two receipts for the sums collected.[281] In a second stage, agreements were

[276] *Op.cit.*, 2.1, no. 141, pp. 213-15. Even in this decree the king expressly renounces the punishment of future transgressions: "seu in viagiis ad dictas partes vel aliquam earum . . . iveritis, portaveritis, comendaveritis vel miseritis." While the first decree referred to transgressions in the past, which were also the subject of an inquiry or would be, and also to transgressions in the future, it was only a temporary renunciation. The latter was a permanent one.

[277] Mon. Hist. Patr. II, c. 376 f.

[278] *Op.cit.*, c. 339.

[279] *Libr. Com.* I, lib. 2, no. 465; Raynaldus-Baronius V, p. 329.

[280] See above.

[281] *Libr. Com.* II, lib. 2, no. 342, and cf. above about the fines imposed at the beginning of the century in Catalonia.

made with the trading nations or there were proposals to this effect. In 1319 the Venetian ambassadors to the Holy See were authorized to offer 5,000 ducats for permission to trade freely (except for war material) with the Moslems.[282] It is not known if the ambassadors reached an agreement. Nor do we know if Pope John XXII granted the Genoese permission in 1326 to carry on trade in Syria for two years, once more for a considerable payment.[283] Since the trading nations offered substantial sums for these permits and the secular authorities, like the king of Aragon, had a long time ago begun to collect fines from those carrying on trade with the Moslems, the Holy See took a further step and also began to grant permits to single traders. From then on, merchants and companies engaged in trade with Egypt and Syria had to allow for certain sums for obtaining such permits, just as they had to pay customs and other fees. The permits were valid for one or more trips to the Moslem Levant.[284] Even if the merchant republic succeeded in obtaining a license, the single trader who was a citizen of the republic had to make his contribution to it. But since so many merchants were eager to carry on lawful trade, the granting and transfer of permits for payment became the object of various transactions. Meanwhile the trade with the dominions of the Mamluks went on, but on a smaller scale.

The Venetians by no means severed their connections with the emporia of Egypt and Syria. Both documents and coin hoards testify to this fact.[285] The two fondachi the Venetians had in Alexandria remained in their hands,[286] and Venetian merchants continued to carry on their activities even in some Syrian towns. By the act of a Genoese notary, drawn up in Beirut in 1344, a Venetian merchant living there manumitted a slave girl.[287] The data in a Venetian Merchant Guide, of the second quarter of the fourteenth century, shed a good deal of light on the Venetians activities in Syria. It shows that they imported industrial goods, such as linen of Reims, cloth of Malines, and scarlets into Damascus from Europe.[288]

The Genoese were much more active in the trade with the Mamluk kingdom, especially in Syria. Several enactments of the Genoese government point to this fact. A decree of 1330 deals with the crews of galleys

[282] *Misti*, ed. Cessi, p. 207.

[283] Raynaldus-Baronius V, p. 329. The ship captains were to take an oath that they would not load "prohibited articles."

[284] See J. M. Madurell Marimón, "Contabilidad de una compania mercantil trescentista barcelonese (1334-1342)," *Anuario de historia del derecho español* 36 (1966), p. 469.

[285] See my paper "Observations on Venetian Trade," p. 535; *Dipl. Ven.-Lev.* I, no. 96 (of a. 1324).

[286] *Art. cit.*, p. 539.

[287] Domenico de Oddo, f. 4a.

[288] *Tarifa*, p. 57.

going to Syria,[289] and in 1344 additional rules were added to it.[290] A decree of 1331 forbids the shipment of precious metals on cogs to Syria.[291] Then, in 1333, the dimensions of the galleys sailing to Greece and Syria were fixed.[292] Finally, in 1341, it was ruled that galleys should sail to Syria in convoys only.[293] Among the articles the Genoese imported into Syria in that period, cloth was relatively important. A Genoese document bears on the activities of the brothers Ansaldo, Giovanni, and Giacomo de Olivera, who had founded a company in 1330 or 1331 and exported French cloth to Syria and Persia (Tebriz). One of them had travelled from Naples to Syria.[294] The Genoese also carried on trade between Southern France and the Moslem Levant. In 1334, for example, a Genoese galley loaded falcons in Nice for Syria.[295] The Venetian Merchant Guide quoted above lists among the commodities imported into Damascus Genoese linen and cloth of Narbonne.[296] Part of the latter was certainly shipped to the Levant by the Genoese. A commenda contract made in 1344 in Genoa also refers to the export of French cloth to Syria.[297] The acts of a Genoese notary, drawn up in 1344 in Damascus and in Beirut, testify to the import of cloth. Francesco Ultramare, owner of a cog, had shipped, in addition to falcons and mastic, cloth from Southern France to Syria. By one of these acts he appointed Ettore Spinola captain of his ship, but by another he appointed another Genoese to sail back with the ship to Aigues-Mortes. In one deed, which is drawn up in Damascus, the names of six witnesses of Genoa and one of Narbonne appear. The company of Jean Vidal, whose goods Francesco Ultramare had shipped to Syria, is represented there by Pierre Bonet & Cie of Marseilles, who had made a certain payment for Ultramare to a trader of Montpellier, Hugo Fornier, evidently in Syria.[298] In one of the acts of the said notary, one finds the signature of the "French consul in Beirut" (the Christian name being Jean, the family name not readable). But most of the witnesses and other Europeans mentioned in his acts drawn up in Damascus and Beirut in 1344 are Genoese or from the small neighboring towns. One of these documents is the will of Antonio di Ghisolfi,

[289] Mon. Hist. Patr. II, c. 323 f.
[290] *Op.cit.*, c. 325 f.
[291] *Op.cit.*, c. 343 f.
[292] *Op.cit.*, c. 312 f.
[293] *Op.cit.*, c. 334.
[294] Liagre-De Sturler, no. 212.
[295] Baratier, p. 221 f.
[296] *Tarifa, l.c.*
[297] Liagre-De Sturler, no. 163.
[298] Domenico de Oddo, f. 3b f., 5b, 6a., and cf. Baratier, p. 222, who erroneously has 1343. That Pierre Bonet made the payment in Syria is clear because of the kind of money used: it was paid in dirhams. Jean Vidal was, according to Baratier, a merchant of Narbonne.

a Genoese; five other Genoese are witnesses.[299] Some Genoese merchants for whom this notary drew up acts lived in Beirut but were also engaged in business in Damascus.[300] One lived in Beirut and his brother lived in Damascus. From the handful of documents that have come down to us from this notary we learn also that at the same time another Genoese cog, called "Sant' Antonio," anchored in the port of Beirut.[301] The Genoese were also engaged in trade between Syria and Crimea, as they had been in the second half of the thirteenth century, for there can be no doubt that a ship that came to Caffa in 1343 from Syria was Genoese.[302]

The Catalan trade with Egypt and Syria also continued in that period, according to many documents. The character of the Catalan trade in the Near East and of Levantine trade in general is illuminated by the accounts of a firm that carried on trade in Cyprus and Egypt from 1334 to 1342. A glance at the accounts is sufficient to make one aware of the great importance that the export of textiles to the Near East had as early as the first half of the fourteenth century. These records also show convincingly that the Near Easterners eagerly acquired the cloth imported from Western Europe, undoubtedly considering it to be of better quality than their own. The company was founded by Arnau Elpazer, Bernat de Puigmoradell, and Pere de Mijavilla. The latter was surely the same Pere de Mijavilla who in 1327 went to Cairo as ambassador of the king of Aragon. Even Eymerich Dusay, who had been the Aragonese ambassador to the sultan several times, joined the company. The original capital was no more than 545 fl., and when others joined the company it rose 991 fl.; so it was not a rich company and it carried on its activities with the help of local agents (factors). It purchased licenses from the Holy See to ship its goods to the ports of Syria and Egypt. The goods exported to Egypt comprised lead from England, tin, coral, mirrors of Sardinia. Falcons, furs, partly bought in Flanders, saffron, honey of Catalonia, and hazelnuts were exported to both Egypt and Syria. But most of the capital was invested in the export of cloth. The company exported to Syria cloth of Bellpuig and Puigcerda and Flemish cloth of Dixmude, and to Egypt cloth of Barcelona, Bellpuig, Châlons-sur-Marne, and Dixmude, and English serge. The purchases made in the Levant were mostly of spices like ginger and cinnamon, dyes like indigo, and cotton of Little Armenia. In Cyprus, the company sold cloth of Barcelona, Valencia, Bellpuig, Châlons-sur-Marne, Banyokes, and Tournai.[303] Most of the cloth was a cheap variety, one piece being worth 6-13 fl. That means that it was

[299] f. 2b f.
[300] f. 5b, 6b.
[301] f. 4b.
[302] L. Balletto, *Genova, Mediterraneo, Mar Nero*, p. 139.
[303] Madurell Marimón, *art. cit.*, p. 480 ff.

cloth offered to the middle class, which preferred it to the products of the domestic industry, which was already in decline.

Valuable information about the activities of merchants of Catalonia in the Near East in those years is also to be found in the records of the royal treasurer, who collected the fines from those who travelled to the dominions of the sultan without having a license. In the year 1337, King Pedro IV granted pardon to a merchant of Barcelona, Bernardo de Pares, who had travelled to Alexandria and carried on trade with the Moslems. Two years later he pardoned one of his Moslem subjects, called Mahomedello, who went to Egypt in 1333 on the ship of Pere Comite of Barcelona. In 1338 Guillem Campis, a merchant of Barcelona, had to pay a fine for having travelled from Famagusta to Syria.[304] In the records of the year 1341, there are notes concerning the fines imposed on the widow of a Jew of Cervera who ten years before had travelled to Syria and other Moslem countries of the Near East. Further, the treasurer collected fines from the Jewish merchants Cresque Alfaquim, Benvenut de la Cavalleria, Samoligo Avenpesat, Mosse de Leyda, and Prefet Bonafos, all of Barcelona, and Vidal de Monço, a Jew of the district of Tarragona, who in the same year had travelled from Cyprus to Syria. The royal treasurer also notes fines imposed on Jucef Astruch Alfaqui, a Jew of Barcelona, who as a young boy went to Alexandria and brought merchandise from there. The records of 1344 contain notes on fines paid by Bonjuha de la Cavalleria, another Jew, for himself and his son Bonant, because they had collaborated with people engaged in trade with the dominions of the sultan.[305]

These records show not only that the king, who had in 1338 solemnly renounced the levying of fines on merchants who had carried on trade with the dominions of the sultan, collected them again a short time after he had collected an indemnity for the renunciation from the town council of Barcelona, but they also point to the fact that many of those who set out for the dominions of the Mamluks had to travel there from Cyprus. Apparently the number of ships licensed by the Holy See was not very great. The accounts of the company quoted above give data concerning the freight of three ships bound for Beirut and one sailing to Alexandria. This is a rather small number for the eight years that the company existed, but certainly the traffic between the great ports of Catalonia and those of Egypt and Syria was not sporadic. A Genoese chronicler recounts, for instance, that

[304] A. López de Meneses, "Florilegio documental del reinado de Pedro IV de Aragon," *Cuadernos de historia de España* 13 (1950), nos. II (p. 182 f.), IV (p. 184 f.); de Mas Latrie, *Histoire* III, p. 734.

[305] F. Baer, *Die Juden im christlichen Spanien* I (Berlin 1929), no. 212 (records from the Archivo del Real Patrimonio).

in the year 1334 two ships of Tarragona were attacked in an Egyptian port by their fellow countrymen.[306]

Just as Catalan merchants applied individually to the Holy See with the request for licenses for trade with Egypt and Syria, the Provençals also submitted such applications. In the 1330's several ships sailed from Marseilles to Alexandria. In 1332 André de Casals, a citizen of Marseilles, went to Egypt to claim the restitution of his merchandise from the sultan. A year later, a merchant of Toulouse, Pierre Miège, had obtained licenses for two ships and sailed to Alexandria, carrying with him merchandise of many traders of Montpellier, Clermont l'Héraut, and Marseilles. Among the articles loaded was coral. But in those years the traffic between the ports of Provence and the Moslem Levant was to a great extent carried on by Genoese ships, which sailed from Marseilles or from another port of Southern France to the emporia of the Near East, although sometimes the Provençal merchants embarked elsewhere. In 1334, for instance, the Genoese galley "Santa Maria" visited Nice and Marseilles, before going to Syria. A merchant loaded 50 falcons there.[307]

Collecting and combining bit by bit the accounts that have a bearing on the Levant trade of that period in the archives of various commercial towns, one is left with the feeling that the result is somehow unsatisfactory. The reason is very simple: countless contracts were purposely styled not clearly, so they would not reveal the true character of the transaction or the destination. So the reports of some Arabic authors on disorders in Alexandria in the year 1327 supply us valuable additional information. Surely one must read between the lines of the medieval chronicles.

The Arabic writers narrate that a brawl broke out between a European merchant and an Alexandrian, and that a general scuffle between the Moslems and the European Christians ensued, with both sides using weapons. The gates of the town were closed, so that people of the villages in the neighborhood could not join those fighting with the Christians, and when they were opened in the evening, in order that inhabitants of the town could return to their homes, there was such a crush among the Alexandrians that some were killed. Thereupon the crowd again attacked the foreign merchants, and although the governor sent troops to stop the fight, they could not push the people back. The crowd even attacked the state prison, and the governor had to apply to the sultan for help; whereupon a vizier and a general were despatched to Alexandria to quell the uproar. They had

[306] Pietro Bizaro Sentinati, *Senatus populique Genuensis rerum . . . historiae* (Antwerp 1579), lib. V, p. 116. The question of whether the Catalans had consulates in Egypt and Syria at this time must for the moment be left open. According to Capmany, 1, pp. 246, 377, there was a Catalan consul in Alexandria in 1344 and another in Beirut in 1340. But he does not indicate sources for these statements.

[307] Baratier, p. 221 f. See also Pardessus, *Collection* III, p. CXI.

detailed orders as to how to punish those who had taken part in or supported the fight.

The interesting point in the accounts of the Arabic authors is the report about the fighting between the Moslems and the European merchants. For it shows that in that period, in which the Church had categorically forbidden travel to the dominions of the sultan, there were so many European merchants in Alexandria that they could fight with the Moslem inhabitants. In one account, it is even specifically stated that they were Venetians.[308]

According to these reports of the Arabic chroniclers, the Mamluk government severely punished those who had instigated the rioters. The contemporary historian adh-Dhahabī says that the Kārimī merchants were heavily fined, and the globetrotter Ibn Baṭṭūṭa, who some years later visited Alexandria, mentions the family Ibn Kuwayk. The Kārimīs were a group of wholesale traders engaged in international exchanges and the Ibn Kuwayk family belonged to that group. ʿAbdallaṭīf b. Aḥmad Ibn Kuwayk, who was then the head of the family (he died in 1334), was a rich and enterprising merchant.[309] Clearly the Mamluks seized the opportunity to punish the Kārimīs, as the rulers coveted their riches, and any pretext to mulct them was welcome. But it is also reasonable to believe that the Kārimīs had indeed supported the rioters. From other sources we know that there was antagonism between the European merchants and the Kārimīs, who tried, not without success, to establish a trust of spice traders and to control other branches of Alexandria's international trade as well.[310] Since the Levant trade of the European trading nations was in that period at an ebb and, on the other hand, the great Egyptian spice traders, i.e., the Kārimīs, could market their merchandise elsewhere, they were not inclined to make concessions or to acquiesce in attempts to break their domination of the spice trade. Egypt's economy was still flourishing, and the Egyptian demand for Far Eastern goods, which the Kārimīs offered, was great so that the latter felt no need to bow to the claims of the European merchants. The favorable attitude toward the Europeans adopted by the sultan's government, which was interested in maintaining the commercial exchanges with Southern Europe and the supply of war material, was considered by the Kārimīs as such an attempt.

adh-Dhahabī recounts that the weavers were also fined, and Ibn Ḳāḍī Shuhba, quoting the contemporary al-Kutubī, says that they had to pay the great sum of 100 dinars for every loom.[311] That the weavers were

308 I.J.H.P. Herzsohn, *Der Überfall Alexandrias durch Peter I, König von Jerusalem und Cypern* (Bonn, 1886), p. XXI.

309 See J. Sublet, "ʿAbd al-Laṭīf al-Takrītī et la famille des Banū Kuwayk, marchands Kārimī," *Arabica* IX (1962), p. 193 ff.

310 See below.

311 *al-Iʿlām*, MS. Bodleiana, f. 209b.

hostile to the European merchants can also be easily understood. The European merchants imported foreign cloth! The economic basis of the conflict, which resulted largely from the import of European textiles, is clearly shown by the report of other Arabic authors on the punishment of Ibn Rawwāḥa. He was accused of having incited the Moslem mob and of having supplied the rioters with weapons, and was therefore executed. According to al-Maḳrīzī, he was the manager of the royal manufactures of textiles in Alexandria (the so-called *ṭirāz*).[312] Since the royal manufacturers sold their products to private customers too (besides supplying the royal court),[313] the reason Ibn Rawwāḥa fomented the fight against the European merchants is perfectly clear. As farmer of the royal manufactures he looked upon the Europeans as his great competitors.[314]

The second quarter of the fourteenth century, when the Holy See insisted on a general prohibition of trade with Egypt and Syria and a high fee had to be paid for every license, was certainly a period of flourishing international trade for Cyprus and Little Armenia. The rulers of these countries, aware of the favorable constellation, did their best to reap the greatest benefit from it.

The king of Cyprus granted privileges to the trading nations of Southern Europe, which had none before, to the Florentines, and to the merchants of Montpellier,[315] and complied with the requests of the others as far as he could. The limitations he imposed upon unlawful trade with the Moslems and the measures he took against it were double-dealing. When the pope had forbidden trade with the dominions of the sultan altogether, the king of Cyprus sent galleys to intercept those who sailed there[316] and, on the other hand, the European merchants were encouraged to come to Famagusta, although it was clear that many of them continued their travels to Egypt and to Syria and that the Oriental commodities offered in the Cypriot emporium came from these countries. The purchase of the spices imported into Cyprus from Syria and Egypt was contrary to the policy of the Church, which aimed at weakening the Mamluks. However, the policy of the king of Cyprus proved a complete success. The data on the convoys of the Venetian State galleys, which visited Cyprus and Little Armenia every year, bear witness to this. At the beginning of the fourteenth century, their number had been six, whereas in the 1330's and 1340's they usually numbered eight.

312 *Sulūk* II, p. 284 f.; Ibn Baṭṭūṭa, *Voyages* (Paris, 1853-1858) I, p. 45 ff.
313 See my *Social and economic history*, p. 150.
314 Other Arabic accounts are: adh-Dhahabī, *Duwal al-islām* II, p. 182 f.; *Continuation of Baybars al-Manṣūrī*, f. 243a f.
315 Heyd II, pp. 11 f., 13 f.
316 Capmany, 1, pp. 260-61; de Mas Latrie, *Histoire* II, p. 121 f.

Table II Venetian Romania and Cyprus-Armenia galleys
in the first half of the XIVth century

Year	Romania	Cyprus-Armenia	sources
1328	10	8	Archivio Veneto 18, p. 318, 321, 334
1329	8	8	Art. cit., p. 321, 336
1330	6	8	Arch. Ven. 18, p. 323, 337
1331	6	8	Cessi-Sambin I, p. 433
1332	10	7	Thiriet, Rég.I, p. 24, 25
1333	10	10	Op. cit., p. 29; Misti 16, f. 20a
1334	8	8	Op. cit., p. 32; Misti 16, f. 71a
1335	10	8	Misti 17, f. 15a, 17b
1336	8	8	Thiriet, op. cit. p. 36; Misti 17, f. 64a
1337	8	4[a]	Misti 17, f. 74a
1338	10	8	Thiriet, op. cit., p. 38
1339	10	8	Op. cit., p. 41; Misti 18, f. 57a
1340	8	6	Op. cit., p. 43
1341	8	6	Misti 19, f. 72a, 73a; cf. Blanc, *Le flotte mercantili di Venezia* (s.l., s.d.) p. 76, 78
1342	8	-	Misti 20, f. 49a
1343	7	7	Misti 21, f. 29b; cf. Thiriet, p. 57
1344	2 to Trebizond	11	Op. cit., ibidem[b]

[a] These four galleys should sail as far as Negroponte and then go to Cyprus.

[b] In addition two communally operated galleys should go to Constantinople and two others to Cyprus, see F. C. Lane, The Venetian galleys to Alexandria, 1344, (in) Wirtschaftskräfte u. Wirtschaftswege, Festschrift H. Kellenbenz I (Nürnberg 1978), p. 432.

These data show that Venetian trade with Cyprus and Little Armenia was not much less in that period than the old, established commercial exchanges with the formerly Byzantine territories. The great sums which the auctions of the Cyprus-Armenia galleys yielded in some years of the 1330's and the 1340's are another clear evidence of the role played by these territories as places of transshipment for the merchandise coming from the Moslem Levant.[317]

The consequences of the papal embargo on trade with the Mamluks were even more tangible in Little Armenia than in Cyprus. More than ever, the little kingdom fulfilled the role of a bridgehead for Western Christianity

[317] Giomo, according to note 259; Thiriet, "Quelques observations sur le trafic des galées," p. 505 f.

to the Near East. The increase in its trade was also the consequence of a change in the trade routes between the ports on the Persian Gulf and the shores of the Mediterranean. After the conquest of Baghdad by the Tatars in 1258 and the fall of the Crusader principality of Antioch in 1268, the caravan route connecting the Persian Gulf with the east coast of the Mediterranean was transferred to the north. Baghdad was no longer a great trading center, as before, and by transporting the spices north of Mamluk Syria, the payment of high customs could be avoided. The change of the trade route, however, was not abrupt, and through the second half of the thirteenth century the Basra-Baghdad route was still a major line of traffic.[318] But in the first half of the fourteenth century, when Tebriz had become a great commercial town, the bulk of the merchandise unloaded in the ports of the Persian Gulf was transported to this town and from there part of it was sent to Little Armenia.[319] The data in other Merchant Guides of that period, as well as Pegolotti's account, point to the importance of the Lajazzo-Sivas-Erzindjān-Tebriz route in the first half of the fourteenth century.[320] The king of Armenia encouraged the South European trading nations, granting them new privileges, and various conflicts were settled by patient negotiations between the royal authorities and the permanent representatives or special envoys of the trading nations. Venice was granted a privilege in 1321, sent an embassy to the king of Little Armenia in 1329, and obtained new privileges in 1333.[321] The traders of Montpellier made a treaty with the king in 1314 and then in 1321; the Sicilians obtained a privilege in 1331.[322] Lajazzo, the main port of the kingdom, was a meeting point for the European merchants and the Moslem traders of Syria and Iraq. Contemporary Arabic authors recount that when the Mamluks raided Little Armenia in 1335 the inhabitants of Lajazzo revenged themselves by setting fire to a khan where 2,000 merchants of Baghdad and others stayed.[323] On the other hand, Venetians and other South European traders came to Lajazzo to carry on trade with the Moslems of Damascus and other towns of Syria and probably went there quite often.[324] Even Egyptian merchants visited Little Armenia and sold their merchandise there. A letter of Leon

[318] See my *Social and economic history*, p. 265.

[319] Heyd II, p. 77 ff.

[320] *Zibaldone da Canal*, p. 110.

[321] V. Langlois, *Le trésor des chartes d'Arménie ou cartulaire de la chancellerie royale des Roupéniens* (Venice, 1863), p. 182 ff., 193 f.; *Misti*, ed. Cessi, I, p. 408.

[322] Langlois, *op.cit.*, pp. 178 ff., 184 f., 186 ff.

[323] Ibn al-Wardī, *Continuation of Abu 'l-Fidā* (Constantinople, A. H. 1286) IV, p. 119; Ibn Ḥabīb, *Durrat al-aslāk*, MS. Bodleiana I, 819, f. 113a; *Continuation of Baybars al-Manṣūrī*, f. 274a; adh-Dhahabī, *Duwal al-islām* II, p. 187; Ibn Ḳāḍī Shuhba, *al-I'lām*, MS. Bodleiana, f. 268a.

[324] *Libr. Com.* II, lib. 3, no. 202.

V, king of Little Armenia, to the doge of Venice deals with the debts four Venetian merchants and two *fattori* of another owed four Moslem merchants of Fuwwa. The letter is dated 1341.[325]

When the South European trading nations had to bow to the papal prohibition of trade with the lands of the sultan of Cairo and had to have recourse to alternative trade routes, their commercial activities in Persia were intensified. The rulers of the country, the Tatar Īlkhāns, were very much interested in fostering trade with the nations of Southern Europe, always hoping that political alliances would result. The customs they levied were much lower than those collected by the Mamluks, 4-5 percent as compared with 10-20 percent in Egypt,[326] and transport of the most precious spices on the land routes had always been preferred, insofar as possible. Further, the European traders could purchase in Tebriz, the great emporium of Persia, the raw silk of the Caspian borderlands, a highly appreciated raw material for the developing silk industry of Italy.

The trading nation that first entered into close contacts with the realm of the Īlkhāns and was most active in this new artery of transcontinental trade was Genoa. Since her colony Caffa had itself become a great emporium and Genoese merchants carried on trade in various ports of the Black Sea, soon after the conquest of Persia and Iraq by the Tatars, they began to visit the major towns of these countries. In the 1270's and 1280's they carried on a lively trade in Tebriz. They travelled there either from Trebizond, where they had a very active colony, or from Lajazzo. In the 1280's, apparently, the transfer of money from Caffa to Tebriz was quite an ordinary transaction.[327] Sivas, on the route from Lajazzo to Tebriz, was very often visited by Genoese merchants. In 1274 the Genoese notary Federico di Pizzalunga drew up contracts there for several Genoese merchants. Some of them lived there a long time, for other contracts made by Genoese in Sivas date to 1280.[328] Other Genoese carried on trade in Erzindjan, also a great trading town on the route to Tebriz. At the end of the thirteenth century, certainly not later than the 1280's, Genoa established a consulate in Sivas.[329] Just as much of the spices and the dyes the Venetian merchants purchased in Egypt and Syria was paid for by the proceeds from the sale of European textiles, so the Genoese exported cloth and linen from European countries to Tebriz via Trebizond and Sivas. Contracts made in Genoa in

[325] *Op.cit.*, no. 532.

[326] See Pegolotti, p. 27 f., 72; *Notices et extraits* XI, p. 36; *Secreta fidelium crucis*, p. 24.

[327] G. I. Brătianu, *Actes des notaires génois de Pera et de Caffa de la fin du treizième siècle*, no. CCLXXIX.

[328] Brătianu, *Recherches*, p. 166, appendices I, II, XII, XIII.

[329] "Statuti della colonia genovese di Pera," ed. V. Promis, in *Miscellanea di storia italiana* XI (Turin, 1870), CCXLVIII, p. 761.

1292 refer to the export of linen of Reims to Tebriz.[330] Notarial acts drawn up in Genoa in 1313, in 1330, and in 1336, too, testify to the export of linen of Reims to the Persian emporium. The first of these contracts also refers to cloth of Châlons-sur-Marne.[331] At the beginning of the fourteenth century, the Genoese had a consulate in Tebriz.[332] The Genoese were highly in favor at the court of the Īlkhāns. Most of the Īlkhāns' envoys to the pope and the kings of Europe were Genoese.[333]

The Venetian Pietro Viglioni, who made his will in Tebriz in 1263, was certainly a pioneer. The fact that he appointed the Venetian *bailo* in Acre executor and that there are no Venetian witnesses in this deed indicates the absence of fellow-countrymen in the Persian emporium. It is clear that Viglioni could not find Venetians so that he had to call on other Europeans, two of them Pisans and one a Frenchman. Viglioni was an agent of a company of several merchants and of his father. The inventory of his merchandise, included in his will, is truly representative of European exports to the Near East and Persia in the later Middle Ages. He had with him linen of Germany, Venice, and Lombardy, Stanforte cloth manufactured in Malines, and crystal.[334] The "linen of Venice" was certainly linen imported into his home town from elsewhere, for Venice is not known to have been a producer of this textile. The export of linen to Persia must have been very profitable, as it is also mentioned by Pegolotti;[335] that of crystal is one of the earliest cases known to us of the export of this Venetian product into the Middle East.

Some time after Pietro Viglioni made his will, other Venetians came to Tebriz and settled there. Like the Genoese, they also began to play a role in the political contacts between the Tatars and Western Europe. In the 1270's a Venetian, Giacomo Vassallo, fulfilled a diplomatic mission for the rulers of Persia in Europe.[336] A papal letter of 1288 is addressed to nine

330 Brătianu, *op.cit.*, appendix, XVIII, and see other contracts for trade in Tebriz made in 1292, nos. XVII, XIX, XX.

331 Doehaerd, *Relations*, no. 1808; Liagre-De Sturler, nos. 63, 72. Even in deed no. 212 quoted above, trade in Tebriz in the 1330's is mentioned. On the investments of the Genoese in Tebriz, see M. Balard, "Precursori di Cristoforo Colombo: i Genovesi in Estremo Oriente nel XIV secolo," in *Atti del Convegno internazionale di studi colombiani*, Genova, 1973 (Genoa, 1974), p. 151.

332 M. I. Candioti, *Historia de la institución consular* (Buenos Aires, 1925), p. 745.

333 Brătianu, *Recherches*, p. 187; L. Lockhart, "The relations between Edward I and Edward II of England and the Mongol Īl-Khāns of Persia," *Iran* VI (1968), p. 26.

334 [B. Cecchetti], "Testamento di Pietro Vioni veneziano fatto in Tauris (Persia) MCCLXIV, X decembre," *Archivio Veneto* 26 (1883), p. 161 ff.; A. Stussi, "Un testamento volgare scritto in Persia nel 1263," *L'Italia dialettale*, N. S. 11 (1962), p. 23 ff., and see p. 24 on the date.

335 P. 30; cf. above p. 25 about the present sent in 1306 by the sultan of Cairo to the king of Aragon.

336 Carabellese, *Carlo d'Angiò*, p. 114.

European Christians in Tebriz, three of them Venetians.[337] Probably the number of the Venetians carrying on trade in Tebriz increased at the beginning of the fourteenth century, but they were also engaged in trade in Sultaniyya and Ormuz.[338] After the final prohibition of trade with the dominions of the Mamluks, Venetian merchants, who formerly operated in Alexandria, transferred their activities to Persia, mostly to Tebriz.[339]

The development of Venetian trade with Persia made it necessary for the Serenissima to enter into diplomatic contacts with the Tatar rulers of the country. The government of Venice sent several embassies to the Īlkhāns, in 1305, 1320, 1323, 1327, 1328, 1329, and again in 1342.[340] The reason it was necessary to send these embassies to Tebriz was in part the lack of discipline in the Venetian colony and the misdeeds of some merchants who had left Persia without paying their debts to the Moslems. Most Venetians had come to Tebriz from Trebizond, where they had established a very active colony, not later than in the second decade of the fourteenth century. From 1320 on they had an organized colony in Tebriz headed by a consul. The latter bore the title *maçor*, and from Venetian records we know that Marco Molin held the post beginning in 1324. However, the consul did not succeed in imposing his authority. Even in the first years of the fourteenth century, the Venetians had conflicts with the authorities of the Īlkhān,[341] and in 1332 and again in 1335 a Persian merchant came to Venice to claim payment of certain sums due him and some fellow countrymen.[342]

Not only did the Genoese and the Venetians carry on trade in Tebriz, but merchants of other Italian towns were also involved. Some of the Italians, who certainly came to Persia as merchants, once there embarked on political and military careers. At the end of the thirteenth century and the beginning of the fourteenth, the Pisans Isol and Giovanni di Bonastro were highly esteemed personalities at the court of Tebriz and one of them was entrusted with a diplomatic mission for Ghāzān Khān.[343] There were also Florentines and Sienese, who had won the favor of the Persian court

[337] Brătianu, *Recherches*, p. 186.

[338] See the text of the Mag. Cons., Clericus Civicus quoted by Thiriet, *Délibérations des assemblées* I, p. 304; *Mostra Venezia e la Persia, testimonianze e documenti* (Venice, Archivio di Stato, 1971), no. 5 (a. 1339).

[339] *Libr. Com.* II, lib. 3, no. 155.

[340] See Heyd II, p. 123 ff.; *Misti*, ed. Cessi, I, p. 286; *Libr. Com.* I, lib. 2, no. 255; II, lib. 3, no. 155; Thiriet, *Régestes* I, p. 50. The treaty made with the Īlkhān in 1320 has been printed by L. de Mas Latrie, "Privilège commercial accordé en 1320 à la République de Venise par un roi de Perse," *Bibl. Ec. des chart.* 31 (1871), p. 72 ff., and then in *Dipl. Ven.-Lev.* I, no. 85.

[341] *Libr. Com.* I, lib. 1, no. 252; *Mostra Venezia e la Persia*, no. 3.

[342] *Libr. Com.* II, lib. 3, no. 254; Thiriet, *Régestes* I, p. 35.

[343] L. Petech, "Les marchands italiens dans l'empire mongol," *JA* 250 (1962), p. 565 f.; J. Richard, "Isol le Pisan," *Central Asiatic Journal* 14 (1970), p. 186 ff.

and were sent as ambassadors to the pope and the kings of Western Europe.[344] Two powers of attorney given in Tebriz in 1328 and 1332 bear the signatures of a Genoese merchant, a Pisan, and not less than four witnesses of Piacenza.[345] However, the number of the merchants of these Italian towns in Tebriz cannot have been very great. Undoubtedly the Genoese were the most numerous. Among the merchants who testified in an inquiry made in Tebriz in 1333 about the heresy of some Franciscans, there were one Piacentine, one Pisan, one from Milan, one man from Asti, two Venetians, and five Genoese. Pegolotti compares the weights of Tebriz only with those of Genoa and Venice.[346]

One consequence of the activities that the Italians carried on in Tebriz was that they began to trade with the Far East. But also the colonies on the Crimean coast and those on the Sea of Azov served as points of departure for travels to China, then known as Cathay, where some of the silk offered on the Middle Eastern markets originated. Some Italian traders set out from Tebriz,[347] others from Tana, and from there they travelled to Astrakhān and Urganč.[348] Pegolotti's well-known account of the security on the transcontinental routes is certainly exaggerated, but it is true that Italian traders not infrequently travelled on them. At the beginning of the fourteenth century, a small colony of Italian merchants was formed in Zayton (Chwan-chau), then a great port of China, in the province of Fu-Kien.[349] Most of them were apparently Genoese, some were probably Florentines. Venetians, too, travelled both by land and by sea to China. Documents of the first and the fifth decade of the fourteenth century support this statement.[350] An inscription on a tombstone of 1342 testifies to the presence of Venetians in China in that period.[351] The Genoese merchants, in the 1330's exported French cloth to China[352] and purchased Chinese silk. Most of the Chinese silk sold in Italy and France in the middle and the second half of

[344] Petech, *art. cit,.* p. 566.

[345] See R.-H. Bautier, "Les relations économiques des occidentaux avec les pays d'Orient," in *Sociétés et compagnies de commerce en Orient*, p. 326.

[346] Golubovich, *Biblioteca bio-bibliografica della Terra Santa e dell' Oriente francescano* (Quaracchi 1906 ff.) III, p. 437; Pegolotti, p. 30 ff.

[347] R. Morozzo della Rocca, "Sulle orme di Marco Polo," *L'Italia che scrive* 37 (1954), p. 122, note 27.

[348] See Heyd II, pp. 189, 226 f., 240.

[349] A. van den Wyngaert, *Sinica Franciscana* I (Florence, 1929), p. 375 f.; Petech, *art. cit.*, p. 553 f.

[350] Golubovich, *op.cit.* III, p. 90. R. Morozzo della Rocca, "Catay," in *Miscellanea Roberto Cessi* (Studi e testi 71-73) (Rome, 1958), I, p. 301 ff.; R. S. Lopez, "Nuove luci sugli Italiani in Extremo Oriente prima di Colombo," *Studi Colombiani* (Genoa 1952), III, p. 392 f., B. Z. Kedar, "Chi era Andrea Franco," *ASLSP*, N.S. 17 (1977), p. 374 ff.: an embassy of the Mongol emperor of China to the pope consisted almost exclusively of Genoese. About Piacentines in China see Balard, "Precursori di Cristoforo Colombo," p. 158.

[351] Petech, *art. cit.*, p. 557.

[352] Liagre-De Sturler, no. 212. Catagium is certainly Cathay i.e. China.

the thirteenth century had probably been acquired by the Italian traders in Little Armenia, in Tebriz, and in the emporia on the coasts of the Black Sea and the Sea of Azov. But at least some of the silk offered in Western Europe at the beginning of the fourteenth century was probably brought from China itself, by the European traders. In 1304 the Florentine firm Frescobaldi sold Chinese silk in London.[353]

Tebriz was also the point of departure for travels to India. Marino Sanuto (the Elder) maintains that many European merchants travelled from Persia to India.[354] Is this a reasonable statement, or is it a gross exaggeration? In both the Genoese and the Venetian archives, documents that testify to commercial travels to India in the first half of the fourteenth century have been found. The hope to enter into direct contact with the regions from which most of the spices came and to continue on to China certainly induced some enterprising Italian merchants to venture upon visits to Northwestern India and to the southern part of the west coast of the subcontinent. The Genoese Benedetto Vivaldi and Percivallo Stancone set out for India in 1315, and Benedetto died there in (about) 1320.[355] Venetian documents refer to a company founded in Venice in 1338 for trade with India. Six Venetian merchants travelled to Delhi and sold their merchandise to Sultan Muḥammad Ṭughluḳ.[356] That the number of Western traders who carried on trade in Indian emporia was not altogether insignificant is a fact that is emphasized in a letter of a Dominican who went to India and wrote form there to Tebriz in 1321.[357] The Genoese were apparently the most numerous of these merchants and of other Europeans who travelled to India and China.[358] The names of some of them are known. In the year 1343 a Genoese merchant, Tommaso Gentile, came to Ormuz to sail from there to China, but decided to return.[359] There were also Pisans among the European merchants who went to India in the first half of the fourteenth century.[360] Some of the Western merchants stayed in India a long time. Philippe de Mézières recounts that in the 1360's a Genoese who had been in India fifty

353 R. S. Lopez, "Chinese silk in Europe in the Yuan period," *JAOS* 72 (1952), p. 73 f.; *idem*, "Nuove luci," doc. XII. That the import of Chinese silk in Western Europe was not insignificant is emphasized by Balard, "Precursori di Cristoforo Colombo," p. 159 f.

354 *Secreta fidelium crucis*, p. 23.

355 Heyd II, p. 143; R. S. Lopez, "European merchants in the medieval Indies: the evidence of commercial documents," *JEH* III (1943), p. 171.

356 Lopez, "European merchants," p. 174 ff.; idem, "Nouve luci," p. 361 ff., 393 ff.; idem, "Venezia e le grandi linee dell'espansione commerciale nel secolo XIII," in *La civiltà veneziana del secolo di Marco Polo* (Florence, 1955), p. 53 ff.

357 Golubovich, *op.cit.* II, p. 71.

358 See *Analecta Francescana*, III (Quaracchi, 1897), pp. 609, 612.

359 Lopez, "European merchants," p. 182.

360 *Analecta Francescana*, III, p. 611.

years came to Cyprus.[361] In dealing with the travels of European merchants to China and India, we must keep in mind that even as these travels are concerned in many contracts, the commercial goal of the journey to be made was purposely not indicated. There were many merchants who concealed their purpose, if only for fear of competition.[362] On the other hand, many of those documents that explicitly refer to such travels date to the second quarter of the fourteenth century, when the Holy See had laid a strict embargo upon trade with the Moslem Levant and compelled the merchants to look for alternative channels for obtaining the Oriental commodities in which they were interested.[363] This cannot be mere chance.

In this period, the Italian merchants certainly made an effort to trade directly with India and the Far East. The French bishop Guillaume Adam, who wrote his treatise *De modo Saracenos extirpandi* in 1317, says that the Genoese have their own ships in the Indian Ocean.[364] This is supported by a curious passage in a work of the famous Arab sailor Ibn Mādjid. Writing in 1462, he quoted "those who have knowledge of the matters of the Franks" according to whom, in bygone times the latter sailed to Madagascar, India, and East Africa.[365] Although Ibn Mādjid cautiously hints that he does not take responsibility for this account, it sounds reliable. But it would be rather risky to conclude from it and from another passage in the writings of Guillaume Adam that the Italian merchants sailed so far to the south that they no longer could see the North Pole, but saw the South Pole 54° high, which would mean they sailed 34° south of the equator.[366] Guillaume Adam did not say that the merchants who travelled there were Europeans.[367]

So there are a considerable number of texts, in different sources, that

[361] E. Blochet, "Neuf chapitres du 'Songe du vieux pèlerin' de Philippe de Mézières," *ROC* IV (1899), p. 375. The king under whose reign the Genoese came to Cyprus was evidently Peter I (1358-1369).

[362] Lopez, "European merchants," p. 168.

[363] Petech, *art. cit.*, p. 549.

[364] RHC, Documents arméniens II, p. 553. On the date of the treatise, see Kohler, p. cxc. According to Kohler (see there in the footnote) the passage refers to the galleys built by order of Arghūn Khān aiming at a blockade of Egyptian trade with India, see above p. 12. But the French author says: *naves faciunt*, and consequently it is unlikely that he had in mind those galleys whose construction in 1290 resulted in a great failure. Certainly the interpretation of J. Richard, who considers the passage as evidence of Genoese commercial shipping in the Indian Ocean, is more convincing; see his paper "Les navigations des Occidentaux sur l'Océan Indien et la mer Caspienne," *Sociétés et compagnies de commerce en Orient*, p. 358.

[365] G. Ferrand, "Une navigation européenne dans l'Océan Indien au XIVe siècle," *JA* 1922, II, p. 307 ff.

[366] *Directorium ad passagium faciendum*, RHC, Doc. armén. II, p. 383 f., and see p. clxi that the author was not Raymond Etienne but Guillaume Adam and cf. Ferrand, *art. cit.*

[367] Cf. R. Hennig, *Terrae incognitae*, 2nd ed. (Leiden, 1944-1956) III, p. 153 f. (who, however, attributes to Ferrand the assumption that the passage in Ibn Mādjid's work referred to the travels of Guillaume Adam himself!).

show that the Italian merchants went to China and to India in that period and were engaged in shipping on the Indian Ocean. To judge from all these sources it could be inferred that, at least in the second quarter of the fourteenth century, the number of such merchants was not very small. But what was the economic importance of these exchanges? What could have been the volume of direct trade between the South European trading nations and India and the Far East?

For a quantitative estimate of these exchanges, the relatively high expense of such lengthy journeys should be taken into consideration. The cost of transportation from India over the land route through Persia and on to the coast of the Black Sea of the Mediterranean must have been exceedingly high. So only the transport of the most expensive spices would have been profitable. Chinese silk, on the other hand, had a lower value on Western markets than that coming from some Caspian provinces and from Northern Persia.[368] Therefore, direct trade between Southern Europe and the Far East and India could not become a viable alternative to trade with the Moslem Levant, insofar as an extensive trade of commodities destined for mass consumption was concerned. But trade with Persia and the emporia on the coasts of the Black Sea and the Sea of Azov had become rather important alternative routes. Not insignificant quantities of spices could be shipped from there to Southern Europe. When the Tatars attacked the Italian merchants in Tana in 1343, the losses of the latter must have been substantial. According to the Florentine chronicler Villani, the losses of the Venetians amounted to 300,000 fl. and those of the Genoese to 350,000 fl. Here we have valuable, though not absolutely reliable, data concerning the volume of the commercial exchanges carried on along this artery of Levantine trade for one may safely suppose that these figures represent more or less the annual investment of the two great Italian trading nations. The Florentine author also recounts that the disaster of Tana resulted in a rise of spice prices in Italy of 50-100 percent.[369]

[368] See Lopez, "Chinese silk in Europe in the Yuan period," *JAOS* 72, p. 72 ff.; *idem*, "L'extrême frontière du commerce de l'Europe médiévale," *Le Moyen Age* 69 (1963), p. 485.
[369] Villani XII, 26.

II
Back to Egypt and Syria (1345-1370)

A. The Renewal of Regular Trade (1345-1364)

In the fifth decade of the fourteenth century there was a great change in the political situation in two areas that served the Italian traders as alternative supply centers of Oriental commodities. In fact, trade with Persia and the Tatar kingdom in Southern Russia had to be discontinued.

After the death of Abū Saʿīd in 1335, the reign of the Īlkhānid dynasty over Persia came to an end, and a long period of anarchy and struggle among various princes and generals ensued. Ādharbaydjān, whose capital was Tebriz, fell to the Chūpānid prince Ḥasan "the Little." Another pretender to the heritage of the Īlkhāns, Ḥasan "the Tall," tried in vain to reunite the kingdom, which had fallen apart, but he succeeded in founding a new dynasty, that of the Djalāʾirids, and his son Uways (1356-1374) ruled over both Iraq and Ādharbaydjān. However, security in Western Persia became so precarious that it was impossible for the Italian traders to carry on their activities and to visit Tebriz, where they purchased spices, silk, precious stones, and the pearls of the Persian Gulf.[1] In 1338 the Venetian government decreed that trade in Persia should be discontinued, and Genoa issued such a prohibition in 1340 and again in 1341.[2] The rulers of Ādharbaydjān themselves, who were interested in the income from the customs, approached the Italian merchant republics and invited them to take up their activities in Tebriz. In 1344 al-Ashraf, then prince of Tebriz, sent an embassy to Genoa and they also had talks with the Venetian *bailo* in Constantinople. Then in 1357 Uways, in a letter to the government of

[1] See Thiriet, *Régestes* I, p. 55 (of a 1344). Lopez, "Nuove luci," append. XIII. Balard says in his paper "Precursori di Cristoforo Colombo," p. 152, that the Genoese colony still existed in Tebriz in 1344 and adduces as proof the report on the inquiry made there on the heresy of some Franciscans, but the result of this inquiry was presented to the Holy See in March 1334; see Chapter I, p. 60.

[2] Thiriet, *op.cit.* I, p. 39.

Venice, once again suggested that the trade with his kingdom should be renewed. But the negotiations and the attempts actually made by some Genoese and Venetian merchants to return to Tebriz resulted in complete failure.[3] There were also other reasons for the interruption of trade with Persia. The relatively great distance between Tebriz and Trebizond, where the merchandise bought in Persia was loaded on the ships, had always been a hindrance to the development of this artery of Levant trade. The cost of transport was a significant factor. But during the period of anarchy in Ādharbaydjān, conditions became difficult in Tebriz too. Even there the Italian traders were no longer secure, as is indicated by the decrees of the Venetian Senate concerning the measures to be taken.[4] In 1344 the Senate left to the Council of the Venetian colony in Constantinople the decision of whether or not the "galleys of Romania" could safely continue their travel to Trebizond.[5] Even relations with the Greek emperor of Trebizond had become strained.[6]

Then, as a result of a conflict in 1343 between the Venetians of Tana and the Tatars, for some years the activities on this alternative route of Levant trade also had to be discontinued. The Genoese too had suffered losses and some had been killed by the Tatars in the Crimea. In fact, in 1344 Venice forbade her citizens to trade with the Tatars.[7] Then it was decided to send an embassy to Djānī Beg, the ruler of the Tatars, and when Genoa proposed approaching him in common, Venice agreed. Thereupon Genoa, too, forbade her subjects trade with the Tatar Kingdom.[8] The steps taken by the two Italian trading nations were successful to the degree that Djānī Beg made new concessions.[9] In any case, in 1347 the Venetian galleys abstained from visiting Tana.[10] The tension between the Venetians and the Tatars continued for some years, for in 1350 the Venetian Senate ordered the merchants to leave Tana.[11]

When these two alternative routes of Levant trade were closed, the Italian merchant republics decided to insist that the Holy See lift the embargo on trade with Egypt and Syria. A request submitted by Venice to the pope in

[3] See Heyd II, pp. 129, 131.
[4] Thiriet, *op.cit.* I, pp. 44, 57.
[5] *Op.cit.* I, p. 55.
[6] *Ibidem.*
[7] *Op.cit.* I, p. 54.
[8] *Op.cit.* I, pp. 55, 56; *Libr. Com.* II, lib. 4, nos. 125, 128, 152, 164, 167, 169; *Dipl. Ven.-Lev.* I, p. 333 f.
[9] L. de Mas Latrie, "Privilèges commerciaux accordés à la république de Venise par les princes de Crimée et les empereurs mongols du Kiptchak," *Bibl. Ecole des chart.* 29 (1868), pp. 584 f., 587 ff.
[10] Thiriet, *op.cit.* I, p. 61 f.
[11] *Op.cit.* I, p. 71.

1338 had been turned down,[12] but this time the Holy See changed its attitude. On one hand, the Church could not overlook the urgent necessity that the trading nations had of maintaining the exchanges with the Near Eastern markets, for otherwise the whole system of world trade, as built up by long, tenacious, and patient efforts, would have collapsed. On the other hand, the Curia and those connected with it wanted to extract more and more money from the trading nations, which were ready to pay for the licenses (*gratia*) directly to the papal treasury or by bribing high-ranking persons who had influence on the decisions of the Curia. From 1344 the Holy See periodically began to grant the trading nations permits to send some ships to the ports of Egypt and Syria, while merchants and government plenipotentiaries had to take an oath before the bishop of their towns that they were not loading war material. Sometimes, however, the ecclesiastical authorities refused to accept these affirmations. On the other hand, these licenses were made temporary—that is, valid for a few ships and a limited time—so that they served only as a palliative. Time and again the trading nations had to intervene in Avignon, to plead the absolute necessity of trading with the dominions of the Mamluk sultan and to spend considerable sums to obtain permission to send some galleys and "round ships" (cogs) to Egypt or Syria. But the Holy See also granted such licenses to powerful noblemen who were not engaged in Levant trade at all, and the latter in turn sold them to merchants. The licenses were transferred to the Genoese and the Venetians, who paid huge sums of money for them.[13] Even churchmen who were entrusted with important tasks by the pope were granted permission to engage in trade with the dominions of the sultan of Cairo, so that they could defray their expenses.[14] The copious information in the rich archives of Venice conveys a clear picture of the diplomatic interplay between the great Adriatic seapower and the Holy See, which conditioned Levant trade in the middle of the fourteenth century, but there can be little doubt that the other trading nations had recourse to the same devices.

In 1344 the pope granted Venice the right to send six galleys and four round ships to the dominions of the Mamluk sultan, in a five-year period.[15] But, since the tonnage of the cogs was much greater than that of the galleys, in 1345 the Venetians requested and obtained permission to send seven

[12] See my paper "Observations on Venetian Trade," p. 538.

[13] See Heyd II, p. 46 ff.; *Libr. Com.* II, lib. 5, no. 45, lib. 6, no. 258.

[14] Setton, *Papacy and Levant* I, p. 234.

[15] *Dipl. Ven.-Lev.* I, no. 144; *Libr. Com.* II, lib. 4, no. 122, has 4 galleys and 6 round ships in every four years, whereas Heyd II, p. 45, quoting *Dipl. Ven.-Lev.*, says 6 galleys and 6 cogs. I checked the original and found that the text is rightly published in *Dipl. Ven.-Lev.*

galleys to the Levant in place of every four cogs.[16] In the course of time the Holy See granted these permits almost every year, as the registers of the Venetian Chancery (the *Libri Commemoriali*) of the 1350's show. However, questions arose as to how the permits should be interpreted, and from time to time these questions were submitted to the doctors of canon law. These consultations referred to the validity of the permits: e.g., were they invalidated by the death of the pope who had granted them; or did the permit begin from the date they were granted or the date they were put to use; or which articles fell under the papal embargo?[17] The need for these consultations resulted from the rigidity of the Holy See with regard to the trade of war material (or articles considered as such, e.g., linen for sails). Transgression of the strict prohibition to sell the Moslems these articles was the pretext for again issuing a general embargo of trade with the dominions of the Mamluks.[18] But, despite all these difficulties, the permits were much coveted. Permits obtained by Frenchmen were sold to Italians, and the Genoese transferred them to Venetians, of course for an adequate payment.[19] Even for the rich merchant republics it was not easy to cover the expenses incurred in obtaining them, either from the Holy See or from other grantees, and for the honorarium of those canonists to be consulted. So the governments were compelled to impose new taxes for this purpose on the Levant traders.[20]

The minutes of the deliberations of the Venetian Senate shed a good deal of light on the hesitations and the apprehensions of the merchant class engaged in overseas trade, concerning the renewal of direct and regular trade with Egypt and Syria. They show how complicated the situation had become after a long suspension of these exchanges and when economic life in Europe itself had begun to undergo a great change. To the perspicacious traders of Venice and Genoa it seemed not at all easy to renew trade with the dominions of the sultan.

Anyhow, in 1344 Venice sent Niccolò Geno as ambassador to the Mamluk sultan. He had orders to request the confirmation of the old privileges, especially those granted Venice in 1302. He was also to ask for a reduction in the import customs amounting to 20 percent for merchandise, 4.5 percent for gold and 3 percent for silver. If the customs in Syria were lower, he was to obtain a reduction in them too. Further, he was to request that a good part of the customs, possibly as much as half, be accepted in silver.

[16] *Dipl. Ven.-Lev.* I, no. 162; *Libr. Com.* II, lib. 4, no. 172. Venice had asked for the substitution of every cog by 8 or 10 galleys.

[17] *Libr. Com.* II, lib. 5, nos. 116, 117; lib. 6, nos. 164, 479.

[18] Raynaldus-Baronius VII, p. 46; *Libr. Com.* II, lib. 6, no. 153.

[19] On the transactions connected with the trade of licenses, see also Setton, *op.cit.* I, p. 263.

[20] ASV, Mag. Cons., Novella, f. 171a (a. 1359): a tax of 1 percent on trade with Egypt and Syria.

He was to ask for the establishment of a mint to strike silver coins in Alexandria so that the Venetian traders could have their ingots coined as dirhams. Since there was no Venetian consul in Alexandria, although Venice still had two *fondachi* there, he was to remain as consul, if he had reason not to return.[21] The sultan was very pleased by the coming of the Venetian embassy, since he hoped that a new period of intense commercial exchanges would begin again. The ambassador did obtain a reduction in the customs for import and export of merchandise to 10 percent and for gold and silver to 2 percent. The import of pearls, coral, and furs was to be custom-free. Further, the Venetians were promised freedom of trade and in particular there would be no compulsory purchases and sales, e.g., purchases of sugar from the sultan's refineries, which had apparently been established in Alexandria a short time before. In addition, the treaty, concluded by Niccolò Geno, included the promise that the Venetians would not be made responsible for the misdeeds of others and primarily not of Christian pirates. This latter promise had been made to the Venetian embassy in 1302, but reconfirmation was considered necessary. The concessions of the sultan were contained in three documents, one in Arabic, a second in Latin, and a third in Venetian. They were drawn up successively in January and February 1345.[22] The sultan also agreed to open a mint in Alexandria, and he fulfilled his promise. Coins that have come down to us show that the Mamluks began to strike dirhams in Alexandria.[23]

Immediately upon the return of Niccolò Geno, in 1345, another Venetian ambassador, Angelo Serbi, went to Cairo. He obtained agreement from the sultan that Venice could appoint consuls in other towns besides Alexandria.[24] At the same time the Venetian authorities appointed a new consul in Alexandria. To judge by the instructions he was given for the administration of the colony, the number of the Venetians then residing in Alexandria was still very small. For, in the case that he could not find twelve nobles, as required by law, he was permitted to set up a council that would include commoners or even non-Venetian subjects of the republic (*fedeli*).[25] In the year 1346, additional rules for the colony in Alexandria were laid down by the Senate and, at the same time, the consul was in-

[21] Misti 22, f. 44, 45a ff., and cf. 90b.

[22] *Dipl. Ven.-Lev.* I, nos. 153-155; cf. my paper "Observations on Venetian Trade," p. 540.

[23] P. Balog, *The Coinage of the Mamlūk Sultans of Egypt and Syria* (New York 1964) (American Numismatic Society, Numismatic Studies 12), no. 493. That Niccolò Geno did not remain (as consul) in Egypt is known from the titles of the sultanian privileges: see *Dipl. Ven.-Lev.* I, pp. 290, 292, and from the decision of the Senate concerning the appointment of a new consul, to be quoted below. (I have checked the originals of the document quoted in first place and found that they read indeed q' add' etc.)

[24] *Dipl. Ven.-Lev.* I, no. 155, and cf. "Observations on Venetian Trade," p. 540.

[25] Misti 22, f. 90b 23, f. 24a.

structed to protest to the Moslem authorities against abuses prejudicial to the Venetian merchants.[26]

Upon the change in policy of the Holy See the other trading nations also took measures to renew the contracts with the Mamluk court. At the end of 1345 Pedro IV, king of Aragon, again sent Pere de Mijavilla as ambassador to Cairo. He was to ask for the relics of Saint Barbara, for the liberation of some captives, and for the reduction of the custom duties which the Catalan merchants had to pay in the dominions of the sultan, so that they should enjoy the same status as the Venetians. In fact, direct trade between Catalonia and Egypt was taken up immediately. In 1344 the king of Aragon had already allowed Pere de Mijavilla and Arnaldo Llorens, both of Barcelona, to send a ship to Alexandria. They had previously obtained a license from the pope. Undoubtedly, regular trade began again, and in the middle of the fourteenth century Catalan ships frequently visited the ports of Egypt and Syria. At the end of 1347 a Florentine merchant wrote from Alexandria to Venice that a Catalan cog that was due to come from Messina with a rich cargo of merchandise from Catalonia was being awaited every day. The writer of the letter emphasizes that the shipment had a license from the pope.[27]

The accounts in the archives of Venice about her Levantine trade in the middle of the fourteenth century shed much light on these commercial exchanges.

In the year 1345 the Venice-Alexandria galley line was re-established. In that year two state galleys were sent to Alexandria; in 1346 three, and in 1347 again two. However, there were fears in Venice as to the success of the expeditions to Egypt. In 1345 the consul had instructions to tell the sultan that few merchants had come to the spice fair, because it was uncertain that they would find a sufficient quantity of merchandise, but if there would indeed be enough, many more would come the next year. But in Venice the interest in the expedition of the galleys and in direct trade with Egypt was very great. The Senate ordered very big galleys to be prepared and so much merchandise was loaded that a great part of it had to be unloaded.[28] The hesitations and doubts prevailed also in subsequent years. It was feared in Venice that the shipments of the galleys to Alexandria would be a failure and the "patrons" of the galleys were allowed to load cheap articles, such as powdered sugar, cassia, senna, dates, and alkali, instead of the precious spices.[29] But these misgivings proved to be unjus-

[26] *Dipl. Ven.-Lev.* I, no. 164.

[27] López de Meneses, "Florilegio documental," *Cuadernos de historia de España* 13, no. XI (p. 188 ff.) 14, no. XIV (p. 183 ff.); *Pignol Zucchello*, p. 111.

[28] Misti 23, f. 30b; F. C. Lane, "The Venetian galleys to Alexandria, 1344" in *Festschrift H. Kellenbenz*, I, p. 435 f.

[29] Misti 23, f. 55a 24, f. 20b f.

tified. The first galley trips to Alexandria were very successful, for one reads in a merchant letter that in 1347 the Venetians acquired great quantities of spices and other articles in Alexandria. By the beginning of August, the Venetian agents had bought so much that they bought no more, feeling that much of what they had already bought would be left in the port, because the galleys would not have enough space to load it all.[30]

However, the proceedings of the Venetian Senate make it very clear that for a long time many of its members had doubts about whether or not trade with Egypt and Syria should be developed. It may even be safely concluded that a not insignificant number of the Venetian merchant class was opposed to fostering trade with the dominions of the Mamluk sultan. There cannot be the slightest doubt that such opinions also existed in Genoa and other trading towns of Italy.

When a proposal was made to the Venetian Senate, in 1352, to send a cog instead of the galleys to Alexandria, there were long deliberations about the advantages of the expedition.[31] Suggestions to send cogs to Alexandria in 1354, when the galley line was still suspended, were not carried.[32] In the year 1357, there was strong opposition to the intensification of trade with Egypt. This is clearly shown by the number of those in the Senate who voted for the despatch of the galleys, against, or abstained.[33] Then, in 1358, the opposition to trade with Egypt was particularly strong. On 4 May in four votes there was no majority for the despatch of the galleys, and on 16 May no less than 10 votes were necessary to obtain a majority—of one![34]

How could the opposition to trade with the Moslem Levant be explained? Despite various conflicts in which Venice was involved in the middle of the fourteenth century, its position in international trade was very strong. In 1345, a new treaty had been concluded with Ancona and once more Venice had confirmed its privileged status vis-à-vis its weaker competitor in the Adriatic.[35] Three years later, in 1348, a new treaty with Nürnberg, the leading commercial town of Southern Germany, guaranteed the Venetians there freedom of trade.[36] Then, in 1349, Venice obtained an agreement form the Visconti that the Milanese would henceforth not acquire certain articles anywhere but in Venice.[37] So the political situation of Venice could

[30] *Pignol Zucchello*, p. 87.
[31] Misti 26, f. 56b, 57a, 85a, 86a, 89a.
[32] Misti 27, f. 21a.
[33] See my paper "Observations on Venetian Trade," p. 543.
[34] Misti 28, f. 47b.
[35] *Libr. Com.* II, lib. 4, no. 158.
[36] *Op.cit.* no. 248.
[37] A. Sorbelli, "La lotta tra Genova e Venezia per il predominio del Mediterraneo," in *Memorie della R. Accademia delle scienze dell'Istituto di Bologna, Cl. di scienze morali*, ser. I, t.V (1910/11), *Sez. di scienze storico-filologiche*, p. 103.

not be the reason for the opposition to the development of trade with the Moslem Levant.

The havoc wrought by the Black Death should certainly not be overlooked. Venice itself had suffered great losses in population, and measures had to be taken to induce foreigners to come to the town to settle there. Various privileges were granted them.[38] In the years subsequent to the Black Death, there was a series of particularly bad harvests in several European countries, and the disarray that followed the great pestilence everywhere may also have kept many people from embarking on what they considered in those circumstances as adventurous activities. But it is borne out, both by Italian and by Arabic sources, that even in the years in which the pestilence was at its height the trade between the emporia of Southern Europe and the Levant was not discontinued. There is little doubt that seaborne traffic slowed down in 1348, when the plague was at its worst. According to Arabic authors, there was a great scarcity of foreign merchandise in Near Eastern markets, and the custom offices in Alexandria were closed.[39] These accounts must not be exaggerated. But the Venetian galley service to Alexandria was not suspended, and an Arabic chronicler mentions the arrival of another European merchantman in Alexandria in 1348.[40]

The opposition to the intensification of trade with the Moslem Levant could be attributed to the general economic situation in many European countries. According to some economic historians, the economies of most parts of Europe suffered from a general depression in the period following the Black Death. When populations decreased by a third or more and the demand for basic food diminished, prices fell, and the volume of trade and production became much smaller. Those who hold this view maintain that the output of the textile industries, the most important sector of mediaeval industry, declined very greatly. Everywhere a large number of villages was abandoned by their inhabitants, grain prices were low for a long period, and in many countries a considerable part of the cultivated area became pasture land. This was true for Spain, the coastal plain of Latium, Northern Apulia, and, in Northern Europe, for England. The export of wool from England diminished very markedly, and the volume of production of woolen cloth in Flanders, a leading center of this industry, declined. So it might be concluded that those in the Italian towns who opposed the development of trade with the dominions of the Mamluks feared, perhaps rightly, that

[38] ASV, Mag. Cons., Novella, f. 91b f., and cf. 117a ff. Cf. S. Romanin, *Storia documentata di Venezia* III, p. 16.

[39] *Sulūk* II, p. 777; Ibn Iyās I, p. 191; cf. M. Dols. *The Black Death in the Middle East* (Princeton, 1977), p. 279.

[40] *Sulūk* II, p. 777 f.

owing to the general economic depression it would be impossible to sell additional ship loads of Oriental spices and drugs and that as a result prices would have to be lowered and losses would ensue. It is possible that such were indeed the motives of this sector of public opinion, so strongly represented in the legislative bodies of the great Italian emporia.

Against this hypothesis it might well be argued that the long decline in grain prices does not necessarily prove general pauperization and decay. Because of the reduced demand for grain the peasants went over to growing other crops, such as high quality foodstuffs or industrial crops, like flax or woad.[41] In some regions of Western Europe there was a great upswing in the production of wine, in others, of fruit growing or the production of dairy products.[42] Whereas the wool industry of Florence and Flanders had a smaller volume, production in the same sector of the textile industry probably increased in Brabant, Normandy, the Rhenish towns, Switzerland, and several towns of Lombardy and Tuscany, and even in Silesia and Poland. The retrogression of English wool exports was closely connected with the great development of England's own woolen industry[43] in the same period; the production of linen stuffs developed considerably in Flanders, Brabant, France, Switzerland, and Southern Germany.[44] The silk industry of Upper and Central Italy certainly did not decline in the second half of the fourteenth century.[45] So it seems exaggerated to speak of an industrial decline. If production in some sectors or some countries declined, it grew in others. The production of some mining centers and siderotechnical industries of Northern Europe certainly grew.[46] In fact the phenomenon most characteristic of economic life in many parts of Europe was the shifting of investments into other directions.

But even if the total of both the agricultural and industrial production decreased, there is good reason to believe that after the terrible losses of population, people were better off than before. The per capita income probably grew substantially. This is surely a very good criterion for judging the economic situation and for weighing the reasoning that opposition to the development of Levantine trade stemmed from fears that it would be difficult to market the costly Oriental spices. Production of grains had to be reduced, because there was less demand. But as in the course of a short time people inherited the fortunes of relatives and there was a great shortage

[41] Th. Abel, *Die Wüstungen des ausgehenden Mittelalters*, 2nd ed. (Stuttgart 1955), p. 39 ff.; R. W. Dowd, "The economic expansion of Lombardy 1300-1500," *JEH* 21 (1961), p. 147, 155.

[42] R.-H. Bautier, *The economic development of mediaeval Europe* (London 1971), pp. 195, 197 f.; E. Pitz, "Die Wirtschaftskrise des Spätmittelalters," *VSWG* 52 (1965), p. 357 f.

[43] Bautier, *op.cit.*, p. 212; M. Postan, "The trade of mediaeval Europe: the North," in his *Mediaeval trade and finance* (Cambridge, 1973), p. 161.

[44] Bautier, *op.cit.*, p. 213.

[45] Dowd, *art. cit.*, p. 155.

[46] See Postan, *art. cit.*, p. 171; Bautier, *op.cit.*, p. 221.

of labor in the towns, the price of labor rose everywhere and people began to spend much more for food and clothing.[47] The decrees against luxurious clothing and the fixing of maximum wages, which date to the years immediately subsequent to the Black Death, are a clear proof of this trend. Everywhere the food basket changed; butter was substituted for lard. Housing improved almost everywhere, and rich townspeople built themselves spacious and comfortable dwellings.

So one will conclude that although certain strata of the peasantry (those who grew, for example, corn) and townspeople (those living from the ground rent) suffered from the economic development of the post-plague period, most people lived better and could afford Oriental spices. The shrewd and well-informed Venetian merchants could not have doubted the good chances of selling the Oriental articles, and consequently it is very unlikely that many of them opposed the development of trade with the Moslem Levant for this reason.

Therefore it could be assumed that those who were against the intensification of trade with Egypt and Syria were the spokesmen of groups of traders who had investments in Greece, in the colonies on the Black Sea, and in Cyprus.[48]

However, it is true that the Italian merchants who came to Egypt and Syria in the middle of the fourteenth century to buy Indian spices and drugs there encountered great difficulties. One serious obstacle was the domination of the spice market by the powerful Kārimīs. They were a rather loosely connected and interconfessional group of rich merchants who were most active in the trade between the Near East, on one hand, and Yemen and India, on the other. Their number was not great, but their great riches made it possible for them to control the international trade of Egypt and Syria to a very great degree. They also engaged in trade with Ethiopia and the Western Sudan, where they bought slaves and gold. One of them, Sirādj ad-dīn ʿAbdallaṭīf b. Aḥmad Ibn Kuwayk, who died in 1334, travelled to the Western Sudan for forty years (and died there on one of his travels).[49] But they specialized in the spice trade, and through the reign of the Baḥrī dynasty (1250-1382) they enjoyed the protection of

[47] This is the line of reasoning of the economic historians who oppose the hypothesis of a great depression in the later Middle Ages: see C. M. Cipolla, "Economic Depression of the Renaissance," *Ec. Hist. Rev.* N. S. 16 (1963/64), p. 523; *Idem*, *Storia economica e sociale dell'Europa pre-industriale* (Bologna, 1974), p. 259; Fr. Lütge, "Das 14/15. Jahrhundert in der Sozial- u. Wirtschaftsgeschichte," *Jahrbücher für Nationalökonomie u. Statistik* 162 (1950), p. 190; J. van Klaveren, "Die wirtschaftlichen Auswirkungen des Schwarzen Todes," *VSWG* 54 (1967), p. 195; G.A.S. Rodgett, *A social and economic history of mediaeval Europe* (London, 1972), p. 214 ff.

[48] Cf. my paper "Observations on Venetian Trade," p. 543.

[49] J. Sublet, "ʿAbd al-Laṭīf at -Takrītī et la famille des Banū Kuwayk, marchands Kārimī," *Arabica* IX (1962), p. 193 ff. and see also above p. 53 and, further, my monograph *Les métaux precieux*, p. 19 f.

the Mamluk government, which was interested in the customs collected from them. A Florentine merchant writes from Alexandria to Venice at the end of 1347 that "quisti chermi" (Kārimites) will soon go to Mecca, so that the caravan from Mecca will be in Alexandria at mid-April and that there will be a great offering of merchandise. It is evident that spices are meant. The Mamluk rulers, however, also had another reason for protecting them: the rich Kārimīs were great bankers and could grant the sultan of Cairo and the king of Yemen substantial loans. Arabic historians speak of the fabulous riches of the Kārimī families of the Ibn Musallam, al-Maḥallī, and al-Kharrūbī, which flourished in the middle and the second half of the fourteenth century. This was indeed the period in which the Kārimīs reached the apogee of their economic power and their political influence. It was in 1351 that they gave huge loans in Cairo to a Yemenite king and provided the Mamluk sultan with the funds he needed by the purchase of his stocks.[50] Since they supplied the market with the Indian spices and were on very good terms with the Mamluk authorities, their control of the exchanges in Alexandria, and probably in some other ports, was almost total, so that they could also fix the prices.

The Italian traders intervened with the Mamluk government, asking that the exchanges be free. In 1363 the Venetian Senate deliberated on the matter. First it was proposed that the Venetian consul in Alexandria should protest to the sultan about the domination of the market by the Kārimīs. From instructions which ought to be given to the consul, according to this proposition, one learns that the Kārimīs controlled the sale of the European merchandise offered by the Italian traders, so that the latter were prejudiced. The proposition was turned down, because the question seemed to be too important to be dealt with by a consul. So it was decided to send an ambassador to Cairo. He was to obtain a decree from the sultan to the effect that the exchanges would be free. In view of the importance attributed to the matter, he was allotted 1,500 ducats for bribing influential people.[51] It seems, however, that the decision to send an ambassador to the sultan was not carried out.

In any case it is highly improbable that the steps taken by the Venetians were successful. For it is a matter of record that spice prices on the Near Eastern markets were rather excessive in the middle of the fourteenth century and remained high up to the end of the century. In Alexandria a sporta (225 kg) of pepper cost not less than 150 dinars in 1345 and, in

[50] See my "The Kārimī Merchants," in my *Studies on the Levantine Trade*, IV, where, p. 56, other papers are listed. That the Kārimīs of that period were an interconfessional group is seen from the letter published in my paper, "A private letter of the Mamlūk period," *Kiryath Sepher* 18 (1941-1942), p. 199 ff. See, further, *Pignol Zucchello*, p. 111.

[51] Misti 31, f. 2a, 2b f., and cf. the letter of Mr. Naura in *JESHO* 15 (1959), p. 233 (which quotes only the passages referring to the Kārimīs).

1347, 110-116 dinars. Since the rise had begun before the great plague, it could not be a consequence of it. Further, the price remained high many years after the plague. In 1355 a sporta cost 163 dinars, in 1366 about 80, and in 1373 more than 87.[52] In 1347 a ḳinṭār (180 kg) exported from Central Syria to Cyprus cost 176 dinars in Famagusta. The prices of other spices too were very high. In the same year, a Damascene ḳinṭār of Mecca ginger cost about 144 dinars in Famagusta, a Damascene raṭl of cloves 8 dinars. Although these were C.I.F. prices of commodities coming from Syria, they point to a level 100 percent higher than at the end of the fourteenth century.[53] The spice prices given in a list compiled in Famagusta, apparently in 1349, are very high too.[54] The dearth of spices in the middle and second half of the fourteenth century cannot be explained by the control of the Near Eastern markets by the Kārimīs only, however, as the price of pepper, the most important of these articles, was apparently rather low in Egypt at the beginning of the fourteenth century,[55] and the Kārimīs were already very powerful in that period. Changes in the price level in India itself, whence most spices were imported into the Near East, must have been another reason. However that may have been, the high level of prices of spices on the Levantine markets was certainly considered by many Italian merchants as an obstacle to the development of trade with the dominions of the Mamluks.

All these difficulties are clearly reflected in the sources that contain data about the development of Venice's Levantine trade in the middle of the fourteenth century. The renewal of regular trade between the South European emporia and the dominions of the Mamluks was not easy; it was also hampered by other factors. In fact the vicissitudes of the political relations between the Mediterranean powers sometimes caused the commercial exchanges with the Moslem Levant to be discontinued.

As a consequence of a new war between Venice and Genoa in the years 1351 to 1354, the Venetian galley line to Alexandria did not function. But

[52] See below, Table X.

[53] See my "La découverte de la voie maritime aux Indes et les prix des épices," in my *Studies on the Levantine Trade* XII, p. 35, 47f. (where it should be: a quintal of Famagusta was equal to 125 raṭls of Damascus), and cf. my *Histoire des prix*, pp. 410, 415, 417. It is true that the spices were packed in Famagusta in parcels of 40 local rotuli, equal to 50 raṭls of Damascus; cf. Pegolotti, p. 85. The custom prevailing in Famagusta to pack the spices in such parcels is an obvious indication that most of them came from Damascus.

[54] *Pignol Zucchello*, p. 123 ff.

[55] According to a Catalan source, a sailor offered in 1303 in Barcelona 3.5 quintals of pepper for 50 pounds; see *Histoire des prix*, p. 324. Since the pound of Barcelona then had the value of a Maghrebin dinar, worth about 1,1 Oriental dinar (see Ch. E. Dufourcq, *L'Espagne catalane et le Maghreb aux XIVe et XIIIe siècles*), p. 529, and 3 quintals were equal to 420 light Venetian pounds (see Pegolotti, pp. 122, 127, 129), it may be concluded that a sporta of 225 kg cost 84 Egyptian dinars. Since this was a CIF price, this datum points to a low FOB price in Alexandria.

since this war was the effect of the tension that prevailed between the two trading nations on the northern coast of the Black Sea and on the coast of the Sea of Azov—and it had again shown the precarious situation of the Venetians in that region—it could only strenghthen the sector of public opinion in Venice that favored the development of trade with the Moslem Levant. The Genoese, in fact, claimed that the Black Sea was an area where they had a privileged position and that other trading nations should pay them a tax for the right of conducting activities there. Further, they tried to impede the access of the Venetians to Tana.[56] Probably not a few Venetians were induced by the Genoese policy to change their minds and became aware of the fact that Venice's commercial future was closely tied to trade with Egypt and Syria. In the treaty of peace with Genoa, Venice had to oblige herself to suspend the trade of Venetian subjects with the Tatar kingdom of the Golden Horde for three years. However, after the war, Venice sent an embassy to Djānī Beg, the ruler of that kingdom, and to the prince of Soldaia, in order to make it clear that after this delay it would resume the exchanges with their dominions.[57] But in 1356 the Venetian authorities were not sure whether conditions in the Black Sea were such as to render possible the sailing of the galleys even to other (southern) regions of this area. They left the decision to the bailo and to the Council of the Venetian colony in Constantinople, with whom the captain of the Romania galleys was to consult.[58] In 1358, towards the end of the three-year period, Venice sent an embassy to Berdī Beg, the new khan of the Golden Horde, and to the ruler of Crimea, to obtain the renewal of the old privileges and new concessions.[59] The Tatar princes granted the Venetian request and reduced the customs to be paid in Crimea.[60] But nevertheless Venetian trade in the Black Sea area and in Greece itself was on the decline. Trade with Trebizond came to a standstill in the 1350's and was not taken up again before 1364.[61] In Constantinople there was an almost permanent tension between the Greek authorities and the Venetians; there were mutual claims and counter-claims. The Venetians complained that they did not enjoy liberty of trade and were the victims of endless vexations; the Greeks claimed that the Venetians interfered in their rights of sovereignty.[62] Consequently, in some years the auctions of the Romania galleys were a

[56] Sorbelli, "La lotta tra Genova e Venezia per il predominio del Mediterraneo," pp. 99 f., 105; Thiriet, *Régestes* I, p. 70.

[57] Thiriet, *op.cit.* I, p. 77.

[58] *Op.cit.*, p. 81.

[59] *Op.cit.*, p. 87 f.

[60] de Mas Latrie, "Privilèges commerciaux," (see n. 9 above), p. 589 ff.; cf. Heyd II, p. 200 ff.

[61] Heyd II, p. 105 f.; Thiriet, *op.cit.* I, p. 107.

[62] Thiriet, *op.cit.* I, pp. 79 f., 80 f., 88, 90, 99.

great failure, e.g., in 1355, 1361, and 1363.[63] So the Venetians had many reasons to intensify their trade with the dominions of the Mamluk sultan. The conquest of Lajazzo by the Mamluks in 1347 was another blow to the Italian merchants, since for a long time this town had served as a great supply center of Oriental articles and as a starting point for an alternative trade route to the Middle and Far East. Certainly this was a strong impetus to develop trade with Egypt and Syria. But meanwhile other events put a strain on the resources of Venice. In 1356 the contest between the Serenissima and Louis the Great, king of Hungary, resulted in a war which forced the Adriatic republic to a great political and economic effort. Naturally, this struggle interfered with commercial activities.

However, Venice continued the development of its trade with Egypt and Syria with great tenacity. When peace had been made with Genoa, an embassy was sent to Cairo in 1355 to pave the way for the renewal of regular trade. The Venetians were indeed not sure as to the attitude of the Mamluk government. An attack of the Genoese on Tripoli (in North Africa) had stirred up the feelings of solidarity in Egypt and Syria. So the Venetian ambassador, Ermolao Venier, was to try to influence the sultan to avoid reprisals against the Venetians. Further, he was instructed to demand that the levy on the merchandise of the Venetians be no greater than 10 percent. Ermolao Venier did obtain confirmation of the privilege granted in 1345, and the government of the sultan promised that the Venetian merchants would be well treated.[64] In the years subsequent to this embassy, Venetian trade with Egypt increased. The number of galleys sent to Alexandria in 1358 was four, and in 1359 it rose to six. But at the end of 1359 the pope revoked the licenses already granted and once again forbade trade with the dominions of the sultan.[65] So the Venetian galley line to Alexandria had to be suspended in 1360. When the papal embargo was lifted, Venice applied to the Holy See, at the beginning of 1361, with the request that the number of galleys allowed to visit Alexandria should be increased. If the ambassadors at the Curia could not obtain licenses for more galleys, they should, according to their instructions, ask for licenses for more cogs.[66] In fact, the Holy See, for a substantial payment, granted Venice licenses for a greater number of galleys, namely six, which could visit Alexandria four times each.[67] The advance of Venetian trade in the dominions of the sultan, however, was not smooth. The Moslem authorities, despite all promises,

[63] *Op.cit.* I, pp. 76, 99, 105, and see the paper of J. Chrysostomides, "Venetian commercial privileges under the Palaeologi," *Studi Veneziani* XII (1970), p. 267 ff.

[64] See my paper "Observations on Venetian Trade," pp. 541, p. 541 f. (where the sources are quoted).

[65] See above, note 18.

[66] Misti 29, f. 97b, 100b, 102b, 104a, 104b, 108a, 111a.

[67] *Libr. Com.* II, lib. 6, nos. 233, 241, 244-246; *Dipl. Ven.-Lev.* II, p. 73 ff.

again began to exact higher export dues. So it was decided to take another step in Cairo. In the same year, 1361, the Senate ordered Niccolò Contarini, who was appointed consul in Alexandria, to go first as ambassador to Cairo and to ask the sultan to keep the promises so often given. He obtained another confirmation of the old privileges and some new concessions.[68]

Meanwhile in Alexandria a colony of Venetian traders had come into being. The acts of Giovanni Campiano, who served as chaplain of Niccolò Contarini and notary of the Venetians in Alexandria, render it possible to catch a glimpse of the composition of the colony in 1362-1363. There were Venetian patricians, who had lived in the Egyptian emporium several years and maintained households with slave girls.[69] But there were also Venetian *popolani* in Alexandria.[70] In addition, people who hailed from small towns near Venice, like Treviso, and who were not merchants, belonged to the colony too.[71] However, it seems that within this colony the Cretan subjects of Venice outnumbered those from the metropolis. The Venetian merchants living in Alexandria not only engaged in the spice trade, but also imported honey and cheese into Egypt. A notarial deed of 1362 refers to the import, by Venetians, of mirrors. This is a very early text testifying to the export of glassware to the Levant.[72] There was already a full-fledged consulate at the head of the colony. Immediately upon the renewal of regular trade with Egypt, the Venetian Senate had laid down strict rules for the administration of the colony in Alexandria. The main purpose of these rules was to avoid friction with the Moslems and to make sure that the decrees of the government of the metropolis and the orders of the consul would be kept.[73] To judge from the acts of Giovanni Campiano, the consulate fulfilled its tasks satisfactorily. The consul had an office and several servants.[74]

Despite the opposition of the papacy and other factors unfavorable to the development of trade with the Moslem Levant, the number of Venetian galleys that visited Alexandria grew, whereas the Romania line declined. In the 1330's every year 8-10 galleys went to the ports of Greece and of the Black Sea; from 1345, their number amounted to no more than 4-5, and sometimes it was even less. The convoy to Cyprus and Little Armenia

[68] Misti 30, f. 5a; *Dipl. Ven.-Lev.* II, no. 47; Heyd II, p. 48; C. Poma, "Il consolato veneto in Egitto," *Bollettino del Ministero degli affari esteri* 1897, p. 469 ff. In the minutes of the Venetian Senate, which are quoted here, sadro is ṣādir, the export due.

[69] Nicoleto Bembo: I, f. 102a and see *Nicola de Boateriis*, no. 45; Antonio Michiel: I, f. 102a, 103b, and see *Nicola de Boateriis*, no. 128; Johan Cocco: I, f. 103b, and see *Nicola de Boateriis* no. 42 and cf. 44, 45; Bernardo Duodo: I, f. 102a, and see Misti 32, f. 82b, 127b, and cf. G. P., Sent. II, f. 32a.

[70] I, f. 102a, 102b.

[71] I, f. 102b.

[72] I, f. 103a, 103b.

[73] *Dipl. Ven.-Lev.* I, no. 164.

[74] I, f. 102a, 103a.

Table III Eastbound Venetian galley lines in the middle of the XIVth century

	number of galleys			source
year	Romania line	Cyprus line	Alexandria line	
1345	2	8	2	Misti 22, f. 81a; 23, f. 11b; Thiriet I, p. 57
1346	4	9	3	Misti 23, f. 57b, 59a; Thiriet, p. 60
1347	4	5	2	Misti 24, f. 22b, 24a; Thiriet, p. 61 f.
1348	first muda: 3	5	3	Thiriet, p. 62; Misti 24, 51a, 52b
1349	5	5	3	Op. cit. p. 64
1350	5	8	3	" p. 69
	1351-54 war			
1355	2	3	3	Op. cit. p. 76
1356	2	3	3	" p. 81
1357	2	3	4	" p. 85
1358	4	3	4	" p. 88 f.
1359	4	3	6	" p. 92
1360	5	5	-	" p. 96
1361	4	-	6	Misti 29, f. 121b; Thiriet, p. 99
1362	4	4	4	Misti 30, f. 74a, b; Thiriet, p. 101
1363	5	4	2	Misti 31, f. 6a, b; Thiriet, p. 105
1364	5	4	4	Misti 31, f. 65b, 66b, 67a; Thiriet, p. 108
1365	4	4	4	Misti 31, f. 96a, 97a; Thiriet, p. 110
1366	5	2[a]	4 + suppl. galley	Misti 31, f. 141a, 141b; Thiriet, p. 112; Libr. Com. III, lib. 8, no. 234
1367	4	4	4 + suppl. galley	Misti 32, f. 130b; 131b; 70a, 84a; Thiriet, p. 114 Libr. Com. III, lib. 8, no. 351
1368	6[b]	3	4	Misti 32, f. 130b; 131b; Thiriet p. 119; Libr. Com. ibidem
1369	4	3	-	Misti 33, f. 28a Thiriet, p. 121

a) These galleys should anchor 2 days in Cyprus and 18 in Beirut

b) Five leased by auction, one fitted out by the government.

before 1345 had consisted of 6-10 galleys; in the middle of the century it numbered 3-5. The sums paid for the lease of the galleys at the yearly auctions show even more clearly the decline of Venetian trade with the Greek territories and the upswing of the commercial exchanges with Egypt. From the end of the 1340's the amount yielded by the auction of the Romania galleys declined, whereas that obtained for the Alexandria galleys increased. In 1350 the sum paid for the lease of the Alexandria galleys was already greater then that paid for both the Romania and Cyprus galleys. In 1355 the amount obtained for the three Alexandria galleys surpassed the total of the rents paid for the Romania and Cyprus galleys together. But the galley line to Cyprus and Little Armenia in the 1350's was still a very important artery of Venice's Levant trade. Both in 1356 and 1357, the auction of these galleys yielded more than those of the Romania and Alexandria galleys respectively. At the end of the 1350's (in 1358 and 1359) and then at the beginning of the 1360's (especially in 1363), when the Cyprus line had been suspended, there was again an upswing of Venetian trade with the formerly Byzantine territories, but it was only temporary.[75]

Cyprus remained a great market of Oriental articles in the middle of the fourteenth century. The small Christian kingdom, an outpost of the Catholic world in the Near East, did not lose the role it had played before the Holy See had partially lifted the embargo on trade with the dominions of the Mamluks. It still served as a meeting place of European and Oriental traders and Greeks of Cyprus itself and of other regions, who were not concerned about the papal decrees and carried on a lively trade with the Moslem territories. In Famagusta there were many Genoese and Venetian merchants and also traders of Florence,[76] Ancona,[77] Messina,[78] and other Italian towns. The market of Famagusta was always well supplied with Indian spices, and sugar and cotton of Syria, as is shown by a price list of 1349.[79] Notarial acts drawn up in Famagusta in 1360 refer to the import of Syrian sugar and flax into Cyprus.[80] Commercial exchanges between Cyprus and Egypt were intense, so that a Venetian trader in 1361 obliged himself to pay a debt out of the amount realized by the sale of the first shipload he would receive from Alexandria or Venice.[81] Certainly spices held first place among the Oriental commodities imported into Cyprus from the Mamluk dominions. Another notarial act of 1360 deals with the pur-

[75] See the table of Fr. Thiriet, *La Romanie vénitienne au moyen âge* (Paris, 1959), p. 344.
[76] *Nicola de Boateriis*, no. 118.
[77] *Op.cit.*, nos.85, 86, 145, 177.
[78] *Op.cit.*, nos. 21, 22, 84; "Sicilians": no. 178.
[79] *Pignol Zucchello*, p. 123 ff., and cf. above, p. 75.
[80] *Nicola de Boateriis*, no. 59, and cf. 159, 98.
[81] *Op.cit.*, no. 82.

chase of pepper in Alexandria.[82] Other towns of Cyprus were also markets of the Levant trade. A judicial act of 1366 refers to the loading of pepper in Limassol.[83] A great part of the Oriental articles was certainly supplied by Levantine merchants, either Greeks or Moslems.[84] According to notarial acts, Venetian merchants carried on trade in Damascus by means of Cypriot *fattori*.[85] So there is good reason to believe that much of the sugar and cotton shipped from Cyprus to Venice[86] originally came from Syria. On the other hand, the Venetians and other Italian traders exported via Cyprus to Alexandria cheese,[87] furs,[88] copper,[89] and other articles.

Crete too was an intermediate point between the Moslem Levant and the South European emporia, even after the Holy See had allowed direct trade. But the island was predominantly a base for Venetian trade. Merchant letters and notarial acts drawn up in Candia and in Alexandria in the middle of the fourteenth century indicate the intensity of the traffic between Crete and Egypt. They refer to travels from Candia to Alexandria and to investments made there in trade with Egypt or to ships sailing from Alexandria to Seteia (Crete).[90] Other documents mention travels to Damietta[91] and Syria.[92] Traders of Crete exported wine to Alexandria[93] and, on the other hand, Candia was a great market for spices, drugs, and Oriental dyes. Ginger, ammoniacal salt and safflower from Egypt were shipped from Crete to Venice. Also, milk was exported from Alexandria via Crete to Venice.[94] Further the Venetian traders exported cotton and flax from Egypt to Crete.[95] As in Cyprus, Greek merchants and shipowners played a prominent role in these exchanges.[96]

Another channel for commercial exchanges between Southern Europe and the Moslem Levant was the trade that the merchants and shippers of Ragusa carried on with Egypt and Syria, either directly or indirectly. Several records, which have come down to us in the archives of this town, relate

[82] *Op.cit.*, no. 42.
[83] G. P., Sent. II, f. 8b f.
[84] About the trade of the Greeks with Egypt, see *Nicola de Boateriis*, no. 174.
[85] *Op.cit.*, no. 43.
[86] *Op.cit.*, nos. 14, 16; G. P., Sent. Int. V, f. 41b, 42a.
[87] *Op.cit.*, no. 143, and cf. above.
[88] *Op.cit.*, no. 128.
[89] *Op.cit.*, no. 125.
[90] *Pignol Zucchello*, p. 46 (a. 1345), 73 (a. 1347); *Zaccaria de Fredo*, nos. 40, 41, 42 (a. 1352). See also G. P., Sent. Int. V, f. 56b: Venetian merchants go from Candia to Alexandria and ship merchandise to Egypt.
[91] *Zaccaria de Fredo*, no. 91 (a. 1357).
[92] *Op.cit.*, nos. 71, 72 (a. 1352).
[93] *Pignol Zucchello*, p. 54 (a. 1346), 73 (a. 1347), 116 (a. 1348).
[94] *Op.cit.*, pp. 61 f. (a. 1346), 76 f. 88, 105, 108 (a. 1347).
[95] Giovanni Campiano I, f. 103a.
[96] *Ibidem*, f. 102a.

to these activities. In 1354 a cog carrying spices from Alexandria arrived in Ragusa; and in 1366 a Ragusan hired sailors for a ship bound for Alexandria.[97] However, Ragusa's Levantine trade was only a minor artery of the South European exchanges with the dominions of the Mamluks. The smaller emporia of the Adriatic could not compete with Venice and had to find their place in the framework of intercontinental trade as established by the Serenissima, which dominated the commerce of the Eastern Mediterranean.

The copious information that the rich Venetian archives provide should not, however, mislead us nor blur our view of the role that the various commercial powers played in the exchanges with the Moslem Levant. In fact, in the middle and second half of the fourteenth century, the Genoese still had a most important place in the trade between Western and Southern Europe and the dominions of the Mamluks, although a shift in the main line of their international trade had begun. This was a consequence of their increasing investments in trade with Northwestern Europe and, on the other hand, of their unchallenged supremacy in the trade with the Black Sea. The possession of the great emporium of Caffa and the privileged status in the Tatar kingdom of the Golden Horde, where they paid lower customs than others,[98] were great advantages and made competition with them in this area difficult. Therefore the Genoese traders became more inclined to invest in transactions in this region than elsewhere. The acquisition of the island of Chios in 1346 gave the Genoese a solid base for trade in the Aegean and with the Turks of Asia Minor, where they purchased cotton and marketed Western textiles. The colony in Pera, another great Genoese emporium in the Near East, was enlarged in 1348. But although the Genoese merchants became more and more interested in the exchanges with other areas, their activities in Egypt were still intense.

However, they no longer held the privileged position there that they had had in the second half of the thirteenth century, because relations between the Mamluk sultans and their neighbors had changed. Whereas in the second half of the thirteenth century there was bitter enmity between the sultan of Cairo and the Tatar rulers of Iraq and Persia, and the military slaves, or at least a very great part of them, destined to fill the ranks of their army had to be brought from Southern Russia via Constantinople by the Genoese, at the turn of the century the Īlkhāns of Persia became Moslems and thereupon the wars between them and the Mamluks came to an end. Henceforth the military slaves could be transported to Syria and Egypt by land, and the sea route through the straits was no longer the main artery of supply. Consequently, there was also a change in the com-

[97] Krekić, nos. 235, 237.
[98] Thiriet, *Régestes* I, p. 121.

position of the slave regiments in the army of the sultan of Cairo. The number of the Circassian slaves transported to Egypt and Syria via Upper Mesopotamia increased steadily, whereas the number of Turks of Southern Russia declined. From the middle of the fourteenth century, the Circassians became the strongest element within the ruling military caste of Egypt and Syria. In 1382 they took over the government and there began the reign of the second Mamluk dynasty, the so-called Burdjites or Circassians. Certainly, through the fourteenth century and even in the first half of the fifteenth century, the sultans of Cairo bought slaves in Southern Russia for service in their army and therefore employed Genoese agents. Barḳūḳ, the first Circassian sultan, had himself been bought in the Crimea. But the rulers of Cairo obtained military slaves elsewhere too. They were no longer dependent on the supply by the Genoese as they had been before. Consequently, Genoese influence diminished in Egypt and Syria in the middle and second half of the fourteenth century.

Genoa lost her privileged status for other reasons as well. The frequent conflicts between various factions in Genoa and the struggle for power resulted several times in the expulsion or exodus of a defeated party. The exiled group then embarked on military activities and privateering in some regions of the Mediterranean. The Genoese government could not prevent them from attacking Christian and Moslem ships alike. It could only warn the governments of those powers with which it wanted to remain on good terms. For instance, at the beginning of 1357 the doge of Genoa informed the government of Venice that four galleys of Genoese exiles, who had entered the service of the Angevin king of Naples, were about to embark on piracy off the Syrian coast.[99] But the Moslems blamed the Genoese government itself for the misdeeds of the exiles. Further, throughout the fourteenth century and later, the Genoese were inclined to adopt an aggressive attitude toward the Moslems, sometimes toward the rulers of Genoa themselves, sometimes the Genoese authorities outside the metropolis. On the other hand, the hold the government of Genoa had on her colonies was rather loose. The attitude of the Genoese was diametrically opposite to that of the Venetians, who distinguished themselves by great patience and who consistently pursued a policy of appeasement toward the Mamluks. There can be no doubt that in the long run this inclination to aggressiveness was prejudicial to Genoa's position in the dominions of the sultan of Cairo.

However, in the middle and second half of the fourteenth century, the Genoese were still very active in Egypt and ranked first among the European trading nations. There are no statistical data that would make it possible

[99] *Libr. Com.* II, lib. 5, no. 213.

to compare the volume of their trade in the Moslem Levant with that of the Venetians and other trading nations in the years subsequent to the renewal of direct exchanges; but it seems that in that period they had not yet lost their supremacy. They enjoyed the privilege of paying customs of only 10 percent (like the Venetians), whereas other foreign merchants paid 15 percent.[100] The Genoese colony in Alexandria must have been rather populous and had its own church.[101] Great commercial companies of Genoa invested a part of their capital in trade with the dominions of the sultan of Cairo. For instance, the company of Domenico Oltremarino, Gioffredo Grillo, and Eliano Camilla, which was founded in 1350 and whose capital amounted to 30,000 pounds (24,000 ducats), decided to invest some of its capital in Syria. Genoese galleys and cogs often visited Alexandria, Beirut, and other parts of the Mamluk dominions. Some were licensed by the Holy See, others not. In 1345 no less than four Genoese galleys, licensed by the pope, were ready to depart from Marseilles for Alexandria and Beirut. Provençal merchants also embarked on these ships and loaded cloth, linen, coral, and saffron. The commercial fleet of Genoa also served the Catalan trade with the Moslem Levant. In the year 1362 or 1363 a Genoese cog, whose captains were Bernardo Botardo, Andrea Muzo, and Orestito de Vento sailed, apparently from a Spanish port, to Alexandria, and had as passengers Tomas Lleopart, a merchant of Barcelona, and Silvestre Ubach. Neither the patrons of the ship nor the said Catalan merchants had a license from the king, which was required in his dominions for trade with Egypt and Syria. But the king granted them pardon. Records of the Royal Chancery of Aragon show that in 1365 the same Tomas Lleopart travelled on the Genoese cog "La Picona" from Genoa to Alexandria, without royal license. In that period Genoese ships frequently sailed between the Egyptian and Syrian ports, on one hand, and those of Cyprus and Crete, on the other. A notarial act drawn up in Famagusta in 1360 refers to two Genoese galleys, those of Luchino Cigala and Leonardo del Rosso, which had come there from Alexandria.[102] In the middle of the fourteenth century the Genoese engaged in trade with the hinterland of the Syrian coast too. From the account of an Arabic chronicler we see that they had a colony in Damascus in the 1360's.[103]

The commercial exchanges between the Provençals and the dominions of the Mamluks were rather irregular in the middle of the fourteenth

[100] Capmany, 2.1, no. 167, p. 248.

[101] Giovanni Campiano I, f. 101b.

[102] Liagre-De Sturler, no. 254 (on the value of the Genoese pound, see Cipolla, "I movimenti dei cambi," p. 42); Baratier, p. 221 f.; López de Meneses, "Los consulados," pp. 126, 127; *Nicola de Boateriis*, no. 42.

[103] Ibn Kathīr 14, p. 322. See also G. P., Sent. Int. V, f. 44a about the trade carried on in Alexandria by the Genoese Domenico de Campo Fregoso (about a. 1350).

century. It seems that in that period Genoa had the lion's share of the trade between the towns of Languedoc and the Provence and the Moslem Levant. The Ligurian republic had more ships and obtained from the pope more licenses. But there are documents that show that the direct trade of the Provençals with the dominions of the Mamluks was not discontinued altogether. In 1360 the council of Marseilles held discussions concerning three galleys belonging to citizens of the town and having a cargo of French cloth. They had departed for the Near East and after suffering shipwreck off the coast of Southern Italy had been seized by the authorities of the king of Naples.[104] From the minutes of the deliberations of the Council in 1365, we see that Marseilles also applied to the Holy See for licenses to trade with the dominions of the sultan of Cairo. In that year her representative at the Holy See had obtained licenses for a galley and a cog.[105] There was a fondaco of Marseilles in Alexandria in the middle of the fourteenth century, but there was no consul there to represent the interests of the merchants.[106] However, in a notarial act drawn up in 1362 in Alexandria there is a passage referring to the tavern of the fondaco,[107] so that it cannot have been abandoned altogether.

Trade between Catalonia and the Moslem Levant was certainly very lively in this period. A papal bull of 1348 indicates that it was never discontinued. Clement VI promised absolution to those traders who had engaged in trade with the Moslems (i.e., without having a permit), if they would use the profits for the war with the Turks. Michael, bishop of Barcelona, was directed to grant absolution to the Catalan merchants guilty of this illegal trade.[108] The Aragonese chronicler Jeronimo Zurita emphasizes the intense commercial activities the Catalans pursued in the 1360's in Egypt and in Syria.[109] Records included in various sources support this statement. A decision of Rabbi Nissim of Gerona, who lived in Barcelona (1310-1375), deals with the activities of a Jew, a merchant from Catalonia, who travelled in the Eastern Mediterranean and visited Cyprus and Alexandria.[110]

On the other hand, Catalan mariners always engaged in privateering in the eastern basin of the Mediterranean, and some documents bear witness to acts of piracy committed in 1360 off the Syrian coast by a Catalan

[104] Baratier, pp. 221 f., 226 f.

[105] *Op.cit.*, p. 228 f.

[106] *Op.cit.*, p. 223.

[107] Giovanni Campiano I, f. 102b.

[108] Raynaldus-Baronius, VI, p. 474 (why the papal legate for Denmark, Sweden and Norway, is given the same task is not clear, however). Ships of Barcelona in Beirut and Catalan merchants in Damascus in the 1440's, see Madurell-Garcia, nos. 98, 102-105.

[109] Lib. IX, cap. 64. A Catalan ship sailing in 1361 to Alexandria, see Madurell-Garcia, no. 114.

[110] *Responsa* (Königsberg, 1862), no. 43.

galley.[111] In this case, merchandise belonging to Venetian merchants was seized by the pirates, for in general they indiscriminately attacked both Christian and Moslem merchantmen. According to these documents, those Catalan privateers had the backing of the king of Aragon. However, it does not seem that their misdeeds prejudiced Catalan trade in Egypt and Syria. There was always a Catalan colony in Alexandria with a consul at its head. Usually a Barcelonan trader was appointed to this post by the Council of the township. Documents of 1347, 1360, 1361, and 1362 deal with the Catalan consulate in Alexandria. In 1360 the Council of Barcelona removed Bernardo Badutii from the post and appointed Bonanato Gil. In 1361 the latter was replaced by a new appointee. Royal letters of 1362 direct the Catalan consul in Alexandria to intervene with the sultan on behalf of the Franciscans in Bethlehem. So sometimes he fulfilled the task of an ambassador.[112]

The king of Aragon took various measures to foster trade with the Moslem Levant and also approached the sultan of Cairo. The purpose of most of his embassies and dispatches to the sultan was to obtain certain rights for the Franciscans and for the Catholics in general at the Holy Places. But these contacts certainly had a favorable influence, at least indirectly, upon the status of the Catalan merchants. Sometimes the king approached the sultan expressly on behalf of the latter.

In 1361 King Pedro IV sent an embassy to the sultan[113] and in 1362 he sent him several letters,[114] claiming certain rights for the Catholics at the Holy Places. The embassy that went to Cairo in 1361 was also to ask the sultan to grant the concessions that the Catalan consul in Alexandria would submit to him;[115] undoubtedly the requests of the merchants were met. It seems, however, that the Catalan colony in Alexandria itself took steps to obtain privileges. In the year 1353 the sultan granted the Catalans the same status as that of the Venetians and the Genoese, namely, that they should pay only 10 percent customs (instead of the 15 percent they had paid before). Thereupon the Council of Barcelona requested that the king impose a 1 percent tax on trade with Alexandria to cover the expenses of obtaining this privilege, and the king agreed to the request.[116]

[111] *Nicola de Boateriis*, nos. 59, 155.

[112] López de Meneses, "Los consulados," p 93, 95, 96, 98, 140 (according to the document quoted in the first place, the Council of Palma de Majorca also had been granted the right by the king of Aragon to appoint a consul in Alexandria, but it seems that it made no use of it); see also Capmany, *Memorias* 1, pp. 245-46.

[113] Rubió i Lluch, *Diplomatari*, p 737 ff.

[114] López de Meneses, *art. cit.*, pp. 98 f., 138 ff , 140, A. Arce, *Estudios orientales, judíos y de Tierra Santa* (Jerusalem, 1974), p. 156 ff.

[115] Rubió i Lluch, *op.cit.*, p. 735 ff. (the requests are not specified).

[116] Capmany, 2.1, no. 167, p. 248. The privilege is mentioned by Heyd, without indicating the exact date.

The attitude of the king of Aragon toward trade with the dominions of the Mamluks was double-faced, however, as it always had been. He again imposed fines on those who carried on trade with the Moslems without having a license,[117] but he readily granted himself such licenses. An enterprising trader of Barcelona, Frances Ça-Closa, got licenses from King Pedro IV for trade with Alexandria in 1355 and then in 1361, 1366, 1371, and 1373.[118] Another, Berenguer Beltran, was granted permits for travels to Egypt in 1363 and 1368. No less than six royal licenses have come down to us from the year 1365. One of them was granted to Leon March, who for forty years engaged in trade with the Levant. He was influential at the courts of the Lusignan kings of Cyprus and was also highly esteemed by the king of Aragon, serving both of them as a go-between. In 1365 he obtained a license from the king after the Council of Barcelona had transferred permission received from the pope to him.[119] So the ecclesiastical and secular authorities granted licenses, and traders like Leon March, who attached great importance to carrying on only legal trade, applied to both of them. Four of the royal licenses granted in 1365 were given to single traders and companies of Barcelonans and one to the consuls of Perpignan, whose ship was scheduled to depart from Collioure. As the destination of this ship and one of the other grantees only Alexandria is given. The others obtained licenses to sail to Damietta or Beirut also, or to both these ports.[120] That the Catalans carried on commercial activities in Syria is also attested to by the account of an Arabic chronicler, who mentions the Catalan traders in Damascus in the 1360's. According to the records of the Royal Chancery of Aragon, apparently there was already a Catalan consulate in Beirut in 1347.[121]

In the middle of the fourteenth century the number of European merchants who resided in the Levantine emporia a longer or shorter time cannot have been insignificant. On Palm Sunday of 1351 the European merchants

[117] M Sáez Pomés, p. 365 f.

[118] *Art. cit.*, p. 375. The destination of the journey in 1361 was supposed to be the Holy Places; the purpose of that mentioned in last place was the request from the sultan to grant the king the relics of Saint Barbara, but all these missions were connected with commercial activities. As the destination of the other travels, the "Soldania" (lands of the sultan) is indicated.

[119] *Art. cit.*, p 366, 373. Apparently also the king of France gave some kind of licenses for trade with the dominions of the sultan to shipowners who had already obtained a permit from the Church. For, otherwise, how could one explain the passage in a document referring to the two galleys of Pierre Miège (see above p. 52) where one reads: "receptos in salvagardia domini Francorum regis"; see Baratier, p 222

[120] Sáez Pomés, p. 367

[121] Ibn Kathīr 14, p. 322; López de Meneses, "Los consulados," p. 93, and cf. p. 126. Capmany, 1, p. 377, says that a Catalan consulate existed in Beirut in 1340, but does not quote a source.

in Acre made a public procession and aroused the anger of the Moslems.[122] So they cannot have been very few.

B. The Sack of Alexandria and its Aftermath (1365-1370)

In the early 1360's the Levantine trade of the South European trading nations developed, despite various obstacles. The increase in the volume of Venice's trade with Egypt and Syria is clearly shown by several data. The number of the galleys sent to Alexandria rose in the quinquennium 1361-1365 to 22, and the auction in 1365 was a great success.[123] It is true that the Venetian galley line to Cyprus had been suspended from 1361 to 1363, but the fact that, notwithstanding the revolt in Crete in 1363-1364, the galley service to Alexandria could be maintained is certainly a proof of the profitable exchanges with the dominions of the sultan. The attitude of the Holy See toward trade with the Moslem Levant had become more lenient. In the year 1365 Venice obtained licenses for eight galleys and six cogs.[124]

But meanwhile the skies of the Eastern Mediterranean were clouded again. King Peter I of Cyprus, a romantically minded knight whose ideas did not fit the political circumstances of his times, was eager to renew the Crusades. The nations of Western and Southern Europe were not inclined to join his adventurous policy or to wage war against the Moslem rulers of the Near East; the worldly interests of a rising bourgeoisie and secularly minded kings prevailed. But the chivalrous and warlike king was sustained by the popes of Avignon, Innocent VI and Urban V, aspiring to the restoration of the greatness of the papacy to those bygone times, and both the king and the popes were supported by some enthusiastic priests, who were sincere and fanatic. The French bishop Pierre Thomas, legate for the Crusade, and Philippe de Mézières, chancellor of Cyprus, were untiring champions of the war against the infidels.[125]

At the end of 1362 Peter I set out for a long journey to the west to negotiate personally with the rulers of the Christian powers for their participation in the forthcoming Crusade. But even before he completed his preparations, the military activities had begun. In 1360 the Cypriots occupied Corycus on the Cilician coast, and in 1361 Adalia, and then in 1363 Christian privateers attacked Abūkīr and Rosetta.[126] The response of the two great Italian merchant republics, Venice and Genoa, to the requests of

[122] A. S. Atiya, "A fourteenth century fatwa on the status of the Christians in the Mamluk empire," *Studien zur Geschichte und Kultur des Nahen und Fernen Ostens, Paul Kahle überreicht* (Leiden, 1935), p. 55 ff.

[123] See my "Observations on Venetian Trade," p. 558.

[124] *Libr. Com.* III, lib. 7, no. 227, 234.

[125] Setton, *Papacy and Levant* I, pp. 258, 259, 260.

[126] G. Hill, *A history of Cyprus* (Cambridge, 1940-1952) II, p. 320 ff.

the king of Cyprus were rather lukewarm. After some hesitation, Venice agreed to transport a part of the Crusader hosts to their destination, then withdrew her undertaking; and, on the other hand, the Venetian government ordered its war fleet to keep an eye on the king's moves. It seems that the king and his agents did conceal their real target Alexandria, from the Venetians.[127] Genoa promised the king three galleys after long negotiations which were rather painful for him. He had to make several concessions to the Genoese.[128] The attitude of the merchants of Venice and Genoa was less diplomatic than that of their governments. They openly showed their ill-will and even contempt for the knightly enterprise.[129]

The Venetian government took precautionary measures. The ships and the merchants should not be exposed to dangers, but if possible the trade with the dominions of the Mamluks should not be discontinued. In 1364 the government gave the consul in Alexandria instructions to this effect. He was ordered to remain there as long as he could without obvious danger, because if he were to leave (Alexandria) and there were no consul present, the galley travel would be in vain (there would be no spice fair), to the detriment of the merchants, "a trade we would not like to lose unless absolutely unavoidable."[130] Then in 1365 the captains of the convoys of the Cyprus and Alexandria galleys were ordered to sail together as far as Candia.[131] There the captain of the Alexandria galleys was to consult the Venetian authorities as to whether or not it was sage to go on to Egypt.[132]

However, all these precautions were in vain, for meanwhile the king of Cyprus assembled his followers in Rhodes and set out for Alexandria. He had brought together a formidable fleet. According to Arabic sources, the fleet that attacked Alexandria consisted of 70-100 ships, whereas Philippe de Mézières speaks of more than a hundred, and the Greek chronicler Makhairas even of 165.[133] Among these ships were some Genoese galleys too, but the data concerning the number are contradictory.[134] The number of the Christian force must have been relatively great. According to Philippe de Mézières it numbered more than 10,000 men. However, even this en-

[127] L. de Mas Latrie, *Histoire* III, p. 744 ff., 751 f.; Setton *op.cit.*, pp. 248, 252, 253, 262, 263 f.

[128] Setton, *op.cit.*, p. 260 f.

[129] Philippe de Mézières, *Life of Peter Thomas*, ed. Smet (Rome, 1954), p. 130.

[130] ASV, Collegio, Secreta 1363-1366, f. 77a, letter to the commander of the war fleet, orders to be transmitted to the consul in Alexandria.

[131] *Ibidem*, f. 123a.

[132] Misti 31, f. 112a, quoted by Setton, *op.cit.*, p. 262.

[133] *Sulūk* III, p. 105; an-Nudjūm az-zāhira, V, p. 194; Ibn Iyās² I, part 2, p. 21; P. Kahle, "Die Katastrophe des mittelalterlichen Alexandria," in *Mélanges Maspéro* III (Cairo, 1935-1940), p. 151; Setton, *op.cit.*, p. 264.

[134] According to Christian sources, three galleys, see Setton l. c., but al-Maḳrīzī, *Sulūk* III, p. 107, and Ibn Iyās² I, part 2, p. 23, say that there were only two and, on the other hand, 24 Venetian galleys. This latter datum is completely mistaken.

thusiastic champion of the Crusade confessed that many of them came to Rhodes for other than idealistic reasons.[135] The Crusaders succeeded in conquering the Egyptian port on 10 October 1365, but held it only a few days, and the conquest resulted only in a terrible plundering of the town. The sack of Alexandria is described very eloquently by a contemporary Arabic author, an-Nuwayrī,[136] whose account is confirmed by several documents referring to the losses and the suffering of the Venetian and Catalan merchants. The documents in the Catalan archives shed bright light on the happenings in Alexandria and on the character of Levant trade in that period.

In fact the European merchants suffered great losses. When the Cypriots attacked the town, the Moslem authorities arrested all the European traders they could seize. An Arabic author says that there were fifty of them and that they were brought to Damanhūr.[137] So it appears that the number of the European traders who resided in the great Egyptian harbor in that period was still small. Among those who were marched off were several Catalan traders, such as Fermin Tarrega, and two citizens of Perpignan, Hugo de Cantagrills, a rich merchant, and Juan Capdinat, an industrialist.[138] The Venetian Alexandria galleys had remained in Famagusta, so that the losses of the Venetians were much smaller.[139] Those of the merchants belonging to other nations were considerable, but both Genoese and Catalan seamen took part in the looting. According to Venetian records, the house of the consul was sacked by the Crusaders, and an Arabic writer recounts that the fondachi of the Genoese, the Catalans, and the traders of Marseilles were put to fire.[140] According to Philippe de Mézières, at the time of the raid there were six Genoese merchantmen in Alexandria and the crews took part in the sack of the town.[141] Catalan documents prove that the

[135] *Life of Peter Thomas*, pp. 126, 127.

[136] The account of Muḥammad b. Ḳāsim an-Nuwayrī has been elaborated in a doctoral thesis: Herzsohn, *Der Überfall*, and recently the Arabic text has been printed: *Kitāb al-Ilmām fīmā djarat bihi al-aḥkām wa 'l-umūr al-maḳḍiya fī waḳʿat al-Iskandarīya* (Hyderabad 1968 ff.) The story of the sack of Alexandria is to be found in vol. II, p. 130 ff. an-Nuwayrī's account is one of the sources of Ibn Ḳāḍī Shuhba, 1598, f. 177a f. A short report is to be found in Ibn Duḳmāḳ, *al-Djawhar ath-thamīn*, MS. Bodl. I, 648, f. 168b f.

[137] *Sulūk* III, p. 106; Ibn Iyās² I, part 2, p. 23; al-Maḳrīzī speaks about fifty merchants and says that they were brought to Damanhūr. But certainly among the imprisoned Europeans there were some who were not merchants, such as the servants of the consuls, or the consuls themselves. an-Nuwayrī says indeed: the consuls and the merchants, see Kahle, *art. cit.*, p. 147. al-Maḳrīzī also says that the merchants spoken of "were in the prison of the governor." But undoubtedly this is a lapsus linguae, and the Europeans were those who were seized upon the landing of the Cypriots.

[138] Sáez Pomés, pp. 370, 381

[139] G. P., Sent. II, f. 63b.

[140] Misti 33, f. 77a, Kahle, *art. cit.*, p. 149.

[141] de Mas Latrie, *Histoire* II, p. 389. According to this author the Genoese took booty worth 100,000 fl., but this is certainly exaggerated.

Catalan seamen looted the house of the Venetian consul and those of many European merchants, among them the Catalans, like that of the Majorcan Jorge Brondo. An inquiry made by the royal authorities of Catalonia showed that merchandise owned by him was brought to Cyprus.[142] The sailors of the Catalan ship "San Nicola" also joined in the pillaging. The ship's captain, Arnaldo Guerau, seized another ship on which the sailors had loaded their booty. Having appropriated to himself all the merchandise, he sailed to Rhodes and from there to Syracuse, but feared to return to Barcelona.[143] Some of the merchandise was brought to Collioure and, since the Aragonese king himself had claims to it, he gave orders to the governor of the province to send all the goods to Barcelona. In the course of the inquiry, it was established that the sailors who looted in Alexandria had revolted against the captain. But finally the royal magistrates, as they did so often, pardoned Arnaldo Guerau, his brother Ramón, and the sailors of the ship exacting the payment of fines, which were registered in the records of the exechequer of the year 1366. Part of the fines was allotted to the son of the king, the duke of Gerona. One of those pardoned was Antonio Farell, the king's tailor, who had travelled on a ship with 180 pots of honey and other merchandise so as to sell it and buy gold-embroidered linen and silk stuffs in Cyprus and Damascus for the royal wardrobe. However, in 1367 new charges were brought before the royal magistrates. A mandatory of the king of Cyprus claimed that Arnaldo Guerau had seized a Cypriot ship in Alexandria, and that the sailors of another Catalan ship, the "Santa Eulalia," engaged in pillaging. The crew of this ship was accused of having looted the stocks of the Catalan traders Leon March and Jaime Margens. Pablo de Montaras, the captain of the ship, had received a deposit from a Catalan trader, but instead of giving it back, he sold it. Then the sailors lost their minds, and the ship consequently suffered shipwreck.[144]

Alexandria was quitted by the Crusaders, who were incapable of holding the town, within a matter of days, but the consequences of the Cypriot raid was a long political crisis in the Eastern Mediterranean, and the trading nations encountered great difficulties in continuing their exchanges with the dominions of the Mamluks.

The rulers of Egypt and Syria, upset by the temporary success of the Cypriots, took measures of precaution against other raids and wrought vengeance on their Christian subjects and on the European traders. On the other hand, they too were interested in the continuation of the trade with

[142] Sáez Pomés, p. 368.

[143] *Art. cit.*, p. 368 ff.

[144] *Art. cit.*, p. 376 ff., and the documents IV, V, in the appendix. However, the ship was apparently later attacked by the Moslems, sixteen Catalans were killed, and the ship itself seized. This is learned from the claims submitted to the sultan by a Catalan embassy in 1366, see below, p. 94.

the South European commercial powers, in view of the substantial income from customs. The king of Cyprus, supported by the Holy See, did not renounce new assaults on the Moslems, while the trading nations put heavy pressure on both of them not to interfere in their commercial activities. In various European sources, there is copious information about the interplay that ensued among the various powers, and there are also many accounts in the Arabic chronicles, some written by eyewitnesses and some based on their accounts.

After the retreat of the Crusaders, the Mamluks imprisoned the European merchants they could find, both in Egypt and in Syria. Some of them succeeded in escaping from their place of confinement in Alexandria at the beginning of 1366,[145] but others remained in prison a long time. Some of them, like the rich Hugo Cantagrills of Perpignan, embraced Islam. However, he later fled to Cyprus, became Christian again, and returned to his town, whereupon he obtained a pardon from the king.[146] Since the goods of the Christian merchants were seized and not a few remained in confinement in Egypt and in Syria, there were long lawsuits in their homelands. Several documents in the Catalan archives refer to them.[147] The losses of the Catalans must have been substantial; for example, a ship, carrying merchandise of Pedro Prixana and other merchants of Barcelona was sequestered by the Mamluks altogether.[148]

Fearing other raids, the Mamluks sent troops to the Egyptian coast to reinforce the garrisons.[149] Frequently the commanders made inspections of the coast, both in Egypt and in Syria,[150] and sometimes foreigners were arrested on suspicion that they were preparing new raids.[151] The Mamluks also built a new war fleet, and the construction of a great number of warships was begun immediately after the retreat of the Cypriots and finished within a year.[152] So there was an atmosphere of apprehension and great tension.

However, the sultan was afraid of the losses that would result from a total rupture with the trading nations. So he let the two great merchant republics and the king of Aragon know, through his envoys, that he was interested in concluding peace.[153] The trading nations were even more eager than he to put an end to the crisis. Immediately upon the return of the Crusaders to Cyprus, Venetians and other European merchants had taken

[145] *Sulūk* III, p. 114.
[146] Sáez Pomés, p. 382 and doc. XV.
[147] *Art. cit.*, doc. XL.
[148] *Art. cit.*, doc. XVI.
[149] *Sulūk* III, pp. 114 f., 133; Ibn Iyās² I, part 2, p. 33f.
[150] Ibn Kathīr 14, p. 323.
[151] See below.
[152] *Sulūk* III, pp. 113, 129 f.; Ibn Iyās² I, part 2, pp. 37, 44, 46.
[153] See Heyd I, p. 53; Zurita, lib. IX, cap. 64.

up trade with Egypt and sailed from Famagusta to the Egyptian ports.[154] The experienced Italian traders feared lest an interruption of the commercial exchanges with Egypt and Syria result in a great dearth of Oriental merchandise in European markets and entail great losses to themselves. In fact there was a shortage of spices in Europe after the raid on Alexandria.[155]

At the same time, there was a growing demand for cotton in the Italian markets. Just in the 1360's, a new cotton industry had come into being in Southern Germany and the raw material had to be obtained from Venice and other emporia of Italy. The development of this new German industry was apparently brought about, at least partly, by the policy of the Luxemburg emperor Charles IV. The war between Venice and Louis the Great, king of Hungary, during which Charles IV and the foremost trading towns of Southern Germany—Nürnberg, Augsburg, and Regensburg—sided with the king of Hungary, had induced the Germans to found a cotton industry of their own, instead of remaining the customers of the North Italian fustian manufactures. The war of Charles IV against Barnabò Visconti, ruler of Milan, had the same consequences. The German traders who could not import fustian from Lombardy began to found factories in their own country.[156] We see that they existed in several towns of Southern Germany from the end of the 1360's: in 1369 in Vienna, in 1372 in Augsburg, in 1373 in Nördlingen, and in 1375 in Landshut. So it seems that the wave of industrial initiative began in about 1365.[157] The raw cotton was mainly acquired in Venice.[158] The projects of Charles IV, who in a certain period planned to change the routes of transcontinental trade, must have had influence upon the channels by which the raw material was brought to Southern Germany. He planned to transfer the main axis of transcontinental trade from Lombardy to the east along a route leading from Venice through Austria to Prague and the Elbe.[159] Since the North Italian fustian industry was still flourishing, the strain put on the cotton trade of Venice must have been heavy. In 1367 there was, indeed, a shortage of cotton in Venice, so that the Senate decided to send another cog to Alexandria in order to ship cotton from there.[160]

So the Venetians and the Genoese gave a sympathetic hearing to the approach of the sultan, and in March 1366 two Venetian ambassadors, Francesco Bembo and Pietro Soranzo, came to Cairo. Their primary task

[154] Philippe de Mézières, *Life of Peter Thomas*, p. 134 f., 141.
[155] See the sources quoted by Heyd II, p. 52.
[156] W. v. Stromer, *Die Gründung der Baumwollindustrie in Mitteleuropa* (Stuttgart 1978), pp. 32, 128 f.
[157] *Op.cit.*, pp. 30 f. 43, 79.
[158] *Op.cit.*, p. 32.
[159] *Op.cit.*, p. 129 f.
[160] Setton, *op.cit.*, p. 277.

was to influence the sultan to the continuation of commercial exchanges. They also tried to obtain the freedom of the merchants who had been imprisoned. In addition, they asked the sultan to reopen the Church of the Holy Sepulchre in Jerusalem, which had been closed after the Cypriot raid on Alexandria. The sultan agreed to the first request only.[161] Some months later a Genoese embassy came to the Egyptian capital. It brought 60 Moslem prisoners, who had been sent to Genoa, and claimed that the government of Genoa had not had any knowledge of the real objectives of the king of Cyprus (which may have been true).[162]

The king of Aragon, too, dispatched an embassy to the sultan. Of course, the ship on which the embassy travelled was also loaded with merchandise, for diplomacy and trade were not strictly separated. From the documents that have been preserved in the archives of Aragon, it seems that two ships were sent to Alexandria. The king himself and his first-born son sent merchandise on them to Egypt. The merchants who took part in this expedition had to pay 3 percent of their investment for the expenses of the embassy, and later the king even imposed on them payment for the cost of the presents to be offered the sultan. Like the ambassadors of the two great Italian merchant republics, the ambassadors of the king, Humberto de Fellonar and Jaspert de Camplonch, were to request the liberation of the imprisoned merchants and the lifting of the sequestration of their merchandise.[163] In addition, they were to ask for permission for the Catalans to carry on trade in the sultan's dominions, as before. The embassy departed in August 1366.[164] Two months later the king also sent an embassy to the

[161] See Heyd II, p. 53 (whose interpretation of the text in the *Libri Commemoriali* is correct; that of Predelli II, lib. 7, no. 268 is not clear); *Sulūk* III, p. 118 f.; Ibn Iyās² I, part 2, p. 35 f. According to the latter author, the sultan even agreed to the second request, but this account is certainly mistaken (see below). Ibn Iyās recounts the coming of this embassy among the happenings of the summer (June) 1366, confounding it with another one. Neither of the authors who are quoted here says that it was a Venetian embassy, but the Christian sources (as quoted by Heyd) leave no doubt about it. al-Maḳrīzī says that the sultan refused to enter upon negotiations of peace with Cyprus and told the ambassadors that the Church of the Holy Sepulchre must be destroyed. This latter passage in the account of al-Maḳrīzī is a bit clumsy, but nevertheless clear. He says: *wa-sa'ālū tadjdīd aṣ-ṣulḥ wa-anna yumakkanū tudjdjāruhum min ḳudūm ath-thaghr wa-anna tuftaḥ kanīsat al-ḳiyāma bi-l-Ḳuds wa-kānat ḳad ghuliḳat . . . fa-adjābahum bi-annaha la budda min ghazw Ḳubrus wa-takhrībiha*. Undoubtedly *takhrībiha* refers to the Church (and not to Cyprus). The "ṣulḥ" the ambassadors had asked for could be the confirmation of the old privileges of Venice, but, since the renewal of the commercial exchanges is spoken of subsequently, it probably meant the conclusion of peace with Cyprus.

[162] *Sulūk* III, p. 122 f.; Ibn Ḳāḍī Shuhba 1598, f. 179a; Ibn Iyās² I, part 2, p. 40. Whereas al-Maḳrīzī gives no exact date, Ibn Ḳāḍī Shuhba says that the embassy came in the month of Shawwāl, i.e., 11 June to 10 July 1366. All these authors, in fact, quote the same source. From the account of Ibn Iyās, one would conclude that the embassy came in the month Dhu 'l-ḥidjdja (9 August to 6 September 1366).

[163] Sáez Pomés, doc. III.

[164] *Art. cit.*, p. 371 ff. and docs. II, VI-VIII, XII, XIII.

Holy See to ask the pope for licenses for two ships of Barcelona and two of Majorca, so that the merchants be set free and their merchandise could be transported home. The instructions King Pedro IV gave his ambassadors are very interesting, since they include data on the volume of Catalan trade with the Moslem Levant in the 1360's. In this memorandum, dated 1 October 1366, the king claimed that 300-400 Catalans had been imprisoned in the dominions of the sultan after the Cypriot raid on Alexandria and that the material losses of the Catalan merchants through the sequestration of their goods and in other ways amounted to 400,000 fl.[165] If these claims are correct, they would point to a relatively great volume of trade between the Levant and the South European nations in the seventh decade of the fourteenth century. Likewise, they would indicate the supremacy of the Catalans in this branch of world trade in that age, for it is unlikely that the commercial exchanges of either the Genoese or the Venetians with the Moslem Levant reached such dimensions in that period. But the figures may be exaggerated and, even if they are precise, they do not necessarily refer to investments in one year. Merchandise shipped by the Catalans to the Levant and not yet sold in 1365 may have been included in the king's estimate. Further, we must realize that the king represented not only the Catalan merchants but also other subjects of the crown of Aragon. When he made this point, he obviously had also the Sicilian traders in mind.

The Catalan embassy was not only to ask the sultan to set the merchants free and to lift the embargo on their sequestered goods, but also to try to get a reduction or, if possible, abolition of the customs to be paid by the Catalans.[166]

The sultan rightly insisted on having peace with all the Christian powers and was not inclined to allow the trading nations to carry on their activities in his dominions, while at the same time the king of Cyprus was preparing new attacks. In March 1366 he sent an ambassador of his own, the Emir Ṭakboghā, to Cyprus, and there negotiations between the two courts began. But, despite the efforts of the Venetian ambassadors who accompanied the Egyptian envoy and mediated between him and the Cypriots, the negotiations were a failure.[167]

Although the king of Cyprus planned new raids on the coasts of Egypt and Syria and his supporters in the Church had not yet renounced their projects, the trading nations tenaciously continued their efforts to maintain regular commercial exchanges with the Mamluk dominions. The attitude

[165] *Art. cit.*, p. 381 ff., and doc. IX.

[166] López de Meneses, p. 141 ff., appendix VI.

[167] *Sulūk* III, p. 120, and cf. Heyd II, p. 54; Setton, *op.cit.*, p. 275. The king of Cyprus sent fifty Moslem prisoners, who had been carried away from Alexandria, back to Egypt, as a sign of good will; see Ibn Ḳāḍī Shuhba 1598, f. 182a.

of the Holy See wavered, and in some years a series of vicissitudes checked the activities of the trading nations. In June 1366 Venice obtained new licenses from the pope for four cogs and eight galleys, and the Holy See also encouraged the Adriatic republic to continue her endeavors to bring about peace between the king of Cyprus and the sultan.[168] But two months later, the pope again prohibited trade with the dominions of the sultan, revoking all licenses already given. He did allow those ships that had departed to continue their journeys.[169] In that year Venice established a new galley line to Beirut, and this route soon became a major artery of her maritime trade. The captain of the Alexandria galleys was ordered to apply to the Mamluk government with the request that the Moslem authorities in Damascus, Beirut, and Tripoli be instructed to deal fairly with the Venetians. The captain of the Beirut galleys were instructed to send an envoy to Damascus to ask the Venetian consul, who was already taking care of the interests of the Serenissima, to take similar steps.[170]

Thus, the renewal of the Levantine trade was making good progress when the Moslems' hostility, which had been aroused by the sack of Alexandria, burst out again and resulted in various attacks on the Christian traders. Undoubtedly justified apprehensions of new raids by the Cypriots were another reason for the Moslems' aggressiveness. The reports of Ibn Kathīr, a Damascene chronicler who died in 1373, contain many accounts of the vexations of the European merchants. The last pages of his chronicle are actually a diary in which he noted such happenings almost every day.

Ibn Kathīr recounts that on 21 October 1366 the authorities of Damascus promulgated a general prohibition of trade with the Venetians, the Genoese, and the Catalans.[171] Tension was high, because at the beginning of the month rumours of a raid on the Syrian coast had spread.[172] Some days later, during the yearly spice fair, the Moslems in Alexandria claimed that some Cypriots were among the merchants who arrived on one Genoese, one Catalan, and five Venetian galleys, and even that one of the galleys was Cypriot. When the Christian merchants denied this claim and refused to hand anyone over to them, the Moslems attacked them on the sea and there were some casualties. The galleys departed, but the Mamluks took their revenge on the European merchants who were on land. Ibn Kathīr relates that the events in Alexandria became known in Damascus on 15 November, and that thereupon the European traders were imprisoned and

[168] *Libr. Com.* III, lib. 7, nos. 267, 273.

[169] *Libr. Com.* III, lib. 7, no. 274. The account given by Heyd II, p. 54 f., should be corrected in this sense.

[170] *Libr. Com.* III, lib. 7, no. 234, and see my paper "Observations on Venetian Trade," p. 547, where the sources are given.

[171] *al-Bidāya wa 'n-nihāya* 14, p. 322.

[172] *Ibidem.*

their goods sequestered. But, according to an-Nuwayrī, whose account is quoted by Ibn Ḳāḍī Shuhba, a Cypriot embassy had come to Egypt on a galley which anchored in the port of Alexandria between two Genoese and two Catalan cogs. When the negotiations between this embassy and the Mamluk government failed, the clash in Alexandria ensued. This Arabic author gives the date as the month of Rabīʿ I 768, i.e., 7 October to 4 November 1366.[173] However that may have been, the European merchants were everywhere imprisoned. In some Syrian ports they had already been arrested earlier than in Damascus; in Beirut not less than forty-six were seized. A letter of the Venetian bailo in Cyprus, which deals with the imprisonment of the Venetians in Tripoli, is dated 12 November 1366.[174] At the end of the year, the Cypriots retaliated with a raid on Tripoli and set fire to a Moslem ship in the port.[175]

In the two years 1367 and 1368 the scenario of successive diplomatic interventions by the Italian merchant republics aiming at the conclusion of peace and of Cypriot onslaughts on the coasts of Egypt and Syria repeated itself. The attitude of the Holy See changed from time to time.

At the beginning of 1367 once again the two great Italian merchant republics dispatched embassies to Cairo. In the month of February an embassy of Genoa, with Pietro de Cassano (or Canale) at its head, came to Cairo to ask the sultan to allow her merchants to take up trade with Alexandria, and the Mamluk government agreed. The response was favorable, just as the Genoese embassy of 1366 had been well received.[176] A short time later a Venetian embassy came to the sultan. Having obtained from the pope permission to send two galleys to Egypt, in order to bring home the merchants who had been imprisoned in October 1366, the Venetian government sent a new embassy to the Mamluk court in February 1367. The main purpose of the ambassadors, Francesco Bembo and Domenico Michiel, was of course to foster the negotiations between the sultan and the king of Cyprus. The embassy should obtain the liberation of the

173 *Op.cit.*, p. 323; Ibn Ḳāḍī Shuhba 1598, f. 182a.

174 *Libr. Com.* III, lib. 7, nos. 301, 302. But, already on 10 November 1366, the Venetian Senate deliberated on the steps to be taken in this matter; see Misti 32, f. 22a. The résumé of Predelli (lib. 7, no. 302) is faulty. From the original one learns that the Venetians who wrote to the captain of the Beirut galleys were merchants detained in Syria, because of the happenings in Alexandria. Further Zuan Michiel, Zuan Vido, and forty-four others wrote to Zuan Bembo and Niccolò Zorzi.

175 Ibn Kathīr 14, p. 323 f. His account apparently points to an earlier date than that indicated in the Christian sources; see Setton, *op.cit.*, p. 278. Ibn Kathīr mentions the raid before recounting that on 20 December 1366 the murder of Yelboghā al-Khāṣṣakī became known in Damascus. Even according to Ibn Ḳāḍī Shuhba, f. 182b, the raid took place in Rabīʿ II 768, i.e., 5 December 1366 to 2 January 1367. The Christian authors indicate the month of January 1367.

176 *Sulūk* III, p. 141; Ibn Ḳāḍī Shuhba, f. 182b; Ibn Iyās² I, part 2, p. 59 (the three accounts are identical).

imprisoned merchants and make sure that trade could go on. In fact the permission granted by the pope was a revocation of the prohibition of trade with the Mamluk dominions, and the two galleys certainly loaded merchandise.[177] The Venetians, whose subtle policy vis-à-vis the Mamluks distinguished itself by great patience, were certainly much more acceptable to the Mamluks than other European trading nations.[178] This was probably the reason why Galeazzo Visconti, ruler of Milan, had applied to the doge of Venice with the request for help for a mission to Egypt. The Milan representatives travelled together with the Venetian embassy and envoys of the sultan who were returning to Egypt. The Milanese envoy, Pietro di Castiglione, was to offer gifts to the sultan, among them a common-falcon, and in exchange acquire some precious articles for the ruler of Milan.[179] Although the embassies of the trading nations did not reach their goal—that is, the conclusion of peace between the sultan and the king of Cyprus—and the negotiations by another Egyptian embassy accompanied by the Genoese and Catalan ambassadors and the king of Cyprus failed, they continued their efforts and meanwhile trade went on.[180]

In May 1367 the Holy See granted Venice more licenses than ever before; no less them twelve galleys and four cogs were permitted to sail.[181] Five galleys actually came to Alexandria that year. The Senate had first decided to send only four to the spice fair in Alexandria, but as the amount of merchandise loaded on them in Venice was so great that it was thought that the Oriental commodities acquired in return for the proceeds in Alexandria would be much more than the galleys could transport and that even the supplementary galley (*galea de rata*) would not be sufficient, five galleys were sent to the Egyptian port. On the other hand, because of the tension resulting from the military activities of the Cypriots, there were fears as to the security of the merchants in Alexandria, so that the Senate ordered the Venetian authorities in Candia to decide if the galleys could safely go to Egypt.[182]

But again King Peter I of Cyprus interfered with the activities of the commercial powers. All the pressure brought upon him by Venice and Genoa did not move him from his warlike attitude, and in September 1367 the Cypriots raided Tripoli, Anṭarṭūs (Tortosa), Bulunyās, and Lajazzo.

[177] *Libr. Com.* III, lib. 7, no. 319; cf. on this embassy my paper "Observations on Venetian Trade," p. 548.

[178] Rightly stated by Setton, *op.cit.*, p. 276.

[179] *Libr. Com.* III, lib. 7, no. 320, 346. If the ambassadors of the sultan were those who had come to Italy a short time after the sack of Alexandria (see above) or others, we do not know.

[180] Hill, *History of Cyprus* II, p. 346 f.

[181] *Libr. Com.* III, lib. 7, no. 351.

[182] Misti 32, f. 84a, 84b, 87a.

According to an Arabic source, a fleet of 130 ships attacked Tripoli, which was taken by the Cypriots.[183] But the government of Venice persisted in continuing the commercial exchanges with the dominions of the sultan and on soothing the excited Moslems. In October 1367 the Senate decided to send Pietro Grimani to Alexandria and to hand over to Marino Venier, the consul in Alexandria, letters to the sultan in which he was requested to set free the merchants imprisoned in Beirut. If the request should be granted and it should not be considered too risky, he was to proceed to Beirut in order to handle the matter on the spot and to bring the Venetians to Crete.[184]

In 1368 a new wave of hostilities occurred. At the beginning of the year, the Moslems arrested at least 150 Europeans in Alexandria, according to the Arabic sources; those arrested were suspected of not being merchants at all, but of having other less peaceful purposes.[185] Then, in April, Genoese corsairs captured a Moslem ship in the port of Alexandria and another in Damietta, while the Cypriots made a raid on the Palestinian coast.[186] The Egyptians retaliated by attacks on Christian ships on the high seas and by the seizure of a Venetian merchantman.[187]

Still the trade with the Moslem Levant and the endeavors to bring about peace were not discontinued, despite the fighting and the acts of hostility by both sides, and notwithstanding the fact that European merchants were still being detained by the Mamluks. In May 1368 the pope granted Venice more new licenses,[188] and in June a joint embassy of Venice and Genoa departed for Cairo. The ambassadors were Niccolò Giustiniani and Pietro Marcello of Venice and Cassan Cigalla and Paolo Giustiniani of Genoa. They travelled with two galleys, especially licensed by the pope for bringing home the imprisoned merchants whose liberation they were to obtain. King Peter I agreed to make peace but put forward many requests, among which was the demand that Cypriot merchants should enjoy liberty of trade in Egypt and Syria, that Cyprus should have consulates there, and that Cypriot interests should be safeguarded, especially those of traders who had suffered shipwreck or had a lawsuit with Moslems. To show his good will, he gave

[183] *Sulūk* III, p. 149 f.; Ibn Iyās² I, part 2, p. 64 f. Bulunyās is Valania; see Guy Le Strange, *Palestine under the Moslems* (London 1890), p. 279. Ibn Ḳāḍī Shuhba 1398, f. 186a f., whose account is very detailed, recounts that the Cypriots tried to liberate a nephew of the king, who was imprisoned in Tripoli, and that the consequence of the raid was a conflict between them and the Genoese. He again quotes an-Nuwayrī, but apparently other sources too.

[184] Misti 32, f. 87a; *Libr. Com.* III, lib. 7, no. 351.

[185] *Sulūk* III, p. 156; Ibn Iyās² I, part 2, p. 74 (the reading 150 ships is obviously a mistake).

[186] Setton, *op.cit.*, p. 279.

[187] *Sulūk* III, p. 159; Ibn Iyās² I, part 2, p. 75f.; Setton *l.c.* The dates given by the two Arabic authors are different. al-Maḳrīzī says that the Moslem ships came back in April, whereas Ibn Iyās gives the date Ramaḍān 769, that is, 20 April to 19 May. Probably the date given by al-Maḳrīzī is the right one.

[188] *Libr. Com.* III, lib. 7, no. 422.

orders to set free Moslem prisoners,[189] but again the negotiations were unsuccessful. According to Christian sources, a powerful group of Mamluks opposed the conclusion of a treaty of peace.[190]

King Peter I was murdered in January 1369, but the policy of Cyprus did not change immediately. In June and again in July 1369 the Cypriots made new raids on the coasts of Syria and of Egypt, sacking first Batrūn and Anṭarṭūs and then attacking Moslem ships in the port of Alexandria and shelling the town.[191]

How great the tenacity of the trading nations and their eagerness to carry on trade with the Moslems were is borne out by the fact that in those years of fighting and acts of retaliation the commercial exchanges with the Mamluk dominions were never discontinued. Notwithstanding the dangers the traders ran in travelling to Egypt and Syria, the Genoese, Venetian and Catalans sent their galleys and cogs to the ports of these countries and continued to carry on their commercial activities.

In the years 1366-1368, Venice sent 16 galleys altogether to Alexandria and Beirut[192] and in addition, in 1366, also established the state line of the Syria cogs. This meant that henceforth the shipment of Syrian cotton and alkali to Venice was carried on by convoys of cogs, licensed and supervised by the government, and sailing every year at the same time to the Levantine ports.[193]

Genoese trade with the Mamluk dominions was intense too. The registers of the custom authorities of Genoa of the second half of the fourteenth century comprise a series of authentic data about the volume of Genoese trade with the Moslem Levant in the 1360's, and the beginning of the 1370's. In the year 1364 the imposition of 1/2 percent on trade with Alexandria yielded 3850 l, so that the volume of these exchanges was estimated to be 616,000 ducats. The whole of Genoa's foreign trade in that year was estimated to be 1,963,325 l, i.e., 1,570,000 ducats. The records of the payments for the "Drictus Alexandrie," a duty of 1 percent imposed in 1367, contain data on Genoese trade with Egypt and Syria in 1367-1371. The impost was levied on ships coming from Egypt and Syria. The data referring to the years 1367-1369 are summed up in Table IV.[194]

[189] *Op.cit.*, nos. 421, 425, 426, 434; de Mas Latrie, *Histoire* II, p. 302 ff.

[190] See Setton, *op.cit.*, p. 281.

[191] Setton, *op.cit.*, p. 282; *Sulūk* III, p. 175 f.; Ibn Iyās² I, part 2, p. 90.

[192] See above, Table III.

[193] See my "Observations on Venetian Trade," p. 547, where sources are given.

[194] For the custom revenues in 1364, see H. Sieveking, "Aus Genueser Rechnungs- und Steuerbüchern" (see Ch. 1, n. 32), pp. 52, 56. In the accounts of the *Drictus Alexandriae* (in the ASG) we add the data concerning the ships coming from Cyprus (as they are given in the records of the *Drictus*), because they carried merchandise which had come from Egypt and from Syria. The records of 1367 contain only data of the second half of the year; that is, they refer to ships that departed from the Levantine ports not earlier than the summer of

Table IV Genoese trade with Egypt and Syria 1367-69

year	ships		value of merchandise	
1367	from Egypt	1 galley		
		3 cogs	167,639 ducats	
1368	from Egypt	4 cogs	109,273 "	
	Syria	1 galley	34,757 "	
				144,030 ducats
1369	from Egypt	2 galleys		
		5 cogs	387,178 ducats	
	from Syria	1 cog		
		1 panfilo	6,884 "	
				394,062 ducats
	from Cyprus	2 galleys	86,118	

From these data it can be seen that in the years 1367-1368, although the Cypriots continued their raids on the coasts of Egypt and Syria, the Genoese still shipped merchandise from there worth 150,000-170,000 ducats a year. In 1369 the volume of Genoese trade with the dominions of the Mamluks reached almost 400,000 ducats, and actually this figure refers to the first half of the year only, as in the second half of the year the commercial exchanges were discontinued, owing to a new political crisis. The data quoted here from the Genoese custom registers point to two facts: they show that Genoa's trade with Egypt and Syria was in that period the most important sector of its seaborne trade and, secondly, they induce us to suppose that its volume was then much greater than that of Venetian trade in the Moslem Levant.

But although the trade with the realm of the Mamluks developed on a satisfactory scale, the trading nations of Southern Europe considered their relations with the Moslem authorities to be unbearable. The numerous outbreaks of hostility and the repeated seizure of merchants and their goods and the refusal of both the sultan and the Cypriots to make peace made travels in Egypt and Syria dangerous. So, in June 1369, Genoa and Venice made an alliance against the Mamluk sultan and decided to break off their relations with Egypt and Syria. The Holy See at the same time promulgated a new prohibition of trade with the dominions of the Mamluks.[195] Obviously

that year. A full summary of the data in the records of the *Drictus* is given in my paper "Il volume del commercio levantino di Genova nel secondo Trecento," in *Saggi e documenti* I (of the Civico Istituto Colombiano, Genova, Studi e testi, serie storica II) (Genoa 1978), p. 397 ff.

[195] Setton, *op.cit.*, p. 282 f.

the two Italian merchant republics hoped that the interruption of their commercial activities in the Moslem Levant would compel the sultan to come to an agreement with the king of Cyprus and to establish a general peace in the Eastern Mediterranean. The Arabic chroniclers write that at the beginning of July 1368 four Christian ships shelled Alexandria and that a naval battle with the Mamluk fleet ensued.[196] The attacking force must surely have been Cypriot. In fact the two Italian merchant republics did not act wholeheartedly when they obliged themselves mutually to discontinue trade with Egypt and Syria and not to conclude a separate peace. Again, their real interests, which lay in carrying on direct and regular trade with the Moslem Levant, prevailed. Peaceful relations with the sultan of Cairo really constituted an urgent need for them, for meanwhile new difficulties had arisen in the commercial exchanges with the Tatars in Southern Russia.[197] Even Italian trade with the Greek territories was not prosperous. The relations of the Venetians with the imperial authorities were strained.[198] The auction of the Venetian Romania galleys in 1367 and in 1369 yielded very small sums.[199] So only a year after the alliance had solemnly been made and consecrated by the pope's prohibition of trade with the Mamluk dominions, peace was finally concluded. According to the Arabic chronicles, an embassy came to Cairo in August 1370, and another in December 1370, together with Moslem prisoners brought back to Egypt. Thereupon peace was concluded.[200] From Venetian sources we learn that it was a joint Genoese-Venetian embassy that succeeded in concluding the overall peace treaty. The Venetian ambassador was Pietro Giustinian.[201] The Arabic author Ibn Ḳāḍī Shuhba emphasizes that peace was concluded with the Cypriots, Venetians, Genoese, and Catalans, and that thereupon the European merchants who were still imprisoned in Damascus were released.[202] The treaty itself has so far not been found in any source.[203]

[196] *Sulūk* III, p. 175 f.; Ibn Iyās² I, part 2, p. 90.

[197] Thiriet, *Régestes* I, p. 119, 120.

[198] *Op.cit.* I, p. 122 f., 123.

[199] See my "Observations on Venetian Trade," p. 558.

[200] *Sulūk* III, pp. 189, 190, 191; Ibn Iyās² I, part 2, pp. 100, 101. Certainly the interpretation de Mas Latrie, *Histoire* II, p. 337, gives of this text is right. The Arabic sources leave no doubt that Cypriot ambassadors are spoken of. After the conclusion of the treaty, the Church of the Holy Sepulchre in Jerusalem was reopened; *Sulūk* III, p. 191, and cf. Heyd II, p. 57.

[201] See my "Observations on Venetian Trade," p. 551.

[202] See Weil, *Geschichte der Chalifen* IV, p. 524.

[203] de Mas Latrie, *Histoire* II, p. 348, is inclined to believe that the treaty made in 1403 between the Knights of Rhodes and the sultan was in great measure a repetition of this one. This is also the opinion of Hill, *History of Cyprus* II, p. 376. What S. Labib, *Handelsgeschichte Ägyptens im Spätmittelalter*, p. 342, says, namely that the treaty is contained in *Ṣubḥ al-aʿshā* 13, pp. 315-17 is mistaken. This is only the oath taken by the king of Cyprus!

III
A New Period of Growth (1370-1402)

A. No More Alternative Routes

The conclusion of peace between the sultan and the king of Cyprus was followed by the renewal of intense trade between Southern Europe and the Moslem Levant. The trading nations increased their activities in the dominions of the sultan, and the volume of their transactions reached new peaks. The new flourishing of European trade with these countries was to a great extent the result of changes in other trade routes, which for a long time had served as alternatives.

In the second half of the fourteenth century Persia was no longer of any importance as a market where the European traders could obtain the spices and other products of the Far East. The Djalā'irids were not capable of reuniting the kingdom of the Īlkhāns, which had fallen to pieces. They ruled only over Iraq and Ādharbaydjān, and their hold even on the latter was not secure. In 1357 Djānī Beg, the Tatar ruler of Southern Russia, invaded and conquered Ādharbaydjān and until his death in 1359 it was under his control. The provinces of Fars and Kirman and a part of Media were ruled by the Muẓaffarids (1353-1387); Khorasan was divided between the Karts of Herat, the Sarbadārs, whose capital was Sabzawār, and other local dynasties. In the eastern provinces of Asia Minor, the town of Sivas had become the seat of an independent prince in 1341. There was rivalry and sometimes actual fighting between these successor states of the Īlkhāns and civil wars were not infrequent. After the death of the Djalā'irid Uways (1356-1374), his kingdom split into two parts, and even these principalities were torn by the struggle among various pretenders to the throne.

Whereas in the days of the Īlkhāns the foreign merchants had enjoyed great security in Persia, there was general anarchy in most provinces of the big country in the middle and the second half of the fourteenth century. When Venetian merchants tried to take up trade in Tebriz, they were robbed on the highway.[1] European trade with Egypt and Syria had to be intensified. But the shrewd Italian merchants understood very well that concentrating all the Levant trade in the dominions of the sultan of Cairo would result in being dependent upon his good will. In 1392 this argument was put forth in the Venetian Senate, and it was proposed that an embassy be sent to Tebriz and that trade with Persia be resumed. But, because of the insecurity that obtained in the country, the apprehensions were too great and the proposal was turned down by four votes.[2] Two years later the same proposition was made in the Senate, and again it was rejected.[3]

However, even if conditions in Persia had been better, the country could no longer fulfill the same role it had in the first half of the fourteenth century. Then its big towns had been not only the extreme points of a trade route that connected it with India, but also that of another transcontinental route, which led to China—the famous silk route. But in 1368 the Mongol khāns of China, whose rule was favorable to the Italian merchants, were replaced by the Ming, a new national dynasty, which was inclined to cut down contacts with the West.

In the 1370's the European merchants lost another alternative trade route that connected the Mediterranean with the ports of the Persian Gulf. For a long time the small Armenian kingdom of Cilicia ("Little Armenia") had been the starting point of a caravan route that, via Upper Mesopotamia, reached Tebriz and also Baghdad, where the Indian spices arrived from the Persian Gulf.[4] In the second half of the thirteenth century and the first half of the fourteenth century, Lajazzo, the main port of Little Armenia, was a major emporium of the Levant trade. But Little Armenia was at the same time the target of several raids of the Mamluks, and in 1347 part of it was conquered by them. Ten years later, Lajazzo fell to the Mamluks and in 1375 what had remained of the Christian kingdom was annexed to the Mamluk dominions.

However, the Italian merchants still held another outlet to the Indian spice trade—their colonies on the shores of the Black Sea and the Sea of Azov. In 1365 the Genoese even considerably enlarged the region of the Crimean coast under their control, and Caffa's trade reached its apogee.[5] Surely after the downfall of the Īlkhāns and the great change in the conditions in Persia, the quantity of Indian spices that reached the Italian trading colonies on the Black Sea was more limited than before; but though this artery of the spice trade was no more than a trickle, it enhanced the

[1] Thiriet, *Régestes* I, p. 214.
[2] *Op.cit.*, p. 195 f.
[3] *Op.cit.*, p. 200. See also Kedar, p. 128.
[4] See my *Social and economic history*, p. 264 f.
[5] Lopez, *Storia delle colonie genovesi*, p. 356 ff.

commercial importance of the Italian factories, which were mainly engaged in the trade of Persian silk, furs, salted fish, and hides.[6] Genoese and Venetian traders also carried on trade in inland towns of Southeastern Russia. A judicial act of the Venetian tribunal of the *Giudici di petiziòn* refers to the export of European cloth and paper in which Andrea Giustinian and Daniele Molin engaged in Astrakhān in 1375.[7] Another trickle of Indian spices reached Constantinople, so that the Genoese and Venetian ships coming from the Black Sea and the Greek ports always carried a certain quantity of these articles.[8] However, in the last third of the fourteenth century, the Tatar kingdom of Southern Russia decayed, anarchy prevailed, civil wars brought about insecurity, and finally Tīmūr, the great Mongol conqueror, invaded the kingdom in 1395 and destroyed Tana, the Italian emporium on the Sea of Azov. This was a heavy blow to the Italian traders, and its consequences were felt in Venice and elsewhere.[9] Since the trade in the Black Sea area was considered a vital artery of their world trade by both the Genoese and the Venetians, immediately upon the retreat of Tīmūr measures were taken to repair the damage done and to take up regular trade. Venice sent envoys to the rulers of the Golden Horde in order to gain permission for the fortification of Tana, and the Venetian colony was indeed rebuilt.[10] In the last years of the fourteenth and the beginning of the fifteenth century, Venice still sent her convoys of galleys and cogs to Tana every year. In fact, Tana was the destination of the state line of the "Romania galleys"; in addition, cogs were also sent there. The cog line also functioned in the years in which the galley convoys were suspended, as in 1400-1402. The cargoes these ships carried to Venice were sometimes of considerable value, for they comprised heavy loads of silk.[11] But conditions worsened greatly and it was never certain whether or not the convoys departing from Venice would accomplish their goals.

Even the situation in Constantinople was fairly precarious. The splendid capital of the Byzantine empire, which had once been the foremost commercial town in the world, was poorly supplied with products of the Far East. Arabic chroniclers recount that in 1385 the emperor of Constantinople sent ambassadors to Cairo, asking that the Greek merchants be permitted to carry on trade in Egypt and Syria and that they have a consul in Alexandria.[12] This account probably points to the drying up of Constantinople's supply of spices arriving on other trade routes. The political situ-

[6] See Misti 65, f. 53a f., 132b; Dat 714, letter of Bindo di Gherardo Piaciti of 22 June 1402.
[7] G. P., Sent. IX, f. b f.
[8] See Heers, "Il commercio," p. 169.
[9] Silberschmidt, *Das orientalische Problem*, p. 129.
[10] Thiriet, *Régestes* I, pp. 211, 217; Silberschmidt, *op.cit.*, p. 133 f.
[11] Thiriet, *Régestes* II, pp. 9, 14, 23.
[12] *Sulūk* III, p. 535; al-Djawharī, *Nuzha*, p. 121; cf. Lannoy, *Voyages*, p. 76 f.

ation of the Byzantine State, so much reduced in size, was alarming. At the end of the fourteenth century the great Italian merchant republics were fully aware of the danger that Constantinople would fall to the Turks and they made efforts to strengthen the tottering Byzantine rule, without however, being completely sincere. From the instructions given to a Venetian ambassador to the Ottoman sultan in 1397, it is seen that Venice was ready to acquiesce in the annexation of Constantinople by the Turks, if the latter would recognize the southern Aegean as her sphere of influence.[13] Clearly, the rulers of Venice foresaw the final breakdown of the system of alternative trade routes to the outlets of the Indian spice trade and the collapse of the network of commercial exchanges resting upon Christian, or at least non-Moslem, emporia.

So it is easy to understand why Venice and Genoa intensified their trade with the Moslem Levant in the last third of the fourteenth century. In the emporia of the Mamluk dominions there was a regular and sufficient supply of Indian spices, aromatics, drugs, and dyes, and in addition the agricultural products of the Near East, in which the Italian traders were very much interested. The Indian commodities were carried to the shores of the Mediterranean on different routes connecting the ports of the Red Sea with Cairo and Alexandria and those of the Persian Gulf with the trading towns of Syria. Certainly the Red Sea route was more important, and some of the spices arriving through it were carried to Damascus, but the Syrian capital was also the goal of caravans that brought spices from Basra and Baghdad. The arrival of these caravans is mentioned in several merchant letters as an important event in commercial life. Even in provincial towns of Syria and Palestine, like Jerusalem, it was possible to buy spices.[14] So the trading nations of Southern Europe resumed their activities in both Egypt and Syria with great eagerness. The Venetians, the Genoese, and the Catalans were the most enterprising, but also the other commercial powers of Southern Europe, trading towns on the coast of the Mediterranean and inland towns, had a share in these exchanges. The war between Genoa and Venice in 1378-1381 was an opportunity for the smaller trading nations to increase their activities in the Moslem Levant. When the two great merchant republics of Italy had to concentrate their efforts on the military contest, they could not maintain control of the trade routes they had imposed before, and smaller trading nations, like the Provençals and the Anconitans, considerably increased the volume of their Levant trade.

The jamming of the alternate trade routes from India also had other

[13] Silberschmidt, *op.cit.*, pp. 177, 182 f.

[14] Melis, *Documenti*, p. 330; Heers, "Il commercio," p. 175 (*dallabo* means "from Aleppo"); Dat 928, copy of a letter from Damascus of 22 March 1403; G. P., Sent. IX, f. 17a ff., 186 ff.

consequences, which were favorable to the Levantine trade of the Italian merchant republics.

As long as the emporia on the Black Sea and on the Sea of Azov were regularly supplied with sufficient quantities of Indian spices and dyes, some were sent to Southern Poland on a trade route crossing the Ukraine and leading to Lwów. In the first half of the fourteenth century this town became a flourishing emporium, and in 1356 the king of Poland recognized this fact by granting her the privileges of Magdeburg. In those days, the spice trade on the Caffa-Lwów route must have been intense, so that even Eastern Germany was supplied with the Indian articles arriving that way. But when the flow of the Indian spices from Persia to Tana and Caffa dried up, the merchants of the Polish towns began to purchase supplies elsewhere. The enterprising traders of Nürnberg, who a long time before had carried on exchanges with the emporia of Bohemia and Southern Poland, offered them the spices they had bought in Venice. It was certainly not by chance that Cazimir the Great, king of Poland, granted Nürnberg privileges in 1365. A new axis of world trade came into being: Alexandria-Venice-Nürnberg-Lwów, or Alexandria-Genoa-Milan-Nürnberg-Lwów. The decline of the spice trade of the Italian colonies on the Black Sea, paradoxically, resulted in an increase of the customers of Genoa and Venice.[15] The relatively great volume of trade on the new axis was also due to the fact that the merchants of Nürnberg could supply the Italian trading towns with some commodities they badly needed for their own exchanges with the Moslem Levant: metals, furs, and ambergris. During the whole of the Middle Ages and even later, these commodities were indeed staple goods of the traders of Nürnberg.[16] Among the various trade routes which connected the great Italian emporia with Nürnberg, that crossing the Brenner and reaching Venice was the most important. Trade between Nürnberg, Augsburg, Regensburg, and other towns of Southern Germany with Milan and Genoa had a smaller volume. Further, the commodities which the Germans bought there were predominantly Italian products, such as fustian.[17]

But the Genoese had a greater share in the trade with Flanders and England, which developed extensively in the second half of the fourteenth century. The demand for spices and other commodities of the Levant had also increased very much in England, and Venetians, Genoese, and Catalans imported relatively great quantities. Whereas the Venetians held first place

[15] Fr. Lütge, "Der Handel Nürnbergs nach dem Osten in 15/16. Jahrhundert," in *Beiträge zur Wirtschaftsgeschichte Nürnbergs* I (1967), p. 347.

[16] Lütge, *art. cit.*, p. 353 f.; Ph. Braunstein, "Wirtschaftliche Beziehungen zwischen Nürnberg u. Italien im Spätmittelalter," in *Beiträge* (as above) I, pp. 394, 402.

[17] Braunstein, "Wirtschaftl. Beziehungen," pp. 381, 395; W. v. Stromer, *Oberdeutsche Hochfinanz 1350-1450* (Wiesbaden, 1970) I, p. 68.

in the trade with London, the Genoese and the Catalans ranked first in Southampton.[18] The Genoese, however, surpassed their competitors in the import of raw materials for the industries, such as cotton and alum. The spices and other commodities they offered in England provided the Italian merchants with the means of payment for the purchase of wool and tin. The Venetian galleys were the largest exporters of tin from England,[19] but the Catalan ships also carried heavy cargoes of the metal to the Mediterranean.[20]

Under the pressure of the economic factors, the growing demand for Oriental articles in Europe and the increasing volume of international trade, the Holy See had to change its policy. The pope was compelled to adopt a more lenient attitude in the question of trade with the Moslem Levant. As a matter of principle, the prohibition of trade was maintained by the Church to the end of the fourteenth century. But the Holy See was much more liberal in granting licenses. However, the change was not sudden; it was a rather slow and progressive softening of the attitude of the Holy See.

Even before the conclusion of peace between the sultan of Cairo and the king of Cyprus, Venice applied to the pope with a request that licenses granted in the past be confirmed and when the peace was indeed ratified her envoys demanded that the licenses be valid for a longer time or that new ones should be issued.[21] In the 1370's the opposition of the Holy See to trade with the Moslem Levant was weaker than before. In 1374 Venice obtained permission for two galleys to commute between Crete and Syria within three years.[22] In 1377 Venice asked for permits for 25 galleys,[23] but the Holy See granted her only another permit for traffic between Crete and Syria; and although not all previous licenses had been used, her envoys obtained new ones for 8 galleys and 9 cogs.[24] A month later the Holy See granted Venice licenses for 12 galleys.[25] The smaller trading towns also applied in those years with such requests to the pope. Savona was authorized by Pope Gregory XI in 1371 to send two merchantmen to Egypt and Asia Minor. In 1373 Ragusa, which had had recourse to the good offices of her protector, the king of Hungary, obtained permission from Gregory XI to send 2 ships every year to the dominions of the Mamluks.[26] On the other hand, the government of Ragusa enacted a decree in 1376 which forbade

[18] Ruddock, *Italian merchants*, p. 84.
[19] *Op.cit.*, p. 90 f.
[20] Carrère, *Barcelone*, p. 646.
[21] Misti 33, f. 63b, 75b, 100a.
[22] *Libr. Com.* III, lib. 7, no. 767; *Dipl. Ven.-Lev.* II, no. 96.
[23] Misti 36, f. 15b.
[24] *Libr. Com.* III, lib. 8, no. 35, 36; *Dipl. Ven.-Lev.* II, nos. 102, 103.
[25] *Libr. Com.* III, lib. 8, no. 37; *Dipl. Ven.-Lev.* II, no. 104.
[26] I. Scovazzi-F. Noberasco, *Storia di Savona* (Savona, 1926-1928) III, p. 169 f.; Krekić, nos. 304, 286; cf. p. 116.

the citizens of the town to engage in trade with the Moslems without having licenses.[27]

As time went on, the trading nations ventured to demand far-reaching concessions from the Holy See. In 1384 Venice asked for a permanent license, that is, for the lifting of the embargo.[28] But the pope was not yet ready to take such a step. He granted the great Adriatic republic licenses only for well-defined periods. At first, in 1384, he gave the Venetians a general license for trade with the Moslem Levant, other than that of war material, for one year.[29] Such licenses were granted yearly for 1386 and 1387,[30] but in 1387 the pope granted Venice a license for two years.[31] Then, in 1390, Pope Boniface IX took another step: he allowed Venice to carry on trade with the dominions of the sultan for ten years.[32] Finally, in 1399, Boniface IX gave the Serenissima a license for 25 years.[33] Apparently the government of Venice had not believed that the Holy See would be so liberal and assumed that it would obtain a license for ten years only. So it agreed to pay a high fee for the new decree, not less than 3,000 ducats.[34]

It would be mistaken, however, to conclude from the granting of these extended licenses that the Holy See had renounced its opposition to trade with the Moslems altogether. In the course of time, the applications for and the granting of licenses, the threat of excommunication and absolution, had become a source of revenue for the Church. Like so many social organisms even this one maintained itself, although its time had passed.

Even in this period the Holy See granted licenses not only to the governments of the trading nations, but to individuals,[35] and not only to merchants. Sometimes ecclesiastical bodies received such licenses, as a source of income. For it was understood that they would sell them to merchants. In 1399 Basilio de Levante, prior of the Hospitallers of Messina, had obtained a license for six ships (that means for one travel each), and in 1400 he transferred them to the Genoese merchant Basilio Cattaneo.[36] The pope granted licenses also for a single ship,[37] for a part of a ship,[38] and even for the investment of a certain amount of money in trade with the Moslems. In 1387 two Genoese merchants, Janono Malocello and Oberto Sauli, had

[27] Krekić, no. 314.
[28] Misti 39, f. 16a.
[29] *Libr. Com.* III, lib. 8, no. 181; *Dipl. Ven.-Lev.* II, no. 113.
[30] *Libr. Com.* III, lib. 8, nos. 212, 213; *Dipl. Ven.-Lev.* II, nos. 118, 119.
[31] *Libr. Com.* III, lib. 8, no. 271; *Dipl. Ven.-Lev.* II, no. 125.
[32] *Libr. Com.* III, lib. 8, no. 340; *Dipl. Ven.-Lev.* II, no. 133.
[33] *Libr. Com.* III, lib. 9, no. 169.
[34] Misti 44, f. 120b, 128a.
[35] Misti 35, f. 157a 36, f. 12b.
[36] ASG, Notai 469/2, Foglietta, Ant., c. 28b/29b.
[37] Musso, *Navigazione*, pp. 75f., 76.
[38] Misti 38, f. 1b.

a papal license for the export of merchandise worth 50,000 fl. within two years, to the dominions of the Mamluks.[39] These papal licenses often changed hands. The merchants sold them to another one.[40] However, it was not enough to have a license from the Church. Almost everywhere the secular authorities insisted that the merchants get an additional permit from them, for a fee, of course. This was a law in Venice,[41] Catalonia[42] and Ragusa.[43]

The fact that the Church maintained the prohibition of trade with the Moslems often had serious consequences, entailing long litigation among people who were not engaged in trade at all. It was enough to put forward a claim that a merchant who had left a bequest had carried on trade with the Moslems without having a license in order to impede the delivery of the goods and to make necessary long proceedings.[44] Since many merchants did engage in trade with the Moslem Levant without having permits, time and again applications were submitted to the ecclesiastical authorities for absolution. In 1382 Pope Urban VI authorized Bartolomeo di Cogorno, the cardinal of St. Lorenzo, to grant absolutions to the merchants of Piacenza, Genoa, and Milan who had carried on illegal trade with the Moslem Levant. They were to be required to pay the Church authorities half of the profit obtained from this trade. Notarial acts refer to payments made in 1383 by several Genoese merchants to the chaplain of the cardinal, the Franciscan Simone de Morgano, for their absolution.[45] In any case, at the end of the fourteenth century the opposition of the Church was no longer a great obstacle to the development of European trade in the Moslem Levant.

The attitude of the Mamluk government was also favorable to the intensification of the commercial exchanges. The increase of income from the custom dues was undoubtedly only one reason for the inclination to foster the activities of the Christian merchants. The Mamluks could not overlook the advantage of providing an outlet for the surplus of the agricultural production of their countries, especially of Syrian cotton. Proceedings of the Venetian Senate indicate that in 1382 the Mamluk authorities made an offer to the republic to pay restitution due to Venetian merchants by handing over to them certain quantities of cotton.[46] Obviously the supply of cotton in the dominions of the sultan was greater than the demand. In the history of Mamluk rule over Egypt and Syria the last third

[39] Foglietta, Oberto, Senior III, c. 2.
[40] ASG, Notai 469/2, Foglietta, Ant., c. 80b.
[41] Misti 37, f. 48a, 68b, 92b, 98a 38, f. 1b, 107b.
[42] López de Meneses, "Los consulados," p. 100.
[43] Krekić, nos. 318, 388.
[44] G. Petti Balbi, "Deroghe papali al 'devetum' sul commercio con l'Islam," *Rassegna degli archivi di Stato* 32 (1972), p. 522, note 1.
[45] *Art. cit.*, p. 522 ff.
[46] Misti 37, f. 101a.

of the fourteenth century was one of the relatively calm periods. In 1382 the reign of the so-called Baḥrite dynasty came to an end and the emir Barḳūḳ founded the second Mamluk dynasty, that of the Circassians or Burdjites. Most of the reign of Barḳūḳ (1382-1399) passed without conflicts with other powers and without those revolts that so often shook the rule of the Mamluk sultans. There was one exception: in 1389 the revolt of some powerful emirs compelled Barḳūḳ to flee from Cairo, but in 1390 he overthrew his adversaries and was able to return to his capital. Barḳūḳ himself encouraged the European traders to intensify their activities in his dominions, and until the end of his reign his policy toward the trading nations was distinguished by restraint and good will. It is worthwhile to quote the testimony of an Italian trader who knew him personally. The Sienese Bertrando Mignanelli came to Damascus as a young man and lived there a long time. Having acquired a thorough knowledge of Arabic, he served as an interpreter on various occasions, for instance, when an envoy of the duke of Milan came to visit Barḳūḳ. Mignanelli testifies that Barḳūḳ was fond of the European traders and that, under his reign and that of his son and successor, upon the request of Christian merchants, those who had offended them were severely whipped at the hands of the Mamluks. Mignanelli says that he himself had beaten offenders to the point of shedding blood.[47] This is a trustworthy account of an eyewitness and helps us to understand the first two Circassian sultans who were aware of the adventages the trade with the South European nations had for their dominions and realized that they must adopt a friendly attitude toward them, despite the friction and the conflicts that resulted from the contacts between the Europeans and the Moslems.

Sometimes the position of the European merchants was endangered by acts of aggression perpetrated by Christian corsairs. The Arabic chronicles of the late fourteenth century contain accounts of several naval raids on the coasts of Egypt and Syria and of acts of piracy. Very seldom do the chroniclers indicate who the aggressors were; mostly they say only that they were "Franks." In the year 1393, Christian raiders attacked Nastarū, west of Burullus on the Egyptian coast, killed some people, took others captive, and looted the town.[48] A year later ships that transported grains from Egypt were captured off the Syrian coast by Christian pirates.[49] In 1401 there was another case of piracy; again some Moslem ships carrying wheat to Syria were captured,[50] and in the same year Christian raiders

[47] W. J. Fischel, "A new Latin source of Tamerlane's conquest of Damascus (1400/1401)," *Oriens* IX (1956), p. 229.

[48] Ibn al-Furāt IX, p. 342; *Sulūk* III, p. 787; Ibn Ḥadjar I, p. 454; al-Djawharī, *Nuzha*, p. 362; 'Abdalbāsiṭ 803 f. 161b.

[49] *Sulūk* III, p. 813; Ibn Ḥadjar I, p. 477.

[50] *Sulūk* III, p. 1059; Ibn Iyās[2] I, part 2, p. 624.

made an onslaught on the port of Tripoli. They captured two Moslem ships which had heavy cargoes and took many prisoners.[51] Since the Mamluk authorities probably knew who the attackers were and were not hostile to the European merchants, these acts of aggression did not result in total suspension of the commercial exchanges. The sultan did not make the merchants of other nations responsible for these raids.

But the campaigns of the great Mongol conqueror Tīmūr cast their shadow on the security of the European traders in the Levant and finally resulted in a short crisis.

The danger of an invasion of Syria by Tīmūr's armies was imminent as early as the 1380's. In the years 1386-1387 he had conquered Fars, Iraq, and Ādharbaydjān, and thereupon his armies occupied most towns of Upper Mesopotamia and moved into Asia Minor and farther to the frontiers of Syria, taking Amid, Malatiya, and Edessa. The situation looked so gloomy that in January 1388 the Venetian Senate allowed the consuls in Damascus and Alexandria to leave their seats and to have the merchandise of the traders shipped from the dominions of the Mamluks even on non-Venetian ships.[52] However, this time Tīmūr returned to the east. But in 1393 he put an end to the rule of the Muẓaffarids in Southern Persia and conquered Baghdad, whereupon Aḥmad b. Uways, the Djalā'irid ruler, fled to Syria. Edessa was again occupied by Tīmūr's troops. Bertrando Mignanelli, who wrote a biography of Barḳūḳ and a treatise about the invasion of Syria by Tīmūr, recounts that the Mamluk sultan gave orders that the European merchantmen should leave Syrian ports and sail to Egypt.[53] There was a standstill in the commercial activities in Syria, and in 1394 there were apprehensions in Venice as to the success of the fall cotton fair. A galley was sent to Syria to obtain reliable news. At the beginning of September, it returned to Venice with the good news that the fears were unfounded.[54] The sultan himself went to Syria to take over her defense, but once more Tīmūr returned to Upper Mesopotamia and on to Central Asia. However, after a campaign in India the Mongol conqueror made his final onslaught on Syria.

In the late fall of 1400, Tīmūr conquered Aleppo, moved to the south, and occupied Damascus in January 1401. The European merchants fled from Syria before the advancing army of Tīmūr. The agent of the Venetians in Aleppo, Martino Cipriano, succeeded in leaving the town before her

[51] *Sulūk* III, p. 1079 (copied by Ibn Iyās² I, part 2, p. 642); Ibn Ḥadjar II, p. 199. The account of this latter author stems from a source other than that of al-Maḳrīzī. From his account, one learns that only one group of the raiders attacked a village in the area around Tripoli, and failed. This means that the other departed with the booty and the prisoners.

[52] Misti 40, f. 101a.

[53] W. J. Fischel, ed. "Ascensus Barcoch," *Arabica* VI (1959), p. 166.

[54] ASV, Mag. Cons., Leona, f. 72b, Dat 797, letter of Zanobi di Taddeo Gaddi of 31 Oct. 1394.

occupation by the Mongols;[55] the Venetians who carried on trade in Sarmīn, the center of a cotton growing district, likewise fled precipitously.[56] Some of the merchants who left Syria did not pay their debts to the Moslems. Since most of the Venetian traders had gone to Famagusta, it was proposed in the Senate of Venice that those who had debts to Moslems in Syria should deposit monies with the Venetian authorities in Cyprus, but the proposition was turned down.[57] The Venetian consul of Damascus, too, fled to Famagusta, and even the consul of Alexandria left the town for Candia.[58] In some places, as in Damascus, the merchants handed over their stocks of merchandise to Moslem traders, to keep for them.[59] On the other hand, much of the merchandise shipped to Syria in 1400 was sent to Cyprus and elsewhere.[60] Nevertheless, the losses of the Italian merchants were considerable.[61] Merchandise that the Venetians had left in Tripoli was robbed by Genoese, who sent a galley there from Cyprus.[62] In Venice there was great excitement. The letters that the agents and friends of Francesco Datini sent him from Venice reflect the anxieties. According to these letters, people feared that Tīmūr would push forward and invade Egypt too. There were even rumors that he had already occupied Cairo,[63] and although the Venetians had made large purchases of cotton in 1400 (surely Turkish) in Rhodes, cotton prices were very high in Venice.[64] In 1401 the galley service to Syria was suspended, although news that Tīmūr had retreated from Damascus had already been received in May. There were grave doubts about his plans. So it was decided to send again a ship to the coast of Syria to obtain news of his moves.[65] But very soon it was heard that people had returned to Syria to their homes and taken up their normal activities. However, much of Damascus was destroyed, as is vividly depicted by Mignanelli,[66] and during the anarchy resulting from Tīmūr's retreat, the Bedouins made the caravan routes insecure. Further, the struggle between the various factions of the Mamluks began again. So at first the Italian merchants hesitated to

[55] G. P., Sent. II, f. 41a ff.

[56] G. P., Sent. VIII, f. lb f.

[57] Misti 45, f. 59a (to be corrected apud Jorga, *ROL* IV, p. 237 where one reads that a decision was taken to that effect).

[58] Thiriet, *Régestes* II, p. 14.

[59] As 57.

[60] Misti 45, f. 119b.

[61] *Anonymous Venetian Chronicle*, Bibl. Naz. Florence, MS. Gino Capponi 1853, CCLVIII, vol. II, f. 302a; *Chron. Dolfin*, f. 268a; Dat 1082, letter of Paris Soranzo of 7 Feb. 1400. See also Dat 797, letter of Simone di Lappacino & Cie. of 15 Jan. 1401: merchandise of the Venetians worth 50,000 fl. was robbed in Damascus and other towns of Syria.

[62] Misti 45, f. 8b, 71b 46, f. 27b; Delaville de Roulx II, p. 106 and cf. I, p. 419.

[63] Dat 927, letter of Commess. of Zanobi di Taddeo Gaddi of 9 Oct. 1401; Ainaud, doc. I.

[64] Dat 713, letter of Simone di Lappacino of 8 Jan. 1401; Dat 797, letter of the same of 15 Jan. 1401; Dat 927, letter of Bernardo Bon of 17 Febr. 1401.

[65] Dat 927, letter of Commess. of Zanobi di Taddeo Gaddi of 25 May and 23 July 1401.

[66] Fischel, "A new Latin source" (see n. 47 above), p. 229.

return to Syria. Obviously, in that year little cotton was grown in Syria, so that only insignificant purchases could be made. Even the offer of spices in Damascus was very poor.[67]

However, the invasion of Syria by Tīmūr was an interlude. After his retreat, the intense activities of the South European merchants in Syria and Egypt went on as before. While the Mamluks endeavored vainly to rebuild their shaken government, the trading nations enjoyed unchallenged supremacy on the sea. Their naval power assured the success of their commercial activities; they had more and better ships than the Moslems and were incomparably stronger in naval warfare. Ships of the Italian merchants carried victuals from Palestine to Egypt[68] and much of the seaborne traffic between Egypt and the countries of the Maghreb was in their hands. Further, the great trading nations of Southern Europe had colonies and points of support on the Christian islands in the Eastern Mediterranean. In 1373 the Genoese succeeded in making the king of Cyprus dependent upon them and to establish their control over the trade of the island.[69] It was to serve them as a base for their trade with all the countries of the Near East. Chios was another important base of Genoese trade; it was the starting point of ship lines that connected it with Pera and the Genoese colonies on the shores of Crimea, on one hand, and Northwestern Europe, on the other. Being so near to the coast of Asia Minor, it served the Genoese as a port for Turkish products to be shipped to the west. The port of Rhodes fulfilled the role of a point of support for both the Catalan and Provençal traders. It was the destination of most galleys and cogs sailing from Barcelona and Marseilles to the Levant. The Venetians had the facilities of Candia and Modon, where they could store and shift cargoes arriving from the dominions of the Mamluks and from Greek ports. It would be an exaggeration to say that at the end of the fourteenth century the Eastern Mediterranean and the Aegean had become a Christian sea, because the power of the Ottoman Turks on the sea was steadily increasing, but the European trading nations had built up a very efficient network of colonies and ports that enabled them to carry on regular and wholesale trade with the Moslem Levant.

B. Venetian and Genoese Trade

Immediately upon the conclusion of peace between the sultan of Cairo and the king of Cyprus the trading nations of Southern Europe began to renew

[67] Dat 927, letter of the same Commess. of 9 Oct. 1401. According to Mignanelli, *l.c.* there was also a locust plague that year in Syria.

[68] Vat. sub 5 Febr. 1400.

[69] Heyd II, p. 409 f.; Lopez, *Storia delle colonie genovesi*, p. 370 ff.

their activities in Egypt and Syria. But the share they had had in this trade and the sectors in which they engaged underwent a change. Venice took the lead; she replaced Genoa as the first trading nation in the Moslem Levant.

Even before peace had been concluded, the Senate of Venice decided to dispatch galleys to Alexandria and to send a new consul there.[70] The Genoese also sent a new appointee to the consulate there.[71] But the Venetians concentrated their efforts upon developing their trade with the dominions of the Mamluks. From 1370 on, their galley line to Alexandria functioned regularly, except for the years of war; and in 1376 another line, that connecting Venice with Beirut, was established.[72] In the 1370's and 1380's, every year two galleys went to Alexandria and three or four to Beirut, and then in the 1390's, when the boom in the Levant trade reached a peak, three were sent to Alexandria and four or five to Beirut. The galley line to Cyprus was suspended when Famagusta became a Genoese port and the Romania line declined. Whereas at the beginning of the 1370's these latter convoys consisted of four to five galleys, at the end of the century they numbered no more than two or three.

In addition to the galley lines, Venice also had cog lines to Egypt and Syria. These cogs were either owned by the State or were private ships, licensed and supervised by the government. They sailed on fixed dates and were intended for the transport of heavier and cheaper merchandise than the spices carried by the galleys. The Alexandria cogs replaced the galleys in some years, but generally only one of these cogs sailed to Egypt every year. The cog line to Syria was much more important. Every year at the end of January or the beginning of February a convoy of cogs departed from Venice to collect the cotton purchased in Syria, and at the end of July a usually smaller convoy made the same trip. This line, which functioned from the time trade with the dominions of the Mamluks was taken up in the 1370's, fulfilled a very important role in the commercial exchanges with the Moslem Levant. In the 1390's the two convoys comprised at least ten ships. The data on this line, which have come down to us (or are known to the present writer) from the end of the fourteenth century, are not complete.[73]

The amounts of the rents that the auctions of the galleys yielded show more clearly than other data the development of the various sectors of Venetian Levant trade in that period. They point to the great decline in

[70] Misti 33, f. 81a, and cf. 82a, 83b.

[71] See there, f. 53b.

[72] Misti 35, f. 115a, 115b. In the years 1374-1375, two galleys commuted between Crete and Syria; see Thiriet, *Régestes* I, pp. 132, 138 and cf. above p. 108.

[73] See my paper "Observations on Venetian Trade," p. 560 f. and appendix A and, further, Marino Sanuto, *Vite de' duchi*, c. 680.

Table V Levantine galley lines of Venice in the late XIVth century

year	Romania	Cyprus	Alexandria	Beirut	source
1370	4 + 1	2 + 1[a]	-	-	Thiriet, Rég. I, p. 123
1371	4 + 1	4	5	-	Op. cit., p. 126; Misti 33, f. 80b, 81a
1372	4 (2 to Tana, 2 to Trebizon)	4[b]	4	-	Op. cit., p. 127 f.
1373	2 + 2[c] (2 to Tana, 2 to Trebizond)	-	-	-	Op. cit., p. 130
1374	3 + 1[d]	-	3	-	" " p. 134
1375	3 + 1[e] (3 to Tana, 1 to Trebizond)				
1376	2 + 1[f]	-	4	3	Op. cit., p. 144
1377	2[g]	-	4	3	" " p. 146
		1378-1381 war with Genoa[h]			
1382	2[i]	-	2	3	" " p. 153
1383	2	-	2	3	" " p. 158
1384	2 + 1[j]	-		4	" " p. 164
1385	2 + 1[k]	-	-	4	" " p. 168
1386	2	-	2	5	" " p. 171
1387	2	-	2	5	" " p. 175 f.
1388	3	-	2	4	" " p. 178
1389	3	-	2	4	" " p. 181
1390	3	-	2	2 + suppl. galley	" " p. 187; Misti 41, f. 110a f.
1391	3	-	2	3	Op. cit., p. 190; Misti 42, f. 3a
1392	3	-	3	4	Op. cit., p. 195
1393	3	-	3	4	" " p. 198
1394	3	-	3	4	" " p. 202
1395	3	-	3	5	" " p. 207
1396	2	-	3	5	" " p. 213
1397	2	-	3	5	" " p. 218 f.
1398	-	-	3	5	" " p. 220

Venice's trade in Greece and in the Black Sea area and, on the other hand, the growth of her trade with Egypt and Syria. They also shed light on other phenomena.[74]

As early as the 1370's, Venice's trade with the dominions of the sultan was incomparably greater than her trade with the territories that formerly

[74] The data of 1395-1402, see in Fr. Thiriet, "La crise des trafics vénitien du Levant," in *Studi Melis* III, p. 65. Fr. Thiriet has also compiled a similar table in his *La Romanie vénitienne*, p. 344 f., but summing up the rents yielded from all the convoys, so that the trend of development of the different lines cannot be distinguished.

Table V (continued)

year	Romania	Cyprus	Alexandria	Beirut	source
1399	2	-	3	5 + suppl. galley[l]	Op. Cit. p. 223; Misti 44, f. 132a ff.
1400	-	-	3	6	Op. cit. II, p. 11 f.
1401	-	-	3	-	" " p. 19
1402	-	-	4	2	" " p. 29

a) This galley and one Romania galley were run by the State.

b) According to Misti 33, f. 109b - five galleys, but according to the auction only four.

c, d, e, f) Run by the State.

g) Three were offered, but nobody was interested. Later the traffic was suspended for that year because of insecurity, see p. 146 f.

h) According to Libr. Com. III, lib. 7, no. 669, two galleys went to Alexandria in 1381, but see Dipl. Ven.-Lev. II, no. 96, that this refers to the year 1377.

i) Run by the State.

j, k) Departing from Candia.

l) The supplementary galley was sent to Alexandria at the beginning of 1400 to collect merchandise that had remained there.

m) See note b to Table VI.

belonged to the Byzantine empire. In the ninth decade of the fourteenth century, when Venice suffered from the consequences of the war of Chioggia, the volume of trade in all sectors was apparently more limited, but at the end of the century the rents obtained for the Alexandria and Beirut galleys peaked, whereas auctions of the Romania galleys yielded small sums. The data in the table also show the great development of Venetian trade in Syria. In several years, the auction of the Beirut galleys yielded more than that of the Alexandria galleys. This was the case in 1388, 1396, 1397, 1399, and 1400. In other years, as in 1386, the sums obtained for the two convoys were almost equal.

Surely the decline of Venetian trade in the formerly Byzantine territories was not only a consequence of the jamming of the Persian route to India and of conditions in Southern Russia. The trade with Trebizond declined too.[75] The relations between the rulers of Trebizond and the Venetians were not smooth at all. The Venetians made naval demonstrations off Trebizond or tried by negotiations to obtain an undertaking that they could carry on their trade without suffering damages.[76] In fact, the Romania

[75] See Thiriet, *Régestes* I, p. 133.

[76] Thiriet, *op.cit.* I, pp. 134 f., 135 f., 137, 139 f., 143 f., 149, 211.

Table VI Auctions of the Levant galleys of Venice
in the late XIVth century

(in lire di grossi)[a]

year	Romania	Cyprus	Alexandria	Beirut	source
1370	221^{3}	265^{7}	-	-	Thiriet, Rég. I, p. 124
1371	64^{3}	643^{13}	1096^{1}	-	Op. cit., p. 126; Misti 33 f. 111a
1372	53^{4}	662^{14}	801	-	Op. cit., p. 128; Misti 34, f. 7a, 8b
1373	221^{3}	-	-	-	Op. cit., p. 131
1374	6 s	-	803^{11}	-	Op. cit., p. 134
1375	62^{5}	-	609^{10}	-	Op. cit., p. 139
1376	25^{3}	-	785^{1}	462^{15}	Op. cit., p. 144; Misti 35, f. 114b, 115a, 118b
1377	25^{2}	-	449^{5}	145^{12}	Op. cit., p. 146; Misti 36, f. 15a, 16a
		1378 - 1381 war with Genoa			
1382	-	-	291^{2}	258^{11}	Op. cit., p. 153; Misti 37, f. 78b., 79b
1383	206	-	373^{9}	237^{7}	Op. cit., p. 148; Misti 38, f. 13a ff.
1384	1 galley:85	-	-	160^{4}	Op. cit., p. 160; Misti 38, f. 113b, 131b, 133b
1385	20^{4}	-	-	580^{15}	Op. cit., p. 168; Misti 39, f. 83a, 86a
1386	202	-	320	319^{20}	Op. cit., p. 171; Misti 40, f. 29b, 32a
1387	242^{5}	-	387^{13}	297^{1}	Op. cit., p. 176; Misti 40, f. 72a
1388	191^{1}	-	125^{10}	496^{3}	Op. cit., p. 178; Misti 40, f. 121a
1389	91^{2}	-	402^{12}	241^{10}	Op. cit., p. 181; Misti 41, f. 10b
1390	55^{3}	-	352^{13}	-	Op. cit., p. 187; Misti 41, f. 85a, 91a
1391	202	-	341^{5}	501^{6}	Op. cit., p. 190; Misti 41, f. 142a, 42, f. 3a f
1392	424^{6}	-	677^{11}	298^{11}	Op. cit., p. 195; Misti 42, f. 62b ff.

galleys did not go to Trebizond at all in some years.[77] The relations of the Venetians with the Greek authorities in Constantinople were also very strained, and the volume of their transactions in the Greek capital decreased. Numerous decrees of the Venetian Senate of the last third of the fourteenth century deal with the conflicts with the emperor and the difficult negoti-

[77] Cf. Silberschmidt, *Das orientalische Problem*, p. 141.

Table VI (continued)

year	Romania	Cyprus	Alexandria	Beirut	source
1393	363^{6}	-	551^{4}	367^{11}	Op. cit., p. 198; Misti 42, f. 113a ff.
1394	437^{5}	-	586^{18}	178^{4}	Op. cit., p. 202; Misti 43, f. 8a f., 9b
1395	332^{15}	-	726^{1}	593	Op. cit., p. 207; Misti 43, f. 63a f., 64a f.
1396	51^{2}	-	590	637^{17}	Op. cit., p. 213; Misti 43, f. 129a, 132a, 135b
1397	204^{19}	-	647^{9}	809^{11}	Op. cit., p. 218; Misti 44, f. 4a f., 6b
1398	-	-	635^{14}	485^{7}	Op. cit., p. 220; Misti 44, f. 44b, 46a, 48a
1399	143	-	642^{2}	758^{6}	Op. cit., p. 223; Misti 44, f. 107b f., 109b
1400	-	-	629^{17}	643^{1}	Op. cit. II, p. 11; Misti 45, f. 17b
1401	-[b]	-	64^{14}	-	Op. cit., p. 19; Misti 45, f. 90a f., 91a
1402	-	-	830^{5}	75^{4}	Op. cit., p. 29; Misti 46, f. 31a, 32a f.

a) 1 lira di grossi = 10 ducats, 1 lira = 20 soldi.

b) In this year two galleys were dispatched to Candia and Negrepont; their auction yielded 104 pounds, see Misti 45, f. 90b f.

ations that went on for many years.[78] The Venetians accused the emperor of actively collaborating with the Turks,[79] but the Serenissima herself began to form a connection with the latter, although very cautiously.[80] Certainly the Venetians could not overlook the possibility of trading with the growing dominions of the Ottomans. On the other hand, Turkish piracy in the Aegean increased; the Turkish corsairs threatened the network of Venetian traffic in the whole of the Eastern Mediterranean and the Ionian Sea[81] and even the rule of Venice on some Greek islands. Time and again measures had to be taken to safeguard Venetian shipping and the security of the Greek colonies.[82] So the Venetians realized that, despite the enmity of the Greeks, their rule in Constantinople meant having a point of support and a check against Turkish power. Consequently the envoys of the Serenissima

[78] Thiriet, *Régestes* I, pp. 128, 136, 140, 142 f., 143 f., 149, 149 f., 152, 159, 160 f., 182 f., 186, 187, 191, 193, 196.

[79] *Op.cit.*, p. 194.

[80] *Op.cit.*, pp. 162, 163, 164, 177 f., 179, 183, 184 f., 210 f.

[81] *Op.cit.*, II, p. 23.

[82] *Op.cit.*, I, pp. 208, 210, 214, 214 f., 215, 221 f.; II, pp. 11, 12, 13, 14, 19, 23, 24, 31.

began to encourage the Greek emperor not to leave Constantinople, to promise him help,[83] and to adopt a more lenient attitude toward the Greek authorities.[84] But meanwhile Venetian trade in Constantinople decreased more and more. This is clearly borne out by the decrees of the Senate concerning the number of days that the Romania galleys going to Tana should stop in the Greek capital. In the 1370's and the 1380's their stop should last no more than two days.[85] In 1398 it was impossible to obtain a majority in the Senate for the proposition to send galleys to Constantinople and the Black Sea ports.[86] The Genoese supremacy in Cyprus was another impetus for the Venetians to concentrate their commercial activities in the Levant in the dominions of the Mamluks. Famagusta could not serve them as an alternative market for the acquisition of spices any more. Sometimes the Senate of Venice forbade her subjects to buy spices there,[87] or even imposed a total embargo on trade with Cyprus.[88]

Several data point to the increase of Venetian trade with Egypt and Syria at the end of the fourteenth century. The registers of the Venetian Senate contain decisions to send galleys to Crete or to Modon, where great quantities of spices had remained because there was no more place in the galleys and cogs returning to the metropolis.[89] In 1374 it was necessary to send two cogs to Candia to collect the spices that had been stored there. Previously two galleys had been sent there, but they were not sufficient.[90] In 1378 the consul in Damascus was ordered to send the merchandise that had remained in Beirut after the departure of the galleys to Tripoli, where the danger of a Genoese attack would be smaller.[91] In 1394 a great sum of money, which the merchants had taken with them to Alexandria and Beirut, could not be invested, because there was no more place in the galleys for more commodities.[92] In 1395 it was permitted to ship spices from Modon to Venice on cogs, although normally they would be loaded on galleys.[93] Then in 1398 it was thought in Venice that two supplementary ships would be necessary to transport the merchandise remaining after the departure of the galleys from Beirut.[94]

The rate of Venetian trade was particularly lively in Syria. In some years

[83] *Op.cit.*, I, pp. 202, 203 f., 205, 216, 218; II, p. 10 f., 19 f.
[84] *Op.cit.*, II, p. 15 f.
[85] *Op.cit.*, I, pp. 134, 171, 175, 181.
[86] *Op.cit.*, I, p. 220.
[87] Misti 45, f. 85a.
[88] Thiriet, *Régestes* I, p. 154.
[89] *Op.cit.*, I, p. 134; Misti 44, f. 26b, 122a, 130a 45, f. 99b.
[90] Misti 34, f. 123b.
[91] Misti 36, f. 56b.
[92] ASV, Mag. Cons., Leona, f. 76b.
[93] Misti 43, f. 41b.
[94] Misti 44, f. 61a.

the investment in the trade with this country was greater than in the trade with Egypt.[95] In Northern Syria the Venetians made great purchases of cotton and also bought silk coming from Persia. So the Senate decided in 1385 that one of the Beirut galleys should visit Tripoli and Latakia.[96] Two years later it was decided to establish a consulate in Sarmīn,[97] a small town in Northern Syria.[98] The appointee was to visit Aleppo once a year. In the latter town the Venetians entrusted their affairs to an agent, who was an Oriental Christian. But in 1395 it was decided to establish a Venetian factory there and to appoint a Venetian as manager. He would have his post for three years, and his house would serve his fellow-citizens for lodging. At first, at least, a candidate could not be found.[99] A Venetian consul in Latakia is mentioned in deliberations of the Senate in the late 1370's,[100] and in 1384 the sultan was asked to recognize his status by granting him a salary.[101] In Beirut too, there was a Venetian consul at the end of the fourteenth century.[102] All these consuls were placed under the consul in Damascus; they were vice-consuls.[103]

However, the Italian traders encountered far more difficulties and suffered more from extortion by the local authorities in Syria than in Egypt. Whereas in Egypt they carried on their activities almost exclusively in Alexandria and rarely went to Cairo, they were accustomed to travel a good deal in Syria. Most of the spices were acquired in Damascus and had to be transported to Beirut. The purchase of cotton made visits to the plantations necessary.[104] So it happened that the merchants were attacked[105] and that the camel- or donkey-drivers (*mucro*, from the Arabic *mukārī*) stole a part of the merchandise. Further, the local custom officers and prefects were more inclined to highhanded proceedings than in Alexandria, which was much nearer to the seat of the central government and therefore better supervised. So there were many complaints, and time and again the Venetian consuls and ambassadors protested against the ill-will of the Syrian authorities. Often they had to protest against forced purchases and forced

[95] *Ibid.*, f. 54a.
[96] Misti 39, f. 132b.
[97] Misti 40, f. 117b. About Venetian trade in Sarmīn, see also Misti 37, f. 48b, 49a.
[98] On the name of this town, see below, note 474.
[99] Misti 43, f. 40b, 41a.
[100] Misti 36, f. 59b.
[101] Misti 39, f. 25b.
[102] Frescobaldi, p. 164; Misti 45, f. 30b. What the French pilgrim Ogier d'Anglure says, namely, that at the time of his visit in 1395 there were no European merchants living in Beirut, is obviously an error: see *Voyage*, p. 10.
[103] The consul of Sarmīn is indeed sometimes called vice-consul; see Misti 42, f. 68a, but see there f. 107b, where he is called consul.
[104] G. P., Sent. 15, f. 48a ff.
[105] Misti 35, f. 14a.

sales of merchandise,[106] a proceeding of the Mamluk authorities that caused the European merchants great losses. But in Alexandria there were also conflicts with the customs officers, and in 1371 it was decided in Venice that the future consul should take the necessary steps in Cairo immediately upon his arrival in Egypt. He was instructed to act together with a Genoese ambassador in case an embassy should come to Cairo from Genoa.[107] In 1376 the Senate left it to the judgment of the consul in Alexandria whether he should go to Cairo and ask for the dismissal of the governor of Alexandria. But then it was decided that he should indeed go there and also demand that the sultan keep certain promises made to the consul of Damascus and, secondly, forbid sales on credit to Venetians.[108]

However, the interventions of the consuls did not carry enough weight to bring about a change in the attitude of the Moslem authorities. So Venice sent several embassies to the sultan in the last thirty years of the fourteenth century. Venetian diplomacy had two principles: on the one hand, the Serenissima did not renounce any claim, however small it was. Every subject of Venice had to be sure that the government would safeguard his interests even if a very small sum of money was involved. On the other hand, Venice tried to diminish as far as possible friction with the Moslem merchants and the Mamluk authorities. She took measures to avoid accusations that Venetians caused damage to Moslems, or even captured them and sold them as slaves.[109] But, first of all, Venice endeavored to remain on friendly terms with the Mamluk government.

In 1375 Giovanni Barbarigo was sent as ambassador to the sultan. His instructions contained a long list of claims and demands. He was to demand that contracts between Venetians and Moslem merchants be made by four clerks, one for each cadi,[110] and that they should be kept. Litigations resulting from such contracts should be brought before secular judges (the *ḥudjdjāb*). The ambassador was asked to obtain binding promises of freedom of trade in Syria and make sure that there would not be sales and purchases of merchandise by compulsion. He was also to raise the question of bequests left by Venetians, who died in the dominions of the sultan, and of the goods of ships which had suffered shipwreck. Further, he was to obtain an undertaking that Venetians would not be made responsible for acts of piracy

[106] Misti 43, f. 10a 44, f. 133b f.

[107] Misti 33, f. 118b, 122a.

[108] Misti 35, f. 113a, 113b. The Venetian authorities, on their part, forbade such transactions, but their orders were not obeyed; see Misti 35, f. 120b 46, f. 162b.

[109] Misti 43, f. 53b 44, f. 38b.

[110] From the reign of Baybars there were four chief judges in Egypt and Syria, for every *madhhab*, and they had deputies in the quarters of the big towns and in smaller towns. The claim put forward by the Venetian embassy should make it impossible that a contract drawn up by a clerk (i.e., a notary) appointed by the judge of one madhhab should not be recognized by another.

committed by non-Venetians. Finally, he should demand that the Venetians could live in Damascus outside the fondachi, as they had become too small.[111] The mission of Giovanni Barbarigo proved a success. The sultan agreed to most of his requests. He ordered that goods left by Venetians should be handed over to the consuls. He also decreed that lawsuits between Moslems and Venetians be brought before secular judges, who did not apply the canon law of Islam and consequently could be more lenient toward non-Moslems. The ambassador was promised that the Venetians would not be required to make compulsory purchases, and finally the sultan undertook to enlarge the places of residence which the Venetians had in Damascus. On this occasion, the sultan also recognized the official status of the consul in Damascus.[112] However, as so often was the case, the solemn promises of the sultan were not kept. In 1376 the Venetians suffered from extortions by the governor in Damascus, some merchants and the consul were imprisoned, and merchandise was sequestered.[113] So the Senate decided to send another embassy to the sultan to ask for the release of the merchants and put forward other claims.[114] However, the embassy did not have full success or was altogether suspended.[115] The sultan sent the government of Venice a letter explaining that the goods of the Venetians had been sequestered as reprisal for the misdeeds of Venetian merchants, one of them the former consul of Damascus, Marco Brici, who had taken merchandise from Moslems and departed without paying for them. Thereupon, in August 1377, the Senate once more found it necessary to dispatch an embassy to the sultan and gave it full instructions. The embassy consisted of Niccolo Loredan and Baldo Quirino.[116] It should demand the release of the goods of the Venetians in Damascus and also intervene on behalf of the king of Little Armenia, who was held a prisoner in Cairo. If necessary, bribes amounting to 15,000 ducats could be offered for the restitution of the sequestered goods. Further, apologies were to be made for the embezzlement of which some Venetians were guilty. The ambassadors should explain that it would be unjust to punish some people for the misdeeds of others. They should also once more demand from the sultan that he forbid sale of merchandise to the Venetians on credit.[117]

When trade with Egypt and Syria was resumed after an interruption of four years, owing to the war with Genoa, the extortions and robbery of merchandise began once more. In 1382 another Venetian embassy went to

[111] Misti 35, f. 9b ff., and see my paper "Observations on Venetian Trade," p. 553.
[112] *Libr. Com.* III, lib. 7, no. 787.
[113] Misti 35, f. 146b, 151b, 152a, and cf. *JEEH* V, p. 554.
[114] Misti 35, f. 146b, 152*b*, 153b.
[115] See *JEEH l.c.*
[116] Misti 36, f. 37a ff., cf. 34b.
[117] Misti 36, f. 35a, 35b.

Cairo; it consisted of the same Baldo Quirino and Piero Grimani. The ambassadors were instructed to protest against the robbery of merchandise of Venetian merchants in Damascus, where furs, tin, and copper had been taken from them, and when they had protested the Moslems had threatened to beat them and to imprison them. The ambassadors were also to insist that the duties levied on the Venetians should not be higher than those fixed in the treaties. As usual, they were also to claim payment for merchandise taken away from Venetian merchants by force. Finally, they should also ask the sultan to agree to the establishment of a Venetian consulate in Damietta.[118] This latter demand certainly is evidence of the growth of the Venetian trade in Egypt. Characteristically, the ambassadors were ordered to raise the question of the liberation of the royal family of Little Armenia, after they had dealt with all the claims of the Venetians. Obviously, this demand was not a first priority on their agenda. In 1384 the Venetian Senate again decided to send an embassy to the sultan, but it is not clear if this decision was realized.[119] Then in 1391, when Barḳūḳ had re-established his rule, Venice sent him an embassy consisting of Niccolò Valaresso and Marino Caravello. The first was an experienced diplomat, who had previously represented the republic at the Holy See and later was sent to the court of Sicily.[120] The object of the embassy was to protest against the extortions from which the Venetians suffered in Syria.[121] In 1398 the Venetian merchants suffered once more from reprisals both in Egypt and Syria for the crimes of a Greek and others accused of acts of robbery. In the Senate the prevailing opinion was that to safeguard Venetian interests it was necessary to establish a consulate at the seat of the Mamluk government. Luca Bragadin and Jacob Suriano were sent as ambassadors to the sultan to obtain his agreement. Like so many other embassies, this one was also to claim restitution for merchandise taken by force from the Venetian merchants. Again, they were instructed to ask the sultan to forbid once and for all the compulsory sale of merchandise imported by the Venetians. One of the instructions given to the embassy sheds light on the relations between the various European trading nations in the Levant. The Venetian embassy was to demand that the Venetians have their own weights in the exchange at Alexandria, as the Genoese had.[122] This shows that for a long time the Genoese had enjoyed the status of most-privileged trading nation in Alexandria. The instructions given to this embassy contain another significant passage: in the matter of a claim of a Turk who had

[118] Misti 37, f. 99b ff., and cf. my paper in *JEEH* V, p. 555 note 124.
[119] Misti 38, f. 135a f.
[120] Misti 42, f. 15a, 77b.
[121] *Ibid.*, f. 2a f.
[122] Misti 44, f. 39b, 42a, 49b, 54b ff.

travelled on a ship of a Moslem and had suffered from an attack by Venetians, the ambassadors should point to the fact that Venice was on very friendly terms with the Mamluk sultanate, whereas the Turks were her enemies.[123] This was not a mere phrase. It points to a far-reaching view of political alliances. By the end of the fourteenth century, Venice had already embarked on a policy aiming at a de facto alliance with the Mamluks.

But meanwhile there were new conflicts between Venice and the Mamluks. In 1399 the Venetian bailo in Cyprus had confiscated a load of iron and timber shipped to Egypt by a Greek. This was war material according to the laws of the Church, and Venice maintained the embargo. The sultan lodged a protest with the Venetian government.[124]

The demand of the Venetian embassy in 1398 to have a consulate in Cairo was obviously rejected and, as the extortions and compulsory sales went on, the Venetians were looking for another way of carrying on their trade in the dominions of the sultan without being the object of ill-will and greed. In 1401 it was proposed in the Senate that the consul in Alexandria should ask the sultan if he would be ready to sell Venice the island of Arwad off the Syrian coast for 10,000 ducats, so that it might serve as an extraterritorial factory.[125] The proposition was turned down, but it shows that even in those days commercial expansion in underdeveloped regions raised the question of founding colonies.

The account of the long and difficult negotiations and the deliberations that preceded them in Venice illustrate the patience of Venetian policy. By concentrating the commercial activities in the Levant in Egypt and Syria and by relentlessly insisting on their claims, by the end of the fourteenth century the Venetians had succeeded in acquiring the greatest share of the trade of these countries with Southern Europe. But they had not yet achieved supremacy in the Levant trade.

The number of Venetian ships that cast their anchors in the ports of Egypt and Syria was not the greatest of the European trading nations. This is shown by the mention of ships or their captains ("patrons") in the acts that have come down to us from notaries in Alexandria, dating from the last years of the fourteenth and the beginning of the fifteenth centuries.[126] Neither had Venice the largest colony in Alexandria, which was the greatest emporium of the Moslem Levant. By chance, the protocols of the Council of the Venetian colony in Alexandria dating from 1401-1402 have been preserved. They contain exact data about the number of the Venetian

[123] Cf. Silberschmidt, p. 189. See also Misti 42, f. 22a: the Venetian government forbids the "Duke of the Archipelago," a Venetian, to attack the subjects of the sultan.

[124] Misti 44, f. 122b.

[125] Misti 45, f. 93b. Cf. Jorga, *ROL* IV, p. 243.

[126] See my "The Venetian supremacy," p. 7; "Observations on Venetian Trade," p. 565.

merchants who then lived in Alexandria. On 17 October 1401 a proposition made in the general assembly of the colony (not in the council) was carried by 26 persons.[127] A year later, on 21 October 1402, the number of those taking part in the assembly was 47.[128] The Genoese colony in Alexandria was certainly much more numerous at that time, as indicated by the number of the merchants mentioned in notarial acts.[129]

Nevertheless, the Venetians were in the first place in the commercial exchanges of the Moslem Levant with the European countries, as far as the amount of the investment was concerned. This was a result of their concentration on the spice trade, that is, the export of the most precious articles. Among the spices they shipped to Venice, two articles outweighed all the others: most of the investment in the trade with Egypt was for the purchase of pepper and ginger. In Syria, every year they spent a great deal for the purchase of cotton. The records, which have been preserved in the archives of Francesco Datini and which are included in the Venetian chronicles, show in fact that the cotton purchases of the Venetians in Syria were so sizable that in some years the price paid for this commodity was equal to or even surpassed the investment in spices there.

Among the articles which the Venetians imported into the Moslem Levant, cloth, metals, and agricultural products were the most important. The textiles, both cloth and linen, the Venetians offered in the Levant were products of various European countries. The Venetians pursued a prohibitionist policy only with respect to their own textile industries.[130] Chief among the metals exported to the Near East was copper, which was shipped in the greatest volume. Great quantities of it were bought by the agents of the sultan and the governors of the provinces, who needed it for the mints, their industrial enterprises, and other purposes.[131] A great part of the commodities exported by the Venetians to the Levant stemmed from Germany. The commercial exchanges between Venice and the German countries had indeed already reached a volume which was probably not surpassed during the fifteenth century.[132] The agricultural products were mostly olive oil, fruits, and honey bought in Apulia and transported to Egypt and to Syria on cogs. The export of agricultural goods to the Moslem Levant was an important sector of Venice's Levant trade. Some time before

[127] Verb. Cons. XII, s.d.; the number of those who opposed the proposition or abstained is not given.

[128] *Ibid.*, s.d.

[129] See below.

[130] What Heers says, "Il commercio," p. 167, namely, that the Venetians exported the products of their own industries, like textiles, should be modified; see below. Export of Venetian cloth was custom free; see Coll., Not. V, f. 82b.

[131] See Heers, *art. cit.*, p. 167; Misti 43, f. 10a, and see below.

[132] Schulte, *Geschichte des mittelalterl. Handels* I, p. 355.

1403 a Venetian company shipped honey valued at 2,400 ducats to Alexandria.[133]

Genoa's trade with the dominions of the Mamluks was already different from that of the Venetians in that period. For the Genoese, the trade with Egypt and Syria was not the main artery of their international trade, as it was for the Venetians and, secondly, they concentrated their activities less than did the Venetians on the purchase of spices.

Being in control of an extended territory in Crimea and of the alum mines of Phocea, which was a Genoese colony from the end of the thirteenth century, the Genoese were more and more interested in the trade of raw materials, which were in demand in Northwestern Europe. The great artery of Genoese trade with the Levant was the line connecting the metropolis with Chios, Pera, and Caffa. At the end of the fourteenth century Pera was a great emporium from which Persian silk was shipped to the west, and cloth of Western Europe and other products of its industries were exported to the colonies in Crimea.[134] The export of alum of Phocea and other mines was then a flourishing sector of Genoese trade. Genoese ships carried it from Pera and Chios to Genoa, Catalonia, Flanders, and England. Some Genoese companies monopolized this great international trade.[135] But the Genoese also bought cotton in Turkey and exported it to the west. On the other hand, they did not have a great market where they could sell spices without encountering competition, whereas the Venetians had almost a monopoly in the export of these commodities to Central Europe. Although the Genoese had the greatest share in the Italian trade with England, even there they were not its only suppliers of spices. Certainly they shipped great quantities of spices to England, but they also shipped heavy cargoes of alum and other commodities.[136] So they bought raw materials in Egypt and Syria, which could be profitably marketed in Northwestern Europe.

The supply of military slaves for the Mamluk army, owing to which the Genoese had enjoyed a privileged status at the beginning of the rule of the Baḥrites and even later, was still a business in which they engaged. Until the middle of the fifteenth century, Genoese were the agents of the sultan in Caffa, where they purchased slaves for his army,[137] but Moslem merchants also carried on this lucrative trade. The names of some of them are mentioned in notarial acts and in Arabic sources of that period. Barḳūḳ, the first Circassian sultan, had a Moslem agent in Caffa, and when the

[133] Misti 34, f. 47b; G. P., Sent. VII, f. 80b f.

[134] Lopez, *Storia delle colonie genovesi*, p. 286.

[135] Liagre-De Sturler, no. 521; Vat. sub 16 Dec. 1400. Cf. M.-L. Heers, "Les Génois et le commerce de l'alum a la fin du moyen âge," *Revue d'hist. écon. et sociale* 32 (1954), p. 33 f.

[136] Ruddock, *Italian merchants*, pp. 79, 84.

[137] See Bertrandon de la Broquière, p. 68, and cf. Heers, *Gênes*, p. 370.

latter died, the Genoese in Alexandria had to indemnify the sultan for what this merchant had left there.[138] There can be no doubt that these Moslem merchants purchased the slaves in other countries too and brought them to Egypt not only via the Straits but on other routes as well. In an earlier period of Mamluk rule, the Genoese had also been the Mamluks' main suppliers of timber, which they imported into Egypt from some provinces of Asia Minor,[139] but in the middle and the second half of the fourteenth century, after the downfall of the kingdom of Little Armenia, the timber was transported to Egypt on Moslem ships.[140] Another reason for the progressive decline of Genoese trade with Egypt and Syria and the loss of their privileged status which the Genoese had enjoyed so long was their aggressive policy toward the Moslem rulers. Whereas the Venetian policy distinguished itself by leniency and patience, the Genoese were inclined to reprisals against the extortions by the Mamluk authorities and to military action. In 1383 the uncompromising position of the Genoese resulted in a major conflict with the Mamluks.

At the end of 1381 or at the beginning of 1382, news was received in Venice and Genoa that the Italian merchants and their consuls in Alexandria, Damascus, and elsewhere had been injured, beaten, and imprisoned. The Senate of Venice decided to suggest to Genoa that they act in common at the court of Cairo, but the Genoese had already decided to send an embassy of their own to Egypt. The ambassadors Cosma Italiano and Marchione Petrarossa departed in March 1382, and at the beginning of May were in Alexandria; they were there a second time in August-September. In the meantime, they visited Beirut and Famagusta three times. These cruises, a strange activity for an embassy, which would have been expected to be going to Cairo, immediately upon its arrival in Egypt, was perhaps connected with attempts to contact the Mamluk governor of Damascus or any other high-ranking emir and to combine action against the sultan with them. If such attempts were made, they must have been a failure. Anyhow, in November 1382, the embassy was back in Genoa. Then, in May 1383, a new doge, Leonardo Montaldo, took over the government of Genoa and embarked on a firm policy. He sent Pietro Piccono with two galleys to Syria in order to negotiate with the Mamluk governor of Damascus. If the

[138] Vat. sub 18 Jan. 1400. A certain Sālim sold to Barḳūḳ the future emir Yelboghā as-Sālimī, born in Samarkand; see aḍ-Ḍaw' al-lāmi' X, p. 289; Khawādjā Maḥmūd Shāh al-Yazdī brought the future sultan al-Malik al-Mu'ayyad Shaykh to Egypt and sold him there in 1380; see *an-Nudjūm az-zāhira* VI, p. 322; Bashbughā sold mamluks to Barḳūḳ, see *ibid.* VI, p. 455. Barḳūḳ himself was brought to Egypt by the slave dealer 'Uthmān Ḳarādjā; see Ibn Khaldūn, al-'Ibar (Cairo 1284) V, p. 472. The brother of the latter, Khawādjā 'Alī, brought some relatives of Barḳūḳ to Egypt in 1388; see Ibn Ḥadjar I, pp. 352, 364 and cf. below. See also Piloti, pp. 52 ff., 143.

[139] See Heers, *Gênes*, pp. 373, 394.

[140] Ibn Baṭṭūṭa II, p. 257.

latter should not be ready for that, Piccono was to send him letters destined for the sultan and wait fifteen to twenty days for an answer. These orders, which would have been rather strange for an ordinary embassy, point to a projected attack on the Syrian coast, probably on Beirut. But upon the arrival of Piccono in the Levant, the situation was already very different from what had been known in Genoa when he had been given his instructions. In May 1383 the Genoese merchants had fled from Alexandria; there had ensued a naval battle between them and the Moslems who pursued them; and those who had remained in the town and the other European merchants were imprisoned.[141] The Genoese retaliated by an attack on the coastal town of at-Tīna, in the eastern delta, and there captured some Moslems. This raid had certainly been made upon the decision of local Genoese authorities, very probably those of Famagusta. In fact, it meant the beginning of a war. Whereas the Venetian and Catalan traders, who had been imprisoned in Alexandria, were set free, owing to diplomatic steps taken by their representatives, and could carry on their commercial activities in the second half of 1383, Piccono went to Beirut. After he had handed over the letter to the Mamluk government, a squadron of ten Genoese galleys under the command of Niccolò Maruffo arrived in Cyprus. Sent by him back to Beirut, Piccono was informed that the sultan was not inclined to make peace with Genoa, before having an undertaking that piracy and naval raids would be stopped. Although Maruffo, according to the report that he later submitted to the Genoese government, had apparently had orders to attack the Egyptian coast, he decided to make a raid against the coast of Southern Syria. In August 1383 he took Sidon by assault, and thereupon approached Beirut, but departed when he became aware of the strength of the Moslem defenders. However, the Genoese brought other galleys and more battalions from Cyprus, landed in Beirut, and planted a flag, as if the place had become Genoese territory. They were once more repelled. In October 1383 they made a second attack on Beirut and were again pushed back. Thereupon, Maruffo returned to Genoa, whereas the Mamluks sent reinforcements to several places on the coast of Egypt. In the year 1384 the war went on. In May the Genoese attacked Rosetta and Damietta, and in June there was a naval encounter between them and an Egyptian squadron. In 1385 a Genoese embassy, consisting of the same envoys who had been sent to Egypt in 1382, concluded peace with the sultan.[142] But from Arabic sources we learn that there was still a state of

[141] *Sulūk* III, p. 487 f.

[142] Ant. Com. 17, c. 61, 72, and cf. 120, 246. According to these registers, the news of the conclusion of peace came to Genoa from Venice on 24 July, whereas one reads in *Libr. Com.* III, lib. 8, no. 204, that on 22 July the doge of Genoa wrote to the Venetian government to thank them for the transmission of the good news. (I have checked the date in the original and found that it is indeed 22 July.)

war between Genoa and the sultan after this date and that another treaty of peace was made in July 1386.[143] The Genoese ambassador who finally concluded peace with the sultan was Simone Lecavello, a veteran Levant trader.[144]

However, there were other Genoese raids on the coasts of the Mamluk dominions after the conclusion of this treaty of peace, and Genoese corsairs attacked Moslem ships. In 1388 some Genoese captured a ship off the Syrian coast. On board there were Moslem merchants (probably with slaves) and some relatives of the sultan, coming from Circassia. The sultan gave immediate orders to seize all Genoese merchants and to sequester their goods; he also decreed that Genoese merchants should not be allowed to enter his dominions. Thereupon, the Genoese set the captives free and sent them to the sultan, together with an embassy which apologized for what had been done.[145] Then, in 1390, Christian forces tried to attack Tripoli. The Arabic chroniclers speak, as they so often did, of "Franks" without specifying who they were. But as they say that subsequently the same Franks attacked al-Mahdiyya, it is clear that the raid was a part of the joint Franco-Genoese expedition against Tunis made in that year. According to a merchant letter, the Genoese found in the dominions of the Mamluks were again imprisoned in 1396, when their compatriot Giovanni Spinola attacked the Moslem ships. In the fall of 1401 and again in the fall of 1402 the Genoese of Cyprus raided Tripoli.[146]

As a matter of fact, the government of Genoa tried time and again to reduce the tension these acts of hostility engendered. In 1402 another Genoese embassy came to Cairo. It consisted of Giovanni de Lagneto and Niccolò Campanaro.[147] But certainly these raids and acts of piracy were

---

[143] See E. Ashtor-B. Z. Kedar, "Una guerra fra Genova e i Mamlucchı neglı anni 1380," *ASI* 133 (1975), p. 3 ff. and especially p. 31. In a letter wrıtten in Venice on 25 May 1385, and quoting letters from Damascus, one reads indeed that the negotiations failed, see Dat 548, letter of Zanobi di Taddeo Gaddı s.d. This points to the dıfficultıes that the Genoese ambassadors encountered before reaching an agreement, apparently in May or June 1385.

[144] Ant. Com. 18, c. 16, 57, 143, 156. These texts have been erroneously interpreted by Musso, *Navigazione*, p. 71, as if Lecavello took part ın the embassy of 1385; but see c. 156 of 18 April 1386, "ıturo," the ambassador who ıs about to depart for Egypt. Also, what Musso says, p. 76, about the Florentine cloth handed over to Lecavello ıs mıstaken. These were the presents for the sultan.

[145] Ibn al-Furāt IX, pp. 33, 38; *Sulūk* III, p. 581; Ibn Ḥadjar I, pp. 352, 364; ʿAbdalbāsıṭ 803 f. 141a. Cf. Silvestre de Sacy, *Chrestomathie arabe* III (Parıs 1826), p. 51.

[146] Ibn al-Furāt IX, p. 221; *Sulūk* III, pp. 723, 725; al-Djaiharī- *Nuzha*, p. 312; Ibn Ḥadjar I, p. 402. The account of the attack in 1390 by the contemporary chronicler Ibn al-Furāt ıs the most complete, that of Ibn Ḥadjar stems from another source. Ibn al-Furāt says that the squadron that attacked Tripoli numbered 70 ships. On the Franco-Genoese expedıtıon, see Setton I, p. 333 ff. Dat 797, letter of Zanobi di Taddeo Gaddı of 23 Sept. 1396. About the raid in 1401, see *Sulūk* I, p. 1079, copied by Ibn Iyās² I, part 2, p. 642; Ibn Ḥadjar II, p. 199; ʿAbdalbāsıṭ f. 186b. About the raid ın 1402, see Delaville le Roulx II, p. 408; Musso, *Navigazione*, p. 80.

[147] Ant. Com. 26, c. 46 and cf. 43, 48, 50. See also Musso, *Navigazione*, pp. 72, 77.

detrimental to Genoese trade with the dominions of the sultan. It would be an oversimplification to suppose that as a consequence of acts of aggression the Mamluk government adopted a hostile attitude toward the Genoese. The Mamluks were too much interested in the revenue from the customs and other dues and payments. But there is good reason to believe that in the course of time the Genoese merchants themselves were less and less inclined to invest in trade with countries where tension prevailed and reprisals were always imminent. But at the end of the fourteenth century, Genoese trade in Egypt and Syria was still flourishing.

It was very different from the Venetian trade, which was largely conducted by means of the galleys and cogs, sailing to the Levant in convoys according to a fixed timetable. The Genoese too employed both galleys and cogs. A convoy of state galleys, called the Syria galleys, visited Cyprus and Beirut of Alexandria every year. Although this service had been established to serve political and military purposes connected with the role of Genoa in Cyprus, it was also used for commercial activities. But the number of these Genoese galleys that visited the ports of Egypt and Syria every year was much smaller than that of the Venetian galleys. The convoys numbered no more than two or three galleys.[148] Further, they did not depart from Genoa on fixed dates. Sometimes they sailed to the Levant in spring,[149] sometimes at the beginning of the fall.[150] The bulk of the merchandise that the Genoese imported into the Moslem Levant and exported from there was carried on cogs, whereas the Venetians used these ships only for the transport of cheap articles. The Genoese indeed built much bigger cogs than the Venetians. They had many cogs which could carry 700-800 tons.[151] It is obvious that the Genoese already preferred these big cogs in that period for trade with the Levant. Whereas it was a principle of Venetian trade that spices and other precious commodities should be carried preferably by galleys, the Genoese did not make this distinction. They used the galleys for the transport of cotton also, and regularly shipped spices on cogs. The cargo of spices which a big cog could transport sometimes had a very great value. According to an anonymous Venetian chronicle, in 1379 the Genoese cog called the "Pidagrossa" was seen off Modon with spices worth 200,000 ducats.[152] Even if this is an exaggeration, it must represent a significant sum.

There was another great difference between Genoese and Venetian trade in the Levant.

[148] Musso, *op.cit.*, p. 73 f.

[149] Cf. Heers, "Il commercio," p. 170, who maintains that the Genoese ships always left at the end of the winter, but this is an over-statement.

[150] Musso *l.c.*

[151] Heers, *Gênes*, p. 273.

[152] Bibl. Naz. Firenze, Memorie varie di Venezia, II, f. 180b.

A basic principle of Venice's commercial policy was that merchandise acquired anywhere by Venetians must be shipped first to the metropolis and could then be re-exported. In the fourteenth century this law was applied to the Oriental spices only, but later it was extended to commodities bought in Western Europe. The Venetians could not transport spices directly from the Levant to Northwestern Europe nor export cloth from there to the Levant. In 1334 the Senate decreed that since it was forbidden to export spices from the Levant directly to the west those who did so should be fined up to 50 percent of the value of the merchandise.[153] Then, in 1387, a proposal made in the Senate to revoke or change the law was turned down.[154] This law, however, did not forbid the export of cotton and alkali from the Levant to the west. In 1388 it was laid down that for the direct export of these articles to Northwestern Europe the same dues should be paid as if they had first been shipped to Venice.[155] But the principle that spices, the most precious commodities, should first be shipped to Venice was upheld. This was confirmed in 1413 by a decree, which was to make it impossible to export spices to other trading towns in the Mediterranean, or to disguise the shipments as those of foreigners. It was also forbidden to use foreign ships for this purpose.[156] The law forbidding export of spices directly from the Levant to Western Europe was reconfirmed in 1440, and at this time it was also forbidden to re-export Oriental articles on non-Venetian ships.[157] The direct export of cloth, furs, and tin from England and Flanders to the Levant was still allowed for payment of the customs that would have been due if the merchandise had first been shipped to Venice. However, this was forbidden to all Venetian subjects (that means both the Venetians and inhabitants of the colonies) in 1424.[158] The direct export of copper from Greece to the Moslem Levant, on the other hand, was already forbidden at the end of the fourteenth century.[159]

The Genoese carried on direct trade between the Levant and Northwestern Europe. A main artery of Genoese trade was the line connecting Pera and Chios with England and Flanders. The big Genoese cogs transported the alum of Phocea directly to Flanders,[160] and much of the spices bought in Damascus and Alexandria was shipped there directly, without transporting it first to Genoa. Every year some cogs sailed from Alexandria

153 Misti, ed. Cessi, II, p. 379 f.
154 Misti 40, f. 66a.
155 Misti 40, f. 115a f.
156 Misti 50, f. 39a.
157 Misti 60, f. 192a, 193b.
158 Misti 40, f. 114b f. 55, f. 35b.
159 Misti 42, f. 21b.
160 Liagre-De Sturler, no. 521; Doehaerd-Kerremans, nos. 1, 2; Vat. sub 16 Dec. 1400.

to Southampton and Sluys, the busy port near Bruges.[161] Sometimes, of course, merchandise destined for Flanders or England was first shipped to Genoa.[162] Under Genoese rule, Famagusta did not become a great emporium of the Levantine trade, but Chios was an important trading town and served the Genoese as a point of support for their trade in the whole eastern basin of the Mediterranean. Their ships commuted between Chios and the ports of Syria and Egypt. One imported mastic and also sulphur from Chios to Egypt. Spices and dyes were shipped there from Alexandria before being exported to the west.[163] Rhodes too served the Genoese as a point of support for their trade in the Eastern Mediterranean.[164]

At the end of the fourteenth and the beginning of the fifteenth century the number of Genoese ships that visited Alexandria was certainly much greater than that of the Venetians. In the last third of the fourteenth century often ten Genoese ships or even more visited in one year the port of Alexandria or Beirut and departed for Genoa, Flanders, the Maghreb, or the Greek islands.[165] The number of the Venetian ships that came to the ports of Syria, where the volume of Venetian trade was relatively greater, were equal to or greater than those of the Genoese.[166]

In Alexandria there was a big Genoese colony, which outnumbered the Venetians and other European traders. On 9 March 1401, no less than thirty-four Genoese traders chartered three Genoese ships in Alexandria; the ships were sailing to Flanders.[167] Many of them were merchants who lived in Alexandria a long time. Seven of them were of the Lomellino family (Niccolò Antonio, Battista, Morello, Pietro, Francesco, Bartolomeo, and Ambrosio). The Lomellino were indeed very much involved in the trade with Egypt and played an important role in the Genoese colony in Alexandria. In 1405 half of the Council of the colony were members of this family.[168] Pietro Lomellino, who took part in the transaction in March 1401, was a member of the Genoese Council in Alexandria in 1400 and died in Cairo at the beginning of 1402.[169] Morello Lomellino belonged to

[161] Liagre-De Sturler, nos. 355, 521, 542, 543, 548, 550, 553, 558-560, 562, 563, 593; Vat. sub 5 March 1401; Melis, *Doc.*, p. 184.

[162] Liagre-De Sturler, no. 611.

[163] Musso, "Armamento," pp. 13, 14; sulphur was employed for refining gold, see Pegolotti, p. 336 f. and was one of the commodities imported into the Levant by the Italian merchants, see price list of Alexandria of 1386, published by Melis, *Doc.*, p. 320; Vat. sub 6 May 1401; Leonardo de Valle sub 13 Sept. 1402, 18 Nov. 1402; Musso, *Navigazione*, pp. 63, 68.

[164] Musso, *Navigazione*, p. 68.

[165] See my "Observations on Venetian Trade," p. 565, and Appendix A6.

[166] F. Melis, "Note sur le mouvement du port de Beyrouth d'après le documentation florentine aux environs de 1400," in *Sociétés et compagnies*, p. 371 ff.

[167] Vat. s.d.

[168] Vat. sub 3 Aug. 1405. Ant. Lomellino was already in 1397 a merchant in Alexandria; see Melis, *Origini*, p. 67.

[169] Vat. sub 24 Sept. 1400; Leonardo de Valle sub 20 Feb. 1402.

the Council in 1400 and in 1401.[170] Another of those Genoese merchants who chartered the ships in 1401 was Brancaleone Grisulfi, who lived in Alexandria at least from 1400 to 1406.[171] He was a business partner of Pietro Italiano, another Genoese trader in Alexandria, at least from 1401 to 1405,[172] and member of the Council of the colony in 1402, 1403, 1405, and 1406.[173] Pietro Italiano himself was a member of the Council in 1404.[174] He conducted trade in Cairo.[175] Another member of that group of thirty-four merchants was Paolo Grillo, who lived in Alexandria at least from 1400 to 1405.[176] In the year 1404 a son of his was also in Alexandria.[177] In addition there were Lucchino Grimaldi;[178] Rafaele Potunaro;[179] Pietro Calvo, who conducted a good deal of trade with Flanders;[180] Pietro Antonio de Murta, who had been the consul of the Genoese in Alexandria in 1399 and 1400;[181] Zanuto Rizzo, who lived in Alexandria at least until 1404;[182] Paolo Rizzo, the acting consul;[183] and Babilano Rizzo who had been consul for a short time in 1399 and held the post later in 1401 and 1402.[184] The numerous data in the notarial acts show that in the last years of the fourteenth century at least thirty Genoese merchants lived in Alexandria, some of them together with other members of their families.[185] There were also Genoese notaries in Alexandria.[186]

The Genoese also engaged in trade in other Egyptian and Syrian towns. Genoese merchants lived in Damietta[187] and their ships anchored in the port. At the end of 1399 or the beginning of 1400, a Genoese ship was

[170] Vat. sub 17 Jan. 1400, 1 Apr. 1401.

[171] See Vat. sub 21 Apr. 1400 and 20 Sept. 1406.

[172] Vat. sub 29 May 1401, 6 Febr. 1405.

[173] Leonardo de Valle sub 20 Febr. 1402, 20 Oct. 1403; Vat. sub 9 and 29 Dec. 1405.

[174] Leonardo de Valle sub 13 Apr. 1404.

[175] Vat. sub 13 Oct. 1401, consul of Valle sub 13 Sept. 1402.

[176] Vat. sub 17 Jan. 1400, 24 Apr. 1400, 9 March 1401, 20 Apr. 1401, 17 Jan. 1405.

[177] Vat. sub 18 Apr. 1404. He carried on trade in Rhodes; see there.

[178] He was a member of the Council in 1404; see Leonardo de Valle sub 13 Apr. 1404.

[179] He was a member of the said Council in 1400-1401; see Vat. sub 24 Sept. 1400, 1 Apr. 1401.

[180] Vat. sub 5 Jan. 1401 (should be 5 March 1401). He was a member of the Council in 1401; see there sub 1 Apr. 1401.

[181] Vat. sub. 2 Dec. 1399, 17 Jan. 1400, 24 Sept. 1400, 22 Oct. 1400.

[182] See Vat. sub 30 Oct. 1404. He was a member of the Council in 1402-1403; see Leonardo de Valle sub 20 Febr. 1402, 5 March 1403, 20 Oct. 1403.

[183] Vat. sub 29 Dec. 1400, 18 Jan. 1401, 20 Apr. 1401. As Pietro Antonio de Murta he remained in Alexandria as a merchant when he was no longer consul; see Vat. sub 6 Febr. 1405.

[184] Vat. sub 1 Sept. 1401. He died in Cairo on 23 Jan. 1402; see Leonardo de Valle sub 11 Febr. 1402 and cf. Musso, *Navigazione*, p. 75.

[185] Two brothers in Alexandria: Leonardo de Valle sub 18 Jan. 1402.

[186] ASG, Notai 409, Parisola, Guirardo, III, c. 6b where Antonio Clavo, a Genoese notary in Alexandria, is quoted.

[187] Vat. sub 14 Jan. 1400, 5 Febr. 1400.

shipwrecked there.[188] Several notarial acts refer to the activities of the Genoese in Damascus. From these acts we learn, for example, that at the beginning of the 1370's ("usque in ann' 1373 vel circa") Augusto Adorno made three trips to the Moslem Levant, two to Damascus, and one to Alexandria, and for every trip had a commenda of 1,000 pounds from Pietro Bachanelli.[189] Other records refer to the activities of the Genoese in Tripoli and Damascus in the 1380's and 1390's[190] or to Genoese traders who died in Damascus in the last years of the fourteenth century.[191]

Since merchants of other towns of Liguria also belonged to the Genoese colonies in Egypt and Syria, sometimes merchandise was shipped directly from there to the Levantine emporia and vice versa.[192] The merchants of Savona were particularly active in the Levantine trade. According to a treaty made in 1251, the citizens of this town enjoyed the protection of the Genoese authorities overseas, just as the Genoese themselves did. Some notarial acts drawn up in Savona show that traders of these towns travelled to Syria in the 1370's and purchased cotton there. A notarial act drawn up in 1401 in Alexandria refers to the charter of a ship by merchants of Savona for the export of merchandise to Egypt.[193]

The Levantine trade of the Genoese and the other Ligurian merchants distinguished itself from that of the Venetians not only by the direct traffic between the Near Eastern ports, and those of England and Flanders. The Genoese also exported spices from Egypt to Sicily[194] and Naples.[195] The trade with Egypt and Syria in that period was a very important sector of Genoese economy and Alexandria was a pillar in the network of her international traffic. Rich Genoese companies, which did not specialize in the trade with the Levant, invested great sums in it.[196]

The range of commodities that the Genoese brought to the Near East was not greatly different from those offered by the Venetians. They shipped great quantities of French cloth[197] and linen[198] and of olive oil; the latter

[188] Vat. sub 14 Jan. 1400.

[189] Parisola, Guirardo, III, c. 195b f.

[190] Misti 42, f. 15b; Vat. sub 11 May 1400, 1 June 1400.

[191] ASG, Notai, Gatto, Bart., a. 1395, f. 153a f.; a. 1401-1406, f.; 54b and cf. 69a.

[192] Merchants of Savona: Liagre-De Sturler, no. 617, Vat. sub 26 Febr. 1401; of Chiavari: Leonardo de Valle sub 18 and 26 Apr. 1402; shipping to Savona, Vat. sub 25 Febr. 1401.

[193] I. Scovazzi-F. Noberasco, *Storia di Savona* I, p. 344 (quoting *Liber Jurium* I, col. 1044 ff.) III, p. 166; Vat. sub 25 Febr. 1401; see also Musso, "Armamento," p. 17.

[194] See my "Il volume del commercio levantino," p. 403: galea di Niccolo Struppa; p. 414: cog of Oberto Squarzafico.

[195] *Art. cit.*, p. 403: galea di Nic. Struppa; galea di Lodisio Belaveo; p. 414: cog of Novello Vespera.

[196] Liagre-De Sturler, no. 360.

[197] About cloth of Beauvais, see "Il volume del commercio levantino," p. 409.

[198] Linen of Reims, Compiègne, and Champagne: Liagre-De Sturler, no. 326.

was purchased in Southern France[199] or more often in Andalusia and in the Campania.[200] They sent considerable quantities of metals, mainly copper, to the Levant although the quantity was less than that offered there by the Venetians. The Genoese could obtain certain quantities of copper, tin, and lead at the fairs of Geneva, Zurzach, and Strassburg.[201] Certainly coral ranked much higher on the list of commodities that the Genoese shipped to the Moslem Levant than that of the Venetians. But it would be an exaggeration to say that it was their most important means of payment for the Oriental spices.[202] Both of the two great Italian merchant republics made their greatest investments in the Levant in the purchase of spices.

But there was a difference between their purchases of the other Levantine commodities. The Genoese exported much less cotton and alkali from Syria, whereas they bought great quantities of cotton and alum in Egypt. It looks as if they had a monopoly in the export of Egyptian alum.[203] Since the Genoese exported great quantities of cheaper commodities from Egypt, the volume of their trade with the dominions of the sultan was smaller than that of the Venetians, although their numbers, at least in Alexandria, were still greater. But the importance of this trade for Genoa's economy was very great. It amounted, at the end of the fourteenth century, perhaps to 15 percent to 20 percent of the whole of Genoa's foreign trade.[204]

c. The Other Trading Nations

In the last third of the fourteenth century even the minor trading nations made a great effort to intensify their commercial exchanges with the dominions of the Mamluks. Some of them were inland towns and therefore had recourse to ports over which they had no control. The volume of their transactions was incomparably smaller than that of the two great Italian merchant republics, but the total of their investment in the Levant trade was considerable.

In that period Pisa still had a share in the Levantine trade. The Pisans used the shipping lines of other nations. Some of them loaded their merchandise—cloth, linen, and other—on Genoese and Catalan ships sailing to the Levantine emporia,[205] but others went to Egypt and Syria themselves.

[199] Vat. sub 1 Sept. 1401.

[200] ASG, Notai 312, Caito, Andr., IV, c. 211a/b, 216b V, c. 87a/b.

[201] Much German copper was available in Milan: see Schulte, *Geschichte des mittelalterl, Handels* I, pp. 572 ff., 694.

[202] Vat. sub 11 Apr. 1401 and see Heers, *Gênes*, p. 378.

[203] See "Il volume del commercio levantino," pp. 423, 424, 431; Heers, "Il commercio," p. 171; *id.*, Gênes, p. 394 ff.

[204] "Il volume del commercio levantino," p. 420.

[205] See *art. cit.*, p. 412: cog of Andaro de Monellia (a. 1377); Rubió i Lluch, no. 388 (a. 1378).

The Florentine traveller Giorgio Gucci, who visited Egypt in 1384, recounts that there were Pisans in Alexandria.[206] During the conflict between Genoa and the sultan in 1383, the goods of Pisan traders were sequestered. Pisa sent an embassy to Cairo and obtained a promise that they would be given back. But since the governor of Alexandria did not return all the goods, in 1385 another embassy headed by Niccolò Vivaldi went to the sultan.[207] The merchants of Lucca also engaged in trade with the Moslem Levant at that time. Upon the conclusion of peace between the sultan and the king of Cyprus, the town applied to the Holy See for a license for trade with the dominions of the Mamluks, and Gregory XI granted permission to send there two ships every year.[208] This license was used, for in notarial acts drawn up in Provence in 1391 it is stated that a ship of Luccans, the "Santa Maria," loaded merchandise in Aigues-Mortes and in Marseilles to be delivered in Alexandria.[209]

The Florentines were then the most active in Tuscany in the trade with the Levant. In the last two decades, Florentine merchants and bankers lived in Alexandria and Damascus. Giorgio Gucci mentions in his travelogue that Florentines lived in Alexandria,[210] and his fellow-traveler Lionardo Frescobaldi recounts that he had bills of exchange from the bank of the Portinari, which was represented in Alexandria by Guido de' Ricci and in Damascus by Andrea da Prato.[211] There can be little doubt that the Portinari engaged not only in banking in Alexandria but also in the export of cloth and other business. In fact they also had a bank in Venice and carried on a lively trade in Florentine cloth in the great Adriatic emporium.[212] The firm of Giovanni Portinari in Venice collaborated with the firm of Datini in the 1390's and obviously engaged in trade with the Levant.[213] In another letter, sent to Catalonia from Alexandria in 1401, one reads that a Florentine merchant arrived there and sold Florentine and Catalan cloth. A Florentine merchant, Luca del Biondo, who sojourned in Alexandria corresponded with the Datini firm in Valencia in 1397.[214] Andrea di Sinibaldo, who was to pay Lionardo Frescobaldi a bill of exchange in Damascus, was a great merchant. He lived there from 1382 and together with a Venetian merchant founded a company. When the latter died, Sinibaldo had claims against his brothers and applied to the Moslem authorities, apparently in 1397, or a

[206] *Visit to the Holy Places*, p. 94.
[207] Amari, *Diplomi*, p. 315 f. (who believed that the goods were sequestered in 1365).
[208] de Mas Latrie, *Hist.* II, p. 347.
[209] Baratier, p. 235.
[210] *Visit to the Holy Places*, *l.c.*
[211] Ed. Angelini, p. 48; cf. pp. 56, 162.
[212] Records of the first half of the 15th century: ASF, IIIa serie Strozziana CXIII, c. 7; same series, c. 77, 85.
[213] Dat 926, letter of 25 Dec. 1397; Dat 927, letter of 11 March 1400.
[214] Ainaud, "Quatre doc." I; Dat 962, letter of Luca del Biondo of 28 July 1397.

short time before.[215] But the Florentines not only engaged in trade in Egypt and Syria. The enterprising merchants of Florence exported commodities considered by the Church as was material to Egypt.[216] On the other hand, they exported spices from Egypt to Flanders, through Genoese agents and their ships.[217] However, Heyd was certainly right in stating that at that time the Florentines engaged much more in banking in the Levant.[218] The fact that the European gold coins in circulation in Egypt, Syria, and other Levantine countries were called *ifrantī* in Arabic points to the preponderance of the florin over the ducat during a certain time. al-Maḳrīzī says that the European gold coin called *ifrantī, iflūrī, bunduḳī,* or ducat circulated there from the year 1388, whereas they had been unknown before.[219] This is certainly a very exaggerated statement, for Lionardo Frescobaldi states that at the time of his visit to Egypt in 1384 only the ducat was accepted in Cairo. Piloti makes a similar statement.[220] al-Maḳrīzī says in another passage that in 1398 the *ifrantī* was the gold coin most used for payment "in all the cities of the world, such as Cairo, Old Cairo, Damascus, Asia Minor, Iraq, and Yemen."[221] Although the Arabic author distinguishes between *iflūrī* and *ifrantī,* it is very probable that they were two Arabic names of the florin, for what else could *ifrantī* mean?[222] But the accounts of Frescobaldi and Piloti and the fact that in 1422 the Florentines had to ask the sultan to permit the florin to be legal tender in his dominions like the ducat[223] show that the expansion of the Florentines did not last a long time. In any case, the reports of the Arabic chroniclers are evidence of the intensive activities of Florentine bankers in Egypt and Syria.

Another of the minor trading nations of Southern Europe that carried on trade with the Moslem Levant was Naples. At the end of the fourteenth century and at the beginning of the fifteenth there was already a consulate and a fondaco of Naples in Alexandria.[224] Merchants of other towns of the Campania, such as Gaeta and Amalfi, also belonged to the colony of the merchants of Naples. One of them, Domenico de Albito of Gaeta, was

[215] Misti 44, f. 56a.

[216] Vat. sub 14 Oct. 1400, and cf. sub 5 Nov. 1400, where one reads that the same Florentine merchant carried on trade in Zara, where he bought iron, and in Venice.

[217] Liagre-De Sturler, no. 591.

[218] S. Heyd II, p.478.

[219] *Sulūk* IV, p. 305.

[220] Ed. Angelini, p. 75; Piloti, p. 108.

[221] *Sulūk* IV, p. 708, and cf. *an-Nudjūm a ā Zāhira* VI, p. 596 (transl. Popper IV, California Univ. Press, 1958, p. 30); see, further, *Sulūk* III, pp. 967, 968 f., 1041, 1059.

[222] This was indeed the opinion of Wüstenfeld, *Chroniken der Stadt Mekka* IV, p. 273; Gaudefroy-Demombynes, *La Syrie à l'époque des Mamelouks* (Paris 1923), p. 135. The explanation of al-Ḳalḳashandī, *Ṣubḥ al-aʿshā* III, p. 441: *ifrantī* comes from *ifransī,* is evidently wrong.

[223] Amari, *I diplomi arabi,* p. 333.

[224] Ogier d'Anglure, p. 78; Lannoy, p. 76f.

consul of Naples in Alexandria from 1399 to 1401,[225] and his successor was another merchant of Gaeta, Jacobo Mostacha.[226] The agricultural and industrial products of the Campania, mainly olive oil, hazelnut, and soap, were exported to the Moslem Levant by Genoese and Catalans, whose ships frequently anchored in Naples and Gaeta,[227] but the merchants of these towns also shipped them on their own vessels. The activities of Antonello de Letera de Scala, or "de Seliglis," of Amalfi, a merchant and captain of a ship, are referred to in several notarial acts drawn up in Alexandria. In 1400, he transported merchandise of Venetians from Tunis to Alexandria.[228] In 1402, he chartered a Catalan ship, "Santa Clara & Sanct Felix," in Alexandria for a journey to Syria and then on to Gaeta, Naples, and Sicily. The ship was to sail to Acre, Beirut, Tripoli, Latakia, and Candia before going to Italy.[229] Obviously the purpose of the charter was to transport cotton and alkali from Syria to Gaeta, where the latter material was needed for the flourishing soap industry. The merchants of Gaeta also engaged in trade between Rhodes and Egypt, for instance exporting figs from Rhodes to Egypt.[230] But they occupied themselves mainly with the export of products of their own country to the Moslem Levant. In 1402 Antonello de Letera exported hazelnuts worth 4,954 dinars and other merchandise worth 1,689 dinars to Egypt. A merchant of Gaeta, Bicoli Lumbito, imported olive oil and soap worth 2,079 dinars to Alexandria in the same year.[231] These shipments, however, were all that the merchants of Gaeta imported into Egypt in that year; that means these merchants acted probably as agents of their fellow-citizens.[232] But these transactions together with those of the merchants of Naples add up to a not insignificant total.

The commercial exchanges between Sicily and the Moslem Levant at the end of the fourteenth century were mainly in the hands of the Catalan traders. Since the island had come under Catalan rule, many of the enter-

[225] Vat. sub 13 Dec. 1399, 13 Oct. 1401. He remained in Alexandria as a merchant; see Leonardo de Valle sub 18 March 1402. Camera says that Domenico de Albito was consul until 1399 and in that year removed from his post, but no source is given for this statement; see M. Camera, *Memorie storiche-diplomatiche dell'antica città e ducato di Amalfi* (Salerno, 1878-1881) I, p. 593.

[226] Leonardo de Valle sub 4 Nov. 1401, 3 Jan. 1403.

[227] See "Il volume del commercio levantino," pp. 408, 409, 411; Rubió i Lluch, no. 388; Dat 876, letter of Antonio e Doffo degli Spini & Cie of 16 Apr. 1400; Dat 509, letter of Sandro Mazzetti e Guido Pilestri & Cie of 23 Apr. 1388.

[228] Vat. sub 25 May 1400 (where one reads *nave castellana,* but see sub 22 May: *nave neapol*), 25 Sept. 1400, 4 Nov. 1405. On 22 Nov. 1405, he made his will in the fondaco of the Neapolitans. See also Vat. sub 9 Aug. 1400: an Amalfitan buys from a Genoese a small watercraft in Alexandria.

[229] Leonardo de Valle sub 1 Sept. 1402.

[230] Vat. sub 16 June 1400.

[231] Vat. w.d., a leaf between the acts of 18 July and 13 Oct. 1406.

[232] The latter deed was drawn up by the notary upon the request of the representatives of the Gaetans to list all the commodities they had imported in 1402.

prising merchants of Barcelona, Valencia, and other towns of Catalonia had settled in its towns and carried on a lively trade with their homeland, with the Italian mainland, and with the Levant.[233] Being the hub of the Mediterranean, Sicily's ports served the Catalan ships sailing to or from the Levant for transshipping their merchandise and, of course, they also became its main suppliers of spices and other Oriental articles. A contract made in Alexandria in 1400 contains the agreement between two businessmen of Barcelona who owned the ship "Santo Antonio," on one hand, and a merchant of Majorca and a citizen of Valencia, on the other hand. The latter chartered the ship for the export of spices to Syracuse and to Aigues-Mortes.[234] In 1402 Italiano Vila and Gabriel Amigo, two Catalan traders, chartered a Venetian cog in Alexandria for the export of 3,300, and possibly more, ḳinṭārs of spices plus a load of cotton, to Syracuse. They stipulated that twenty-five merchants could embark on the ship together with their servants without paying charges. The freight for the 3,300 ḳinṭārs amounted to 2,500 ducats.[235] So the cargo must have had a great value. Ships belonging to subjects of other nations and coming from Alexandria or Beirut visited Syracuse,[236] but also the Sicilians themselves took part in this trade. In Alexandria and in other towns of Egypt and Syria there were Sicilians who engaged in trade with their home country. The Sicilian Simone Amata was a merchant in Alexandria at least from 1401 to 1406. His son Antonio also lived there.[237] They engaged in the export of spices to Sicily and other transactions as well.[238] Notarial acts drawn up at the beginning of the fifteenth century in Alexandria contain the names of several Sicilians who signed as witnesses. Some of them may have been merchants. One was Luciano of Syracuse,[239] another Matteo de Bonifacio, once called of Catania, but mostly "of Trapani."[240] Antonio de Cusentino, of Trapani, carried on trade in Candia and Damietta at the end of the fourteenth and the beginning of the fifteenth century. In 1406, after his death, the Council of Trapani inquired of the Venetian authorities in Candia to confirm that his widow had appointed Giovanni de Aliotti to make claims concerning the bequest.[241]

[233] Carrère, *Barcelone*, p. 635.

[234] Vat. sub 21 Apr. 1400.

[235] Leonardo de Valle sub 14 Apr. 1402.

[236] Misti 42, f. 111b.

[237] Vat. sub 7 June 1401, 13 Oct. 1401, 25 June 1404; Leonardo de Valle sub 9 Nov. 1402, 15 March 1403, 7 May 1403. About Pino Campolo of Messina, who carried on trade with Egypt, see A. Lombardo, *Un testamente*, etc., Bollettino (of) Centro di studi filologici X (1969), p. 46 ff.

[238] See below.

[239] Vat. sub 4 Febr. 1401.

[240] Leonardo de Valle sub 20 Nov. 1401, 21. Febr. 1402, 12, 14 and 18 Apr. 1402, 1 May 1402.

[241] C. Trasselli, *I privilegi di Messina e di Trapani (1160-1357)* (Palermo, 1949), p. 111. Having quoted these data I should emphasize that the Sicilians had no fondaco of their own

On the Adriatic coast of Italy, Ancona was the town whose merchants were the most active in the trade with the Levant at that time. Her good port and her geographical situation were her great assets. Situated not too far from Florence, Ancona could serve this great industrial center as an outlet and, on the other hand, the town always maintained close connections with the ports of Dalmatia, where commodities which were in great demand in the Moslem Levant were obtained. But Ancona had to maintain herself against the heavy pressure of Venice, which considered the Adriatic Sea as being under her control and did everything possible to impede the development of the Levantine trade of other towns situated on the coast. In the middle of the fourteenth century, Venice was already attacking the flourishing soap industry of the March of Ancona by various measures[242] and took steps against the import of spices by the Anconitans to Upper Italy and Central Europe.[243] In 1391 the Senate of Venice granted a subsidy to exporters of soap to the Levant in order to make competition by the Anconitans more difficult.[244] Often Venice accused the Anconitans of acts of hostility and took reprisals against them. In 1377 they were accused of piracy and there ensued a conflict in which the pope, Ancona's protector, intervened on her behalf.[245] Then, in 1393, the Anconitans were again accused of this crime and also of levying higher customs on Venetian commodities than those agreed upon.[246] These charges were accompanied by threats. But despite the heavy pressure that Venice brought upon the small town on the Adriatic coast her trade with the Levant developed considerably. When the resources of Venice were absorbed by the war with Genoa in 1378-1381 and the Venetian galley lines did not function, Ancona supplied a part of Italy, which probably had not always belonged to her customers, with spices, cotton, and other Oriental articles. Commercial treaties with the towns of Dalmatia and one made in 1380 with the Lombards strengthened the position of Ancona. In 1390 the town also applied to the Holy See for permission to carry on trade with the dominions of the sultan of Cairo. A further step in the development of Ancona's trade with the Moslem Levant was made in 1391 when the Statutes of the *consulat de mare* were laid down and finally in a decree of 1393 the dues to be levied

in Alexandria. The suggestion of some scholars to "correct" a passage in the travelogue of Lannoy, p. 110, and to read instead of fondaco "de pèlerins," de Palermo, is not warranted by any document; see Heyd II, p. 432; F. Cerone, "La politica orientale di Alfonso d'Aragona," *Arch. Stor. Prov. Nap.* 27 (1902), p. 25. If there had been such a fondaco, it would have been mentioned in one of the thousands of acts that have come down to us from the registers of the Venetian notaries in Alexandria of the late fourteenth and the fifteenth centuries.

242 See "Il commercio levantino di Ancona," p. 217.

243 *Art. cit.*, p. 216 f.

244 Misti 41, f. 127b, and cf. *art. cit.*, p. 219.

245 *Art. cit.*, p. 218.

246 Misti 42, f. 103b, 104a.

on merchandise shipped to Alexandria were referred to. Anconitan ships began indeed to visit the ports of Egypt and Syria regularly.[247] All these data point to the growth of Anconitan trade in Egypt in the later 1380's and the 1390's. In one of those years, the Anconitan consulate in Alexandria was founded. Since the fondaco of Ancona is not mentioned by Florentine travellers who visited Alexandria in 1384 and since Ogier d'Anglure mentions it in 1395, obviously it must have been founded in one of the years between these two dates. According to an Anconitan tradition, the first consul in Alexandria was appointed in 1386.[248] From then on, the post of the Anconitan consul in Alexandria was filled by one of the citizens of the town, usually a merchant who had experience in the Levant trade.[249] As to the colonies of other major towns of provinces in European countries, merchants of some neighboring towns of the Marches and of Umbria belonged to the Anconitan colony in Alexandria.[250] But the number of its members, i.e., the merchants who were residents of the great Egyptian emporium, was never great.[251] Some Anconitans carried on trade in Syria. Niccolò de Cortesiis, a rich merchant, died in Beirut in 1395,[252] Giovanni de Guidolini engaged in trade with Damascus in about 1390.[253]

Table VII Italian Merchants in Alexandria, 1400 - 1402

year	Venetians	Genoese	Florentines	Anconitans
1400	15	35	6	16
1401	26	62	1	3
1402	48	33	1	10

[247] See "Il commercio levantino di Ancona," p. 220, where the sources are given. See also Dat 1082, letter of Zanobi of 19 March 1396 (a ship comes from Alexandria to Ancona); Dat 844, letter of Scolaio di Giovanni Spini from Ancona, of 26 Nov. 1397: a ship came from Alexandria to Ancona.

[248] See *art. cit.*, p. 221 f. What Natalucci infers from a decree of the Anconitan authorities in 1393, namely, that in that year a commercial treaty was concluded between Ancona and the sultan of Egypt, is not warranted by the source quoted by him; see C. Ciavarini, *Statuti anconetani del mare, del Terzenale e della dogana e natti con diverse nacioni* (Ancona, 1896), p. 263, and cf. M. Natalucci, *Ancona attraverso i secoli*, 2nd ed. (Città del Castello, 1960) I, p. 341 f.

[249] See the names, *art. cit.*, p. 222. *Porelo qd Vitalis de Guidolini* was consul until the end of 1402 (at least); see Leonardo de Valle sub 18 March 1402, 11 Sept. 1402.

[250] E.g. of Matelica: see Vat. sub 13 and 15 Jan. 1400, 15 March 1400; Ascoli: Vat. sub 13 Jan. 1400, 29 March 1401, 22 July 1401; Fano: Vat. sub 14 and 18 Oct. 1400, 8 Nov. 1400; Foligno: Vat. sub 13 Jan. 1400.

[251] The captains of ships and the Venetian consuls who were not allowed to engage in commercial activities, servants, etc., are not included in the following table.

[252] Misti 43, f. 69a.

[253] See "Il commercio levantino de Ancona," p. 223 and also p. 230.

Naturally, Anconitan trade with the Moslem Levant was conditioned by the relations of the town with her Italian hinterland and the Balkans. The Anconitans exported to the Levant soap produced in the Marches[254] and lead from the Balkans.[255] From Greek ports they also shipped copper that came from Turkey to the Levant[256] and olive oil and soap from Gaeta to Alexandria.[257] Through the port of Ancona, cloth of Florence, Lombardy, Flanders, and Catalonia was exported to the dominions of the sultan.[258] Some of the records which refer to these activities also testify to the import of spices by the Anconitans into Italy. However, the market that the Anconitans supplied with spices was rather small; it comprised only some of the provinces of Central Italy. On the other hand, it was much easier for them to market cotton and alkali, raw materials for the fustian and soap industries. A merchant letter which contains information about the cargoes of Anconitan ships returning from Syria and Egypt in 1379 shows that cotton ranked high on the list of merchandise they imported into Italy from the Levant.[259] A contract made in Alexandria in 1402 refers to the charter of a Catalan ship by Giacomo Antonio for a journey to Beirut-Tripoli-Latakia-Ancona. The merchant who chartered the ship stipulated that it should anchor twenty-five days in Tripoli and Latakia and load 350 ḳinṭārs of alkali and a very small quantity of spices.[260]

Ragusa was another of the smaller trading nations of Southern Europe which engaged in commercial exchanges with Egypt and Syria in the last third of the fourteenth century. Not only the township but also single citizens applied to the Holy See for permission to carry on trade with the Moslem Levant, and some of them obtained such licenses.[261] Others engaged in such trade without being licensed.[262] The records in the archives of Dubrovnik show that in that period there was regular trade with Egypt. In some years, two ships sailed from Ragusa to Egypt, e.g., in 1385, 1387, and 1397. In other years, if one can judge from these sources, only one

[254] Misti 41, f. 127b.

[255] Misti 40, f. 135a.

[256] Misti 42, f. 21b. Undoubtedly the Anconitans also engaged in the supply of iron to the Moslems (the Mamluks and the Turks), despite the embargo by the Church; see C. Schalk, "Rapporti commerciali fra Venezia e Vienna," *Nuovo Archivio Veneto* N.S. 23 (1912), p. 64, and cf. Ph. Braunstein, "Le commerce de fer a Venise au XVe siècle," *Studi Veneziani* VIII (1966), p. 288 f. Sometimes they also sold in Alexandria copper refined in Hungary and stamped in Venice ("di bolla"); see Dat 844, letter of Scolaio di Giovanni Spini from Ancona, of 29 May 1399.

[257] See Day, *Douanes*, pp. 272, 527.

[258] See C. Ciavarini, *Statuti anconetani del mare*, pp. 251 ff., 263 ff.

[259] Melis, *Doc.*, p. 142 f.

[260] Leonardo de Valle sub 19 Aug. 1402.

[261] Krekić, *Dubrovnik*, nos. 323, 332, 484.

[262] See above p. 31.

ship left for Alexandria.[263] The Ragusans exported to the Moslem Levant the metals hauled form the mines of Bosnia and Serbia[264] and olive oil of Apulia.[265] Their ships visited the ports of Apulia so often before sailing to Egypt that we can speak of a Ragusa-Apulia-Alexandria shipping line.[266] In Egypt the Ragusan ships sometimes also anchored in Damietta.[267]

The Genoese and Catalans were in the forefront of the trade between the coasts of the Tyrrhenian Sea and the Moslem Levant. But there was a third artery of this long-distance trade, the shipping line connecting Alexandria with Marseilles and Aigues-Mortes. A supplementary line was that leading from Collioure or Leucate to Egypt. Ships of the Provençals and the traders of Languedoc carried on a regular trade on these lines, but Genoese and Catalan ships also used them. In fact, the Genoese had a great share in the trade between Southern France and the Levant. Genoese merchants lived in Montpellier and there engaged in trade with the Levant;[268] on the other hand, the Superba tried to cut down direct trade of the Provençals with the dominions of the Mamluks. But during the war of Chioggia, the Provençals could develop their trade with the Moslem Levant without being encumbered by the Genoese. The ships sailing from the ports of Southern France to Egypt and Syria often visited Gaeta and Naples too. In 1400, for instance, the Genoese cog "Santa Maria and Sant' Antonio" was leased by some merchants in Aigues-Mortes and Savona for a trip to Gaeta and Alexandria. But the captain went to Naples instead of to Gaeta.[269] In the years 1379-1385 the Levant trade of Marseilles flourished; every year three to five ships sailed from its port to Alexandria or Beirut. In those years, Marseilles also served Italian traders of Avignon as a point of support for their trade with the Levant. They chartered ships in Marseilles to sail to the dominions of the sultan.[270] From 1385 to 1391 the merchants of Languedoc, mainly those of Montpellier and Narbonne, were much more active, and every year two or three of their ships sailed to the ports of Egypt and Syria. And they carried on their activities in close connection with the traders of Marseilles, so that the latter could load merchandise on their ships.[271] The Datini archives and the deeds of the notary Antoniello de Vataciis show that even in the 1390's every year one or two ships sailed from Alexandria or Beirut to the ports of Southern France.[272]

[263] Krekić, *op.cit.*, nos. 323, 378, 387, 471, 476, 484, 488, 494.

[264] *Op.cit.*, no. 379.

[265] *Op.cit.*, no. 476.

[266] *Op.cit.*, nos. 476, 484.

[267] *Op.cit.*, no. 494.

[268] Vat. sub 9 Dec. 1399. About a Genoese ship sailing from Alexandria to Pisa, Aigues-Mortes, Barcelona, and Flanders, see Dat 549, letter of Zanobi of 21 May 1394.

[269] Vat. sub 25 Febr. 1401.

[270] See Baratier, pp. 232 f., 235 ff., appendix II.

[271] Baratier, p. 233.

[272] See appendix A 4, the data to be added to these collected by Baratier.

In Alexandria there were three French consulates and fondachi, those of Marseilles, of Narbonne, and that called "of Avignon and France," or simply "of France."[273] For a long time, Simone Regla (or Raia) was the head of the Marseilles colony. He is mentioned in notarial acts of 1399-1402 as consul of Marseilles or "consul of Marseilles and Provence." According to a Catalan document in 1385, he was already consul of Marseilles in Alexandria.[274] His successor was Jean Audibert.[275] Consuls of the "French," of whom the merchants of Montpellier were the most numerous, were Pierre de Podiasco in the 1390's[276] and Pierre Soler of Montpellier in 1400-1402.[277] The number of the French and Provençals in Alexandria was not great, and the colony of the merchants of Narbonne was the smallest. Therefore the pilgrims on the way to Palestine or back from Mount Sinai lived in their fondaco and the consul of Narbonne was also "consul of the pilgrims."[278] In the 1380's, however, the consul of the French held this post.[279] At any rate, merchants of Marseilles, Montpellier and Narbonne always lived in Alexandria, and they carried on a lively trade with their home country. The uninterrupted existence of their fondachi is evidence of this fact.[280] The number of French merchants who are mentioned in the notarial acts drawn up in Alexandria at the turn of the fourteenth century are summed up in the following table.[281]

Table VIII French merchants in Alexandria, 1400 - 1402

		merchants of		
year	Montpellier	Marseilles	Narbonne	"French"
1400	1	4	2	2
1401	3	7	1	4
1402	3	2	3	5

273 See my "The Venetian supremacy in Levantine Trade," p. 9, where the sources are given.

274 Vat. sub 10 Dec. 1399, 1 Dec. 1400, 26 Febr. 1401, 1 June 1401, 26 July 1401; Leonardo de Valle sub 28 Dec. 1401, 3 Jan. 1402; López de Meneses, "Los consulados," p. 106 f.

275 *Les Bouches-du-Rhône*, encyclopédie départementale, II (Paris, 1924), p. 378; Baratier, p. 378.

276 He died before 1400; see Vat. sub 21 Jan. 1400.

277 Vat. sub 2 Dec. 1399, 17 Jan. 1400 (his election); Leonardo de Valle sub 28 Apr. 1402. He died before February 1403: see Leonardo de Valle sub 7 Febr. 1403.

278 Ogier d'Anglure, p. 78.

279 Frescobaldi, p. 84 f.

280 Heyd was wrong in saying that the text of Lannoy's account should be corrected to read, instead of fondaco of the pilgrims, fondaco of the Palermitans. The merchants of Palermo never had a fondaco in Alexandria. As to Heyd's interpretation of Lannoy's account, see above, note 241.

281 This table also includes the consuls, because those of the French (of all colonies) also engaged in trade.

In Syria the number of the French was even smaller, so that they had no consulate of their own and were represented by the Catalan consul of Damascus.[282] This is true even for the French monks in Jerusalem.[283]

The French merchants imported into the Moslem Levant honey, coral, and cloth of their country. The books of a great merchant of Narbonne, Jacme Olivier, who engaged in trade with Egypt and Syria, shed light both on the commodities exported and those imported by the French merchants, and on the volume of their commercial exchanges with the dominions of the sultan. From 1381 to 1390 Jacme Olivier sent honey and cloth worth 500-1000 fl. every year to Alexandria or Damascus. The cloth was a cheap sort, produced by the manufacturers of Narbonne and worth 12-13 fl. a piece. The Oriental commodities he imported were pepper, ginger, and cinnamon.[284] In 1398-1399, Bartolomeo Bera imported cloth of Narbonne (*zahuches*) and honey to Alexandria on a Genoese ship.[285] On the other hand, he exported spices from Egypt to the Provence.[286] The merchants of Montpellier exported to the Moslem Levant the same products as those of Narbonne, sometimes loading them on Genoese ships.[287] The chief commodity exported by the merchants of Marseilles was coral.[288] The articles shipped to France by the merchants of all these towns were mainly spices. In December 1401 four French traders chartered a French ship in Alexandria to go to Rhodes and Aigues-Mortes in order to export spices and cotton. The freight was to be paid in Montpellier. A rich trader of Marseilles, Julien de Casaulx, imported spices worth 5,000 fl. in one year.[289] The enterprising merchants of Montpellier even exported spices from Egypt to England.[290] The French merchants in Alexandria also engaged in trade with Rhodes. Andre Triol of Montpellier, who lived in Alexandria at least from 1398 to 1404 (although he travelled very much),[291] exported fruits from Rhodes to Egypt,[292] carried on trade with Syria, importing grains there together with other French merchants,[293] and of course traded with Southern France.[294] The French ships also sailed between the ports of Tunisia and Egypt, transporting Moslem merchants and their merchandise.[295]

[282] López de Meneses, "Los consulados," p. 129, and appendix XVIII.

[283] See below.

[284] "Le livre de comptes de Jacme Olivier," ed. A. Blanc, in *Bulletin de la commission archéologique de Narbonne*, 1896, 2e sémestre, and see appendix B.

[285] Vat. sub 2 Dec. 1399.

[286] Vat. sub 21 Apr. 1400.

[287] Vat. sub 9 Dec. 1399.

[288] Baratier, p. 246.

[289] Leonardo de Valle sub 23 Dec. 1401; Baratier, p. 247 note 3.

[290] Liagre-De Sturler, no. 564.

[291] Leonardo de Valle sub 5 Jan. 1402, 4 and 6 Oct. 1404.

[292] Leonardo de Valle sub 5 Jan. 1402.

[293] See there sub 14 Apr. 1402.

[294] See there sub 23 Dec. 1401.

[295] Vat. sub 1 Apr. 1401; Leonardo de Valle sub 3 Jan. 1402.

Like the Levantine trade of the Genoese, the trade of the Catalans with the dominions of the Mamluks was prejudiced by their inclination to acts of aggression. The parallel of the situation was even more marked since the king of Aragon and Catalonia in that period largely opposed the acts of hostility and tried to establish friendly relations with the sultan of Cairo. As in earlier times, the king fostered trade with the Moslem Levant, but did not forget his own interests. The fines levied on unlicensed trade with Moslems were always a source of revenue, which the king did not renounce. Several documents of the 1370's refer to inquiries concerning commercial travel to Egypt and Syria made by Catalan traders who had no licenses, either from the pope or from the king. In 1377 the king pardoned Jacme Cantu, a merchant of Perpignan, who had gone to Damascus with merchandise worth 100,000 pounds of Barcelona.[296] In 1373 King Pedro IV had made an agreement with the town of Barcelona concerning the fines to be paid for ships sailing even from a port outside his dominions to Egypt or Syria.[297] The king also insisted that the merchants travelling to the Moslem Levant must have a special license to take gold coins with them.[298] Besides the difficulties made by the Crown, the merchants suffered from the hostility aroused by the acts of aggression committed by their fellow-countrymen against the Moslems. The Arabic chroniclers recount that in 1378 Europeans, who had come on their ships, tried to attack Tripoli. They succeeded in landing, but were pushed back.[299] Who these "Franks" were is not disclosed, but Catalan sources leave no doubt about their identity. From the records of the Royal Chancery of Aragon, one learns that in 1379 Francesce Ça-Closa, a veteran Levant trader, was sent as ambassador to the court of Cairo to request the return of the merchandise of the Catalan merchants; obviously the goods had been sequestered after the attack on Tripoli.[300] His mission was successful, for in the same year the king gave orders that henceforth Egyptian and Syrian ships should not be attacked, since peace had been concluded with the sultan.[301] In 1386 the king sent another embassy to Cairo. It consisted of Jaime Fivaller, Bernat Gualbes, and Bernat Pol, merchants of Barcelona, whose objective was to conclude a new commercial treaty.[302] But in 1395 Catalans again committed acts of aggression which resulted in reprisals by the Mamluks. They attacked some Moslem ships in the port of Beirut and one belonging to the Genoese. The

[296] López de Meneses, "Los consulados," p. 100; Sáez Pomés, p. 365.
[297] Capmany 2.1, no. 198, pp. 292-97.
[298] Rubió i Lluch, no. 539.
[299] *Sulūk* III, p. 335; Ibn Iyās[2] I, part 2, p. 230 (copied from al-Maḳrīzī); Ibn Ḥadjar I, p. 174; 'Abdalbāsiṭ 803, f. 117a.
[300] Sáez Pomés, p. 367. However, according to Zurita, lib. IX, cap. 64, the embassy was despatched in 1373.
[301] Capmany 2.1, no 210, pp. 313-14.
[302] Zurita, *Anales* X, cap. 38.

property of Venetians too was robbed. The Catalans were ready to give back some of the goods, but refused categorically to return those of the Genoese. Thereupon the consul of the Catalan, in Damascus, and five Catalan merchants were imprisoned and their goods sequestered.[303] The assault in the port of Beirut had been made by a Catalan noble, Guillem Ramon de Montcada, who committed acts of piracy in other regions too.[304] In 1400 there was again a conflict between the Catalans and the Mamluk authorities, and the Catalan colony in Alexandria encountered difficulty in making the payment that the Moslem authorities demanded of them.[305]

The Catalan colony in Alexandria was not a big one. In the acts of the notaries who served the European merchants there, fifteen Catalan merchants are mentioned as residing in the town in 1400, 22 in 1401, and five in 1402. The colony consisted of merchants of Barcelona, Tarragona,[306] Manresa,[307] Perpignan,[308] and Majorca.[309] There was another colony of Catalan merchants in Damascus headed by a consul.[310] In various documents the names of these consuls have come down to us from the end of the fourteenth century. Arnaldo Marsells held the post from 1379 to 1382, Arnaldo de Valseca from 1382 to 1385, Bernat Maresa from 1385 to 1390, Anton Ametler from 1390 to 1396 and Pere Quintaner from 1396. In 1402 Michael Gualbes held the post.[311] The Catalan colony in Damascus must have been the most important of the European colonies in that town at the end of the fourteenth century, for the French "guardian of Mount Zion" applied to the Catalan consul when in 1391 four monks were executed in Jerusalem.[312] That Catalan trade in Egypt and Syria was flourishing in the

[303] Dat 710, letter of Zanobi di Taddeo Gaddi of 7 Sept. 1395, quoting a letter from Damascus of 14 June 1395; letter of Bertrando Mignanelli of 2 Aug. 1395, apud Melis, *Doc.*; p. 184. Dat 549, letter of Zanobi di Taddeo Gaddi of 7 Sept. 1395. Another letter of his, Dat 797 of 13 May 1396, quoting news from Damascus of 25 March about attacks by Catalan ships on Moslems probably refers to new acts of hostility.

[304] Rubió i Lluch, p. 658 note 1.

[305] Vat. sub 19 Oct., 25 Oct. and 1 Dec. 1400.

[306] Leonardo de Valle sub 20 Dec. 1401.

[307] Vat. sub 21 Jan. 1400.

[308] Vat. sub 15 March 1401.

[309] Vat. sub 21 Jan. 1401.

[310] Frescobaldi, p. 161.

[311] Fernandez de Navarrete, p. 188b.; Capmany, 2.1, nos. 219, 231, pp. 326, 337; López de Meneses, "Los consulados," pp. 101, 128, 129, 130, 133f., 134; Rubió i Lluch no. 509; Del Treppo, in *RSI* 70, p. 53. Bernat Maresa had in 1387 Maron of Villanova paint a portrait of Saint Catherine for the Monastery of Mount Sinai, where it has remained to this day, see H. L. Rabino, *Le monastère de Sainte Catherine (Mont-Sinai)* (Cairo, 1938), p. 46. Antonio Ametler was later Catalan consul in Alexandria from 1398 to 1402. See Rubió i Lluch, no. 668; López de Meneses, p. 113 f.; a brother of his was a merchant in Damascus in 1397; see Vat. sub 11 May 1400. About Pere Quintaner, see also Ainaud, "Quatre documents," doc. II. This notarial act testifying to the losses the consul suffered when travelling from Damascus to Beirut may refer to his flight from the Syrian capital before it was taken by Timūr.

[312] P. Durrieu, "Procès-verbal du martyre de quatre frères mineurs," *AOL* I, p. 539 ff.,

last third of the fourteenth century is also indicated by the fact that in 1381 the Council of Barcelona laid down the rules for the administration of the Catalan consulates in Alexandria and in 1386 for that in Damascus. The rules refer to merchandise imported by the Catalan merchants into Egypt and Syria from Sicily, Rhodes and Turkey.[313]

Catalan trade with the Levant was carried on by both cogs and galleys. Both of them transported spices. At the end of the fourteenth century, the galleys held a foremost place in the Levantine trade of Catalonia. The Council of Barcelona itself organized convoys of galleys. The line connecting Barcelona with Beirut was undoubtedly more important than the Alexandria-Barcelona line in that period.[314] The documents that have come down to us from the 1370's and the 1380's point to no more than one or two ships sailing in any one of those years from Catalonia to the Moslem Levant. But from 1390 Catalan shipping to Egypt and Syria increased greatly. According to records that have been preserved in various sources, in 1392 and 1394 three Catalan vessels visited the ports of the Moslem Levant; in 1390, 1396, 1398, and 1401, five or even eight a year; and in 1395 there were seven. In other years two or four Catalan ships sailed to Beirut or Alexandria.[315]

In addition to the main line of Catalan traffic with the Moslem Levant, there was another line connecting the territories of the crown of Aragon situated north of the Pyrenees with the dominions of the sultan. In this region, Perpignan was a flourishing industrial and commercial center and its port was Collioure. The merchants of Perpignan not only exported their cloth to the Levant, they also engaged to a great extent in the spice trade and supplied some regions of Southern France with the Oriental commodities. They even sold spices in Barcelona, shipping them there from Collioure.

In the archives of Francesco Datini there have come down to us many letters written at the end of the fourteenth century by Pere Tequin, a great merchant of Perpignan. He traded in cloth, cotton, cheese, and spices and was in close contact with the merchants of Montpellier and the Datini firm in Barcelona. He had a ship of his own, whose captain was Johan Bastier. This ship commuted between the Levantine ports and those of the Tyrrhenian Sea. It visited Pisa, Aigues-Mortes, Collioure, and Tortosa. Pere Tequin had an agent in Damascus who was a Catalan too. His name was

---

the guardian himself was Fr. Gérard Calveti of Aquitaine; see Golubovich, *Serie cronologica dei superiori di Terra Santa* (Jerusalem 1898), p. 88 f.

[313] Capmany 2.1, nos. 214, 231, pp. 319-322, 337-39.

[314] *Op.cit.*, 1, p. 745. The traffic, however, was not exclusively a traffic of galleys, as Heers says, see "Il commercio," p. 173. Heers, *l.c.* exaggerates, when he maintained that the Catalans sailed only to Syria.

[315] See appendix A 3.

Francesc Caralt. When Tīmūr invaded Syria, he succeeded in leaving Damascus in time, to the great joy of Pere Tequin. The greatest profits of Pere Tequin derived from the import of Oriental commodities, spices, Damascene sugar, cotton, dates, and other articles. He supplied the markets of Toulouse and Paris with spices and also shipped certain quantities of these commodities to Barcelona. In the notarial acts drawn up in that period in Perpignan there are mentioned the names of several other merchants who carried on trade with the Levant. Also, merchants and clothiers of some small towns near Perpignan engaged in trade with Syria and Egypt. Of course they exported cloth produced in their province, in Villefranche-de-Conflent and other towns. All these merchants used ships leaving from Collioure, but also ships which sailed to the Levant from Barcelona. On the other hand, ships sailing from the Levant to Barcelona often anchored, on their way to Catalonia, in Collioure.[316]

The ships leaving from Collioure, southeast of Perpignan, visited some ports of Southern France before sailing to the Near East. Most of the Catalan ships made a stop in Rhodes before going on to Beirut or Alexandria. Rhodes served the Catalans as a point of support for their activities in the Levant, because of the friendship between the Aragonese dynasty and the Hospitallers. Cyprus too was very often visited by the Catalan ships. The Catalans were indeed in close contact with the royal house of Lusignan and regularly carried on trade with the island.

The southern provinces of the kingdom of Aragon and even Castile had at the end of the fourteenth century commercial relations with the Moslem Levant. In 1391 a Castilian cog sailed from Barcelona to Jaffa and in 1393 another to Syria. In 1396 a Castilian ship went to Alexandria. An insurance

[316] About the export of spices from Perpignan (via Collioure) to Barcelona, see Dat 1158, no. 126 (of 16 Dec. 1399); about Pere Tequin, see Dat 906: export of cloth to Gaeta, see letter of 21 June 1402, 11 Sept. 1402; his ship, see letters of 19 April 1400, 14 Oct. 1401, 16 May 1402; APO, Proc. Real IV, f. 69b of Sept. 26, 1402 referring to the ship which will return from Alexandria (misinterpreted in *Inventaire sommaire des archives départementales antérieures a 1790, Pyrénées orientales*, série B.C., par B. Alart, I, Paris, 1868, p. 109b); an inventory of its cargo carried in 1401 from Alexandria, see Dat 1171; his agent in Damascus, see Dat 906, letters of 30 Jan. 1400, 2 Febr. 1400; export of dates to Toulouse, see *ibid.*, letter of . . . Aug. 1399; of pepper to Paris, see letter of 27 March 1400; of ginger and dates to Barcelona, see letters of 14 Oct. 1401, 14 Nov. 1401, 25 Febr. 1402, 14 March 1402. See, further, APO, B. 250, liasse 24, act of 23 Sept. 1394. About his affairs with the Crown and the township of Perpignan, see Alart, pp. 103b, 117a. See, further, APO B. 131, Andreas Romeu, f. 78b: a clothier of Villefranche-de-Conflent travels in the early 1370's to Damascus. About shipping from Collioure, P. Ornos, f. 79b f.: the ship "Sant Johan," patron P. Terrasa of Collioure, sails in 1387 to Cyprus and Beirut; APO, B. 250, liasse 24, act of 13 Oct. 1395: charter of a ship Collioure for trip to Beirut; *ibid.*, act of 3 May 1396: a merchant of Perpignan undertakes to embark on a galley sailing from Barcelona to the Levant.

In addition to Barcelona, Valencia, and Collioure, there were in the kingdom of Catalonia other ports from which ships departed for the Levant; see Dat 1159, no. 1141 (of 1397) insurance of the ship "*Santa Maria*," owned by Luca del Biondo, sailing from Denia to Alexandria (about this Florentine merchant, see note 214 to this chapter).

act, drawn up in 1397, refers to the ship (saietta) "Sta Maria" of Luca del Biondo (a Florentine, see above), sailing from Denia to Alexandria.[317]

The commodities exported by the Catalans to the Moslem Levant were mainly the agricultural and industrial products of their own country, honey, olive oil, saphron, hazelnuts, and cloth. The shipments of Catalan honey to the Levant were sometimes substantial. However, among the commodities exported from Catalonia to the Moslem Levant cloth held the first place. In the records of a notary of Barcelona dating to 1398, one finds a commenda, given by a single merchant, of 118 pieces of cloth. Most of the cloth exported by the Catalans to the Levant consisted of products of the local industry. Great quantities of Catalan cloth were shipped to the Near East also on foreign vessels. A Genoese merchantman carried, in 1399, 400 bales of Valencia cloth to Alexandria. But one exported to the Levant also Irish serge and in Catalan freight tariffs of 1374 and 1394 one finds French cloth, Flemish serge, and cloth of Wervicq-sur-Lys and Courtrai.[318] Much coral was also shipped by the Catalans to the Moslem Levant.[319] The shipments of metals were apparently much less important than those carried by the Italian merchantmen, since the Catalans had no access to regions that supplied the Italians with great quantities of copper and lead. What they could offer was mainly tin from England.[320] Like all other trading nations of Southern Europe, the Catalans chiefly purchased spices in the Levant. Some of these spices were intended for Flanders and England. They also purchased considerable quantities of cotton in Syria.[321]

D. THE COMMODITIES

The Levant trade of the South European trading nations was a great export trade. It would have been impossible for them to pay the price of the Oriental spices and dyes in cash, since the volume of imports into the

[317] See appendix for trade and shipping from Rhodes. For Cyprus, see AHPB, Berenguer Ermengol, Manual 2. Jan.-30 Dec. 1378, f. 56a ff.: a Catalan galley chartered to the king of Cyprus; B. Nadal I, f. 37b: Catalan ships visiting Cyprus (a. 1397); ships of Castile, etc.: Del Treppo, p. 608; Dat 1159, draft of insurance act of 19 July 1397.

[318] Pere Marti VI, sub 8 May 1374; Bernat Nadal I, f. 67a f. (a. 1387) II, f. 9b, 14a, 15b, 16b, 17a, 17b, 19a, 19b f., 20b f., 23a, 26a, 27a, 29a, 29b; Dat 777, letter of Agnolo de Ser Pino & Giuliano di Giovanni of 12 July 1399; Vat sub 9 June 1400, 1 Dec. 1400; Leonardo de Valle sub 22 Dec. 1401; Capmany, 1, p. 258; Sáez Pomés, p. 373; Del Treppo, p. 737 f.; Piloti, p. 146. Madurell-Garcia, nos. 141, 144, 147.

[319] Bernat Nadal II, f. 12b; Capmany *l.c.* and cf. Carrère, *Barcelone*, p. 646; Del Treppo *l.c.*

[320] *Carrère, l.c.* It is true that in the Catalan freight tariffs lead is mentioned. This is probably lead from the mines of Tortosa. However, the shipments to the Moslem Levant must have been insignificant.

[321] *Op.cit.*, p. 647; Dat 550, letters of Com. of Zanobi of 1 and 10 Jan. 1401. Purchase of pepper: Pere Marti VI, sub 4 May 1374 and VIII, sub 31 Oct. 1380; Bernat Nadal II, f. 16a, 17a, 20b f.; ginger: *ibid.*, f. 17b, 27b, 29a; cloves: ibid. f. 17a, 27b, 29a; gum lac: *ibid.*, f. 29a.

European countries was increasing more and more. On the other hand, the importance of the Moslem Levant as an outlet for their industrial and even agricultural production was particularly great in a period in which the demand in Europe was decreasing owing to the depopulation after the Black Death. However, even the Moslem Levant could not absorb all that was imported from Europe. Some of the industrial products brought into the Levant were re-exported by the Moslem merchants to Persia, India, and elsewhere.

The most important item of European export to the Near East was undoubtedly cloth. As the Levantine industries had begun to decline, there was an increasing demand for European textiles in the Near East.[322] The woolen stuffs that the European merchants offered in the Levant came from almost all the countries of Europe. Merchants of all the trading nations brought to the Levant the precious Florentine cloth, the so-called tintilani, made of English wool,[323] and other Florentine cloth made of Spanish wool (*di San Matteo*). Venice and Naples were great markets of Florentine cloth and from there it was shipped to the Levantine emporia.[324] A Venetian merchant imported 120 pieces of Florentine cloth, perhaps worth 4,000-5,000 ducats, to Alexandria in 1402.[325] Besides the three kinds of cloth made of Spanish wool, which are simply called "Florentine cloth" on the price lists, the cheaper Florentine stuff called *panni di fontego* was brought in.[326] Florentine cloth of high quality was very much appreciated by the upper classes of Oriental society. Characteristically, in 1386, a Genoese ambassador to the sultan brought him Florentine cloth as a gift.[327]

Another staple commodity which almost all the Western merchants shipped to the Levant was cloth of Flanders and Brabant. Although the ancient textile industries of Flanders had already begun to decline a long time before, other centers had developed and their products were much appreciated in the Mediterranean countries and in the Levant.[328] In Venice, the departure of the Alexandria and Beirut galleys sometimes had to be postponed in

[322] See Dat 928, letter of Commess. of Zanobi di Taddeo Gaddi of 17 Apnl 1402, quoting a letter from Alexandria of 18 Jan. 1402: cloth is in great demand and at high pnces.

[323] See Misti 29, f. 52b, and cf. on this kind of cloth H. Hoshino, "Per la storia dell'arte della lana ın Firenze nel Trecento e nel Quattrocento, un riesame," *Annuario dell 'Istituto Giapponese di cultura a Roma* X (1972-1973), p. 50.

[324] G. P., Sent. IX, f. 65a; Hoshino, *art. cit.*, p. 59.

[325] G. P., Sent. VII, f. 33a f.

[326] See my paper "L'exportation de textiles occidentaux," pp. 313, 315.

[327] ASG, Antico Comune 18, c 16, cf. above note 144.

[328] R. van Uytven, "La draperie brabançonne et malinoise du XIIe au XVIIe siecle, grandeur éphémère et décadence," in *IIa Settimana di studio, Istituto Fr. Datini* (Florence, 1976), p. 85 ff., and, on the other hand, F. Melis, "La diffusione nel Mediterraneo occidentale dei panni di Wervicq e delle altre città della Lys attorno al 1400," ın *Studi A. Fanfani* (Milan 1962) III, p. 217 ff. E. Ashtor, *Europaïsche Tuchausfuhr in die Mittelmeerländer* in Spatmıttealter (Nürnburg, 1982), p. 10 ff.

order to make it possible to load the cloth which was about to arrive or had arrived too late from Flanders.[329] In 1384 and in 1385 an exception was made so that Flemish cloth could be loaded up to the day of the departure of the Beirut galleys, because it was known that a large quantity of cloth was due in Venice.[330] Sometimes the amount of Flemish cloth brought in to Venice was so great that it caused concern. The Venetian textile manufacturers who were interested in fostering the export of their own products intervened with the government and obtained a prohibition against the export of the foreign product on the galleys going to Alexandria. This happened, for instance, in 1372.[331] In the 1380's and 1390's cloth of Ypres and Wervicq-sur-Lys was shipped to the Moslem Levant also by the merchants of Marseilles. Even the Catalan traders exported woolen stuffs of Flanders and Brabant to the Moslem Levant.[332] On the price lists compiled by the agents of Francesco Datini in Alexandria and Damascus the expensive kinds of cloth of Flanders and Brabant rarely appear, although the firm did export it to the Moslem Levant.[333] According to a price list drawn up in Damascus in 1395, cloth of Malines was sold there for 38.5 ducats a piece; the cloth of Wervicq-sur-Lys cost half that amount.[334]

The Italian merchants also shipped cloth of Milan and other towns of Lombardy to the Levant[335] and the Provençals and other merchants of Southern France exported not only woolen stuffs produced in Languedoc, as in Narbonne, Carcassonne, Montréal, Limoux, and Anduze, but also those of Northern France. The cloth manufactured in Southern France was mostly a cheap product. The *zahuches* of Narbonne were sold in Damascus and in Alexandria, according to some price lists, for 9-11 ducats in the 1390's. They rarely fetched a higher price.[336] Commenda contracts made in Marseilles in the 1380's for export to the Moslem Levant refer to cloth of Louviers in Normandy, which was much more expensive, and to cloth of Montivilliers, where high-quality scarlets were woven.[337]

However, to judge from the number of quotations in the price lists compiled for the Datini concern in the Levantine emporia, it was the Catalan

[329] R. Cessi, "Le relazioni commerciali fra Venezia e le Fiandre nel secolo XIV," in his *Politica ed economia di Venezia nel Trecento* (Rome, 1956), p. 110.

[330] Misti 38, f. 156a 39, f. 114a. Usually it was forbidden to load at the eve of the departure.

[331] Misti 34, f. 7b; cf. Cessi, *art. cit.*, pp. 68, 77, and see also my paper "Observations on Venetian Trade," p. 585.

[332] See Baratier, appendix II; Carrère, *Barcelone*, p. 500: a merchant of Barcelona exports cloth of Malines to Beirut in 1396.

[333] H. Laurent, *La draperie des Pays-Bas en France et dans les pays méditerranéens (XIIe-XVe siècles)*, p. 190.

[334] See my paper "L'exportation de textiles," p. 339 f.

[335] Saminiato de' Ricci, p. 121; Frescobaldi, p. 48.

[336] See "L'exportation de textiles," p. 327 f., and see above, p. 146.

[337] *Art. cit.*, p. 330 f.; often "cloth of Languedoc" or simply "French" cloth is spoken of in the contracts; see *art. cit.*, pp. 329, 331.

cloth that was exported to the Near East in the greatest volume at that time. It seems that the shipment of these cheap woolen stuffs surpassed those of all other kinds of cloth. Those of Barcelona and Puigcerda (a town in the province of Gerona)[338] cost 10-12 ducats a piece in the Levant, the cloth of Villefranche de Conflent (in Roussilon),[339] white and colored, a bit more, i.e., 14-15 ducats. Perpignan produced a variety of cloth that was already exported to the Near East in the first half of the fourteenth century.[340] It cost more there than other cloth produced in the territories of the crown of Aragon. Catalan cloth, which at the end of the fourteenth century undoubtedly was, in the Levant, first among the European woolen stuffs of lower quality, was imported there mostly by Catalan merchants, who marketed it mainly in Syria, but it was also brought in by traders of Languedoc and the Provence.[341] At any rate, its export was mainly a business of the Catalans, whom the big towns of Sicily served as markets and ports for transshipping. Cloth comprised the greatest part of the freight of the Catalan ships sailing to Sicily. These shipments of Catalan cloth comprised the most variegated products. On a freight tariff of 1394, cloth of Banyoles is listed as one of the Catalan articles exported to the Levant.[342] The export of cloth to the Levant was one of the most important sectors of Catalonia's economy; her cloth industry was indeed mainly intended for export and its sale made it possible to supply the country with grains.[343]

Relatively large quantities of linen were also imported into the Near East from Central and Western Europe. The import of this article had begun a long time before, but greatly increased in the last third of the fourteenth and at the beginning of the fifteenth centuries. The great volume of this trade is attested by both European and Oriental sources. The Florentine traveller Lionardo Frescobaldi, who was in Egypt in 1384, narrates that the women in this country wore garments made of Reims linen.[344] Arabic chroniclers write that in 1391 the Mamluk authorities took measures against the fashion of excessively long shirts of Venetian linen, worn by rich ladies in Cairo.[345] The linen called "bunduḳī" (Venetian) by the Arabic authors was, however, mostly German linen, which the Venetians re-exported. In the Venetian sources the German linen is simply called *de fontico*, because it was sold in the Fondaco dei Tedeschi.[346] The greatest center of the German

[338] M. Gual Camarena, "Para un mapa de la industria textil hispana en la edad media," *Anuario de estudios medievales* IV (1968), p. 147.
[339] *Art. cit.*, p. 157.
[340] Pegolotti, pp. 37, 55, 58, 79.
[341] "L'exportation de textiles," p. 332 ff.
[342] Carrère, *op.cit.*, p. 638; Del Treppo, p. 738.
[343] Carrère, p. 648.
[344] *Viaggi*, p. 77.
[345] See the sources quoted in my paper in *JEEH* V, p. 582.
[346] Misti 33, f. 58a, 109b, and cf. 34, f. 26b.

linen industry, which supplied Venice (and other Mediterranean emporia) with its products, in that period was Constance. There broad and narrow pieces were manufactured, a piece of the first kind being sold in the Levant for 6-7 ducats, the other for 3.3-4.7. It is very probable that the flourishing linen industry of St. Gallen also supplied Venice and Genoa with its products. In fact, in 1262, merchants of St. Gallen bartered linen for pepper in Genoa. The first document referring to trade between St. Gallen and Venice dates from the 1360's. But often linen of St. Gallen and other towns of the region of the Bodensee was sold as "Constance linen," as the products of this town had a great reputation. St. Gallen became a great industrial center only in the second half of the fifteenth century. The price lists sent to the Datini firm from the Levantine emporia show that the price of the German linen fell progressively.[347] The Venetians apparently had the greatest share in the export of German linen to the Levant, but merchants of Southern France also exported this article to the Near East.[348] The decisions to postpone the departure of the galleys for the Levant so as to have more time for loading the German linen show how important the export of this material was to the Venetians.[349] Both the Venetians and the merchants of Southern France exported also some kinds of French linen to the Moslem Levant, besides that of Reims and of Germany. Even the Genoese took part in this trade. Linen of Champagne, Verdun, Noyon (in the department of Oise), and Vienne were exported. These kinds of linen were cheaper than linen of Reims. Whereas Reims linen was sold in the Levant for 30-40 ducats the 100 pics, the other kinds fetched no more than 8-12.[350] Italian linen, for instance that of Novi Ligure, was also exported to the Moslem Levant. In 1400 a Venetian firm, Pietro Venier & Cie, exported 42 bales of this article to Damascus; 9 bales were sold for 763 ducats. So the whole shipment was worth (C.I.F. prices) 3,560 ducats.[351]

Besides woolen cloth and linen, the South European traders exported precious silken stuffs and serge to the Near East.[352] Much of these cheap woolen stuffs, often called "Irish" serge, was shipped from England and Flanders to the Italian emporia and re-exported to the Levant, sometimes after having been dyed.[353] Serge was apparently much in demand in the

[347] "L'exportation de textiles," p. 356; H. C. Peyer, *Leinwandgewerbe und Fernhandel der Stadt St. Gallen von den Anfängen bis 1520* (St. Gallen, 1960) II, pp. 4, 5, 9, 26, and see there p. 8, I, p. 67: merchants of St. Gallen sell "linen of Constance."

[348] "L'exportation de textiles," p. 356 f.

[349] Misti 34, f. 26b (a. 1372) 38, f. 156a (a. 1384) 42, f. 74a (a. 1392); on the export of linen to Syria, see G. P., Sent. IV, f. 14a (about a. 1375).

[350] "L'exportation de textiles," p. 355. See Misti 41, f. 92b: import of linen of Noyon and Reims to Venice.

[351] G. P. Sent. VII, f. 100a ff. 11, f. 45a ff.

[352] "L'exportation de textiles," p. 368 f.

[353] Misti 55, f. 35b, 60, f. 60a.

Levant. In 1399 it was proposed in the Venetian Senate to allow loading it on the Levant galleys until their departure.[354]

Metals ranked high on the list of the commodities exported to the Moslem Levant by some trading nations; for others they had less importance. For it is clear that only those whose metropolis was not too far from regions from which metals were brought could ship these heavy and relatively cheap articles. Venice had the great advantage of being close to the Balkans and to Central Europe, the regions rich in various ores. The Genoese and Catalans, who had much less easy access to centers of mining, could not easily compete with them.[355] The profits realized in this export trade were then relatively modest, but it should not be forgotten that the market for European textiles in the Levant had its limits and that the heavy metals also served as ballast.

Copper was chief among the metals exported to the dominions of the sultan. Great quantities were needed by the Mamluk government for the coinage of the *fulūs*, the small copper coins which, from the end of the fourteenth century, became the means of payment for most transactions. al-Maḳrīzī recounts that Maḥmūd b. ʿAlī, the major-domo of Barḳūḳ, sent missions to Europe to acquire copper for the Royal Mints.[356] The Arabic author says that the European merchants themselves also imported much copper to Egypt.[357] Since the Mints of the Mamluk sultans had issued large quantities of *fulūs*, the silver dirham disappeared and was replaced by these copper coins.[358] But copper was also needed in Egypt and Syria for the manufacture of kettles, e.g. for sugar-cooking, and other utensils.[359] The agents of the sultan bought copper from the Venetians, in Beirut and elsewhere,[360] but often it was taken by them and others by force.[361] Some of the copper imported into the dominions of the Mamluks was re-exported to India. This was in fact an export trade that had begun a long time before.[362]

The heavy shipments of copper which the Venetian cogs and galleys carried to the Moslem Levant came from various regions. A good deal came from Central Germany and was sold in Venice by auction in the Fondaco dei Tedeschi. The copper production in Central Europe was in that period

[354] Misti 44, f. 120a.
[355] See Ph. Braunstein, "Wirtschaftl. Beziehungen zwischen Nürnberg u. Italien," p. 392.
[356] *Traité des famines*, ed. Wiet (Leiden, 1962), p. 69.
[357] *Shudhūr al-ʿuḳūd*, ed. L.-A. Mayer (Alexandria, 1933), p. 16.
[358] See my monograph *Les métaux précieux*, pp. 43 f., 56.
[359] Misti 44, f. 55a (copper taken by force from the Venetian merchants in order to make kettles for the sugar-boiling plants of the sultan).
[360] Misti 43, f. 10a.
[361] Misti 37, f. 99b ff.
[362] S. D. Goitein, "Letters and documents on the Indian Trade in mediaeval times," in his *Studies in Islamic history and institutions* (Leiden, 1966), pp. 340, 343.

indeed hit far less by the general crisis of mining than that of gold and silver.[363] The merchants who imported it to Venice were mostly the traders of Nürnberg, who were in contact with the rich copper mining centers of Saxony and Bohemia. Mansfeld, in the district of Merseburg in Saxony, was a great center of copper mining from the end of the twelfth century and its ore was exported to various countries. Probably the traders of Nürnberg also obtained copper from the Rammelsberg mines (near Goslar).[364] The mines of Kuttenberg in Bohemia began to supply copper to Nürnberg at least from the 1370's.[365] Another region from which the Venetians obtained copper was Slovakia, where in the districts of Banská-Bystrica (Neusohl), Spišská Nová Ves (Zipser Neudorf), and Smolnik (Schmöllnitz) rich mines had been found in the second half of the thirteenth century and at the beginning of the fourteenth. Later the mines of Lubietová (Libethen) also supplied great quantities of copper. Copper mining had developed greatly in Slovakia in the fourteenth century, since King Robert of Anjou had forbidden the export of gold and silver and foreign capital had been invested in the production and export of copper. A great part of the Slovak copper was sold to the traders of Nürnberg and Venice. Several decisions of the Venetian Senate, dating to the end of the fourteenth century, refer to "Hungarian" copper, that is, the Slovak ore.[366] A part of it was refined in Slovakia, mostly in the refineries of Neusohl (*Fuxine nove*), and transported to the Adriatic via Segna and from there by sea to Venice, or through Styria and Carinthia by land. Another part was refined in Venice.[367] Not infrequently the copper refined in Slovakia was shipped directly from Segna

[363] G. M. Thomas, *Capitular des deutschen Hauses in Venedig* (Berlin 1874) pp. 40 f., 42, 59, 60 ff., 86. Cf. J. U. Nef, *The conquest of the material world* (Chicago, 1964), p. 30.

[364] M. Mück, *Der Mansfelder Kupferschieferbergbau* (Eisleben, 1910) I, pp. 7, 8, 14 f., and cf. II, nos. 3-6; A. Möllenberg, *Die Eroberung des Weltmarktes durch das mansfeldische Kupfer* (Gotha, 1911), p. 10 f.; Fr. Lütge, "Der Handel Nürnbergs nach den Osten," p. 355; R. Hildebrandt," Augsburger u. Nürnberger Kupferhandel 1500-1619," *Zeitschrift für Wirtschafts—u. Sozialwissenschaften* 92 (1972), p. 3; about copper mining on the Rammelsberg, see K. Brüning, *Der Bergbau im Harze u. im Mansfeldischen* (Braunschweig, 1926), p. 104; W. Borchardt, *Geschichte des Rammelsberger Bergbaues von seiner Aufnahme bis zur Neuzeit* (Berlin, 1931), p. 73 ff., but cf. Fr. Rosenheimer, *Die Geschichte des Unterharzer Hüttenwesens* (Goslar, 1968), p. 151.

[365] R. Klier, "Nürnberg u. Kuttenberg," in *Mitteilungen des Vereins f. Geschichte der Stadt Nürnberg* 48 (1958), p. 62; cf. A. Schulte, *Geschichte der grossen Ravensburger Handelsgesellschaft* (Stuttgart, 1923) II, p. 196.

[366] G. v. Probszt, "Der deutsche Bergbau in Nordkarpatenraum," *Ostdeutsche Wissenschaft* IX (1962), p. 158; J. Vlachović, "Die Kupfererzeugung u. der Kupferhandel in der Slowakei vom Ende des 15. bis zur Mitte des 17. Jahrhunderts," in *Schwerpunkte der Kupferproduktion u. des Kupferhandels in Europa 1500-1650*, ed. H. Kellenbenz (Cologne, 1977), p. 148 ff.; P. Ratkoš, "Das Kupferwesen in der Slowakei vor der Entstehung der Thurzo-Fuggerschen Handelsgesellschaft," in Ing. Bog (ed.), *Der Aussenhandel Ostmitteleuropas 1450-1650* (Cologne, 1971), p. 584 ff.; Misti 38, f. 159b (a. 1384) 42, f. 25a/b (a. 1391).

[367] Misti 42, f. 25a 44, f. 16b, and cf. Ratkoš, *art. cit.*, p. 587.

to Syria and other Levantine countries by non-Venetians.[368] The Austrian merchants, those of Vienna and Wiener Neustadt, who, at the end of the fourteenth century, sold copper to the Venetians, offered them ore hauled to a great extent from the Slovak mines. The copper trade of the Austrian merchants was large. One of them exported about 9 t to Venice in 1369, in half a year.[369] The Slovak copper was considered to be of excellent quality. In a price list compiled in Damascus in 1394, its price is higher than that of "Venetian," i.e., German, copper.[370] The Venetians also obtained copper from Flanders[371] and exported it to the Levant.[372] This may have been copper from Sweden, where the rich Stura Kopperberg mines had been discovered in the fourteenth century, or it may have been Slovak copper.[373] Further, the Venetians could offer copper of Bosnia and Serbia, which they obtained from Ragusa.[374] The Ragusans themselves exported the copper of the Balkans to the Levant, sometimes on Venetian ships.[375] Finally, the Turkish copper should be mentioned. Copper brought from the mines of Castamuni and other Turkish mines was shipped to Venice,[376] but much more of it was sold by other Italian merchants in the Moslem Levant.[377] Certainly the Genoese engaged in this trade.[378] In order to hit the competition, Venice had to renounce a basic principle of her commercial policy and allow her subjects to do the same, that is, to ship the Turkish copper directly to the Levant.[379]

The volume of copper exported from Venice to the Levant was great. It was shipped both on galleys and on cogs. In 1355 it was decreed that every Cyprus galley should carry 80 migliaia of copper and tin.[380] Consequently, the Senate took measures to increase the supply and to guarantee the quality

[368] Misti 42, f. 25b, and see Ratkoš, *art. cit.*, p. 587 f. (quoting a Hungarian work of Pauliniy).

[369] Misti 33, f. 46a 35, f. 109a (copper refined in Fuxine nove); see further C. Schalk, "Rapporti commerciali fra Venezia a Vienna," *Nuovo Archivio Veneto* N. S. 23 (1912), pp. 288 f., 298; also merchants of Breslau sold in Venice Slovak copper, see H. Wendt, *Schlesien und der Orient* (Breslau, 1916), p. 48, and see below.

[370] Melis, *Doc.*, p. 384.

[371] Misti 23, f. 54b.

[372] *Les métaux précieux*, p. 61.

[373] J. U. Nef, "Mining and metallurgy in medieval civilization," *C.E.H.E.* II, p 439; Ph. Braunstein, "Le marché du cuivre à Venise à la fin du moyen âge," in *Schwerpunkte der Kupferproduktion und des Kupferhandels*, p. 86.

[374] D. Kovacevic, "Dans la Serbie et la Bosnie médiévales; les mines d'or et d'argent," *Annales E.S.C.* 5(1960), p. 257.

[375] Misti 34, f. 26b.

[376] Misti 42, f. 20a 44, f. 9a, 16b.

[377] Misti 42, f. 21b.

[378] See Verb. Cons. XII sub 9 March 1402.

[379] The decision was taken after some hesitation; see Misti 42, f. 21b; Braunstein, "Le marché du cuivre," p. 85.

[380] Misti 27, f. 28b; see also the freight tariffs for the Alexandria galleys Misti 23, f. 22b 30, f. 17a 38, f. 127a.

of the commodity. In 1382 the Senate reduced the impost on its import to half to keep copper from being shipped from Central and Western Europe to the Levant on other routes.[381] Then, in 1391, the custom dues for the import of Turkish copper were reduced.[382] These decrees were accompanied by measures for safeguarding the quality of the copper exported by Venetians to the Levant. In 1383 the Senate decreed that Venetians should export only copper refined or worked in Venice (i.e., copper vessels).[383] Then it was ordered that the copper refined in Hungary, which came to Venice via Segna and was exported to the Levant, should be marked by a stamp (*bolla*), so that its quality should be considered as warranted. The Venetian authorities forbade the subjects of the republic to sell unstamped copper.[384]

Tin and lead were exported in much smaller quantities. The tin the Italian traders shipped to the Levant came from England or from Germany. The production of tin in Cornwall and Devon had very much increased in the fourteenth century. Despite ups and downs, at the end of the century it was incomparably greater than at the beginning,[385] and both Italian and Catalan merchants shipped it to the Mediterranean. The tin carried to Venice on the Flanders galleys was certainly tin of Cornwall and Devon.[386] But the Venetians obtained tin from Germany as well. Like copper, it was brought to Venice by the merchants of Nürnberg and Austria and sold in the Fondaco dei Tedeschi.[387] The Venetians were already exporting tin to Egypt in the middle of the fourteenth century. In the last third of the century it was shipped to the Levant on both galleys and cogs.[388] It was sold in Damascus, Aleppo, and elsewhere.[389]

The shipments of lead[390] that the Italian ships carried to the Levant came from various regions. Much of the lead offered by the Venetians in the Levant came from the rich mines of Bosnia and Serbia, from Olovo, and other mines.[391] Most of it was shipped to Venice from Ragusa. In 1403 a

[381] Misti 37, f. 82a.
[382] Misti 42, f. 20a.
[383] Misti 38, f. 29a.
[384] Misti 42, f. 25b.
[385] Nef, *art. cit.*, p. 439; G. R. Lewis, *The Stannaries* (London, 1908), p. 252 f.
[386] Misti 23, f. 54b and cf. 55, f. 35b. See, further, Ruddock, *Italian merchants*, p. 91: the Venetians are the largest exporters of tin to the Mediterranean, see also Heers, "Il commercio," p. 177.
[387] Misti 27, f. 102a 35, f. 109a.
[388] Export to Egypt: *Nic. de Boateriis* no. 42 (a. 1360); freight tariffs of the Alexandria galleys, Misti 24, f. 22b (a. 1347) 30, f. 17a (a. 1361); freight tariffs of cogs, Misti 38, f. 127a (a. 1384) 39, f. 91b (a. 1385).
[389] Misti 37, f. 99b; G. P., Sent. II, f. 41a ff., and cf. 15, f. 48a ff.
[390] For the use of tin and lead in the Levant, see my *Les métaux précieux*, p. 84.
[391] D. Kovacevic, *art. cit.*, pp. 253, 257.

convoy of 300 horses carrying lead arrived in Ragusa.[392] But the lead of the Balkans was also exported to the Levant by the Ragusans and the Anconitans.[393] In order to hit the competition, the Venetian Senate, in 1388, permitted its shipping directly from Dalmatia to the Levant; however, payment of the customs which would have been due if it had been sent first to Venice was required.[394] The Genoese probably obtained lead from Sardinia.[395] The Venetians exported the ore regularly to the Levant, as is borne out by many records, for example, freight tariffs for galleys and cogs going to Alexandria and Beirut.[396]

What were the profits from the export of these metals? In the 1390's copper in tablets (*rame di bolla*) cost 82-85 ducats the migliaio grosso in Venice; in Alexandria, a ḳinṭār djarwī (of 90 kg) was sold for 16-20 dinars.[397] So the gross profit amounted to 25 percent. The profits from the export of tin and lead were apparently the same. A migliaio of tin cost 102.5 ducats in Venice in 1395, and at the same time in Alexandria a ḳinṭār djarwī was sold for 20 dinars, and in Damascus a ḳinṭār (of 180 kg.) for 40 dinars. So the gross profit was not more than 20 percent. The data on the prices of lead in Genoa, Venice, Alexandria, and Damascus point to a difference of 30 percent.[398]

Another sector of the export trade to the Levant was the marketing of agricultural products, mainly olive oil, honey, and fruits. The decay of agriculture in the Levant, a consequence of the rapacious methods of Oriental feudalism, was so great that Syria and Tunisia could no longer supply sufficient quantities of these products. Formerly, Egypt had imported them from those countries; in that period they were also imported from Southern Europe. The European olive oil and honey were used by the upper classes of Oriental society, whereas the lower strata of society had to content themselves with the cheaper and poorer quality products of their own countries,[399] for in the late Middle Ages a dual economy had come into

[392] *Art. cit.*, p. 257.

[393] Krekić, nos. 379, 392, and cf. my "Il commercio levantino di Ancona," p. 241 f.

[394] Misti 40, f. 135a.

[395] See the price list of Avignon published by Heers, "Il commercio," p. 162.

[396] Misti 23, f. 32b 24, f. 22b 30, f. 17a 34, f. 76b f. 35, f. 159b 38, f. 127a 39, f. 91b.

[397] Prices of copper in Venice: *Les métaux précieux*, p. 117, and appendix, p. 116 ff., and appendix C 1.; on the form of the copper shipped to the Levant, see Pegolotti p. 381. Prices in the Levant: *Les métaux précieux*, p. 61 f., and, further, appendix C 2.

[398] Tin: Dat 926, letters of Zanobi di Taddeo Gaddi of 26 May and 10 June 1395; *Les métaux précieux*, p. 85; lead: Melis, *Doc.*, p. 304; *Les métaux précieux*, *l.c.*; Dat 926, letters of Zanobi di Taddeo Gaddi of 26 May and 20 Aug. 1395; Verb. Cons. XII sub 20 March 1402. In the fifteenth century and at the beginning of the sixteenth century, the profits were greater; see my "The Profits from trade with the Levant," p. 254, and see also *Les métaux précieux*, p. 64. This was probably the consequence of the technological progress made in mining in the fifteenth century, see Nef, *art. cit.*, p. 457 f.

[399] See my "*Quelques problèmes que soulève l'histoire des prix*," p. 219 ff.

being in the Moslem Levant. All the trading nations of Southern Europe engaged in the export of olive oil to the Levant. Western Andalusia supplied excellent olive oil, which was shipped to the Near East mainly by Genoese.[400] The Venetians too purchased much of it.[401] However, the olive oil they exported to Egypt was mainly from Apulia,[402] but sometimes they shipped to Egypt oil from Tunisia as well.[403] The Genoese exported also olive oil from the Provence to the Levant.[404] The olive oil of the Campania was even more appreciated. It was shipped to the Levant by Gaetans and Genoese,[405] and the Catalans, too, sold great quantities of it in the Levant.[406] The volume of olive oil exported by the Venetians was particularly large. It was carried both by galleys and cogs[407] and they exported it not only to Egypt, but also to Syria.[408] The profits of the merchants engaged in this trade must have been substantial, since the difference between the prices of olive oil in Genoa and Venice, on one hand, and in Alexandria, on the other hand, was 50-100 percent.[409]

The honey which the European merchants marketed in Egypt and Syria came mostly from Greece and the Greek islands and from Catalonia. Honey of Candia, Coron, Mequinanz and other districts of Catalonia, as well as from Lombardy and Provence, is found in the price lists compiled in the Levant emporia by the agents of Italian firms.[410] The Venetians imported into Egypt honey from Apulia;[411] the French [412] and the Catalans of course the products of their own countries.[413] The import of honey into Egypt was by no means an insignificant sector of trade. The Venetian Leone Condulmier in 1402 shipped honey to Alexandria worth 1,698 ducats there[414] and another Venetian merchant sold to a Moslem there, in the same year, honey and nuts for 1,128 dinars.[415]

In addition to olive oil and honey, the Europeans imported considerable

[400] See above, p. 136. Cf. Piloti, p. 146.
[401] G. P., Sent. IV, f. 80b ff.; Collegio, Not. II, f. 162b.
[402] Misti 34, f. 47b.
[403] Vat. sub 25 May 1400.
[404] Vat. sub 1 Sept. 1401.
[405] See above p. 139.
[406] Vat. sub 1 Dec. 1400: a merchant of Barcelona exports to Alexandria olive oil worth 2964 dinars there.
[407] Misti 34, f. 130a 44, f. 6a f., 48a, 108b; see further, 41, f. 92b and Vat. I, f. 5a.
[408] Misti 35, f. 159 b.
[409] See, "Profits from trade with the Levant," p. 252 f. and cf. "Quelques problèmes," *l.c.* The conclusion concerning the price differences in the latter paper is based on data of the fifteenth century, but there is no reason to believe that a great change occurred.
[410] See my "Quelques problèmes," p. 224 f.
[411] Misti 34, f. 47b.
[412] Vat. sub 2 and 9 Dec. 1399.
[413] Leonardo de Valle sub 22 Dec. 1401. Madurell-Garcia, no. 151.
[414] Verb. Cons. XII sub 20 March 1402.
[415] Same records sub 25 May 1402.

quantities of various kinds of nuts, hazelnuts, chestnuts, and almonds[416] into Egypt. The merchants of Naples and the Gaetans were very much engaged in this trade,[417] as were the Catalans.[418] The Venetians exported these products to Egypt and Syria from Apulia and Crete,[419] and, along with others, from Chios and Rhodes.[420]

The quantities of saffron, another agricultural product which the European merchants exported to the Moslem Levant, were very small. But the price of this product, used as a dye and also in pharmacy, was very high; so it cannot be overlooked. It was indeed an important article of world trade in the Middle Ages. Saffron was grown in several provinces of Central Italy mainly in the Abruzzi, the Marches, Umbria, Tuscany, and Lombardy. The zyma saffron of the Abruzzi was held in high esteem and merchants of various countries came to buy it in l'Aquila[421] and exported it everywhere.[422] The Ravensburg Company purchased saffron in Foligno.[423] Another region from which much saffron was exported was Catalonia. At the beginning of the fifteenth century, there were offered mainly four kinds of Catalan saffron: that of Urgel or Balaguer, of Orta (Huerta), mercader, and that called lastet.[424] Milan, Casalmaggiore (in the province of Cremona), and Venice were the great saffron markets.[425] From Venice saffron was exported via Nürnberg to all provinces of Western and Eastern Germany.[426] In the course of time, the saffron trade increased so much that according to some records, the Germans bought a quantity worth more than 100,000 ducats every year in Venice.[427] There, both Italian and Catalan saffron was available. According to the reports of Datini's friends and agents, the saffron of Tuscany was the most expensive in the 1380's and

[416] See Misti 41, f. 92b 46, f. 94a: the *consolacium* to be paid to the Venetian consul in Alexandria for import of these commodities.

[417] See above.

[418] Vat. sub 9 June 1400: a Catalan sells hazelnuts in Tripoli.

[419] Misti 34, f. 47b; G. P., Sent. V, f. 84a f. (Lorenzo Loredan charters a ship for the import of 500-600 staria of chestnuts to Syria), IX, f. 23b f.

[420] Vat. sub 16 June, 1400; Verb. Cons. XII sub 9 March 1402.

[421] G. Mussoni, "L'antico commercio dello zafferano nell'Aquila ed i capitoli relativi," *Bollettino della Società di Storia Patria Anton Ludovico Antinori negli Abruzzi* 18 (1906), p. 248 ff.; L. Bardenhewer, *Der Safranhandel im Mittelalter* (Bonn 1914), p. 15 ff.; A. Petino, Lo zafferano nell'economia del medioevo, *Studi di economia e statistica* (Univ. di Catania, Facoltà di commercio e economia) I (1950-1951), p. 171.

[422] See ASF, Va serie Strozziana, 1746, f. 134a, 142b, 143a, 169b (export to Geneva).

[423] Bardenhewer, *op.cit.*, p. 17.

[424] Horta (Horta de Sant Joan) is a small town northwest of Tortosa and south of Gardesa; cf. E. Morera y Laurado, "Provincia de Tarragona," in Fr. Carrera y Candi, *Geografia general de Catalunya* (Barcelona, s.d.), p. 487 ff. Lastet is a kind of Orta saffron; see Bardenhewer, p. 19 g., and Petino, p. 193. Cf. Madurell-Garcia, nos. 135, 138.

[425] *Op.cit.*, p. 17; Petino, *art. cit.*, p. 183 ff.

[426] Lütge, *art. cit.*, p. 349.

[427] Ph. Braunstein, "Wirtschaftl. Beziehungen zwischen Nürnberg u. Italien," p. 338.

the 1390's, as it had been in the first half of the fourteenth century, according to Pegolotti.[428] Its price was always higher than the price of that of Lombardy and of the Marches, whereas Orta saffron cost more than that of Balaguer.[429] The price at which this article was sold in Damascus and Alexandria was not much higher than in Venice.[430] It may be that the merchandise which was exported to the Levant was of lower quality.

The South European traders exported luxury articles to the Levant too. The three articles most often shipped to the Near East were furs, coral, and ambergris.

The upper classes of Oriental society had always very much liked furs. The Mamluks who came to these countries from Russia and the Caucasus were especially fond of wearing furs. In the winter months they wore garments lined with sable, ermine, marten, beaver, and grey squirrel. The robes of honor given to their officers on various occasions were lined with furs. Even the theologians in the Mamluk kingdom wore coats lined with squirrel and trimmed with beaver.[431] Often the Mamluks took the furs from the Italian merchants by force, without payment.[432] The sultan himself did this.[433] Being so eager to have furs, the Mamluk rulers fostered their import by levying lower customs upon them.[434] The Venetians acquired the furs from German merchants and exported them to the Levant. Hanseatic companies and merchants of Nürnberg supplied them with sable, ermine, squirrel, weasel, and marten, which they themselves had obtained from Russia and Scandinavia.[435] But the furs of Sweden and the Baltic countries arrived in Venice via Flanders also.[436] The volume of the fur export to the Moslem Levant must have been considerable, for according

[428] P. 376.

[429] Dat 709, letters of Antonio Benincasa of 23 Dec. 1387, 15 Apr. 1388, 19 and 25 Jan. 1389, 23 March 1389; Dat 710, letters of Zanobi di Taddeo Gaddi of 27 and 30 March 1395, 10 Apr. 1395; Dat 712, letter of the same of 20 Nov. 1400.

[430] Dat 1171, price lists of Damascus of 6 Nov. 1379, 1 Sept. 1386; Dat 927, letter of Zanobi di Taddeo Gaddi of 5 Oct. 1395 containing prices in Damascus on 12 Aug. 1395.

[431] L. A. Mayer, *Mamluk costume* (Geneva, 1952), pp. 25, 52, 58, 59. The great liking of furs was, however, not a new fashion. In fact the import of furs from Northern Russia and other regions of Northeastern Europe into the Moslem countries of the Near East was already a flourishing trade in the days of the Abbasid caliphs; see al-Mas'ūdī, *at-Tanbīh* (Leyden, 1894), p. 63, and *idem*, *Murūdj adh-dhahab* II, p. 14 (translation Ch. Pellat, *Les prairies d'or* I, Paris, 1962, p. 164), and cf. G. Jacob, *Welche Handelsartikel bezogen die Araber des Mittelalters aus den nordisch-baltischen Ländern*, 2nd ed. (Berlin, 1891), p. 23 ff.

[432] Misti 43, f. 17b 37, f. 99b ff.

[433] Misti 43, f. 10a.

[434] Heyd II, p. 451.

[435] See W. Stieda, *Hansisch-Venetianische Handelsbeziehungen im 15. Jahrhundert* (Rostock, 1894), pp. 49, 90, 102. The furs sold in Venice by the merchants of Nürnberg came mainly from Lübeck; see Braunstein, "Wirtschaftl. Beziehungen," p. 394.

[436] Misti 55, f. 35b.

to the registers of the Venetian Senate the value of the furs taken away from a merchant sometimes amounted to 1,000 or 1,600 dinars.[437]

Coral was imported into the Near East mainly by the merchants of the Campania, Southern France, and Catalonia. The traders of Naples and the Provençals sold the coral found off the peninsula of Sorrento and Capri. In 1276 businessmen of Marseilles were granted a license for fishing coral in these waters. The Angevin king of Naples granted them other privileges for coral fishing in 1305, 1317, 1324, and 1366. In the middle of the fourteenth century merchants of Marseilles engaged in coral fishing also off Lipari.[438] A part of this coral was worked in Naples by skilled craftsmen who used it for the manufacture of knives with handles, chains, and other more expensive objects.[439] The Genoese exported to the Levant coral from Marsa al-Kharaz, near Buna, and also from Ceuta and Sardinia, while the Catalans exported coral of Sicily and Sardinia. The Catalan freight tariffs of 1374 and 1394 contain several kinds of unpolished and worked coral.[440] Also, the Venetians, who obtained coral in Apulia, imported it into the dominions of the sultan.[441] Even the Ragusans, who found it in the neighborhood of their town, engaged in this export trade.[442] The export of coral to the Moslem Levant became a flourishing sector of the Levantine trade, because in fact a great part of it was reexported by the Levantine merchants to Yemen, India, and China.[443]

Ambergris was also much in demand in the Moslem Levant.[444] The Venetians, who purchased it from German traders[445] and in Flanders,[446] exported it to both Egypt and Syria.[447] It was sold in Damascus in the 1390's for 2 ducats the 100 pesi (equal to a light Venetian pound).[448] That means that it was a very expensive article.

Most of the investment in the Levant trade of the South European merchants was put into the purchase of spices, aromatics, drugs, and dyes, which largely came from India. The Europeans bought them in both Egypt

[437] Misti 37, f. 101a 44, f. 55a.

[438] G. Tescione, "L'industria del corallo nel regno di Napoli dal secolo XII al secolo XVII," *Arch. Stor. prov. Nap.* NS. 23 (1937), pp. 338 f., 341.

[439] *Art. cit.*, p. 341 f.

[440] Heyd II, p. 609; Carrère, *Barcelone*, p. 636; Del Treppo, p. 737 f. Cf. above, note 202.

[441] Misti 34, f. 47b, 76b f.

[442] Krekić, p. 122.

[443] M. Clément-Mullet, "Essai sur la minéralogie arabe," *JA*, 1868, I, p. 202.

[444] See Misti 44, f. 120a. By the beginning of the Middle Ages, much ambergris was imported into the Near East from Spain, and the merchants realized high profits, according to an Arabic writer of the tenth century more than 200 percent; see al-Mas'ūdī, *Murūdj adh-dhahab* I, p. 366.

[445] G. M. Thomas, *Capitular*, p. 531.

[446] Misti 55, f. 35b.

[447] As note 441, and add Misti 46, f. 94a.

[448] Dat 927, letter of Zanobi di Taddeo Gaddi of 5 Oct. 1395.

and Syria, as the difference in their prices in these two countries was essentially insignificant. The cost of the spices bought in the greatest quantities was most often the same in Egypt and Syria. Those of some other articles, such as cloves, zedoary, and gum-lac were higher in Syria.[449] At the end of the fourteenth century, one of the most important articles of the Levant trade, namely ginger, was also more expensive in Syria.[450] On the other hand, it seems that for a long time cinnamon was cheaper in Syria than in Egypt.[451] Some of the price differentials were due to the preference given to transport by land for delicate spices, like ginger and cloves. They were preferably sent from Arabia to Damascus, so that the better kind was sold there.

Pepper and ginger accounted for the largest sums of money (or merchandise in case of barter) spent for the purchase of spices. The following table shows the role of these two commodities in the spice trade of the Venetians in that period, that is, the percentage of the total investment in spices. From this table it can be seen that the Venetians allotted 65-80 percent of their investment in spices in Egypt to the purchase of pepper and 10-15 percent to the purchase of ginger. Alexandria was indeed the great pepper market, whereas ginger was preferably transported to Damascus.

Since pepper and ginger had such great importance in the Levantine trade of the European trading nations, the fluctuations of these prices had a decisive influence upon the total of their investments. Both articles were rather expensive in the last third of the fourteenth century. These tables[452] are not complete, but they comprise sufficient data to draw some conclusions.

The price of a sporta of pepper in Alexandria in that period rarely fell below 60 dinars and often it rose to more than 80 dinars. In the 1370's it was still high, as it had been in the preceding decade.[453] In the 1380's it fluctuated. To judge from the prices in Damascus, apparently the price sometimes rose to more than 80 dinars, and sometimes it fell below 60. At the beginning of the 1390's the price rose again. In 1391-1393 it was very high, a sporta costing 80-90 dinars and even more than 100. This was certainly the consequence of conditions in India, for from merchants letters it is learned that the offer of spices in the South European markets was

[449] See my *Histoire des prix et des salaires*, pp. 418, 423, 424.

[450] *Op.cit.*, p. 416.

[451] *Op.cit.*, p. 414.

[452] See, further, appendices C 3 and 4, tables of the prices of pepper in Damascus and of ginger in Alexandria.

[453] Cf. the table of pepper and ginger prices in Genoa in my "Il volume del commercio levantino," p. 428.

Table IX Purchase of pepper and ginger of the Venetians
(according to the freight inventories of the galleys)

year	Alexandria galleys	Beirut galleys
1382	pepper 80% ginger 11.7%	
1386		pepper 65.7% ginger 15.1%
1393		pepper 61.7% ginger 11.2%
1394	pepper 68% ginger 15%	pepper 47.3% ginger 25.8%[a]
1395	pepper 70% ginger 11.6%	pepper 30% ginger 29%
1396	pepper 64.8% ginger 20.5%	pepper 37.4% ginger 20.6%
1399	pepper 84 % ginger 5.2%	pepper 5.2% ginger 34 %[b]
1400		pepper 54 % ginger 9.6%
1401[c]	pepper 49.5% ginger 22.6%	

a) In this year and in the following year ginger was very expensive so that the amount spent for it in Damascus, the great market of this article, increased.

b) In this year, the Venetians spent 37% of their investment in Syria in spices for cloves (and bought much less pepper than usually).

c) These estimates refer to an account of the purchases made until 22 September, see my paper The volume of Levantine trade, p. 582.

very small in those years.[454] The price fell in 1394-1395 to 60-70 dinars, but rose in 1396 again to 80-90. From 1397 to the beginning of the fifteenth century, it was about 70 dinars. The price of pepper in Syria was mostly equal to its price in Egypt,[455] but occasionally, as in 1396, pepper prices were much higher in Syria. In 1400 there was a steep rise because of the invasion of the country by Tīmūr.

The price of ginger was very high in the 1380's; it reached a peak in 1384 and in 1386 was still 50 percent higher than in the second quarter of the century. In the first half of the 1390's it rose very much. In 1393 a spice ḳinṭār (of 45 kg.) of beledi ginger cost 30 dinars in Egypt, 50 percent more than in the period of the Black Death. It rose even more in 1394 and in the following year amounted to double the price of 1348; in Alexandria it cost 45 dinars and in Damascus (a Damascus ḳinṭār) 152-180 dinars. In

[454] See Heers, "Il commercio," p. 208.

[455] See in the table appendix C 3 the data of the years 1386, 1395, 1398.

Table X Price of pepper in Alexandria, (1345 - 1402)

date	price of a sporta (225 kg)	source
1345	20 dinars	Pignol Zucchello, no. 13
Aug.-Nov. 1347	116 "	Op. cit., no. 44, 45, 52, 56
18 Dec. 1347	112 "	Op. cit., no. 57
23 Dec. 1347	110 "	Op. cit., no. 58
fall 1355	163 "	ASV, PSM Comm. miste 153, Com. Michele Boldu
fall 1366	75-86 "	G.P., Sent. II, f. 44a ff.
20 Feb. 1373	87.3 "	ASV, PSM Com. citra 74a, Com. Tom. Sanudo
26 Aug. 1384	63 "	Dat 548, letter of Zanobi di Taddeo Gaddi of 28 Sept. 1384
spring 1386	61 "	Ibid., letter of the same of 15 May 1386[a]
24 July 1386	60 "	Melis, Doc., p. 320
29 Sept. 1386	60 "	Dat 1171, price list
April 1392	88 "	Heers, ASI 113, p. 208
10 Aug. 1392	105 "	Dat 549; letter of Zanobi of 9 Oct. 1392
Sept. 1392	129 "	Braunstein, Rel., p. 269
spring 1393	90 "	Dat 549, letter of Zanobi of 8 May(?) 1393
Aug. 1393	82 "	Dat 710, letter of Zanobi of 25 Oct. 1393[b]
Sept. 1393	82-86 "	Dat 549, letter of the same of 18 Nov. 1393
20 Dec. 1393	81 "	Ibid., letter of the same of 11 March 1394
begin. 1394	61 "	Misti 43, f. 10a[c]
16 Feb. 1394	63 "	Dat 549, letter of Zanobi of 24 Apr. 1394
3 April 1394	60 "	Ibid., letter of the same of 21 May 1394
	60-62 "	Ibid., letter of Agostino di Tedaldo Benozzi of 21 May 1394

1396 the price in Syria rose to 200 dinars and more.[456] In the last years of the century ginger prices fell to the level that they had been in its first half.

The high prices of these spices were certainly due to a large extent to

[456] The discrepancy between the price curves of pepper and ginger, that of pepper going down in 1394 and in 1395, points clearly to the fact that conditions in India were the reason for the dearth of spices in the Levant (and consequently in Europe).

Table X (continued)

date	price of a sporta (225 kg)	source
27 Aug. 1394	61-65 dinars	Ibid., letter of Zanobi of 10 Oct. 1394
1 Sept. 1394	75 dinars, then 75-80	Dat 797, letter of Zanobi of 12 Nov. 1394
Sept.(?) 1394	75-80 "	Ibid., letter of the same of 12 Nov. 1394
begin. Sept. 1394	59-70 "	Ibid., letter of the same of 14 Nov. 1394
14 Oct. 1394	75 "	Ibid., letter of the same of 14 Nov. 1394
29 Jan. 1395	64 "	Dat 710, letter of the same of 30 March 1395
26 March 1395	67 "	Ibid., letter of the same of 17 April 1395
spring 1395	66 "	Dat 926, letter of the same of 13 July 1395[d]
9 July 1395	68 "	Dat 710, letter of the same of 7 Sept. 1395
12 Aug. 1395	69 "	Dat 927, letter of the same of 5 Oct. 1395
23 Sept. 1395	75 "	Dat 549, letter of the same of 4 Nov. 1395
17 Feb. 1396	82 "	Dat 1082, letter of the same of 19 March 1396
26 Feb. 1396	76 "	Heers, art. cit., p. 205
begin. April 1396	85 "	Dat 926, letter of Zanobi of 13 May 1396
June-July 1396	93 "	Ibid., letter of the same of 23 Aug. 1396[e]
Sept. (?) 1396[f]	96 " then 92, then 88	Dat 550, letter of Zanobi of 26 Oct. 1396
13 Oct. 1396	88-90 "	Dat 1171, price list[g]
25 Feb. 1397	75 "	Dat 550, letter of Zanobi of 23 March 1397
28 July 1397	68 "	Dat 962, letter of Luca del Biondo from Alex. to Valencia

conditions in the regions from which they were imported to the Near East. The sudden rise in prices at the beginning of the 1390's shows this clearly. But there were also other reasons for this phenomenon. There was still a great demand for spices in Egypt and Syria themselves; the general price level of foods was high and began to rise even more when by the end of the 1370's the dirham was debased. Secondly, the control of the spice market by the Kārimīs was unchallenged in those years, their power being at its apogee. On the other hand, the demand for spices by the European merchants increased considerably.

Table X (continued)

date	price of a sporta (225 kg)		source
fall fair 1397	63 dinars		Dat 797, letter of Zanobi of 12 Dec. 1397
22 March 1398	70 "		Dat 926, letter of Piero di Giovanni Dini of 7 May 1398
Oct. 1400	70-73 "	but going down to 64-62	Dat 1083, letter of Com. of Zanobi of 29 Nov. 1400
end of 14th century	70 "		Saminiato de Ricci, p. 124
1401	62-73 "		Dat 1171[h]
end April 1401	72 "		Dat 927, letter of Com. of Zanobi of 23 July 1401
Dec. 1401	71.5 "		Verb. Cons. XII sub 22 Dec. 1401
18 Jan. 1402	60 "		Dat 928, letter of Com. of Zanobi of 17 Apr. 1402
Sept. 1402	71 "		Leonardo de Valle sub 13 Sept. 1402
Oct. 1402	67-70 "		Verb.Cons. XII sub 21 Oct. 1402[i]

a) The writer of the letter gives no exact date to which the news refer.

b) As a.

c) The sultan sold by force to the Venetians for 80 din., see also Misti 43, f. 12a.

d) As a.

e) As a.

f) No date is given. The price fell after the arrival of a caravan carrying 3000 loads of pepper.

g) Heers, art. cit., p. 205 quotes this price list, but reads 85.

h) See my paper in JRAS 1976, p. 37 note 27.

i) The assembly of the Venetian colony in Alexandria authorizes the consul to purchase at this price.

The prices on the spice markets in Venice, Genoa, and Barcelona of course corresponded to the fluctuations on the Levantine markets. News of great purchases of pepper made by the Venetians in Alexandria or even about the arrival of large quantities of pepper in the great Egyptian emporium resulted in a fall of its price in Venice.[457] Although the prices of the spices in the great trading towns of Southern Europe depended on the purchases made in the Levant, they were not the same in Genoa and Venice. It seems that pepper prices in Genoa were usually higher than in Venice,[458] probably because the rates of customs and profits were higher and also because the

[457] Dat 714, letter of Bindo di Gherardo Piaciti of 23 June 1402; Dat 927, letter of the commessaria of Zanobi di Taddeo Gaddi of 9 Oct. 1401.

[458] See the tables in my "Il volume del commercio levantino," p. 428.

Table XI Price of ginger in Damascus
1379-1402

date	beledi	Meccan	colombino	source
	price of a ḳinṭā (180 kg)			
end 1379	68 din. (1700 dirh.)	56 din. (1400 dirh.)	160 din. (4000 dirh.)	Dat 1171, price list
8 Apr. 1384	224 (5600)	112 (2800)	208 (5200)	Ibidem
1 Sept. 1386	68 (1700)	34 (850)	64 (1600)	Ibidem
1 Oct. 1391		52 (1300)		Dat 549, letter of Zanobi of 4 Nov. 1391
22 June 1392	100 (2500)	52 (1300)		Ibid., letter of the same of 20 Sept. 1392
begin. July 1392	112-120 (2800-3000)			Ibid., letter of same of 9 Oct. 1392
17 Feb. 1393	140-152 (3500-3800)	80 (2000)		Ibid., letter of same of 18 April 1393
Jan. 1394	144 (3600)	68 (1700)		Dat 797, letter of the same of 24 April 1394
27 Feb. 1394	144 (3600)	68 (1700)		Dat 549, letter of the same of 24 April 1394
7 March "	140-144 (3500-3600)	64 (1600)		Ibid., letter of Agostino di Tedaldo Benozzi of 24 April 1394
13 July "	152 (3800)	68 (1700)		Dat 797, letter of Zanobi of 5 Sept. 1394
1 Aug. "	140 (3500)	152 (1800)		Dat 549, letter of the same of 29 Oct. 1394
29 " "	160 (4000)	84 (2100)		Dat 710, letter of the same of 4 Nov. 1394
begin. Sept. "	160 (4000)	84 (2100)		Dat 549, letter of Zanobi of 4 Nov. 1394
fall 1394	128-140			Dat 549, letter of Zanobi of 29 Oct. 1394
fall 1394[a]		68-104 (1700-2600)		Dat 710, letter of Agostino Benozzi of 27 Nov. 1394
23 Oct. 1394	180 (4500)	88 (2200)	168 (4200)	Melis, Aspetti, p. 384
1394	120-156 (3000-3900)	60-82 (1500-205)	(3000-3900)	Dat 549, letter of Zanobi of 4 Nov. 1394[b]

cost of living in the Western Mediterranean was higher. How much the level of spice prices in the great trading towns of Southern Europe depended also upon demand in Northern and Central Europe is shown by the reports that the agents and friends of Datini sent him from Venice, the greatest spice market of Southern Europe. The main customers on the Venetian spice market, in addition to the merchants who bought the not insignificant quantities destined for Northern Italy, were the Germans.[459] Substantial

[459] Dat 711, letter of Inghilese d'Inghilese & Donato & Cie of 12 Jan. 1398; Dat 713, letter of Bindo di Gherardo Piaciti of 31 Dec. 1401, 21 Jan. 1402.

Table XI (continued)

date	price of a kinṭā (180 kg) beledi	Meccan	colombino	source
20 Nov. 1394	140 (3500)	64 (1600)		Ibid., letter of the same of 4 March 1395
6 Jan. 1395	152 (3800)	75 (1800)		Dat 549, letter of the same of 30 March 1395
28 Feb. 1395	160 (4000)	88 (2200)		Ibid., letter of the same of 17 April 1395
24 March "	180 (4500)	100 (2500)		Ibid., letter of the same of 6 May 1395
8 April "	188 (4700)	100 (2500)		Dat 549, letter of the same of 11 May 1395
10 May "	210[c] (5250)	120 (3000)	210 (5250)	Dat 1171, price list
14 June "	164 (4600)	104 (2600)		Dat 710, letter of Zanobi of 7 Sept. 1395[d]
15 June "	200 (5000)	120 (3000)		Dat 549, letter of the same of 7 Sept. 1395
summer "		72-104 (1800-2600)		Dat 797, letter of the same of 14 Oct. 1395
summer "	196 (4900)	104 (2600)		Dat 549, letter of the same of 7 Oct. 1395
2 Aug. "	200 (5000)	104 (2200)	200 (5000)	Melis, Aspetti, p. 184[e]
13 Aug. "		104 (2600)		Dat 927, letter of Zanobi of 5 Oct. 1395
15 Sept. "	192 (4800)	100 (2500)		Dat 797, letter of the same of 27 Oct. 1395
begin. of 1396	212 (5300)	148 (3700)		Dat 926, letter of the same of 1 April 1396
" " "	212 (5300)	104 (2600)		Ibid., letter of the same of 6 May 1396
Feb.(?) 1396[f]	212 (5300	108 (2700)		Dat 550, letter of the same of 1 April 1396
15 March 1396	208 (5200)	106-108 (2650-2700)		Melis, Doc., p. 154
25 " "	208 (5200)	106.4-120 (2660-3000)		Dat 797, letter of Zanobi of 13 May 1396
8 April "			224 (5600)	Heers, art. cit., p. 205
April(?) "	224 (5600)	112 (2800)		Dat 550, letter of Zanobi of 27 May 1396

purchases by the Germans resulted in high prices and the departure of the Germans resulted in the fall of spice prices.[460] At the end of the fourteenth century all the great firms of Nürnberg already had their agents in Venice.[461] The German merchants not only supplied the great market of Central and Eastern Europe; they also re-exported the spices they bought in Venice to

[460] Dat 713, letter of Bindo di Gherardo Piaciti of 31 Dec. 1401, 18 Febr. 1402; Dat 927, letter of Commess. of Zanobi di Taddeo Gaddi of 20 Aug. 1401.

[461] Kress v. Kressenstein, "Beiträge zur Nürnberger Handelsgeschichte aus den Jahren 1370 bis 1430, "*Mitteilungen des Vereins f. Geschichte der Stadt Nürnberg* II (1883), p. 187 ff.

Table XI (continued)

	price of a ḳinṭā (180 kg)			
date	beledi	Meccan	colombino	source
5 May 1396	200 (5000)	112 (2800)		Dat 926, letter of the same of 23 Aug. 1396
summer 1396[g]	232 (5800)	104 (2600)		Dat 797, letter of the same of 23 Sept. 1396
4 Aug. 1396	224 (5800)	108 (2700)		Dat 550, letter of the same arrived in Pisa on 30 Sept. 1396
15 " 1398	81.6 (2450)	46.6 (1400)	63.3 (1900)	Dat 1171, price list
15 Sept. "			80 (2400)	Heers, art. cit. l. c.
14 Feb. 1399	53.3 (1600)	36.3 (1100)	45 (1350)	Dat 1171, price list
before 1400	1 pondo 56 duc.			G.P., Sent. VI, F. 29b f.
summer 1402	73.3 (2200 dirh.)[h]			G.P., Sent. IX, f. 17a f.
end 1402	83.3[i] (2500)			Dat 928, letter from Damascus of 22 March of 1403

a) This letter was sent together with the price list of 23 Oct. and the inventory of the Venetian Beirut galleys of 1396. Consequently it refers to the prices during the fall fair.

b) These prices were, according to the letter, those at which the Venetians bought through the year 1394 in Damascus.

c) Heers, art. cit., p. 205 reads 30 March 1395 - 5000 dirh.

d) But in his letter Dat 549, same date, one reads: beledi 5000 dirh., Meccan 3000.

e) Letter of Bertrando Mignanelli who adds that in fact it is impossible to find colombino.

f, g) No date is given.

h) Calculated according to the exchange rate 1 dinar = 30 dirh., but the tribunal calculated 1 ducat at 28 dirh. (that means at a higher exchange rate of the dirham) and fixed the price at 78.5 ducats.

i) The dinar was equal to 65 dirh. but the Italian merchants calculated according to an exchange rate of 30 (as before).

Flanders.[462] The Venetians themselves shipped much pepper and ginger to Flanders and England.[463] Even the Datini firm bought pepper in Venice, for export to England.[464] Venice also supplied a great part of Central Italy with pepper, and sometimes pepper was bought in Venice to be sent to

[462] Dat 713, letter of Bindo di Gherardo Piaciti of 26 Feb. 1402.

[463] See Dat 710, letter of Zanobi di Taddeo Gaddi of 1 March 1395: cargo of the Flanders galleys; Dat 926, letter of the same of 10 March 1397: the Flanders galleys carry 1,000 colli spices, two-thirds of them ginger; Dat 797, letter of Zanobi of 5 Apr. 1399: cargo of the Flanders galleys.

[464] Dat 713, letter Bindo di Gherardo Piaciti of 18 Feb. 1407.

Genoa.[465] The Datini firm also sold in Bologna and other towns pepper which had first arrived in Venice.[466]

Among the commodities exported by the South European merchants from the Moslem Levant, cotton was second only to the spices. The importance of this sector of the Levantine trade has been underestimated by Heyd and other historians, who had no access to the rich information in the Datini archives and other sources. The data in these sources amply confirm that the investment of the Venetians in the purchase of cotton in Syria was very large, sometimes equalling the sum spent for the purchase of spices or even exceeding it.

The growth of this trade, especially for the Venetians, was the consequence of the growing demand for cotton in Central Europe, where the fustian industry was fast developing in the last third of the fourteenth century. Because of a new conflict with the duke of Milan, the German emperor Charles IV in 1374 forbade trade with the great Italian emporium, a center of the fustian industry. This embargo on the trade with Milan, which had been the source of supply for the German fustian market, ushered in a new wave of promotion of industry.[467] There was a large increase in cotton weaving in Southern Germany. New manufacturers were founded in towns where none had existed before; in Ravensburg in 1379, in Regensburg and Constance in 1382, in Biberach in 1386, and in Basel in 1392. The fustian industry also spread to Bohemia and Silesia, where Prague and Schweidnitz became its centers. The raw material was obtained in Venice.[468] The other centers of the cotton industry were supplied with raw material from regions outside the dominions of the Mamluks. The Catalans bought a good deal of cotton in Malta, and the Genoese purchased supplies mainly in Turkey,[469] although both of them purchased cotton in Egypt and Syria as well. However, the Venetians concentrated on the export of Syrian cotton, and in the course of time this trade became a mainstay of the economy of Venice. Although the Venetians were not the only European merchants who exported cotton from Syria, the cargoes of cotton exported by other foreign merchants from Syria were incomparably smaller.[470]

[465] Dat 713, letter of the same of 21 Jan. 1402.

[466] Dat 713, letter of the same of 30 May 1400, Dat 549, letter of Zanobi di Taddeo Gaddi of 8 Oct. 1387 and accounts of 23 Jan. 1393 and 28 Jan. 1395: export of pepper to Pisa.

[467] Stromer, *Baumwollindustrie*, p. 128 f.; L. Frangioni, "Sui modi di produzione e sul commercio dei fustagni milanesi alla fine del Trecento," *Nuova Rivista Storica* 61 (1977), p. 535.

[468] Stromer, *op.cit.*, pp. 38 f., 40 ff., 43, 48. See about the purchases of a firm of Regensburg: F. Bastian, *Das Runtingerbuch 1383-1407* (Regensburg, 1935-1944) I, pp. 54 f., 550 f.

[469] Carrère, *Barcelone*, p. 637; Heers, "Il commercio," p. 393.

[470] Also Turkish merchants buy Syrian cotton; see Dat 927, letter of commessaria of Zanobi di Taddeo Gaddi of 23 July 1401.

There is good reason to believe that the cotton plantations of Syria were substantially enlarged during the fourteenth century. After the great decrease in the demand for grains, which must have resulted from the Black Death and subsequent epidemics, the peasants necessarily had to exchange cereal cultivation for other crops. The increasing demand for cotton by the European merchants induced them to engage more and more in this sector of agriculture. Comparing the development of grain prices and cotton prices in Syria and Egypt in the last third of the fourteenth century with those up through the fifteenth century, one sees that cotton prices rose much more than those of grains, which, in fact, after a slight rise at the end of the fourteenth century and the beginning of the fifteenth, dropped.[471] So it was that areas that had not been planted to cotton before, e.g., around Tyre and Sidon, were now so used.[472] Also in Egypt more cotton was grown than before, and the European merchants, mainly the Genoese, exported it to the west. It was known as cotton of Fuwwa or of Alexandria.[473]

In the last third of the fourteenth century the Venetians made the greatest purchases of cotton in Northern Syria, in the districts of Latakia, Sarmīn,[474] and Ḥamā.[475] In that period Latakia was the port from which the greatest shipments of cotton came to Venice.[476] The fact that the price of the Palestinian cotton ("cotton of Acre") is rarely given in the merchant letters from Venice of this period is a clear proof that the purchases of cotton by the Venetians in this region were still limited. But the activities of the Venetian cotton traders in Northern Palestine increased at the end of the fourteenth century. In 1391 the Venetian ambassadors Valaresso and Caravello had orders to ask for the protection of the merchants in this province.

471 See below Table XII, and cf. my "The development of prices in the mediaeval Near East," in *Handbuch der Orientalistik* I, 6, 6, *Wirtschaftsgeschichte des Vorderen Orients in islamischer Zeit*, part 1 (Leiden, 1977), p. 101 ff.

472 Lannoy, *Voyages*, pp. 110, 113, and cf. my "The Venetian cotton trade in Syria," p. 680 f.

473 The hypothesis of Heyd II, p. 613, that the cotton exported from Egypt was Indian cotton is not borne out by the sources, and see, on the other hand, the texts quoted in "The Venetian cotton trade," p. 685 f. The fact that the cotton price in Syria and probably in Egypt rose at the same time in which there was a sharp rise in the prices of spices must not be considered as a proof for the hypothesis of Heyd. The steep rise in the cotton price at the end of the fourteenth and the beginning of the fifteenth centuries was probably the result of a great increase in the demand or of shortage of labor. The lack of any hint to the Indian provenance of the cotton bought by the Italian merchants in the Moslem Levant seems to be a decisive argument against the hypothesis of Heyd. But it may be that the import of cotton fabrics from India into the Near East influenced the cotton price; that means that a rise of the price of these textiles owing to conditions in India resulted in an increase of the price of the Syrian cotton—see ʿAbdalbāsiṭ 812, f. 371b, about the rise of the prices of the Indian cotton fabrics in Mecca. At any rate, this is a mere hypothesis.

474 Sarmīn was called *Siamo* by the Italians because they confounded its name with Shām, the Arabic name of Syria; see my "The Venetian cotton trade," p. 678 f.

475 Misti 39, f. 25 b.

476 Misti 42, f. 116a.

Table XII Price of raw cotton in Venice, 1364-1402
(in Venetian lire di grossi)

date	Hamath	Sarmin	Acre	Egyptian	other & not specified	source
1364					14^{15}	Stromer, Baumwollindustrie, p. 157
1379	14-14 duc.				Turkish	Melis, Doc., p. 144
12 May 1384	6^{10}	5^{10}	6	5		Dat 548, letter of Inghilese d' Inghilese
27 Aug. 1384	5		5			Ibid., letter of Zanobi di Taddeo Gaddi
6 Jan. 1385	6^{5}	4^{15}-5^{10}				Dat 548, letter of Inghilese d' Inghilese e Michele Vai
19 Jan. 1385	6^{10}-7	5^{5}-10				Ibid., price list of Zanobi
26 June 1385	6^{5}-10	5^{5-8}				" "
21 Sept. 1385	7^{5-10}					" "
25 Jan. 1386	6^{10}	5^{10}				Ibid., letter of Donato Dini
25 May 1387	6^{5-10}	5^{5-10}				Dat 549, letter of Gherardo Bartolomeo e Franc. di Ser Stefano
4 June 1387	6^{5-10}	5-10				" "
8 March 1388	6^{15}	5^{10-13}		6^{5}		Ibid., price list of Marchione e Piero Turgiani
13 Jan. 1389	7^{5}	5^{9-10}	6^{5}			Dat 709, letter of Ant. Benincasa
12 Jan. 1390	8-9					Dat 710, letter of Zanobi
18 Nov. 1391		12 gr 4 13				Ibid., letter of the same
2 Dec. 1391		12 - 13	9^{10}-10^{10}			Dat 549, letter of Zanobi
27 July 1392	10^{5-15}	8-9				Dat 549, letter of Zanobi
27 Aug. 1392	10-10^{10}	8^{10}-9				"
16 Nov. 1392	10^{5}	8^{10-15}				"
1 March 1393	9^{10}-10	8^{10-15}				"
31 May 1393	9					"
26 July 1393	8	6^{15}-7^{5}				"
22 Nov. 1393	7^{15}-8	5^{10}-7				"
31 Dec. 1393	8-8^{5} and more	6-6^{15} and more				Melis, Doc., p. 302

Table XII (continued)

date	Hamath	Sarmin	Acre	Egyptian	other & not specified	source
30 Jan. 1394		6^{10}				Dat. 549, letter of Zanobi
11 April 1394	8^{10}	6^{10}-7				Dat 797, letter of the same
12 Nov. 1394	7^{10}	6-6^{5}				"
26 May 1395	7		7^{5}			Dat 926, letter of the same
24 July 1395	5^{10}-7^{10}					"
16 Sept. 1395	6-6^{10}	5-5^{10}				"
21 Sept. 1395	7^{5}	7^{10}		6-6^{10}		Dat 548, letter of the same
17 Nov. 1395	6^{10}-7^{15}	5-5^{10}				Dat 926, letter of the same
23 Dec. 1395	7	5^{10}-6				"
10 Dec. 1396		6^{10}-7^{10}				"
5 March 1397	10	9	9^{10}			"
20 March 1397	7	6^{10}				"
31 May 1397		5^{15}				Dat 711, letter of Inghiles d' Inghilese
7 July 1397		5^{10}				"
4 Aug. 1397	6^{15}	6				Dat 926, letter of Zanobi
1 Dec. 1397		9^{9}				Dat 711, letter of Inghilese d' Inghilese
18 May 1398		9				Dat 926, letter of the same
20 May 1398	9	8^{10}-9^{5}[b]				Dat 712, letter of Zanobi
25 May 1398	10	9				Dat 926, letter of Piero Dini
1 June 1398	10	8^{10}-9				Dat 712, letter of Zanobi
22 Oct. 1398	10^{10}	9^{10}				Dat 926, letter of the same
12 Dec. 1398	9^{10}	9^{4-5}			of Cyprus 7^{10}	Dat 712, letter Inghilese d' Inghilese
6 Sept. 1399	8	6^{10}				Dat 927, letter of Piero Dini
20 Dec. 1399	8 1/2-9	7-7 1/2		8-8 1/2		Dat 712, letter of Zanobi di Taddeo Gaddi
16 Jan. 1400	8 1/2	7-7 1/2				Ibid, letter of the same
9 Feb. 1400	9	7			Turkish 6	Ibid., letter of Nofri d'Andrea
spring 1400		6-6 1/2[c]				Dat 713, letter of Bindo Piaciti of 3 March 1400

Table XII (continued)

date	Hamath	Sarmin	Acre	Egyptian	other & not specified	source
19 July 1400	6^{15}	5 s 10				Dat 927, letter of Bernardo degli Alberti
21 Aug. 1400	6	5-5 s 10				Ibid., letter of Com. of Zanobi di Taddeo Gaddi
20 Oct. 1400		5 1/4-5 3/4				Ibid., letter of the same
6 Nov. 1400		6 1/2-6 3/4				Ibid., letter of the same
end Dec. 1400	6-6^{5}	4 1/2-5				Dat 713, letter of Simone Lappacino of 23 Dec. 1400
1400					5	G.P., Sent VI, f. 46b ff.
8 Jan. 1401		7, before 4^{15}				Dat 713, letter of Simone Lappacino
20 Jan. 1401					8-8^{5}	Dat 927, letter Com. of Zanobi di Taddeo Gaddi
1 April 1401	10	8		9		Ibid., letter of Alessandro Borromei
2 April 1401	10^{5}-11	7^{5-8}-8^{5}		8 1/2-9		Ibid., letter of Nicoluccio di Filippo Vina-ccesi
9 April 1401	10-10^{5}	8^{5}	9^{5}			Ibid., letter of Bindo Piaciti
15 April 1401		8 1/2				Ibid., letter of Com. of Zanobi di Taddeo Gaddi
20 May 1401	7-7 1/2	"low" 5 middle 5 1/2 fine 6				Ibid., letter of the same
29 May 1401					great supply; low prices: good cotton	Ibid., letter of Bindo Piaciti
4 June 1401					6 1/2-7, formerly 8 1/2 - 9	
4 June 1401					good cotton: 6 1/2 - 7	Ibid., letter of the same
11 June 1401		7 1/2 - 8			8 1/2 - 9	Ibid., letter of Com. of Zanobi di Taddeo Gaddi
16 July 1401	8-8 3/4	7-7 1/2		8-8^{15}		Ibid., "
23 July 1401	9	7^{5}-7 1/2		8-8 1/2		Ibid., "[d]
3 Sept. 1401		7 1/2				Ibid., "
17 Sept. 1401		7 1/2				Ibid., "
1 Oct. 1401	9-8 1/2					Dat 713, letter of Bindo Piaciti

Table XII (continued)

date	Hamath	Sarmin	Acre	Egyptian	other & not specified	source
9 Oct. 1401					bad news from Syria, 8-10	Dat 927, letter Com. of Zanobi di Taddeo Gaddi
26 Nov. 1401	9	7^{5-8}				Ibid., letter of Simone Lappacino
11 Feb. 1402		7^{15}	8 1/2			Dat 713, letter of Bindo Piaciti
2 April 1402		$7\text{-}7^{5}$				Dat 928, letter of Com. of Zanobi di Taddeo Gaddi
15 April 1402	9	7-7 1/2	8-8 1/2			Ibid., letter of Bindo Piaciti
6 May 1402					7^{15}-8	Dat 928, letter of Com. of Zanobi di Taddeo Gaddi
13 May 1402	9	7 1/2	8 1/2			Ibid., letter of Bindo Piaciti
5 Aug. 1402		6 - 7				Ibid., letter of Com. of Zanobi di Taddeo Gaddi

a) *The prices are those of 1000 light Venetian pounds, other than those of 1379,* which are for 100 pounds. They are given in Lire di grossi (1 l = 10 duc.) and soldi (1 lira = 20 soldi, 1 s = 12 gr). If the source is a letter of the same date, it is not repeated.

b) The writer of the letter does not specify the kind, but it is clear that it is Sarmin cotton.

c) This is not a report, but a prognostication.

d) The letter contains news about the dearth of cotton in Syria. So these prices point to the fact that there were still great stocks of cotton in Venice.

In the last years of the fourteenth century their purchases of cotton in Northern Palestine amounted perhaps to less than a fifth of the cotton they bought in all provinces of Syria and Palestine.[477]

According to Pegolotti,[478] the best cotton in Syria was that of Ḥamā; that of Sarmīn ranked second, and the Palestinian third. However, the merchant letters of this period require modification of this statement, as far as the last quarter of the fourteenth century is concerned. From these data, it appears that the quality of the Palestinian cotton was considered

[477] Misti 42, f. 15b ff.; Dat 550, letters of Donato di Bonifazio of 30 Apr. and 22 Nov. 1399.

[478] P. 366.

better than that of the Sarmīn cotton, though not up to the Ḥamā cotton. The cost of the Ḥamā cotton in Venice was always 10-20 percent more than that of the Sarmīn cotton, while the price of the Egyptian cotton was a bit lower than that of Ḥamā but more than that of Sarmīn.[479] From the data on cotton prices in Venice[480] it will be concluded that the "normal price" of a North Syrian ḳinṭār (of 217 kg)[481] of Ḥamā cotton at the end of the fourteenth century was 20 dinars (25 ducats). In Egypt a ḳinṭār (of 45 kg) in 1347, when prices were very high, cost 4 dinars,[482] and, in 1386, 3 1/2 dinars.[483] In Venice in the last quarter of the fourteenth century, the price of a migliaio (1,000 light pounds, i.e., 30 kg) of Ḥamā cotton was 60-70 ducats. This was its price in 1387 and 1395-1397 and in the second half of the year 1400. Sometimes it rose to 80 ducats and even more, e.g., in 1393. This was probably the consequence of the advance of Tīmūr: it was feared that the Mongol conqueror would invade Syria and that cotton would not be available at all. The contemporary rise of spice prices had obviously no connection with the dearth of cotton. Pepper was already very expensive in 1391-1392.

At the end of the fourteenth century, Venice was already the largest cotton market of Southern Europe. It supplied not only the German industries, but also those of much of Italy and of Northwestern Europe. The Datini firm exported cotton from Venice to Milan, Mantua, Genoa, Pisa, and Bologna,[484] and also to Majorca and Flanders.[485]

Another raw material that the Italian merchants exported from Syria (and also from Egypt, though on a smaller scale) was alkali. The sale of the ashes of two plants, Salsola soda L. and Salsola kali L., which were burnt by the Bedouins and which they were obliged to deliver to the Mamluk authorities, was a monopoly of the latter, who to a great extent

[479] See Table XII, and see also L. Frangioni, *art. cit.*, p. 508.

[480] Cf. on cotton prices in Syria "The Venetian cotton trade," p. 701 ff. To the data listed there should be added the prices mentioned by Zanobi di Taddeo Gaddi Dat 926, letter of 1 April 1396, quoting news from Syria (without date). According to them the prices there at the beginning of 1396 were: cotton of Ḥamā 800 dirh. (32 dinars) and cotton of Sarmīn, 600 dirh. (24 dinars).

[481] See *art. cit.*, p. 700 f. (note 193).

[482] *Pignol Zucchello*, nos. 56, 57.

[483] Melis, *Doc.*, p. 320.

[484] Dat 713, letters of Bindo di Gherardo Piaciti of 8 and 15 Oct. 1401; see also letter of the same Dat 714, of 26 Aug.; further Frangioni, *art. cit.*, p. 506 f., and appendix; Dat 709, letter of Antonio Benincasa of 30 May 1388. About export to Lombardy, see also Dat 548, letter of Zanobı dı Taddeo Gaddi of 6 Nov. 1386; about export to Pisa, Dat 550, letter of the same of 25 June 1400, and letter of Donato di Bonifazio of 5 Aug. 1399; about export to Bologna, Dat 550, letter of Donato of 14 Aug. 1399; see, further, *ibid.*, his letter of 8 August 1399, about the voluminous purchases that the traders of Lombardy had made of cotton in Venice.

[485] Dat 1082, letter of Zanobi di Taddeo Gaddi of 12 May 1397; Dat 550, letter of Com. of Zanobi of 16 Apr. 1401.

sold the product to the European merchants. This material, containing about 50 percent of sodium oxyde was called *ushnān* by the Arabs (and in the vernacular *kali*) and by the Italians *lume catina*. It was used for the production of both soap and glass.[486] Sometimes it served also as an ingredient for the production of majolica. So it was a raw material which was always very much in demand.[487] This was a cheap product, a Damascus ḳinṭār amounting to no more than 2 ducats in Syria.[488] But since it served as ballast and was very much in demand in the industrial centers of Europe, significant quantities of it were shipped to the Italian ports by the Venetians, Anconitans, and others. The Genoese too engaged in its export from Syria.[489]

A sector of trade which is relatively infrequently mentioned in the sources was that of precious stones. It is not difficult to understand why so few references to this sector of trade are found: the merchants concealed the precious stones for the sake of security. But Egypt had always been a market for precious stones, which were brought there from India and from other countries, and enterprising Italian merchants realized great profits from the trade. An Arabic chronicler recounts that in 1369 precious stones had been stolen from the sultan and that a European merchant offered one of them to the governor of Damascus.[490] Sometimes the merchants could not conceal the stones and had to declare their value. So we find in the Genoese custom registers that in 1377 the cog of Antonio de Vignolo carried jewels worth 2,640 ducats from Alexandria and that of Lucchetto Busenga jewels worth 9,150 ducats.[491]

E. The Volume of Trade

The Genoese customs registers of the 1370's that have come down to us and the freight inventories and merchant letters in the Datini archives make it possible to guess at the total investment of the South European trading nations in the Levantine trade. Although our knowledge of the significance

[486] See A. de Boucheman, *Une petite cité caravanière—Suné* (Damascus, w.d.), p. 77 ff.; J. Cantineau, *Le dialecte arabe de Palmyra* (Beirut, 1935), II, p. 70 ff.; R. Mantran-J. Sauvaget, *Règlements fiscaux ottomans* (Beirut, 1951), p. 22 ff., 69; cf. my lecture "Le Proche-Orient au bas moyen âge—une region sous-developpée," *Xa Settimana di studio, Istituto Fr. Datini*, p. 406 ff. Alkali was exported both from Syria and Egypt; see *Zibaldone da Canal*, pp. 66, 134, and cf. Pegolotti, pp. 141, 419.

[487] In 1394 Venice forbade its export to Milan, whereupon Giangaleazzo Visconti threatened with reprisals; see *Libr. Com.* III, lib. 8, no. 415.

[488] See in the said lecture.

[489] See my "Il volume del commercio levantino," p. 432.

[490] *Sulūk* III, p. 171.

[491] See *art. cit.*, p. 413 f. Also Piloti, p. 136, mentions the export of *balassi* as a sector of the Levantine trade.

Table XIII Venetian spice trade at the end of the XIVth century[a]

year	Alexandria galleys	Beirut galleys	
1382	60,000 dinars		
1386	purchases to 1 Sept. 68,000 din.		
1393		4 galleys	170,000 din.
1394	3 galleys, 1 cog 220,000 din.	4 galleys	110,000 din.
			330,000 din.
1395	3 galleys 200,000 din.[b]	5 galleys	180,000 din.
			380,000 din.
1396	4 " 172,000 din.	5 galleys	150,000 din.
			322,000 din.
1399	purchases up to departure of galleys 175,000 din.	5 "	180,000 din.[c]
			355,000 din.
1400		2 galleys	65,000 din.
1401	purchases to 22 Sept. 302,000 din.		

a) If no other source is given, all the data are quoted from Dat 1171. The same is true for the following tables, which contain data about the volume of trade. Some freight inventories are obviously incomplete. The totals in this table contain the additional cargoes loaded in Candia and Modon.

b) In a letter of Zanobi di Taddeo Gaddi of 4 November 1395 (Dat 549), one finds other data. According to this letter the galleys brought not 2100 sportas pepper but 1700 (and 400 sportas were worth about 27,000 dinars). But this latter inventory is obviously defective, since it quotes news from the beginning of the spice fair in Alexandria (the galleys departed from Alexandria on 28 October).

c) This total comprises the cargo of a pilgrim galley. According to a letter to the Datini firm, the Venetian purchases in Damascus until 22 September were 4500-5000 colli spices, mostly ginger and cloves, see Dat 927, letter of Zanobi di Taddeo Gaddi of 22 November 1399. But the freight inventory of the Beirut galleys comprises only 4313 colli.

of certain parcel units is incomplete and despite other difficulties, the major results should be fairly close to the actual magnitude of these commercial exchanges. For the investments in some commodities, namely pepper, ginger, and cotton, were so incomparably greater than those made in all other articles that a more or less correct estimate of the shipments of these items will prevent gross errors.

The estimates (in Table XIII) refer only to the spices, drugs, aromatics, and dyes. The other commodities carried by the galleys are excluded from the estimates because, on the one hand, the spices represented the greatest part of the merchandise shipped by the galleys and, on the other, the standard parcels used for them are better known. The assumption that at that time the Egyptian pondo weighed 180 kg and the Syrian 90 kg[492] is taken as the basis. The prices summed up are the FOB prices.[493] The Datini records provide us indeed with relatively rich data about their fluctuations at the end of the fourteenth century. Whereas some of these totals can safely be considered as representing the whole of the investments made by the Venetians in a given year for the acquisition of spices, in other years (1386, 1401) only the amount of the purchases (in one country) until a certain date is known to us. We do not know the quantity of spices bought from this date to the departure of the galleys.[494] Further, after the departure of the galleys a large quantity of spices often remained in Alexandria, Beirut or another Levantine port, and consequently, additional ships were sent to collect them or the merchandise was loaded on the cotton cogs. In 1387 there remained in Alexandria almost 1000 colli spices and in 1388 800 colli. In 1393, 700 colli (bales) remained in Beirut and in 1394 (September) in Modon there were 2000 "loads" (carichi) of pepper to be shipped to Venice, and a cog carrying 500 loads was awaited there. An additional cog (*de rata*), whose cargo does not appear here, sailed to Alexandria to collect the merchandise that remained there. From the registers of the Venetian Senate and the letters sent to the Datini firm, one learns that 1,450 colli spices, worth 100,000 ducats, according to perhaps exaggerated views expressed in the said body, remained in Beirut in 1397.[495] In Alexandria there had remained in that year 1,500 colli spices. In 1398, 1,800 colli of pepper,[496]

[492] See my "The volume of Levantine trade," p. 573 ff.

[493] This is one of the differences between the following calculations and those made by J. Heers (who calculated CIF prices in Venice, which include the profits of the merchants). Further, Heers believed that the Egyptian pondo was equal to the Syrian, which is also called collo, and weighed 91 kg. The same assumption was made by Bautier, "Les relations économiques," p. 296 f. Consequently, the cargoes of pepper and ginger, the most important spices, which were exported from Egypt, were underestimated by these authors by 50 percent. Wake, on the other hand, believes that the Egyptian pondo was at the end of the fourteenth century equal to the sporta; see his "The changing pattern of Europe's pepper and spice imports, ca. 1400-1700," *JEEH* VIII (1979), p. 367, and see my remarks, "The volume of mediaeval spice trade," *JEEH* IX (1980), p. 754 f.

[494] See my paper in *JEEH* IV, p. 582 note a.

[495] Misti 40, f. 73b, 120a f.; Dat 549, letters of Zanobi de Taddeo Gaddi of 12 Nov. 1392, 28 Nov. 1393, 29 Oct. 1394; Dat 797, letter of the same of 12 Dec. 1397; Misti 44,.f. 26b f. (it was decided to send two cogs to collect the merchandise, see f. 27b f.). According to the agents of Fr. Datini, the merchandise left in Beirut was only 1,200 colli; see Dat 926, letter of Guido & Giov. Portinari of 25 Dec. 1397. About a cog which came in the fall of 1392 to Modon with spices purchased in Alexandria and Damascus, see the letter published by Braunstein, "*Rel.*," p. 269. Braunstein reads "con le dyte galye che sera aviendo pondy 330 de pip" etc., "che sera vegnudo de Damasco," etc. It should be: "che iera a Modon pondy 330 de pip,' " etc. "che iera vegnudo de Damasco," etc. "con nave."

[496] Dat 926, letter of Zanobi di Taddeo Gaddi of 2 Jan. 1399.

worth about 50,000 dinars, and in 1399, 1,000 colli spices remained in Beirut.[497] In Alexandria, in 1401, 1,700 colli spices remained.[498] So our table is not complete.

In any case, all the data show that in the last decade of the century every year the Venetians bought spices, aromatics and dyes, amounting to 150,000-200,000 dinars, both in Egypt and Syria. This was so in 1395, 1396, and 1399. In some years the investment in these commodities must have reached 450,000 dinars. In 1392 the Alexandria galleys brought 4,400 colli pepper and 400-500 ḳinṭār ginger. So the value of all the spices bought by the Venetians in Alexandria must have been not less than 200,000 dinars. According to another report, this convoy carried 1,800 "loads" (Venetian ones, of 120 kg) of pepper and the Beirut convoy 2,200. Their value may have amounted to more than 250,000 dinars since the prices of pepper and ginger were then very high. We have no cargo inventories of the Venetian galleys of 1398. But a business partner of Datini writes him that up to September 14 the Venetians bought 100,000 pounds cloves and 60,000 pounds nutmeg in Damascus.[499] These purchases amounted to perhaps 33,000 and 16,000 dinars, respectively. Our data point to a very large total of spice purchases, for the Venetians seldom bought such great quantities of these expensive articles. But in the 1380's the Venetian investments in the purchase of spices in Egypt and Syria were much smaller. In some years for which we have information, as in 1382 and probably in 1386, they bought far less spices, perhaps of 80,000-100,000 dinars value in each of the Mamluk countries. An account contained in a work of Marino Sanuto bears out the supposition that one should not consider the investment in years of great boom as characteristic of the volume of Venetian trade in the Moslem Levant, in the last third of the fourteenth century. When, in 1407, a Venetian ship coming from Alexandria suffered shipwreck, the loss was estimated at 35,000 ducats. The cargo consisted of cinnamon, frankincense, Brazil-wood, gum-lac, and indigo.[500]

[497] Dat 927, letter of the same of 5 Jan. 1400; Dat 1082, letter of Donat di Bonifazio of 10 Jan. 1400.

[498] Dat 713, letter of Bindo di Gherardo Piaciti of 19 Nov. 1401. On spices transported by cogs from Syria to Venice, see Dat 548, letters of Zanobi di Taddeo Gaddi of 26 Oct. 1385 and 9 Nov. 1385: a cog which carried 500 pondi spices, in addition to cotton, suffered shipwreck. See also Ainaud, "Quatre documents," doc. I: in February 1401, a Venetian cog carrying 500 pondi spices and another also carrying spices arrived in Candia. In the 1380's, however, the quantities of spices that remained in the Levantine ports and were shipped to Venice on the cogs were relatively small; see Dat 549, letter of Zanobi of 21 May 1387: less than 400 bales of spices remained in Syria.

[499] Dat 797, letter of Antonio Diotifeci & Cie of 28 Nov. 1392; Dat 549, letter of Zanobi di Taddeo Gaddi of 12 Nov. 1392 (the writers of these letters emphasize that the shipments from Beirut comprise much pepper); Dat 926, letter of Zanobi di Taddeo Gaddi of 9 Nov. 1398.

[500] *Vite de' duchi*, c. 838.

However, the galleys also carried other commodities to Venice. The different kinds of sugar loaded on the Beirut galleys in 1394 had perhaps the value of 10,000 dinars; in 1395, of 16,000; and in 1396, of 14,500. In addition, they had cargoes of silk and pearls. In 1395 the Beirut galleys carried pearls worth 60,000 ducats. Further, the cargoes included silken stuffs and bocasin. In the same year, 1395, the Beirut galleys carried 9,000 pieces of this cotton stuff, whose value was about 20,000 ducats.

So there were years in which the total value of the galley cargoes reached 350,000-450,000 dinars and others in which it was worth no more than 200,000. The boom of 1395-1399 was certainly the result of the great decline of trade in the Black Sea area.[501] The year 1401 was an exceptional one. In that year the Venetian galleys did not go to Syria, and in the preceding year the purchase of spices in Syria had been very limited, because of the invasion of the country by Tīmūr.[502]

From the freight inventories of the Venetian galleys one will also draw conclusions as to the share that the Venetians had in the Levant trade at the end of the fourteenth century. For summing up the spice cargoes of the Alexandria galleys one finds that they carried no more than 3,000 pondi even in boom years like 1394, 1395, 1396, and 1399. On the other hand, according to some merchant letters, the great spice caravans brought 10,000-12,000 pondi to Alexandria every year.[503] So the Venetians were still very far from having achieved supremacy in the spice trade in the Moslem Levant, although they already ranked first in the Levant among the European trading nations.

The export of Levantine cotton was a sector of Venetian trade that was strictly separated from the spice trade. The cotton of Syria, where the Venetians made the largest purchases, was carried to the metropolis by two convoys of cogs sailing to the Levant in February and at the end of August.[504] The friends and agents of Francesco Datini included information on the cargoes of these cogs in the letters they sent him from Venice. These data, which were unknown to several excellent historians,[505] must

[501] Rightly stressed by Bautier, "Les relations économiques," p. 295.

[502] See my "The volume of Levantine trade," p. 583, note 35. See, however, Dat 550, letter of Com. of Zanobi di Taddeo Gaddi of 19 Dec. 1400, where one reads that the cargo of four Beirut galleys (two others suffered shipwreck) was estimated at 300,000 ducats, i.e., 250,000 dinars.

[503] Dat 927, letters of the Commess. of Zanobi di Taddeo Gaddi of 25 Oct. 1400, 25 May 1401. In 1400 a caravan brought 8,000 pondi to Damascus; see the letter quoted in first place.

[504] See above and appendix A 1.

[505] Overlooking these data and calculating the Egyptian spice parcel (pondo) at 91 kg. instead of 180 kg., Heers arrived at the conclusion that the late fourteenth century was a period of decline (depression) in the Levantine trade; see his paper "Il commercio," p. 168, 187.

Table XIV Venetian cotton purchases in Syria at the end of the XIVth century

			source
1384	spring fair	5000 sacks raw cotton	Dat 548, letter of Zanobi di Taddeo Gaddi of 21 April 1384
	fall fair	3500 sacks " "	Ibid., letter of Inghilese d'Inghilese & Piero & Cie of 22 Oct. 1384[a]
1385	spring fair	6000 sacks raw cotton	Dat 548, letter of Donato Dini of 19 May 1385[b]
	fall fair	2000 sacks raw cotton	Ibid., letters of Zanobi of 26 Oct., 9 Nov. 1385[c]
1386	spring fair	5900 sacks raw cotton 350 bales spun cotton 150 boxes sugar 160 miglaia alkali 40 boxes pearls	Dat 548, letter of Zanobi of 15 May 1386
	fall fair	4000 sacks raw cotton	Ibid., letter of the same of 6 Nov. 1386
1387	spring fair	4770 sacks raw cotton 366 boxes powdered sugar	Dat 549, letter of Zanobi of 21 May 1387[d]
1388	spring fair	3450 sacks raw cotton 300 bales spun cotton	Dat 709, letter of Ant. Benincasa of 12 May 1388[e]
1389	spring fair	2000 sacks raw cotton 380 boxes sugar	Dat 549, letter of Zanobi of 6 May 1389
1392	fall fair	3500 sacks raw cotton 400 boxes sugar 500 " powdered sugar	Letter of Piero Bicharano of 4 Nov. 1392[f]; Dat 549, letter of Zanobi of 12 Nov. 1392
1393	spring fair	5000 sacks raw cotton 450 bales spun cotton 170 boxes powdered sugar	Dat 549, letters of Zanobi of 29 March and 18 April 1393
	fall fair	3500 sacks raw cotton 150 bales spun cotton	Dat 710, letter of Zanobi of 25 Oct. 1393; Dat 549, letter of his of the same date
1394	spring fair	6058 sacks raw cotton 500 bales spun cotton 486 boxes powdered sugar 790 sacks alkali 323 pondi spices	Dat 707, letter of Zanobi of Zanobi of 24 and 30 April 1394; Dat 549, letter of the same of 24 April 1394[g]
	fall fair	3500 sacks raw cotton 300 bales spun cotton 100 boxes sugar 450 boxes powdered sugar	Dat 710, letter of Zanobi of 4 Nov. 1394 and other letters of his[h]
1395	spring fair	3500 sacks raw cotton 250 bales spun cotton 200 boxes powdered sugar 1200 miglaia alkali	Dat 926, letter of Zanobi of 26 May 1395; Dat 549, letter of his of 17 April 1395[i]
	fall fair	4500 sacks raw cotton 180 bales spun cotton 700 boxes powdered sugar	Dat 549, letter of Zanobi of 27 Oct. 1395[j]
1396	spring fair	4800 sacks raw cotton 500 bales spun cotton	Dat 797, letter of the same of 13 May 1396[k]

Table XIV (continued)

			source
	fall fair	2500 sacks raw cotton 70 bales spun cotton 800 boxes powdered sugar 2000 sacks alkali	Dat 550, letter of same of 26 Oct. 1396; ibid., letter of Inghilese d'Inghilese & Donato di Bonifazio of 17 Nov. 1396[l]
1397	fall fair	little arrived, high prices	Dat 711, letter of Inghilese d'Inghilese of 1 Dec. 1397
1398	spring fair	4000 sacks raw cotton 100 bales spun cotton	Dat 1082, letter of Zanobi of 5 May 1398; Dat 926, letter of Inghilese d'Inghilese of 18 May 1398[m]
1399	spring fair	5000 sacks raw cotton 200 bales spun cotton	Dat 712, letter of the same of 6 May 1399[n]
	fall fair	3000 sacks raw cotton 60 bales spun cotton 1800 boxes sugar	Ibid., letter of same of 22 Nov. 1399; Dat 550, letter of Donato di Bonifazio of 22 and 29 Nov. 1399
1400	spring fair	8000 sacks raw cotton 600 bales spun cotton	Dat 550, letter of Zanobi of 11 May 1400[o]
	fall fair	3800 sacks raw cotton 130-150 bales spun cotton	Ibid., letter of Com. of Zanobi of 1 Jan. 1401[p]
1401	spring fair	1600-1700 sacks raw cotton 30 bales spun cotton but there remained in Syria 1000-1200 sacks raw cotton which would be shipped by a cog so that there would be 3000 sacks	Dat 713, letter of Bindo Piaciti of 26 May 1401[r]
	fall fair	1200 sacks raw cotton 40 bales spun cotton 800 boxes powdered sugar	Ibid., letter of the same of 19 Nov. 1401; Dat 550, letter of Com. of Zanobi of 9 Nov. 1401[s]
1402	spring fair	1300 sacks raw cotton 300 bales spun cotton	Dat 928, letter of Com. of Zanobi of 6 May, 1402
	fall fair	2000 sacks raw cotton	Dat 928, letter of the same of 6 Dec. 1402

a) Fl. Edler, Glossary of mediaeval terms of business (Cambridge, Mass. 1934), p. 190 quotes documents in Dat 124, where the same data are to be found.

b) In a letter of Zanobi di Taddeo Gaddi written on the same day (Dat 548) one finds other data: 6000 sacks raw cotton, 600-800 bales spun cotton.

c) On expected 3000 sacks, see the letter quoted in first place.

d) Dat 549, letter of Gherardo Bartolemei and Francesco de Ser Stefani of 25 May 1387 has: 5000 sacks raw cotton, 250-300 bales spun cotton. Both letters are written before the convoy arrived.

e) Dat 709, letter of Zanobi di Taddeo Gaddi of 12 May 1388 has: 4377 sacks raw cotton, 330 bales spun cotton.

f) See Braunstein, Relations, p. 269.

Table XIV (continued)

source

g) In the letter Dat 797, of 24 April 1394 one reads: 250-300 boxes powdered sugar. Dat 549, letter of Agostino Benozzi of 24 April 1394 has 6000-6500 sacks raw cotton, 450-500 bales spun cotton, but this is a prognostic.

h) In an earlier letter Zanobi writes that there would come 3000 sacks raw cotton, see Dat 549, his letter of 29 Oct. 1394, and the same datum is to be found in his letter to Pisa, Dat 549, of 4 Nov. 1394, and his letter to Genovan Dat 797, of 31 Oct. 1394. Dat 797, letter of Zanobi of 12 Nov. 1394, has 500 boxes powdered sugar and 400 of Cyprus sugar. In a letter Dat 549, of 7 Nov. 1394, he says that there came 3300-3500 sacks raw cotton and 200 bales spun cotton.

i) Dat 549, letter of Alexxandro Borromei of 28 April 1395, has 3500-3600 sacks raw cotton, 250-300 bales spun cotton. This is a prognostic.

j) Dat 797, letter of the same and of the same day and another letter of his, of 10 Nov. 1395, have 200 bales of spun cotton and 800 boxes of powdered sugar. Dat 549, letter of Lorenzo di Giacomo of 27 Oct. 1395: 4000-4500 sacks raw cotton, 200-250 bales spun cotton. This latter communication is a prognostic.

k) In a letter written a day before he says: 5000 sacks raw cotton and 600 bales spun cotton, see Dat 550, his letter of 12 May 1396. In a previous letter he had spoken of 3700 sacks raw cotton, see Dat 926, his letter of 1 April 1396 (written before the arrival of the convoy).

l) Zanobi in his letter quoted above and in others, Dat 797 of 4 Nov. 1396, Dat 1082 of 31 Oct. and 4 Nov. 1396, says: 2000 sacks raw cotton. These letters are obviously written before the arrival of the cogs.

m) In a preceding letter Zanobi spoke of 3500 sacks raw cotton, see Dat 712, his letter of 4 May 1398. In addition 500 sacks were brought from Alexandria, see Dat 797, his letter of 4 May 1398.

n) In another letter, Dat 927, same date, the writer does not mention the spun cotton. According to Dat 550, letter of Donato di Bonifazio of 30 April 1399, there should be added 500 sacks raw cotton bought by the sailors and there were 350 bales of spun cotton. In a letter of the same, Dat 550, of 6 May 1399, one reads: 500 bales spun cotton. Zanobi had in an earlier letter 150 bales of spun cotton, see Dat 797, letter of 4 May 1399.

o) Dat 713, letter of Bindo Piaciti of 3 April 1400, has 7000 sacks raw cotton and 1000 bales spun cotton, whereas Dat 1082, letter of Donato di Bonifazio of 10 June(?) has 6000 sacks raw cotton and 500 bales spun cotton, and cf. Dat 550, letter of the same of 8 May 1400: 8500 sacks raw cotton and 1000 bales of spun cotton. The letter of Bindo Piaciti, quoted in first place, is clearly a prognostication. The same news are, however, to be found in a letter from Milan, see Frangioni, in Nuova Rivista Storica 61, p. 507.

p) Dat 713, letter of Simone Lappacini of 23 Dec. 1400 has 5000 sacks raw cotton and 200 bales spun cotton. According to a letter of the Com. of Zanobi di Taddeo Gaddi Dat 712, of 25 Oct. 1400, the number of the bales of spun cotton was 500 and according to another letter of the same, of 6 Nov. 1400, - 400-500. In two other letters of the Com. of Zanobi, Dat 550, of 18 and 19 Dec. 1400, one reads: 3800-4000 sacks raw cotton and 90 bales spun cotton.

r) See also Dat 550, letter of Com. of Zanobi of 8 May, 1401: one expects from Syria and Cyprus 2000 sacks raw cotton.

s) The letter of Bindo Piaciti superseded another of his written on 8 October. In both letters he emphasizes the small quantity of the cotton purchases in Syria. There is another similar account in Dat 927, letter of Com. of Zanobi of 9 Oct. 1401. According to the letter of the Com. of Zanobi of 9 Nov. 1401 the convoy brought only 1000 sacks of raw cotton and wool.

induce us to change the old idea of the Levant trade. They show how great was the Venetian investment in cotton.

The data in the letters to the firm Datini show that at the end of the fourteenth century the Syria cogs carried every year about 8,000 sacks of raw cotton in Venice. In the 1380's, 5,000 sacks were considered to be an unusually large freight of a convoy. The author of the letters that contain the account of the spring convoys of 1384 and 1385 emphasize, in fact, the great volume of the cargo of the cogs. On the other hand, when a fall convoy was reported to carry only 3,000 sacks, it was considered as a poor one (as it is said in a report on the fall convoy of 1385). In an account on the spring convoy of 1389 (quoted above) one reads that 2,000 sacks raw cotton are a very small shipment, as this convoy usually has 3,500-4,000. When a spring convoy brought, in 1394, 6,000 sacks, one said in Venice that it was a peak not reached in the last ten years (as emphasized in one of the reports quoted above). But in the 1390's the total of the cotton export from Syria increased. According to a report on the fall convoy of 1,400 (quoted above), 5,000 sacks were the average total in fall. In order to calculate the total of the Venetian cotton purchases in Syria one can also sum up the average cargoes of the cogs. In the last decades of the fourteenth century the two yearly convoys numbered (together) 12 cogs or even more and a cog carried on the average 500-600 sacks of raw cotton. So one arrives once more at a total of about 8,000 sacks. Supposing that the cotton was packed in sacks containing 80 (Tripoli) raṭls equal to 150 kg (exactly 144 kg), the total of the yearly shipment amounted to 5,500 North Syrian ḳinṭārs (for the acquisitions were made in the hinterland), worth perhaps 140,000 dinars. But a part (unknown to us) of these shipments came from Cyprus.[506] On the other hand, the cotton cogs transported also weighty shipments of alkali, sugar, and other commodities to Venice.[507]

In some years the purchases were much greater. In 1386 and in 1394 they reached almost 10,000 sacks of raw cotton and in 1400 almost 12,000. The fall convoy of 1399 also carried 1,800 boxes of sugar, worth perhaps 30,000 dinars, so that the price of the cotton and the sugar amounted in that year to 170,000 dinars at least. Together with the 355,000 dinars invested in Egypt and in Syria in spices, there was a total investment of 525,000 dinars. These totals, however, include investments made in Cyprus. Sometimes they were substantial and certainly this is true for the latter year. This is borne out by a letter to the Datini firm that states that the

506 See about the sacks, my "The Venetian cotton trade," p. 700 f., and see about the prices *art. cit.*, p. 701 f. and above p. 179. About export of cotton from Cyprus to Venice see Dat 550, letters of Com. of Zanobi di Taddeo Gaddi of 8 and 19 May 1401.

507 About the shipments of sugar, see, in addition to the data in Table XIV, also Dat 548, letter of Zanobi di Taddeo Gaddi of 26 Oct. 1385: a cog carries 400 boxes of Syrian sugar in addition to other articles.

merchants travelling to Syria on the cogs in fall 1399 took with them 250,000 ducats beside silver money.[508] Even assuming that cotton prices were high that year, one cannot believe that more than 250,000 ducats (200,000 dinars) were spent for the purchase of 3,000 sacks of raw cotton, the said quantity of sugar and a small shipment of spun cotton. The total of the Venetian investment in Egypt and Syria in 1400 must have been 500,000 dinars, 300,000 in spices, and 200,000 in cotton. In the year 1395 the total investment reached 540,000 dinars at least. One should indeed add to the investments in cotton and spices the purchases of spun cotton and alkali. Usually a convoy brought some hundred bales of spun cotton.

Finally, one should take into consideration additional cargoes carried to Venice by cogs that were not part of the cotton convoys and also merchandise shipped on the pilgrim galleys, despite the prohibition against using them for commercial purposes.[509] The registers of the Venetian Senate contain permission given in 1382 (on various dates) to five ships to sail to Alexandria.[510] In 1387, in addition to the convoys, two cogs from Beirut arrived in Venice, and in the protocol of the Senate of May 1398 one reads that "many ships from Alexandria are awaited in Venice."[511] In a merchant letter one reads that in May 1400 a cog came from Alexandria to Venice and that one awaited three others, and, in another letter, of December 1402, two cogs carrying spices from Alexandria were expected.[512] These latter cogs evidently carried the merchandise that had remained after the departure of the galleys (the "rata"). Anyhow it is not likely that the value of the cargoes of all these ships, if added to the totals we have calculated, would change them greatly.

The Genoese trade with the Levant at the end of the fourteenth century is well documented too. The registers of the *drictus Alexandriae* and the general custom registers of 1376/7 contain the following information on the cargoes carried on Genoese ships in 1371 and 1377:[513]

[508] Dat 712, letter of Manetto Davanzati & Cie of 31 July 1399.

[509] Sometimes it was, however, allowed by the authorities; see ASV, Mag. Cons., Leona f. 56a.

[510] Misti 37, f. 48a, 68b, 92b, 97a, 98a. What Sottas, p. 143f. (quoting Riant in whose paper however I do not find the relevant text), says about 7 ships in 1382, 7 in 1383, etc. which should transport pilgrims apparently refers to these ships. It seems that this author has confounded or added the pilgrim galleys and other ships, which were licensed for travel to the Moslem Levant.

[511] Misti 40, f. 54a 44, f. 39b.

[512] Dat 550, letter of Donato di Bonifazio of 15 May 1400; Dat 714, letter of Bindo di Gherardo Piaciti of 9 Dec. 1402. See, further, Dat 797, letter of Zanobi di Taddeo Gaddi of 10 May 1396.

[513] See the full data in my "Il volume del commercio levantino," pp. 403 ff., 416 f. The data of the year 1376 (three ships coming from Egypt) obviously refer only to a small part of the cargoes, and consequently they have been omitted here.

Table XV Genoese Levant trade in the 1370's[a]

year	ship		ducats	in dinars
1371	galley of Nic. Struppa	spices	6,050	4,840
		other	46	36.8
			6,096	5,877
	cog of Lanzarotto Cattaneo	spices	14,466	11,573
		sugar	515	412
			14,981	11,985
	galley of Lodisio Joannisbono mastic	spices	53,381	42,705
		sugar	11,623	9,298
		other	169	135
			65,173	52,138
	cog of Matteo Maruffo	spices	15,853	12,682
		sugar	1,000	800
		cotton	220	176
			17,073	13,658
		total	4 ships	82,658 dinars
1377	cog of Joh. Grillo	spices, dyes	33,149	26,519
		other	9,179	7,343
			42,328	33,862
	cog of Rafaele Moronecio[b]	spices	325	260
		cotton	1,518	1,214
		other	87	70
			1,930	1,544
	cog of Manuele de Vedereto[c]	spices	9,751	7,801
		other	11,268	9,014
			21,019	16,815
	cog of Pietro Dentuti	spices	12,815	10,252
		other	23,281	18,625
			36,096	28,877
	cog of Ant. de Vignolo	spices	30,845	24,676
		other	34,418	27,534
			65,263	52,210

It would be preferable not to draw conclusions from the data of 1371, which cannot be considered as representing the Genoese investment for a whole year. They comprise only the customs levied in the first half of the year and, on the other hand, the peace between the sultan and the king of Cyprus was concluded at the end of 1370, so that the number of the ships returning from the Moslem Levant before the end of June 1371 was small. The cargoes of the 11 ships, which came back in 1377 from the dominions of the sultan, are probably characteristic of the volume of Genoa's Levant

Table XV (continued)

year	ship		ducats	in dinars
1377 (continued)				
	cog of Simone Lecavello	spices	63,513	50,810
		sugar	345	276
		other	3,949	3,159
			67,807	54,246
	cog of Oberto Squarzafico	spices	56,119	44,895
		sugar	361	289
		other	873	698
			57,353	45,882
	cog of Covello Vespera[d]	spices	2,104	1,683
	cog of Lodisio Joannisbono			
		spices	382	305
		mastix c	1,872	1,498
			2,254	1,803
	cog of Lucchetto Busenga	spices	14,207	11,366
		other	36,683	29,346
			50,890	40,712
	cog of Ioffredo Panzano	spices	17,950	14,360
		sugar	15,382	12,305
		other	93,161	74,529
			126,493	101,194
			total 11 ships - 378,829 dinars	

a) All the ships, besides that of Ioffredo Panzano, came from Egypt. The latter came from Syria.

b) The data (customs paid) refer obviously only to a part of the cargo.

c, d) Perhaps like b.

trade in the 1370's. They were estimated at 380,000 dinars. So calculating FOB prices, their value amounted to 250,000 dinars. Sixty to 70 percent of the cargoes were spices; most of the rest was cotton and sugar (in addition to commodities that are not specified).

The Datini archives contain freight inventories of Genoese ships that sailed from Egypt and Syria to Genoa or directly to England and Flanders in the last decade of the fourteenth century and the beginning of the fifteenth century. Unfortunately some of them have no dates. The following table contains those which are dated. The price estimates made here are based on the price lists compiled by Datini's agents and friends, so they are FOB prices. According to these data, in the years of the great boom, 1394-1401, five ships (galleys and cogs) sailed every year from the ports of Egypt and Syria to Genoa, carrying on the average cargoes worth 30,000-40,000 dinars each. Further, two or three Genoese cogs went directly from

Table XVI Genoese Levant trade
1391 - 1401

1391

ship of Buto Squarzafico
Alex.-Genoa

spices	23,000 din.
sugar	3,000
cotton, flax	4,000
	30,000 din.

1394

2 ships: Giorgio Riccio, Crist. Lomellino, Alex.-Genoa

spices	10,000 din.
sugar	3,400
cotton, flax	2,000
	15,400 din.

ship of Pietro Dentuto
Alex.-Flanders

spices	11,000 din.
cotton	500
	11,500 din.

3 other ships to Flanders[a]

spices	170,000 din.
cotton	10,000
	180,000 din.

total 6 ships 206,900 din.

1396

2 galleys
Alex.-Genoa

spices	70,000 din.
sugar	4,500
	74,500 din.

ship Lomellina
Alex.-Genoa

spices	49,000 din.

ship of Paolo Lercaro
Alex.-Genoa

spices	52,300 din.
cotton	2,000
other	3,700
	58,000 din.

1396 (continued)

ship of Rafaele Squarzafico
Alex.-Genoa

spices	20,000 din.
cotton	
flax	3,500
	23,500 din.

1395

2 galleys
Syria-Genoa

spices	75,000 din.
sugar	6,000
cotton, bocasine, silk	14,000
	95,000 din.

ship of Ottaviano Lercaro
Alex.-Genoa

spices	33,000 din.
alum	9,000
sugar	200
	42,200 din.

ship of N...Grillo and another cog
Beirut-Genoa

spices	28,000 din.
sugar	280
	28,280 din.

ship of N... Negro
Alex.-Flanders

spices	28,000 din.
alum	20,000
	48,000 din.

another ship to Flanders[b] (40,000)

total 7 ships 253,480 din.

1399

2 galleys
Beirut-Genoa[d]

spices	50,000 din.
cotton	10,000
	60,000 din.

1400

7 ships to Flanders[e]

1401

2 ships to Genoa and 4 ships to Flanders[f]

spices	200,000 din.

ship of Gabriele Grillo[g]
Alex.-Flanders

Table XVI (continued)

	total	5 ships	205,000 dinars	spices	29,000 din.
				sugar	500
				cotton	4,500
				alum	30,000
					64,000 din.
2 other ships to Flanders[c]				total 7 ships 264,500 din.	

a) Dat 549, letter of Zanobi di Taddeo Gaddi of 21 May 1394 and cf. Bautier, Les relations économiques, p. 297 (whose estimate of the cargoes is mistaken, as he reads in the inventory of the third ship 700 loads of cotton instead of 600 pondi pepper and 200 Meccan ginger).

b) See Heers, Il commercio, p. 171. This estimate is apparently confirmed by an account of the cargo of three Genoese ships which departed in 1395 from Alexandria, two for Bruges and one for Aigues-Mortes. According to this inventory, Dat 549, letter of Zanobi di Taddeo Gaddi, of 17 April 1395, the value of their cargoes amounted to 130,000 dinars.

c) Dat 797, letter of Zanobi of 10 May 1396.

d) Dat 550, letter of Donato di Bonifazio of 4 Dec. 1399.

e) Bautier l.c. According to Heers l.c. only six ships. Two of these ships are mentioned in Dat 1158, no. 127. Their patrons were Luigi Cabella and Battista di Allegro.

f) Dat 713, letter of Com. of Zanobi di Taddeo Gaddi of 6 May 1401, and Dat 550, letter of the same of 8 May 1401. In a letter published by Ainaud, Quatre *documents*, doc. I, *one finds data concerning the cargoes of three Genoese ships* that were to depart from Alexandria in 1401, two for Flanders and one for Spain. They point to a total value of 130,000 dinars.

g) Heers I. c. Grillo's ship, whose cargo inventory is quoted by Heers, was probably one of those which according to the letter of 6 May 1401 (see above note f), came (with three others) to Candia on the way to Northwestern Europe. So its cargo of spices should not be added to that summed up in the said letter, but, on the other hand, the author of this letter has omitted the merchandise other than the most important spices carried by the four ships.

the ports of Egypt and Syria to England and Flanders annually, so that the total of the Genoese investment in the Moslem Levant was 200,000-300,000 dinars a year. The convoy of seven cogs sailing to Flanders in 1400 carried heavy cargoes shipped from the Aegean, to compensate for the smaller purchases made in that year in Syria owing to the Mongol invasion. The five Genoese ships that arrived in the spring of 1401 in Candia (according to the letter quoted in the table) probably included the two ships chartered in Alexandria whose contract has been mentioned above. But there was another Genoese cog sailing from the Egyptian port in that spring (or at the end of winter) to Flanders, so that the total of the Genoese investment in Egypt and Syria in that year reached about 250,000 dinars. There may well have been years in which the Genoese investment in the Mamluk dominions was greater, but in that period it was not greater or even equal to the value of the cargoes carried by the Venetian galleys and cogs from Egypt and Syria. Although the number of the Genoese merchants, at least in Alexandria, was still greater than that of the Venetians, the volume of Genoa's trade with the Moslem Levant was already smaller than that of the Venetian trade. This was certainly the consequence of greater investments in cheap articles. The many Genoese ships that arrived in Alexandria and other ports of Egypt and Syria loaded heavy cargoes of less expensive articles as well as spices. The ship of Negro, for instance, in 1395 carried no less than 3000 ḳinṭārs of alum to Flanders.

The records found in the Datini archives concerning ships returning from the Moslem Levant to the ports of Southern France are not numerous, but they do make it possible to estimate the average volume of their cargoes. According to our estimates, the value of the cargoes of the ships sailing from the Levant to Southern France was smaller than that of the vessels of other trading nations. This may have been connected with the more limited demand of spices in France. For it seems that in France much smaller quantities of spices were consumed than in Italy and in some other European countries.[514] It goes without saying that our table sums up a small part of the shipments to Southern France from the Moslem Levant. But the acts of the Venetian notaries in Alexandria and the freight inventories and accounts in the merchant letters addressed to the Datini firm and other sources make it possible to complete the table compiled by E. Baratier of traffic between Southern France and the Levant in the late fourteenth century.[515] The additional data show that in the 1380's three to five ships from Syria and Egypt arrived in the ports of Southern France every year and in the 1390's mostly 2. Our sources also contain reports about seven ships which came to the ports of Southern France from the Levant in 1401, but almost all of them were foreign merchantmen. As may be inferred from the table, the average value of their cargoes was 25,000-30,000 dinars; therefore, the investment made by the merchants of Montpellier, Narbonne, and Marseilles in the Levant trade in the 1380's amounted to 50,000-120,000 dinars (FOB prices) and in the 1390's to 30,000-60,000.

The freight inventories of Catalan ships in the Datini archives that have dates (or more exactly those known to the present writer) are summed up in the following table. The cogs and the galleys whose cargoes are summed up in this table carried merchandise worth 20,000-40,000 dinars each (FOB prices). If the cargo was worth more than 40,000 dinars, this was due to the high prices of spice in that year. Our table, however, does not contain all the purchases made by the Catalans in those years in the dominions of

[514] See Bautier, "Les relations," p. 351, and cf. the texts I have quoted from an Italian cookbook in my "Profits from trade with the Levant," p. 273.

[515] See appendix A 4.

Table XVII Cargoes of French ships coming from the Levant

1387	ship of Ramon Pons Alexandria-Marseilles	spices	18,000 din.
		cotton, flax	1,000
		other	1,000
			20,000 din.
1394	ship of Paolo de Montesimoli Alex.-Aigues-Mortes	spices	3,000 din.
		cotton, flax	1,250
			4,250 din.
1396	ship of Jac. Ibalvi[a] Beirut-Aigues-Mortes	pepper, ginger	12,300 din.
		sugar	8,000
		other	15,000
			35,300 din.
1397	ship of ... Luziano Alex.-Marseilles	spices	26,470 din.
		cotton, flax	900
			27,370 din.
1399	Catalan galley Beirut-Aigues-Mortes[b]	spices	25,000 din.
		sugar	2,755
			27,755 din.
1400	"ship of Collioure"[c] Beirut-Marseilles	spices	25,600 din.
		sugar	5,675
			31,275 din.
	spinazza of Alvise Giuffrida[d] Alex.-Provence	spices	26,700 din.
1401	ship of Novello Lercaro Alex.-Aigues-Mortes	spices	30,000 din.

a) The inventory in Dat 1171 is completed by another in Dat 797, letter of Zanobi di Taddeo Gaddi of 18 Nov. 1396. This latter inventory comprises an item "448 colli" (not specified) so that the estimate is a guess.

b) See Heers, Il commercio, p. 175.

c) Art. cit., p. 171.

d) Dat 1083, letter of Com. of Zanobi di Taddeo Gaddi of 29 Nov. 1400.

Table XVIII Catalan Levant trade at the end of the XIVth century

	ships from Alexandria		ships from Beirut	
1371	ship from Alex.		ship of Francesco Casasagia	
	spices	10,000 din.	spices	14,000 din.
	sugar	1,000	sugar	3,360
	cotton, flax	4,000	cotton	20,000
		15,000 din.		37,360 din.
			total 2 ships	52,360 din.
1383			ship of Johan Carbi	
			spices	20,800 din.
			sugar	4,200
			textiles	1,000
				26,000 din.
1384			ship of Capo de Bon[c]	
			spices	55,000 din.
			sugar	9,600
				64,600 din.
1386			ship of Johan Manresa	
			spices	22,000
			sugar	1,000
			cotton	2,000
				25,000 din.
1389	ship of Pere Salom			
	spices	26,000 din.		
	sugar	3,000		
	cotton	1,800		
		30,800 din.		
1391			ship of Francesco Casasagia[e]	
			spices	55,700 din.
			sugar	3,800
			cotton, flax, bocasine	2,500
				62,000 din.
			ship of Johan Morella	
			spices	25,220 din.
			sugar	2,080
			cotton, flax, bocasine	1,300
			other	4,000
				32,600 din.
1391			ship of Pere Dertazo	
			spices	20,000 din.
			sugar	8,000
			cotton, flax, bocasine	2,000
				30,000 din.
			total 3 ships	124,600 din.
1394			ship of ... Pascal	
			Beirut-Collioure	
			spices	16,000 din.
			sugar	500
			cotton	3,000
				19,500 din.

Table XVIII (continued)

	ships from Alexandria		ships from Beirut		
1395	4 cogs in Rhodes[f]		3 galleys[g]		
	spices	128,655 din.	spices		28,000 din.
			sugar		3,500
			cotton		1,000
					32,500
			2 unknown ships		
			spices		30,000 din.
			total	9 ships	191,155 din.
1396			5 galleys		
			spices		208,000 din.
			sugar		18,000
			cotton		2,000
					228,000 din.
1397			4 galleys[h]		
			spices		94,600 din.
			sugar		3,400
					98,000 din.
			ship of Johan Manresa		
			Beirut-Collioure		
			spices		27,500 din.
			sugar		2,000
			cotton, bocasine		2,500
					32,000 din.
			total	5 ships	130,000 din.

a) If there is no other indication the ship arrived in Barcelona.

b) The owner (captain) is not mentioned.

c) The freight inventory of this ship and those of the ships of Pere Salom (a.1389) and Johan Morella (a. 1391) have been published by M. Spallanzani, Ceramiche orientali a Firenze nel rinascimento (Florence 1978), p. 145 ff.

d) Dat 705, letter from Valencia to Florence.

e) According to a document quoted by Capmany II, app. III, this ship and that of Johan Morella came from Alexandria.

f) Dat 710, letter of Zanobi di Taddeo Gaddi of 17 April 1395.

g) Besides the freight inventory in Dat 1171 see Dat 797, letter of Zanobi di Taddeo Gaddi of 21 Oct. 1395. That these galleys had little cargoes was probably the consequence of the conflict with the Moslems, see above p.

h) Carrère, Barcelona, p. 644.

the Mamluks. The freight inventory of the four cogs that came to Rhodes on their way to Catalonia in 1395 is not complete. But what is more important, the number of the ships that commuted between the ports of Catalonia and the Moslem Levant was much greater. From Catalan sources we learn that in 1390 at least five ships sailed from Barcelona to the Moslem Levant, in 1391 five, whereas in 1392 only three made this trip and in 1394 three. In 1397 (in addition to those listed above) another cog came from Beirut to Catalonia and a galley to Valencia.[516] In the year 1398 six galleys and two round ships departed from Barcelona for Beirut.[517] We know about four ships which sailed in the year 1400 from the Levantine ports to Catalonia, and there is informaton about two Catalan cogs that returned from Beirut at the beginning of 1401, one on the way to Aigues-Mortes.[518] In the latter year at least five Catalan cogs sailed to the ports of Egypt and Syria. Catalan sources indicate that four sailed to Beirut,[519] and the acts of the Venetian notaries in Alexandria show that at least four other Catalan cogs anchored there in that year.[520] In 1402 at least two Catalan cogs visited Alexandria.[521]

We may conclude, therefore, that in the 1390's almost every year five to eight Catalan ships returned from the dominions of the sultan of Cairo to Barcelona and sometimes to Collioure,[522] carrying merchandise worth 150,000-250,000 dinars (FOB prices).

So we have a great deal of information on the volume of the Levantine trade at the end of the fourteenth century, but it is still not possible to arrive easily at an overall estimate that could be considered as very near to the actuality. The difficulty stems mainly from two facts: the great changes in the volume of the trade in the last third of the fourteenth century, and, secondly, the disproportion of our information.

After an upsurge in the 1370's, the volume of the Levantine trade was rather limited in the 1380's, when the two great Italian merchant republics were exhausted after the war of Chioggia. In the 1390's, and especially in its second quinquennium, it reached a peak. The great investment in the first five years was due to the unusually high prices of spices; that in the second five years was a consequence of the efforts to compensate for the decline in trade with the Black Sea area. The data that has come down to

516 Carrère, *Barcelone*, p. 644, and see appendix A 3.
517 *Ibidem*.
518 Dat 713, letter of Simone di Lappacino of 8 Febr. 1401, letter of Bindo di Gherardo Piaciti of 3 April 1401; Dat 1083, letter of Commess. of Zanobi of 29 Nov. 1400.
519 Carrère, *l.c.*
520 Vat. sub 25 Jan., 11 Apr., 7 June, 18 and 26 July 1401; Leonardo de Valle sub 22 Dec. 1401.
521 See appendix A 6.
522 See above, note 316.

us from the eighth decade of the fourteenth century are unfortunately poor. We have full data for the Genoese Levant trade for only one year and incomplete data for the other years. The records of the 1380's are more numerous, but provide disproportionate information for several years and various trading nations. Full data are available only for the last decade of the fourteenth century. They point to a total investment of 400,000-500,000 dinars (FOB prices) by the Venetians, including a substantial amount of money spent in Cyprus. In the 1390's the Genoese invested 200,000-300,000 dinars a year in the trade with Egypt and Syria; the Catalans 200,000-250,000. Adding the investments of the minor trading nations—i.e., the merchants of Southern Italy, Ancona, Ragusa, and Provence-Languedoc—one arrives at a gross total of a million dinars or a bit more. But it must be emphasized that this great investment was due to two exceptional factors: the dearth of spices in 1391-1395 and the decline of trade with the Black Sea area after 1385. The volume of the Levant trade in the 1380's was much more limited. The connection between the spice prices and the total of the investment is clearly borne out by the fluctuations in the prices of spices. A ḳinṭār of pepper cost 80 dinars in Damascus in April 1386, and on September 1, 1386, 48.6 dinars. The decline of the price of the most important Oriental commodity, just on the eve of the yearly spice fair, shows convincingly that the demand was limited.

———IV———

THE ASCENDANCY OF VENICE (1403-1421)

A. The Decline of Oriental Industries

At the beginning of the fifteenth century a great change took place in the economic structures of the Near East: there was a sharp decline in industrial production. It would perhaps not be an exaggeration to speak of a collapse. Whatever the magnitude of the decrease of industrial production in the Levant may have been, it had far-reaching consequences for commercial exchanges with the European countries. It entailed a considerable increase in the import of industrial products into the Moslem Levant and the returns on this import trade made it possible for the European merchants to acquire great quantities of costly Oriental articles, practically by barter. Otherwise, they would certainly have encountered great difficulties in buying them, especially in periods in which the prices were high.

The crisis of the Oriental industries was not an unexpected phenomenon; it was in fact the end of a long evolution and was brought about by several factors.

A very important reason for the decline of Oriental industries was the rise in the price of labor, itself a consequence of the shortage of working hands after the Black Death and the epidemics subsequent to it. There was such a great increase in wages that a steep rise in the prices of all industrial products followed.[1] Another reason for the industrial decline was the great difficulty in obtaining good raw materials. Some dyes had to be imported from Europe, so that this too caused a substantial rise in production costs. As far as the use of bulky raw materials was concerned, the Near Eastern manufactures had to use those which they had worked with before.[2] On the other hand, a large part of the raw materials produced in the Levantine

[1] See *Sulūk* IV, p. 28; my "L'évolution des prix dans le Proche-Orient a la basse-époque," *JESHO* IV (1961), p. 34 ff.; *Hist. des prix*, pp. 316 ff., 404 ff.

[2] See my "Les lainages," p. 682 f.

countries themselves was not used in their manufacturing, but sold to the European merchants, who supplied them to the industries of various regions of Southern, Western, and Central Europe. The most important of these was cotton. It seems that the cotton plantations in Egypt and Syria were again increased at the end of the fourteenth century and the beginning of the fifteenth century. In Palestine the increase of the cotton plantations must have been particularly spectacular, for Western writers who described Palestine in the late thirteenth century and at the beginning of the fourteenth century do not mention cotton as one of its products. Neither did Ibn Faḍlallāh al-ʿUmarī, writing about 1345, mention it. But an Arabic author, who apparently wrote in the seventh decade of the fourteenth century, dwells on the importance of cotton planting in the district of Acre. The cadasters that the Ottoman Turks made after the conquest of Palestine in 1516 certainly show the great role of cotton-growing in the districts of Acre, Nazareth, Safed, and Jaffa. From the work of an Arabic author, who wrote at the end of the fifteenth century, one learns that Jerusalem then had a cotton market.[3] Although Syria and Palestine had their own cotton manufacturing plants, it seems that the greater part of the cotton crops was exported to Europe.

In addition to the high cost of labor, the importation of high cost raw materials from Europe, and the failure to use their own raw materials, the industrial structure was a decisive factor in the decline of Levantine manufactures. In the days of the Abbasid and Fatimid caliphs, there were royal factories in all Near Eastern countries, which apparently were often rented by industrialists and run as capitalistic enterprises. They employed mostly free, but also some compulsory, labor and produced for export. These factories, the so-called *ṭirāz*, are referred to in various Arabic sources. In addition to the royal manufactures, there was a flourishing private industry.[4] The competition between these industrial sectors induced the managers to introduce innovations, and the relatively large volume of the production made it possible to experiment. But, in the later Middle Ages, the private manufactures suffered so much from tax pressure that many were closed. The management of the royal factories, on the other hand, was corrupt and finally many of them were closed because they were no

[3] See Piloti, p. 69; *Die Pilgerfahrt des Ritters Arnold v. Harff* (Cologne, 1860), p. 159; *Ṣubḥ al-aʿshā* IV, p. 86 f.; B. Lewis, "An Arabic Account of the province of Safed," *BSOAS* 15 (1953), p. 483; *idem*, "Studies in the Ottoman Archives," *BSOAS* 16 (1954), p. 489; *idem*, "Nazareth in the Sixteenth Century According to the Ottoman Tapu Registers," in *Arabic and Islamic Studies in honor of Hamilton A.R. Gibb* (London, 1965), p. 417; Mudjīr ad-dīn al-ʿUlaymī, *al-Uns al-djalīl* (Cairo, A. H. 1283), p. 383.

[4] See the quotations in my "Les lainages," p. 668; my *Social and economic history*, pp. 97, 150 f.

longer profitable.[5] Thus, many of the Levantine industries were reduced to the level of small workshops, which could not afford long and costly experiments, so necessary for technological innovation. Even those royal factories that still functioned did not introduce new and better methods of production, since they had no need of them after they had succeeded in driving out the private manufacturers.

The decay of some important Levantine industries had begun a long time before. Over a period of several generations no innovations were made, and technological stagnation obtained in almost all industrial sectors. At the end of the fourteenth century and at the beginning of the fifteenth, the decay was accelerated by the impoverishment of many of the townspeople. The bourgeois classes could no longer afford high-class products. The frequent civil wars under the first Circassian sultans were fateful for these classes. Faradj, the son and successor of Barḳūḳ, became sultan in 1399 at the age of ten, and during the thirteen years he sat on the throne he had to withstand several revolts and make campaigns time and again against the rebellious governors of the Syrian provinces. Both he and the rebels imposed high tribute on civil servants, merchants, and others and took compulsory loans from the merchants.[6] These extortions had catastrophic consequences for the well-being of the bourgeois classes. Barḳūḳ was compelled to decree that even his courtiers should not wear costly silken garments.[7] In the reign of Faradj, the economic situation of much of the population of the Mamluk realm seriously worsened. Industrial production declined at a rapid rate; technological stagnation and general impoverishment resulted in a cataclysm.

The striking feature of the technological decline of Levantine industries in the later Middle Ages was the failure to use water power for new methods of production. The use of water-driven mills in various sectors of production was one of the great achievements of European industries in the later Middle Ages. Hydraulic power was used in the textile industries, in sugar refineries, in paper mills, and also in sawing and in the production of blades. In the Near East, water-driven mills were not unknown, and in the Persian countries, especially, they were commonly used. But several accounts in the Arabic sources of the later Middle Ages point to the fact that they were rarely used for industrial or even agricultural purposes in the Moslem Levant.[8] The Near Eastern industries used old-fashioned methods, and their products could not compete with those imported from Europe. This was

[5] *Khiṭaṭ* II, p. 98 f., Ibn Khaldūn, *The Muqaddimah* II, p. 67.

[6] *Sulūk* III, p. 1175; IV, pp. 30, 72, 116, 160, 161, 226 f.; Ibn Ḥadjar II, pp. 450, 457, 458.

[7] *Khiṭaṭ* II, p. 228.

[8] Abū Yūsuf, *Kitāb al-Kharādj*, transl. E. Fagnan (Paris, 1921), p. 89, note 2; *Khiṭaṭ* I, p. 248; my "Aspetti dell'espansione italiana," p. 9 f.; *Social and economic history*, p. 368 f.

the main factor in the great expansion of the European nations, which began in that period. A keen observer, who had experience in the economic life of the Levant, was fully aware of the importance of this phenomenon. Piloti says expressly that only the export of many European industrial products to the Moslem Levant made it possible for the Western merchants to make their purchases there.[9] It is sufficient to have a look at the list of European articles for whose import to the Levant duties had to be paid to the consuls of the trading nations,[10] in order to see how just this observation was.

The gradual decline of the textile factories, the most important sector of industrial production in the Middle Ages, is well documented. It had begun at the end of the twelfth and in the first half of the thirteenth century, or even earlier when the great centers of the famous linen industry in Lower Egypt had to be closed. Characteristically, the geographer Yāḳūt, writing in that period, did not know where Dabīḳ, the seat of a once-flourishing textile center, was situated.[11] al-Maḳrīzī recounts that in the third decade of the thirteenth century Tinnīs, another great center of the Egyptian textile industry, stopped production.[12] Probably this was brought about by the rise in the price of labor after the great pestilence in 1201-1202 and the technological stagnation. In fact, in that period the import of Flemish cloth to Egypt and Syria was already beginning.[13] It apparently increased very much in the second half of the thirteenth century, as is borne out by contemporary Arabic and Latin writers.[14] Production methods in the European textile industries had meanwhile improved considerably. The great upswing was mainly the effect of three important innovations: the use of the automatic spinning wheel, the treadle loom, and the water-driven fulling mill.[15] It seems that these innovations were not introduced into the Levantine industries, and the resulting technological stagnation engendered a decline, with the result that there was an ever-increasing import of European products. Various accounts indicate that European cloth and linen were imported into the Moslem Levant through the fourteenth century, but, on the other hand, in the same period there was also an export of Oriental textiles, especially of silken and cotton stuffs, to European countries. Just in the fourteenth century, a flourishing cotton industry had come

[9] P. 110.

[10] See, e.g., Misti 46, f. 94a (a. 1403).

[11] *Mu'djam al-buldān* II, pp. 546, 548.

[12] *Sulūk* I, p. 224; *Khiṭaṭ* I, p. 181.

[13] "Les lainages," p. 667.

[14] See the sources quoted *art. cit.*, p. 673 f.

[15] Lynn White Jr., *Mediaeval technology and social change* (Oxford, 1962), pp. 117, 119; E. M. Carus-Wilson, "An industrial revolution in the thirteenth century," *Ec. Hist. Rev.* 11 (1941), p. 29 ff.

into being in Baalbek and in some towns of Northern Syria.[16] The products of the Syrian cotton industry were exported to Egypt and to Southern Europe, to Catalonia, Genoa, and Venice.[17] Also, Egyptian and Syrian silk products were still very much appreciated in Europe in the fourteenth century. Of course, one cannot be sure that all the textiles called "Alexandrian" or "Damascene" in European documents were really Levantine products and not imitations, but the freight inventories of the merchant fleets of the South European trading nations contain many items that testify to the export of Levantine silken stuffs to Italy and Catalonia in that period. The Venetian Beirut galleys of 1395 carried not less than 800 pieces of camaca,[18] and in 1400 the king of Aragon ordered brocades in Damascus.[19]

However, in the first years of the fifteenth century Egypt and Syria underwent an economic crisis, ushered in by a crop failure and high prices in Egypt in 1403-1404 and aggravated by the long civil war under the reign of Sultan Faradj. The contemporary Arabic writer al-Maḳrīzī recounts that the inhabitants of Egypt changed their way of dressing: instead of costly, fine linen, everyone began to wear cheap European textiles.[20] There was undoubtedly a sharp decline in the industrial production of the Moslem Levant at that time. The account of the sudden change is certainly exaggerated. For the disaster that occurred in the first decade of the fifteenth century was a phase in a long development. According to the results of the census taken by the Mamluk authorities, the number of the looms in Alexandria, then a major center of Egypt's textile industry, had declined from 14,000 in the 1390's to 800 in 1434.[21]

The Levantine textile industries were not closed altogether. They still produced for export, and through the fifteenth century Oriental cotton and silken stuffs were shipped to Europe.[22] But, on the other hand, a true

[16] R. B. Serjeant, "Materials for the history of Islamic textiles up to the Mongol conquest," *Ars Islamica* 11/12 (1946), p. 141; Ḥ. Zayyāt, "The specialities of Baalbek in industry and agriculture in ancient times" (in Arabic), *al-Machrique* 41 (1927), p. 157 ff. The bocasine was a cotton stuff manufactured in Baalbek and other towns of Syria; see Wansbrough in *BSOAS* 28, p. 518.

[17] *Khiṭaṭ* I, p. 107; Dat 1171, freight inventory of ships of Joh. Carbi (a. 1383), Francesch Casasagia (a. 1391), Joh. Morella (a. 1391), Venetian Beirut galleys a. 1393, 1394, 1395, 1399; Dat 928, letter of Comm. of Zanobi di Taddeo Gaddi of 15 Dec. 1403: the Venetians bought bocasine for 20,000 ducats in Damascus; my "Il volume del commercio levantino," p. 425.

[18] Dat 1171, freight inventories of the Venetian Beirut galleys of 1393, 1394, 1395, 1399, ships of Joh. Morella and Pere Dertazo (a. 1391); "Il volume del commercio levantino," pp. 415, 425; on camaca, cf. Ibn Khurdādhbeh, *Kitāb al-Masālik*, ed. de Goeje (Leyden, 1889), Glossaire, p. 7.

[19] Rubió i Lluch, no. 668.

[20] *Khiṭaṭ* II, p. 98, transl. R. Dozy, *Dictionnaire détaillé des noms des vêtements chez les Arabes* (Amsterdam, 1845), p. 128.

[21] *Sulūk* IV, p. 909; *an-Nudjūm az-zāhira* VI, p. 714 (transl. Popper IV, p. 112).

[22] Piloti, pp. 90 f., 136f.; export of bocasine: Misti 48, f. 12b ff., 82a ff., 158a ff. 49, f. 125b f. 50 f. 4b; export of silken stuffs: Misti 48, f. 154a; Accounts Soranzo, c. 90.

dumping of European textiles began when at the end of the fourteenth century, great quantities of Catalan cloth were imported into Egypt and Syria. Catalan, Genoese, Venetian, and other merchants marketed the cloth of Barcelona, Perpignan, Miranda, Puigcerda, and Valencia. Much of it was acquired from the Catalans in Sicily, which was a great exchange for these products.[23] Florentine cloth too was sold in the Moslem Levant by merchants coming from various countries. Some kinds of cloth marketed in the Levant, like bastardo and gilforte, were originally produced in England and later in Italy.[24] All the European merchants imported Flemish cloth into the Levant too,[25] and the Venetians marketed some kinds of precious German cloth, e.g., that of Cologne.[26] That was when the import of English cloth also began. In the first decade of the fifteenth century, cloth of the Cotswolds and Essex was already being sold in Syria;[27] cloth called "of Southampton" is mentioned in a Damascus price list of 1424.[28] From the beginning of the fifteenth century, the European traders also imported silken stuffs, velvets, and other luxury textiles into the dominions of the Mamluks.[29] In 1392 a high-ranking dignitary of the court of Cairo gave a Venetian ambassador 1,000 ducats to buy 10 pieces of velvet for him in Italy.[30] But after the economic crisis in the first decade of the fifteenth century, the import of these costly textiles increased and especially that of scarlets and velvets, which were much in demand.[31] While these articles were intended for the upper classes of society, fustian and serge were sold to the middle and lower strata. The serge came partly from England and Ireland and was marketed by Italian and Catalan traders.[32] The fustian was surely produced by the North Italian industry.[33] A large portion of all these

[23] Nic. Venier B, 2, f. 1a, 10a/11a; Piloti, p. 147 ff.; Giacomo della Torre, no. 14; G. P., Sent. 48, f. 5a ff. 52, f. 94a ff. 54, f. 34a ff.

[24] Misti 52, f. 57b; my "L'exportation de textiles occidentaux," pp. 316, 345 f.

[25] Piloti, p. 144 f.

[26] Misti 50, f. 83b.

[27] G. P., Sent. 18, f. 3b, 30b; "L'exportation de textiles occidentaux," p. 343. In fact, cloth of Essex was already being sold in the Mediterranean countries at the end of the fourteenth century: see Dat 549, letter of Zanobi di Taddeo Gaddi of 27 July 1392.

[28] Melis, *Doc.*, p. 318.

[29] Misti 50, f. 104a 52, f. 57b, 60a 53, f. 89b, 118b. It is true that by the end of the fourteenth century the import of European silk stuffs to Syria had begun; see Dat 797, letter of Zanobi di Taddeo Gaddi of 31 Oct. 1394.

[30] Misti 42, f. 75a.

[31] Misti 48, f. 73b; G. P., Sent. 19, f. 96b ff. 22, f. 34a f. 29, f., 46a ff. 32, f. 5b ff. (Bartolomeo Gardelimo imports in 1420, or thereabout, velvet for 4,500-5,000 dinars to Egypt) 34, f., 37a ff. 39, f. 5a (in 1405 Marco Condulmier imports silken stuffs for 2,500 ducats to Alexandria) 45, f., 46b ff. (Bartolomeo de la Porta and Joh. Contarini ship in 1413-15, to Alexandria, velvet and other silken stuffs for 4,630 ducats).

[32] Misti 41, f. 92b 53, f., 104a, 214a ff. 54, f., 72a ff.; G. P., Sent. 16, f. 55b ff., cf. 65a f. 18, f., 23b ff., 95b ff. 32, f. 92a ff. 45, f., 119b 52, f. 45a; Del Treppo, p. 77.

[33] Import of fustian to Egypt and Syria: G. P., Sent. 19, f., 2a f. 70, f. (a leaf between 11 and 12; Misti 54, f. 74b).

textiles was especially dyed in the colors liked by the Levantine customers.[34] A striking feature of this great export trade, carried on by merchants of several South European trading nations, was the gradual decline of the prices of various textiles.[35] Probably this was connected with the general impoverishment of the Near East at the end of the Middle Ages. There was a downward drift of prices, and the European traders had to adapt themselves to this trend.

The development of another important sector of the Levantine industries, namely, the sugar industry, was very similar to that of textiles. Until the end of the fourteenth century, Egypt and Syria supported sizable quantities of various kinds of sugar. The freight inventories of the Venetian Beirut galleys and the cog convoys in the 1380's and 1390's usually included a certain quantity of sugar, and the same is true for the freights of Genoese, French and Catalan vessels.[36] Likewise, in the letters written in that period by merchants of the great Italian emporia, shipments and trade in Syrian sugar are often mentioned. Venice supplied both Northern and Central Italy with Syrian sugar.[37] Although the greater part of these shipments consisted of powdered sugar, their role in the commercial exchanges between the Levant and Southern Europe should not be minimized. The accounts of the forced purchases of sugar are witness to the growth of this Levantine industry. They show that the Mamluk authorities found no other way of marketing the products of the sugar factories than by compelling the European merchants to purchase some part of them.[38] The cargoes of the European merchantmen consisted mainly of high-class "Damascene" sugar, of middle-quality "Babilonio" and "musciatto" (the so-called twice-boiled sugar), and cheap powdered sugar. Not infrequently, the cheaper sugar of Tripoli is mentioned.[39] Then, at the end of the fourteenth and the beginning of the fifteenth century, something like a collapse must have occurred: many of the sugar factories stopped production. Whereas an

[34] Misti 48, f. 84b.

[35] See my "Les lainages," p. 679; "Some Observations," p. 571.

[36] Dat 1171, freight inventories of the Venetian Beirut galleys of 1382, 1384, 1395, 1399. See also Dat 548, letter of Inghilese d'Inghilese & Piero & Cie of 31 Oct. 1385: the galleys brought 1,200-1,300 boxes sugar. On the sugar loads of the cotton cogs, see above, Table XIV; Heers, "Il commercio," pp. 168f., 171, inventory of the ship of Rafaele Castello a. 1379, and see above, pp. 30, 32, 68, 80.

[37] Dat 548, letters of Zanobi di Taddeo Gaddi of 21 Apr. 1384 and 18 Aug. 1384 (accounts of Damascus sugar sent to the Datini firm in Pisa); letter of the same of 30 July 1384: purchase of sugar by merchants of Lombardy; of Inghilese d'Inghilese & Piero & Cie of 19 Oct. 1384; Donato Dini of 14 Dec. 1385; of Inghilese d'Inghilese & Michele Vai of 21 Febr. 1385, 25 Febr. 1385, 11 Apr. 1395; Dat 549, accounts of Gherardo Bartolomei of 19 Febr. 1396: sale of Damascus sugar to Pisa.

[38] Jorga, "Notes et extraits," *ROL* IV, p. 228; my "Some Observations," p. 553.

[39] Misti 34, f. 110a; price list of Avignon apud Heers, "Il commercio," p. 163; Dat 548, letter of Zanobi of 12 May 1384; Dat 797, letter of the same of 12 Nov. 1394.

Arabic author counted sixty-six sugar factories in Cairo in (about) 1325,[40] their number had declined after 1400 by at least 40 percent. To judge from an account of Ibn Duḳmāḳ, who wrote in the first years of the fifteenth century, at least twenty-eight factories had been closed. The same was true for the sugar refineries in Upper Egypt.[41] The decline of the Levantine sugar industry was certainly the consequence of technological stagnation, brought about by the harassment of private industry and by the mismanagement and the corruption of the royal factories, for a great number of the factories, both in Egypt and in Syria, were owned by the sultan, his sons, and the high nobility.[42] The shortage of labor, following the great decrease in the Levantine populations, resulted in a considerable rise of production costs and of the prices of the various kinds of sugar, so that many customers had to forego the expensive product.[43] At the same time, great changes had been made in the sugar production in Cyprus and Sicily. The most important innovation was certainly the use of water-driven cylinders in the sugar presses.[44] This great innovation resulted in a considerable decrease in production costs.

One should beware of exaggerating and speaking of a complete breakdown of the Levantine sugar industry at the turn of the fourteenth to the fifteenth century. Sugar production was not discontinued altogether; both in Egypt and in Syria there were still plantations of sugar cane[45] and some factories were still working. As in earlier periods, the Mamluk authorities sometimes compelled the European merchants and even pilgrims to buy the products of their sugar factories.[46] Many documents show that sugar was still exported by the European merchants. Numerous decrees of the Venetian Senate refer to the transport of Syrian sugar on the Syrian cogs; sometimes it was allowed and at other times forbidden.[47] It seems, however, that most of this Syrian sugar was powdered sugar,[48] and the article disappears al-

[40] *Khiṭaṭ* I, p. 342.

[41] See my "Levantine sugar industry," p. 239.

[42] See *art. cit.*, pp. 237 f., 241; Misti 44, f. 55a.

[43] See *art. cit.*, p. 250 f.

[44] E. O. v. Lippmann, *Geschichte des Zuckers*, 2nd ed. (Berlin, 1929), p. 338; C. Trasselli, "La canna da zucchero nell'agro palermitano nel sec. XV," in *Annali della facoltà di economia e commercio, Univ. di Palermo* VIII (1953), no. 1, p. 119 ff.; *idem*, "Lineamenti di una storia dello zucchero siciliano," *Archivio Stor. per la Sicilia Orientale* 69 (1973), p. 38 f.; my "Levantine sugar industry," p. 246.

[45] Joos van Ghistele, *Voyage* (Ghendt, 1572), pp. 63, 205; "Levantine sugar industry," p. 258.

[46] Misti 52, f. 76a, 133a.

[47] Misti 47, f. 25b, 56a 48, f. 12b ff., 42a, 82a ff., 158a ff. 49, f. 4b, 32a 52, f. 68a, 101b ff. 53, f. 54a, 158b ff.; Dat 1171, freight inventory of Venetian Beirut galleys a. 1405. (According to Venetian law lump sugar, considered as a precious article, ought to be shipped on the galleys.)

[48] *Aspetti dell'espansione italiana*, p. 13.

together in the accounts of purchases made by the Venetians in Damascus in 1411, 1416, and 1417.[49] On the other hand, the export of sugar from Cyprus increased very much,[50] and sugar and molasses from Sicily and elsewhere began to be imported into Egypt.[51]

Even the production of soap in the Levantine countries declined considerably then, while it had flourished in the days of the caliphs and later; in the tenth century and in the period of the Crusaders, Northern Syria and Palestine had many soap factories, which produced for export.[52] In the fourteenth century too, the soap plants of Sarmīn, in Northern Syria, and Nablus, in Palestine, were well known for their excellent products.[53] The oppressive taxation by the Mamluk authorities and the compulsory purchase of great quantities of olive oil, to which they often had recourse, resulted in the decline of the soap industry.[54] However, the monopoly of alkali was perhaps even more prejudicial to these manufactures. Olive oil and alkali were the two raw materials from which the so-called hard soap (fast-foaming soap, also called soap of Marseilles or of Venice) was produced. Most of the alkali came from the Syrian desert, but it was also produced from the ashes of some plants found in Lower Egypt.[55] The Mamluk (and later the Ottoman) authorities sold a lot of the ashes to the Italian merchants who supplied it to the soap industry of their own country. Its price was very low and, on the other hand, it was very much in demand in Europe. So the export of alkali became a flourishing sector of the Levantine trade.

The Italian merchants shipped great quantities of alkali to Gaeta, Naples, Apulia, the March of Ancona, and Venice, which were the centers of their country's soap industry.[56]

When the misconceived policy of the Mamluks had brought about the decline of the Levantine soap industry, the government of Venice (and

[49] See Arch. Zane, accounts of purchases.

[50] Misti 48, f. 82a ff., 158a ff. 49, f. 31b ff.

[51] Arch. B. Dolfin, Ba 181, fasc. 13 (a. 1418); G. P., Sent. 34, f. 37a ff. cf. "Levantine sugar industry," p. 261; Piloti, p. 147. On the other hand, one began to supply the Italian markets with Spanish sugar; see Dat 550, letter of Com. of Zanobi di Taddeo Gaddi of 19 Febr. 1401; letter of Donato di Bonifazio of 15 May 1400.

[52] al-Muḳaddasī, p. 180; Ibn ash-Shiḥna, *ad-Durr al-muntakhab* (Beirut, 1909), pp. 25, 165, 249 (transl. J. Sauvaget, *Les perles choisies* [Beirut, 1938], pp. 147, 194, 198).

[53] Ibn Baṭṭūṭa I, p. 145 f.; ad-Dimishḳī, *Nukhbat ad-dahr*, ed. A. Mehren (St. Petersburg, 1866), p. 200 (transl. Mehren, Copenhagen, p. 270).

[54] *Aspetti dell'espansione italiana*, p. 15.

[55] P. Belon, *Les observations de plusieurs singularités et choses mémorables* (Paris, 1588), p. 217.

[56] G. P., Sent. 20, f. 122a 71, f. 55a ff. (direct transport to Gaeta by Venetians); ASG, Carat. Vet. 1552, f. 125a (transport to Gaeta and Savona by Genoese); see, further, G. P., Sent. 18, f. 85 ff. 20, f. 122a 23, f. 75b 30, f. 74b f. 71, f. 55a ff.; G. P., Ter VII, f. 12a f. On the volume of this export trade, see my "The Venetian supremacy," p. 45.

Table XVIIIA-Prices of Alkali

Date	Place	Price of a ḳinṭā	Source
before 1408	Tripolo	2,75 duc. (110 dirh.)	G.P., Sent. 18, f.85b ff
1411		2,22 duc.	G.P., Sent. 20, f. 122a
1412	Beirut	2,5 "	G.P., Sent 30, f. 74b f.
1426	Tripoli	2 "	G.P., Sent. 65, f. 129a f.
1440	"	2 "	G.P., Sent. 88, f., 30b ff.
1441	"	1,7-1, 87"	G.P., Sent 97, f. 116b ff.
1450	Beirut	2,3 duc.	G.P., Sent 124, f. 63b ff.
1468	Tripoli	1,2 duc. (60 dirh.)	G.P., Sent. 165, f. 183a
before 1473	"	0,63-0, 725 duc.	G.P., Sent 158, f. 43a ff.
1473	Damascus	1,4 duc. (70 dirh.)	G.P., Sent 161, f. 172b ff.
1476 (or 1477)	Aleppo	2,5 ashrafis[b]	G.P., Ter. IX, f. 13a
1477	Beirut	1,7 duc.	G.P., Ter. III, f. 82a
1479	Damascus	1,8 duc.	G.P., Sent. 188, f. 206a ff.

a) Concerning the ḳinṭā of the various provinces of Syria and Palestine, see my remarks in "The Venetian Cotton Trade," p. 700.

b) The ashrafī generally had the same value as the ducat, see my paper "Etudes sur le systeme monetaire des Mamlouks circassiens," Israel Oriental Studies VI (1976), p. 272.

probably those of other European states) fostered their own manufactures, even by subsidizing export.[57] As early as the fourteenth century, the Italian soap producers exported their products to many countries, and by the beginning of the fifteenth century soap was a sizable part of the cargoes of the Italian merchant fleets, which sailed to Egypt and to Syria.[58] The soap production of Syria was certainly not discontinued, and the soap of Nablus was exported to Egypt up to our own day,[59] but the higher strata of society were the customers of the European factories, and the export of soap to the Levant became a profitable business of the South European merchants.

[57] Misti 41, f. 127b.

[58] See my "Observations," p. 579; "Aspetti dell'espansione italiana," p. 16 and, further, Misti 48, f. 13b f. 55, f. 92a, 123b; *Chron. Morosini*, c. 355 (by Venetians!); Nic. Venier B, 2, f. 18b/19a (from Cyprus), 32b f. (by Genoese).

[59] See M. Meyerhof, "Der Bazar der Drogen u. Wohlgerüche in Kairo," in *Archiv für Wirtschaftsforschung des Orients*, 1918, Heft 3/4, p. 210.

The cause of the decline of the Levantine soap industry appears to be simply the mistaken policy of the Mamluks, whereas in the case of the decay of the paper industry it is very easy to indicate the technological failures. In fact, the decline of this industry shows what a decisive role technological stagnation played in the economic (and political) decline of the Near East in the later Middle Ages.

The production of paper from rags had been introduced into the Near East by Persians in the late eighth century and during the course of the ninth century. From then on, it was a flourishing industry, whose products were exported to many other regions, e.g., to India.[60] However, the Persian and Arab paper-makers exactly imitated the production methods they had learned from the Chinese, without making any innovations. The Levantine paper was glossy and since it was sized with vegetable starch (either of wheat or rice), it contained the germs of its own destruction. In the course of the fourteenth century, the quality deteriorated.[61] Meanwhile, a new paper industry had come into being in Italy, first in Fabriano and then in other towns, where some important innovations were made. Whereas the Arabs pulped the rags in mortars with hand-pestles, the Italian paper-makers used hammers with stone heads, which were arranged in alternately working batteries operated by water power. So the rags were much better triturated and the fibers of the paper had a uniform length. Secondly, instead of vegetable starch they used glue obtained by boiling scraps of animal skins. This animal gelatine did not contain those germs which were so prejudicial to the preservation of the Oriental paper and often brought about its decomposition. Further, for producing the sheets the Italians used metallic wire, instead of the cane or bamboo used by the Arabs. Consequently, the sheets were better stretched and there were regular distances between the chain lines.[62] Since the new kind of paper was of a much better quality than the Oriental product, the Italian merchants began to market it in the Near Eastern countries with substantial profits. From the beginning of the fifteenth century, paper was regularly imported into all Levantine countries by the Venetians and by other South European traders.[63]

[60] S. D. Goitein, *Letters of mediaeval Jewish traders* (Princeton, 1973), p. 196.

[61] J. Irigoin, "Les premiers manuscrits grecs écrits sur papier et le problème du bombycin," *Scriptorium* IV (1950), p. 201; idem, "Les débuts de l'emploi du papier a Byzance," *Byz. Zeitschrift* 46 (1953), p. 319.

[62] A. Zonghi, "The ancient papers of Fabriano," in *Zonghi's watermarks* (Hilversum, 1953) (Monumenta chartae papyraceae historiam illustrantia, III), p. 15 ff.; A. F. Gasparinetti, "Paper, papermakers & papermills of Fabriano," *op.cit.*, p. 63 ff.

[63] To Egypt: G. P., Sent. 45, f. 33a ff. and cf. 52, f. 6a ff. (a. 1419) 66, f. 57b ff. (a. 1412, paper of Fabriano) 70, f. (between 11 and 12); Misti 46, f. 94a (a. 1403) 54, f. 74b (a. 1422); to Syria: Misti 60, f. 47b (a. 1436); to Bursa: (G. P., Sent. 37, f. s. d. 24 Aug. 1403; to Astrakhan: G. P., Sent. IX, f. 58b (a. 1375); to Tana: Misti 45, f. 53a (a. 1401); see also M. Beit-Arie, *Hebrew codicology* (Paris, 1976), p. 32.

There were yet other industrial sectors that declined very greatly in the Levantine countries in the later Middle Ages. The coincidence of the sharp decline of a number of industries points clearly to common causes.

Another such industry was glassmaking. In view of the fact that the Near Eastern glassmakers exported their products to many countries and that the volume of their production was not insignificant, it is not out of place to speak of the breakdown of an industry.

Glassmaking was originally a Syrian craft, at least glassblowing had been invented there. The products of the Syrian and Egyptian glassmakers were renowned in the days of the caliphs; the transparency and thinness of Syrian glass were proverbial. In the middle of the thirteenth century, a new period of growth began in the history of Levantine glassmaking. The Egyptian and Syrian craftsmen produced excellent enamelled glass with fine red contours. The glass vessels produced in their workshops in the fourteenth century show Chinese influences, namely calligraphic and naturalist ornaments. Moslem and European travellers who visited Syria and Palestine in that period praised the glass manufactured in Damascus and in Hebron.[64] Their products were indeed exported to Asiatic and European countries, as far as China, on one hand, and Germany, on the other.[65] Documents referring to the Levantine trade of the South European trading nations contain data on the export of Oriental glass to Europe at the end of the fourteenth century.[66]

This industry too was severely prejudiced by the overpowering competition of the royal factories[67] and by oppressive taxation.[68] The Levantine glassmakers of the later Middle Ages also encountered great difficulties in acquiring good raw materials. Tartar, which was commonly used in glassmaking, had to be imported from Europe. Genoese, Florentine, and Venetian merchants imported it from Italy and Southern France. Some of the documents that refer to the export of tartar from Southern Europe to the Levant point to sizable transactions.[69] Cupric oxide (*ferretto*), verdigris, and realgar were used. All these materials were imported from Europe and

[64] Ibn Baṭṭūṭa I, p. 208; *Itinerarium Symonis Semeonis*, p. 74; Fra Niccolò da Poggibonsi, *Libro di Oltramare (1348-1350)* (Jerusalem, 1945), pp. 68, 92; *Liber peregrinationum di Jacopo da Verona*, p. 95.

[65] Ibn Kathīr 13, p. 120; C. J. Lamm, *Mittelalterliche Gläser u. Steinschmittarbeiten aus dem Nahen Osten* (Berlin, 1930), pp. 246, 259, 483; *idem*, *Oriental glass of mediaeval date found in Sweden and the early history of lustre-painting* (Stockholm, 1941), p. 73; W. Pfeiffer, "Acrische Gläser," *Journal of Glass Studies* 12 (1970), p. 67 f.

[66] Dat 1171, freight inventories of the ship of Franc. Casasagia (a. 1379, 1391), Joh. Morella (a. 1391), Catalan Beirut galleys (a. 1395).

[67] *Ṣubḥ al-a'shā* IV, p. 188 (transl. Gaudefroy-Demombynes, *La Syrie a l'époque des Mamlouks*, p. 151).

[68] See J. Sauvaget, "Décrets mamelouks de Syrie," *BEO* II, no. 11, p. 32 ff.

[69] Nic. Venier B, 2, f. 32a ff.; G. P., Sent. 65, f. 68a ff. 66, f. 57b ff. 68, f. 75a ff. 70, f. between 11 and 12, 141b ff.; Vat. sub 8 Nov. 1404.

some of them were very expensive.[70] Another important ingredient of glass was alkali. By the end of the thirteenth century the Venetian glassmakers were using Syrian alkali.[71] European treatises on glassmaking of the later Middle Ages show convincingly how great the importance of Syrian and Egyptian alkali was for the development of the glass industry in several countries of Southern Europe.[72] So the Mamluk authorities supplied the European glass manufacturers with an indispensible raw material and made their great development possible. Syrian alkali was indeed so indispensible to the manufacture of glass so that the Venetian government rigorously forbade exporting it.[73] On the other hand, glassmaking in the dominions of the Mamluks declined considerably in the fifteenth century. European travellers of that period recount that the quality of the glass produced in Syria and Palestine was very bad.[74] Some modern scholars who have studied Oriental glass of that late period have arrived at the same conclusion.[75] The decline of glassmaking in the Moslem Levant was certainly not brought about by Tīmūr, who exiled many craftsmen from Damascus to Central Asia, for the craft declined in towns where Tīmūr's troops never penetrated. It was mainly the consequence of technological stagnation.

It was at that time that European glassmakers began to employ new and better raw materials and to develop new methods of production. For the production of crystal, the glassmakers of Murano used raw material brought form the Saint Bernard pass, and for coloring the glass cobalt imported from Germany.[76] To increase the transparency of the glass and to improve the coloring, they used pyrousite, called the glassmaker's soap.[77] There was a great development of lustre-painting and production of enamelled glass, and later the Venetian glassmakers produced the famous white lattimo glass. The quality of the Italian glass, especially that of the Murano glass, was so much better than that of the Oriental glass that by the end of the fourteenth century glass was beginning to be exported to the Moslem Levant. In 1396, for instance, the Venetian Antonio Dolfin sold thirteen

[70] Uzzano, p. 112. Other data in my "Le Proche-Orient au bas moyen âge—une région sous-developpée," *X^a Settimana di studio, Istituto Fr. Datini*, p. 419 f.

[71] ASV, Podestà di Murano, Ba 3, fasc. 1, c. 17b.

[72] *Dell'arte del vetro per musaico tre trattatelli*, ed. G. Milanesi (Bologna, 1864), II, 1, 2, 4, 5 III, 18, 65, etc.

[73] Misti 47, f. 161a (a. 1408).

[74] Felix Fabri, *Evagatorium in Terram Sanctam, Arabiae et Aegypti peregrinationes*, ed. C. D. Hassler (Stuttgart, 1843-1849), II, p. 371.

[75] Lamm, *Oriental glass*, p. 72.

[76] W. Ganzmüller, "Hüttengeheimnisse der italienischen Glasmacher des Mittelalters," in his *Beiträge zur Geschichte der Technologie und der Alchemie* (Weinheim, 1956), p. 73; *idem*, "Über die Verwendung des Kobalt dei den Glasmachern des Mittelalters," in the same volume, p. 171.

[77] R. W. Douglas-J. Frank, *A history of glassmaking* (Hanley-on-Thann, 1972), p. 7.

cases of mirror glass for 430 ducats in Alexandria.[78] The cargoes of the Venetian Beirut galleys in 1400 contained five cases of glass vessels,[79] and crystal is mentioned in the work of a contemporary author as one of the articles that the Venetians imported into Egypt.[80] Provençal merchants also marketed glass in Egypt at the beginning of the fifteenth century.[81]

Another aspect of the technological decline of the Moslem Levant in the later Middle Ages was the inferiority in shipbuilding and in nautical skill. This phenomenon too had far-reaching consequences for the economic and political relations between the Near East and Christian Europe.

Actually, the inferiority of the Moslems in shipping dated from the period of the Crusades. As early as the Lateran Council of 1179, there were decrees against the "bad Christians" who served the Moslems as helmsmen.[82] When the big Nordic cogs were introduced into the Mediterranean by the Basque shippers, the superiority of the European fleets increased even more. These were very strong ships and especially useful for sailing in winter. The armament of the European ships with bombards, those mediaeval cannons, gave them another great advantage. It guaranteed them superiority in any naval encounter and enhanced the security of the passengers and the cargoes in the case of attack by pirates. Whereas the Mamluks, typical Turkish knights, despised the use of firearms, all European powers equipped their armies and their fleets with bombards. The Venetian cogs had some pieces of artillery from the 1370's on.[83] The Catalan galleys and Castilian ships had bombards from the beginning of the fifteenth century.[84] Venice went ahead in the perfection and in the use of firearms, so that princes of other countries and the governments of distant commonwealths applied to the Serenissima with requests to lend them bombards and to allow them to acquire munitions. In 1409 even the Genoese *mahona* of Chios addressed such a request to Venice.[85] Certainly, the Moslems still built ships; they had many merchantmen, and from time to time also equipped war fleets. The forests of Cilicia supplied them with the necessary timber.[86] But, because of the undeniable superiority of the European ships and the incomparably greater security, Moslem travellers, and especially merchants, used European vessels to a very considerable extent for trans-

[78] G. P., Sent. VI, f. 65a.
[79] Heers, "Il commercio," p. 168.
[80] Piloti, p. 149 ff.
[81] Leonardo de Valle sub 7 Febr. 1403. See, further, the documents quoted in *Aspetti dell'espansione italiana*, p. 19.
[82] Mansi, *Concilia* XXII, col. 230 f.
[83] See *Aspetti dell'espansione italiana*, p. 23.
[84] Capmany, 1, p. 640; *Le Victorial, chronique de D. Pedro Niño, comte de Buelna*, par Gutierre Diaz de Gomez (Paris, 1867), p. 194.
[85] Secreta IV, f. 12b and cf. *Aspetti dell'espansione italiana*, p. 25.
[86] Piloti, p. 139 f.

port. The fleets of all South European trading nations served the Moslems. Italian ships were leased to them for the transport of merchandise from Syria to Egypt and vice versa. In 1399 the governor of Alexandria chartered an Anconitan ship for the transport of salt to Tripoli (in Syria).[87] The traffic between the Maghrebin countries and Egypt was to a great extent in the hands of Catalan, French, and Italian shippers.[88] It goes without saying that the use of European transport meant a great loss for the Near Eastern economy and considerable gains for the South European trading nations. In 1404 a Genoese ship was chartered to sail from Tunis to Alexandria for 1,800 doblas (worth 1,666 ducats) and in 1405, a shipment of 2,790 oil jars from Seville to Alexandria cost 1,400 dinars.[89]

The sharp decline of industrial production in the Moslem Levant and its general technological backwardness were certainly propitious to the development of the commercial exchanges between the countries of Southern Europe and the dominions of the Mamluks. But in autocratic states like that of the sultans of Cairo, much depended on the attitude of the rulers.

The Circassian sultans who ruled over Egypt and Syria from the end of the fourteenth century were inclined to a rapacious policy, and probably the economic decline of their countries compelled them to employ all means to increase their revenues. Whereas most of the sultans of the first Mamluk dynasty, the Baḥrites, belonged to one family and inherited the throne, the Circassians were self-made men who ascended the throne after having fought with other pretenders and defeated them, or by having successfully plotted against their predecessors. The reign of Faradj was particularly stormy, and even his successor al-Malik al-Mu'ayyad Shaykh (1412-19) had to subdue some revolts. But it seems that neither of them made the European merchants great difficulties. On the contrary, they were apparently rather benevolent toward them. A Christian author stated that Sultan Faradj threatened to expel the Christians (i.e., the natives) from his dominions, on the pretext that the Pact of 'Umar did not safeguard their right to live in the Moslem lands forever and that it was only a limited permission.[90] Apparently this writer referred to rumors that seemed to have spread about 1410 and to talks that were not translated into action. Sultan Shaykh was inclined to make a show of his devoutness in order to curry favor with the orthodox zealots, and from time to time he allowed them to persecute the non-Moslems.[91] At any rate, the European merchants

[87] Misti 47, f. 63a (a Venetian ship); Vat. sub 13 Jan. 1400.

[88] Vat. sub. 13 Jan. 1400, 13 Jan. 1406, 10 Aug. 1406, 2 Sept. 1404; G. P., Sent. 48, f. 85a ff., 102a 52, f. 8b f.

[89] Vat. sub 18 Aug. 1404, 3 Nov. 1405.

[90] Piloti, p. 43 ff.

[91] See my *History of the Jews in Egypt and Syria under the Mamluks* (in Hebrew) (Jerusalem, 1944-1970), II, p. 66 ff.

were not hurt by these sultans. But even under the reign of Faradj there were conflicts with the Moslem authorities and the Europeans had to make those arbitrarily imposed "contributions" to the government, just like other groups of the population of the Mamluk realm. This happened, for instance, in 1411. According to a merchant's letter, at the beginning of that year the Mamluk authorities imposed on the European merchants in Damascus a fine of 5,620 ducats, of which the Venetians had to pay 1,900.[92] Even the frequent revolts sometimes endangered the European merchants. In 1408, when the civil war in Syria was at its height, it was feared in Venice that it would be impossible to make the cotton purchases in time, and there were complaints about the extortions of the Mamluks.[93] Then, in the spring of 1414, when Emir Nawrūz revolted against Shaykh and the latter besieged him in the citadel of Damascus, there was fighting in the streets, and the foreign merchants were threatened by the battalions of the warring factions. The Venetians with their consul Zuan Dolfin, the Genoese, and Catalans found a refuge in the Khān of Tenem. There they resisted the attack until the sultan rescued them.[94] There were other interruptions of the normal course of commercial activities. Sometimes there were fears of an invasion of Syria by foreign armies or there was an actual penetration of such forces. In the spring of 1403 and again in the fall of that year, there was concern that Tīmūr would again invade Syria.[95] In 1413 the Turcoman prince Ḳarā Yuluḳ invaded Syria, and the Venetian merchants suffered great losses.[96] Then in 1418 it was thought that there would be another invasion of his troops, and there was a general flight from Northern Syria. The Venetian merchants too departed.[97]

However, all these occurrences were only episodes. In fact, the commercial exchanges between Southern Europe and the Moslem Levant were carried on quite regularly, and the industrial decline of the Near Eastern countries gave them a new impetus. Even the increasing activities of the Turkish corsairs[98] and the raids of Cypriot fleets[99] did not interfere very much with the activities of the trading nations in the Levant. The Church

[92] ASV, Arch. Zane, fasc. V, letter of Benedetto Dandolo of 26 March 1411.

[93] Misti 48, f. 38a, 42a.

[94] *Chron. Morosini*, c. 281; Jorga, "Notes et extraits," *ROL* IV, p. 543, and cf. *an-Nudjūm as-zāhira* VI, p. 337 f. (transl. Popper III, p. 25f.). The number of the Venetians was 95, according to Morosini. The Venetian chronicler states that the merchants saved themselves by paying a ransom.

[95] Dat 928, letter of Comm. of Zanobi di Taddeo Gaddı of 20 April 1403 and letter from Damascus of 22 March 1403; Dat 714, letter of Paris Soranzo of 24 Nov. 1403; *Chron. Morosini*, c. 154.

[96] *Chron. Morosini*, c. 270. There are no accounts of this invasion in Arabic sources.

[97] See Jorga, "Notes et extraits," *ROL* IV, p. 595; *Sulūk* IV, pp. 457 f. 458 f., 460.

[98] Thiriet, *Rég.* II, pp. 80, 93, 177.

[99] Hill, *History of Cyprus* II, p. 469.

no longer put obstacles in the way of trade with the Moslems. The supplications submitted to the Holy See by some Genoese merchants in 1418-1423 to obtain absolution for having carried on such trade in the past and for permission to engage in it in the future were no more than an expression of personal devoutness.[100]

B. The Aggressiveness of the Genoese and the Catalans

The extent to which the various European trading nations benefitted from the new possibilities in the exchanges with the Levant was very unequal. The share of some declined, both absolutely and relatively. This was in part due to their reactions when they encountered difficulties in their commercial activities in the Moslem countries and to their inclination to pursue an aggressive and expansionist policy in the Levant. Their readiness to support schemes of expeditions against the Moslems and actually to join those who undertook them, on the one hand, and the hopes to get a foothold in the Moslem Levant by the occupation of some port, on the other hand, played a great role in the policy of these nations and necessarily had negative consequences for regular trade with the dominions of the sultan of Cairo. This was especially true for the Genoese and the Catalans. The policy on which they embarked also resulted in conflicts between themselves and much more so in conflicts with other trading nations of Southern Europe.

Relations between Genoa and Venice were very tense at the beginning of the fifteenth century. Some Venetian ships had been captured by the Genoese in Famagusta, in Rhodes, and elsewhere. On the other hand, Genoa accused Venice of supporting the king of Cyprus, who tried to recover the full suzerainty of the island.[101] But, since both powers were essentially interested in avoiding a conflict, there was an exchange of embassies, and negotiations were carried on in Genoa and in Venice. However, meanwhile, at the beginning of 1403, the Genoese made a raid on Tripoli and the Venetians suffered losses.[102] Nevertheless, in April 1403 an agreement was reached by which the Genoese obliged themselves to pay restitutions.[103] During the negotiations the Serenissima had shown good will, her ambassador in Genoa had orders to be flexible, and the request of the king of Cyprus to be granted at least financial help for his undertaking against Genoa was turned down.[104]

[100] L. Baletto, *Genova, Mediterraneo, Mar Nero (sec. XIII-XIV)*, p. 33 ff.

[101] An account of the Venetian losses owing to Genoese aggression, see Coll., Not. III, f. 93b f.; see, further, *Libr. Com.* III, lib. 9, no. 253; Genoese claims: Secreta I, f. 81a ff.

[102] Delaville le Roulx I, p. 419.

[103] *Libr. Com.* III, lib. 9, no. 262.

[104] Secreta I, f. 87a f. and cf. Thiriet, *Rég.* II, p. 25. See, further, Delaville le Roulx II, p. 414.

But there was still great apprehension in Venice as to what the attitude of the Genoese government would be in the future and as to its actual projects. Genoa, a French protectorate since 1396, was embroiled both with the king of Cyprus and the sultan of Cairo. At the beginning of 1403 a Genoese ambassador, Carozzo Cigalla, was in Egypt to negotiate with the Mamluk government in the matter of the restitution due for losses that Moslems had suffered from Genoese pirates.[105] But what mattered much more than the general tension in the Eastern Mediterranean was the character of Marshal Boucicault, the French governor of Genoa. He was a typical knight, always inclined to warlike activities and imbued with personal hatred against the Moslems after having taken part in the battle of Nicopolis and been taken a prisoner by the Turks. So there were various rumors in Italy when just in the month of April 1403, before the negotiations with Venice were finished, Boucicault departed with a war fleet for the Levant. Although officially the goal of the expedition was Cyprus, in Genoa and Venice it was feared that Boucicault would attack the Mamluks and the Venetians too.[106] Public opinion in Genoa was against the expedition. Having made an agreement with Venice, the Genoese were against further attacks on Venetian ships. They suspected the ambitions French governor of even coveting the crown of Cyprus.[107] Despite the mistrust of Boucicault's projects, the Venetian government gave orders to the admiral of the war fleet, Carlo Zeno, to do his best to avoid conflict with the Genoese. The admiral, who was cruising with his fleet in the Greek waters, was instructed to attack the Genoese only if they did great damage to the Venetians.[108]

However, within a very short time the apprehensions of the Venetians proved to be justified. Boucicault, with the help of the grandmaster of the Knights of Rhodes, succeeded in coming to an agreement with the king of Cyprus. Thereupon he began action against the dominions of the Mamluks.

The French marshal tried to lull the sultan of Cairo into security by sending him an embassy. There were talks in Alexandria, but the representatives of the sultan soon became aware of the bad faith of the Genoese envoys.[109] There can be little doubt that the Mamluks had been warned by the Venetians that an attack by the Genoese was impending. This is what one reads both in a source friendly to Boucicault and in another which is

[105] Leonardo de Valle sub 21 Febr. 1403.

[106] See the letters to the firm Datini in Valencia quoted by R. Piattoli, "La spedizione del maresciallo Boucicault contro Cipro ed i suoi effetti nel carteggio di mercanti ficrentini," *Giornale storico e letterario della Liguria*, N.S. V (1929), p. 134.

[107] Ant. Ceruti, "Lettere di Carlo VI, re di Francia e della Republica di Genova relative al maresciallo Bucicaldo," *ASLSP* 17 (1885), p. 360 ff.; *Memorie varie di Venezia*, MS. Bibl. Naz. Florence, II, f. 201b.

[108] Secreta I, f. 94a ff.

[109] Piloti, p. 193.

outspokenly pro-Venetian.[110] In an official document, the registers of the Venetian Senate, we see that Carlo Zeno wrote to the consul of Alexandria to warn him of the danger of an attack by the Genoese.[111] Even if the Venetian authorities had only warned their subjects in the Levantine ports, the news must have been transmitted to the Mamluks. The Genoese merchants in Alexandria were arrested, the other Europeans departed,[112] and the sultan sent troops to Alexandria and Damietta. According to Piloti, they numbered 4,000 knights, but Arabic authors say that there were only 400. This happened at the beginning of July 1403.[113] Boucicault himself made a raid against the port of Alaya, on the southern coast of Asia Minor with a part of his forces and sent a squadron to Alexandria. However, his plan failed.

In fact, the Genoese commanders opposed the project of Boucicault and returned when they encountered adverse winds. Piloti, who recounts this story, adds a particularly interesting detail: he says that, together with the Mamluk troops that awaited the Christian forces, the sultan had sent to Alexandria a rich spice merchant who had a great deal of experience in working with the European traders. He reports that this merchant had half a million ducats with him, so that he could eventually buy off the attackers. This is a trustworthy account, since the Christian author writes that he himself accompanied the merchant, who was his friend.[114] His account is confirmed by some Arabic authors of that period. An Arabic chronicler stated that the well-known Kārimī merchant Burhān ad-dīn al-Maḥallī asked for permission to take part in the expedition to the coast "because of his love of glory."[115] According to this author, al-Maḥallī was even given the post of a commander. Since it would have been very unusual in the realm of the Mamluks to appoint a civilian to a military command, the account of his secret mission, as given by Piloti, is much more convincing. Other Arabic chroniclers say expressly that al-Maḥallī was ordered to join the expedition.[116] However, it is not necessary to consider the various accounts of the mission of al-Maḥallī as contradictory. The Kārimīs were hostile to the European merchants, because of their interest in dominating the spice market and establishing cartels. So the sultan would trust the great Kārimī.

[110] Delaville le Roulx II, p. 438; Piloti, p. 192. See also Vertot, *Histoire des chevaliers* II, p. 382.

[111] Secreta I, f. 102a.

[112] Piloti, p. 193.

[113] *Sulūk* III, p. 1106; ʿAbdalbāsiṭ 803, f. 192a; Ibn Iyās² I, part 2, p. 672; Piloti, p. 195.

[114] Piloti, *l.c.*

[115] Ibn Ḥadjar II, p. 234.

[116] *Sulūk* III, p. 1116; Ibn Iyās² I, part 2, p. 682. al-Maḳrīzī (whose account is quoted by Ibn Iyās) in fact recounts the expedition to Alexandria twice, under June and September 1403. The participation of al-Maḥallī is mentioned in the second text.

After the failure of the expedition against Alexandria, Boucicault made a raid against the coastal towns of Syria. On 1 August 1403 he attacked Tripoli without much success and departed three days later. Then on 8 August he launched an attack against Beirut. The civilians had left the town in time, while the Mamluk garrison, the Lebanese feudals, and voluntaries opposed with a strong resistance. Finally the Genoese attacked Sidon, and once more there was heavy fighting in which the governor-general of Syria also took part. The Genoese were repulsed and sailed back to Famagusta.[117]

Two Arabic chroniclers, Ibn Ḥadjar and al-ʿAynī, report that the Genoese sacked Sidon and found there a large quantity of spices belonging to the Catalans. But this is a mistake. Ṣāliḥ b. Yaḥyā, an eyewitness, is better informed. He says that this happened in Beirut and that the spices belonged to the Venetians. Piloti states that the Genoese were against the sack of Beirut[118] and tried to avoid a conflict with the Venetians. They were overruled by Boucicault, however. According to Venetian sources, some Venetian merchants went to Boucicault and asked him to give orders that their property be safeguarded.[119] Whatever the case may have been, all these interventions were ineffectual. Boucicault wrought vengeance on the Venetians, who in his belief had spoiled his undertaking, and he had the stolen merchandise sold at an auction in Famagusta.[120]

A naval battle off Modon followed, and the Genoese were defeated by the Venetians, with long negotiations as to the mutual claims of restitutions and damages ensuing. Although both of the two merchant republics had great interest in concluding peace, there was still great animosity and ran-

[117] *Sulūk* III, p. 1114, 1115; Ibn Ḥadjar II, p. 258; al-ʿAynī, *ʿIḳd al-djumān*, MS. Istanbul, Čarullah 1591, f. 672a; ʿAbdalbāsiṭ 803, f. 193a f., Ibn Iyās² I, part 2, p. 680 f.; Ṣāliḥ b. Yaḥyā, *Taʾrīkh Bairūt* (Beirut, 1969), p. 32 ff. The report of the latter author is the most valuable, as it is that of an eyewitness. In fact, Ṣāliḥ b. Yaḥyā took part in the fighting. Whereas the Egyptian chroniclers say that the governor of Syria arrived in Beirut when the battle was still going on, he says explicitly that the attack was over when the governor came. According to the Christian sources, the attack on Tripoli began on 7 August and that on Beirut on 10 August. But the Arabic authors, who also mention the day of the week, are more reliable. They say that Tripoli was attacked on 12 Muḥarram 806, which was a Tuesday, and Beirut on 20 Muḥarram, which was a Thursday. The latter date is correct, whereas the 12 Muḥarram fell on a Wednesday. Morosini recounts that the sack of Beirut was on 9 August. This reliable account confirms the Arabic reports.

[118] P. 197.

[119] *Chron. Dolfin*, f. 266a f.; Marino Sanuto, *Vite de' duchi*, c. 801; *Chron. Morosini*, c. 143a; cf. Fr. Surdich, "Genova e Venezia fra Tre e Quattrocento," *ASLSP* N.S. VII (1967), p. 259; *Memorie varie di Venezia* II, f. 300a.

[120] Delaville le Roulx II, p. 443; Musso, *Navig.*, p. 78. A Venetian chronicler maintains that Boucicault had promised the Venetians of Beirut that they will not be attacked; see Cod. Marciana 2034, f. 277a. Another Venetian chronicler reports that in addition to the Venetian merchants others also (Europeans) suffered losses; see the anonymous chronicle Marciana 7293, f. 77b.

cor. The losses of the Venetians in Beirut, according to their claims, amounted to 30,000 ducats, and in addition the Genoese had captured a ship of the Venetian Marco delle Chiodere in the port of Alexandria.[121] Also, the approach to the negotiations by the Genoese and the French governor was not the same. The latter still cherished hopes of revenging his defeat in the naval battle and planned new expeditions against the Moslems. In March 1404 an agreement was reached;[122] but its implementation caused problems. In June 1406 a Venetian ambassador concluded a new treaty with the Genoese government which referred to all the losses that both sides had suffered during, before, and after the expedition of Boucicault.[123] However, even then some questions remained open and had to be laid before arbiters. The Florentines, who were chosen, declined, and the verdict of the Count of Savoy, who replaced them, was rejected by the Genoese.[124] But still the will to peace prevailed.

The expedition against the Syrian ports and its great failure were a heavy blow to the position of Genoa in the Levant. Once more the Genoese had gone to war against the Mamluks and had aroused their enmity. Obviously, waging war with the sultan of Cairo was incompatible with enjoying freedom of trade. Piloti maintains that the Genoese almost discontinued their trade with the Mamluk dominions. From then on, so he says, when a Genoese had caused grief to Moslems, e.g., when corsairs had attacked Moslems, the Genoese merchants in Alexandria were imprisoned, sent to Cairo and compelled to pay 20,000-30,000 ducats or even half a million.[125] But the account of the Cretan author is exaggerated. Both the sultan and the Genoese were interested in the continuation of the commercial exchanges.

Boucicault himself sent an embassy to Egypt to conclude peace. Piloti writes that before departing from Rhodes, on his way to Genoa, he despatched Paolo Arqua and Pietro Naton of Savona to Alexandria with big cogs and that they began to attack the Moslems. Then, he says, they proposed to the Mamluks to conclude peace, and after long negotiations agreed to pay restitution amounting to 30,000 ducats for the damages done to the Moslems.[126] But even after this new agreement Genoese-Mamluk

[121] *Chron. Morosini* I, p. 25 ff.; Marino Sanuto, *op.cit.*, c. 790; Dat 714, anonymous letter of 9 Febr. 1404.

[122] *Libr. Com.* III, lib. 9, no. 276.

[123] *Libr. Com.* III, lib. 10, no. 19.

[124] Secreta III, f. 133a, 134a IV, f. 10a, 38a (these texts were misunderstood by Thiriet, *Rég.* II, p. 83a).

[125] Piloti, p. 200.

[126] Piloti, p. 199 f. Although he says that Boucicault sent the two cogs to Egypt while he was still in Rhodes, it is improbable that the second report of al-Maḳrīzī about the despatch of troops to Alexandria refers to this expedition. In fact, the Arabic author says that the news

relations were not easy. The Genoese were always inclined to aggressiveness, and time and again there were conflicts between them and the Mamluk authorities, although both governments tried to smooth over the friction.

According to the acts of a notary in Alexandria, there was another such conflict at the beginning of 1405. All the Genoese merchants in Alexandria were imprisoned, and they had to pay a great sum for their liberation.[127] Their liberation was obtained by a Genoese ambassador, Paolo Lercaro. According to other acts of the same notary, eight Genoese merchants stood surety for the payment of the ransom, but six of them fled from Egypt.[128] When Genoa had again become independent in 1409, various diplomatic moves were made to establish peaceful relations with the sultan. In June 1411 the Genoese authorities in Famagusta addressed a letter to the Mamluk government to show their good will. They informed them about the steps they had taken against corsairs who threatened Moslem ships and ports and stated that they had liberated Moslems taken prisoners by the corsairs. They also let the Mamluk government know that they had restored a shipment of soap to the merchant who had sold it to them and from whom it had been taken.[129]

However, a short time after this, there was a new outbreak of hostilities, and the relations between the Genoese and the Mamluks again worsened.

In the summer of 1411 there was a naval battle between the Genoese and the Catalans in the port of Alexandria, another of the numerous acts of hostility in the long conflict between Genoa and the Catalans. According to Arabic sources, the Genoese attacked the Catalan ships they found there, and in the heavy fighting many were killed. In Genoese sources, one finds that the Catalans lost four or five merchantmen. From the Arabic sources, it seems that finally the Catalans had the upper hand, for they succeeded in capturing a well-known corsair who was their great enemy. The Arabic chroniclers call him "the Biscayan," and Piloti also says that he was a Biscayan. But, according to other sources, he was a Castilian or even simply a Genoese. In any case, he was one of the commanders of the Genoese ships. The Catalans delivered him to the Mamluks, and before the sultan accused him of being a great enemy of the Moslems; the Arabic chronicles state that he was requested to pay a great ransom. When the Genoese

---

of the arrival of the Genoese ships came to Cairo on 15 August. This early date suggests that al-Maḳrīzī refers to the same expedition; cf. above, note 116.

[127] Vat. sub 23 May 1405.

[128] Vat. sub 28 June 1405, 3 Aug. 1405.

[129] *Ṣubḥ al-aʿshā* VIII, p. 124 f., transl. H. Lammens, "Correspondances diplomatiques entre les sultans mamlouks d'Egypte et les puissances chrétiennes," *ROC* IX (1904), p. 365 ff. In the translation the name should be corrected from Savignone or Silvio Bono to Centurione. Further, *khāzin* is not the shop but the merchant (from whom the soap had been bought).

refused to pay it, they were imprisoned, sent to Cairo, and their goods were sequestered.[130]

Thereupon the Genoese revenged themselves by new acts of aggression. They attacked the small coastal town of at-Tīna, east of Alexandria, and captured some of the inhabitants.[131] In February 1412 they raided Damietta, and in March they made another attack on at-Tīna, where, according to Arabic sources, they were pushed back after heavy fighting.[132]

As so often happened in the history of Genoese-Mamluk relations, after the hostilities in 1411 and 1412, trade was taken up, the Genoese merchants returned to Alexandria and once more the government of Genoa embarked on a policy of appeasement. In 1413 it decreed that Genoese subjects should abstain from attacks on the inhabitants of Egypt and Syria.[133] But in 1415 there was another conflict. Because of acts of aggression committed by the Genoese ruler of the island of Mytilene, the consul of Genoa in Alexandria was called to Cairo and there imprisoned. The Genoese merchants too were put into prison.[134] Then, in 1420, the Genoese exile Giovanni Ambrosio Spinola, with a small corsair fleet, attacked Venetian ships in Greek waters and endangered trade with the dominions of the Mamluks.[135] His activities induced Venetians and Mamluks to joint action.

The relations between the Catalans and the Mamluks in that period were no less stormy. Time and again acts of flagrant piracy and aggression resulted in reprisals, and the normal course of commercial exchanges was interrupted.

At the beginning of 1406, Antoni de Sori, a merchant of Barcelona, who lived in Alexandria, was called to Cairo and compelled to pay restitution for the damages caused Moslems by a privateer of Majorca. The said pirate had captured a Catalan ship, transporting grain and olive oil to Egypt, and brought it to Cagliari.[136] Then, in 1408, a similar act of piracy again entailed

[130] *Sulūk* IV, p. 182; Ibn Ḥadjar II, p. 491 f.; ʿAbdalbāsiṭ 803, f. 218b (who has the date Rabīʿ I 814, i.e., 23 June to 22 July 1411, and recounts that Ibn an-Naḥḥās, see below, fell in Alexandria); Ibn Iyās² I, part 2, p. 813 (the latter account is mistaken, being a second-hand report); according to most Arabic sources the encounter took place in Rabīʿ II 814, i.e., 23 July to 20 August, whereas the Genoese chronicler Stella says that the fighting went on from 26 July to 25 August; see Joh. Stella, *Annales* apud Muratori *Rer. It. Scriptores* 17, col. 1238; Piloti, p. 219 ff.; see, further, Jorga, "Notes et extraits," *ROL* IV, p. 517 f., Pero Tafur, *Andanças y viajes*, ed. Jimenez de la Espada (Madrid, 1874), p. 112 ff.

[131] al-Maḳrīzī and Ibn Ḥadjar *l.c.*, ʿAbdalbāsiṭ 803, f. 220a, and see also as-Sakhāwī, *aḍ-Ḍaw al-lāmiʿ* I, p. 203 f., about the death of Ibn an-Naḥḥās, who fell in the fighting (where it should be 13 Rabīʿ II instead of 13 Djumādā II).

[132] *Sulūk* IV, p. 596; Ibn Ḥadjar II, p. 492.

[133] Musso, *Navig.*, p. 72.

[134] Jorga, "Notes et extraits," *ROL* IV, p. 543; Arch. Zane, letter from Cairo of 5 March 1416.

[135] *Chron. Morosini*, c. 374, 377, 379 f., 381; Secreta VII, f. 183a, 204a VIII, f. 7b, 5a f., 9b, 10b f., 13a, 16b, 17b ff., 19b, 22a, 23a and cf. Thiriet, *Rég.* II, p. 185 f., 186.

[136] Vat. sub 19 March 1406.

reprisals and conflicts. Piloti reports that Moslem merchants who embarked with their merchandise on a Catalan ship in Alexandria for a trip to Tunis were brought to Barcelona by the captain and sold as slaves. When their parents applied to the sultan of Cairo, he accepted the argument of the Catalan consul, who maintained that they ought to apply to the ruler of Tunis, their own country. But in 1411, Piloti says, after the death of Faradj, his successor, Shaykh, condemned the Catalan traders to pay 30,000 ducats as restitution, half of the sum in Alexandria and the other half in Damascus. The Catalan consul of Alexandria wrote to his fellow-countrymen in Damascus, advising them to flee, but the latter sent 4,000 ducats to the sultan and handed him the letter of the consul. Thereupon, the sultan had the consul beaten, and all Catalan merchants left his dominions. The consul himself was sent to Alexandria to remain in confinement. This story, as told by the Cretan author, has been quoted by several modern scholars as authentic,[137] but it should be corrected according to more reliable sources. In fact, the reprisals against the Catalans began two years before the death of Sultan Faradj. According to the letter of a Catalan merchant, written in Alexandria on April 1, 1410, a fine had been imposed on the Catalans at the beginning of that year. They were fined because a Catalan ship's captain, Marti Vicens, had taken two ships of Moslems with merchandise belonging to native Christians and Turks in the port of Damietta.[138] The fine of 30,000 ducats was indeed imposed upon the Catalans in 1411 (but by Sultan Faradj who reigned until 1412!). From the acts of a notary in Damascus we learn that on 5 October 1411 the chief interpreter of the sultan, a Genoese renegade, came to the Syrian capital with an order to sequester spices bought by the Catalans up to the value of 15,000 dinars. The spices purchased by the Catalans had already been loaded on a Venetian galley and had to be discharged.[139] This document is confirmed and completed by a merchant letter written in Damascus in the same month. A Venetian agent writes to his firm in Venice that the sultan imposed a fine of 30,000 dinars on the Genoese and Catalans (sc. of Damascus) for having broken the peace and committed acts of violence in the port of Alexandria. So the fine was a consequence of the Genoese-Catalan encounter in Alexandria, and both parties were punished.[140]

In May 1412 the Venetian merchant whose letter has been quoted before reported to his firm in Venice that the sultan had taken a great quantity

[137] Piloti, p. 229 ff., Heyd II, p. 472 f., Labib, *Handelsgeschichte*, p. 347 f. (who gives the date of the payment of the fine as 1415!); N. Coll Julia, "Aspectos del corso catalán y del commercio internacional en el siglo XV," *Estudios de historia moderna* IV (1954), p. 160 ff., Del Treppo, p. 30.

[138] Ainaud, "Quatre doc.," doc. III.

[139] Giacomo della Torre, no. 2, cf. no. 7.

[140] Arch. Zane, letter of Benedetto Dandolo of 7 October 1411.

of spices from the Catalans and that they discharged 12,000 pieces of cloth and 200 boxes of coral in Rhodes (instead of shipping them to Syria).[141] Piloti wrote that the Catalans departed from the dominions of the sultan after the events in Alexandria in 1411. This may have been true, since the Moslems were enraged with the Catalans. When the Catalan Antoni de Sori, a veteran Egypt trader, arrived in Alexandria on his ship, he was imprisoned and detained more than two years. But a short time later the Catalans attempted to re-establish friendly relations and regular trade with the Mamluk dominions. At the end of 1412, Fernando I, king of Aragon, addressed a letter to Emir Nawrūz, the actual ruler of Syria, and asked him to take measures so that the Catalan merchants could carry on their activities in Syria. He also wrote a letter to the sultan on behalf of a Catalan noble who went to the latter's dominions. A year later he gave Francesch Zatrilla, who had been appointed Catalan consul in Alexandria, letters of recommendation to the Egytian authorities.[142] In 1414 the consul obtained a letter from the sultan promising that the Catalan merchants would be well treated, and Catalan trade was taken up in both Egypt and Syria.[143]

In the year 1415, however, there was a new conflict between the Catalan merchants and the government of the sultan. Maghrebin merchants demanded the payment of 120,000 dinars form the Catalans as restitution for damages caused them by flagrant robbery. The Catalan consul was summoned to Cairo, condemned by a High Court of the four chiefs cadis, and put into prison.[144] A merchant letter indicates that at the beginning of March 1416 the Catalan merchants and their consul were still imprisoned.[145] The king of Aragon had tried to curb the activities of the Catalan corsairs and had given orders in this sense to the authorities in Sicily in March 1415. But, seeing that leniency did not prove successful, the Catalans again chose aggression. They decided to act against the Mamluks *manu militari*. In August 1416 eight big Catalan cogs anchored in the port of Alexandria, the crews landed, attacked the Moslems, took many prisoners, and killed about twenty men. Then they besieged the town, whose gates had been closed in time. When a Maghrebin ship loaded with olive oil arrived in the port, the Catalans captured it and massacred the crew. Many inhabitants of the town fled, and troops were despatched from Cairo to fight the Cat-

141 *Ibidem*, letter of 14 April 1412.

142 ACA, Cancill. Real, 2359, f. 71b 2384, f. 96a/b. Quoting these documents, A. Boscolo speaks about two embassies sent by the king of Aragon to Cairo in 1413 and 1414, see his "La politica italiana di Fernando I d'Aragona," *Studi Sardi* XII-XIII (1952-1954), parte II, p. 92 f. This statement is not supported by the said letters. As to the king's intervention for Antoni Sori see Cancill. Real, 2397, f. 127b f.: he writes in February 1414 to the sultan, asking him to restore to Sori his sequestered goods, since he had suffered great losses.

143 Capmany, 2.1, no. 283, pp. 419-20; about Zatrilla see *op.cit.*, II, app. p. 59.

144 *Chron. Morosini*, c. 295; Jorga, "Notes et extraits," *ROL* IV, p. 543.

145 Arch. Zane, letter of 5 March 1416 from Candia.

alans, but, when they arrived, the Catalans had already departed.[146] The reports of the Arabic chroniclers and of Piloti are completed by a detailed account of a Venetian chronicler. He recounts that three Catalan cogs with merchandise worth 75,000 dinars came to Alexandria and that the merchants actually engaged in trade. Then the Catalans set fire to four Moslem ships, whereupon the Moslems rose against them, and all the European merchants were imprisoned. Then the Catalans departed, carrying with them a Genoese and a Venetian ship and eighty Moslem captives. A month later, says the author, the Venetians were set free and could return to their fondaco.[147]

This attack had grave consequences for the Catalan trade in the Mamluk dominions. At that time, the sultan and his government were irate with those European powers who collaborated with and supported the activities of corsairs, and the Catalans were indeed very active in privateering and raiding the coasts of the Moslem Levant. The Cypriots and Rhodians, apparently with the help of the Catalans, raided the coasts of Syria and Egypt time and again. In 1410 four Christian ships captured a Moslem merchantman in the port of Jaffa.[148] Two years later, corsairs landed on the Lebanese coast, at the mouth of the river Damur, but were repulsed.[149] Then in May 1416 the small Egyptian coastal town of Nastarū was attacked,[150] and a month later Jaffa was raided and fifty Moslems captured. In the same month, there was a brawl between European merchants and Moslems in Alexandria, and they captured a Maghrebin ship.[151] The Arabic authors who report these acts of hostility speak generally of Franks, but Piloti specifically details the aggressive policy of the Cypriots and the ransoming of Moslem prisoners brought to Cyprus.[152] al-Maḳrīzī reports that in 1415 not less than 535 Moslem captives were ransomed from the Cypriots,[153] and an act drawn up by a Venetian notary in Damascus refers to

[146] ACA, Cancill. Real, 2429, f. 42a/b; *Sulūk* IV, p. 360 ff.; Ibn Ḥadjar, III, p. 94; 'Abdalbāsiṭ 803, f. 236b. The Arabic authors do not say who these "Franks" were, but al-Maḳrīzī remarks that the ships were those "of the Atlantic Ocean." Weil V, p. 135, mentions these accounts and explains that they were "pirates." Neither did Labib, *op.cit.*, p. 350 f. identify the attackers. According to Piloti, p. 232 f., the Catalan attack took place "about three years" after the punishment of the Catalans for the capture of the Maghrebins and the imprisonment of the consul. Once more the Cretan author's account is not exact. Further, he says that the Moslem ship which they captured in Alexandria was a Turkish one.

[147] *Chron. Morosini*, c. 323.

[148] *Sulūk* IV, p. 143.

[149] Ṭannūs ash-Shidyāḳ, *History of the personalities of Lebanon* (in Arabic) (Beirut, 1954), p. 47 (it is not said in this account that they were Cypriots, although it is very probable; cf. Ch. Schefer, *Le voyage d'Outremer de Bertrandon de la Broquière*, p. XLIX).

[150] *Sulūk* IV, p. 353; Ibn Ḥadjar III, p. 90.

[151] *Sulūk* IV, p. 357; Ibn Ḥadjar III, p. 93; 'Abdalbāsiṭ 803, f. 236a.

[152] Piloti, p. 174 f.

[153] *Sulūk* IV, p. 300; Ibn Ḥadjar III, p. 53; 'Abdalbāsiṭ 803, f. 230b. f. (who has 550 captives).

the ransoming by a Jew of poor Moslems who had been captured by Catalans and brought to Rhodes.[154] Catalan pirates intercepted the Moslem ships going between the southern coast of Asia Minor and Egypt.[155] The intense activities of the Catalan privateers is also witnessed by many notarial acts drawn up in the ports of Sicily. Moslems taken captives by Catalans in Syrian waters were sold as slaves in Sicily. Several acts of notaries of Messina refer to this.[156] In the year 1416, when the Catalans attacked the Moslems in Alexandria, a Catalan pirate, Nicholau Sampier, cut the lines of communication in the Eastern Mediterranean and captured ships in the ports. In the month of July he captured a Venetian cog in Beirut: then in 1417 he cruised off the southern coasts of Greece, awaiting the Venetian cotton cogs, sailed to Acre, and captured two Venetian cogs there.[157] At the same time, Biscayan pirates infested the Central and Eastern Mediterranean.[158] So there was a great tension, and the Moslems feared new attacks, especially in Alexandria.[159] In 1417, when the excitement in Alexandria was high, Catalan merchandise was sequestered.[160] In fact, after the attack on Alexandria in 1416, the sultan had forbidden the Catalans to carry on trade in his dominions, and they had to entrust other European merchants with the marketing of their merchandise.[161] But the Catalan pirates were not influenced by these measures. In 1419 a Catalan pirate, Moncoffa, captured a Rhodian ship carrying merchandise of Moslems in the port of Beirut. Thereupon the Venetian, Genoese, and Anconitan merchants in Beirut and Damascus were imprisoned and their goods sequestered. The Moslem authorities threatened them if they would not disclose the whereabouts of the goods of the Catalans.[162] Again orders were given to sequester all Catalan goods in Syria.[163] In 1423 the embargo on the import of Catalan commodities was still in force.[164] Meanwhile, the Catalan corsairs continued their activities. In 1421 the Catalan Guillem de Montagna captured, off Rhodes, a French ship sailing to Egypt.[165]

[154] My "New data for the history of Levantine Jewries in the fifteenth century," *Bulletin of the Institute of Jewish Studies* III (1975), pp. 83, 101 f.

[155] Piloti, p. 139.

[156] Andreolo sub 14 Sept. 1419, 18 Sept. 1419; M. Alibrandi, "Messinesi in Levante nel medioevo," *Arch. Stor. Sic.*, ser. III 21/22 (1972), p. 108 f.

[157] *Chron. Dolfin*, f. 301a ff.; Misti 52, f. 2b f., 15b f., 39a; G. P., Sent. 29, f. 67a f.; Thiriet, *Rég.* II, p. 163; Cod. Marciana 2034, f. 329a/b.

[158] *Chron. Morosini*, c. 238, 263, 290, 323; Anonymous chronicle, Cod. Marciana 7293, f. 102a, and Cod. Marciana 2034, f. 309b: Biscayan pirates capture in 1413 three Venetian ships, one of them returning from Alexandria and carrying merchandise worth 20,000 ducats.

[159] *Sulūk* IV, pp. 386, 394; Ibn Ḥadjar III, p. 138.

[160] Misti 52, f. 39a.

[161] Piloti, p. 148 f.

[162] Nic. Venier B, 2, f. 14b ff., 16a f.

[163] *Ibid.*, f. 17a f., 18a.

[164] G. P., Sent. 33, testimonies of 24 Jan. 1424, 1 March and 14 March 1424 34, f. 12a f.

[165] Nic. Venier B, 2, f. 42b/43a.

The aggressiveness of the Genoese and the Catalans was undoubtedly prejudicial to the development of their trade in the dominions of the Mamluks. The frequent interruptions of the regular exchanges and the reprisals by the Mamluk authorities certainly resulted in considerable losses and must have induced many merchants to invest their capital elsewhere. The inclination to attack the Moslems was one of the factors that brought about the decline of the Levantine trade of these nations, whereas the Venetian leniency and patience certainly contributed to their ascendancy. But we must be careful not to exaggerate the impact of this factor. Piloti, who, though not always exact, was a good observer and an expert in all the problems connected with the Levant trade, emphasizes that the Catalans could carry on their trade despite the privateering. There were, however, various other factors that brought about the decline of Genoese and Catalan trade with the Levant.[166] It was connected with the commercial activities of these nations and the economic condition in their own countries. The acts of aggression, prejudicial though they were to their trade with the Mamluk dominions, did not entail their immediate discontinuation or even a rapid decline. In fact, many documents show that there was a substantial volume of Genoese and Catalan trade in the Moslem Levant in the first quarter of the fifteenth century.

The Genoese even tried at this time to get a greater part of the trade between Central Europe and the Mediterranean. When King Sigismund put an embargo on trade between Germany and Venice, the Genoese tried to intensify their own commercial exchanges with the great trading towns of Upper Germany. In 1417 emissaries of Genoa and Milan came to Constance and promised the German merchants that they would enjoy better conditions in Genoa as compared with Venice. They even declared that the Germans could ship their merchandise from Genoa by sea, whereas Venice never allowed foreigners to use her port for this purpose. Then, in 1420, the archbishop of Milan submitted to the Diet of Breslau the agreement reached between envoys of the German traders and the authorities of Genoa.[167]

The Genoese colony in Alexandria was fairly numerous in the first decade of the fifteenth century. There can be no doubt that its size declined, but, to judge from notarial acts drawn up in 1405 and 1406, the Genoese were still more numerous than the Venetians. The acts of 1403 indicate that there were more Venetians, but Piloti says that forty Genoese were imprisoned when Boucicault moved to the Levantine coasts.[168] Further, they

[166] See, for the Catalan trade, J. Vicens Vives, "Evolución de la economia catalana durante la primera mitad del siglo XV," in *IV Congreso de historia de la Corona de Aragón*, 1955, ponencia 3, and cf. below; Piloti, p. 234 f.; see also Del Treppo, pp. 29 f., 40.

[167] A. Schulte, *Geschichte des mittelalt. Handels* II, no. 381 (p. 256 ff.), and see I, p. 515 ff.; *idem*, *Geschichte der grossen Ravensburger Handelsgesellschaft* I, p. 260 ff.

[168] See Table XVIII and Piloti, p. 192.

still maintained two fondachi[169] and the consulate was always filled by a competent Genoese merchant.[170] However, in the second decade of the fifteenth century the number of Genoese in Alexandria greatly decreased; certainly the acts of aggression had their consequences. In 1406, a tax of 6 percent for import to Alexandria and of 1 percent for export had to be imposed by the Genoese authorities to pay the debts of the colony, and a part of the sum yielded by this impost was assigned to the payment of restitution for the capture of a Moslem ship by the Genoese Marco Malocello.[171] As before, the Genoese also engaged in trade in Syria and had a colony in Damascus, with a consul at its head. In 1407 the post was held by Benedetto Ciba and in 1419 by Benedetto Paravesini.[172] The commercial activities of the Genoese were supervised by the *Officium Alexandriae*, also called *Officium Syriae et Cypri*.[173] This office in the metropolis and the consulates in Alexandria and Damascus established and collected the special taxes that were almost regularly imposed on the Genoese trade with the Levant. In 1403 a tax of 1 percent for trade with Alexandria was established,[174] and in the same year a *drictus Syriae* was imposed.[175] In 1404 once more a tax of 1 percent for the shipping of merchandise to and from Alexandria on Genoese vessels was imposed for two years. For gold and silver, however, the impost was 3 percent.[176] At the end of 1405, the tax was imposed once again.[177]

The number of Genoese ships that anchored in the port of Alexandria was still considerable. The convoy of the Cyprus-Alexandria galleys consisted of three galleys in 1403,[178] and in notarial acts drawn up in Alexandria in 1405 six Genoese ships are mentioned.[179] Genoese documents refer to ships sailing to Alexandria in 1408 and in 1414.[180] Also, merchants and ships of Savona apparently visited the great Egyptian emporium rather often in this period. A notarial act drawn up in Genoa in 1408 refers to the charter by a Genoese merchant of a ship of Savona, the "Santa Maria-Stus Nicolaus-Stus Theramus." The ship was to sail to Gaeta, Naples,

[169] Nic. Venier B, 2, f. 30a (a. 1421).

[170] Ilario Cattaneo was consul, 1404-1406; see Vat. sub 8 July 1404, 29 Dec. 1405, 29 Jan. 1406, 13 Aug. 1406. Carlo Iustiniano succeeded him in 1406; see Vat. sub 15 Aug. 1406, 13 Oct. 1406. Azelino Gentile was consul until mid-summer 1421; see Nic. Venier B, 2, f. 26a/b, 30a, and his successor was Gabriele Cattaneo, see there f. 37b/38a.

[171] Vat. sub 15 Aug. 1406.

[172] Musso, *Navig.*, p. 75; Nic. Venier B, 2, f. 23a/b.

[173] Musso, *Navig.*, p. 76 f.

[174] Ant. Com. 26, p. 43 cf. p. 132.

[175] Musso, *Navig.*, p. 78.

[176] Vat. sub 5 and 18 June 1405.

[177] Vat. sub 23 Dec. 1405.

[178] Ant. Com. 26, p. 36.

[179] See my paper in *JEEH* III, p. 7.

[180] Musso, *op.cit.*, p. 76.

Table XIX Catalan merchants in the Moslem Levant, 1403 - 1413

year	Alexandria	Damascus
1403	14	
1404	19	
1405	20	
1406	21	
1412		6
1413		6

Castellamare, Salerno, Rhodes, and Alexandria and to anchor in the Egyptian port twenty-five days. Then it was to sail back to Rhodes, Chios, visit Phocea, Mytilene, and once more Chios, and finally go to Sluys.[181] In 1409 a ship of Savona was chartered in Alexandria by Florentine merchants for a journey to Aigues-Mortes, but the captain sailed to Savona, where, according to their claims the merchandise was stolen. Its value amounted to 25,000 ducats.[182] Another line of shipping on which the Genoese and other Ligurian merchants still engaged in a lively trade in the first quarter of the fifteenth century was the line Pera-Chios-Alexandria. Genoese ships sailed from Pera to Alexandria,[183] and Genoese merchants of Pera and Chios imported their merchandise to Egypt. In 1419 two Genoese merchants of Pera sold timber for 1,170 ducats to the Mamluk authorities in Alexandria.[184] The import of mastic of Chios to Egypt was still an exclusively Genoese business. In 1405 it was farmed out by the Genoese authorities to eight merchants.[185]

The line Chios-Alexandria was the main artery of Genoese shipping in the eastern basin of the Mediterranean, and many ships commuted on it.[186] Since the Genoese had many and big ships, they served not only their own commercial activities. Often their ships were chartered by merchants belonging to other trading nations. In the year 1414 Giovanni Griffo, a Pisan living in Genoa, chartered the cog of Antonio Oxelo de Vulturis for a trip

[181] ASG, Notai 405, Gatto, Bart. 10/2, sub 27 Nov. 1408.

[182] G. P., Sent. 21, f. 19a ff., 21a (litigation concerning the assurance); Chron. Morosini I, p. 300 (the records of the proceedings of the litigation before the Giudici di petiziòn and the account in the chronicle undoubtedly refer to the same case. According to the said proceedings, where no date of the journey is given, Boucicault was still in control of Genoa, so it cannot have been after 1409).

[183] Vat. sub 26 July 1404.

[184] Nic. Venier B, 2, f. 37b ff.; see also Leonardo de Valle sub 4 Febr. 1404: Jacobus Lomellino di Circassia.

[185] ASG, Notai 436, 1, Ravellino, Crist. c. 70/71; see, further, Leonardo de Valle sub 10 March 1403; Piloti, p. 155 f.

[186] Nic. Venier B, 2, f. 40a ff.; Musso, *Navigazione*, p. 135.

to Castellamare, Trani, from there to Granada or Flanders, and finally, via Modon, to Rhodes or Chios or Alexandria.[187]

As in earlier periods the Genoese imported great quantities of olive oil to Egypt,[188] especially from Andalusia.[189] The inventory of the goods left by a Genoese merchant who died in 1421 in Alexandria comprises olive oil, soap, and paper.[190] The Genoese imported hazelnuts from Ventimiglia into Egypt,[191] and, as always, marketed coral in both Egypt and Syria.[192] Of course, they imported a good deal of cloth, the products of the Italian and Catalan manufacturers and of many others.[193]

At the beginning of the fifteenth century the volume of Genoese trade in the Moslem Levant was still considerable, but already smaller than that of the Venetian trade. In 1403 an impost of 1 percent on Genoese trade with Egypt was farmed out for 5,240 l.[194] As the tax, which undoubtedly comprised the tax paid for trade with Syria, was collected both for import to and export from Egypt, the volume of the Genoese investment could not have been very much greater than perhaps 250,000 ducats. Comparing this sum with the total of the 1 percent impost collected in the port of Genoa, one arrives at the conclusion that the Genoese investment in trade with Egypt amounted then to about 28 percent of the total investment in foreign trade.[195] So the importance of the trade with the Moslem Levant as compared with other sectors of Genoa's foreign trade was even greater than in the 1370's.[196] But probably the estimate of the volume of the Levantine trade of Genoa was made according to the data of the years of boom in the late 1390's. It does not show the decline after the unfortunate expedition of Boucicault.

From the data on the Levantine trade of the Catalans in the first quarter of the fifteenth century, similar considerations will be drawn. In the first decade of the century, its volume was still sizable, certainly it then was not smaller than in the 1380's and the 1390's. But later it declined greatly. The intensity of Catalan trade with the Moslem Levant in the first years of the century is borne out by the numbers of Catalan merchants who are

187 Doehaerd-Kerremans, no. 179.

188 Vat. sub 19 and 22 Dec. 1405; Musso, "Armamento," p. 14 f.

189 Vat. sub 3 Nov. 1405 (worth 6382 dinars!).

190 Nic. Venier B, 2, f. 32a f.

191 Piloti, p. 149.

192 Nic. Venier B, 2, f. 2a-4a, 39b (a merchant imports coral worth 682 ducats; another, coral worth 600; a third, coral worth 978).

193 See above, note 23. It goes without saying that some Genoese did not abstain from importing timber into Egypt; see Tur V, f. 30a (referring to a transaction in 1414 approximately).

194 Ant. Com. 26, p. 43 and cf. 132.

195 H. Sieveking, "Aus Genueser Rechnungs-u. Steuerbüchern" (see ch. 1, n. 32), p. 52.

196 See above.

mentioned in the acts of the notaries of Alexandria and Damascus. These data point to an increase in the number of Catalan merchants in Alexandria at the beginning of the fifteenth century.[197] Fewer acts of the Alexandrian notaries have been preserved from the second decade of the century, but nevertheless one may conclude from them that the Catalan colony became smaller, as a consequence of the conflicts with the Moslem authorities. Some of these acts refer to the sale of slave girls by Catalans; in others, Catalans appear as witnesses.[198] The fact that in the acts of Niccolò Venier the Catalans are missing altogether points clearly to the decline of their trade in Egypt, for this notary served all the European merchants.

In the Catalan trade with the Moslem Levant, the merchants of Barcelona held first place. Most ships sailing from Catalonia to the Levantine ports belonged to citizens of Barcelona, and they were the largest investors in this trade. But, also, Tortosa and Perpignan were commercial centers which had direct relations with the Moslem Levant. They were maintained by ships owned by merchants of Perpignan or by inhabitants of Collioure, and also by ships of Barcelona which visited Collioure on their way to Sicily and the Levant (and on the return voyage).[199] A "ship of Tortosa" which arrived from Alexandria in 1403 in Aigues-Mortes is mentioned in a letter to the Datini firm in Barcelona. It discharged in Aigues-Mortes a great quantity of spices. Perpignan was still a great market for Levantine articles. It supplied Languedoc with spices. After the death of Pere Tequin (in 1405-1408), his sons Tomaso and Johan carried on his business. They still had their ship, whose patron was Johan Bastier, and also agents in Damascus and in Alexandria. In the Syrian capital, Johan Fagio was their agent. Another enterprising merchant and clothier of Perpignan was Jean Fabre, who too engaged in the first years of the fifteenth century very much in the spice trade and had an agent in Damascus. Even he carried on business with the Datini firm in Alexandria and with some towns of Southern France. The brothers Guillem and Georges Campredon, who carried on (together or separately) a lively trade with France, Barcelona, Aragon, Valencia, the Balearic Islands and Sicily, also engaged in trade with the Levant. Guillem Campredon exported in 1416 to the Moslem Levant cloth worth 1,433 pounds of Barcelona (1,910 ducats) and in 1417 cloth worth 2,208 pounds (2,944 ducats). The two brothers had also ships of their own. In 1413 two ships of Georges Campredon sailed for the Mamluk dominions.[200]

[197] Cf. above.

[198] Crist. Rizzo sub 8 Nov. 1414: Joh. de S. Pedro sells a slave girl; *idem* sub 6 June 1416: Nic. Sampier sells another one, sub 6 Aug. 1416.

[199] Investments by traders of Perpignan: Real Patr. 2910/1, f. 18b (and see below); by merchants of Tortosa, *ibid.*, f. 20b.

[200] Dat 844, letter of Andrea di Giovanni Brandi, fom Aigues-Mortes, of 7 May 1403; about the activities of Tomaso Tequin, see Dat 907, his letters to the Datini firm in Barcelona of

The Catalan merchants who lived in Alexandria in the first decade of the fifteenth century came from various provinces of their country. There were merchants of Valencia,[201] Gerona,[202] Ampurias,[203] Perpignan,[204] and Majorca.[205] Some of them lived in the Egyptian emporium for a long time.[206] From 1402 to 1406 Michael Galbes was the head of the colony;[207] from 1406 to 1408 it was Guillem de Cabanyells,[208] and after him Pere Oliver. When in 1413 Francesch Zatrilla was appointed consul, the king of Aragon ordered Oliver to leave the post, adding threats to his order.[209] Piloti writes that the Catalan consul who had tried to counteract the order of the sultan in 1411 and had been confined to obligatory domicile in Alexandria fled from there during the Catalan attack in 1416.[210] Since Oliver was apparently an unruly and stubborn man and the king of Aragon had to threaten him in 1413 to get him to leave his post, the account of Piloti may refer to him (and not to Zatrilla). In any case, after the events of 1416 the post of the Catalan consul in Alexandria was not filled for many years.

---

12 Dec. 1409, 3 and 23 Apr. 1410 (the ship), 30 Apr. 1410 (the agent in Damascus); and see Ainaud, "Quatre documents," doc. IV (an agent in Alexandria); see also Dat 929, letter of Luigi di Manetto Davenzati and Luca di Matteo & Cie of 27 Nov. 1406: "the son of Pere Tequin returns on the ship of Collioure from Beirut"; about the death date of Pere Tequin, see Dat 907, letter of his of 22 Nov. 1409; Tomaso Tequin was still active in 1431, when he borrowed from the Royal authorities arrows for the equipment of his ship; see AOP, Proc. Real IX, f. 60a, cf. Alart, p. 156b, 157a.

See, further, the letters of Jean Fabre, *ibid.*, and especially those of 2 June, 18 Oct., 26 Oct., 20 Nov. 1403, and 24 Jan. 1404. See also APO, Consulat de mer, Rég. a. 1417: Tomaso Tequin and Jean Fabre cash imposts for the "Consulate of the sea"; see, further, R. Ferrer 196, f. 37a; APO, notary Paytavi 859, sub 15 Apr. and 27 May 1422.

See, further, APO, Proc. Real IV, f. 126b f.: Bernat Jou, merchant of Perpignan, undertakes in 1404 to pay all the imposts due for the ship "Santa Maria-Santa Eulalia," which was scheduled to depart for Alexandria; APO, B. 250, liasse 24, act of 9 Febr. 1407 and R. Ferrer 98, f. 11b about the Levant trade of Georges Barbariga of Perpignan; see also F. Bosqueros 731, f. 33a, 42a (a. 1404) 735, f. 1a, 2a, 4b f., 5a, 5b, 6a, 6A f., 6b f., 7b, 8b f. (a. 1406) (all of them referring to the export of cloth, by merchants of Perpignan, to the Moslem Levant) and *ibid.*, 8a (export of furs).

About the activities of the brothers Campredon, see Ant. Guitard 1552, f. 70a 1553, f. 16a 1554, sub 1 March 1417 1550, p. 30 1560, f. 15a ff.; APO b. 199, Manual of Jaume Nadal 72, f. 21b (misinterpreted by Alart P. 143b).

201 Leonardo de Valle sub 24 March 1403, 12 Oct. 1403; Vat. sub 8 Febr. 1405, 29 Dec. 1405, 3 March 1406, 15 March 1406.

202 Leonardo de Valle sub 2, 15 and 20 Oct. 1403; Vat. sub 19 March 1406.

203 Vat. sub 13 April 1405, 2 May 1405.

204 Leonardo de Valle sub 10 March 1403.

205 Vat. sub 19 Jan. 1405, 8, 9 and 29 Dec. 1405, 29 Jan. 1406, 8 Febr. 1406, 3 March 1406.

206 Antoni de Sori of Barcelona lived in Alexandria at least from 1400 to 1406; see Vat. sub 11 May 1400 and 14 March 1406. Berenger Vidal of Gerona lived there from 1403 to 1406; see Leonardo de Valle sub 23 March 1403, Vat. sub 19 March 1406.

207 Leonardo de Valle sub 4 July 1403, 29 Apr. 1404; Vat. sub 19 Jan. 1405, 3 March 1406; Del Treppo, RSI 70, p. 53.

208 Vat. sub 7 June 1406; López de Meneses, "Los consulados," p. 114.

209 López de Meneses, *art. cit.*, p. 114f.

210 Piloti, p. 232.

Acts of the Italian notaries in Damascus include data about the Catalan merchants who lived in the Syrian capital, in Beirut, and in Tripoli in the second decade of the fifteenth century.[211] Some Catalans even lived there for several years.[212] Among them were merchants of Barcelona, Perpignan, and Majorca.[213] They imported into Syria saffron, coral,[214] Catalan and French cloth, e.g., cloth of Miranda,[215] and engaged in the trade of precious stones.[216]

However, data in various documents show that in that period the Catalans carried on much more trade with Egypt than with Syria, although many Catalan ships visited both countries. Those that went to Jaffa probably transported mainly pilgrims.[217] These data culled from the registers of the customs offices and the acts of notaries in Barcelona and Perpignan leave no doubt as to the increase in the number of the Catalan ships that sailed to the ports of the Moslem Levant in the first decade of the fifteenth century. In those years, Catalan traffic to the Moslem Levant increased by 50 percent as compared with the 1390's.[218] In addition, there should be added to the Catalan ships Biscayan and Castilian vessels that went to Egypt and Syria and on the way visited Barcelona or another Catalan port, loading merchandise there. Several notarial acts of Barcelona refer to them.[219] But these data are not complete. The acts of the notaries of Alexandria mention other

[211] Giacomo della Torre, nos. 14, 16; Nic. Venier B. 2, f. 5a ff., 16a ff. About the activities of the Catalans in Beirut see Ainaud, "Quatre doc.," doc. I.

[212] Joh. Chanal of Barcelona, a representative of several firms of his town, lived in Damascus from 1410 to 1418 (at least); see Giacomo della Torre, no. 3, 8, 18; Nic. Venier B, 2, f. 5b/6a, 6a/b. Some of them carried on trade first in Alexandria and then in Damascus, e.g., Pericono Casasagia, who was in Alexandria in 1403, see Leonardo de Valle sub 4 July 1403, and in 1418 in Damascus, see Nic. Venier B, 2, f. 5a, 5b/6a.

[213] Giacomo della Torre, no. 3, 20.

[214] Nic. Venier B, 2, f. 6a/b, 17a/b, 18a.

[215] Giacomo della Torre, no. 14. This was probably cloth of Miranda in the département of Gers.

[216] Nic. Venier B, 2, f. 5b/6a.

[217] Our table sums up the data collected by Carrère, p. 851 ff., Del Treppo, p. 608 ff. But non-Catalan ships are excluded, and some corrections have been made according to the registers of the Real Patr. and Ainaud, "Quatre docs.," doc. IV (ship of Borrell from Collioure to Alexandria in 1410); Carrère, *Barcelone*, p. 165 (ship of Bernat Gualbes in 1411). Data about the shipping from Collioure to the Levant have been added from F. Bosqueros 731, f. 33a, 34a; APO, Proc. Real IV, f. 126b f. ("Santa Maria-Santa Eulalia," patron Ant. Sallels, a. 1404, cf. note 200); F. Bosqueros 735, f. 1a, 4b f., 5a, 5b, 6a, 6a f., 8b f., 9a (ship of Johan Bastier); Ant' Guitard 1553, f. 12b, 16a (ship "Spindola"). Sub a. 1413 Del Treppo, p. 612, lists three ships sailing to the Moslem Levant, those of Johan Pi, Johan Bonet, and Guillem Campredon. But, according to APO B. 199, Manual of Jaume Nadal 72, f. 21b, the ships whose patrons were Johan Pi (of Collioure) and Johan Bonet were owned by Guillem Campredon.

[218] This is rightly emphasized by Del Treppo, p. 31.

[219] See Del Treppo, p. 610, 612 and cf. p. 26. Also, some Genoese and Florentine ships visit Barcelona on their way to the Moslem Levant, see *op.cit.*, p. 616.

Table XX Catalan shipping to the Moslem Levant, 1403 - 1421

year	to Alexandria	to Beirut	to Jaffa	to several ports or to the "Levant
1403	4	2	1	3
1404	9	1	1	
1405	7	2		1
1406	4	1	1	3
1407		2		
1408	4	1		2
1409	3	2		
1410	3			
1411				7
1412	1			
1413	2	1		1
1414	3	1		
1415	2	1		1
1416				2
1417	3			2
1418	7			
1419	9		2	
1420	2			
1421	3			

Catalan ships that anchored in the great Egyptian port in those years.[220] The same data also emphasize the fact that after the encounter with the Genoese in the port of Alexandria in 1411, Catalan trade in Egypt declined. They confirm, on the other hand, the account of Piloti, who dwells on the continuation of Catalan trade with the dominions of the Mamluks after the acts of hostility in Alexandria in 1416. In fact, the number of the Catalan ships that anchored in the ports of Egypt in 1418 and 1419 was much greater than before. So our data also point to the irregularity of Catalan shipping in the Moslem Levant. This was due to economic conditions in Catalonia, but of course the piracy and the other acts of aggression prejudiced Catalan trade in the Levant.

As at the end of the fourteenth century, Rhodes served the Catalans as a base for their commercial activities in the Eastern Mediterranean. Because of the close relations between them, the Catalans could always be sure of enjoying the help and protection of the Knights Hospitallers.[221] In 1403

[220] In 1405, seven ships, and in 1406, four; see appendix A 6.

[221] See Vat. sub Sept. 1404 (no exact date): Bernat Laurenzii, a Catalan trader in Alexandria, gives the ambassador of the Knights a loan of 1,000 dinars.

the knights concluded a treaty with the sultan of Cairo and obtained freedom of trade in his dominions for their subjects, with the right to appoint consuls in Alexandria, Damietta, and Jerusalem.[222] From then on, there were Rhodian consuls in Alexandria and in other towns.[223] Rhodian ships anchored in the ports of Egypt, and the Greek merchants of Rhodes carried on trade in Egypt and Syria.[224] However, the trade between Rhodes and the dominions of the sultan was mainly in the hands of other merchants, among whom the Catalans ranked first. The Catalans supplied the Order of the Hospitallers with great quantities of spices purchased in Alexandria and engaged in trade between Syria and Rhodes.[225]

The commenda contracts drawn up in Barcelona at the beginning of the fifteenth century and other sources contain much data about the commodities which the Catalans exported to Egypt.

Even in that period, the Catalans imported into the Moslem Levant great quantities of olive oil, that of Tarragona, of Majorca, and of other provinces ruled by the kings of Aragon.[226] They marketed the excellent honey of Mequinanza, Tortosa, Prades, Penades, and Banyoles, as well as honey of some districts of Languedoc.[227] The export of Catalan cloth to the Moslem Levant was still a flourishing trade in that period, and Sicily was the great exchange from whence it was shipped to Egypt and to Syria. In Palermo, Messina, and in other towns of Sicily, great quantities of cloth of Barcelona, Valencia, Gerona, and Perpignan were sold and shipped to the Levant. Sicily also serves as an exchange for Flemish cloth.[228] But much Catalan cloth was shipped directly from Barcelona and other ports of Catalonia to Egypt and Syria.[229] In the first quarter of the fifteenth century, coral was

[222] Jorga, "Notes et extraits," *ROL* IV, p. 238 f.

[223] Georgius Melli was consul in Alexandria from 1400 to 1404; see Vat. sub 2 March 1400, Leonardo de Valle sub 20 Oct. 1404; Petrus de Lise in 1405, see Vat. sub 4 Nov. and 29 Dec. 1405.

[224] See appendix, A 6.

[225] Del Treppo, p. 86; Giacomo della Torre, no. 4. It goes without saying that also Sicily served the Catalans as a major base for their trade with the Moslem Levant, see Real Patr. 2910/1, f. 6a, 9a, 17b; see also f. 5b: a merchant of Perpignan carries on trade with Egypt from Rhodes and Sicily. Sometimes Candia fulfilled this role, see *l.c.*, p. 62.

[226] Vat. sub 10 Jan. 1406; Del Treppo, p. 73 f. Madurell-Garcia, nos. 174, 182.

[227] Del Treppo, 1. c.; Piloti, p. 147 f. See also Real Patr. 2910/1, f. 19b.; Tomas de Bellmunt IV, f. 19b. About export of almonds, *ibid.*, f. 18b; Tomas de Bellmunt IV, f. 4a f., 8b f. (to Alexandria), 26b (to Jaffa).

[228] Real Patr. 2910/1, f. 17b, 18a, 18b, 19a, 19b; ASPal, Gravezze 352, f. 193b: import of cloth by Catalan galleys (a. 1408); Notai 762, Di Marco, Giacomo, 1415-1426, sub 9 March 1416; sale of cloth of Barcelona; Notai 604, Rubeo, Paolo, c. 67a/b (a. 1412): cloth of Gerona sold by a Genoese, c. 154a: cloth of Valencia sold by a merchant of Valencia (a. 1414); Andreolo sub 22 Sept. 1419: a merchant of Perpignan sells cloth. Cloth of Wervicq-sur-Lys: ASPal, Notai 762, Di Marco, Giacomo sub 17 March 1416; Rubeo, Paolo, c. 158a: sold by a Genoese.

[229] Commenda contracts in Barcelona: Tomas de Bellmunt IV, f. 4a f., 10a, 11a, 19b (cloth of Villefranche exported to Jaffa), 20a, 20b (cloth of Olot exported to Jaffa), 21a, 26b f.

another article the Catalans sold in the Moslem Levant in considerable quantities.[230] Antimony sulphide (*cofolo*) was a typical Catalan chemical, and through the whole of this period it was exported to the Moslem Levant, where it was used as a cosmetic and for collyrium.[231] When Egypt suffered from a scarcity of grain, the Catalans brought in grains from Sicily, which served as a granary for several Mediterranean countries in the later Middle Ages.[232] The commenda contracts drawn up in the towns of Catalonia (and in Perpignan) very often comprise instructions as to the merchandise to be bought for the price obtained by the sale of the Catalan export goods. Most often spices are mentioned, such as ginger, cloves, and others. The agents were requested to ship the goods to the Catalan ports or to Aigues-Mortes.

How great the volume of the Catalan Levantine trade was in the first decade of the fifteenth century can be judged from the accounts of some chroniclers. A Genoese chronicler recounts that two ships, which the Catalans lost in 1411 in Alexandria, carried merchandise worth 80,000 ducats. A Venetian chronicler has left us an account of the shipwreck of a Catalan cog in 1415. The cog which sailed to Damietta suffered shipwreck off Abūkīr. It carried a cargo of saffron, cloth, olive oil, coral, and almonds, worth 60,000 dinars. But other Catalan ships carried cargoes which were worth 25,000-30,000 ducats.[233] The cargoes of the ships sailing from Collioure to the Levant had, of course, a lesser value than those departing from Barcelona. This can be seen by adding the amounts of the commendas which have come down to us in the acts of the notaries of Perpignan.

c. The Small Trading Nations

Whereas the volume of the Levantine trade of the Genoese and the Catalans in the first quarter of the fifteenth century was very irregular, the smaller trading nations continued their activities as before and even intensified them. They certainly enjoyed the new possibilities resulting from the breakdown of the Oriental industries.

The number of the Tuscan merchants in Alexandria increased in that period, although they did not become a big colony. The Florentines, who

[230] Piloti, p. 108, 147 f.; export of coral by Catalans from Sicily: Real Patr. 2910/1, f. 3b. Shipping directly from Barcelona to Jaffa: Tomas de Bellmunt IV, f. 5a.

[231] Del Treppo, "Antimonium, Stibium, Alcofoll," *Atti dell' Accademia Pontaniana*, N. S. VIII (1958-1959), p. 187; *idem*, *I mercanti catalani*, p. 75; according to another opinion it was lead sulphide used in ceramics. About his import into Egypt, see Piloti, p. 148; commenda contracts: Tomas de Bellmunt IV, f. 5a, 19b (shipped to Jaffa), 26b f. (to Beirut); see, further, Vat. sub 20 May 1401 (imported by Genoese); Tur II, f. 21a ff.; import to Damascus: G. P., Sent. 162, f. 25b ff. But Germany also produced alcohol; see G. P., Sent. 129, f. 36a.

[232] Vat. sub 22 June 1405 (a very great quantity is spoken of, as the freight amounted to 1568 fl.).

[233] Stella, col. 1240; *Chron. Morosini*, c. 295; Del Treppo, p. 69.

were the majority, had no fondaco of their own and lived in those of other trading nations, e.g., in that of the Anconitans.[234] In addition to the Florentines, there were Pisan and Sienese merchants in the dominions of the Mamluks. The names of several Pisans appear as witnesses on notarial acts drawn up in Alexandria,[235] and at least some of them may have been merchants. A Sienese is mentioned in an act drawn up in Damascus in 1413.[236] Florentine firms had their agents in Alexandria, and even Pandolfo Malatesta, through the Florentine firm Giovanni Bonaccorsi, engaged in trade in Egypt. The Florentine agents in Alexandria had close connections with Florentine merchants in Avignon. One of them, Francesco Manelli, lived for some time in southern France, in Montpellier.[237] The enterprising Florentine merchants engaged in trade between all the countries of Southern Europe and the Moslem Levant. They imported into Egypt from the Provence olive oil, honey, tartar, linen, and other commodities. In a letter written by a Florentine in 1406, one reads that some of his compatriots returned from Syria on a Catalan ship and brought spices with them.[238] At the same time, they exported the Oriental articles to the Provence.[239] As in many other countries, the Florentines also engaged in the insurance business[240] and in banking. The Florentine Jacob Cappone was a banker in Alexandria in the first years of the fifteenth century.[241]

The Neapolitan colony in Alexandria, including the merchants of Gaeta and Amalfi, then had its own fondaco,[242] and the post of consul was regularly filled by an experienced merchant. Jacobo Mostacha, who held the post in 1403, was succeeded by Anello de Albito, another merchant of Gaeta,[243] and then by Filippo Cruscone.[244] But much of the trade between Naples and the dominions of the Mamluks was carried on by merchants and ships of other trading nations, the merchants of Naples, Amalfi, and Gaeta exporting to the Moslem Levant mainly victuals, such as olive oil and hazelnuts.[245] They had, of course, ships that visited the Levantine ports; in 1406 at least two Gaetan ships anchored in Alexandria, that of Andrea

[234] Vat. sub 8 Nov. 1404.

[235] Leonardo de Valle sub 26 May 1403; Vat. sub 3 and 28 July 1404, 14 Aug. 1404.

[236] Giacomo della Torre, no. 22.

[237] Vat. sub 8 Nov. 1404; cf. Baratier p. 240. In one of the notarial acts drawn up by Vat. on 8 Nov. 1404, there appears together with Manelli, Roberto Aldobrandini and cf. Baratier *l.c.* about Michele Aldobrandini.

[238] Vat. *l.c.*; Dat 929, letter of Com. of Zanobi oí 27 Nov. 1406.

[239] G. P., Sent. 21, f. 19a ff., 21a.

[240] G. P., Sent. 21, f. 21a.

[241] Leonardo de Valle sub 4 Febr. 1404, and cf. Vat. sub 9 Sept. 1406. See also Vat. sub 11 July 1404: Paolo Cappone, a merchant in Alexandria.

[242] Leonardo de Valle sub 31 Jan. 1403; Vat. sub 8 and 18 July 1405.

[243] Vat. sub 21 Apr. 1405, 8 and 9 July 1405.

[244] Vat. sub 19 Aug. 1405, 8 Aug. 1406.

[245] Vat. sub 2 July 1404, 19 Aug. 1404.

Buchana and that of Antonio Bocsina.[246] In 1408 another Gaetan ship sailed to Alexandria.[247]

Several acts drawn up in Messina and in Alexandria refer to the ships that sailed between Sicily and Egypt in the first quarter of the fifteenth century. Some of them are contracts made by Sicilian merchants with the captains of these ships and indicate the character of the commercial exchanges between these regions.

In 1404 Simone Amato, the Sicilian merchant whose name is known from many documents, chartered the ship of Pascal Pauli of Messina in Alexandria, for the export of pepper to Augusta and Messina.[248] A ship called "San Niccolò" coming from Messina anchored in Alexandria in 1404.[249] This ship was again in the Egyptian port in 1405, and Simone Amato chartered it for the export of flax and hides. The plan was that it would first sail to Candia, where the flax would be discharged and malmsey (*malvasia*) loaded. From there it would sail to Syracuse, then to Messina and Palermo, where the wine would be discharged. Finally, the ship would carry merchandise loaded in Palermo by Amato's agent back to Alexandria.[250] However, before the ship departed, Amato changed his mind and made a new contract with the captain. The ship should sail to Modon, and an agent of Amato who would embark there, should inquire which town of Apulia would be the most convenient market for the hides, Brindisi or Taranto. There the captain was to load whatever Amato's agent designated and sail back to Alexandria.[251] The "Santa Maria della Scala," Pascal Pauli's ship, was again in Alexandria in 1405, and was chartered by two merchants of Candia for a journey to Crete and from there to Damietta.[252] One of the witnesses who signed a contract with Amato in July 1405 was the captain of another Sicilian ship anchored in Alexandria. Another ship sailed in April (or May) from Alexandria to Syracuse, and Simone Amato loaded merchandise on it.[253] The ship "Santa Maria della Scala & Santo Villano," belonging to a merchant of Messina, Antonio Porzello, was sold in Alexandria in 1405 for 3,500 ducats.[254] So, in 1405, at least five Sicilian ships, three of them ships of Messina, anchored in Alexandria. But it goes without saying that many other ships sailed between the ports of Sicily and the Moslem Levant. Neta, a Jew of Syracuse, exported honey and hazelnuts

[246] Vat. sub 8 Aug. 1404; Vat. a. 1406, without exact date, a leaf between acts of 18 July and 13 October, and an act w. d. before 28 July.

[247] M. Del Treppo-A. Leone, *Amalfi medioevale* (Naples, 1977), p. 167.

[248] Vat. sub 28 July 1404.

[249] Leonardo de Valle sub 21 Apr. 1404.

[250] Vat. sub 1 July 1405.

[251] Vat. sub 18 July 1405.

[252] Vat. sub 9 Apr. 1405.

[253] Vat. sub 13 Apr. 1405.

[254] Vat. sub 12 Oct. 1405.

to Alexandria in 1405 on the ship of a Maltese.[255] Of course, Catalan ships commuted between Palermo and Messina, on one hand, and Alexandria, on the other hand.[256] But the share of Sicilian ships in this traffic was not insignificant. In 1406 there was a ship of Trapani, belonging to Andrea Mariranga and Antonio Fardella, in Alexandria. The latter was a patrician and high dignitary in Trapani, and Andrea Mariranga is known from Sicilian sources as his close friend and business partner.[257]

In the year 1417 the ship "Santa Maria Della Scala-Santo Jacobo-Santo Cristoforo-Santo Juliano," belonging to Antonio Falanga of Messina, was chartered for the export of grains from Eastern Sicily ("from Catania to Augusta") to Northern Africa and Syria.[258] In 1419 the ship again sailed to Syria, and the patron received several sea loans.[259] Another ship, called "Santa Maria della Scala-Santo Juliano," sailed in the same year from Messina to Agrigento and then to Syria.[260] The conditions on which the sea loans were given in Messina to merchants and captains were purposely drawn up in a very general way. But if in 1419 Jolpicius de Bartolomeo, patron of the ship San Niccolò, received a loan "for several and different travels to any place, both allowed and forbidden of the lands of the believers and the unbelievers" and for six months,[261] there is good reason to suppose that he sailed to Egypt or Syria. In another contract, made in Messina about two weeks later, Syria is explicitly mentioned as a destination. The contract refers to a loan given to Damiano de Marbilistio(?), captain of the ship "San Niccolò" (another San Niccolò).[262] These data allow us to conclude that although the registers of the notaries of Messina and Alexandria (not to speak of Syracuse) that have come down to us from that period cover only a few years, every year several Sicilian ships plied between the ports of the island and those of Egypt and Syria.

But the greater part of the trade between Sicily and the Moslem Levant was carried on by the Catalans, Genoese, and Venetians. The Italian merchants and others bought Catalan cloth in Palermo and molasses produced in the Sicilian sugar factories and exported them to Egypt.[263] In Alexandria,

[255] See my paper "New data," p. 81.
[256] Vat. sub 22 June 1405.
[257] Vat. sub 25 June 1406; C. Trasselli, "Antonio Fardella, viceammiraglio di Trapani," in his *Mediterraneao e Sicilia all'inizio dell'epoca moderna* (Cosenza, 1977), pp. 15 ff., 26. Data concerning people of Trapani who lived in some emporia of the Eastern Mediterranean in those years certainly point to the fact that there were commercial exchanges between the Sicilian port and these towns. See ASTrap, Notai, de Nuris, Giovanni, f. 88a f. (of April 1421) about a man of Trapani who died in Rhodes and left a bequest there.
[258] Andreolo sub 13 May 1417.
[259] *Ibid.* sub 5 Sept. 1419.
[260] *Ibid.* sub 7 and 9 Sept. 1419, 3 Oct. 1419.
[261] *Ibid.* sub 16 Sept. 1419.
[262] *Ibid.* sub 4 Oct. 1419.
[263] ASPal. Gravezze 352, f. 80b; G. P., Sent. 48, f. 5a f.

the Sicilians had no fondaco of their own and used the protection of the Catalan consul.[264] But there were always Sicilians among the European merchants who lived in Alexandria in that period. The names of some witnesses who are of Messina appear in an Alexandrian notary's acts dated 1405,[265] and from the work of a Sicilian author of the fifteenth century one learns that Pietro Rombulo of Messina went to Alexandria in 1403, lived there three years as a merchant, associated with a Genoese, and then spent a year in Cairo, and finally went to Ethiopia.[266]

The commercial exchanges between Ancona and the dominions of the Mamluks were never discontinued in the first quarter of the fifteenth century, although the small republic had to withstand the predominance of Venice in the Adriatic. Since Florentines, Genoese, and Catalans used the facilities of the port of Ancona and Anconitan ships for their trade with the Levant, Venice had reason to fear that Ancona could serve as an alternative point of support for the Levantine trade of her competitors and tried to curb Anconitan activities as much as she could.[267] In fact, even Venetians used Anconitan ships for the export of their commodities to the Levant, either because they shipped "forbidden" articles (war material) or to pay less in customs. So the Venetian government ordered the war fleet to sequester merchandise of Venetians transported on Anconitan ships.[268] Further, there were those incidents and conflicts between Venetian and Anconitan ships that are almost unavoidable between neighboring states and that resulted in reprisals.[269] In addition, the small towns of the Marches from time to time tried to play off Venice against Ancona.[270] Finally, Venice sometimes imposed an embargo on trade between Ancona (and other Adriatic towns) and Segna.[271] Since this small town was an outlet for the timber of Croatia and the metals of Slovakia, the prohibition to sail there was a heavy blow for the Anconitans. So there were many reasons for friction and for frequent conflicts. However, when Ancona had to sustain a war against Carlo Malatesta, prince of Pesaro and Cesena, the small republic had to apply for help to Venice, and the Serenissima intervened to bring about peace.[272] The Anconitans were so utterly dejected by the attack of the prince of Pesaro that they asked henceforth to be the protectorate of the Serenissima, that is, that Ancona would be a vassal town, and the Anconitan

[264] Vat. sub Febr. 1405 (without exact date); Trasselli, *art. cit.*, p. 86.

[265] Vat. sub 21 Apr. 1405, 22 June 1405.

[266] C. Trasselli, "Un italiano in Etiopia nel XV secolo," *Rassegna di studi etiopici* I (1941), p. 173 ff., especially p. 176 f.

[267] Secreta I, f. 131a (a. 1404).

[268] *Ibidem.*

[269] Misti 51, f. 126a (a. 1416) 52, f. 52a, 60b (a. 1417) 173b, 174a (a.1419) 53, f. 25a (a. 1420), 123a (a. 1421).

[270] Misti 48, f. 79a (a. 1409, Fermo) 51, f. 125b (a. 1416, Recanati).

[271] Misti 53, f. 162a, 177b, 182b f., 195b f. (a. 1421).

[272] Secreta VI, f. 16a f., 26b f. (a. 1414); *Libr. Com.* III, lib. 10, no. 207 (a. 1414).

ships flew Venetian flags.[273] Then, in 1416, Carlo Malatesta again waged war against Ancona, and once more the little town applied to Venice for help.[274]

From various data, one may infer that despite the precarious political status of their republic, the Anconitans carried on a regular trade with Egypt and Syria. Anconitan ships sailed every year between Alexandria and their home port. On 1 October 1403 a ship coming from Alexandria arrived in Ancona;[275] in the spring of 1404, two ships departed from Ancona to Alexandria;[276] and at the beginning of the summer a ship returned there from Egypt, carrying pepper and cotton. Another ship returned from Syria in October. In 1405, in October, a *panfilo* from Alexandria and Syria returned with a freight of cotton, whereas a Catalan ship chartered by Anconitans for carrying cotton from Syria and sugar from Cyprus to Ancona was lead away by the captain.[277] There is no reason to believe that in most of the other years, from which no documents have been preserved, the traffic was discontinued.[278] The inventory of the bequest of an Anconitan merchant who died in Alexandria in 1421 is illustrative of the activities of the Anconitans in the Levant. The merchant left olive oil, soap, paper, and tartar.[279] The Anconitans also imported into Egypt and Syria camlets and exported pepper, ginger, mace, and cinnamon from Alexandria and Damascus. Further, they were much engaged in the import of Syrian cotton to Italy.[280] Sometimes they shipped their merchandise not directly to Ancona, but to Rhodes, which served them, like the Catalans and other trading nations, as a point of support in the Eastern Mediterranean.[281]

Although the Anconitan residents in Alexandria were few (as far as one can judge from the number of those mentioned in the notarial acts), their consuls held an esteemed position among the European merchants who lived in the Egyptian emporium at the beginning of the fifteenth century.[282] In addition, there were always some Anconitans living in Damascus, and the family name Baruti, given to a well-known Anconitan family, testifies to trade carried on in that Syrian port.[283]

[273] Secreta VI, f. 26a, 26b f., 34a, 38b.
[274] *Ibid.* f. 87a, 88a.
[275] Dat 928, letter of Com. of Zanobi di Taddeo Gaddi of 10 Nov. 1403.
[276] Secreta I, f. 131a.
[277] Dat 715, letter of Giovanni di Ser Nigi and Gherardo Davizi of 28 June; letter of the same of 31 Oct. 1404 (in this letter it is not said where the ship came from, but since it brought 435 sacks cotton, it certainly came from Syria); Dat 929, letter of the same of 17 Oct. 1405; letter of Com. of Zanobi di Taddeo Gaddi of 14 June 1404.
[278] On other ships see my "Il commercio levantino di Ancona," p. 228.
[279] Nic. Venier B, 2, f. 32a/b.
[280] "Il commercio levantino di Ancona," p. 231. As to the cotton trade, see above, note 277.
[281] Leonardo de Valle sub 20 Nov. 1401.
[282] "Il commercio Levantino di Ancona," p. 222.
[283] *Art. cit.*, p. 252.

Table XXI Italian merchants in Alexandria at the beginning of the XVth century

year	Florence	Naples	merchants of Gaeta	Amalfi	Ancona
1403	3	2	-	-	-
1404	8	1	2	4	4
1405	2	5	3	3	1
1406	5	1	3	1	5

The Levantine trade of Ragusa went on in the first quarter of the fifteenth century at the same pace as before. According to the documents preserved in the archives of the Dalmatian town, in some years, as in 1405, 1408, 1415, and 1418, only one ship sailed to Alexandria or a Syrian port[284] and, in others, as in 1409 and 1410, two or three.[285] There may have been years in which no Ragusan ship went to the ports of Egypt and Syria, but, on the other hand, we see from the registers of the Venetian Senate that Venetian merchants used the services of the Ragusan ships for sending their merchandise to the Moslem Levant.[286] However, the volume of the Levantine trade of Ragusa was very modest, compared with that of the Levantine trade of the great trading nations and even with that of the Sicilians and Anconitans. Even a great Ragusan merchant like Andreas Volćević invested no more than 1,300 ducats in the trade with the Levant in 1409, and in 1410, 700.[287] Neither did the transactions of Constantin, a Greek merchant living in Ragusa, reach the volume of those of the rich merchants of Venice and Genoa. When in 1408 he undertook to pay 360 ducats freight for his merchandise to Syria, that of his partners was included. Then in 1409 he paid 350 ducats for freight.[288] Even the Ragusan ships were small, if the number of the sailors mentioned in various documents is any criterion.

The merchants of Ragusa exported to the Moslem Levant olive oil, nuts,[289] wheat from Apulia,[290] and coral.[291] Cloth, a staple of the Levantine trade of the major trading nations, is not mentioned in the contracts which date of the same period and refer to Ragusan shipping to the dominions of the sultan of Cairo.

The merchants of southern France maintained the volume of their ex-

[284] Krekić, nos. 526, 556, 616, 649.
[285] *Op.cit.* nos. 565, 576, 579, 585, 586.
[286] Misti 47, f. 2a.
[287] Krekić, no. 579.
[288] *Op.cit.*, nos. 556, 573.
[289] *Op.cit.*, no. 616.
[290] *Op.cit.*, nos. 556, 573, 576.
[291] *Op.cit.*, no. 585.

Table XXII French merchants in Alexandria 1403 - 1406

year	Montpellier	merchants of Marseilles	Narbonne	"French"
1403	9	1	4	5
1404	10	3	7	4
1405	2	-	4	2
1406	1	-	2	2

changes with the Moslem Levant in the first decade of the fifteenth century, but later it declined.

When the attack of Boucicault on the coasts of the Mamluk realm was impending, all the merchants of Montpellier and Narbonne found in Alexandria and their consuls were imprisoned. They remained in prison two and a half months, and four of them died there.[292] Then, at the end of November 1403, an attempt was made to come to an agreement concerning the restitution to be paid to the Moslem merchants, who had suffered losses by the Genoese-French attack, but the negotiations failed. Thereupon the merchandise of the French in Alexandria was sequestered and the merchants sent to Cairo. Later they were confined to their fondachi in Alexandria for some time.[293] But, after this crisis, the trade between the Provence and Languedoc, on one hand, and the dominions of the Mamluks, on the other, was taken up. The Levantine trade of Marseilles declined, but the merchants of Montpellier were still very active in the emporia of the Moslem Levant. In the years subsequent to the expedition of Boucicault, the number of French merchants in Alexandria was even greater than before. There were consulates of the "French," of Narbonne and Marseilles, in Alexandria as before.[294] Some French merchants also lived in Damascus.[295]

In the first decade of the fifteenth century, every year some ships, either

[292] One of them was Raymond Afrian of Montpellier; see Leonardo Valle sub 5 Sept. 1403 and cf. Baratier, p. 240. He had come to Alexandria in that year; *op. cit.*, see appendix.

[293] Leonardo de Valle sub 14 Dec. 1403.

[294] At the beginning of 1403, Raymond Gali was consul of the "French"; see Leonardo de Valle sub 9 March 1403, where he is called "of Marseilles," but see there sub 25 Aug. 1402 and 7 Febr. 1403: Raymond Gali of Narbonne. His successor was Jean Fornier, who held the post from 1403 to 1406; see Leonardo de Valle sub 5 Sept. 1403, Vat. sub 12 May 1406. In a document of 14 Dec. 1403 he is called "consul of Montpellier and Narbonne"; see Leonardo de Valle *sub data*. If that be so, he was succeeded as consul of Narbonne by Bernard Sasera; see Vat. sub 8 Nov. 1404. Sasera was a Majorcan; see Vat. sub 18 Dec. 1406, referring to his bequest. Before, in 1403, he had been consul of Marseilles; see Leonardo de Valle sub 5 and 24 March 1403. After him the post was filled by Pancrace Nicolini; see Vat. sub 20 Sept. and 8 Nov. 1404. He went to the Levant in 1395 (see Baratier p. 247 note 3) and was a merchant in Alexandria in 1401 (see Leonardo de Valle sub 30 Nov. 1401) and remained there until 1407 (see Baratier, p. 239).

[295] Giacomo della Torre, nos. 7, 9, 10 (a. 1412-13).

French or others, sailed between the ports of the Provence and Alexandria. The Provençal ports mentioned most often in the contracts of charter and in other documents are Aigues-Mortes and Marseilles. A ship of Marseilles, the "Saint-Jacques," sailed in 1403, 1405, 1406, and 1408 to Alexandria and carried cloth of Languedoc, French and German linen, olive oil, honey, hazelnuts and coral.[296] The registers of the notaries of Alexandria mention other ships. In 1403 Nado Cavoni and Berengar Content, both of Montpellier, shipped olive oil, honey, hazelnuts, rice, and cloth to Alexandria on a Catalan ship, owned by Pere Michael. A part of the merchandise had been loaded in Marseilles.[297] In 1404 two ships were chartered in Alexandria to sail to Aigues-Mortes, that of Michael Bera of Marseilles was leased to Pierre Fabre of Narbonne,[298] and the Biscayan ship "Santa Eulalia" was chartered by seven Catalans and by the French merchant Armand Durat of Montpellier for a journey to Aigues-Mortes and Barcelona.[299] The same French merchant imported honey and cloth from Languedoc to Egypt.[300] In 1405, François Vialar of Narbonne chartered the ship of Bernat Fustier of Barcelona in Aigues–Mortes to go to Alexandria, where it arrived on 30 October. It carried the commodities usually marketed by the French merchants in the Levant—olive oil, honey, and cloth of Languedoc. In December 1405 the ship was chartered in Alexandria by Garin Barduc, a merchant of Montpellier.[301] Vialar himself had embarked on the ship and travelled to Alexandria. Then, in April 1406, together with Garin Barduc and François Tignerol of Narbonne, he made a contract with the Genoese Rafaele Squarzafico, captain of the ship "Santa Maria & San Julian." The ship was to carry spices to Rhodes and Aigues-Mortes, and the merchants stipulated that it should also visit Sicily, if they wished.[302] In addition to Aigues-Mortes and Marseilles, few towns of Southern France served as ports for the traffic with the Moslem Levant. One of them was Nice. Sometimes ships coming from Alexandria visited its port.[303]

These data indicate the intense activities of the French merchants in Egypt and the regular traffic on the line Aigues-Mortes–Alexandria. In addition to metals, the French exported all the standard articles to the Levant. Once more it is worthwhile to quote the inventory of the bequest a merchant left in Alexandria in 1403. The inventory of the goods of Raymond Afrian is characteristic of the commodities imported by the French

[296] Baratier, p. 239, appendix.
[297] Leonardo de Valle sub 24 March 1403.
[298] Vat. sub 11 Aug. 1404. On the way to France, it was to visit Rhodes.
[299] Vat. sub 27 Sept. 1404.
[300] Vat. sub 4 Oct. 1404.
[301] Vat. sub 9 Oct. 1405, 6 Nov. 1405, 9 Dec. 1405, 12 May 1406.
[302] Vat. sub 28 Apr. 1406.
[303] Dat 907, letter of Jean Fabre of 20 Nov. 1403.

into the Levant: he had many bales of cloth, linen, a great quantity of honey, and hazelnuts.[304] Even soap was imported into Egypt by the traders of Marseilles.[305] As for so many other South European traders, Rhodes served the French as a point of support, and some of them exported fruits, such as raisins, from there to Egypt.[306] Some French merchants also engaged in trade between Pera and Alexandria.[307]

Like the Genoese and Catalan trade with the Levant, the commercial activities of the Provençals and the traders of Languedoc declined in the second decade of the fifteenth century. To judge from the acts of the notaries of Marseilles, only a few ships sailed from the Provence to Egypt and to Syria in those years.[308] However, the commercial exchanges were not totally discontinued. An act of an Italian notary in Alexandria refers to the import of honey by a merchant of Narbonne in 1421,[309] and undoubtedly there was indirect trade between Southern France and the Moslem Levant.

D. The Venetian Ascendancy

The leniency, patience, and diplomatic skill of the Venetians put them a priori in a favorable situation in their relations with the Moslem Levant, but at first even they could not derive all the advantages resulting from the industrial decline of the Near East.

The expansion on the Terraferma undoubtedly put a great strain on Venice; the conquest of Padua, Vicenza and Verona in 1404-1406 involved a great financial effort. The long conflict with Sigismund, king of Hungary and Germany, was a great nuisance to the Venetians and disturbed the normal course of their international trade. As early as the 1390's the representatives of great commercial companies in Nürnberg took over the direction of the mints, custom services, and mining activities in Hungary and removed the Italian company, *Societas participum montaneorum a ramine Hungariae*, from its position in Slovakia. This company, which had marketed the Slovak copper, that of Vieri de Cambi de' Medici, represented both Venetian and Florentine capitalists.[310] Since copper was one of the staple goods that the Venetians exported to the Near East, the loss of their

[304] Leonardo de Valle sub 5 Sept. 1403.

[305] *Ibid.* sub 7 Febr. 1403.

[306] Vat. sub 7 Sept. 1405.

[307] Guillaume Morin of Montpellier imported grain in 1404 from Pera to Alexandria; see Vat. sub 26 July 1404.

[308] Baratier, p. 241.

[309] Nic. Venier B, 2, f. 42b/43a (The ship on which the merchandise was carried to Alexandria was certainly a French one).

[310] W. v. Stromer, "Nürnberger Unternehmer im Karpatenraum, ein oberdeutsches Buntmetall-Oligopol 1396-1412," *Kwartalnik Historii Materialnij* 16 (1968), p. 649; "König Siegmunds Gesandte in den Orient," *Festschrift für H. Heimpel* (Göttingen, 1972), p. 604.

position in the mining centers of Upper Hungary was a great blow for them. In 1405 the free export of copper from Hungary was forbidden and a royal monopoly was established.[311] Some years later, in 1412, however, Hungary ceded the province of Zips to Poland, but in the same year King Sigismund proclaimed an economic war against Venice and forbade any trade with her. Having the communications and continuous commercial exchanges with South Germany cut off was certainly another heavy blow for Venice, for Germany was a great market for the Oriental spices and the cotton imported from the Levant. King Sigismund pursued a policy which was consistent, though not very rich in prospects. To replace the sources of supply, he tried to foster trade with the Genoese colonies in Crimea and other emporia on the Black Sea, where spices and cotton could be obtained.[312] He also made attempts to come into direct contacts with some Near Eastern rulers. The agents of some important commercial companies of Southern Germany served him as ambassadors to the rulers of the Oriental countries, with which he hoped to establish regular trade.[313] In the long run, the embargo on trade with Venice, once again proclaimed in 1417 and in 1418, and the attempt to replace the supply from the Genoese colonies on the Black Sea, was a hopeless undertaking.[314] The flourishing South German fustian industry would have been compelled to increase the costs of production very much by purchasing raw materials in so distant a region as the Crimean or Moldavian coast. But certainly the prohibition of trade with Venice by the German king had to be reckoned with.

The civil war that raged in Syria in the first decade of the fifteenth century was another factor that prejudiced the development of Venetian trade in the Levant. Even in Cyprus, where the Genoese were in control, the Venetians encountered great difficulties. In order to avoid conflicts with the Genoese, in 1408 the Venetian government forbade its subjects to visit the island.[315] In 1412 similar measures were taken.[316] Although these orders were only threats, they show that the position of the Venetians in Cyprus was precarious. For all these reasons Venice tried to develop her trade in the Black Sea area, but in 1410 Tana, the great Venetian emporium on the Sea of Azov, was sacked by the Tatars, and the Venetians suffered very

[311] v. Stromer, "Nürnberger Unternehmer," p. 654.

[312] H. Heimpel, "Zur Handelspolitik Kaiser Siegmunds," *VSWG* 23 (1930), p. 145 ff.

[313] v. Stromer, "König Siegmunds Gesandte," p. 603.

[314] Another opinion is expressed by W. v. Stromer, "Die Schwarzmeer u. Levante-Politik Sigismunds von Luxemburg," *Miscellanea Charles Verlinden* (Rome, 1974), p. 607. On the failure of the embargo see H. Klein, "Kaiser Sigismunds Handelssperre gegen Venedig und die Salzburger Alpenstrasse," *Festschrift Th. Mayer* (Constance, 1954-1955) II, pp. 324, 327. Klein proves that the trade between Salzburg and Venice was troubled, but never discontinued.

[315] Misti 48, f. 20a, 21a, 21b.

[316] Thiriet, *Rég.* II, p. 117.

serious losses.[317] The colony was rebuilt and fortified again in 1411.[318] But the maritime routes in the Greek waters were endangered by the ever-stronger Turkish fleets and, on the other hand, what the Venetian galleys and cogs brought from Tana and other ports in this area could not replace the supply from Egypt and Syria. They carried mainly silk, furs, wax, and slaves, and far less spices.[319] Then in 1418 Tana was again sacked and burned by the Tatars and the Venetian losses amounted to 60,000 ducats.[320] Venice again took measures to rebuild the colony,[321] but the great reverses in this area necessarily induced the Venetians to concentrate their activities in the Levant in the dominions of the sultan of Cairo and to make great efforts to establish friendly relations with the Mamluk government.

This was certainly not easy, and all the resources of Venetian diplomacy had to be used. The extortions by the Mamluk authorities sometimes brought the Venetian merchants to despair, and the registers of the Venetian Senate and other documents contain many accounts of the measures taken to surmount the difficulties.

Piloti states that in 1404 ("about that year") the Venetian consul of Alexandria, Andrea Giustinian, went to Cairo to lodge a protest with the sultan against the bad treatment of the Venetian merchants and to threaten that they would leave Egypt altogether.[322] In 1407 there was a brawl between the Moslems and the European merchants in Latakia, from which great quantities of cotton were shipped to the west. There were six Venetian ships in the port, and, when the Turcomans who had quarrelled with the Europeans did not succeed in capturing them, they sacked the port and some Venetians were killed. Thereupon the European merchants had to ransom themselves, paying 250, 500, or even 800 ducats each. In Damascus, all the European traders were imprisoned and had to pay ransoms.[323] A year later, the Mamluk authorities in Alexandria did not allow the Venetian galleys to depart before the consul and the merchants agreed to send an envoy to the "Duke of the archipel" and to ransom Moslem captives sold to him by the pirate Pietro de la Randa.[324] In the same year in Syria too, the Venetians encountered difficulties in carrying on their trade and suffered from extortions by the Moslem authorities. There was great apprehension in Venice that it would be impossible to make the cotton purchases in the

[317] *Chron. Dolfin*, f. 278b; *Chron. Savina*, f. 257b.
[318] Misti 49, f. 14a; Thiriet, *op.cit.* II, p. 96 f.
[319] *Chron. Morosini*, c. 304, 310, 374.
[320] *Chron. Dolfin*, f. 301a; *Chron. Zancaruola*, f. 490b.
[321] Thiriet, *Rég.* II, p. 172, 181.
[322] Piloti, p. 188 ff.
[323] *Chron. Morosini*, c. 205.
[324] Piloti, p. 201 ff.

fall.[325] In the spring of 1410 the Venetians were beaten in Syria, the sum of 100,000 dirhams was taken from them by force, a fine amounting to the same sum was imposed upon them, and many merchants returned without making the cotton purchases.[326] In that year there was also tension in Egypt between the Mamluk authorities and the European merchants. When the Moslem zealots raised the question of the non-Moslems' right to live in the Moslem countries after eight-hundred years of the Moslem era had elapsed (see above), the sultan threatened to expel the European merchants from his dominions. He also required the Venetians to pay restitution for the misdeeds of others. He had claims against them as well, concerning the delivery of certain commodities. The Venetians were maltreated; the consul of Alexandria and some other merchants were imprisoned and brought to Cairo and apparently beaten. In Damietta, too, the Moslem authorities took measures against them. In January 1410 the Venetian Senate had ordered Lorenzo Capello, appointee to the post of consul in Alexandria, to go to the sultan, to protest against the mistreatment of the merchants and to argue that Venice could not obtain the commodities demanded because she was at war with the countries where they were produced.[327] But later it was apparently decided to write a letter of protest to the sultan.[328]

In the reign of Sultan al-Malik al-Mu'ayyad Shaykh (1412-1421), there were the same conflicts, and time and again the normal course of trade was interrupted. In 1415 there was a revolt of all the governors in Syria, and the Venetians fled to the seacoast, especially to Beirut, to escape from the dangers of the civil war.[329] However, these were not very momentous misadventures. The extortions by the Mamluk authorities caused the Venetians much more damage and when they became more and more frequent, the Venetian Senate decided in May 1415 to send a solemn embassy to the sultan. Lorenzo Capello and Santo Venier were appointed ambassadors.[330] The Arabic chroniclers report that in August 1415 a Venetian embassy arrived in Cairo, and one of them mentions the presents brought to the sultan. They were cloth (surely scarlets and velvet), a crystal goblet dec-

[325] Misti 48, f. 38a, 42a.

[326] *Chron. Morosini*, c. 222 and cf. Jorga, "Notes et extraits," *ROL* IV, p. 318 f. concerning the extortions from a Venetian merchant in Beirut.

[327] Jorga, *op.cit.*, *ROL* IV, pp. 315, 318. The commodities that the Venetians failed to deliver may have been metals.

[328] *Ṣubḥ al-aʿshā* VIII, p. 123 f.; Lammens, in *ROC* IX, p. 363 f., 390 f. (text and translation). The letter was received in Cairo in June 1411. The text has been misinterpreted by Labib, *Handelsgeschichte*, p. 347: "Nicola" was not an ambassador but apparently a subaltern employee, for an embassy to the sultan in that year is not mentioned in Venetian sources. Further, the Venetian government did not address the sultan with the request that he should influence the consul to treat the merchants well. The sultan himself was requested to treat them more gently.

[329] *Chron. Morosini*, c. 290, and cf. Weil V. p. 134.

[330] Jorga, *op.cit.*, pp. 543, 544.

orated with silver and faced with glass beads, four trays with four waterpots, five plates with other goblets and drinking cups, all of them of silver and lined with glass beads, plus other glass objects. Another chronicler recounts that the presents were sold to use the sum obtained for the construction of the sultan's mosque.[331] These accounts show clearly how great the superiority of the production of the European industries had already become, especially that of the textile and glass industries. The instructions given to the embassy by the Venetian Senate, on the other hand, shed light on the development of Venetian trade in the dominions of the sultan, on the problems of the commercial exchanges, and of the Mamluks' policy.[332] The ambassadors were to protest against sales of merchandise by force and against the habit of the Moslems to return merchandise they had bought a long time before. They were to draw the attention of the sultan to the extortions against the Venetian merchants in Acre and the payments extorted arbitrarily from the captains of Venetian ships. Like so many embassies, this one was also to raise the question of the goods of vessels that had suffered shipwreck and of the bequests of merchants who had died in the dominions of the sultan. Further, the embassy was to insist that litigation between Venetians and Moslems should be brought before secular judges, and not before the religious courts. They were also to claim the restitution of losses suffered by Venetian merchants. The ambassadors also had orders to protest against the injuries of pilgrims in Jerusalem and Ramla and to ask the sultan for the right to appoint a consul in Jerusalem who would possibly have a salary from the Mamluk government. This claim shows that in that period Venice began to play the role of the leading European power in the Moslem Levant. Whereas the Genoese had fulfilled the role of the protectors of the pilgrims in the fourteenth century and obtained the right to have a consul in Jerusalem for this purpose, at the beginning of the fifteenth century the Venetians began to replace them.[333]

Another question with which the ambassadors were to deal was the forced purchase of pepper. Both in Alexandria and Damascus, the two most important spice markets of the Moslem Levant, the custom had been established of imposing on the Venetians every year, during the spice fair in the fall, the obligatory purchase of a certain quantity of pepper from the sultan's agent and an auction. Before these transactions were completed,

[331] *Sulūk* IV, p. 325; Ibn Ḥadjar III, p. 75.

[332] Misti 51, f. 41b ff., and cf. Jorga, *op.cit.*, p. 545 f.

[333] See W. Heyd, "Les consulats établis en Terre Sainte au Moyen Age pour la protection des pèlerins," *AOL* II, p. 355 ff. It is, however, possible that the Venetians demanded official recognition in 1415, having already appointed such a consul before. In fact, a Venetian consul in Palestine is mentioned in a travelogue of 1413: "Viaggio a Gerusalemme di Nicolò da Este," in *Miscellanea di opusculi inediti e rari dei secoli XIV e XV, Prosa*, I (Turin, 1861), p. 118 f., 128. But it may also be that this was the Venetian vice-consul of Ramla; see below.

they were not allowed to buy any pepper. The price of the stated quantity was arbitrarily (that means not by bargaining) fixed by the Moslems.[334] The pepper was bought by the consulate; the Council of the colony (the Council of XII) fixed a minimum price for an auction and when, as frequently happened, the sum yielded was smaller than that paid to the Moslems, the difference was imposed upon all the merchants as "the pepper loss" (*danno del pepe*), as a kind of tax. This practice dated from at least the end of the fourteenth century, as it is already mentioned in the registers of the Venetian Senate of 1397, but it may have been older.[335] The pepper sold by auction to the Venetians was that of private Moslem merchants, as is clearly borne out by the registers of the Venetian consulate in Alexandria of 1418.[336] This procedure caused losses and aroused strife.[337] The fixing of the price (surely by a cartel of big merchants, sc. the Kārimīs) raised the price to be demanded in the subsequent free trade and, on the other hand, there were Venetian merchants who tried to shirk paying the *danno del pepe* and left Alexandria; and there were also others who secretly made agreements with Moslem merchants. In addition, the Moslems purposely delayed fixing the price of the pepper to a date close to the departure of the galleys, so that the pepper had to be bought in a hurry and there was no time for bargaining.[338]

So for the Venetians this was a very important question and the ambassadors had orders to insist upon the request that the pepper trade be free. In any event, they obtained promises from the sultan that almost all their claims would be reckoned with and their demands fulfilled. They were also assured that the Venetians would in future not have to pay more than the dues established by the treaties, and officials in some towns of Palestine who had extorted higher payments from them would be punished. They were also promised that they would not be compelled by the Moslem authorities in Acre to ransom Moslems captured by corsairs who belonged to other nations. The sultan also made an undertaking that pilgrims would not be mistreated in Jerusalem. Since the Venetians engaged a great deal in the transport of pilgrims, this too was an important matter for them. The sultan also agreed, apparently, to the appointment of a Venetian consul

[334] "frangere vocem" in Latin and "rompere la voxa" in Venetian, a translation of the Arabic; see Jorga in *ROL* IV, p. 552; J. Wansbrough, "A Mamluk commercial treaty," p. 75 is mistaken in presuming that this indicated perhaps the regal monopoly of spices; see below.

[335] Misti 44, f. 3b (a. 1397) 51, f. 42b: "Est usitatum q' in Alex' et Damasco tempore galearum datur nostris mercatoribus certa quantitas piperis per vim p' frangendo vocem quod est in damnum mercatorum," 53, f. lb: the price for the auction of the pepper bought by compulsion from the sultan is fixed by the Council of XII.

[336] Published in my "The Volume of Levantine Trade," p. 598 f.

[337] Misti 53, f. 86 b.

[338] Misti 54, f. 36b, 118b ff. 55, f. 30b 56, f. 35b 57, f. 12b.

in Jerusalem. Further, he also gave orders that the Venetians could stay in his dominions as long as they wished and, finally, that they should not be compelled to buy spices.[339] There was only one request the sultan rejected: the abolition of the forced purchase of a certain quantity of pepper.[340]

But under Mamluk rule promises of the government were very often not carried out. In 1418 the Venetian consul of Alexandria, Fantin Viaro, was already reporting to his government that the merchants were again suffering from extortions and had to pay the debts of relatives. He complained that agreements made with the Moslems were not kept, that there had again been cases of forced purchases of sugar, and that customs had been levied before the merchandise imported by the Venetians was sold. The Senate decided to address letters to the sultan, to his major-domo,[341] and to the chief of the customs services in Alexandria.[342] In addition, the consul was asked to protest personally to the sultan in Cairo.[343] However, it was not only the rapacity of the Mamluks that interfered with the normal course of the commercial activities of the Venetians. In that year, Venetian trade in Syria was discontinued for some time for another reason. When a new invasion of the country by Ḳarā Yuluḳ was impending, the Venetian merchants fled to the coast in order to depart.[344] But, it is true, the extortions by the Mamluk authorities were much more troublesome and sometimes almost unbearable. Even when there were no conflicts between the authorities and the Venetian merchants, the consuls were summoned and had to make substantial payments, which had to be covered by imposts on the merchants.[345] The forced purchases of various commodities were another method of extortion. In 1419 the Mamluk authorities in Alexandria compelled the Venetians to buy 150 sportas pepper at the price of 150-160 dinars, whereas the commercial price was no more than 100. Further, the Moslems penetrated into a Venetian fondaco in Alexandria, broke the wine casks, beat the crew of the galleys. The customs officers again requested

[339] Jorga, *op.cit.*, p. 551 ff.; *Libr. Com.* III, lib. 10, nos. 209, 210; *Dipl. Ven.-Lev.* II, p. 304 ff. There was a Venetian consul in Jerusalem in 1422, see Brancacci, p. 179, and in 1434, see Tur V, p. 15a ff., and cf. my paper "The Venetian supremacy," p. 51.

[340] The text reads as follows: "e di quelli che constrenze i merchadanti a la vegnuda de le suo galie en le parti di Alexandria e di Soria che i non possa comprar ni vender fin a tanto che non i habia rota la voxe de le spetie, e intende di venderli le spetie per forza . . . nu commandemo che non sia constrecti a far cossa alguna che i sia di danno in questo e no altro etc." That means that it (trade) should be allowed before the fixing of the pepper price (here even "the spices" are spoken of!) but the forced purchase of a certain quantity of pepper is not abolished. Also, the texts quoted in notes 335, 337 and 338 dating to 1415 and the 1420's prove that this custom was not abolished.

[341] Stendar i.e., Ustādār.

[342] "cadi of Alexandria."

[343] Jorga, *op.cit.*, p. 587.

[344] *Chron. Morosini*, c. 354 f., and cf. Weil V, p. 142.

[345] Collegio, Not. IV, f. 157a (a. 1414, Damascus).

the payment of a part of the imposts immediately upon the arrival of the galleys, took furs from the merchants by force and said they would be returned if they would agree to buy a certain quantity of pepper. The compulsory purchase of pepper was certainly a very grave matter; it foreshadowed the interference of the Mamluk government in the pepper trade. When these occurrences were reported to the Venetian government, the Senate ordered the consul to appear before the sultan in Cairo, claim restitution of the losses, and demand that orders should be given against the mistreatment of the Venetians.[346] It is not known what answer he received, but from the registers of the Venetian Senate it is known that in 1420 the customs officers in Alexandria again took furs and honey from the merchants by force, so that the consul was ordered to demand restitution.[347] The Venetian government did its best to improve the relations with the Mamluks. In the same year, 1420, it forbade its subjects to buy slaves other than negroes who were natives of the sultan's realm, and it decided to ransom Moslem captives in Cyprus.[348] But the good will of the Venetian authorities was often not repaid. Therefore it was proposed in the Senate in 1421 not to send the galleys to the dominions of the Mamluks. The proposal was turned down, but it was decided that the galleys should ply the route between Modon, Crete, on one side, and the ports of Egypt and Syria, on the other side. Further, the galleys were to anchor in the Moslem ports only a few days.[349] This meant the abolition of the yearly spice fair, which gave the Moslems so many occasions to put pressure upon the Venetian merchants.

Despite all these disturbances and the frequent conflicts with the Mamluk authorities, the Venetians succeeded in the first two decades of the fifteenth century in remaining on friendly terms with the rulers of Cairo and in increasing trade with their dominions. The Venetians seemed never to act in anger, and they abstained from acts of retaliation. In fact, Venice was considered by other powers to be an ally or at least a state very friendly with the Mamluks.[350] Sometimes, the Genoese and Catalans turned to the Venetians for help, asking them to carry on trade on their behalf in Egypt and Syria and to declare that the merchandise was their own.[351] On the other hand, the sultan applied to the Venetians to obtain certain commodities.[352]

[346] Misti 53, f. 25b f.; partly quoted by Jorga, *op.cit.*, p. 615.
[347] Misti 53, f. 72a.
[348] Jorga, *op.cit.*, p. 617.
[349] Misti 53, f. 102b ff.
[350] Cf. "Aspetti dell'espansione italiana," p. 28 and the papers quoted there in note 140.
[351] Misti 47, f. 113a (a. 1407).
[352] Jorga, *op.cit.*, p. 316; cf. above. al-Malik al-Mu'ayyad Shaikh was considered by the Venetians as their friend; see *Chron. Savina*, f. 265a.

Table XXIII Venetian and Genoese merchants in Alexandria and in Damascus 1403 - 1422

	Alexandria		Damascus	
year	Venetians	Genoese	Venetians	Genoese
1403	37	22		
1405	35	45		
1406	17	30		
1415	28	5		
1416	29	-		
1418	36	-	28	7
1419	43	-	41	10
1420	41	2		
1421	27	23		
1422	42	9		

The success of the Venetians was also to a very great extent the effect of the excellent management of the galley service. Despite unfavorable political circumstances and the increasing danger of attacks by Turkish fleets, the galley service functioned regularly, so that the Moslem merchants, on one hand, and the Italian and German customers, on the other, could always make their plans for their transactions. On the average, twenty-eight to thirty-four galleys visited the ports of the Moslem Levant in every quinquennium.[353] Transport on the galleys was sure, and the Venetian government's prohibition against importing spices in the same period of the year on other ships safeguarded the merchants from competition.[354]

The development of Venice's trade in the dominions of the Mamluks is clearly shown by the data on the growth of the Venetian colonies in Alexandria and Damascus. Venetian names in notarial and judicial acts point to an essentially progressive increase.

The Venetian expansion in Syria must have been even greater than in Egypt. At the beginning of the fifteenth century there were Venetian vice-consuls (sometimes called consuls) not only in Beirut, but also in Acre and Ḥamā.[355] Ḥamā was not only a great cotton market, but spices could also be purchased there.[356] Venetian trade in Acre flourished in that period. Actually, in the last twenty years of the fourteenth century the Venetians

[353] See my "The Venetian supremacy," p. 18 ff.

[354] F. C. Lane, *Navires et constructeurs à Venise pendant la renaissance* (Paris, 1965), pp. 13, 22.

[355] Beirut: Misti 47, f. 117b f. (a. 1407) 48, f. 82a ff. (a. 1409), Acre: Misti 51, f. 141b ff. (a. 1415); Ḥamā: Misti 47, f. 35b (a. 1406).

[356] Sassi, *Scritture*, pp. 145, 151.

had already been engaged in a lively trade in Acre, mainly purchasing cotton there. But in 1398 they began to send one of the Beirut galleys there, for the town had also become a market for spices.[357] From 1419 one of the Beirut galleys went there and remained for six days. However, even in the first half of the fifteenth century Acre was mainly a cotton market, and it was for this reason that a small colony of Venetians had come into being then.[358] In Ramla, too, there was a Venetian colony; in the treaty concluded between Venice and the sultan in 1415 a paragraph refers to their houses in Ramla and Lydda.[359] Both spices and cotton were purchased there.[360]

The growth of Venetian trade in Syria was closely connected with the upswing of the cotton export. It appears reasonably sure that despite many difficulties, especially the shortage of working hands, the cotton plantations in Syria and Palestine even in this period increased. The testimony of a Burgundian traveller, who describes the Valley of Esdraelon in 1434 as one big cotton plantation, is noteworthy.[361] Surely the Venetians also purchased cotton regularly in the former Byzantine territories, in Salonica, Euboea, Modon, Coron, and Chios,[362] and even Crete supplied them with this article.[363] But Northern Syria was the most important center of cotton cultivation. The decisions of the Venetian Senate concerning the number of days that the cotton cogs should anchor in Acre, and in Latakia, leave no doubt about this fact.[364]

The service of the cogs, which transported the cotton to Venice, functioned as regularly as the galleys. The spring convoy numbered on the average five to seven cogs, but in some years there were four and in others nine to eleven. The fall convoy consisted mostly of four to five ships.

Transport of these big ships carrying 400-600 tons[365] was much cheaper than on the galleys, because the crews were incomparably smaller, often no more than a tenth of that of the galleys.[366] Cotton was the bulk of their cargoes, but they transported both alkali and spices (if it was allowed by the Senate). Because of the lack of space on the galleys or because of the lower freight charges, certain quantities of spices were indeed readily shipped by the cogs. However, in order to safeguard the monopoly of the galleys

[357] Misti 44, f. 54a 56, f. 41a ff.; G. P., Sent. 85, f. 158a ff. 86, f. 20b ff.
[358] Misti 52, f. 180b f.; G. P., Sent. 25, f. 69b ff. 28, f. 92a f. 29, f. 67a f.
[359] *Dipl. Ven.-Lev.* II, p. 314.
[360] Sassi, *Scritture*, pp. 162, 163; G. P., Sent. 21, f. 37a ff. (a. 1408) 22, f. 104a f., 109b 19, f. 2a f. (a. 1410), 28b f. (a. 1411); G. P., Sent. Int. VIII, f. 41b f. (a. 1408).
[361] de la Broquière, p. 185.
[362] Misti 46, f. 147b 51, f. 72b; Thiriet, *Rég.* II, pp. 54, 56, 63, 65, 84.
[363] Thiriet, *op.cit.*, p. 46, and cf. idem, *La Romanie vénitienne au moyen âge*, p. 321 f.
[364] Misti 47, f. 13b, 25b (2 days in Acre, 20 in Latakia).
[365] Lane, *Navires et constructeurs*, p. 44.
[366] *Op.cit.*, p. 37.

Table XXIV Venetian cotton cogs, 1403 - 1421

year	Syria cogs	Alexandria cogs	source
1405	spring 3		Dat 929, letter of Domenico di Andrea of 15 Jan. 1405; Morosini c. 173; Misti 47, f. 7a f.
	fall 6		
1406	spring 3		Morosini c. 193; Misti 47, f. 25b; Coll., Not. III, f. 141a.
1408	spring 4		Bautier, Relations, p. 320.
	fall 4	2	Morosini c. 208.
1413	spring 5		Misti 49, f. 143b.
1414	spring 6[a]		Morosini c. 275.
1415	spring 10-11[b]		Op. cit., c. 292.
1416	spring 11-12[c]	2	Op. cit., c. 311; Misti 51, f. 88b.
	fall 5		
1417	spring 7[d]		Op. cit., c. 326
	fall 5		Op. cit., c. 331; Misti 52, f. 24a ff.; Coll., Not. V, f. 75b
1418	spring 9[e]	2	Morosini c. 345; Misti 52, f. 110b; Coll., Not. V, f. 88b
1419	spring 7	4[f]	Morosini c. 355
1420	spring 10-11		Op. cit., c. 367
	fall 4		Op. cit., c. 373
1421	spring 5[g]		Op. cit., c. 377
	fall 3		Op. cit., c. 380

a) In addition a cog was sent to Cyprus.

b) The chronicler gives names of 12 captains, however.

c) But there are only eight names of captains.

d) Chron. Dolfin f. 301b, 302b has 6 cogs. This chronicler says, however, that the cogs departed on 17 June, but the value of the cargoes indicated by him tallies with that given by Morosini for the spring cogs.

e) Misti 52, f. 110b has 10 cogs.

f) These cogs were sent to "Alexandria and Candia".

g) Later only four cogs are spoken of.

as spice carriers, a part of the freight paid for the spices transported by the cogs was apportioned to the galleys or to the Venetian government.[367] In any case, the cog line became a new artery of Venice's Levantine trade in that period.

In order to evaluate the importance of the cotton purchases within the total of the Venetian investments in the Levant, the considerable rise of the cotton prices in that period must be taken into account.

[367] Misti 40, f. 12a f. 41, f. 10a 42, f. 4a f. 47, f. 25b.

Table XXV Cotton prices in Syria,
end of XIVth-beginning of XVth century[a]

date	place	price of a ḳinṭā	source
1379	Damascus	57 duc. (1000 dirh.)	Dat 1171, price list[b]
March 1354		17.5 duc. (350-400)	Dat 797, letter of Zanobi di Taddeo Gaddi of 24 April 1394[c]
July 1394		of Hamath 32-34 duc. (640-680) of Sarmin 12.5-22.5 duc. (250-450) of Acre 22.5-27.5 duc. (450-550)	Dat 549, letter of the same of 31 Oct. 1394, quoting a letter from Damascus of 1 Aug.
fall fair		of Hamath 37.5 duc. (750) of Sarmin 20 duc. (400) of Acre 30 duc. (600)	Dat 549, letter of the same of 4 Nov. 1394
23 Oct.	Damascus	25 duc. (500)	Melis, Aspetti, p. 384.
30 May 1395	"	of Hamath 26.5 duc. (550) " Sarmin 24 duc. (500) " Latakia 24 duc. (500) " Acre 29 duc. (600)	Dat 1171, price list
2 Aug. 1395	Damascus	of Acre 25-31 duc. (500-650)	Ibid.[d]
begin. 1396	Damascus	of Hamath 33.3 duc. (800) of Sarmin 25 duc. (600)	Dat 926, letter of Zanobi di Taddeo Gaddi of 1 April 1396[e]
Feb. 1396		25-33.3 duc. (600-800)	Dat 550, letter of the same date, news without date
March 25, 1396		29-33.3 duc. (700-800)	Dat 797, letter of the same of 13 May 1396.
1397 (?)		of Latakia 37.4 duc.	G.P., Sent. VI, f. 46b ff.[f]
15 Aug. 1398	Damascus	of Acre 37.5 duc. (900)	Dat 1171, price list.
Sept. 1407	Hamath	with expenses 65.6-67.6 duc.	Accounts Soranzo c. 18b; Sassi, Scritture, p. 182.
1408	Hamath	with expenses 50, 51, 53.6 duc.	Sassi, op. cit., p. 80, 82, 109, 184.
March 1408	"	delivered on the ship 53.8 duc.	Accounts Soranzo, c. 11b
Sept. 1408		50-51.2 duc.	Ibid. f. 18b.
March 1409	"	45 duc.	Ibid. f. 21a.
1410	Latakia	33.7 duc. (800)	G.P., Sent. VIII, f. 66b f., 80a f.
March 1412		of Hamath, delivered on the ship 43 duc.	Accounts Soranzo, c. 35a

Table XXV (continued)

date	place	price of a ḳinṭā	source
1413		" Hamath 47.5-48.6 duc.	ASV, Miscell. di carte non appartenenti a nessun arch., Ba 8, fasc. 1
		" " , delivered on the ship 56.7 duc.	Accounts Soranzo, c. 41a.
		" Hamath, delivered on the ship 59 duc.	Ibid. c. 46b.
1416		32.5 duc.	Sassi, op. cit., p. 88 ff.
March 1417		of Acre, delivered on the ship 38-39 duc.	G.P., Sent. 29 f. 68a f.

a) In some documents the place is not given and in others the range of prices is indicated without specifying those of the various kinds. As to the ḳinṭārs of Syria see my paper The Venetian cotton trade, p. 700 f.

b) See art. cit., p. 701, note 200.

c) The news about the cotton price does not refer to a certain date, but undoubtedly the spring fair of cotton is meant.

d) See The Venetian cotton trade, p. 702, note 201.

e) The writer of the letter quotes news from Damascus without date.

f) See The Venetian cotton trade, p. 702, note 202.

As can be seen from this table, cotton prices in Syria were higher by at least 50 percent at the beginning of the fifteenth century than in the last quarter of the fourteenth century. The scarcity which had begun in 1397 lasted until the mid-1420's.

But the high prices of the Syrian cotton did not prejudice its import into Europe. It still had a large market in Italy and Germany. A middling rank Venetian merchant bought thirty to forty sacks a year, and during the dearth of cotton such a shipment cost 1,200-1,600 ducats.[368] Rich merchants (and agents of several firms) bought eighty to one-hundred, the companies one-hundred to two-hundred.[369] There were some companies in Venice that specialized in the trade of Syrian cotton (however, not excluding other transactions). In the first half of the fifteenth century one such company was the firm of Soranzo & Brothers. Its accounts[370] contain full data on the transactions in the Moslem Levant.

The data summed up in this table show that the firm usually invested 2,000-3,000 ducats a year in the purchase of Syrian cotton, most of it sold

[368] Cf. my "The Venetian supremacy," p. 41.

[369] See *art. cit.*, p. 42.

[370] ASV, Miscellanea Gregolin 14, and cf. my paper in *JEEH* III, p. 42, where some data are quoted from the account books of the Soranzo firm and where the net prices are given.

Table XXVI Levant trade of the firm Soranzo[a],

(a) Cotton trade (including bocasine)

1407		
spring fair		
8 sacks cotton	622 duc.	136 pieces bocasine
bocasine	98 duc. (15.7%)	516 duc.
		prof. 132.5 duc. (26.5%)
fall fair		
12 sacks cotton	546 duc.	
		total investment 1304 duc.
1408		
spring fair		
47 sacks Hamath cotton	1985 duc.	
profit	383 " (19.3%)	
fall fair		
25 sacks Hamath cotton	1052.5 duc.	
profit	187.5 " (17.8%)	
		total investment 3367.5 duc.[b]
1409		
spring fair		
44 sacks Hamath cotton net price	1386 duc.	
fall fair		
20 sacks Hamath cotton net price	703 duc.	77 pieces bocasine 255.5 duc.
profit of both purchases	276.5 duc. (13.2%)	total investment 2344.5 duc.
1410		
22 sacks Hamath cotton	1136.1 duc.	79 pieces bocasine 255.5 duc.
profit	231.4 " (20.3%)	
		total investment 1391 duc.
1411		
fall fair		
10 sacks Hamath cotton	490.5 duc.	3 bales bocasine 452 duc.
profit	141.5 " (28.8%)	profit 162.5 " (35%)
		total investment 942 duc.
1412		
spring fair		
11 sacks Ramla cotton	291 duc.	179 pieces bocasine of Hamath 403 duc.
profit	99 " (34%)	profit 176.5 duc. (44%)
28 sacks Hamath cotton	1012 duc.	
profit	374 " (37%)	
		total investment 1706 duc.

Table XXVI (continued)

1413			
spring fair			
1 sack Hamath cotton	43.5 duc.		
1 " " "	39 "		
5 sacks " "	225.5 "	60 pieces bocasine	157.6 duc.
profit of these 5 sacks	9.5 duc. (4.2%)	141 pieces bocasine	291.5 duc.
17 sacks of Hamath cotton	780.5 "		
28 " Sarmin cotton	707 "	profit	126 duc. (43%)
profit	212 " (27%)		
5 sacks Ramla cotton	183 "		
profit	21 " (11.4%)		
		total investment	2464 duc.
1414			
spring fair			
17 sacks Acre cotton	753.5 duc.	3 bales spun cotton	191.5 duc.
profit	40.5 "		
1 sack Hamath cotton	45 duc.		
fall fair			
1 sack Hamath cotton	45 duc.	3 bales bocasine	548 duc.
		145 pieces bocasine	377 "
		total investment	1960 duc.
1415			
spring fair			
69 sacks Hamath cotton	2573 duc.	120 pieces bocasine	304.5 duc.
profit	462 " (17.9%)		
		total investment	2878.5 duc.
1416			
spring fair			
66 sacks Hamath cotton	2200 duc.	127 pieces bocasine	344 duc.
profit	917 " (41%)	profit	73 " (21%)
fall fair			
31 sacks Hamath cotton	1077 "	total investment	3621 duc.
profit	123 " (11.5%)		
1417			
spring fair			
32 sacks Hamath cotton	2470.3 duc.		
profit	299.5 " (12.5%)		
1418			
spring fair			
22 sacks Sarmin cotton	478.5 duc.	244 pieces of Hamath bocasine	239 duc.
28 " Hamath "	929.5 "		
128 " " "	2294.5 "		
profit (of latter)	(28%)		

Table XXVI (continued)

fall fair			
103 sacks Hamath cotton	1828 duc.		
profit	734.5 " (40%)		
		total investment	5869.5 duc.
1419			
spring fair			
45 sacks Hamath cotton	1513 duc.	bocasine	458 duc.
profit	1055.5 " (70%)		
fall fair			
72 sacks Hamath cotton	1816 duc.		
profit	852.5 " (47.3%)		
		total investment	3707 duc.
1420			
spring fair			
77 sacks Hamath cotton	1797 duc.	bocasine	692.5 duc.
		profit	70.5 duc. (10.2%)
		total investment	2498.5 duc.
1421			
spring fair			
9 sacks Hamath cotton	243 duc.		
profit	110 " (45%)		
fall fair			
5 sacks Hamath cotton	272.5 duc.	4 bales bocasine	48.2 duc.
profit	42.5 " (15%)	profit	99 "(20%)
		10 pieces of Hamath bocasine	18 "
		profit	13.5 " (78%)
		total investment	1015.5 duc.[b]
1422			
3 sacks Hamath cotton	117 duc.		
profit	15 " (12.8%)		
22 sacks Djabala cotton	98 "		
profit	58 " (59%)		
		total investment	1104 duc.
1423			
spring fair			
25 sacks Hamath cotton	939 duc.		
profit	101 " (10.7%)		
4 sacks Djabala cotton	204.5 duc.		
profit	(6.5%)		
18 sacks Acre cotton	1077 duc.		
profit	15 (1.5%)		
		total investment 2220 duc.	

Table XXVI (continued)

1424				
spring fair				
85 sacks Hamath cotton				
net price	2578.5 duc.			
1 sack of Acre cotton	51.3 "			
profit	9 " (18%)			
fall fair				
19 sacks Hamath cotton	682.5 duc.			
profit	53.5 " (7.8%)		total investment	3312.3 duc.

(b) Spice trade

1411			
c. 30a	pepper bought in Alexandria	895.5 duc.	
	profit	823.5 "	(92%)
1412			
c. 36a	pepper bought in Alexandria	430 duc.	
	profit	93.5 duc.	(21.7%)
1413			
c. 41b	pepper bought in Damascus	729.5 duc.	
	profit	67	(9.1%)
1424			
c. 118	pepper bought in Damascus	1230 duc.	
	profit	293.5 "	(23.8%)
	ginger bought in Damascus	1490 duc.	
	profit	556 "	(37.3%)

a) If there is no other indication, the prices given here are the gross prices, including all expenses, both in Syria (Egypt) and in Venice. When only the net price is quoted, the data referring to the investment and the profits have only relative value.

b) In this year, the firm invested a great amount in the purchase of Damascene silken stuffs. This was perhaps the reason for a smaller investment in cotton.

to South German customers with greatly varying profit rates. The typical rate of profit seems to have been 20 to 30 percent. The range of profit may have been smaller than in earlier and later years, when cotton prices were lower.[371] But the small profits in 1413-1417 also point to the consequences of the economic war waged by King Sigismund against Venice and his proclamations prohibiting trade.

Although the striking feature of Venice's Levantine trade was the reg-

[371] See my, "Profits," p. 271.

Table XXVII Auctions of the Venetian Levant galleys, 1403 - 1421[a]

year	Alexandria	Beirut	Romania	source
		line of		
1403	-	-	115[5]	Misti 46, f. 85b f.
1404	118[13]	108[13]	93	Misti 46, f. 138b, 144a
1405	339	331[2]	-	Misti 47, f. 9b, 10a
1406	498[3]	310[6]	293[4]	Misti 47, f. 55b, 56a, 56b
1407	362	104[5]	281[9]	Misti 47, f. 118b
1408	477[7]	87[7]	160[2]	Misti 48, f. 12b, 13b f.
1409	429[15]	54[10]	184[2]	Misti 48, f. 83a, 84a, 88a
1410	158	136[18]	300[6]	Misti 48, f. 150a, 159a
1411	636[3]	389[8]	246[12]	Misti 49, f. 33a, 34a
1412	92[14]	260	160[5]	Misti 49, f. 126a, 127a, 118a
1413	522[16]	301[12]	162[16]	Misti 50, f. 3b, 4a, 5b, 55b
		suppl. galley 160		
1414	602[10]	421[14]	285[2]	Misti 50, f. 119b, 134b, 135b
1415	507[5]	493	10[19]	Misti 51, f. 28b, 30a, 31a
1416	282[9]	76	52	Misti 51, f. 136a ff.
1417	387[14]	371[9]	131[17]	Misti 52, f. 21a, 22a, 22b
1418	471[10]	502	93[16]	Misti 52, f. 102b, 103a
1419	421[16]	331[8]	155[3]	Misti 52, f. 175a f., 181a, 181b
1420	275[11]	295[6]	138[4]	Misti 53, f. 48a f., 53b, 54b
1421	335[10]	665[3]	301[12]	Misti 53, f. 150a f., 159b, 160b

a) The amounts of the rents paid are given in lire and soldi as in the preceding tables. The same data are quoted by Thiriet, Rég. II, p. 39f., 47, 52, 59, 69, 77, 86, 91, 92, 101, 108, 113, 114, 124, 126, 135, 144, 155, 166, 175, 176, 181.

ularity of the galley and cog services and the keeping of the timetable of the fairs in the Levant, it did not develop in a straight line. There were ups and downs in the trade with the various Levantine countries. This is clearly shown by the sums the auctions of the galleys yielded.[372]

The sums yielded by the yearly auctions of the Alexandria galleys in the first decade of the fifteenth century were certainly smaller than those obtained in the years of the boom of 1395-1400. But, compared with those of the Alexandria galleys in the 1380's, they were on the average greater (2382 1., so 340 per annum, against 2253 1, so 322 per annum). But there

[372] The data of the years 1405-1421 have been published in tables by Thiriet, *La Romanie vénitienne*, p. 42 f.; those of 1403-1412 by the same author, "Quelques observations," *Studi Fanfani* III, p. 511, and those of 1403-1407 also in his, "La crise des trafics vénitiens au Levant dans les premières années du XVe siècle," *Studi Melis* III, p. 65.

was in those years a very great decline in the auctions of the Beirut galleys. This was surely connected with conditions in Syria, where civil war raged throughout the reign of Sultan Faradj. Obviously, the Venetian merchants were less inclined to invest in the spice trade with this country under these conditions. Even when the offer of spices on the Syrian markets was abundant, the Venetians were sometimes reluctant to purchase, because of the great insecurity. This is convincingly shown by a merchant letter reporting conditions in Damascus in 1403. On the other hand, it became difficult to sell European articles at profitable prices in the Levant. The civil war was connected with heavy taxation and compulsory purchases imposed by the Mamluk authorities, so that the market was very dull. Merchant letters of those years dwell on this phenomenon. In 1406 both the Alexandria and the Beirut galleys returned with rather poor freights. Even the spring convoy of the Syrian cogs came back with little cargoes of cotton and other articles. The merchants reported that there was civil war and famine in Syria and that the offer of spices in Egypt and in Syria was very small. The same was true for the year 1407. The three Alexandria galleys brought only 1133 colli spices. In 1408 the merchants reported that conditions in Syria were very bad. In that year the volume of the Venetian cotton trade in Syria was probably at its lowest ebb.[373] At that time efforts were made to intensify Venetian trade with the Black Sea area, as shown by the increases in the rents paid for the Romania galleys in 1406, 1407, and 1410. That the crisis of the Syrian spice trade was not the consequence of greater investments in cotton[374] is shown by the results of the auctions in the second decade of the fourteenth century. When the Moslem Levant again had a stable government and Syria was no longer a war area, the auctions of the Beirut galleys again yielded very substantial sums.[375] Comparing the number of cogs in the cotton convoys in the first decade of the fifteenth century with that in the second, one sees that they increased considerably in the second decade. On the other hand, the Romania line of the galleys declined very considerably. In some years, no one would lease the Trebizond galley (in 1412-1414, 1418), and in 1415 it was leased for the symbolic payment of five shillings. In several years only two galleys were offered for the Romania line (in 1403, 1406, 1409, 1417, 1419). The trip of the

[373] Dat 928, letters of Com. of Zanobi di Taddeo Gaddi of 24 Nov. 1403, 15 Dec. 1403; *ibid.*, letter from Damascus of 22 March 1403; Dat 929, letters of Com. of Zanobi di Taddeo Gaddi of 14 Aug. 1406, 24 Nov. 1406, 27 Nov. 1406; letter of Gianozzo e Antonio degli Alberti of 7 Aug. 1406, Dat 930: letter of Gianozzo e Antonio degli Alberti of 26 Nov. 1407; letter of Com. of Zanobi of 18 May 1408; letter of Perluccio del Maestro Paolo of 12 Nov. 1408; Ainaud, "Quatre doc.," doc. III.

[374] As Thiriet believes, "Quelques observations," p. 515.

[375] The new upsurge of the galley auctions, however, was not connected with the export of grains, timber, and fustian on the galleys, as maintained by Thiriet, "La crise des trafics vénitiens," p. 67. It would be difficult to prove this assertion.

Romania galleys in 1408 was a complete failure. So one cannot speak of a general crisis in the Venetian Levant trade at the beginning of the fifteenth century; one should distinguish between Venice's trade with the various Levantine countries. Actually the volume of Venetian trade in Egypt and Syria became so great then that very often the galleys did not have sufficient space for the spices, and supplementary galleys and cogs had to be despatched to ship the merchandise to Venice.[376]

Various data in merchant letters and in chronicles make it possible to draw some conclusions as to the volume of the Venetian investments in the Levant at this time. They are compiled in Table XXVIII. A discussion of these data must begin with the statement that they are not complete. The quantity of spices that the Venetian merchant actually purchased in the Levant must often have been much greater than foreseen. For time and again one finds accounts of hundreds of bales that had remained in the ports of Egypt and Syria and of supplementary cogs that had to be despatched to collect them.[377] The accounts of the pepper sold by the Venetian consul in Alexandria in some years constitute additional evidence of the growth of the Venetian spice trade in the Levant. In 1418 the consulate auctioned 201 sportas, worth about 20,000 dinars. Another account refers to the purchase of 411 sportas, which the Venetians bought in Alexandria in the same year.[378] A document of 1419 contains information on the purchase of pepper in Alexandria for 115,000 dinars.[379] The data provided by Morosini clearly point to the sum of 300,000 ducats as the "average" investment in spices; that means the cash and the merchandise taken by the Venetian merchants who embarked on the galleys. This was apparently true for the second decade of the fifteenth century, when the long civil war in the Mamluk realm was over. Additional purchases may have been financed with money transferred earlier or by drafting bills of exchange. Further, certain shipments carried by the pilgrim galleys should be taken

[376] On the Romania galleys in 1408, see Dat 930, letter of Perluccio del Maestro Paolo of 22 Nov. 1408. As to the supplementary galleys and cogs, see the table in my paper, "The Venetian supremacy," p. 18 f., to which there should be added the following data: 1406, 1407, 1411, 1412, and 1420, a supplementary cog to Alexandria, see *Chron. Morosini*, c. 191, 205, 232, 238, 374; in February 1421 a supplementary galley was sent to Alexandria, see *Chron. Morosini*, c. 377; in 1413 a supplementary galley to Beirut, see Misti 50, f. 54b ff. and *Chron. Morosini*, c. 272. Further, in 1417 the number of the Beirut galleys was six, according to *Chron. Dolfin*, f. 267a and according to *Chron. Zancaruola*, c. 490b, five.

[377] In 1417, 800-1,000 bales remained in Beirut, according to *Chron. Morosini*, c. 342 (*Zancaruola*, f. 490b and *Dolfin*, f. 304b: 1000), worth perhaps 100,000 ducats. Then in 1420 a cog sent to Alexandria was not sufficient for collecting the merchandise that remained there, so a supplementary galley was despatched. It was to travel between Alexandria and Modon until the transport was achieved. The supplementary cog had shipped 1520 bales to Corfu; see *Chron. Morosini*, c. 377, 378.

[378] See my, "The Volume of Levantine Trade," p. 598, 599.

[379] See my, "The Venetian supremacy," p. 39.

Table XXVIII Volume of Venice's Levantine trade, 1403 - 1421[a]

year	galleys: Alexandria	galleys: Beirut	Syria cogs	source
1403			cargo of spring convoy 300 sacks raw cotton 200 bales spun cotton[b]	Dat 928, letter of Zanobi di Taddeo Gaddi of April 28, 1403
1404			cargo of fall convoy 2000 sacks raw cotton 100 bales spun cotton 400 boxes powdered potash	Dat 715, letter of Giovanni di Ser Nigi of 25 Nov. 1404; Dat 929, letter of the same, of 18 Dec. 1404.
1405	value of cargoes 100,000 duc.[c]		fall 320,000 duc.	Morosini c. 173, 191
1406	cash and merchandise 370,000 duc.		cargo of spring convoy 1400 sacks raw cotton 140 bales spun cotton 340 boxes powdered sugar 500 sacks potash	Op. cit., c. 196; Dat 929, letters of Zanobi of 14 & 21 Aug. 1406; letter of Giannozzo Antonio degli Alberti of 7 Aug. 1406
1407	cargo of a suppl. cog 35,000 duc.			Morosini c. 205
1408			cargo of spring convoy 2500 sacks raw cotton 300 bales spun cotton	Dat 930, letter of Com. of Zanobi of 18 May 1408
			cargo of fall convoy 1050 sacks raw cotton	Dat 930, letter of Paoluccio del Maestro Paolo of 12 Nov. 1408
1410			cargo of spring convoy 4000 sacks raw cotton 300 bales spun cotton	Dat 930, letter of Bindo di Gherardo Piaciti of 31 May 1410[d]
1411		cargo of 4 galleys and a suppl. cog 4000 bales[e]		Morosini c. 232
1413	cash 80-100,000 duc. merchandise[f]	210-220,000 duc. merchandise[g]		Op. cit., c. 266 267
1414	160,000 duc.[h]	160,000 duc.		Op. cit., c. 881
1415	160,000 duc.	cash 180,000 duc. merchandise 40,000 duc.	spring 135,000 duc.	Op. cit., c. 292, 296
			total 515,000 duc.	
1416	140,000 duc.	160,000 duc.	spring (with 2 ships to Flanders and one to Greece) cash 150,000 duc. merchandise 50,000 duc. fall 30,000 duc.	Op. cit., c. 311, 314, 320
1417	210,000 duc.	180,000 duc.	spring cash 150,000 duc. merchandise 100-150,000 duc. fall 180,000 duc.	Op. cit., c. 326, 331 Chron. Dolfin, f. 301b, 302b
			total 845,000 duc.	

Table XXVIII (continued)

year	galleys		Syria cogs		source
	Alexandria	Beirut			
1418	120,000 duc. suppl. 1 galley 40,000 duc.		spring	60,000	Morosini c. 345, 351, 353
			fall	35-40,000 duc.	
			total 350,000 duc.		
1419	80,000 duc.	160,000 duc.	spring	80,000 duc.	Op. cit., c. 355, 359
			Candia Alex. cogs	20,000 duc.	
			fall	150,000 duc.	
			total 490,000 duc.		
1420	130,000 duc.	120,000 duc. cargo of 2 suppl. cogs 130-140.000 duc.	spring	80-100,000 duc.	Op. cit., c. 367, 368, 369/70, 373, 377
			fall	65-70,000 duc.	
		duc.	total 410,000 duc.		
1421	suppl. galley cash 120,130,000 duc. merchandise 50,000		fall	185,000 duc.	Op. cit., c. 377, 380
	85,000 duc.	190,000 duc.	total 550,000 duc.		

a) Most of the data are taken from the Morosini chronicle and Datini letters. When Morosini does not specify the amount of cash and the value of the merchandise carried by the galleys that depart for the Levant, he gives an estimate of both. The Datini letters give us data about the cargoes the cog convoys brought back to Venice.

b) The writer of the letter does not say that this will be the quantity of cotton arriving from Syria, but that this will be the cotton available in Venice. However, as before this passage, he says that there is no fear of another invasion of Syria by Timur; he apparently is referring to the Syrian cotton. But according to a document stemming from the archives of the family Soranzo and published by Bautier, Relations, p. 320, the cargo of the Syria cogs coming from the spring muda consisted of 1809 sacks raw cotton, 263 sacks spun cotton, 294 sacks potash and 34 sacks powdered sugar.

c) This is an estimate of the value of the merchandise shipped by both galley convoys. When Morosini reports the value of a cargo he has in mind the FOB price, see c. 205 where he says that a cog suffered shipwreck and that it carried merchandise worth 35,000 duc., which would have yielded a profit of 20%.

d) A letter written on the same day by Paolo Giovanni, ibid., states, however, that the cargo contained 4500 sacks raw cotton.

e) The value of a bale can be assumed to have been about 100 duc., see Morosini c. 205; 300 colli spices are worth 35,000 duc.

f, g) Value not indicated.

h) According to a freight inventory published by Bautier l.c. the value of the cargo brought back by these galleys would have amounted to the same sum or to a bit more.

i) Cf. the letter of Nic. Contarini quoted in my paper in JEEH IV, p. 592. There is no contradiction between these two documents, as Contarini may refer to all the money the merchants who came with the cogs and the galleys had brought with them to Damascus where they stayed.

j) Dolfin has 260,000 duc., Marino Sanuto, Vite, c. 1015 has: cash 360,000 ducats and merchandise 160,000 ducats.

into consideration. Sometimes the Venetian authorities forbade the use of these galleys for the transport of merchandise to the Levant[380] but at other times it was allowed,[381] and rather often they served as supplementary carriers for the transport of spices.[382] A pilgrim galley that went to Palestine in 1404 was supposed to carry merchandise and money amounting to 100,000 ducats.[383]

The amount of cash and the value of the merchandise carried by the two convoys of Syrian cogs was quite different in each year, but it probably would not be very much in error to figure 200,000 ducats as the average investment in the second decade of the fifteenth century. The data provided by the Datini letters show that the cotton purchases, and consequently the investment, in Syria were much smaller in the first decade. But certainly there were exceptions, as in 1405. The unusually great convoy of cotton cogs in spring 1416 transported merchandise and cash amounting to perhaps 150,000 ducats. A peak was apparently reached in 1417, when the spring convoy departed from Venice with 250,300 ducats in cash and merchandise. Part of the cash and the merchandise shipped by these convoys, however, was for purchases in Cyprus, where these ships regularly anchored. In fact, sugar bought in Cyprus was carried by these cogs to Syria and then shipped to Venice.[384] Another part of the money (and merchandise) sent to Syria on the cogs was for the purchase of spices. In 1421 a Syrian cog carrying spices and other commodities estimated to be worth 100,000 ducats was awaited in Venice.[385] So the role of the cog convoys as a major artery of Venice's Levantine trade in that period, almost equal to the role of the galleys, should not be underestimated.[386] To estimate the total Venetian investment in the Levant trade, the direct shipment to the Levant of merchandise from Spain, such as olive oil of Seville,[387] various articles from the Campania, e.g., soap of Gaeta,[388] and olive oil from Apulia,[389] should also be taken into account.

All these facts point to an average investment of 500,000 dinars a year. This conclusion would be in full keeping with the data provided by Tommaso Mocenigo in a famous speech delivered in 1421 or 1423. According to him,

380 Misti 48, f. 28a (in addition to French and Venetian cloth).

381 Misti 46, f. 140b.

382 Misti 47, f. 117b f. 48, f. 209a 51, f. 29a, 137a, 181a 53, f. 129b f.

383 Thiriet, *Rég.* II, p.153.

384 *Chron. Morosini*, c. 296; Misti 48, f. 82a ff. 49, f. 125b f. 50, f. 4b; Secreta I, f. 81a ff.

385 Secreta VIII, f. 7b, 10b, 17b ff.

386 As is done by Thiriet, "La crise des trafics," p. 72 (where we read "Amman," to be corrected into "Ḥamā," so called by the Italians).

387 *Libr. Com.* III, lib. 10, no. 19.

388 *Chron. Morosini*, c. 340.

389 G. P., Sent. 34, f. 39a ff.

the Venetians sold spices and cotton valued at almost a million ducats every year in Italy. If the difference between FOB and CIF prices is taken into account, these sales point to an investment of 450,000 ducats. To this amount should be added 150,000-200,000 as the price of the commodities sold to the Germans and in Northwestern Europe. So these data imply a yearly investment of 600,000-650,000 ducats, i.e., 480,000-520,000 dinars.[390] Although the increase of the Venetian investment in the Levant in the second decade of the fifteenth century was partly due to the high prices of the spices and the cotton in the first quarter of the century, the difference between the average volume of the Levant trade in those years and at the end of the fourteenth century is conspicuous; it had risen from 300,000-500,000 dinars to an average investment of half a million and more. In some years, as in 1417, the investment of the Venetians in the Levant trade reached peaks never heard of before.

As the Venetians became the foremost trading nation in the Eastern Mediterranean in that period, the shipments of cloth they exported into the Moslem Levant probably increased very greatly. They exported Florentine cloth, precious German cloth, English gilforte, and, of course, the products of their own textile industry to Egypt and Syria. They also exported Catalan cloth of Barcelona, Valencia, and Perpignan to Syria.[391] The Venetians benefitted more than all other trading nations from the decline of the Levantine industries and imported into the dominions of the Mamluks soap, paper, and other industrial products.[392] Piloti mentions as the most important articles of the Venetian export to the Levant soap, cloth, silken stuffs, and saffron of Lombardy.[393] But they also marketed great quantities of copper and lead in Egypt and in Syria.[394] In 1404 the firm Pietro Pisani & Sons sold 101 t copper in Alexandria;[395] Marco Giustinian sold, in 1405, 14½ t; a partner of his, 3½ t; and his brother Andrea, 5, 7 t.[396] They also engaged very much in the import of foodstuffs, such as olive oil, honey, almonds, raisins, etc., as they did in earlier times.[397] In 1406 a

[390] Cf. "The Volume of Levantine Trade," p. 594 f.

[391] Florentine cloth: G. P., Sent. 20, f. 12b ff. (a. 1408) 25 f. 6b ff., 24b (a. 1413); German cloth: G. P., Sent. 38, f. 66a ff. Misti 55, f. 117b; see further the freight tariffs: Misti 56, f. 32a ff. 57, f. 11b, 13b, 117a 58, f. 70b 59, f. 57a, 119b 60, f. 157a ff.; gilforte: G. P., Sent. 22, f. 24a ff. 46, f. 63a f. 77, f. 139b ff. Dat 929, letter of Antonio Contarini to Luca del Ferro in Florence, a. 1404, without exact date.

[392] See above, pp. 209, 210.

[393] Piloti, p. 149 ff.

[394] Misti 48, f. 76b 51, f. 181a 53, f. 71a 58, f. 63a f.; G. P., Sent. 15, f. 37a ff.

[395] G. P., Sent. 16, f. 30a ff.

[396] G. P., Sent. 18, f. 15a ff.

[397] Olive oil: *Chron. Morosini*, c. 290; Misti 55, f. 122b; Coll., Not. II, f. 162b V, f. 171b; G. P., Sent. 34, f. 11a ff and cf. above notes 388, 389; honey: G. P., Sent. II, f. 18a f.; Arch. B. Dolfin Ba 181, fasc. 13; Misti 53, f. 72a.

Venetian ship carried olive oil worth 25,000 ducats to Syria. Most of the olive oil was shipped directly from Tunisia, Spain, the Campania, and Apulia. The honey had been purchased in Lombardy or in Rhodes.[398] Even the export of hazelnuts to the Levant was not insignificant. The Venetian merchant Paolo Michiel imported 1,987 sacks of hazelnuts into Alexandria in 1418 after the departure of the galleys.[399]

All these articles were practically bartered for the spices, dyes, aromatics, and cotton of the Near and Far East. Venetian trade in the Levant in that period had become not only much greater but also more varied. The Venetian merchants also exported cheap commodities, such as salt, from Egypt. True, very often it served as ballast, but not necessarily always.[400]

[398] G. P., Sent. Int. VIII, f. 24b ff. See also Arch. B. Dolfin, Ba 181, fasc. 23 (oio di Barberia); G. P., Sent. 34, f. 37a ff., 39a ff. (from Apulia).

[399] Arch B. Dolfin Ba 181, fasc. 13.

[400] Coll., Not. III, f. 100b (a. 1403) IV, f. 1b (a. 1406), 78a (a. 1408), 83b (a. 1410) V, f. 6a (a. 1414), 15a (a. 1414, export to Bologna and Romagna), 82b (a. 1417, from Alexandria Damietta), 144a (export to Verona). See, further, J.-Cl. Hoquet, *Le sel et la fortune de Venise* (Lille 1978-1979) I, pp. 100, 256 (other references of the same period) and *op.cit.*, II, pp. 206, 260, about the export of salt from Egypt by the Venetians in earlier periods.

V

A New Crisis (1422-1452)

A. The Downfall of the Kārimīs

In the third decade of the fifteenth century once more the social structures of Near Eastern society underwent a change that had a great impact on the Levantine trade of the South European trading nations. It was the decline of the powerful group of wholesale merchants who were called Kārimīs. At first their downfall meant a deterioration of the conditions in which the Europeans carried on trade in the Moslem Levant, for it was the sultan of Cairo who took over the role of these merchants, and it was much more difficult to deal with him, but in the course of time a modus vivendi was established between the Europeans and the sultan, who renounced his project of monopolizing the spice trade, and instead of a trust of rich merchant princes, henceforth the Europeans dealt with middle-class traders, who, of course, did not have the power to impose conditions. So in the long run the downfall of the Kārimīs was a great advantage for the European merchants.

When the Mamluk sultan decided to break the power of the Kārimīs, they already had a long history. In fact, they had established their domination of the Egyptian international trade a long time before. The term "Kārim" appears first in Judaeo-Arabic merchant letters of the third and fourth decades of the eleventh century. In these letters it meant the ship captains and merchants (often the same person) who dealt with the export of spices from India to the Near East.[1] The Kārimīs are also mentioned in a Moslem (literary) source referring to the seventh decade of the eleventh century.[2] It seems that these first Kārimīs were not yet a company, but a group of ship captains travelling in a convoy,[3] and often the totality of the

[1] S. D. Goitein, "New lights on the beginnings of the Kārimī merchants," *JESHO* I (1958), p. 176 f.; as to the literal meaning of Kārim, see Goitein, *art. cit.*, p. 182, and S. Y. Labib, art. *Kārimī*, in *Enc. Isl.* 2nd ed., IV, p. 640.

[2] H. Rabie, *The financial system of Egypt 1169-1341* (London, 1972), p. 97.

[3] Goitein, *art. cit.*, p. 181.

India travellers was called Kārim (not yet Kārimi).[4] The Fatimid caliphs of Egypt, who had a great interest in fostering the trade of Egypt with India and in diverting the major route of the Near Eastern trade with India from the Persian Gulf to the Red Sea, took the Kārimīs under their wings, granting them military protection. A squadron of their war fleet cruised the Red Sea to safeguard the merchantmen of the Kārimīs,[5] and the dynasties that succeeded the Fatimids adopted the same attitude. They even granted them their protection but, on the other hand, levied various dues on them. These dues were a not insignificant source of revenue for the rulers of Egypt, and in their administration there was a special department, with a branch in Damascus, dealing with the Kārimīs.[6] Until the end of the fourteenth century, there were indeed two major routes of the Kārimī trade, one connecting the Red Sea port of ʿAydhāb via Ḳūṣ in Upper Egypt with Cairo and Alexandria and the other connecting the trading towns on the Red Sea with Damascus, i.e., the caravan route from the Ḥidjāz to Central Syria.[7]

In the fourteenth century the Kārimīs had become a very rich and influential group of merchants who engaged in various sectors of international trade. In the way of mediaeval authors, the Arabic historians dwell on the wealth of the Kārimīs, who built splendid houses for themselves and made bequests for mosques, madrasas, and other religious establishments. They also relate how in times of famine the government required the Kārimīs to feed a certain number of the poor.[8] It goes without saying that one seldom finds data about the volume of the Kārimī trade in the writings of the mediaeval authors. But in a biography of ʿAbdalʿazīz 6, Manṣūr of Aleppo, who travelled to China five times, there is a statement that he came to Egypt in 1305 with merchandise worth a million dinars.[9] This is certainly an exaggeration but a significant one. On the other hand, the same Arabic historians hint strongly at the political influence that the Kārimīs had upon the courts of Cairo and Yemen.[10] It was a consequence of their financial power.

The Kārimīs were merchants who hailed from various countries and from a very varied strata of society. Some of them had been born in Syria, others

[4] Goitein, *Letters of mediaeval Jewish traders*, p. 214.

[5] *Ṣubḥ al-aʿshā* III, p. 524.

[6] *Op.cit.*, IV, pp. 32, 187; XI, p. 321; and cf. Gaudefroy-Demombynes, *La Syrie a l'époque des Mamelouks*, p. LXXIV, 149 f.

[7] G. Wiet, "Les marchands d'épices sous les sultans mamlouks," *Cahiers d'histoire égyptienne* VII (1955), p. 94, 96; Labib, *Handelsgeschichte*, p. 376.

[8] *ad-Durar al-kāmina* no. 2450, 3670; *Khiṭaṭ* II, p. 253, 368f. 427; Ibn Duḳmāḳ IV, p. 98 F.; *al-Manhal aṣ-ṣāfī*, MS. Paris 2068, f. 23b f.; ʿAbdalbāsiṭ 803, f. 104a.

[9] *Sulūk* II, p. 132 f.; *al-Manhal aṣ-ṣāfī* 2071, f. 70a.

[10] *ad-Durar al-kāmina* no. 5020; al-Mufaḍḍal b. Abi 'l-Faḍā'il, ed. Blochet, p. 644; W. J. Fischel, "Über die Gruppe der Kārimī-Kaufleute," in *Studia Arabica* I (Analecta Orientalia 14) (Rome, 1937), p. 80.

in Iraq, in Yemen, or even in Ethiopia.[11] There were Kārimīs who were born poor and had made their fortunes themselves, true parvenus; others had inherited riches from their parents.[12] But there were among them some families which in their days held the foremost place in the economic life in Egypt and Syria. Such families were the Ibn Kuwayk in the first half of the fourteenth century and the al-Kharrūbī in the second half.[13] Under the rule of the Mamluks, however, it was almost impossible that a family of great merchants could remain rich through several generations. Careful study of the data that has come down to us in the collections of Arabic biographies of the later Middle Ages shows that mostly such a family comprised three generations of rich merchants.[14] The methods of the Mamlūk fisc and the compulsory purchases of the stocks of the sultan's commercial agencies, which were imposed time and again upon the merchants, ruined them. The Kārimīs were by no means a purely Moslem group of merchants. Just as several geniza documents of the eleventh and the twelfth centuries testify to the participation of Jews in their activities, in a Judaeo-Arabic letter of the Mamluk period the names of some Kārimī merchants appear, which point to their being Jews or Christians.[15] So the Kārimīs were a very heterogeneous group as far as their origins are concerned, and they were only a loosely knit partnership. The Arabic sources do not contain data that would justify the use of such expressions as corporation, etc., in connection with the Kārimīs.[16] True, sometimes the Mamluk government appealed to them as a group and conferred the title "Head of the merchants" or the like on the most successful and influential of them,[17] but it would be a mistake to conclude that these leading Kārimīs were heads of an organized association. It was the custom of the Mamluks, as it was of other Moslem governments, to confer such titles upon leading men of certain

[11] Fischel, *art. cit.*, p. 164.

[12] E. Ashtor, "The Kārimī merchants," p. 47.

[13] Wiet, *art. cit.*, p. 105 ff.; Ashtor, *art. cit.*, p. 49 (to be added, Nūr ad-dīn Ibn al-Kharrūbī al-Kārimī, who died in 1412; see *Djawāhir as-sulūk*, MS. Br. Museum, Or. 6854, f. 345a).

[14] See my "The Kārimī merchants," p. 48 f., and see below.

[15] See my "A private letter of the Mamlūk period," *Kiryat Sepher* 18 (1941-1942), p. 199ff., and see there, p. 200, Naṣrallāh ibn al-Kārimī and, p. 201, Faradjallāh al-Kārimī. When I published this letter, I still had doubts as to whether these Kārimīs were non-Moslems. But in Geniza documents that I published later, and which date from the Mamluk period, there are references to many Jews named Faradjallāh: see my *History of the Jews in Egypt and in Syria under the rule of the Mamlūks* III (Jerusalem, 1970), pp. 134, 135 (beginning of the sixteenth century) and, further, p. 135, Faradjallāh Netifa, *ibidem*, Shams Faradjallāh, p. 94, Faradjallāh Ibn ad-Damīrī (no date) and *l.c.* Yūsuf Faradjallāh, p. 125 f., Faradjallāh b. Ya'ḳūb Ibn Shams (second half of the fifteenth century), and see also *op.cit.*, II (Jerusalem, 1951), p. 423, Faradjallāh of Rosetta (in Cairo, a. 1481), and p. 555 Faradjallāh b. Mūsā (in Cairo, a. 1442). So the assertion that the Kārimīs were exclusively Moslems can be dismissed; see Fischel, "The spice trade in Mamlūk Egypt," *JESHO* I, p. 166; Wiet, *art. cit.*, p. 130.

[16] Fischel, "The spice trade," p. 165.

[17] *Sulūk* III, p. 539; 'Abdalbāsiṭ 803, f. 135a.

classes or professional groups. Then, in case of necessity, the government applied to them either for counsel or for levying financial contributions.

The Kārimīs were active in several branches of trade and industry. They traded in wheat,[18] precious stones and jewels,[19] cloth,[20] and slaves,[21] and they invested great sums of money in the sugar industry. The Kharrūbī family had three sugar refineries in Cairo. In addition, Badr ad-dīn Muḥammad al-Kharrūbī (d. 1361), a great sugar industrialist, had some factories in the countryside.[22] In his account of the sugar factories in Fostat, the Arabic historian Ibn Duḳmāḳ also mentions those of Madjd ad-dīn Maʿālī al-Kārimī and of Ibn al-ʿAdjdjān *as-simṣār bi 'l-kārim* (the spice broker).[23] However, the Kārimīs were first of all spice traders, who imported spices, dyes and aromatics from India and Yemen into Egypt and Syria.[24] So they had ships of their own.[25] In the fourteenth century, they mostly bought the spices and other Indian articles in Yemen and therefore commuted between this country and Egypt a great deal. They had large storehouses for the Indian commodities in some of the towns of Yemen,[26] but one should not infer from the numerous data concerning their journeys from Yemen to Egypt and vice versa that they did not travel to India in that period.[27] Indeed, they were always great travellers, and some of them visited both India and China, while others sent their agents there.[28] Because of their important role in the Yemen trade, they were held in high esteem there and became go-betweens of its royal court and the sultans of Egypt.[29] Their influence was enhanced by the fact that they also fulfilled the role of bankers and gave loans to merchants and princes.[30]

[18] *an-Nudjūm az-zāhira* V, p. 121; Labib, *Handelsgeschichte*, p. 393.

[19] al-Mufaḍḍal b. Abi 'l-Faḍā'il, p. 621; al-Khazradjī, *History of the Resuliyy dynasty* (ed. Redhouse) IV, p. 350.

[20] A well-known Kārimī of the Mamluk period is called *al-bazzāz*—the cloth merchant; see Wiet, *art. cit.*, p. 87.

[21] See my "The Kārimī merchants," p. 55 f., and see above p. 73.

[22] Ibn Duḳmāḳ IV, pp. 42, 46; *Khiṭaṭ* II, p. 369 f.

[23] Ibn Duḳmāḳ IV, p. 44, l. 12-15, and ultima.

[24] *Ṣubḥ al-aʿshā* III, p. 461.

[25] Ibn al-Furāt IX, p. 7; al-Khazradjī, *op.cit.*, IV, p. 289, 321; Wiet, *art. cit.*, p. 93.

[26] al-Khazradjī, *op.cit.*, IV, p. 374; al-Mufaḍḍal b. Abi 'l-Faḍā'il, p. 549 f.; Ibn al-Furāt IX, p. 434; *an-Nudjūm az-zāhira* V, p. 117.

[27] As does Fischel, "Über die Gruppe der Kārimī-Kaufleute," p. 72; cf. Wiet, *art. cit.*, p. 130. See, further, in a letter of the Venetian merchant Niccolò Bernardo, written in Alexandria on March 16, 1424:" E 'l fo detto per mori eser a chamin con gran suma di spezie Cheren le qual a niun modo de qui a tempo de le gallie quel aremo per el suo lungo navegar; chredo de qui le aremo uno altr'ano a 'sto," Melis, *Doc.*, p. 190.

[28] See my "The Kārimī merchants," p. 56. See also Ibn Iyās[2] II, p. 98 f. about the death of an Egyptian Kārimī in India.

[29] al-Khazradjī, *op.cit.*, IV, p. 435 V, pp. 193, 198, 283; Ibn al-Furāt IX, p. 458; *an-Nudjūm az-zāhira* V, p. 571; Ibn Iyās[2] I, part 2, pp. 485, 487; *Ṣubḥ al-aʿshā* VIII, p. 72 ff.; cf. Fischel, "Über die Gruppe," p. 81.

[30] Ibn al-Furāt VIII, p. 62; *Sulūk* I, p. 739, and see above.

The rule of the Baḥrī Mamluks brought the Kārimīs renewed success, as the first sultans of this dynasty took measures to intensify the commercial relations between their countries and the Far East. Sultan Ḳalā'ūn issued safe-conducts for the Far Eastern merchants to encourage them to come to Egypt,[31] and the Rasūlī kings of Yemen fostered international trade, suppressing piracy off the coasts of Southern Arabia and sending embassies to the rulers of India.[32] How great the benevolence of the Baḥrī sultans towards the Kārimīs was is shown by the fact that they very rarely imposed upon them the compulsory loans or extorted from them those "contributions" (*muṣādarāt*) from which other rich people suffered so much, although, in 1300, in a case of great emergency, they did do so.[33] Further, under their rule the commercial agency of the sultan very seldom interfered with the activities of the Kārimīs. There was one exception: Karīm ad-dīn ʿAbd al-karīm, the director of the sultan's Royal Department—that is, head of the agency that sold the goods produced on the fiefs allotted to him and in fact a powerful finance minister under the rule of al-Malik an-Nāṣir Muḥammad (1309-1341)—also dealt with spices. A contemporary Arabic writer narrates that until his downfall in 1323 one could not sell or buy the articles in which he was interested either in Egypt or in Syria. We are told that he also sent his agents to "the Kārim" and to other countries; that means that he engaged in the spice trade.[34] But this was an exception under the rule of the Baḥrī Mamluks. In fact, the second half of the thirteenth century and the first half of the fourteenth century was a period of growth and success in the history of the Kārimīs. The Arabic authors emphasize that their number was then large,[35] and the biographical data of this period point to their great role in the Egyptian economy[36] and their lively trade with the European merchants.[37]

Even in the second half of the fourteenth century, when the economy of the Mamluk dominions began to decline, the Kārimī merchants distinguished themselves by their intense activities and their great riches. Nāṣir ad-dīn Muḥammad Ibn Musallam, who died in 1375, was considered to be extremely rich and the greatest merchant of his time. He was the son of a porter and in his youth had travelled to India, Ethiopia, and the Western Sudan. According to the Arabic chroniclers, he had ships of his own and

[31] *Ṣubḥ al-aʿshā* XIII, p. 339 ff.

[32] Wiet, *art. cit.*, p. 88.

[33] *Sulūk* I, p. 899, and cf. *ad-Durar al-kāmina*, no. 1905.

[34] Ibn aṣ-Ṣuḳāʿī, *Tālī Kitāb Wafayāt al-aʿyān*, ed. J. Sublet (Damascus 1974), p. 194 (translation p. 224).

[35] *ad-Durar al-kāmina*, no. 1905; *Sulūk* II, p. 103.

[36] *Sulūk* II, p. 340, and cf., above, about ʿAbdalʿazīz b. Manṣūr.

[37] See *Sulūk* II, p. 103 f: a Kārimī gives a commenda to a European merchant; but see *ad-Durar al-kāmina*, no. 1037: the European had a debt to the Kārimīs for merchandise he had bought.

his numerous agents travelled in many countries. When he died, he left 200,000 dinars to each of his sons.[38] His contemporary Zaki 'd-dīn al-Kharrūbī (d. 1385) had been born poor too and became a leading merchant. In his old age he was the "head of the merchants of Egypt."[39] Another very successful Kārimī of this period was Nūr ad-dīn ʿAlī b. ʿAnān, who died in 1387.[40]

But the last quarter of the fourteenth century was already a period of transition in the history of the Kārimīs. When the stocks of bullion in the royal mints dwindled and the silver dirham had to be devalued and the resources of the Royal Exchequer diminished, the government began to enlist the help of the Kārimīs. The economic decline compelled the Mamluk kingdom to draw on all sources. The attitude towards the Kārimīs too had to be changed. In 1381 the vizier Ibn Makānis imposed fines upon various groups, such as the high officials and the Kārimīs.[41] Then, in 1394, Sultan Barḳūḳ applied to three rich Kārimī merchants, Shihāb ad-dīn Aḥmad Ibn Musallam, Nūr ad-dīn ʿAlī al-Kharrūbī, and Burhān ad-dīn al-Maḥallī, for a loan of a million dirhams.[42] During the long civil war under the reign of Sultan Faradj, large amounts of money were extorted from all those who were known for their riches, nor were the Kārimīs spared. The sultan confiscated much of the wealth that Nāṣir ad-dīn Ibn Musallam and Burhān ad-dīn al-Maḥallī had left to their sons.[43] Another step that led to the decline of the Kārimīs was the participation of the sultan in the spice trade. Under the rule of the last Baḥrī Mamluks and under the first Circassian sultan, Barḳūḳ, the leading Kārimīs were requested to carry on trade for the Royal Exchequer. They became "the sultan's merchants," although they continued their private commercial activities. An account referring to an event in the year 1369 states that Nāṣir ad-dīn Ibn Musallam was already "trader" of the sultan at that time.[44] There cannot be the slightest doubt that when the great Kārimīs took over trade for the sultan, they also invested his money in spices, a trade in which they specialized. In the same story about an event in the life of Nāṣir ad-dīn Ibn Musallam, it is not said explicitly that he traded in spices for the sultan; that would be inferred from the mention of merchandise of India that he had gone to collect in Ḳūṣ. Another text refers to someone employed in 1396 in "the mint, the

[38] al-Bayrūtī, MS. Bodl. 712, f. 95b.; *ad-Durar al-kāmina*, no. 4575; *Khiṭaṭ* II, p. 401; Ibn Ḥadjar I, p. 99 f.; *al-Manhal aṣ-ṣāfī* s.v.; *an-Nudjūm az-zāhira* V, p. 281; ʿAbdalbāsiṭ 803, f. 104b.

[39] *ad-Durar al-kāmina* no. 1205; *Khiṭaṭ* II, p. 427; *Sulūk* III, p. 539.

[40] *an-Nudjūm az-zāhira* V, p. 442.

[41] *Sulūk* III, p. 444.

[42] Ibn al-Furāt IX, p. 378 f.; *Sulūk* III, p. 811; *an-Nudjūm az-zāhira* V, p. 562; Ibn Iyās² I, part 2, p. 468, has 200,000 dinars; that means much more.

[43] *Khiṭaṭ* II, p. 369; *aḍ-Ḍaw al-lāmiʿ* I, p. 112 f.

[44] *Sulūk* III, p. 174 f.

sultan's commercial agency, and the Kārim (the spice trade)."[45] Also Burhān ad-dīn al-Maḥallī held the position of the "sultan's trader" (*tādjir al-khāṣṣ*).[46]

Probably the Kārimīs' hold on the international trade of the Moslem Levant was also considerably weakened by the economic crisis that Egypt underwent in the first years of the fifteenth century. During the recession and inflation that shook Egypt's economy in those years, some clever and lucky merchants may have made great profits by shrewd speculation, but others certainly lost a great deal. Characteristically, the Arabic historians call the leading Kārimīs of the end of the fourteenth century "the last Kārimīs." Zaki'd-dīn al-Kharrūbī,[47] Nūr ad-dīn ʿAlī al-Kharrūbī, who died in 1401,[48] and Burhān ad-dīn al-Maḥallī (d. 1403)[49] are referred to in this way.

On the other hand, the ever-growing financial difficulties of the Royal Exchequer, resulting from decreasing revenues from the royal estates, which suffered from the shrinking of the cultivated area and the land-flight of the peasants, made it necessary for the sultan to fasten his grip on every possible source of income. The customs levied on the spice trade were one of them, but the spice trade itself seemed to be even more promising. When the Royal Exchequer was depleted of savings and regular income after the exhausting civil war in the first decade of the fifteenth century, the sultan began to engage much more than before in the spice trade.

al-Malik al-Muʾayyad Shaykh (1412-1421) began to invest money in the spice trade immediately upon his accession to the throne. He had recourse to the services of a Kārimī merchant, ʿAlā ad-dīn ʿAlī b. Muḥammad al-Ghīlānī, a Persian who after long travels settled in Mecca in 1398, but who commuted regularly between the Ḥidjāz and Egypt. In the business circles of his day, he was known as Shaykh ʿAlī.[50] From the acts of a litigation brought before a Venetian law court, one learns that Shaykh ʿAli sold, together with other merchants, spices for not less than 56,000 dinars to Clario Arcangeli in Cairo in 1412.[51] In the year 1413 the sultan entrusted him with his spice trade. He ordered him to buy spices in the Ḥidjāz to be sold in Egypt. The first transaction resulted in a great success. Shaykh ʿAlī bought pepper in Mecca at the price of 25 dinars the 100 mann

[45] Ibn al-Furāt IX, p. 445 (he died on 2 Djumādā I 798, i.e., 12 Febr. 1396, and was employed by ʿAlā ad-dīn Ibn at-Ṭablāwī, who was appointed to the post of mintmaster and commercial agent of the sultan in Ramaḍān 797 i.e. July 1395). See Ibn al-Furāt IX, p. 411.

[46] *Ṣubḥ al-aʿshā* VIII, p. 72 (Fischel, "Über die Gruppe," p. 81) interprets this text as referring to his being purveyor of the sultan. This is a misinterpretation.

[47] Ashtor, "The Kārimī merchants," p. 54.

[48] *al-Manhal aṣ-ṣāfī* 2071, f. 132a.

[49] *aḍ-Ḍaw al-lāmiʿ* I, p. 112 f.

[50] Wiet, *art. cit.*, p. 124, no. 40; *aḍ-Ḍaw al-lāmiʿ* V, p. 313 (no. 1034).

[51] See my "The Venetian supremacy," p. 27.

and, as the spice prices were then very high in Egypt and Syria—a sporta of pepper amounting to 220 dinars in Alexandria—he sold for 12,000 dinars what he had bought for 5,000.[52] Needless to say, the sultan continued his spice trade.

The modalities of the pepper trade in Alexandria had been established a long time before, and al-Malik al-Mu'ayyad Shaykh did only modify them. Every year at the beginning of the spice fair in October, the Venetian merchants first had to buy a certain quantity of pepper from the sultan, at a price higher than the commercial price. Then the pepper auctions began, with initial prices fixed by negotiations between the Venetian consul and the commercial agent of the sultan in Alexandria. Before the latter allowed the pepper of the private merchants to be put to the hammer, the Venetian consul had to pay him a high fee. This procedure is clearly reflected by the papers of the Venetian consulate in Alexandria from the years 1418 to 1420. Among the names of those from whom the Venetians bought pepper at the successive auctions, the commercial agent of the sultan does not appear. These documents show that in the second decade of the fifteenth century the sultan's commercial agency contented itself with imposing upon the Venetians the purchase of a certain quantity of pepper. After this purchase and the auctions, the pepper trade was free. Every Moslem merchant could sell his stocks to the Europeans.[53] Other spices were also sold first by auction and later by free exchange. Since the auctions resulted in a rise of prices, the Moslem merchants delayed them as long as possible, so that they were held a few days before the end of the fair, i.e., the departure of the Venetian galleys. The Venetians protested many times against this maneuver.[54] Despite the obligatory purchase of a certain quantity of pepper and the pressure brought upon the Venetian merchants by the private merchants, the spice trade was still free in those days. But when Sultan Barsbāy ascended the throne in 1422, he embarked on a new commercial policy.

Both mediaeval chroniclers and modern historians characterize Sultan Barsbāy as not only cruel, but also extremely avaricious. This is certainly true, but his economic policy was undoubtedly the consequence of the progressive decline of several sectors of Egypt's (and Syria's) economy and the decrease of the Crown's revenue. Depopulation and land-flight; neglect of the dams and the water canals through which the water of the Nile flowed for irrigation; decrease of the yield rate; and, on the other hand,

[52] Ibn Ḥadjar II, p. 521. About the pepper price, see below, p. 313 ff.

[53] See the documents published in my "The Volume of Levantine Trade," p. 598 f.; for the payment made to the *nāẓir al-khāṣṣ* for any auction, see Arch. B. Dolfin, Ba 181, fasc. 23 (a. 1417); on the fixing of the initial price at the auctions, see Misti 53, f. 216a.

[54] Misti 54, f. 76b (a. 1422), 118b (a. 1423) 55, f. 33b (a. 1424) 56, f. 35b (a. 1426) 57, f. 12b (a. 1428).

low grain prices, as an effect of reduced demand—all necessarily brought about the continuous decline of the sultan's income. In 1425 Barsbāy devalued the gold dinar, diminishing its weight from 4.25 gr. to 3.45 gr. However, this was not a sharp change in the monetary system of the Mamluks, as the value of the gold dinar had been declining from the beginning of the century and the confidence in its alloy had been vanishing.[55] Striking a new gold coin, equal to the ducat, Barsbāy had adapted the monetary system of his kingdom to the diminishing supply of bullion and put an end to the spread of the ducat. In order to cope with the decrease of the Crown's revenue, he began to establish monopolies in various sectors of Egypt's economy. He tried to make a monopoly of the sale of cotton fabrics, produced in Syria or imported from Iraq,[56] and in some years he made great efforts to exclude private enterprise altogether from sugar production. In 1423 Barsbāy proclaimed that henceforth only his own sugar factories should continue production. In 1427 he even forbade the planting of sugarcane on estates other than his own. This decree was again promulgated in 1430.[57] But establishing a sugar monopoly meant hitting the interests of the powerful Mamluk oligarchy and it aroused fierce opposition. The resistance the spice traders could offer was much weaker.

Because of changes in the political and commercial conditions in the countries around the Red Sea, in the 1420's the establishment of a pepper monopoly became possible. In the year 1424 Ḥidjāz had come under the rule of the Mamluk sultan,[58] and, at the same time, the captains of the ships coming from India began to shun the port of Aden, where they suffered extortion by the Yemenite authorities. The Mamluk officials, on the other hand, did their best to receive them in a friendly fashion, so that Djidda replaced Aden and became the terminus of the Indian ships.[59] The revenue that the sultan had from the customs levied on the spice trade in the port of Djidda and in Mecca was very great and induced him to derive advantage from it in other ways too.

Sultan Barsbāy tried to make the pepper trade a monopoly at the end of 1426, for the first time. No one but his commercial agents were allowed to sell pepper, the most important of the spices, to the European merchants in either Egypt or Syria.[60] Once more Shaykh ʿAlī was the sultan's agent.[61]

[55] See my "Etudes sur le système monétaire des mamlouks circassiens," *Israel Oriental Studies* VI (1976), p. 268.

[56] Darrag, *Barsbay*, p. 155 f.

[57] See M. Sobernheim, "Das Zuckermonopol unter Sultan Barsbai," *Zeitschrift f. Assyriologie* 27 (1912), p. 75 ff.; my "Levantine sugar industry," p. 242 f.

[58] Weil V, p. 178 f.

[59] Heyd II, p. 445; Ibn Shāhīn, *Zubdat kashf al-mamālik* (Paris, 1894), p. 14.

[60] *Sulūk* IV, p. 735.

[61] Concerning the activities of Shaykh ʿAlī in Mecca, see *Chroniken der Stadt Mekka*, ed. Wüstenfeld, III, p. 208.

In Mecca and Djidda he bought pepper and other spices imported from India and shipped them to Egypt, where they were offered to the Europeans. This monopoly meant the exclusion of the Kārimīs from the spice trade, which had been dominated by them through many generations. A year later the sultan took an additonal step to tighten his grip on the spice trade: he ordered merchants of Syria and Iraq who had bought spices in Mecca to travel from there to Egypt to pay the customs.[62] When the merchants protested against this decree, the sultan renounced it, but imposed customs to be paid first in Mecca and a second time in Damascus.[63] Then, at the beginning of 1428, he revoked this concession.[64] Before the spice fair of 1428 Barsbāy officially proclaimed a monopoly of all spices. However, it was not the trade of the spices that was declared the exclusive right of the sultan, but the privilege of making his transactions before others. He forbade private merchants the sale of pepper to the Europeans before he had sold his stocks.[65] At the beginning of 1430, Barsbāy once more forbade the Moslem merchants to sell spices (*sic*) and, on the other hand, decreed that the customs levied on the Indian merchants in Djidda be paid in pepper.[66] Two years later the sultan had recourse to an expedient which the Mamluks used very often in order to fill their cash-boxes—the compulsory purchase of his stocks by the private merchants, the so-called *ṭarḥ*. He sold his pepper to the Egyptian merchants for seventy dinars the sporta and then compelled them to sell him the same commodity for fifty. At the same time, he reenacted the decree conferring upon him the monopoly of its sale to the Europeans. This time it was an absolute monopoly, for the sultan proclaimed that only he had the right to buy pepper from the Indian merchants in Djidda and to sell it to the Europeans.[67] This was a heavy blow for the Egyptian merchants, and the contemporary Arabic authors emphasize that they suffered great losses. But this was indeed one of the aims of the sultan, for he set out to break the power of the Kārimīs and to replace them by his agents. It was a well-conceived project and the sultan made a great effort to make envasion impossible. In fact he did not content himself with monopolizing the pepper trade of Egypt; he tried to dominate the spice

[62] *an-Nudjūm az-zāhira* VI, p. 624 f.

[63] *Sulūk* IV, p. 768.

[64] *Sulūk* IV, p. 791; according to *an-Nudjūm az-zāhira* VI, p. 628, he revoked the decree at the beginning of 1428.

[65] *Sulūk* IV, p. 791; Ibn Ḥadjar III, p. 423; Labib, *Handelsgeschichte*, p. 382, says that the decree was promulgated in 1429, but since it is dated Muḥarram 832, it should be 1428. al-Maḳrīzī speaks about spices in general, whereas Ibn Ḥadjar says that the sultan forbade selling to the European merchants before his agency had sold its stocks. This author speaks only of pepper; this account looks more probable.

[66] *Sulūk* IV, p. 824.

[67] *Op.cit.*, IV, p. 869; Ibn Ḥadjar III, p. 473. The latter author speaks of spices in general and says that the sultan had sold the pepper for 70 dinars.

markets of the neighboring countries also. In 1434 he decreed that Egyptian and Syrian merchants who bought the Indian spices in Aden were to pay customs amounting to 20 percent in Djidda, and Yemenite merchants coming there with spices were to lose them altogether by confiscation. This order was intended to punish the Egyptian and Syrian merchants who went to Aden to buy spices and to exclude the Yemenites from trade in Ḥidjāz. The sultan also took measures to make it impossible to export pepper against his will from Ḥidjāz to Syria. Further, his agents compelled the Indian merchants to buy coral, copper, and other articles from them, and some Mamluk dignitaries did the same on their own behalf.[68] During the spice fair the sultan re-enacted the decree that only he could sell to the Europeans.[69] The spice fair in the fall of 1435 did not pass without a new promulgation of the pepper monopoly.[70] In his endeavors to make the pepper trade a monopoly, Sultan Barsbāy was consistent and unrelenting. In November 1435 Damascene merchants who had transported pepper from Ḥidjāz to Syria were summoned to Cairo, and their stocks in the Egyptian capital were sequestered until they appeased the sultan by the payment of a fine. At the beginning of 1436 the sultan imposed upon the spice traders of Cairo and Damascus the purchase of 1,000 loads (*sportas*) of pepper at the price of one hundred ashrafīs each. At the end of the year the purchase of the same quantity and at the same price was imposed upon the merchants of Alexandria.[71]

The measures taken by Sultan Barsbāy to establish a monopoly of the pepper trade resulted in the downfall of the Kārimīs. In fact, the policy of Sultan Barsbāy was in agreement with that pursued by other Moslem dynasties in the Middle Ages. It was a policy aimed at the maximal exploitation of the economic resources of their countries and characterized by a continuous and reckless encroachment on the development of agriculture, industry, and trade. Its final effect was the decline of their countries, with their economic and political submission to the Western powers. The immediate consequence of Barsbāy's policy was the ruin of the upper stratum of the Levantine bourgoisie, the merchant princes that were the Kārimīs. They lost their supremacy in the wholesale spice trade of Egypt and Syria. No longer could they impose their will on the market and fix the prices; their power was broken.

Certainly, the Kārimīs did not disappear. Even in the chronicles of the middle and second half of the fifteenth century they are sometimes men-

[68] *Sulūk* IV, p. 929 f.; Ibn Ḥadjar III, p. 539 f.; Labıb, *Handelsgeschichte*, p. 383 f., has the date 1435, but this is a mistake.

[69] *Sulūk* IV, p. 935.

[70] *Op.cit.* IV, p. 935.

[71] *Op.cit.* IV, pp. 965, 972, 1004; as-Sallāmī, p. 156.

tioned. Such Kārimīs were ʿAbdarraḥmān an-Nāṣirī (d. 1485), [72] Ṣalāḥ ad-dīn Muḥammad (d. 1490), [73] and the Damascene ʿĪsā al-Ḳārī (d. 1490).[74] But the biographical information in the Arabic sources shows clearly that these later Kārimīs were men of moderate wealth. They were no more merchant princes like the great spice traders of the fourteenth century. Some of them were in fact commercial agents of the sultan. The sultan usually confiscated their goods after their death, so that the families of these late spice traders did not last even two generations.[75] Several Kārimīs left Egypt and also Ḥidjāz, then under the control of the Mamluks, and settled in some towns of India, where they could continue their trade without encountering the opposition of the mighty sultan of Cairo,[76] and others became "traders of the sultan."[77]

The plight of the family Ibn al-Muzalliḳ was characteristic of the great change in the social structure of the Near Eastern society, which was the downfall of the Kārimīs. Shams ad-dīn Muḥammad Ibn al-Muzalliḳ (d. 1444) was one of the richest merchants of Syria at the beginning of the fifteenth century. He engaged in the spice trade, but also traded in other commodities. In the Arabic sources there is plenty of information about his activities. He had come to Damascus from Aleppo, travelled several times to India, and on one of these journeys earned 1.8 mill. dirhams. He was also renowned as a great benefactor who made pious endowments for Mecca and Medina.[78] When, in 1408, the governor of Damascus imposed

[72] Abdalbāsiṭ 812, f. 349a.

[73] *Op.cit.*, f. 396b.

[74] *Op.cit.*, f. 397a, and see *aḍ-Ḍaw al-lāmiʿ* VI, no. 523; Ibn Ṭūlūn, *Mufākahat al-khillān* I, p. 128. Some of his descendants travelled to Egypt because of his bequest; cf. I. M. Lapidus, *Muslim cities in the later Middle Ages* (Harvard Univ. Press, 1967), p. 215. The name of these merchants should be added to those listed by Wiet, *art. cit.*, p. 127 ff. See also al-Djawharī, *Inbā al-haṣr*, p. 211.

[75] See the account quoted in the two preceding notes.

[76] See the biographies of ʿAlī b. Maḥmūd Ibn Ḳawwān (d. about 1490), *aḍ-Ḍaw al-lāmiʿ* VI, no. 105; ʿUmar b. Aḥmad al-Baṭāʾūnī, emigrated to Cambay in 1453, *op.cit.*, VI, no. 244; Ḳāsim, the son of Shaykh ʿAlī, emigrated to Cambay in 1448, *op.cit.*, VI, no. 627.

[77] See the biographies of Fakhr ad-dīn Abū Bakr at-Tibrīzī (d. 1455), *aḍ-Ḍaw al-lāmiʿ* XI, no. 244; Muḥammad b. Mūsā, see al-Djawharī, *Inbā al-haṣr* (Cairo, 1970), p. 478, and *aḍ-Ḍaw al-lāmiʿ* X, p. 64 f. (even his bequest was confiscated by the sultan); Burhān ad-dīn ʿAbdalḳādir b. Ibrāhīm Ibn ʿUlaiba (d. 1485), *aḍ-Ḍaw al-lāmiʿ* IV, p. 259f. and cf. Ibn Iyās III, p. 115, 216; Ibrāhīm al-Barantīshī (d. 1475), see as-Sakhāwī, *Dhail*, MS. Bodl. 853, f. 115a, *aḍ-Ḍaw al-lāmiʿ* I, p. 72f., ʿAbdalbāsiṭ b. Khalīl, *ar-Rawḍ al-bāsim*, MS. Vaticana 729, f. 109b; ASG 2774 cf. 24b; Muḥammad b. Abi ʾl-Ḳāsim al-Barantīshī (d. 1487), *aḍ-Ḍaw al-lāmiʿ* VIII, p. 288 ff. and see about Ghālib Rufāʾīl in my "The Venetian supremacy," pp. 27, 29. Both the Barantīshī and Ghālib Rufāʾīl were Spaniards; and see further about the latter Tur II, f. 6a f. (a. 1455); Cristoforo del Fiore V, f. 17b f. (a. 1456). Finally, Sharīf Ḳāsim, merchant of the sultan in 1441, is mentioned in notarial acts, Tur II, f. 21a f., Serv. Pecc. sub 5 Oct. 1448. His successor was Badr ad-dīn Ḳāsim, a veteran merchant hailing from the Maghreb; see Serv. Pecc. *l.c.* and G. P., Sent. 46, f. 25b ff.

[78] *aḍ-Ḍaw al-lāmiʿ* VIII, no. 429; Sauvaire, "Description de Damas," *JA* 1895, II, p. 261 ff.; as-Sallāmī, p. 41 (certainly the laḳab Bahā ad-dīn is a mistake).

a fine on the judges and the merchants of the town, he ordered Shams ad-dīn Ibn al-Muzalliḳ to levy the sum requested from the latter. He was indeed the "head of the merchants of Damascus."[79] His son Aḥmad (d. 1468) too was a great merchant. An act drawn up by a Venetian notary in Damascus in 1418 refers to his activities. He imported coral and saffron into Syria from Catalonia.[80] Most of the notarial and judicial acts that have come down to us in the Venetian archives and refer to the activities of this family of Kārimīs mention only the family name, so that one cannot know if Muḥammad or his son Aḥmad is meant. From these acts one learns that the Ibn al-Muzalliḳ sold the European merchants spices, such as cloves, exchanging them for textiles,[81] and had many other dealings with them.[82] When the sultan began to engage in the spice trade, Shams ad-dīn Ibn al-Muzalliḳ made various transactions for his agency. As a reward for the services he had rendered the sultan, he was granted exemption from imposts for merchandise up to the amount of 200,000 dirhams (probably a year).[83] But he was still a private merchant. In 1421 the Venetian Senate gave orders to an embassy to the sultan to protest against the encroachment of Ibn al-Muzalliḳ upon the liberty of trade. The embassy was to maintain that this was not the right of a private merchant.[84] But in documents of the time subsequent to the establishment of the pepper monopoly by Sultan Barsbāy, time and again the name of "Ibn al-Muzalliḳ" appears as the "sultan's trader" in Damascus. As such he sold pepper and ginger to the Europeans in 1434, 1436, and 1440,[85] and threatened the Venetian consul Marco Zane that if he did not pay the debts of a Venetian merchant all the Venetians would be imprisoned and their goods sequestered.[86] However, even in the service of the sultan, the Ibn al-Muzalliḳ made transactions of their own. They exported indigo, cloves, and frankincense to Constantinople and bartered them for scarlets, Florentine and other cloth.[87] Aḥmad Ibn al-Muzalliḳ sold diamonds to Genoese merchants at the end of the 1430's.[88] But, whereas Muḥammad and Aḥmad Ibn al-Muzalliḳ had been great merchants, the third generation of the family were government officials.[89]

Not only the documents which refer to the activities of the Ibn al-

[79] *Sulūk* IV, p. 72.

[80] Nic. Venier B, 2, f. 6a/b; *aḍ-Ḍaw al-lāmi'* II, no. 415.

[81] G. P., Sent. 46, f. 63a ff.

[82] Giacomo della Torre, nos. 16-18.

[83] *Ṣubḥ al-a'shā* XIII, p. 40.

[84] Jorga, *ROL* V, p. 115.

[85] G. P., Sent. 66, f. 103b f. 76, f. 51b ff. 90, f. 133A.

[86] Jorga, *ROL* VII, p. 93 (of a. 1443). See also *BSOAS* 28, p. 492.

[87] Badoer, c. 12, 13, 16, 26, 27, 28, 32.

[88] ASG, Notai, Branco Bagnara 10, no. 20. In this act the name Aḥmad Ibn al-Muzalliḳ is explicitly mentioned.

[89] See "The Venetian supremacy," p. 28f.; Sauvaire, "Description de Damas," *JA* 1895, I, p. 272; *al-Manhal aṣ-ṣāfī* s.v. Badr ad-dīn Ḥasan b. Muḥammad Ibn al-Muzalliḳ.

Muzallik, but also other Venetian documents of the fifteenth century mention the commercial agency of the sultan (*al-matdjar as-sulṭānī*) or the "sultan's trader" (*tādjir as-sulṭān*).[90] However, from these documents it also becomes clear that in the course of time the sultan had to give up his monopoly. A late Portuguese author gives a most interesting account of the trade carried on by the sultan's agency: the Indian merchants were obliged to sell the sultan in Djidda a large part of the pepper at the cost price in Calicut. On the other hand, the sultan's agent imposed the purchase of copper upon them.[91] In Cairo any merchant who had bought pepper from an importer had to buy a proportionate quantity from the sultan at much more than the commercial price.[92] That means that, other than the acquisition of a certain quantity of pepper from the sultan's stocks, the spice trade had become free. In fact, notarial acts drawn up in Alexandria in the mid-thirties of the fifteenth century testify to this fact.[93] Thus the downfall of the mighty Kārimīs was a great advantage for the European merchants. Further, the disappearance of a group of wholesale traders, who totally dominated the spice market and also engaged in other branches of trade, opened up sectors in which the role of the European merchants had been secondary as compared with that of the Egyptians.[94]

But before the sultan renounced the monopoly of the pepper trade and a modus vivendi with him had been reached, the European merchants had to withstand heavy pressure, and the Levant trade underwent a great crisis.

B. The Sultan versus the European Merchants

The contest between the sultan and the European trading nations did not begin immediately upon the accession of Barsbāy to the throne, but from the time of the abdication of al-Malik al-Mu'ayyad Shaykh there were signs of the approaching crisis.

After the short reign of al-Malik al-Mu'ayyad's son, Aḥmad (13 January to 29 August 1421), the influential emir Ṭaṭar seized the reins of government, and during his short reign of three months (he died on 30 November 1421), he decreed that the European merchants should no longer enjoy the

[90] In Arabic sources, he is also called *wakīl as-sulṭān*; see *Ḥawādith*, p. 507. In the Venetian documents, he is often called "ṭawāshī," or "toresi," meaning eunuch, perhaps because sometimes one of the sultan's eunuchs had been entrusted with this office; see G. P., Sent. 74, f. 130b; Jorga, *ROL* VI, p. 417, 422; Tur V. f. 2a f.: "toresinus saracenus cozie sultani" (the Khawādjā, i.e., the trader of the sultan). Also in the accounts of Badoer, there always appears this latter title: Choza Muxalach (Khawādja was a title given to the rich merchants; see *Ṣubḥ al-a'shā* VI, pp. 13, 38, 41, 42).

[91] Fernam Lopez de Castanheda, *História do discobrimento e conquista da India pelos Portuguezes* (Lisbon, 1833), libro II, cap. 75, p. 249; cf. *JA* 1920, II, p. 19.

[92] *Op.cit.*, p. 250; cf. *JA* 1895 II, p. 21.

[93] Tur V, f. 55b f., 56b f., 63a f.

[94] "The Venetian supremacy," p. 29.

right of unlimited sojourn in his dominions.[95] That the sojourn of foreign traders should be limited to some months was a principle upheld from the old days by the Moslem jurisconsults and especially by the Shāfiʿī school of law, the latter fixing it at four months. It was a Byzantine law transmitted to the Moslems; however, it seems that it was rarely enforced.[96] Therefore, its enactment by the sultan aroused apprehensions in Venice.

In December 1421 the Senate of Venice decided to send an embassy to Cairo and gave the ambassadors Bernardo Loredan and Lorenzo Capello instructions. They were to request that the sultan revoke this decree or at least that a longer sojourn be conceded to the foreign merchants. Secondly, they were to demand that the spice trade be absolutely free and not be held up until after an auction of pepper (or more correctly some successive auctions). Of course, they were to demand the confirmation of the old privileges and, as usual, the ambassadors were also to submit various claims concerning the restitution of goods of Venetians.[97] Since the Senate considered the decree of Sultan Ṭaṭar a very serious matter, it was decided for the present not to ship merchandise and precious objects (havere capselle) to Syria. But after long deliberations, the Senate changed its mind and decided to send two galleys to Syria in March (*di trafego*) to ship the goods of the Venetians from there. The ships were to visit Beirut and Latakia, carry the merchandise to Modon, and then return once more to Beirut. They departed from Venice with heavy cargoes of merchandise.[98] When these decisions were taken in Venice, Ṭaṭar was already dead, and, after a short reign of one of his sons, Barsbāy ascended the throne on 1 April 1422; it was he with whom the embassy had to negotiate. Since he had conceived the plan to replace the Kārimīs by his commercial agency from the beginning of his reign apparently, he had a great interest in encouraging the exchanges with the trading nations of Southern Europe, certainly under the conditions that he would establish, and consequently he agreed to most of the Venetian requests. In fact, the sultan confirmed the treaty made with the Venetians in 1415 by his predecessor al-Malik al-Mu'ayyad Shaykh, and issued special decrees to the governors of Alexandria, Damietta, Gaza, Ramla, Jerusalem, Safed, Acre, Damascus, Ḥamā, Tripoli, and Aleppo, admonishing them to safeguard the rights of the Venetians. He also explicitly allowed the Venetians to stay in his dominions as long as they wished. In

[95] *Chron. Morosini*, c. 382.

[96] See my paper "Il regime portuario nel califfato," (in *XXV Settimana di studio del Centro italiano di studi sull'alto medioevo*, Spoleto, 1977), p. 666 f.

[97] *Dipl. Ven.-Lev.* II, no. 176; Misti 54, f. 36b; Jorga, *ROL* V, p. 115 f.

[98] Misti 53, f. 213b, 214a ff.; *havere capse* (or *capselle*) means pearls, gold, and precious stones; see Misti 34, f. 21a 46, f. 57a. From the registers of the Senate it would appear that various proposals made to this effect were turned down, but see *Chron. Morosini*, c. 384/5 and see below about the cargo of the galleys.

a letter to the government of Venice on 30 April 1422, Barsbāy stated that he had given orders to dismiss some officials who had prejudiced the interests of the Venetian merchants. As to the request of the Venetians that the spice trade should not be conditional upon a preceding auction, he included in the new privilege the clause contained in the treaty of 1415, viz., a general promise that the Venetians' interests should not be prejudiced. On the other hand, the Venetian chronicler Morosini explicitly says that the sultan did not agree to revoke the residence limitation;[99] however, it seems that the decree was not implemented.

In the year 1422, Barsbāy concluded another commercial treaty with a European trading nation—Florence. The versatile Florentine merchants had carried on trade in Egypt and Syria for a long time before they approached the sultan with the request to receive privileges like those granted other South European trading nations. But at the beginning of the 1420's Florence made a great effort to take her place in the international trade beside the other great trading nations whose financial and industrial power was no greater than her own. Of course, the main purpose of these efforts was to save the profits accruing from the export of Florentine cloth for the Florentine themselves. One of the measures taken was the despatch of embassies to various rulers of Greece and also an embassy to the sultan of Cairo.[100] The ambassadors Carlo Federighi and Felice Brancacci were instructed to claim for Florence as the successor to Pisa, occupied by its forces in 1406, the same rights as the major trading nations, Venice and Genoa, had had a long time. They were to ask for equality with the Venetians, the most privileged trading nation, as to customs, and the right to have a consulate in Alexandria, a fondaco, bath, and church of their own, and especially that the florin, which had just been made equal to the ducat, be legal tender in the Mamluk dominions. The embassy was to refuse an undertaking that Florence would extradite her subjects guilty of a crime committed in Egypt or in Syria, or at least insist that the extradition should be delayed for a year from their arrest.[101] After a visit to Rhodes, where the embassy obtained from the Great Master exemption from customs for the Florentine merchants,[102] they sailed to Egypt and concluded a treaty with the sultan in September 1422. He recognized Florence as a trading nation; granted

[99] *Libri Com.* IV, lib. 11, no. 94, 126 (Predelli's résumé is not exact. The third document is an order to return to the Venetians a certain amount of money); *Dipl. Ven.-Lev.* II, no. 174. This text, dated 30 April 1422, is in fact a copy of the privilege of 1415. It may be that it is no more than a draft used to prepare a new treaty, see Wansbrough, "A Mamlūk commercial treaty," p.45 f. The letter of the sultan *Lib. Com.* 11, f. 77b, is summed up by Predelli IV, p. 40, rather inexactly; *Chron. Morosini*, c. 387.

[100] Scipione Ammirato, *Istorie fiorentine* (Florence, 1647-1649) I, part 2, p. 997.

[101] Amari, *I diplomi*, p. 331 ff.

[102] D. Catellacci, *Diario di Felice Brancacci*, p. 163.

her the right to have consuls in Alexandria, Damascus, and other towns; and also agreed that the florin, which had gone out of use in his territories, should be legal tender. The privilege granted the embassy comprised the usual promises of freedom of trade, the renunciation of the *ius albinagii* and *ius naufragii*, but the clause referring to the customs is styled in a very general way, establishing that the Florentines should pay "like the other trading nations." That means that the Florentines were not given the privileged rate paid by the Venetians. The question of extradition was not mentioned in the treaty at all.[103] The sultan also gave orders to the governor of Alexandria to concede the Florentines a fondaco.[104] The embassy was very satisfied with the concessions that the sultan had made.[105]

So the relations of Venice with the new sultan had begun under good circumstances, and a new trading nation had won official status. The Catalans, on the other hand, embarked on another policy toward the sultan. Under the reign of Alfonso V (1416-1458), the Catalans pursued a policy of expansion aimed at establishing their supremacy in the whole of the Mediterranean. King Alfonso V set out not only to oust the Angevins from the kingdom of Naples but also to counterbalance the rising power of the Turks. Since the diplomatic relations of his kingdom with the Mamluks had been broken off some years earlier and trade with Egypt and Syria nevertheless could be continued,[106] the king saw no reason to stop the activities of Catalan pirates. Rhodes and Cyprus served them as bases from which they attacked Moslem ships and made raids on the coasts of Egypt and Syria. The Catalan pirates also attacked Christian ships, and time and again Venice had to take measures to protect her ships.[107] Florentine and Genoese ships were also often attacked by them.[108] But Moslem merchantmen and the coasts of the Mamluk dominions were the favorite targets of the Catalans, and their attacks had grave consequences for the Catalan trade. Since the Moslem fleets suffered from technological and nautical inferiority, the Catalans often won easy victories.

The continued aggression of the Catalans against the Moslem ships and the coasts of Egypt and Syria began immediately upon Barsbāy's accession to the throne. In April 1422 an embassy of the king of Aragon had come

[103] Amari, *op.cit.*, p. 336 ff. That the florin had gone out of use in Egypt and Syria is borne out by the testimonies of Frescobaldi, p. 75, and of Piloti, p. 108.

[104] *Op.cit.*, p. 341 f.; *Libr. Com.* IV, lib. 11, no. 121.

[105] See their report, Amari, *op.cit.*, p. 345: "Appare (sc. from the text of the privilege) essersi ottenuti molte piu cose non avemmo in commissione." The reception of the Florentine embassy is also mentioned by al-Maḳrīzī, *Sulūk* IV, p. 618.

[106] See above.

[107] Thiriet, *Rég.* II, pp. 193 (a. 1422), 209 (a. 1423); Jorga, *ROL* VII p. 389 (a. 1444); Secreta IX, f. 169a XI, f. 26b, 54b XIII, f. 53b XVI, f. 191a; *Chron. Morosini*, c. 383, 402, 403, 499, 506; *Chron. Dolfin*, f. 415a.

[108] *Chron. Morosini*, c. 393, 428.

to Cairo, but the subject and the outcome of this mission are not known to us.[109] However, some months later the Catalans again began to attack the coasts of Egypt and Syria. In August 1422 two galleys attacked the port of Alexandria at night and, after the fighting of some hours, their crews fired a Moslem merchantman with a rich cargo. The Arabic chroniclers state that the Moslems who fought with them were helpless, as they had only arrows, which did not reach the Christian ships. The attackers sailed from Alexandria to Barca and after raiding her coast turned to Syria and continued their attacks there. Morosini recounts that the Catalan galleys attacked a Moslem ship, on which there was an envoy of the sultan to the prince of Caraman, in the port of Beirut, and they also attacked a Genoese merchantman. In reprisal, the Mamluks imprisoned all the European merchants found in Latakia.[110] Further, the sultan ordered that the Church of the Holy Sepulchre in Jerusalem and the church in Bethlehem be closed. The Franciscans in Jerusalem were arrested and sent to Cairo. The sultan considered the attacks as a protest of the Catalans regarding his commercial policy, and he asked the Florentine ambassadors who came to him immediately upon these raids to influence the Catalans to agree "to sell his merchandise."[111] Barsbāy was so enraged that he threatened to expel all the European merchants from his dominions. He summoned the consuls of Venice and Genoa from Alexandria to Cairo and urged them to guarantee the security of the Moslem ships. By giving his promises that their governments would intervene with the king of Aragon, and supporting their diplomacy by substantial payments, they succeeded in calming the sultan.[112] But in Venice there was great excitement, and in the month of December it was decided to ship the goods of the Venetians from the dominions of the sultan.[113] The sultan proclaimed an embargo on Catalan merchandise, insisting that other European traders should not sell them.[114] Another measure of retaliation for the Catalan attacks was the imprisonment of pilgrims from Catalonia who came to Jerusalem in 1423, disguising themselves as Georgians.[115]

[109] Ibn Ḥadjar III, p. 270.

[110] *Sulūk* IV, p. 617; *an-Nudjūm az-zāhira* VI, p. 561; Ibn Shāhīn, *Zubdat kashf al-mamālik*, p. 138. (The Arabic authors do not say that the raiders were Catalans, but this results from their reports about the subsequent happenings. The date is Shaʿbān 825, i.e. 21 July to 18 Aug. 1422), *Chron. Morosini*, c. 389, and cf. Jorga, *ROL* V, p. 128, note 1. Lannoy recounts that he met Venetian, Genoese, and Greek merchants in Beirut but he does not mention Catalans; see *Voyages*, p. 156.

[111] *Diario di F. Brancacci*, pp. 179, 180; *Sulūk* IV, p. 619.

[112] *Diario*, pp. 166, 168.

[113] Jorga, *ROL* V, p. 128.

[114] G. P., Sent. 33, f. testimonies on 24, 26 January, and 14 March, 1423; G. P., Sent. 34, f. 17a f., Brancacci, *Diario*, p. 168; and cf. Chapt. IV, note 231.

[115] *Sulūk* IV, p. 637.

The conflict aroused by the Catalans in 1422 was one of those incidents in the relations between the South European trading nations and the sultan of Cairo to which they had probably become accustomed. The violent reaction of the sultan disclosed, however, that he had decided to usher in a new period in the foreign trade of his countries and that he would not relax in his endeavors. In 1424 he began to pursue his policy with great tenacity.

Before the spice fair of 1424, the sultan sent one of his agents to Damascus with orders to buy all the spices available, while it was forbidden to others to buy or to sell before he had finished his transactions. The Venetian consul in Alexandria, Marco Morosini, received orders from the Senate to protest to the sultan, especially if Venetians had been compelled to buy from the agent. He was to ask for a formal undertaking that this should not be done again, particularly since upon a preceding protest by Venice there had been a promise that the spice trade would be free. The consul was also to protest against the arrest of Venetian merchants and the sequestering of their goods, after a raid organized by the Genoese ruler of Mytilene and directed against the port of Damietta.[116] When the consul, who had just been appointed, went to hand over his credentials, the sultan threatened him, but the clever diplomat succeeded in appeasing his wrath. Barsbāy gave orders to liberate those who had been imprisoned and sent word to Damascus that the spice trade should be free.[117] But the Venetian Senate had no great confidence in the intentions of the sultan. In January 1425 it was decided that the goods of the Venetian merchants should be shipped from Syria on the cotton cogs sailing to the spring fair and on two additional cogs.[118] A month later, fearing an attack by the Catalans on the Egyptian coast and reprisals by the Mamluks, secret orders to the same effect, i.e., clearing away the Venetian goods and evacuation of the Venetians themselves, if they wished, were given to the consul of Alexandria, some ships being sent to Alexandria for this purpose.[119] At the end of March 1425 the consul of Alexandria was instructed to hand over to the sultan a letter of protest against the attitude toward the Venetian merchants. The letter was sent to Alexandria by a special galley.[120] Then in May and

[116] Misti 55, f. 59b and cf. Jorga, *ROL* V, p. 176 f. In 1423, the government of Venice had dispatched galleys to Syria to ship the goods of the merchants who were in danger, see Morosini, c. 393.

[117] *Chron. Dolfin*, f. 328b; Marino Sanuto, *Vite*, c. 980.

[118] Misti 55, f. 81b cf. 88b, 91a; *Chron. Morosini*, c. 420; Jorga interprets this decision concerning the cotton cogs as if the Senate would have forbidden trade with Egypt and Syria: see *ROL* V, p. 184, but it was only forbidden to ship precious articles then. See also Morosini, c. 419.

[119] Misti 55, f. 90a, 95a, and cf. Thiriet, *Rég.* II, p. 224.

[120] de Mas Latrie, "Nouvelles preuves de l'histoire de Chypre," *Bibl. Ecole des chartes* 35 (1874), p. 133 f.

June again there were fears in Venice that the sultan would compel the merchants to buy spices from his stocks. Consequently, the Senate decided to send three galleys to Alexandria and Beirut immediately to load with the greatest speed all the spices in possession of the Venetians. In addition, orders were given to the consul of Alexandria again to demand a written undertaking from the sultan that there would be no compulsory purchases. He was also to protest against extortions and make clear that the sultan had no right to make the Venetians responsible for the acts of piracy and raids committed by others.[121] Meanwhile the sultan began to prepare his expedition against Cyprus. He called the consuls of Venice and Genoa to Cairo once more and accused their governments of supporting the king of Cyprus, who, together with the Catalans, raided the coasts of Egypt and Syria. But the skill of the consuls prevailed and the sultan promised them that the activities of their merchant colonies could be continued and that they would enjoy freedom of trade, if the two republics would abstain from helping the Cypriots.[122]

When Barsbāy in 1426 established his pepper monopoly which was the death knell of the Kārimīs' trade, the great crisis in the relations between the sultan and the trading nations began, and Venice had to bear the brunt of the pressure brought upon them. In fact, owing to the retrogression of Genoa's trade in the Moslem Levant, Venice was already the foremost European trading power in the Levant. During the spice fair the Europeans had to buy the sultan's pepper by compulsion, and, after the departure of the Venetian galleys, he declared that the price was higher and compelled the consuls (sc. of Venice and Genoa) to pay the difference. Further, he raised the customs to be paid by the Venetians for the import of European commodities from 10 percent to 13 percent.[123] In the year 1427 the trade of Venice with the Mamluk dominions was already in full crisis. The Senate decreed at the beginning of the year that the cotton cogs sailing to the spring fair in Syria should not carry any merchandise. Because of the extortions and the injuries (the merchants had been beaten) caused by the Moslem officials, trade should be limited to a minimum. It was also forbidden to the inhabitants of the Venetian colonies in the Levant (Crete, Modon, etc.) to travel to Egypt and Syria, or to ship merchandise there on foreign ships. The consul in Damascus received instructions to arrange that the spices bought by the Venetian merchants be loaded on the cotton cogs. Later in March, orders were given to the commander of the squadron of the war fleet to sail to Alexandria in order to ship the goods of the Venetians

[121] Misti 55, f. 117a; cf. Jorga, *ROL* V, p. 198, and Misti 55, f. 121a ff.
[122] *Chron. Morosini*, c. 428; Arch. Lor. Dolfin, letter of Jacomo de Zorzi to Lor. Dolfin of 8 Aug. 1425.
[123] *Sulūk* IV, p. 735; *Chron. Morosini*, c. 455.

from Egypt and to take on board those Venetian merchants who would like to depart. In that year the galley service to Alexandria and to Beirut was suspended.[124]

Then in 1428 the situation worsened greatly. The sultan compelled not only the Egyptian merchants but also all the Europeans—Venetians, Genoese, Florentines, and Provençals—to sell him their merchandise and at very low prices (a fifth of their commercial value), and, on the other hand, he imposed upon the Venetians the purchase of his pepper stocks. He sold it to them for 120 dinars (ashrafis) the sporta, although the commercial price was 80 dinars. The Arabic chronicler al-Maḳrīzī recounts that the Venetians offered resistance and departed from Alexandria with much of their merchandise.[125] In 1429 they were again compelled to buy pepper from the sultan, and, in addition, he sold them cotton by force and levied a special fee for every sack. In Alexandria, they had to buy 520 sportas for 100-120 dinars per sporta from him. But there was an abundant supply of spices on the Levantine markets, and the Venetian galleys came back from the fair with heavy cargoes.[126]

In the year 1430 the tension reached a peak. In January the Senate of Venice again decided to ship the goods of the Venetian subjects out of the Mamluk dominions, and orders were given to all merchants to leave Egypt and Syria until the end of June. The consuls too were to depart. The cotton ships sailing to the spring fair in Syria were not to carry money. The sultan, on the other hand, remained intransigent. At the same time, in February, he again compelled the Venetian merchants to buy pepper from him at the price of 130 dinars (ashrafis), then twice its commercial price; but later the sultan's agent reduced the price to 100, as he had done in 1428.[127] In April the Venetian consul in Alexandria, Benedetto Dandolo, appeared before the sultan to lodge a protest against the extortions, but Barsbāy replied that the Venetians could leave. He also had many merchants arrested and their houses closed. When the consul complained that he put pressure only on the Venetians, the sultan said that he would establish a monopoly in all the other spices and even of commodities imported from Europe.

The Senate of Venice reacted in May 1430 by a decree by virtue of which trade with Egypt and Syria was allowed only by special permission.[128] In fact, the Venetians found themselves in a very difficult situation, for at the

[124] Misti 56, f. 71a ff., 104a ff.; *Chron. Morosini*, c. 458; Secreta X, f. 30b; Jorga, *ROL* V, p. 350.

[125] *Chron. Morosini*, c. 498; *Sulūk* IV, p. 791; Marino Sanuto, *Vite*, c. 1021.

[126] *Chron. Morosini*, c. 512, 515.

[127] Misti 57, f. 184a ff.; Secreta XI, f. 64b f., 65a; *Chron. Morosini*, c. 516; Sanuto, *Vite*, c. 1021, 1022; cf. the texts quoted by Jorga, *ROL* VI, p. 71. The order to depart from Syria was repeated in August; see Misti 57, f. 243a; *Sulūk* IV, p. 824. Cf. Weil V, p. 183.

[128] Jorga, *ROL* VI, p. 71; *Chron. Morosini*, c. 520, 522; Misti 57, f. 214b, 222a ff.

same time another war with Genoa had begun. The Genoese began to capture Venetian ships and, on the other hand, Venice despatched a squadron of war ships to the Ligurian coast. Nevertheless, the yearly purchases on the Levantine spice markets were not given up. The Senate, however, decreed that trade should be carried on aboard the galleys, depriving the sultan of the customs. This decree was also to be valid for the fall convoy of the cotton ships. However, there was strong opposition to this decree, and many merchants did not conceal the fact that they would not accept it. At the same time, measures were taken for the final evacuation of the Venetians from Egypt and Syria, even though it was feared that the sultan would not allow it. But when the galleys came to Alexandria, the merchants had a surprise: the Moslem officials behaved in very friendly fashion. The orders given them had been changed.[129] The sultan, on the other hand, did not allow the Venetians living in Egypt to depart.[130] At the beginning of 1431 the Senate decreed once more that the merchants embarking on the cotton cogs to Syria should carry on trade on the ships. Various proposals were made in the Senate to send an embassy to the sultan, but they were not carried. Venice was indeed very much interested in coming to an agreement with the sultan, as the war with Genoa went on and preparations were being made to attack Chios, the great base of Genoa's trade in the Eastern Mediterranean. Finally, it was decided to charge the consul of Alexandria to hand over to the sultan a letter containing the requests of Venice. He was to ask for new privileges and a binding undertaking that there would be no more compulsory purchases of spices,[131] and indeed the consul reached a new agreement with the sultan.[132]

The patience and tenacity of the Venetians for that five-year period paid off. The leniency of Venice, however, was also a necessity. It corresponded to her economic interests, for the Indian spices bought in Alexandria and Damascus were the life blood of Venice's trade, since their marketing enabled the Venetians to carry on trade with almost the whole of Europe. At the same time, the Serenissima was engaged in a long war with Milan from 1424; in fact, it was a great contest over the supremacy in Upper Italy, and every year it cost more. It was not only a financial burden, but it also made necessary a shift in the arms policy. The Arsenal had to build new types of ships which could be used for warfare and transport on the rivers and

[129] *Chron. Morosini*, c. 531; *Zancaruola*, c. 536b; Misti 57, f. 218b ff., 222a ff., 225a f., 244a; Marino Sanuto, *Vite*, c. 1008. This author says c. 1010 f. that only after the departure of the galleys the attitude of the Moslem authorities worsened. Cf. Thiriet, *Rég*. II, p. 276. The repetition of the order that the merchants should depart from the dominions of the sultan shows that it had not been kept.

[130] Misti 58, f. 32a.

[131] Misti 58, f. 44a; *Chron. Morosini*, c. 534.

[132] Marino Sanuto, *Vite*, c. 1018, 1023 f.; *Chron. Morosini*, c. 548.

lakes of Lombardy.[133] As, under the leadership of Francesco Foscari, Venice had embarked on an expansionist policy and aimed at imposing her rule on a great part of Lombardy, she could not, at the same time, pursue an aggressive policy toward the sultan, which would entail the cutting off of the main line of her Levant trade, the major artery of her commercial exchanges. So other interests had to be subordinated and alternative options to be discarded. When the king of Cyprus, seriously threatened by the sultan, applied to Venice for help in 1425, he was refused. Even the grant of a loan was refused. Five years later, the king applied to Venice with the same request and received the same answer.[134] In 1444 Venice joined the Christian powers in a Crusade against the Turks, but the Serenissima ordered the commander of her squadron of warships to refrain from any embroilment with the Mamluks so that the trade with their dominions should not be disturbed.[135]

The reaction of the Genoese and the Catalans to the economic policy of Barsbāy was very different because their needs and interests were unlike those of Venice. Genoa was less interested in the spice trade, since she did not have such great markets as Venice, which supplied spices and aromatics to the whole of Central Europe and to other regions. Secondly, the flourishing colonies in Chios and Pera had become great centers of Genoese trade in the Eastern Mediterranean, so that Genoa could afford the decline of her trade with Alexandria. Pera, Chios, and Rhodes served the Genoese as supply centers for spices too. On the other hand, the relations of Genoa with the sultan of Cairo often became strained for other reasons, in addition to his monopolization of the pepper trade. Genoa did not have strong control of her colonies and of territories ruled by Genoese. The republic itself was shaken by frequent revolts and had to suffer the consequences of the activities of the rebels and outlaws. When in 1424 Biscayan ships coming from Mytilene committed acts of aggression on the Egyptian coast, the Genoese merchants in Alexandria were, of course, the first to be held responsible. They were imprisoned and their goods sequestered. The Genoese government applied to the sultan with the request to liberate the merchants and asked the captain of Famagusta and the ruler of Mytilene to refrain from acts of aggression. The conquest of Cyprus by the Mamluks, which resulted in the capture of Genoese in Famagusta, caused new problems. The Genoese demanded their liberation from the sultan, and Genoa also sent an embassy to Cario in 1427, to explore the plans of the sultan. New assaults on the island and on its Genoese colony were feared.[136]

[133] Lane, *Venice, a maritime republic*, p. 230.
[134] de Mas Latrie, *Hist. de Chypre* II, p. 516 f.; Secreta XI, f. 11a f.
[135] Setton, *Papacy and Levant* II, p. 85 note 14.
[136] Jorga, *ROL* V, p. 197 f.; Bănescu, *Le déclin de Famagouste*, p. 18 f. and append. IV,

Another problem that strained Genoa's relations with the Mamluks from time to time was the purchase of military slaves (i.e., slaves destined for military service) by the sultan's agents in Caffa, a great slave market. In 1428 the sultan imposed a fine of 9,000 ducats on the Genoese merchants in Alexandria because some slaves bought in Caffa by an agent of his had been taken away by the authorities of the Genoese colony. To cover this payment, the Genoese in Alexandria established an impost of 3 percent of the value to be levied on merchandise imported or exported by subjects of the republic in Egypt.[137] In addition to these conflicts, the Genoese, like the Venetians, suffered from the extortions by the Mamluk authorities. An Arabic chronicler recounts that in August 1429 the Genoese left Alexandria, because they could no longer stand the pressures put upon them. He says that merchants who had lived a very long time in Alexandria and even some who had been born there departed. According to him, they left debts to the Moslems amounting to 20,000 ashrafīs. Two Genoese ships awaited them not far from the coast. The Arabic author also emphasizes that the sultan was very fearful when he heard about their departure.[138] Thereupon Genoese trade with Egypt was discontinued.[139] But a year and a half later the commercial interests prevailed, and the government of Genoa decided again to take up relations with the sultan. It was decided to send an embassy to Cairo to negotiate with the sultan. The ambassadors were ordered to protest against the compulsory purchases of spices and cotton and to insist on an undertaking that trade be free. They were also to make sure that the merchants would not be made responsible for acts of piracy committed by others, e.g., rebels against the Genoese government or the independent Genoese rulers of Mytilene or of other territories. Further, they were to demand that there be only a Genoese consul in Jerusalem and Damietta, as there had been before. In addition they were to claim restitution for the sum, which had finally amounted to 16,000 ducats, extorted from the merchants for the sultan's losses in Caffa. The embassy consisted of Ciriaco Colonna and Andrea Pallavicino, who were instructed to try to have the peace treaty concluded in Famagusta.[140] The results of this mission, which received its instructions in February 1431, are not known to us, but apparently an agreement was reached.

XXII (the request to liberate the captives had been made in 1426 by the consul of Caffa, clearly in order to profit from the sultan's interest in good relations with the authorities of this great slave market).

[137] Jorga, *ROL* V, p. 372, f. VI, p. 55 f.

[138] Ibn Ḥadjar III, p. 420 f. (misinterpreted by Labib, *Handelsgeschichte*, p. 360 f.); 'Abdalbāsiṭ 803, f. 308b.

[139] Misti 57, f. 162b.

[140] Silvestre de Sacy, "Pièces diplomatiques tirées des archives de la république de Gênes," *Notes et Extraits* XI (1827), p. 71 ff.; Jorga, *ROL* VI, p. 95 ff.

The attitude of the Catalans toward Sultan Barsbāy remained defiant and even aggressive through the 1420's. The acts of aggression were considered a means to obtain from the sultan renunciation of his commercial policy, but they also served political purposes as well. Some of the corsair activities were conducted by true privateers; others were bailed by the king or high dignitaries of the Aragonese-Catalan kingdom. Since, starting in 1421, a Catalan, Antonio Fluvian, was Great Master of the Knights of Rhodes, the pirates and raiders could always count on their help. But Cyprus also served them as a base, and because of the close contacts and the collaboration one cannot always discern who attacked the Moslems. The Catalans could afford the aggressive policy for various reasons. One was their great superiority in naval warfare, which guaranteed the success of their attacks and often rich booty. Another was the fact that they had a strong commercial base in Rhodes, where they could obtain great quantities of spices. They also counted upon the interest of the sultan in the continuation of trade with his dominions, despite the piracy and the raids on their coasts. The merchants of Catalonia, on the other hand, tried time and again to induce the king to a more friendly policy toward the sultan. Because of this interplay of various (and conflicting) interests and tendencies, the acts of aggression alternated with diplomatic steps. Often both aggression and diplomacy were used at the same time as a means of influencing the sultan.

In March 1424 the Catalans came to an agreement with the sultan, so that they could take up regular trade in his dominions.[141] But some months later the acts of aggression began once more. The Arabic chronicles contain a long series of accounts of Catalan assaults. In June 1424, off Damietta, the Catalans captured two ships, which carried rich cargoes, and took prisoner more than one hundred Moslems, passengers and crew. Thereupon the sultan gave orders to imprison the European merchants and to sequester their goods. A comtemporary Arabic author narrates that a merchant of Damietta, Aḥmad Ibn al-Hamīm, had a big ship and had brought a heavy load of soap and other commodities in it from Tripoli. He says that the corsairs were Biscayans and that they captured the ship near the mouth of the Nile (i.e., the branch of Damietta).[142] The Mamluks knew, of course, that the corsairs were based in Cyprus and enjoyed the support of the king. So the sultan intensified his armaments for the onslaught on the island, which resulted in its conquest by his forces in 1426. Meanwhile, the aggression on the coasts of Egypt and of Syria went on. In April 1425 there was

[141] *Chron. Morosini*, c. 410. The Venetian chronicler says that the news of this agreement came to Damascus on 24 March 1424.

[142] *Sulūk* IV, p. 665 f.; *an-Nudjūm az-zāhira* VI, p. 578 f.; Ṣāliḥ b. Yaḥyā, *Ta'rīkh Bayrūt*, p. 219 ff.; 'Abdalbāsiṭ 803, f. 281b.

a raid on Tyre and another north of Tripoli. These attacks, however, were made by the Cypriots themselves.[143]

The Mamluk war fleet patrolled along the Syrian coast, but nevertheless Moslem ships were captured by the corsairs.[144] In February 1426 the Catalans attacked the port of Alexandria and captured a Venetian ship and a Moslem merchantman,[145] and in the month of June there was a naval battle between a squadron of the Mamluk war fleet and four Christian galleys sailing to Alexandria.[146] The submission of the king of Cyprus to the Mamluk sultan was a heavy blow to the corsairs, and the sultan tried to exploit his success for inducing the king of Aragon to put an end to aggression.[147] But, although the corsairs had been deprived of an excellent base, the attacks went on. In 1427 their activities were intense. A squadron of corsair ships captured eight Moslem merchantmen not far from Alexandria, the last of these being two ships coming from ʿAlāya (on the Cilician coast) carrying timber.[148] Then in 1428 Catalan ships again attacked the port of Alexandria. According to an Arabic author, thereupon the Genoese and the Catalans were arrested both in Egypt and in Syria.[149] Another flotilla captured a Moslem galley, which carried a cargo worth 12,000-15,000 ducats, and also a Turkish ship. Thereupon the sultan decreed that henceforth the Catalans should not be allowed to visit Alexandria or Beirut. Nevertheless, trade was not discontinued, and Catalan ships visited Alexandria by virtue of safe-conducts. But in 1428 some merchants who came on one of them were arrested and jailed in Cairo.[150] Meanwhile the war went on. Also in 1429, the Catalans attacked the port of Alexandria, but encountered strong resistance by Moslem troops which were on the alert. As a consequence, Catalan trade with Egypt and Syria was for some time suspended.[151]

However, the sultan was very much interested in renewing the commercial exchanges with Catalonia, and he made the first move to bring

[143] *Sulūk* IV, pp. 684, 686; Ibn Ḥadjar III, p. 346; ʿAbdalbāsiṭ 803, f. 286a, and see also *op.cit.*, f. 285b, about the despatch of Mamluk troops to the Egyptian coast because of the fear of an impending attack; Ibn Iyās² II, p. 97. Hill, *History of Cyprus* II, p. 471.

[144] *Sulūk* IV, pp. 668, 589; *an-Nudjūm az-zāhira* VI, p. 580; ʿAbdalbāsiṭ, 803, f. 286b.

[145] *Sulūk* IV, p. 718 (the Arabic author speaks of *Ḳaṭarāniyūn*, that is, Catalans.

[146] *Op.cit.*, p. 720; ʿAbdalbāsiṭ 803, f. 293 f.

[147] This was probably the purpose of the letter written by the sultan to Alfonso V; see Darrag, *Barsbay*, p. 337.

[148] *Sulūk* IV, p. 744.

[149] *Op.cit.*, p. 780; Ibn Ḥadjar III, p. 405; ʿAbdalbāsiṭ 803, f. 303b; and cf. Labib, *Handelsgeschichte*, p. 354.

[150] *Chron. Morosini*, c. 490. About the incident in 1428 see ACA, Cancill, Real 2647, f. 147b ff. a letter of the king to the sultan.

[151] *Sulūk* IV, p. 802 f.; Ibn Ḥadjar III, p. 420; *an-Nudjūm az-zāhira* VI, p. 644; ʿAbdalbāsiṭ 803, f. 307a f. The Arabic authors again speak in a general way about "Franks," but since subsequently Ibn Ḥadjar mentions the departure of the "Genoese Franks," it is clear who is meant in this account. About the suspension of trade, see *Morosini*, c. 498.

about peace. He sent a Franciscan monk of the Monastery of Mount Zion in Jerusalem to Barcelona in order to make suggestions. Naturally, the merchants of Barcelona gave serious attention to them, and they intervened with the king, influencing him to agree to negotiate with the sultan. The Great Master of the Knights of Rhodes was helpful, and, thanks to his mediation, ambassadors of the king of Aragon and of the sultan met in Rhodes.[152] The Catalan embassy consisted of Rafael Ferrer and Luis Sirvent, the latter one of the most active and experienced Levant traders of Catalonia. The negotiations were successful and at the end of May 1430 a treaty of peace and commerce was concluded.[153] The treaty contained several clauses, which one finds in all similar contracts, e.g., that customs should be paid only for merchandise actually sold and that litigation between Catalan merchants and subjects of the sultan should be brought before secular judges (and not *cadis*). It also contained an undertaking of the sultan that there would not be compulsory purchases and sales of any commodity. Other clauses were connected with the special character of Catalan trade and traffic and the activities of the Catalan corsairs. Since often Catalan ships were chartered by Moslem merchants, it was stipulated that the latter might ask for guarantees (that the Moslem passengers should not be kidnapped, etc.). The Catalan embassy also undertook that the Catalan merchants in Egypt and Syria would be responsible for acts of piracy committed by Catalans and even by others, if the latter had been supported by Catalans.[154] The jurisdiction of the consul within the Catalan merchant colony was recognized as binding only if he would administer justice in the presence of a Moslem official; thus his status was restricted as compared with that of the Venetians and Genoese consuls. On the other hand, the Catalans were granted a right of preference as far as loading of their merchandise was concerned.[155] Certainly this treaty contained clauses favorable to the Cat-

[152] Del Treppo, p. 37 f.; Coll Juliá, "Aspectos del corso catalan," p. 162. The credentials and instructions for the ambassadors are in ACA, Cancill. Real 2647, f. 149b ff., and see there, f. 153a f., an order to stop aggression against the subjects of the sultan; see, further, ACA, Cancill. Real 2648, f. 21b ff., another decree on behalf of the ambassadors.

[153] The Arabic text with a Spanish translation and a commentary has been published by R. Ruiz Orsatti, "Tratado de paz entre Alfonso V de Aragon y el Sultan de Egipto al-Malik al-Ašraf Barsbay," *al-Andalus* IV (1936-1939), pp. 333-389; the same text and translation (with slight corrections) was printed again in Alarcón-García, *Documentos*, no. 153. Unfortunately, the translation of several passages is faulty, so that both the translator and other scholars, who relied on it, have drawn from it far-reaching conclusions which are unfounded. Why Labib, *op.cit.* p. 356, says that the whole of the treaty is unknown is not clear.

[154] This clause has been misunderstood by the translator, and consequently erroneous conclusions have been drawn from it.

[155] Further, by clause no. 24, the sultan undertakes to build a new fondaco, but according to the translator he allowed the merchants to build one (Del Treppo, p. 37, interprets the clause as an undertaking of the sultan to give the Catalans a second fondaco). But this is not said and would have been in contradiction to the international law that had developed in the course of time and that regulated the relations between the Moslem rulers and the colonies

alans, but the latter did not obtain the privileged status of the Venetians. According to the treaties between Venice and the sultan concluded in 1415 and in 1422, a Venetian was not obliged to appear before a law court, if the Moslem litigant had not previously proved his claim. Finally the purely political claims of Alfonso V, such as an undertaking of the sultan to keep peace with Rhodes and to safeguard the rights of the Franciscan monks in Jerusalem, had not been agreed to by the envoys of the sultan, and there is no mention at all of restitution for losses during the hostilities.

So in the course of the year 1430 and the first half of 1431 the three major trading nations of Southern Europe had made agreements with the sultan. Apparently he had given up his monopoly of the pepper trade, and the Italian and Catalan traders could hope that a new era in the commercial exchanges would begin. Their hopes were very soon frustrated. In the second half of his reign, Barsbāy made new efforts to establish the monopoly of pepper trade, and the reaction of the trading nations was very firm.

In 1432 Barsbāy proclaimed once again that only he had the right to sell pepper to the European merchants.[156] In 1434 the Venetian merchants suffered from various extortions. In Damascus they were compelled to buy pepper from the sultan, and when they came to the ports, they were not allowed to depart before buying another quantity of spices from his stocks. When they tried to resist the pressure, the sultan expelled them altogether from his territories. This was an unheard-of offense and a great blow for the Venetians. They left merchandise worth 235,000 ducats in Egypt and Syria.[157] But the desire of the Venetians to continue their activities in Egypt and Syria was so great that the trade with these countries was not suspended. In the Venetian Senate there were long deliberations about proposals to send a new embassy to the sultan. Finally it was decided, in April 1435, to order the consul of Alexandria (who apparently had remained there) to lodge a protest with the sultan. It was also decreed by the Senate that in the future the consuls in Egypt and Syria should not buy pepper

of European merchants. The fondachi were built and owned by the Moslem sovereign. Clause 26 refers to the right of the consul to be arbitrator if a Moslem and a Catalan chose him as such, although the Moslem was granted the right to appeal his verdict to the Moslem authorities. This was by no means a great concession to the Catalans. Clause 30 grants the consul the right to appoint the warden of the fondaco, but as the translator read عوقوا instead of غرقوا ; he believed that the consul was authorized to establish a fondaco. In an additional clause the Catalan envoys declare that the treaty would be valid only if the sultan returned the goods of the ship of Nicolau Julia and liberated the passengers (or crew) who had been imprisoned. (The translator read instead of عوقوا , who were detained; غرقوا , who drowned.) See also ACA, Cancill. Real 2648, f. 21b ff. that Luis Sirvent should supervise the maintenance of the peace; 2521, f. 100a/b a decree imposing a tax of 2 percent on trade with Alexandria in order to pay him a remuneration.

[156] *Sulūk* IV, p. 869; Ibn Ḥadjar III, p. 473; al-Maḳrīzī speaks about pepper, Ibn Ḥadjar about spices in general.

[157] Jorga, *ROL* VI, p. 135.

or other commodities for the merchants, as had been done at every spice fair from the end of the fourteenth century.[158] But a month later there was apparently good news from Alexandria. The Senate sent a letter to the sultan thanking him for the liberation of a pilgrims' galley and asking him once again not to enforce compulsory purchases of pepper. At the same time, trade with the sultan's dominions, which had been suspended, was again allowed.[159]

However, during the spice fair of 1435 there were again the same conflicts. The Venetians refused to submit to the demands of the Mamluk authorities and were expelled. Spices bought by the Venetians were sequestered in Beirut.[160] The consul in Alexandria left for Rhodes, and the consul in Damascus went to Nicosia in Cyprus. But the Venetian government was keen to continue the trade with Egypt, despite all the pressure brought upon the merchants and notwithstanding the offenses. In February 1436 the Senate ordered the consul of Alexandria to return to his post if he should receive a conciliatory letter from the sultan.[161] After long deliberations, it was also decided to send an embassy to the sultan. The ambassador Marco Geno was instructed to ask the sultan to revoke the expulsion of the merchants and to allow free trade, without compulsory purchases. If he succeeded in his endeavors, he was to call the consuls and merchants back to Egypt and Syria and wait there to see if they could trade freely and ship out their merchandise. But if the sultan insisted on his pepper monopoly, he was to tell him that the Venetians would buy the spices elsewhere, in Constantinople, Bursa, and Trebizond. In case the sultan should be unaccommodating, he should be requested at least to allow the Venetians to ship their goods from his dominions and grant permission for some Venetians to return to Egypt and Syria for a certain time to settle their affairs. In any case, if absolutely necessary in order to make possible the renewal of trade and the return of the merchants, the ambassador could buy 1,000 sportas pepper for 100 ducats each from the sultan. If the sultan intended to forbid the spice trade in Damascus altogether, he was to be asked to fix a date for the end of the transactions.[162] The interest of Venice in the continuation of the trade with the Mamluk dominions was so great that even before receiving news from the ambassador it was decided to despatch the galley convoy to Beirut that year (but not to Alexandria).[163]

[158] Misti 59, f. 105a.

[159] Jorga, *ROL* VI, p. 136 f.

[160] *Sulūk* IV, p. 966; Coll., Not. VI, f. 155b, 165a; Misti 59, f. 187b. According to Marino Sanuto, *Vite de' duchi*, c. 1041 this happened in 1435.

[161] *Sulūk* IV, p. 966; Misti 59, f. 144a; *Chron. Dolfin*, f. 373b.

[162] Jorga, *ROL* VI, p. 371 f. The readiness to purchase a great quantity of pepper certainly referred to a single purchase (and not to an undertaking of regular, i.e., annual purchases).

[163] Misti 59, f. 169b ff.

The reply of the sultan was indeed negative. He was not ready to renounce the pepper monopoly. Once more, in August 1436, there were long debates in the Venetian Senate, and it was proposed that an attempt be made to reach a compromise, offering to buy from the sultan 1,500 sportas for 100 ducats each. It was suggested that this offer be made by the Venetian merchants in Alexandria (who apparently had returned), pretending that they were not proceeding according to orders from Venice. The agreement should contain an explicit obligation that trade could be continued by the Venetians and that the goods that had been sequestered in Beirut would be given back. There were also propositions that went further. It was proposed that the Venetians accept the pepper monopoly on the condition that the sultan fix the price once and for all.[164] The result of the mission of Marco Geno is not known to us, but it may be assumed that some agreement was reached, for instructions were given to the merchants who left the dominions of the Mamluks to return and to collect their goods,[165] and trade went on, but the question of the sequestered goods remained. In March 1437 a special envoy, Filippo Quirino, was ordered to go from Crete to Cairo to negotiate the restitution; later, Francesco Correr was entrusted with this mission.[166] Since he had no success, the Senate decreed that if these goods were not given back by the time of the arrival of the galleys in Alexandria and Beirut, trade should be carried on only on board the ships. Then, for fear of new extortions and conflicts, orders were given that the captain of the Beirut galleys should not allow trade at all, if the spices had not been given back.[167] Meanwhile, another envoy, Leone Contarini, was sent to the sultan.[168] However, during the spice fair both in Alexandria and in Syria, new pressure was brought upon the Venetians.[169] All the precautions were futile. In the month of November, the sequestered spices were finally restored to the Venetians.[170] But once more the merchants were compelled, both in Syria and in Egypt, to buy pepper from the sultan, and they suffered great losses. In Syria they were required to buy pepper from the sultan for 70,000 ducats and, when they refused, they were imprisoned, and the spices bought by them sequestered.[171] In Alexandria, the Venetians had been compelled to buy 1,000 sportas for 100 ducats each during the spice fair.[172] The Mamluk authorities even had

164 Misti 59, f. 172a ff.
165 *Ibid.*, f. 173a.
166 Misti 60, f. 3b, 4b.
167 *Ibid.*, f. 29a, 36a f.
168 *Ibid.*, f. 31a.
169 See below.
170 Misti 60, f. 46b.
171 Jorga, *ROL* VI, p. 396 f.; *Chron. Dolfin*, f. 379a.
172 See also *Zancaruola*, f. 568b. Jorga, *ROL* VI, p. 406, quoting the Zancaruola chronicle, says that the agents of the sultan demanded from the Venetians in 1438 in Damascus 103

recourse to new methods of compelling the Venetians to buy the pepper of the sultan's stocks; in 1437; during the fall cotton fair in Syria, they allowed the Venetians to ship cotton only if they purchased a certain quantity of pepper from the sultan.[173] Consequently, there were again long deliberations in the Venetian Senate in February 1438. It was proposed that the Venetians should leave the dominions of the sultan altogether and that trade with them should be suspended.[174] Then, in May 1438, a decision was taken to address a letter to the sultan (to be sent by a special galley) to protest against another sequestration of Venetian goods and against the arbitrary arrest of merchants. Until an answer was received, it was forbidden to sail to the sultan's dominions, to send merchandise there, or even to import commodities from there to Venice. Characteristically, these proposals were carried against strong opposition: 74 members of the Senate voted for them, 31 were against, and 11 abstained.[175] However, the senators did not know that Barsbāy was in his castle, dying, and that the stormy period of his reign had come to an end. For the Levant traders of Venice it had been a great trial.

In fact Venice had won the game; the vicissitudes of the long contest and the concessions made from time to time should not blur the picture. The attempt to establish a monopoly of the pepper trade sank to the grave with Barsbāy, although his successor did try to take up his policy. It failed for two reasons: one was the stubborn opposition by the Venetians to accept the principle of compulsory purchase. On this point the Serenissima held firm, although she was ready to make concessions sometimes and agreed to the obligatory purchase of a certain quantity. Clearly, Venice could not dictate to the sultan what his policy should be toward the Egyptian and Syrian merchants. But there the sultan failed too. Several documents that have come down to us in the Venetian archives and some accounts in Arabic chronicles show how the sultan's officials and the Egyptians and Syrian merchants infringed the sultan's decrees and sold pepper to the Europeans.[176]

---

ducats for a sporta pepper. But in Zancaruola, *l.c.*, one reads that in 1437 the Venetians in Syria were imprisoned and their goods sequestered after having been requested to buy 350 ḳinṭārs pepper for 100 ducats each and having refused. Further, one heard in Venice that the Venetians in Alexandria had been compelled to buy 1,000 sportas for 100 ducats each and even their goods had been sequestered.

[173] Misti 60, f. 36a f.

[174] *Ibid.*, f. 54a f.; Jorga, *ROL* VI, p. 396 f., was mistaken in quoting this text as a decision. It was only a proposal.

[175] Misti 60, f. 77b f.

[176] Another opinion about the outcome of Barsbāy's policy and the attitude of the Venetians (and the other trading nations) has been expressed by Darrag, *Barsbay*, pp. 307, 318, 331. As to the Venetian documents that refer to the disobedience of the Mamluk officials and the Moslem merchants, see my "Le monopole de Barsbay d'après les sources vénitiennes," *Anuario de estudios medievales* IX (1974-1978), p. 551 ff.

The Genoese and the Catalans suffered no less from the extortions by the officials of Barsbāy and from his pepper monopoly, although the envoys of Venice sometimes accused the sultan of compelling only her subjects to buy spices from his stocks. But since Genoa's Levant trade was much less concentrated on the purchase of spices, it was not as vital a problem of her international trade as it was for Venice. However, in 1436 Genoa sent the sultan an embassy, headed by Filippo Pinello, which probably was to protest against the encroachment on free trade.[177]

The reaction of the Catalans to the stubborn policy of Barsbāy, who stuck to his monopolism until the end of his reign, was violent; the peace concluded in 1420's was short-lived. Again there were acts of piracy and raids on the coasts of Egypt and Syria, which resulted in reprisals and long conflicts. In the 1430's they were no longer the activities of privateers, but were organized by the king of Aragon himself and by the princes and dignitaries who sided with him in his contest for the crown of Naples. The policy of Alfonso V towards the Mamluks in the 1420's was part of his great scheme of Catalan domination of the Mediterranean. His diplomatic contacts with the Negus, directed against the sultan of Cairo, had the same objective.[178] He probably considered the treaty he had made in 1430 with the sultan an expedient to permit the continuation of trade; the basic policy had not been changed.

In 1432 Alfonso V waged war against the ruler of Tunis and at the same time his allies attacked the Mamluk dominions. In September of that year, corsairs assailed the port of Tripoli and captured a ship with many Moslem passengers and a rich cargo; a ship that came there from Damietta was captured too. This raid had been organized by the prince of Taranto, who was allied with Alfonso V. When the news of the raid came to Cairo, the sultan ordered the arrest of the Catalans and the Genoese and the sequestering of their goods, explicitly excepting the Venetians from these reprisals.[179] Two months later the king of Aragon made a diplomatic move on behalf of the trade of his subjects with the dominions of the sultan. In November 1432 a Catalan ambassador appeared at the court of Cairo and handed over a protest against the sultan's commercial policy. In this note the king declared that the Catalans would under no circumstances submit to the pepper monopoly and would cut off the commercial exchanges. In his verbal message, the ambassador referred to the great fleet that the king had assembled in Sicily. The Arabic authors, who have left us an account

[177] Tur V, f. 68a, 71b, 72a ff., 72b ff., 76a ff., 78a, 79a f.

[178] See F. Soldevila, *Historia de Catalunya*, 2nd ed. (Barcelona, 1962) II, p. 676 f.; G. Wiet, "Les marchands d'épices," p. 120 ff.; Darrag, *Barsbay*, p. 338 ff.

[179] *Sulūk* IV, p. 882 (quoted by as-Sallāmī, p. 41); Broquière, pp. 55, 66; ʿAbdalbāsiṭ 803, f. 322b (who speaks about some ships coming from Damietta).

of this embassy in their chronicles, say that the sultan gave a very unfriendly reply.[180] To have recourse to military action and diplomatic steps at the same time was indeed an integral feature of the policy of Alfonso V toward the Mamluks.

Since this embassy had no success, the king of Aragon sponsored other acts of aggression, and the Mamluk forces had to be on the alert.[181] On the other hand, the Catalan merchants visited the ports of Egypt and Syria as if there were no conflict between war and trade. In 1434 the Catalans launched an intense attack on the coasts of Egypt and Syria and on the shipping of the sultan's subjects. In the spring of that year the corsairs captured five ships, with many passengers and heavy cargoes, off Beirut. The king of Aragon also sent to the governor of Damietta a letter for the sultan written in a very offensive style. By this letter he again protested against the pepper monopoly. The Arabic chroniclers recount that the sultan became very angry and tore up the letter of the king. Its contents are not known to us, but it is not improbable that King Alfonso intended to attack Egypt himself in 1434.[182] Summing up the results of the naval war in the year 837 (August 1433 to August 1434), al-Maḳrīzī reports that the corsairs captured eighteen Moslem ships, taking much booty, and killing or carrying away those whom they found on board.[183] The Mamluks retaliated by capturing a Venetian galley, with coral and other merchandise, in the waters of Beirut, and a Genoese ship off Tripoli. They set fire to this latter ship, after having taken as prisoners more than twenty persons found on it. According to an Arabic chronicler who reported this event, the government of the sultan was embarrassed by the action of its naval forces, since both the Venetians and the Genoese were then on peaceful terms with the Mamluks.[184] The attitude towards the Catalans was intransigent. Georgian pilgrims to the Holy Sepulchre in Jerusalem were imprisoned and brought to Cairo, when it was suspected that Catalan nobles were among them.[185] In 1435 there was a lull in the Catalan aggression against the Mamluks, undoubtedly because in that year Alfonso V made a supreme effort to

[180] *Sulūk* IV, p. 885; *an-Nudjūm az-zāhira* VI, p. 682; ʿAbdalbāsiṭ 803, f. 323b. According to Ibn Ḥadjar III, p. 518, this embassy came to Cairo in 837 (1433-1434), but al-Maḳrīzī's account is more reliable, because in 1432 Alfonso V had indeed assembled a great fleet. The Arabic authors say that the king of Aragon also protested against the commercial activities of the Mamluk dignitaries.

[181] *Sulūk* IV, p. 915; Ibn Ḥadjar III, p. 307 and cf. p. 303.

[182] *Sulūk* IV, p. 914 (copied by as-Sallāmī, p. 108); Ibn Ḥadjar III, p. 518 (who adds that these Moslem captives were sold as slaves); ʿAbdalbāsiṭ 803, f. 332a, and cf. C. Marinescu, *L'île de Rhodes et l'ordre de Saint Jean de Jérusalem au XVe siècle d'après des documents inédits* (Studi e testi, 125) (Città del Vaticano, 1946), p. 386.

[183] *Sulūk* IV, p. 921, and cf. Weil V, p. 184 (inexact).

[184] *Sulūk* IV, p. 919.

[185] *Op.cit.*, p. 928 (copied by as-Sallāmī, p. 117 f.); ʿAbdalbāsiṭ 803, p. 334a.

conquer Naples and assembled all his naval forces for a decisive fight. It ended with his defeat in the naval battle of Ponza, and he was captured by the Genoese.

But in 1436 the Catalans took up military action against the Mamluks. In the month of August three galleys attacked two Moslem ships and captured them off Abūkīr on the Egyptian coast. The Mamluk garrison of Alexandria succeeded in recovering one of them, while the other was burned by the Catalans. The next day a Catalan ship attacked a Genoese merchantman in the port of Alexandria. The Moslems supported the Genoese, and the Catalan ship departed.[186] However, since the Catalan trade in the Moslem Levant was at stake and the sultan had forbidden the Catalans to visit the ports of his countries, in October 1437 the Council of Barcelona applied to the king with a request to embark on negotiations with the sultan.[187] Catalan shipping to the Mamluk dominions was indeed at a low ebb in 1436-1438, just as Venice had suspended the service of the galley lines to Egypt and Syria in 1438.

So the Levant trade of the European trading nations was truly in crisis when Barsbāy died on 7 June 1438.

Sultan Djaḳmaḳ, who succeeded him on the throne of Cairo in September 1438 (he reigned until February 1453), after the short reign of Barsbāy's son Yūsuf, did not renounce the pepper monopoly, and those interminable conflicts with the European trading nations continued. But this sultan was less violent, so that it was a bit easier to come to terms with him.

In the spring of 1438 Venetian merchants had again been imprisoned in Egypt and the question of the spices that had been bought by Venetians and had been sequestered in 1437 in Damascus had not yet found a solution.[188] In addition, the Venetians had again suffered from extortion.[189] But an effort was made to bring about a reconciliation, and when the imprisoned merchants had been liberated, at the end of the year the Senate of Venice revoked the embargo on the trade with the dominions of the sultan. In May 1439 it decided to appoint new consuls for Alexandria and Damascus.[190] So it seemed that under the reign of Sultan Djaḳmaḳ a new era in the Levant trade would begin, but very soon the hopes of the European trading nations were dashed. In April 1439 the news in Venice was that the sultan

[186] *Op.cit.*, p. 994; Ibn Ḥadjar, MS. Yeni Čami 814, f. 259b; cf. Weil, *l.c.*, (mistaken).

[187] Capmany, 2.1, no. 319, pp. 466-467. The statement in the letter of the town council of Barcelona concerning the sultan's prohibition of visits of Catalans to his dominions is substantiated by a passage in the travelogue of Pero Tafur, *Andanças e viajes*, p. 73. Pero Tafur was in Egypt in September 1436.

[188] Jorga, *ROL* VI, p. 408, VII, p. 45.

[189] Misti 60, f. 107a.

[190] *Ibid.*, f. 114a; Jorga, *ROL* VI, p. 407.

would allow the Europeans to sojourn in his dominions six months only,[191] and at the end of the year there was news that the sultan had again established a monopoly of all spices.[192] Europeans who had bought pepper from private traders in Damascus were called before the governor and accused of having transgressed the law.[193] Venice reacted vigorously: in January 1440 the Senate decided that the cogs sailing to Syria to the spring cotton fair should be used for shipping the goods of the Venetians from that country and that the merchants should leave both Syria and Egypt. Trade with the Mamluk dominions was once more forbidden altogether.[194] But some months later there were second thoughts and it was decided to despatch the galleys to Alexandria and Beirut, although the sultan had arrested the Venetian merchants in reprisal for the capture of some Moslems by a Venetian in Rhodes.[195] The merchants who went to the dominions of the Mamluks that year had bad experiences. In Damascus, they were compelled to buy pepper at a very high price and then they were expelled. Consequently, in September 1441, the Senate addressed a protest to the sultan.[196] Already in May 1441 there was news in Venice that the sultan had firmly decided to keep up the pepper monopoly[197] and that he would allow the European merchants to stay in his countries only four months.[198] It was also said that the merchants had been beaten and money extorted from them. At first people in Venice were inclined to agree to the new law, i.e., that the merchants should stay only four months in Egypt and in Syria, and orders were given accordingly. But then it was decided that the galley lines in Alexandria and Beirut should be suspended in that year. The goods of the Venetians were to be shipped to Candia, Modon, and Corfu on the cotton ships,[199] and in October the merchants were to leave Egypt and Syria. But, in fact, it was not really intended to cut off trade with these countries. It was decreed that those who would go there could stay four months; in other words, Venice was yielding to the sultan. However, there was the pretense that permission to go to Egypt and Syria was exceptional.[200] The suspension of the galley service was surely a heavy blow for the sultan, for the revenue he had from the customs levied on the spices (the cargo of the galleys) was much greater than that accruing from the cotton purchases. But of course the Venetians bought spices in

[191] Jorga, *ROL* VI, p. 414.
[192] *Ibid.*, p. 422. See also ʿAbdalbāsiṭ 812, f. 31b.
[193] Misti 60, f. 212b.
[194] Jorga, *ROL* VI, p. 422.
[195] *Ibid.*, p. 429.
[196] Jorga, *ROL* VII, p. 46.
[197] *Ibid.*, p. 42.
[198] *Ibid.*, p. 42f.; Senato Mar I, f. 45a.
[199] Senato Mar I, f. 45b.
[200] *Ibid.*, f. 46a; Jorga, *ROL* VII, p. 42 f.

Egypt and Syria in 1441 too, and, as was so often the case, the effort was made to compel them to buy from the sultan and, when they refused, they were imprisoned.[201]

However, the suspension of the galley lines proved to be a successful ploy. In June 1442 Sultan Djaḳmaḳ changed his tactics; he approached the Venetians in a friendly way. In a letter to the Venetian government he promised that henceforth there would not be compulsory purchases or sales.[202] Since he also hinted that he would like an embassy to come to him, it was decided to try the art of diplomacy again. The embassy to be sent to the sultan was to protest against the compulsory purchases and the extortions, especially in Syria. If the sultan should insist on the purchase of pepper from his stocks (beside the quantity one had agreed upon to buy every year), the ambassador was to ask why the sultan imposed this ruling only on the Venetians and not on the Genoese and Catalans. At the same time, when it was decided to send an embassy to the sultan, new consuls to Alexandria and Damascus were appointed. On the other hand, the Senate empowered the ambassador to agree to the sultan's wish that the merchants should stay in his dominions no more than four months.[203] The ambassador, Andrea Donato, concluded a commercial treaty with the sultan, including various undertakings in which Venice was very much interested. The sultan promised again that there would not be compulsory purchases of spices, cotton, and alkali. By virtue of this treaty, the Venetians could live everywhere in the dominions of the sultan and were assured that they would not be compelled to pay customs twice. The various dues and fees were fixed exactly. Venetians were not to be held responsible for the debts of others, and some officials who had mistreated them were removed from their posts. Several clauses in the treaty testify to the great upswing of Venetian trade in Syria. These are the clauses referring to the customs to be paid in some towns of Syria and especially to the right of the Venetians to travel, dressed as Moslems, over the countryside; since the Venetians often visited the estates where cotton was planted, this was indeed an important concession. On the other hand, the question of the compulsory purchase of pepper is styled in a very general way. Further, the treaty contained many clauses which had been agreed upon in 1415 and in 1422, and there were added undertakings of the Mamluk government concerning the restitution of a Venetian ship and the liberation of Venetians who had been imprisoned.[204]

[201] Jorga, *ROL* VII, p. 66 f.
[202] *Ibid.*, p. 62 f.
[203] *Ibid.*, p. 58, 62 f., 66 f.
[204] Amari, *I diplomi arabi*, serie II, no. 42; *Dipl. Ven.-Lev.* II, no. 189, and see there nos. 190-197 the additional documents; the letter of the sultan to the doge also *Libr. Com.* IV,

It is almost superfluous to state that a short time after the conclusion of this treaty the Mamluk authorities again began to squeeze the Venetians. In 1443 there were again compulsory purchases in Beirut. When the galleys were about to depart, the Venetians were compelled to buy a certain quantity of pepper at double the commercial price, and the captain of the convoy was imprisoned.[205] Therefore, Venice used a new means. In February 1444 the sultan was asked to agree to the appointment of a permanent Venetian representative in Cairo.[206] But the request was turned down, and in the winter of 1444-1445 the merchants were again compelled to buy pepper in Damascus, so that the Venetian government once more had to lodge a protest with the sultan.[207] In June 1445 the Venetian government another time addressed the sultan in the same matter.[208] A year later the sultan again restricted the right of the European merchants to sojourn in his dominions, this time limiting them to six months. The Venetians agreed,[209] but a short time later a new crisis arose. There is good reason to believe that the fall of the price of pepper (and other spices) because of the great supply and the risk of being left with large, possibly unsaleable, stocks, induced the sultan to enforce the monopoly or at least to impose the purchase of great quantities on the European merchants. The losses that the Venetians suffered in 1446 as a consequence of the compulsory purchase of pepper were apparently substantial.[210] So it was proposed in the Venetian Senate that trade with the dominions of the sultan be suspended for a year and that the merchants and the consuls should leave. But then it was decided that the cotton cogs should sail to Syria. A sharp note was addressed to the sultan, reminding him of his promises and requesting him to allow the departure of the merchants.[211] The sultan's reply was negative: he insisted on the compulsory purchase of pepper from his stocks. Thereupon the Senate decided again that the merchants should depart from Syria, where the extortions by the Moslem officials were particularly frequent, and that in 1447 the galley service to Beirut should be suspended. However, this decision was not taken wholeheartedly, and a proposal to suspend trade with the Mamluk dominions altogether obtained only a third of the votes.[212] The cotton cogs were allowed to sail to Syria to the fall fair, on the condition

lib. 13, no. 223; J. Wansbrough, "Venice and Florence," p. 487 ff.; Marino Sanuto, *Vite de' duchi*, c. 1107.

[205] Jorga, *ROL* VII, pp. 381, 401 f.

[206] *Ibid.*, p. 390 f.

[207] Jorga, *ROL* VIII, p. 7 f.

[208] Senato Mar II, f. 79b.

[209] *Ibid.*, f. 170b f.

[210] Thiriet, "Quelques observations," p. 520.

[211] Senato Mar II, f. 185a ff.; Jorga, *ROL* VIII, p. 35 f.

[212] It was proposed to forbid for the moment (until a new decision) travels to Egypt and Syria and import of merchandise from these countries, Senato Mar III, f. 21a f.; Jorga, *l.c.*

that trade should be carried on on board the ships. Privately owned ships were also allowed to sail to Alexandria.[213] In 1448 the galley line to Beirut was suspended, and after the return of the cotton cogs from the spring fair and the return of the consul of Damascus, it was decided to lay an embargo on trade with Syria until mid-November. That means that the convoy to the fall cotton fair was suspended and it was forbidden to import any merchandise from Syria (by other ships) until the end of May 1449.[214] On the other hand, in that year five galleys were despatched to Alexandria (instead of three of four, as in the preceding years). Proposals made in the Senate to write a letter to the sultan threatening that the Venetians would transfer their activities to Turkey were not carried.[215]

All these deliberations and decisions make it very clear that Venice was not really inclined to break off trade with the dominions of the sultan. In February 1449 it was decided, indeed, to send Lorenzo Tiepolo as ambassador to Cairo. He was to explain to the sultan that Venice was interested in the continuation of regular trade with his dominions, but he was also to threaten that the trade would be transferred to Turkey if the sultan should not change his attitude. If the sultan should be intransigent, the ambassador was to ask him to allow the merchants to depart. From the instructions he was given, it appears that the merchants encountered especially great difficulties in Syria, where the officials behaved to them with less restraint than in Egypt. So Lorenzo Tiepolo was to demand an undertaking that additional dues (beyond those established in the treaties) should not be levied in the Syrian ports and that certain officials should be removed from their posts. Until the return of the ambassador, trade with Syria was suspended. In fact, his instructions point clearly to the fact that in Alexandria the Venetians were no longer compelled to buy pepper from the sultan (of course in addition to the quantity purchased every year collectively).[216] Apparently the sultan's reply to the ambassador was satisfactory, but he insisted on the compulsory purchase of alkali, another royal monopoly. Finally a compromise was reached, insofar as the Venetians undertook to buy from the governor of Tripoli a certain quantity of this commodity every year. Thereupon the sultan issued decrees to the governors of all provinces of Syria, admonishing them to render it possible for the Venetians to carry on trade freely.[217] Needless to say, this under-

[213] Senato Mar III, f. 23b f.
[214] Senato Mar III, f. 54b f.
[215] Senato Mar III, f. 80a f.; Jorga, *ROL* VIII, p. 38 f.
[216] Jorga, *ibid.*, p. 56 ff.
[217] Senato Mar III, f. 101a ff., 135b; Jorga, *l.c.*; *Libr. Com.* IV, lib. 14, nos. 83, 87-89; *Dipl. Ven.-Lev.* II, no. 205. In his orders to the governor of Ḥamā the sultan referred explicitly to the cotton trade. In the decree addressed to the governor of Tripoli he ordered that there should not be compulsory purchase of alkali. The Venetians should at first buy a certain

taking of the sultan was not kept. In the same year, 1449, the Venetians were compelled to buy alkali against their will in Tripoli.[218]

However, the agreement between Venice and Djaḳmaḳ in 1449 meant the final renunciation of the pepper monopoly by the sultan. This was a great victory for Venice, which had consequently abstained from any act that could be interpreted as hostile to the sultan. In 1445 the Serenissima refused to grant help to the Knights of Rhodes against the sultan,[219] and the Senate forbade the supply of weapons both to them and to the king of Cyprus.[220] At the end of Djaḳmaḳ's reign, Venice had not only won the long contest with the sultan, but had also become the first commercial power in the Mediterranean and obtained unchallenged supremacy in the Levant trade. When the war with Milan came to an end in 1454, Venice was in control of the greatest part of Lombardy, one of the most advanced countries of mediaeval Europe, which supplied her with considerable quantities of agricultural and industrial products marketable in the Near East.

The commercial exchanges between Genoa and Catalonia with the dominions of the sultan were also often disturbed under the reign of Djaḳmaḳ because of various conflicts, in addition to the attempts of the sultan to monopolize the spice trade. Again the Genoese were made responsible by the sultan for any encroachment by the authorities of Caffa on the purchase of slaves for his army. In 1452 the sultan requested the Genoese in Alexandria to send an envoy to Caffa, because the shipping of slaves from the Genoese colony to Egypt had been disturbed.[221] The Catalans suffered from the reprisals for the activities of the corsairs, who were supported or even armed by the king. The merchants of Barcelona represented by the Council of the town continuously tried to smooth away the conflicts. At the end of the reign of Barsbāy the relations between the Catalans and the Mamluks were very strained. In 1437 the Catalans suffered from extortions, and their consul in Alexandria was mistreated by the Mamluk authorities, so that he died of his wounds, before the sultan had altogether forbidden Catalan ships to visit the ports of his dominions. Having addressed the king in November 1437, concerning the establishment of peaceful relations with the sultan, the Town Council of Barcelona asked the king in April 1438 to appoint Pere Muntros as consul in Alexandria and also as royal

---

quantity from the sultan's agent and thereupon trade of this article should be free (to be added to Predelli's résumé). As to the undertaking to buy a certain quantity of alkaki from the sultan, there was a quarrel between the ambassador and Marino Priuli, the consul of Alexandria, who accomplished the mission together with him. Tiepolo opposed this undertaking; see *Libr. Com.* IV, lib. 14, no. 120.

[218] Senato Mar III, f. 157a.

[219] Thiriet, *Rég.* III, p. 123 f.

[220] *Op.cit.*, p. 134.

[221] Tur II, f. 14b ff., 17b f.

ambassador to the sultan. The Council asked that the king curb the activities of the corsairs and abolish the customs levied on export to Egypt.[222] King Alfonso V agreed to the first request and gave Muntros the credentials. Meanwhile Sultan Barsbāy died; his successor, Djaḳmaḳ, received the Catalan envoy with courtesy and also addressed a friendly letter to the Town Council of Barcelona.[223]

However, at the same time there was fear in Egypt of new attacks by the Catalan war fleet on the Syrian coast,[224] and in August 1439 there was indeed a raid on Rosetta.[225] A month later there was a naval battle between the corsairs and Moslem forces off Beirut, resulting in a crushing defeat of the latter.[226] So the naval war had begun again. In August 1440 the Mamluk government despatched fifteen galleys against the corsairs, who had captured Moslem merchantmen.[227] Certainly one cannot be sure that all these acts of piracy and raids were really activities of the Catalans, but many of them probably were. In 1441 a Castilian galley captured a Moslem ship in the port of Beirut. The inhabitants of Tripoli fled to the mountains, fearing an attack, but the raiders sailed to the coast of Egypt and attacked at-Tīna, where they captured two ships.[228]

But the Catalan merchants tenaciously continued their trade with the dominions of the Mamluks, and the post of Catalan consul in Alexandria was always filled by a competent person. In 1444 the Town Council of Barcelona appointed Johan Gavarro to the post of consul in Alexandria.[229] In the 1440's there were fewer attacks by the Catalans on the coasts of Egypt and Syria, and the Mamluks took the initiative in the contest over political supremacy in the Eastern Mediterranean, making several expeditions against Rhodes, which was always supported by the king of Aragon. But, nevertheless, the commercial exchanges between Catalonia and the dominions of the sultan of Cairo did not go on unhampered. They suffered from the reprisals provoked by the misdeeds and acts of violence committed by some merchants. At the end of 1445 some Catalan merchants were imprisoned in Alexandria because they were guarantors for other Catalans

[222] López de Meneses, "Consulados," p. 118; Capmany, 2.1, no. 321, pp. 468-469.

[223] Capmany, 2.1, no. 316, p. 463. The date 1437 is obviously mistaken. The signature of Djaḳmaḳ proves that instead of Shawwāl 840 it should be Shawwāl 842, i.e., 1439, for Djaḳmaḳ ascended to the throne on 9 September 1438; cf. Darrag, *Barsbay*, p. 347.

[224] *Sulūk* IV, p. 1112; Ibn Iyās[2] II, p. 208.

[225] *Op.cit.*, p. 1165, copied in *an-Nudjūm az-zāhira* VII, p. 106.

[226] *Sulūk* IV, p. 1170; Ibn Ḥadjar, MS. Yeni Čami 814, f. 274b. See also as-Sakhāwī, Cont. to *Duwal al-islām* of adh-Dhahabī, MS. Bodl. 843, f. 180a.

[227] *Sulūk* IV, p. 1,205 f.; *an-Nudjūm az-zāhira* VII, p. 112; ʿAbdalbāsiṭ, MS. Vat. Arab. 728, f 5b, 8b; ʿAbdalbāsiṭ 812, f. 32b; Ibn Iyās[2] II, p. 224.

[228] *Sulūk* IV, p. 1,227; ʿAbdalbāsiṭ, MS. Vat. Ar. 728, f. 17a.

[229] Coll Juliá, "Aspectos del corso catalan," p. 163; López de Meneses, "Los consulados," p. 119.

who had bought spices from the "merchant of the sultan" and had departed without paying the price, amounting to not less than 9,000 ducats. Luis Sirvent and some other merchants had apparently bought these spices for the Great Master of the Knights of Rhodes and had departed for the island. Johan de Camos, probably vice-consul of the Catalans in Alexandria, therefore appealed to the Town Council of Barcelona on 23 October 1445, to take measures for the settlement of the affair.[230] At the end of the same year another Catalan merchant provoked a new conflict with the Mamluk authorities. It was Gabriel Ortigues, who was also a veteran Levant trader.[231] He came with a galley of his own to Alexandria and not far from the port captured a Moslem ship, taking prisoner the merchants who were travelling on it. Thereupon Johan de Camos, Pere Dez Pla, and other Catalans were arrested in retaliation, and the galley of Johan de Camos and its cargo were sequestered. This galley was a state galley and its cargo had a very great value, amounting to more than 70,000 ducats, according to Johan de Camos. Further, the merchants had put merchandise and money amounting to 10,000-12,000 ducats in the Catalan fondaco. Despite the intervention of the Great Master of Rhodes, Johan de Camos and the other merchants remained in jail until December 1446, when they could escape.[232]

In 1446 the king of Aragon, always stimulated by the merchants of Barcelona, made a new bid to conclude peace with the sultan, perhaps hoping to check the Ottomans by his forces. But, in the tradition of his predecessors, he made very demanding proposals of the sultan. He asked for not less than 200,000 ducats as reparations for his expenses during the hostilities. Further, he claimed the right to send two round ships and two big galleys of his own to the dominions of the sultan every year to carry on trade (clearly without paying customs).[233] Needless to say, the proposal was turned down. Then, in 1448, the Town Council of Barcelona again asked the king to take the initiative to conclude peace with the sultan.[234]

Meanwhile the naval war went on. At the end of the 1440's Catalan corsairs were very active in all regions of the Mediterranean and endangered commercial shipping everywhere. Time and again Venice had to despatch her warships against them.[235] The recrudescence of the corsairs' activities was connected with the policy of Alfonso V. From 1440 he protected King

[230] Capmany, 2.1, no. 350, pp. 507-08.

[231] He already engaged in trade in Alexandria in 1428; see Tur IV, f. 62a, 62b f.

[232] Coll Juliá, *art.cit.*, p. 163 f. On the galley of Joh. de Camos, see Del Treppo, p. 627 f., cf. p. 438. About the escape of Camos from the prison in 1346, see *Dietari del Capella d'Anfos el Magnanim*, ed. J. Sanchis i Sivera (Valencia, 1932), p. 187.

[233] ACA, Cancill. Real 2653, c. 123b/124a and cf. C. Marinescu, "Alfonso le Magnanime, protecteur d'un rival du commerce catalan, Jacques Coeur. Pourquoi?" *EHM* III (1953), p. 47 f. About the political requests of King Alfonso V, see Marinescu, *L'île de Rhodes*, p. 390; answer of the king to the sultan's letter: ACA, Cancill. Real 2542, f. 18a f.

[234] Capmany, 2.1, no. 363, pp. 526-27.

[235] Thiriet, *Rég.* III, p. 142 f., 148.

John II of Cyprus, and in 1447 he intervened on his behalf with the sultan. The sultan was inclined to peace.[236] But his efforts were frustrated. The Catalans stuck to their aggressive policy. In 1450 four Moslem ships which had come from Turkey and carried heavy cargoes of wheat, flour, and other commodities were captured off Rosetta. According to Arabic sources, the cargoes had the value of 100,000 ducats. Then, in 1451, a Christian flotilla raided Tyre and sacked the little town. Finally, having been repulsed, the raiders sailed to the Egyptian coast and attacked at-Tina.[237] The Catalan forces under the command of Bernat Villamari also attacked the port of Alexandria in 1451 and captured a Moslem ship there. The Catalan consul in Alexandria tried to negotiate its restitution.[238]

As at other times in the same year, the king of Aragon offered the sultan peace, though making proposals in the tradition of the kings of Aragon. He sent Luis de Sant'Angelo as ambassador to Cairo to propose peace (or a truce) for five years on the following conditions: the sultan should oblige himself to buy from the king every year 10,000 quintals of soap worth 100,000 ducats, 5,000 djarwī ḳinṭār hazelnuts for 125,000 ducats, and 3,000 butts of olive oil for 90,000 ducats. The commercial agents of the king should enjoy freedom of trade, e.g., they should not be compelled to buy or to sell, and this undertaking should also apply to precious stones. The Catalan merchants should pay the same customs as the subjects of the sultan in the dominions of the Crown of Aragon. Finally the sultan should oblige himself not to wage war against Cyprus and Rhodes.[239]

One can easily imagine what an impression such proposals made on the sultan. They were, indeed, another facet of the expansionist and aggressive policy of Alfonso V. It was a policy diametrically opposite to that which the Venetians pursued, and it was certainly one of the reasons for the decline of Catalan trade with the Moslem Levant.

c. Successful Trade Despite Pressure

Just as Venice had withstood the brunt of the sultan's onslaught on the freedom of trade, she also derived the greatest profit from the increase of the commercial exchanges with the Levant. The second quarter of the fifteenth century was a period of great growth of her Levant trade despite the almost endless vexations by the Mamluk authorities.

[236] Bānescu, *Le déclin de Famagouste*, p. 29, 30.

[237] *Ḥawādith*, pp. 96, 109; as-Sakhāwī, *at-Tibr al-masbūk* (Būlāḳ 1896), p. 323 f. 350 f. Egypt suffered from scarcities at that time; see my "Quelques problèmes que soulève l'histoire des prix dans l'Orient médiéval," p. 208. Therefore wheat was imported, as-Sakhāwī, *op.cit.*, p. 350 f.

[238] Tur II, f. 24b; Soldevila, *Historia de Catalunya* II, p. 677. Marinescu, *L'île de Rhodes*, p. 394.

[239] ACA, Cancill. Real 2697, c. 103b-105b; cf. Marinescu, "Alfonso le Magnanime," *l.c.*

The upswing of the Levant trade of Venice was probably to a great extent the effect of the abundance of spices at relatively low prices on the Levantine market, a factor which facilitated their marketing in Europe. This is a fact alluded to or explicitly stated in several contemporary sources.[240] Speaking of the year 1430, the chronicler Morosini says: "I would like to remark that for many years so much spice and other commodities had not come to Venice."[241] Not only the galleys, but also the cogs, carried heavy loads of spices to Venice.[242] As in earlier periods, very often hundreds of parcels of spices for which no place had been found in the galleys remained in Alexandria and Beirut.[243] The statement of the chronicler about the abundance of spices is also borne out by the fact that very often special galleys had to be despatched by the Venetian government to collect those that had been shipped to Candia and Modon or even to Rhodes and Corfu and to transport them to the metropolis.[244] The stocks of spices kept in the storehouses of the Venetian colonies were indeed very great. In 1430, 1,600 parcels (pondi) of spices had been brought to Candia and Modon.[245] In 1441, three galleys were sent to Candia and three others to Modon to collect spices.[246] In 1448 one galley was despatched to Modon to collect spices and another to Cyprus.[247]

The abundance of spices was certainly one of the reasons for the remarkable decline of their prices on the Levantine markets. But it was only one of them. Another reason was the deflationary trend of the Near Eastern economies and the decline in the demand for these relatively costly articles in the Levantine countries. The decline of domestic prices certainly induced the merchants to be more flexible when dealing with the Europeans. The curve of the pepper price in Egypt in the first half of the fifteenth century sheds a good light on this phenomenon.

From this Table XXIX it can be seen that the price of pepper, which had risen greatly from 1410, remained high in the 1420's. In 1423-1425 it even reached a new peak, viz. 120-130 dinars. Then from 1428 it went down and was 70-100 ashrafis the sporta until the 1440's. The high price of pepper in the 1430's, however, was caused by the transactions of the sultan. When the commercial price was 70 ashrafis, he compelled the Moslems

[240] *Chron. Morosini*, c. 550, 559; *Zancaruola* c. 546a; Mag. Cons. Uursa f. 55b.

[241] *Chron. Morosini*, c. 515.

[242] *Op.cit.*, c. 516.

[243] Marino Sanuto, *Vite*, c. 1021; *Chron. Morosini, c. 506.*

[244] *Chron. Morosini*, c. 434 (a. 1426); Misti 56 f. 119a (a. 1427) (but cf. f. 126a f.) 57, f. 27a f. (a. 1428) 137b f. (a. 1492), 181b (a. 1430), 60, f. 51a (a. 1438) (cf. Thiriet, *Rég.* II, p. 247, 252). About the cargo of these galleys, see *Chron. Morosini*, c. 515: a galley carried 1,300 colli spices from Modon in 1430.

[245] *Chron. Morosini*, c. 525.

[246] Thiriet, *Rég.* III, p. 89 f.; see also there p. 94 about the measures taken in 1442.

[247] *Op.cit.*, p. 146 (in that year, however, the service of the Beirut galleys had been suspended).

Table XXIX Price of pepper in Alexandria[a], *first half of the XVth century*

date	price of a sporta	source
April 1403	75 din.	Dat 928, letter of Com. of Zanobi di Taddeo Gaddi of 9 May 1403
29 Sept. 1403	75 "	Ibid., letter of the same of 17 Nov. 1403[b]
Oct. 1403	74 "	Ibid., letter of the same of 24 Nov. 1403
Nov. 1403	74 "	Dat. 714, Anonymous letter of 9 Feb. 1404
begin. May 1404	86 "	Dat 715, letter of Ser Giov. di Ser Nigi & Gherardo Davizi of 28 June 1404
(Sept.?) 1404	81 "	Ibid., letter of the same of 31 Oct. 1404
begin. of XVth cent. 1405 (?)	140 "	G.P., Sent. VII, f. 76b ff[c]; same series 27, f. 59a ff.[d]
March 1410	75 "	Ainaud, Quatre doc., doc. III
Nov. 1410	110 "	Art. cit., doc. IV
1411	95-96 din.	G.P., Sent. 32, f. 114b f[e].
1411	104.8 "	Accounts Soranzo c. 30b
1412	170.25 "	Ibid. c. 36a.
fall fair 1412	the Moslem merchants want 240 then 220 din.	Ibn Hadjar II, p. 521
1412	225 din.	G.P., Sent. 19, f. 88a f.[f]
March 1413	220 "	Suluk IV, p. 253
2 March 1414	160 "	Arch. B. Dolfin, Ba 180, fasc. 14
fall fair 1416	110 "	G.P., Sent. 78, f. 99b
1417	120 "	Accounts Zane
1418	97 "	Arch. B. Dolfin, Ba 181, fasc. 13, 23[g]
1418	98 "	Ibid.
1418	99 "	Ibid.
1418	100 "	Ibid.
1418	101 "	Ibid.
29 Aug. 1418	106 "	Arch. B. Dolfin, Ba 181, fasc. 15
1418	150 "	Ibid. fasc. 23
18 Oct. 1418	100 din.	Ibid.
1 Nov. 1418	98 "	Ibid.
31 March 1419	97-101 din.	Ibid.
18 Nov. 1419	160 din.	Ibid.
1419	160 "	Arch. B. Dolfin, Ba 180, fasc. 15
1421	70 "	G.P., Sent. 34, f. 37b
1421	85 "	same series 56, f. 38a ff. cf. 41a
1421	82 "	same series 38, f. 39b ff[h]
2 May 1422	108 "	price lists Lor. Dolfin
summer 1422	110 "	G.P. 34, f. 11a ff.

Table XXIX (continued)

date	price of a sporta	source
Nov. 1422	120 "	Sapori, Studi III, p. 21[i]
" "	120, 122, 123, 125 dinars	ASF, Accounts Bened. Strozzi
1433	125-126 din.	Morosini c. 394 f. 2a, 33a
2 Feb. 1423	121-124, 130 "	price lists Lor. Dolfin
16 March 1424	130 din.	Arch. Lor. Dolfin, letter of Nic. Bernardo, of the same date[j]
1425	Cairo by barter 110 din., commercial price 107-108	Crist. del Fiore I, f. 19a
25 July 1425	delivered on the ship 113 din.	Ibid. f. 2a[k]
4 Oct. 1425	delivered on the ship 130 din.	Ibid. f. 4a f.
1426	72 duc.	G.P., Sent. 52, f. 142b f.
fall fair 1426	by barter 80 duc.	same series 54, f. 34a ff., 36a ff.[l]
1426(?)	1 pondo 80 duc.	same series 45, f. 108b f.[m]
3 May 1427	by barter 80 duc.	Tur IV, f. 18b
4 June 1427	76 duc., delivered on the ship 78	Ibid., f. 23b ff.
Sept. 1427	100 duc.	Ibid., f. 40a ff.[n]
Nov. 1427[o]	77-79 duc.	Ibid., l. c.
20 Nov. 1427	76-77 "	l. c.
6 Dec. 1427	76-78 "	Ibid., f. 40b f.
26 Aug. 1428	55 duc.	" f. 77b
26 Aug. 1428	72 "	" f. 78a
1428(?)	70 "	G.P., Sent. 46, f. 25b ff.[p]
Oct. 1428	80 ashrafis	Suluk IV, p. 791
before 1432	109 duc.	G.P., Sent. 60, f. 177a ff
1429	70 "	same series 69, f. 66a f.
Feb. 1430	in Cairo 50, in Alex. 59-64 ashr.	Suluk IV, p. 824
Jan. 1432	73.5 duc.	Morosini c. 569
1432(?)	70 duc.	G.P., Sent. 86, f. 39a f.
1432	110 "	same series 64, f. 8a f[r]
1433	100 "	same series 66, f. 136a ff.
Sept. 1434	80 "	Tur V, f. 8b ff.
1435	125 "	G.P., Sent. 70, f. 37a ff. 102a
1436	Ven. embassy empowered to buy at 100 duc.	ROL VI, p. 372
Begin. of 1436	86 duc., delivered on the ship 90 bought secretly at less than 90	G.P., Sent. 74, f. 51b ff.
1436	70 duc.	same series 125, f. 181a
fall fair 1436	100 "	same series 76, f. 46a ff., 61b ff.
1437	108 "	G.P., Sent. 82, f. 9a f.
before 1440	100-120 din.	Uzzano, p. 111
1439	70 duc.	ROL VI, p. 422
before 1442	61.25 duc.	G.P., Sent. 87, f. 98b ff.[s]
1440	40.5 "	same series 100, f. 6a ff.[t]

Table XXIX (continued)

date	price of a sporta	source
spring 1442	60 "	Krekié, no. 989[u]
1442(?)	56 "	G.P., Sent. 97, f. 60a ff.[v]
1443	38-40 duc.	same series 96, f. 106b f.
1443(?)	48 "	same series 98, f. 117b ff.[w]
1443(?)	delivered on the ship 50 duc.	same series 100, f. 40a[x]
1443	1 collo 100 duc.	same series 102, f. 84b f.[y]
1444	55 duc., delivered on the ship 59	same series 117, f. 206a ff.[z]
Oct. 1444	delivered on the ship 60 duc., but also 97 was paid	same series 107, f. 188 ff.[a']
1444(?)	70 duc.	same series 114, f. 77a[b']
1444(?)	58.5 duc.	same series 102, f. 84b f.[c']
1445	68.6 duc.	Carat. Vet. 1552, f. 128a
1445	55 "	G.P., Sent. 105, f. 136b ff.
1445	delivered on the ship 45 duc.	G.P., Straordnario Nod. 18, f. 30b[d']
1445	1 pondo 75 duc.	G.P., Sent. 102, f. 79a f.[e']
1445	1 collo 70 "	same series 104, f. 101b f.[f']
1447	55 duc.	Arch. Bouches-du Rhône, Verdillon 143, f. 101-102
1448	delivered on the ship 45 duc., by barter 55	G.P., Sent. 107, f. 129a ff.[g']
1448	56 duc.	same series, 108, f. 68a ff.[h']

a) This table contains only commercial prices, those referring to the prices at which the sultan sold to Moslems and Europeans by force have been omitted. The notes to data quoted in my paper Spice prices are not repeated here. For the meaning of pondo, see my paper The Volume of Lev. trade, p. 574 ff.

b) It is not said in the letter that the price in Alexandria is given, but there can be no doubt about it.

c) This is quoted from the proceedings of a law suit in 1405.

d-f) See Spice prices, Table I and the notes.

g) The document from which the following data of 1418 are quoted has been published in my paper The Volume of Levantine trade, p. 598. It bears the date of 27 Oct. 1418, another copy of it has the date 18 Oct. 1418.

h-i) See Spice prices, Table I and notes.

j) Melis, Doc., p. 190 quoting this letter has 125-130, but I found in the original 130.

k-m) See Spice prices, Table I and notes.

n) This is not the commercial price, but an offer made due to exceptional conditions.

o) This is the price at which the Genoese bought after the departure of the Venetian galleys.

p-t) See Spice prices, Table I and notes.

u) This price includes the expenses in Alexandria and also the freight.

v-z, a'-c') See Spice prices, Table I and notes.

d') The pepper had been bought from another Venetian.

e'-h') See Spice prices, Table I and notes.

and the Europeans to buy it for 100. In the fifth decade of the century, the price was very low, 50-60 ashrafis or even less. The curve of the prices of ginger, second only to pepper among the spices exported by the European merchants, was similar. In the later 1430's it cost half the price that it had been in the preceding two decades. The prices of several other spices and aromata moved in the same direction: they went down in the middle of the fifteenth century.[248]

The decline of the spice prices on the Levantine markets in the middle of the fifteenth century was certainly an advantage for the Venetians, who had become the suppliers of the Indian articles to the greater part of Europe. It must have stimulated them to greater investments in this branch of the Levant trade. This does not mean that other sectors of Venice's international trade were neglected or that the merchants who had engaged in it went over to the export of spices from Egypt and Syria. Venetian trade in the formerly Byzantine territories flourished again in the second quarter of the fifteenth century. A Venetian chronicler recounts that in 1425 the Romania galleys came back with a cargo of silk, spices, and slaves worth 300,000-350,000 ducats[249] and that the cargo of the Romania galleys in 1430, too, had a value of 350,000 ducats.[250] The cargo in 1432 (in fact, they arrived in Venice in 1433) comprised 800 pondi spices and more silk, slaves, 400 sacks cotton, plus wax and other commodities. Merchandise worth 50,000 ducats (mostly furs and slaves) had remained in Tana. The value of the merchandise bought in Trebizond alone amounted to 400,000 ducats. According to this chronicler, the total value of their cargoes, without that of the silk purchased in Tana and that of the slaves, amounted to not less than 750,000 ducats.[251]

But, as in preceding periods, the cargoes of the Romania galleys consisted predominantly of furs and slaves and of rather small quantities of spices.[252] In any case, the data quoted above show that the second quarter of the fifteenth century was indeed a period of great economic expansion in the history of Venice. Even the commercial exchanges of Venice with the Balkans increased considerably.[253] The main artery of Venice's trade in Europe was still the axis Venice-Nürnberg, and many data point to the fact that despite the attempts of King (then Emperor) Sigismund to cut off trade between Venice and the towns of Upper Germany it went on. The great

[248] Ashtor, "Spice prices," p. 32, 33 (ginger, cloves); *Hist. des prix et des sal.*, p. 419 (frankincense), 420 f. (nutmeg), 421 f. (cubeb, cardamom); for the influence of the sultan's transactions see *Sulūk* IV, p. 1004.

[249] *Chron. Morosini*, c. 494.

[250] *Op.cit.*, c. 522.

[251] *Op.cit.*, c. 593.

[252] *Op.cit.*, c. 403, 527; Misti 60, f. 87b ff.

[253] See *Libr. Com.* IV, lib. 11, no. 125 lib. 13, no. 262.

merchant families of Nürnberg, the Rummel, Imhof, Koler, Kress, and others, had their permanent agents in Venice, and the number of the German merchants residing in Venice became so great that in 1434 a special chapel with a German chaplain was founded there. The traders of Nürnberg marketed the spices bought in Venice not only in Upper Germany, but also in Northwestern Europe, in Northern Germany, and in the countries of Eastern Europe.[254] The war in Lombardy sometimes interfered with the Levant trade, but the difficulties arising from this were successfully overcome.[255]

Despite the long contest with the sultan, Venice maintained the galley services to Alexandria and Beirut. Both lines functioned quite regularly, except in some years when they were suspended to retaliate against the sultan. If we compared the totals of the galleys that visited the ports of Egypt and Syria in the second quarter of the fifteenth century[256] with those of the end of the fourteenth century and the beginning of the fifteenth century, it will be seen that they were greater in the 1390's and in the

[254] See Thiriet, *Rég.* III, p. 69. About the contacts of Sigismund with the Levantine rulers, see W. v. Stromer, "Eine Botschaft des Turkmenenfürsten Qara Yuluq an König Sigismund auf dem Nürnberger Reichstag im März 1431," *Jahrbuch für fränkische Landesforschung* 22 (1962), p. 431 ff., and about his embargo upon trade with Venice and the implementation and the steps made by the merchants of Nürnberg, see H. Simonsfeld, *Der Fondaco dei Tedeschi* I, nos. 334, 335, 336, 350, 359 II, p. 45, 46; v. Stromer, *Die Nürnberger Handelsgesellschaft Gruber-Podmer-Stromer im 15. Jahrhundert* (Nürnberg, 1963) (Nürnberger Forschungen VII), p. 108; about the trade of the merchants of Nürnberg in Venice, see the list of merchants of Nürnberg in Venice apud Simonsfeld, *op.cit.* II, p. 74 ff. and see, further, v. Stromer, *op.cit.*, p. 69, about sale of spices by the traders of Nürnberg in Leipzig, p. 119; see, further, H. Ammann, *Die wirtschaftliche Stellung der Reichsstadt Nürnberg im Spätmittelalter* (Nürnberg, 1970), (Nürnberger Forschungen 13), p. 173; about the trade of the merchants of Nürnberg in Leipzig, see E. Kroker, *Handelsgeschichte der Stadt Leipzig* (Leipzig, 1925), p. 41 f.; of course merchants of other towns of Germany also carried on trade with Venice; see A. Dietz, *Frankfurter Handelsgeschichte* (Frankfurt-on-the-Main, 1910-1925) I, p. 253 ff.; about the trade between Ulm and Venice, partly by interposition of agents of the traders of Nürnberg, see G. M. Thomas, "Beitrage aus dem Ulmer Archiv zur Geschichte des Handelsverkehrs zwischen Venedig und der deutschen Nation," *SBW der Kgl. Bayr. Akademie* 1869, I, pp. 285, 286.

[255] The opposition of the Church to trade with the Moslems was no longer a great obstacle, although Venice (like the other trading nations) still applied for licenses. But this had become a formality. In 1425 Venice obtained permission to trade with the Moslems for 25 years, see *Libr. Com.* IV, lib. 11, no. 199. Then, in 1445, the Senate gave orders to the ambassador at the Holy See to intervene with the pope, who had laid an embargo on the trade with the Moslem Levant because of the attack of the Mamluks on Rhodes; see Jorga, *ROL* VIII, p. 8.

[256] The following table sums up the data contained in my "The Venetian supremacy," p. 18, and see there Table V. The following corrections have been made: in 1424, 1426, and 1434, a supplementary galley (*galea di rata*) was dispatched to Beirut; see *Chron. Morosini*, c. 412; Jorga, *ROL* V, p. 327, and Misti 58, f. 67b. The joint convoys in 1429 and 1432 (actually sailing in January 1433) were supplemented by a *galea di rata*; see *Chron. Morosini*, c. 504 and Misti 58, f. 159b ff., 181a f. In 1436 4 galleys were sent to Alexandria and 3 to Beirut, see Misti 59, f. 170b ff., 173a. In 1437 4 galleys were despatched to Alexandria, see Misti 60, f. 29a ff.

Table XXX Decennial totals of Venetian Levant galleys, 1381-1450

	Alexandria	Beirut	Joint convoy	total
1381-1390	14	35		49
1391-1400	29	46		75
1401-1410	30	28		58
1411-1420	34	37		71
1421-1430	23	31	7	61
1431-1440	25	24	13	62
1441-1450	34	27		61

decade 1411-1420. But at the end of the fourteenth century, the number of the Beirut galleys considerably surpassed that of the Alexandria galleys, which were much bigger.[257] In the second quarter of the fifteenth century, the number of the galleys commuting on the two lines was equal (82 on each).

That Venice's trade with the dominions of the Mamluks flourished in this period is convincingly shown by the results of the auctions of the galley lines to the Levant (Table XXXI). These data give evidence of the great upswing of the Venetian spice trade in 1422-1426, followed by a crisis which was particularly oppressive in 1435-1439. In the 1440's Venice's spice trade prospered again. The comparison of the data in Table XXXI with the amounts yielded by the galley auctions at the end of the fourteenth century and in the first two decades of the fifteenth century is very instructive.[258] One sees that in the immediately preceding period the auctions of the Alexandria and Beirut galleys (together) rarely yielded 1,000 lire di grossi or more. In the 1420's and the 1440's they often yielded 1200-1600. The sums obtained in those years were equal to those reached in the years of the great boom in the 1390's or even more.

From the various data referring to the Venetian cotton trade in Syria, one would draw similar conclusions. The activities of the Venetians in Syria were hampered by the interminable extortions by the Mamluk officials, who were much more daring in provinces distant from the capital. Secondly, cotton prices were high until the 1440's. However, in the fifth decade of the fifteenth century, a North Syrian ḳinṭār of cotton cost 16-20 ashrafis, against 50-60 in the first two decades of the century, and 30-40 in the 1420's.[259] But, unlike spice prices, cotton prices were not elastic because one could purchase cotton in several other countries: in Turkey, in Cyprus,

[257] See my remark in "The Venetian supremacy," p. 22 note 78.
[258] See above, Tables VI, XXVII.
[259] See below Table.

Table XXXI Auctions of the Venetian Levant galleys[a], 1422 - 1452

year	Alexandria	line to Beirut	Romania	source
1422	521[11]	643[14]	454[3]	Misti 54, f., 35b, 36b; Thiriet, Rég. II, p. 195
1423	624[6]	955[12]	89[12]	Misti 54, f. 116b, 117b, 118b, cf. Thiriet II, p. 204
1424	314[19]	1295[7]	214	Misti 55, f. 28a, 32a, 33b, 46a; Morosini c. 411, 412; Thiriet II, p. 217.
1425	June convoy	856[5]	66[10]	Misti 55, f. 120a, 122b; Morosini c. 422/3; Thiriet II, p. 228
	203[6]	360[19]		Misti 55, f. 150b; Morosini c. 424
1426	779[8]	632	30[8]	Misti 56, f. 34a, 36a; Morosini c. 448; Thiriet II, p. 235
1427	-	-	34[7]	Thiriet II, p. 243
1428	723[6]	495[18]	80[13]	Misti 57, f. 13a, 15a; Morosini c. 485; Thiriet II, p. 249
1429	1176[5]		246[10]	Misti 57, f. 104b, 118b; Morosini c. 502; Thiriet II, p. 260
1430	166[1]	359[14]	-	Misti 57, f. 225b
1431	587[14]		55[7]	Misti 58, f. 71a; Thiriet III, p. 13f.
1432			242[5]	Misti 58, f. 119a, cf. Thiriet III, p. 22
1433	January convoy 1045[8][b]			Misti 58, f. 160a
	1 additional galley 60[12][c]			Ibid. f. 181b
			241[2]	Misti 58, f. 204a, cf. Thiriet III, p. 30
	additional galley 182[19]			Misti 58, f. 214b.
1434	728[7]	1013[9]	332[2]	Misti 59, f. 53a, 57b, 59a, 67b
		spring convoy 206[15]		Misti 59, f. 90b
	286[3]	249[10]	440[10]	Misti 59, f. 120a, 121a; Thiriet III, p. 47
1436	520[2]	552[18]	180[12]	Misti 59, f. 170b, 171b, Thiriet III, p. 51 f.
1437	713[18]		384[6]	Misti 60, f. 29; Thiriet III, p. 58.
1438	-	-	394[17]	Thiriet III, p. 68.
1439	385[7]	527[19]	415[5]	Misti 60, f. 148a, 224a, 224b; Thiriet III, p. 83.
1440	536[11]	753[5]	252[1]	Misti 60, f. 213b, 224a/b.
1441			393[6]	Thiriet III, p. 88.
1442	770[12]	427[12]	495[12]	Mar I, f. 103b, 104a; Thiriet III. p. 93.
1443	810[12]	766[11]	568[19]	Mar I, f. 171b, 177a, 178a; Thiriet III, p. 102

Table XXXI (continued)

date	Alexandria	line to Beirut	Romania	source
1445	952^{3}	768^{18}	Cyprus: 130^{8} 73^{6}	Mar. II, f. 77a, 85a, 85b; Thiriet III, p. 125
1446	744^{1} duc.	717^{9} duc.	539^{6} duc.	Mar. II, f. 153b, 154b; Thiriet III, p. 131.
1447	595^{14} duc.	-	737^{7} duc. 60^{1} duc.	Thiriet III, p. 138.
1448	1033^{13} "	-	751^{8} duc.$_{5}$	Mar III, f. 72a; Thiriet III, p. 144, 146.
1449	569^{9} "	667^{10} duc.	580^{15} duc.	Mar III, f. 142a, Thiriet III, p. 150.
1450	612^{6} "	383^{9} duc.	649 33^{8} duc.	Mar III, f. 142a; Thiriet III, p. 156, 157.
1451	264^{9} "	600^{7} duc.	297	Mar IV f. 63a, 64b; Thiriet III, p. 165f.
1452	729^{10}	715^{2} duc.	596^{6} duc. 61^{3} duc.	Mar IV, f. 118a, 134a, 135a; Thiriet III, p. 174.

a) The amount yielded by the auctions are given in lire di grossi, equal to 10 ducats each. From 1446 the fractions are given in ducats. The figures given by Thiriet have been corrected according to the sources.

b) Six of these galleys should transport spices, four cotton.

c) Two additional galleys were auctioned, one for the transport of spices and one for cotton. One yielded 61, the other 60^{4} pounds of grossi.

in Sicily, and elsewhere. Not only the Genoese but also the Venetians themselves still exported cotton from Egypt in the 1440's.[260] In addition, the conflict between Venice and Emperor Sigismund sometimes impeded the export of cotton to Southern Germany. So the total of the purchases of cotton in Syria decreased in that period as far as the quantity was concerned. When the spring convoy of 1428 brought 4,000-4,500 sacks of raw cotton to Venice, a Venetian chronicler remarked that this was an exceedingly rich cargo. In the fall of 1431 the great Venetian merchant Andrea Barbarigo expected that a convoy of six cotton ships would carry 3,000 sacks to Venice.[261] In the preceding period such a shipment was not considered extraordinary. But the cotton trade in Syria was still a flourishing branch of Venice's trade. In the spring of 1426, 1,300 sacks of cotton, which had been bought by the Venetians and could not be shipped to Venice because there was no place in the cogs, remained in Syria.[262] The two convoys of cotton ships sailed regularly every year to Syria, one late in January and the other at the end of July. Table XXXII shows that in this period the spring convoy of the Syria cogs consisted mostly of seven to nine ships and that of the fall of two to four. Sometimes a convoy of cotton

[260] Misti 58, f. 167b.

[261] *Chron. Morosini*, c. 487; Lane, *Barbarigo*, p. 63.

[262] Misti 56, f. 25a f.

Table XXXII Venetian cotton cogs[a], 1422 - 1452

year		Syria cogs	Alexandria cogs	source
1422	fall	2		Morosini c. 388
1423	spring	8		Morosini c. 393
	fall	2		" c. 400
1424	spring	7-8		Morosini c. 406; Misti 54, f. 184b
1425	spring	8		Morosini c. 419
1426	spring	7		Coll., Not. VI, f. 16b; Morosini c. 432; Zancaruola c. 517a; Misti 55, f. 181a ff.
	fall	4		Morosini c. 444, 447[c] Misti 56, f. 16b f., 25a f.
1427	spring	9		Coll. Not. VI. 27b[d]; Morosini c. 459; Misti 56, f. 71a ff.
	fall	7	2	Coll., Not. VI, f. 36b; Morosini c. 469[e]; Misti 56, f. 104a ff.; ROL V, p. 361.
1428	spring	7	2	Coll., Not. VI, f. 45b; Morosini c. 478 cf. 487[f]; Misti 56, f. 141b, 154b.
	fall	6		Morosini c. 487.
1429	spring	9		Morosini c. 495 cf. 506.
	fall	2	1	Op. cit. c. 504; Misti 47, f. 139a, 139b.
1430	spring	3		Morosini c. 522.
	fall	3	1	Coll., Not. VI, f. 84a; Morosini c. 523; Zancaruola c. 536b; Misti 57, f. 232a cf. ROL VI, p. 81[g]
1431	spring	6		Coll., Not. VI, f. 92a; Morosini c. 534; Zancaruola c. 537b[h]; Misti 58, f. 22a.
	fall	6		Coll., Not. VI, f. 99b; Morosini c. 544, 549; Misti 58, f. 60a ff. 62a, 66a, 72b, 74a; Secreta 12, f. 20b ff.[i]
1432	spring	5		Morosini c. 574.
	fall	6		Zancaruola c. 550a
1433	spring	4 galleys		Misti 58, f. 159a f.
	fall	6		Coll., Not. VI, f. 121b; Morosini c. 606; Misti 58, f. 213a[j]

Table XXXII (continued)

year		Syria cogs	Alexandria cogs	source
1434	spring	free shipping, no convoy		Misti 59, f. 18a
	fall	3		Misti 59, f. 68a.
1438	spring	6		Misti 60, f. 120b
1439	spring	6		Misti 60, f. 119a, 119b, 120b.
1441	spring	6		Coll., Not. VII, f. 23a.
1442	fall	6	2	Zancaruola c. 581a; Chron. Dolfin f. 391b
1443	spring	9		Coll. Not. VII, f. 59a[k]
1444	spring	9		Secreta 16, f. 75a f.
1446	spring	12(?)		Coll., Not. VIII, f. 32b[l]
1447	fall	9		Coll., Not. VIII, f. 61b; ROL VIII, p. 35f.; Senato Mar III, f. 23b
1449	fall	2		Coll., Not. VIII, f. 96b.
1450	spring	14(?)		Coll., Not. VIII, f. 104b[m]

a) The primary source for information on the convoys of the cotton cogs are the registers of the Notatorio of the Collegio, where the ships offered and admitted are booked. Those which had been licensed were marked by a sign (i.e. the names of the patrons). Sometimes galleys were despatched instead of the cogs. The data in the chronicles of Morosini have been summed up by F.C.Lane, The merchant marine of the Venetian Republic, (in) Venice and history, p. 148.

b) But two cogs sailed at an earlier date to Acre and Lattakia, see Misti 55, f. 182a.

c) Coll. Not. VI, f. 23a has only 3 names of patrons.

d) Morosini has 8-10 and 9 names of patrons. The Misti have the names of 5 patrons and Coll. Not. those of 3.

e) Morosini has the names of the patrons of only six ships sailing to Syria and of two sailing to Alexandria.

f) Coll., Not. and Morosini have only 7 names of patrons, probably those who sailed to Syria.

g) Misti has only two ships to Syria and one to Egypt.

h) The convoy sailed both to Egypt and to Syria.

i) Thiriet, Rég. III, p. 14 has only 5.

j) Misti 58, f. 211b, 213a, 228a have 6 ships, but 212a - 7.

k) The patrons cancelled their offer and were obliged by the authorities to sail, but there is no sign of approbation.

l-m) No signs of approbation.

cogs was also sent to Syria in July;[263] and, in addition to the licensed cogs sailing in the convoys, which had certain privileges, there was free shipping.[264] The traffic of private ships cannot have been insignificant altogether, though the bulk of the spices and the cotton was carried by the convoys.

Some important Venetian merchants specialized in the export of cotton from Syria, e.g., the Soranzos. Even in this period, every year they purchased great quantities of cotton in Ḥamā, Latakia, and Tripoli.[265] The heavy loads of Syrian cotton carried to Venice were mainly intended for the fustian industries of Lombardy and Southern Germany, but it was also exported to France and Flanders.[266]

In addition to alkali, the cotton cogs and the other Venetian ships carried various other Syrian commodities, which were industrial products of Syria herself, especially sugar[267] and silk fabrics.[268] Although both the sugar and the silk industries had seriously declined in Syria, the European merchants still bought certain quantities of these products. In addition to these products, spices were the most important group of commodities that the Venetians and other Europeans purchased in Syria. The spices arrived in Syria not only from the Red Sea ports but also from the Persian Gulf. In several letters of this period the Venetian *fattori* in Syria mention the spice caravans coming from Basra.[269] Spices must have been carried to Syria from Ormuz too, as it was then already an important port.[270] They were transported

[263] Misti 56, f. 16b f. (a. 1426).

[264] *Chron. Morosini*, c. 401, 424.

[265] Lorenzo qd. Vettore Soranzo lived from 1432 until 1448 in Northern Syria, mostly in Ḥamā, see Broquière, p. 77; G. P., Sent. 70, f. 26b ff. 107, f. 149b ff. 111, f. 76b f. (but also in Latakia and Tripoli, see G. P., Sent. 107, f. 79b 124, f. 36b f.). Lorenzo fil. Antonio Soranzo carried on trade in Tripoli in 1434, see G. P., Sent. 70, f. 132a ff. Luca Soranzo made large purchases of cotton in Tripoli (and imported velvet) in 1443 and in 1444; see G. P., Sent. 104, f. 84b ff. Vettore, son of Donato Soranzo, bought through agents, cotton in Latakia in 1446 (approximately): see G. P., Sent. 107 f. 185a ff., 192a ff., 109, f. 225a ff., G. P., Straordinario Nodari 18, without pagination, of 9 Sept. 1449. He even exported velvet and camlets to Syria in 1440; see G. P., Sent. 86, f. 74 ff. But he also carried on trade in Alexandria in the 1440's; see G. P., Sent. 86, f. 76a ff. 108, f. 68a ff.

[266] Export to Flanders: *Chron. Morosini*, c. 424 (a. 1425); Misti 57, f. 75a (a. 1429); export to France by the galleys of Aigues-Mortes: Misti 56, f. 15b, 26a, 81a, 159a.

[267] Alkali was exported directly to Turkey; see Badoer, c. 314; about sugar, see *Chron. Morosini*, c. 494, 515.

[268] *Op.cit.*, c. 568; *Libro di mercatantie*, pp. 142, 146.

[269] Arch. Lor. Dolfin, letter of Nic. Bernardo of 8 Febr. 1422 (4,000 pondi spices came from Basra to Damascus); *ibid.*, letter of Zorzi Loredan of 27 March 1424 (the caravan of Basra with 1,200 loads was awaited); Melis, *Doc.*, p. 330 (of 24 March 1425). About the supply of spices from the Ḥidjāz, see Sulūk IV, pp. 755, 791, 965; *an-Nudjūm az-zāhira* VI, p. 624 f., and see also the letter published by Melis, *Doc.* p. 190, and Weil V, pp. 181, 182.

[270] ʿAbdarrazzāḳ b. Isḥāḳ as-Samarḳandī, a diplomat in the service of Shāh Rūkh and author of *Maṭlaʿ as-saʿdayn wa-madjmaʿ al-baḥrayn*, who was in Ormuz in 1441, says that merchants of all countries came there, from Egypt, Syria, and Iraq; see Quatremère, "Notice de l'ouvrage persan . . . Matla-assadein," *Notices et Extraits* 14 (1843), part I, p. 429. The statement may have been exaggerated, but it points to commercial relations with the countries

through Northern Mesopotamia to Northern Syria, and the Venetians also bought spices in Latakia and Ḥamā.[271]

The second quarter of the fifteenth century was a period of great expansion of the Venetian trade in Northern Syria. The Venetians were especially active in Ḥamā, Latakia, Tripoli, and Sarmīn. Ḥamā and Sarmīn were centers of regions where much cotton was planted and there was a Venetian vice-consul in Ḥamā.[272] Latakia was one of the busiest ports of Syria in the 1420's, more important than Tripoli. All the cotton cogs as well as galleys visited it and Venice had a vice-consul there.[273] In 1442 a new Venetian consulate was founded in Tripoli. The new consulate also represented the Venetians in Ḥamā, Latakia, Sarmīn, and Aleppo. Its foundation was considered an important step (since it was clearly planned as a true consulate and not a vice-consulate, like those in other towns of Northern Syria, although their appointees sometimes went by the title of consul). Consequently the Senate asked the sultan to give orders concerning it to the Mamluk governors in Syria.[274] In Palestine too the activities of the Venetians increased considerably in that period. They purchased great quantities of cotton planted in the valley of Esdraelon,[275] and Acre became an important port for the shipping of the cotton of the region. But the Venetians also purchased cotton of the district of Jaffa.[276] The number of days that the Venetian cotton cogs were to anchor in these ports, according to the rules laid down by the Senate, kept increasing. In 1430 a cotton convoy was to anchor five days in Acre, as against six to ten in Latakia; and in 1431, eight days in Acre, against ten days in Latakia and eight days in Tripoli.[277] Some of the Beirut galleys also began to visit Jaffa and Acre. Jaffa is first mentioned in the orders given to the captain of the galley convoy in 1407, when he was to send a galley there for one day. In 1418, this galley was to anchor seven days in Jaffa; in 1434, it was sent to Acre for six days and twice to Jaffa, the first time for one day and the other for six days.[278] The Venetians carried on a lively trade in Acre. Andrea Bar-

---

of the Fertile Crescent. Similar statements were made by Afanasij Nikitin; see *Il viaggio al di là dei tre mari*, Russian text and Ital. transl. by Carlo Verdiani (Florence, 1963), p. 26, and by Giosafa Barbaro, who visited Ormuz in 1475-76, see *I viaggi*, p. 147. Cf. Heyd II, p. 457.

[271] Misti 55, f. 182a, 191b f., 56, f. 41a ff., 141b ff., 159a.

[272] Senato Mar III, f. 31a (a. 1447), and cf. "The Venetian Supremacy," p. 31; for Sarmīn, see above, p. 179.

[273] Misti 55, f. 191b f., 56, f. 41a ff., 104a ff., 57, f. 13b ff., 227a ff., 243a, 58, f. 159a ff. (instructions given to the captains of the convoys of galleys and cotton cogs as to the number of days they should stay in the various Syrian ports).

[274] Senato Mar I, f. 125a ff., and cf. Jorga, *ROL* VII, p. 77.

[275] About the cotton plantations in the Valley of Esdraelon, see Broquiere, p. 185.

[276] Misti 56, f. 17b (a. 1426).

[277] *Chron. Morosini*, c. 520 (a. 1425); Misti 57, f. 243a, 58, f. 22a; Senato Mar III, f. 23b f.

[278] Misti 47, f. 117b ff., 52, f. 101b ff., 59, f. 57b ff.

barigo exported Florentine and English cloth worth 332 ducats to Acre in 1431; in 1433 Venetian, Mantuan, and English cloth whose cost price was 1183.5 ducats; in 1434 Mantuan and English cloth worth 564 ducats. He bought 1881 ducats worth of cotton in Acre in 1434.[279]

The range of commodities that the Venetians imported into the Moslem Levant at that time underwent certain changes. Certainly they continued to market a great deal of copper both from Central Europe and Turkey,[280] soap,[281] molasses,[282] olive oil,[283] chestnuts and hazelnuts and other fruits[284] and also sold weapons in Egypt and Syria, as in earlier periods.[285]

They also continued to import into Egypt and Syria great quantities of cloth of the most different kinds, but in this sector of the Levant trade a new phase began.

Like the other European merchants, the Venetians imported cloth produced in Venice itself,[286] cloth of Florence and Lombardy,[287] Flemish[288] and German,[289] French[290] and Catalan.[291] They shipped velvets, brocades,[292] and other precious silk fabrics to Egypt and Syria, so that in 1450 a German traveller could hear in Damascus that all the silken stuffs offered there were indeed imported from Venice.[293] The fine scarlets were always very much appreciated by the upper classes of the Near Eastern society and, accordingly, they were offered as presents to the sultans and to the high dignitaries.[294] In addition, the Venetians marketed fustian of Cremona and Milan[295] and linen of the latter town.[296]

But the Moslem Levant was then suffering from an economic depression;

[279] Sassi, pp. 222 ff., 236 ff., 242, 248, 250. Cf. Lane, *Barbarigo*, p. 61 ff. and my "Europäischer Handel im spätmittelalterlichen Palästina," *Das Heilige Land im Mittelalter*, (Erlangen, 1980), p. 112 ff.

[280] Tur V, f. 70b f.; Misti 60, f. 143b; Badoer, c. 198, 227, 228, 291.

[281] Misti 55, f. 123b; *Chron. Morosini*, c. 437, 531.

[282] G. P., Sent. 48, f. 5a f., 54, f. 31b ff., 34a ff.; Tur IV, f. 22b, V, f. 70a.

[283] Tur V, f. 31a ff. (imported from Tunisia); Misti 56, f. 104a ff. 57, f. 140a 60, f. 114a; G. P., Sent. 34, f. 11a ff., 48, f. 85a ff., 52, f. 8b f. (from Tunisia) 56, f. 78b ff. (1,100 ḳinṭār for 5.75 din. each!), 58, f. 57b, 74, f. 51b ff.; *Chron. Morosini* c. 493, 499, 503, 519.

[284] *Chron. Morosini*, c. 406, 437, 493, 519, 604; Tur V, f. 29b (from Naples). 63a f. See also Amari, *Dipl. arabi*, p. 202: the commodities characteristic of the Venetian import trade in the Levant are olive oil, soap, almonds, honey, and hazelnuts.

[285] Jorga, *ROL* VIII, p. 21.

[286] Misti 60, f. 204 f.

[287] Uzzano, p. 110, 114; *Libro di mercatantie*, pp. 73, 142, 146.

[288] Misti *l.c.*, and 224a f.

[289] Misti 56, f. 32a ff., 57, f. 13b, 117a, 58, f. 70b, 59 f. 57a, 119b.

[290] *Libro di mercatantie*, *l.c.*

[291] *Op.cit.*, p. 73.

[292] Misti 60, f. 52b, 53a; Tur V, f. 20b; Uzzano, p. 110.

[293] Senato Mar II, f. 33a; Travelogue of Stephan von Gumpenberg in *Reyssbuch des Heyligen Lands* (Francfort, 1609), p. 451.

[294] *Chron. Dolfin*, f. 394a; *Zancaruola*, c. 583b ff.

[295] Misti 60, f. 249b.

[296] Uzzano, p. 110; *Libro di mercatantie*, p. 146.

its economy was characterized by deflation and the impoverishment of broad sections of the population. The decline of prices of various commodities was a striking feature of the economic life, so that the European merchants, among whom the Venetians were most prominent, had to lower the prices of the European cloth they marketed in the Near East and to offer cheap articles. Almost all the data concerning the prices of European cloth sold in Egypt and Syria in that period point to a slow decline.[297] The German cloth that the Venetians offered in the Moslem Levant was generally very cheap, and this was certainly also true of the Polish cloth.[298]

Another phenomenon of the Levant trade in that period was the spread of the use of English cloth. In the second quarter of the fifteenth century, the Venetian merchants (and others too) began to import various kinds of English woolen stuffs into the Moslem Levant, on a large scale. In fact, its import into the Near East had already begun at the beginning of the century, but in the second quarter it increased greatly, and its continuously growing volume was to have far-reaching consequences for the industries and the trade of all Mediterranean countries. The cloth industries of several countries began to decline, so that there ensued unemployment, reduced demand for wool, and a crisis in certain sectors of trade. In some regions, especially in the more industrialized ones, these phenomena had fateful consequences.

Cloth of the Cotswolds was already being imported by Venetians to Damascus in 1405;[299] cloth of Essex (*panni di sex*) figures on price lists of Damascus of the years 1416 and 1417. This cheap article was marketed in the 1440's both in Syria and in Egypt.[300] The cloth called "bastard" was first produced in England and later imitated in Padua and in other towns of Italy.[301] It is mentioned on price lists drawn up in Damascus in 1413, and judicial acts refer to its sale by Venetians in Damascus in 1427 and in the 1440's, in Alexandria in 1441, and in Tripoli in 1452.[302] The cloth called *loesti* is mentioned on price lists of Damascus of 1413 and of Alexandria of 1424, whereas judicial acts refer to its import into Beirut in 1417. Other acts testify to its sale by Venetians in Syria in 1425, 1426 (approximately), 1440 (in Damascus), 1441 (in Latakia and Tripoli), and 1442. Of course it was also imported into Egypt. That it was sold in this country in the 1420's is borne out by some letters of 1423.[303] Cloth of Southampton (*Soantona*) figures on a price list of Damascus dated 1416, and another document

[297] See my "L'exportation de textiles occidentaux," p. 316; and "Observations on Venetian trade," p. 171 f.

[298] Misti 56, f. 32a ff., 57, f. 13b, 117a.

[299] "L'exportation des textiles occidentaux," p. 342 f.

[300] *Art. cit.*, p. 343 f.

[301] Senato Mar IV, f. 161a, V, f. 152b; Pasi c. 57b.

[302] "L'exportation des textiles occidentaux," p. 345 ff.

[303] *Art. cit.*, p. 348 f.

indicates its sale in Acre in 1439.[304] The price lists which contain data about English cloth of these various kinds point clearly to the downward economic trend. This phenomenon was in keeping with the general trend of the Near Eastern economies.

The spread of English cloth[305] ushered in a new period in the commercial exchanges between Western and Southern Europe, on one hand, and the Moslem Levant, on the other. Its import increased progressively, certainly replacing the products of other countries.[306] The increasing volume of the import of English cloth was an important phenomenon, since the import of textiles from Europe into the Near East had become a major branch of the Levant trade. Indeed, it had a sizable volume; for instance, the Venetian firms J. M. Contarini-Fr. Geno-M. Giustinian sold cloth worth 1180 ducats in Alexandria in 1444, and Domenico Trevisan cloth worth 4000 ducats in Tripoli in 1435 (approximately).[307]

Data in various sources make it possible to draw some conclusions as to the total volume of Venice's trade with the dominions of the Mamluks in the second quarter of the fifteenth century.

When the Venetian Senate deliberated on the declarations made by the merchants concerning the value of their merchandise shipped by the galleys in 1431 to the Moslem Levant, namely that it amounted to 250,000-260,000 ducats, it was maintained that they were fraudulent. Some members of the Senate stated that the cash and the value of the merchandise carried by the galleys to Alexandria and to Beirut usually amounted to 400,000-450,000 ducats.[308] However, these assertions, perhaps influenced by the growth of the Levant trade in the immediately preceding years, were certainly exaggerated. The reliable accounts of the Venetian chroniclers concerning the yearly investments and the values of the cargoes brought back from the Levant and some other data contradict them. The data contained in Table XXXIII show that the yearly investment in the spice trade then (during the spice fair, not in the whole of the year) amounted to 250,000-350,000 ducats (see sub anno 1422, 1424, 1429, 1431, 1446). However, in some years, for instance in 1430, it was much greater. The investment in the cotton purchases amounted to 300,000-400,000 ducats. However, this does not indicate the total of the Venetian investment in the Moslem Levant. But, conclusions from these data should be taken *cum grano salis*, for sometimes the merchants already had money in the Levantine trading towns

[304] *Art. cit.*, p. 341 f. About the spread of English cloth in other Mediterranean countries in that period, see Ph. Wolff, "English cloth in Toulouse," *Ec. Hist. Rev.*, 2nd ser. II (1949-1950), p. 291 ff.

[305] See also Uzzano, p. 114.

[306] See Misti 60, f. 60a, 224a.

[307] "L'exportation des textiles," pp. 372, 373.

[308] Misti 58, f. 145b.

Table XXXIII Volume of Venice's Levant trade, 1422 - 1452

year	galleys to Alexandria	Beirut	Syria cogs		source
1422		460,000 duc.[a]			Morosini c. 384 f.
	160,000 duc.	180-200,000 duc.	fall	21-25,000 duc.	Op. cit., c. 387,388
			total	835,000 duc.	
1423		150-152,000 duc.[b]			
	55-90,000 duc.	50-60,000 duc.	fall	70-75,000"	Op. cit., c. 393, 399,400
			cash merchandise	20-25,000"	
			total	400,000 duc.	
1424	100,000 duc.	160-170,000 duc.			Op. cit., c. 411
1425	first convoy	580,000 duc.			Op. cit., c. 423
1426	60,000 duc.	60,000 duc.	spring	150-180,000"	Op. cit., c. 432, 444, 447, 448
		-	fall	160-180,000"	
			total	455,000 duc.	
1427	-	-	spring	-	
1428	85,000 duc.	145,000 duc.	2 Alex. cogs	200,000 duc.	Op. cit., c. 478, 486, 487, 494
	cargoes of Alex. and Beirut galleys (including ad. cog) 650-660,000 duc.		cargo of spring convoy 4000-4500 sacks cotton		
			total investment	430,000 duc.	
			total of cargoes	7 0,000(?) duc.	
1429		240,000 duc.	spring	150-160,000 duc.	Op. cit., c. 495, 502, 504, Zancaruola c. 534a
			fall	300,000 duc.[c]	
				250,000 "	
			total	700,000 duc.	
1430	150,000 duc.	350,000 duc.			Op. cit., c. 523, 532
			total of galleys		
1431	250-260,000 duc.			500,000 duc.	Op. cit., c. 551
1432	spring, cargoes of 2 galleys & 5 cogs from Syria[d]			250-300,00 duc.	Op. cit. c. 574, 590
			fall cargo	120,000 "	
			total of cargoes	400,000 duc.	
1433	galleys of summer cash 550-600,000 duc.[e]				Op. cit. c. 604, 606
	galleys in fall		*fall*	*80-100,000 duc.*	
	cash 278,000 duc.	cash 182,000 duc.			
	merchandise 380,000 duc.[f]				
			total	1.5 mill. duc.	
1442			fall	400,000 duc.	Zancaruola c. 582b; Chron. Dolfin f. 391b

Table XXXIII (continued)

year	galleys to Alexandria		galleys to Beirut		Syria cogs	source
1446	cargo	190,000 duc.	cargo	150,000 duc.	total of galley cargoes 340,000 duc.	Germanisches Museum Nürnberg, Imhoff Arch. F.VIII 20[g]

a) This was the value of the cargoes of the "trafego galleys", despatched to Syria in March 1422, see above p.

b) Galee di trafego, see above note 113.

c) This was the value of the cargoes of 4 cogs, two of them sailing to Syria, one to Alexandria, and one to Candia.

d) The galleys were pilgrims' galleys, see Misti 58, f. 113b f. The account of Morosini is quoted by Lane, A. Barbarigo, p. 65.

e) From the account of Morosini it is not clear if this amount was carried by the galleys alone or by them and the cogs.

f) It may be that a part of the merchandise was destined for Corfu, Modon, and Crete, as the chronicler says before that, besides cash merchandise worth 160,000 ducats was shipped to these Venetian colonies.

g) This is an evaluation of the cargoes of the convoys that arrived in Venice on 22 December 1446. The freight inventories had obviously been sent to the firm Imhoff by their Venetian business partners.

and, in addition, the *fattori* made purchases throughout the year. But the bulk of the purchases were made during the fairs.

To judge from these data, one would infer that the investment in spices had not increased very much from the beginning of the century. Since spice prices fell considerably from the end of the 1420's, the quantity of merchandise bought must have become much greater. The fact that such large investments were made in the cotton trade, not smaller than the sums of money invested in the spice trade, was a result of the high prices of cotton. At the beginning of the 1420's, when Venice had to take into consideration the difficulties arising from the conflict with Emperor (then still King) Sigismund, the investments in the purchase of this commodity were apparently rather small. But later they very often surpassed the investments in spices (although not all the money shipped to the Levant on the cotton cogs was intended for the purchase of cotton). To a great extent, however, this was the consequence of the high cotton prices in the 1420's and the 1430's.

That our conclusions concerning the great role of the cotton trade cannot be mistaken is borne out by the number of cotton ships that sailed every year to Syria and by the accounts of the value of their cargoes. From various accounts, one learns that a Venetian cotton cog usually carried a cargo worth not less than 30,000 ducats and often much more.[309] Since not less than twelve cogs (i.e., those serving on the state lines) sailed every year to Syria, they carried home cargoes whose total value cannot have been much less than 360,000-400,000 ducats (FOB prices). Surely, these cargoes also included articles bought in Cyprus.

So there is no reason to cast doubt on the data provided by Morosini and those found in other sources referring to the volume of Venice's Levant trade in the second quarter of the fifteenth century. They point to a total investment of 600,000-650,000 ducats on the average, that is 20 percent more than at the beginning of the century. But the value of the merchandise shipped to the Moslem Levant on privately owned ships (in addition to those carried by the convoys of the state lines) and on the pilgrims' galleys should be added.[310]

The information on the Venetian investments also makes it possible to guess at the relation between payments in cash and barter. Unfortunately, only a few accounts of the investments specify the cash and the value of the merchandise shipped to the Levant. According to one account, the cash amounted to 54 percent, according to another to 75 percent. The freight inventory of a ship that sailed in 1419 from Venice to Alexandria shows the exact amount of the cash, whereas the value of the merchandise is not indicated. However, the data in this document point to a total value of 22,000-23,000 ducats, about 75 percent of it in cash.[311]

Trying to evaluate the transactions of the single Venetian traders who engaged in the Levant trade at that time, one finds himself on firmer ground. There are indeed many documents that contain relevant data.

They show that there was a relatively large number of merchants in Venice who bought in Syria every year 30-40 sacks cotton amounting to 600-800 ducats or even less. Many merchants purchased spices for 200-300 ducats in a year.[312] Middle-size traders would invest 1,000-2,000 ducats a year in the Moslem Levant.[313] But these data about the small and middle-sized traders do not mirror exactly the value of their transactions. Often

[309] *Zancaruola*, c. 551b (50,000 duc.), 682b (35,000 duc.), 591b (45,000 duc.). Further, the cotton cogs often carried heavy loads of spices. A passage in the registers of the Senate refers to a cog which brought from Syria 1,660 colli, worth perhaps 120,000 duc., see Misti 60, f. 55a.

[310] See Misti 49, f. 165a, 50, f. 150a.

[311] Melis, *Doc.*, p. 328.

[312] See my papers, "The Venetian supremacy," p. 41, and note 158; "The Venetian cotton trade," p. 696; "The Volume of Levantine Trade," p. 603. Much other data could be quoted: Filippo Malerbi sent merchandise worth 950 duc. to Alexandria on a ship in 1419; see Melis, *Doc.*, p. 328. Maffeo Zane & Cie bought in Latakia in 1425 50 sacks cotton; see G. P., Sent. 38, f. 128a f. Vettor Soranzo Lanzolo de Ca' de Pesaro bought in 1447, by an agent, in Latakia, 60 sacks cotton; see G. P., Sent. 107, f. 185 ff. Bartolomeo Barovier bought in Tripoli for some Venetian firms in 1448, 43 sacks cotton; see G. P., Sent. 176, f. 91b f.

[313] See my papers, "The Volume of Levantine Trade," p. 602; "Profits," p. 269.

they engaged in trade with other regions at the same time and there invested sizable amounts of money. Table XXXIV, containing data concerning the activities of the Venetian firm Giustinian (*Fraterna Giustinian*) in Syria, is a good example.[314] But there were also truly rich merchants and companies that shipped 2,000 and up to 5,000-6,000 ducats a year to the Levant.[315]

D. The Retrogression of Venice's Competitors

Whereas Venice succeeded, despite the conflicts with the sultan, in holding her positions in Egypt and Syria and even in increasing her commercial exchanges with these countries, the activities of most other South European trading nations in the Moslem Levant substantially declined in that period. There were various reasons for their decline. The pressure brought upon them by the sultan was one; and they also suffered from the consequences of their violent reactions to the sultan's policy, from the wars between themselves which resulted in the decline of their shipping, and from the economic difficulties caused by the political conflicts in Southern Europe.

The decline of Genoa's trade with Egypt and Syria was concomitant with and a corollary of her political decline. But to a very great extent, the Genoese transferred their activities to other sectors of the Levant trade, such as the export of alum from Turkey to Northwestern Europe. The marketing of the alum of Phocea became a flourishing sector of international trade, monopolized by the Genoese. In 1449 they exported via Chios 100,000 quintals whose cost price was perhaps 40,000-50,000 ducats.[316] Consequently the shipping line Pera-Chios-Southampton-Sluys became the major artery of Genoa's international trade. On the way to Flanders and England, the Genoese ships most often visited Naples, Gaeta, and Cadiz. Chios served the Genoese even more than before as a base for their trade in the whole of the eastern basin of the Mediterranean, whereas the colonies in Alexandria and in Damascus declined. Even the Indian spices bought in Alexandria were first shipped to Chios. As at the end of the fourteenth century and the beginning of the fifteenth century, the Alexandria-Chios and Syria-Chios shipping lines were other arteries of Genoese trade, and the relations

[314] ASV, PSM, Com. di citra, Ba 91a, fasc. VII, parts 1 and 2. The "fraterna" consisted of Bernardo, Polo and Jeronimo Giustinian, the sons of Giustinian Giustinian. The purchases were made in Damascus in 1317 by Domenico, son of Polo, in 1421 by Jeronimo, and in 1423 and 1425 by Niccolò di Bartolomeo. In 1425 the latter did not return to Venice but remained in Syria two years; see G. P., Sent. 45, f. 117b ff.

[315] See "The Venetian supremacy," p. 42, note 61; "The Volume of Levantine Trade," p. 604. Other data: Lorenzo and Marco Bembo sent 4,400 ducats in cash to Alexandria on one ship in 1419; Natale Canal sent 4,200 duc.; Franco Bon 3,700 duc., Franco Giorgio 2,414 duc. and velvet, ambergris, and honey worth perhaps 1,300 duc., see Melis, *Doc.* p. 328.

[316] M.-L. Heers, "Les Génois et le commerce de l'alun," *Revue d'histoire économique et sociale* 32 (1954), p. 45.

Table XXXIV Trade of the firm Giustinian

1417				
	bought in Damascus and sold in Venice			
	pepper	554 duc.		
	cinnamon	622 "		
	beledi ginger	310 "		
	profit	49.5 " (16%)		
	Meccan ginger	605 "		
	profit	262.5 " (57%)		
	cloves	846.5 "		
	indigo	108 "		
	profit	11.5 " (9.66%)		
	mace	85.5 "		
	profit	3.5 " (4%)		
	cubeb	105 "		
	profit	21 " (16.6%)		
	rhubarb	28 "		
	profit	14 " (50%)		
	galingale	349.5 "	*total of investment*	4322.5 duc.
	brazil-wood	709 "		
	profit	200.5 " (22%)	merchandise sold	2300 "
			profit	662.5 " (28.8%)
1419				
	bocasine	178 duc.		
	gum lac	90	total of investment	268 duc.
1421				
	bought in Damascus and sold in Venice			
	pepper	438 duc.		
		268.5 "		
	cinnamon	292 duc.		
	beledi ginger	67 "		
	frankincense	105.5 duc.	total of investment	1171 duc.
1422				
	cinnamon	335.5 duc.		
1423				
	bought in Damascus			
	pepper	177 duc.		
1425				
	bought in Damascus			
	pepper	226 duc.		

between the Genoese merchants in these two great commercial centers were intense.[317] Rhodes also served the Genoese as a base, and a lively trade was carried on between this emporium and the dominions of the sultan. Often Genoese merchants living in Rhodes engaged in trade in Alexandria. The Genoese exported various commodities, such as coral, from Rhodes to Syria.[318] Genoese ships also carried on intense trade along the coast of Northern Africa, mainly between Tunis and Egypt.[319] And the Genoese still engaged in the slave trade between the shores of the Black Sea and Egypt. Bertrandon de la Broquière met the Genoese Gentile Imperiale, who was the agent of the sultan in Caffa, in Damascus.[320] Attempts made by the Church to curb the Genoese slave trade were fruitless. In 1434 Pope Eugene IV addressed a letter to the government of Genoa, blaming her for the supply of slaves to the Mamluk army. The answer was that only non-Christian slaves were shipped from Caffa to Egypt.[321] Of course, the Genoese not only shipped slaves to Egypt and to Syria from their colonies on the Black Sea; they also engaged in the trade of furs and other Russian commodities, which had a market in the Levant.[322]

But Genoa did not give up her share in the spice trade. When the conflict between King Sigismund and Venice flared up once more at the beginning of the 1420's, Genoa tried again to benefit by it by replacing Venice as a supplier of Levantine articles to Germany. In July 1423 an envoy of Genoa was in Constance; a month before Sigismund re-enacted the prohibition of trade with Venice.[323] The steps taken by Genoa were, of course, in concert with Philip Visconti, the duke of Milan, under whose rule the town had come. In 1422 and in 1423 and again in 1424 and 1431 Genoa and Milan also granted new privileges to the German merchants, to induce them to transfer their activities from Venice to themselves.[324] King Sigismund, on the other hand, proclaimed the prohibition of trade with Venice again in 1425 and then 1431.[325] But all these endeavors had no great success; Genoa

[317] Tur IV, f. 26b, 37a, 55a ff., 60b ff. See, further, insurance acts of 1431 for the ships of Niccolò Pernice sailing from Chios to Alexandria, that of Giuliano Montano sailing from Syria to Chios, and that of Corrado Sansoni going from Chios to Beirut and back to Chios; see Melis, *Origini*, pp. 277, 278.

[318] Tur V, f. 46a. See also Melis, *Origini*, p. 277, about the ship of Pietro Squarzafico, sailing in 1431 from Famagusta to Alexandria.

[319] ASG, Carat. Vet. 1552, f. 45a, 124a (a. 1445).

[320] *Voyages*, p. 68; cf. Heers, *Gênes*, pp. 365, 368, 370.

[321] Setton, *Papacy and Levant* II, p. 47. See, further, A. Bonfante, *Storia del commercio*, parte I, sec. ed. (Rome, 1938), p. 222.

[322] See Heers, *op.cit.*, p. 368.

[323] Schulte, *Der mittelalterliche Handel* I, p. 518 f.

[324] *Op.cit.*, p. 435 ff., 557.

[325] *Op.cit.*, p. 519. Genoa also applied to the pope for permission to trade with the Moslem Levant, see L. Balletto, *Genova, Mediterraneo, Mar Nero*, p. 39 f. (the pope grants Genoa a license for 40 years) and, further, Jorga, *ROL* VII, p. 407 f. (a. 1444); as to single merchants who obtained licenses, see ACA, Real Patr. 2910/1, f. 4b.

could not compete with Venice, which had an unchallenged supremacy in the supply of spices and cotton to Central Europe.

The decline of Genoa's trade with the dominions of the Mamluks is clearly shown by the acts drawn up by the Italian notaries in Alexandria in the 1420's. The number of Genoese ships mentioned in Alexandria is small. In an act of 1425 by a Venetian notary, who exercised his profession in Alexandria, the ship "Santa Maria-Sanct Johan Battista" of the Genoese Giovanni Camporotondo is mentioned as sailing from Alexandria to Perpignan.[326] An insurance act drawn up in Genoa refers to a ship whose patron was an inhabitant of Nice and which sailed in 1429 from Gaeta to Alexandria. Another insurance act, of the same year, testifies to the departure of a Genoese ship from Naples for Alexandria.[327] In the acts of a notary in Alexandria, dated 1427, three Genoese ships are mentioned, all of them sailing to Rhodes.[328] The acts of the same notary refer to one Genoese ship anchoring in Alexandria in 1428 and to two in 1435.[329] Since the acts of this latter notary are very numerous and since all European merchants in the great Egyptian emporium had recourse to his services, the small number of the Genoese ships mentioned in them cannot be incidental. The registers of Genoa's customs service, which have come down to us from 1445, are certainly a very reliable source. From these registers it appears that in 1445 two Genoese ships visited Alexandria and one a Syrian port, probably Beirut. They sailed from there to Chios and finally to Flanders and England. One of them, the ship of Cosma Dentuto, visited Naples and Gaeta, where it unloaded pepper and cotton on its way to Flanders and England. It carried pepper to Bruges and had cargoes of clove stalks, gum lac, frankincense, and slaves (the latter from Caffa).[330] The ship of Gherardo Lomellino, in addition to great quantities of alum, loaded in Chios and destined for Flanders and England, carried cotton from Beirut and delivered it in Gaeta. The ship of Benedetto Doria carried from Syria cinnamon, Brazil-wood, and powdered sugar.[331] On the other hand, the Genoese trade between Crimea and the dominions of the Mamluks was not altogether insignificant. A Genoese ship coming from Caffa, captured in 1434 by Catalans in the port of Tripoli, had carried a cargo worth 48,000 ducats there and had loaded spices.[332]

Although in the second quarter of the fifteenth century the Genoese

[326] Cristofore del Fiore I, f. 6b ff.

[327] Melis, *Origini*, p. 275.

[328] Tur IV, f. 40a ff.

[329] Tur V, f. 37a f., 43b f., 72a ff. See also Melis, *Origini*, p. 278: insurance of merchandise shipped on the vessel of Lazzarino Canettoli from Genoa to Alexandria.

[330] ASG, Car. Vet. 1552, f. 127b, 128a, 128b, 129b, 130a, 281b.

[331] *Ibid.*, f. 132b ff., 134a, 135a.

[332] Marino Sanuto, *Vite*, c. 1036 f.

finally lost first place among the European trading nations in Egypt, their colony in Alexandria was still very active. It had a full-fledged consulate,[333] with a chaplain (serving also as chancellor).[334] Sometimes the number of the Genoese merchants in Alexandria was quite large,[335] and among them there were some who lived a long time in the town.[336] As in an earlier period, there were also merchants of Savona in the colony.[337] The Genoese carried on trade in Damietta too. There were Genoese merchants who lived there, and Genoese ships visited the port.[338] In Syria, too, the Genoese engaged in various sectors of trade. There were apparently always Genoese merchants in Damascus[339] and sometimes also in Acre, like Johan Fatunati at the end of the 1440's.[340] They also carried on trade in Ramla, from whence merchandise was exported via Jaffa.[341] The imposts, which were almost regularly levied by the Genoese government on trade with the Mamluk dominions (*drictus Alexandria*) bear out that the Levantine trade was in that period still a not insignificant sector of Genoa's commercial relations.[342]

The Genoese imported into the dominions of the sultan cloth,[343] cam-

[333] Gabriele Cattaneo was consul in 1421-1422; see Nic. Venier B, 2, f. 37b/38a, 39b, 43b ff., 46b ff., 48b f., 53b f. (the last document in which he is called consul dates of 5 Sept. 1422; so Bart. Lomellino, who is called consul by Brancacci, Diario, p. 168, may have been a vice-consul). Vincenzo Vivaldi in 1425-1426; see Cristofore del Fiore I, f. 9b ff., 13a ff., 15b f., 20a, 23a ff.; degli Elmi Ba 74/75 sub 23 Sept. and 2 Oct. 1426. Dario Calvo in 1427-1428; see Tur IV, f. 4b f., 26b, 27a. Battista Paniza in 1428, see Tur IV, f. 60b ff., 64b ff. Antonio de Puteo before 1431; see Jorga, *ROL* VI, p. 97. Gherardo Calvo in 1434-1436; see Tur V, f. 1b, 30a, 38a f., 45a f., 48a, 72b ff., 76a ff. Percivallo de Camilla in 1442; see Tur II, f. 44b ff. Nic. de Castiglione in 1452; see Tur II, f. 30b.

[334] Crist. del Fiore I, f. 20b; Tur II, f. 14b ff. V, f. 30a, 68a ff.

[335] Tur II, f. 14b f. But the acts of the Venetian notaries who exercised their profession in the 1420's in Alexandria show that the Genoese were usually less numerous than the Venetians. In December 1425, 8 Venetians, 3 Genoese, and 2 Florentines stood surety for a Rhodian knight who had been released by the Mamluks on condition that he would have liberated 4 Moslem captives; see Cristofore del Fiore I, f. 13a ff.

[336] Gherardo Calvo, consul in 1434-1436, was in Alexandria at least from 1404 (see Vat. sub 8 July and 18 Oct. 1404, 20 June 1405) and in 1432 in Rhodes (see Nic. Venier B, 2, f. 50b). Nic. de Castiglione, consul in 1452, was already in Alexandria in 1428; see Tur IV, f. 53a. So Ibn Ḥadjar could say, exaggerating a bit, that the Genoese who left Alexandria in 1429, had lived there many years or were born there; see Inbā III, p. 420 f.

[337] Nic. Venier B, 2, f. 43b f.; Serv. Pecc. sub May 1448.

[338] Tur II, f. 30b.

[339] Broquière met Jacopo Pallavicino in Damascus; see p. 30 and see, further, pp. 32, 66, and see above, p. 333. Teramo and Leonardo Lomellino were merchants in Damascus in 1445; see Branco de Bagnara 10, no. 20. Rafaele Grillo in (about) 1448; see Fazio, Ant. 13 (part 2), no. 64 and cf. Heers, *Gênes*, p. 377. About Genoese in Damascus in 1440, see G. P., Sent. 84, f. 122a f.

[340] Fazio, Ant., *l.c.*

[341] A bill of exchange to Jaffa in 1432; see Musso, *Navigazione*, p. 76.

[342] See about these imposts in 1428, 1438, and 1444, Jorga, *ROL* VI, p. 404 VIII, pp. 6, 7 f.; about imposts in 1447, see Bănescu, *Le déclin de Famagouste*, pp. 31 ff., 37 ff.

[343] Rizzo, Borromeo 1, no. 74; cf. Heers, *Gênes*, p. 378.

lets,[344] and others, but apparently much more olive oil[345] (from Tunisia and elsewhere), and dried fruits, such as raisins from Rhodes,[346] and hazelnuts[347] and honey from Catalonia.[348] They bought a great deal of pepper[349] and other spices in Alexandria and exported them to the Maghreb and to Northwestern Europe.[350] In 1425 a Genoese merchantman carried from Beirut a very great quantity of spices, which was believed by the Catalans to be worth much more than 100,000 ducats.[351] But they also purchased cotton in Syria. For instance, in 1422 a Genoese ship loaded cotton in Beirut.[352] In 1434 a Genoese merchantman loaded, in Tripoli, 600 colli spices and 250 sacks cotton, worth altogether 48,000 ducats, and was captured by Turks.[353] In order to load cotton, Genoese ships also anchored in the port of Acre.[354]

Although the Catalans, who evaluated the spices loaded on a Genoese ship in 1425 in Beirut at 300,000 ducats, were certainly wrong and exaggerated, the various data quoted above show that the volume of Genoese trade in the dominions of the Mamluks was still considerable. Another report of the Venetian chronicler Morosini is more accurate. In 1432 a French ship departed from Alexandria for Southern France with a cargo of spices worth 40,000 ducats, most of it owned by Genoese.[355] From other sources it is known that at least three Genoese ships visited Alexandria every year, and, adding to them those that anchored in Syrian ports, one arrives at a rather substantial total of the values of their cargoes.

The commercial exchanges between Catalonia and the Moslem Levant underwent a great change in this period. In the beginning they were still flourishing but declined greatly from (about) 1435.

In the 1420's Catalan shipping to the dominions of the sultan was still intense. In that decade, it even increased. Although in 1422 the sultan had forbidden the Catalans to visit his dominions, their ships anchored regularly in their ports. This proves that some time after its promulgation this decree was not enforced or was revoked. In fact, Catalan shipping to the ports of

[344] Jorga, *ROL* VI, p. 97.
[345] Heers, *Gênes*, p. 374.
[346] Nic. Venier B, 2, f. 43b f.
[347] Jorga, *ROL* VI, p. 97.
[348] Tur V, f. 45b. Of course they also sold weapons to the Mamluks. In 1444 the Knights of Rhodes captured a Genoese ship carrying weapons to them; see Juan Augustin de Funes, *Cronica de la ilustrissima milicia y sagrada religión de San Juan* (Valencia, 1626-1639), p. 247.
[349] Tur V, f. 78a.
[350] Tur V, f. 48a.
[351] *Chron. Morosini*, c. 428.
[352] *Op.cit.*, c. 389.
[353] Marino Sanuto, *Vite*, c. 1036-1037.
[354] Senato Mar III, f. 102b. About the Genoese cotton purchases in Syria, see also Heers, *Gênes*, p. 377, note 2.
[355] *Chron. Morosini*, c. 428, 590.

Egypt and Syria was not discontinued after the raids in 1422.[356] Until 1433, every year five to seven Catalan ships visited the ports of Egypt and Syria, as against two to four in most of the preceding years. But from 1435 on there was a sharp decline. From that year until 1444 only two to three Catalan ships a year anchored in the ports of the Mamluk dominions. From 1445 there was again an upswing, the number of the Catalan merchantmen that came to Alexandria and other ports of Egypt and Syria usually being four to five a year. Although Table XXXV is most probably not complete,[357] it shows that altogether Catalan shipping to the Moslem Levant declined greatly in that period, if compared with the activity at the beginning of the fifteenth century.

The Catalan ships that visited Alexandria and other ports of the Mamluk dominions were of different kinds. Most of them were privately owned ships; others were government ships. In the later 1430's, when Catalan shipping to the Moslem Levant was at a very low ebb, most of the ships sailing to Egypt and Syria were those of the government. In the year 1435 there were two ships of the Generalitat among them; in 1437 also two; in 1438 and in 1439 all the ships sailing there were those of the government. Most of the ships that sailed between the ports of Catalonia and the Moslem Levant were cogs, but not a few of them were galleys. In the first half of the 1440's the galleys were even predominant among the Catalan ships sailing to the Moslem Levant. Most of the Catalan ships sailing to the Levant departed from Barcelona or were owned by Barcelonans. However, galleys of Valencia, Majorca, and Perpignan also took part in this traffic. Like all other merchantmen of the South European trading nations, the Catalan ships sailing to the Moslem Levant visited several ports of other countries on their way, where they unloaded and loaded a part of their cargoes. Usually the Catalan merchantmen sailing to Egypt made a stop at Palermo and Rhodes, the two most important bases of Catalan trade in the Central and Eastern Mediterranean. Sicily was a Catalan dominion, and the relations of the Catalans with the Knights of Rhodes were close, especially in the days when the Catalan Antonio Fluvian was their Great Master (1421-1437). Often they anchored in Cagliari, Gaeta, Naples, and Syracuse. In the 1420's the Catalan ships sailed almost exclusively to Alexandria; from 1433 on they also began to visit Beirut. The pilgrims' galleys, whose destination was Jaffa, served commercial interests, since they also carried merchandise.[358]

[356] Del Treppo, p. 35 f.

[357] See, for instance, Funes, *op.cit.*, p. 248; in 1444 a convoy of Catalan ships came to Rhodes from Syria.

[358] Vertot, *Histoire des Chevaliers* II, pp. 416, 435; ACA, Real Patr. 2910/1, f. 2a, 4a; Marinecsu, *L'île de Rhodes*, p. 383 f.

Table XXXV Catalan shipping to the Moslem Levant, 1422 - 1452

year	to Alexandria	to Beirut	to Jaffa	to several ports or to the Levant
1422	7		1	
1423	5 [b]			
1424	4			
1425	5			
1426	3			
1427	6 [c]			
1428	5			
1429	5 [d]			
1430	7 [e]			
1431	5 [f]			
1432	7			
1433	5	1 [g]		
1434	1 [h]			
1435	1			3 [i]
1436	-			
1437	2			1 [j]
1438	3 [k]			
1439	1			2
1440	4 [l]			
1441	3			
1442	2			
1443	2			
1444	2			1
1445	2			3
1446	4			1 [m]
1447	2	1		1 [n]
1448	1 [o]			1
1449	3			
1450	1			3
1451	1			3
1452				1

a) This table contains the data collected by Del Treppo p. 616 ff., compared with those of Carrère p. 855 ff. If Syria was indicated a ship's goal, it has been registered in the column "Beirut" in this table. Some corrections have been made by adding data from the acts of Venetian notaries.

b) Four ships are the same in the tables of Del Treppo and Carrère, the fifth was according to Del Treppo that of Berenguer Sauri and according to Carrère that of March Figueret.

c) Del Treppo has (certainly by error) three times the ship of Anthoni Roig whereas Carrère has in addition that of Jacame Sorroll and Esteva Torres.

d) Both Del Treppo and Carrère have five ships. The name of the patrons of four is the same. The fifth was that of Johan del Buch, according to Del Treppo, and according to Carrère that of Anthoni Roig.

Table XXXV (continued)

e) Six names of patrons are the same in the tables of Del Treppo and Carrère, the seventh, according to Del Treppo, is Johan Alco, and according to Carrère Nicholau Julia.

f) Carrère has six.

g) In 1433, the ship of Jacob Pascual of Majorca was in Beirut, see Vat III, f. 4a f.

h) The ship of Esteva Torres, which departed from Barcelona in the fall of 1434, was scheduled to sail to Rhodes and Greece, see Del Treppo, p. 622 f.; but it also went to Alexandria where it anchored in May 1435. Then it sailed (probably a second time) to Rhodes, see Tur V, f. 48b f., 49b f., 52b.

i) Carrère has three to Alexandria and one to the "Levant".

j) Carrère has in addition a galley of Pere Dusay to the "Levant".

k) Carrère has another galley of Majorca to Alexandria.

l) Carrère has, instead of the balenier of Joh. Mandrench sailing to Alexandria, three ships sailing to the "Levant".

m) Carrère has 8 ships altogether.

n) " " 6 " "

o) Carrère has another ship to Alexandria.

Just as most of the ships belonged to Barcelonans, so most of the Catalan Levant traders were merchants of the same town. Others were merchants of Tortosa,[359] Saragossa,[360] and Valencia. Perpignan too still kept its relations with the Levant, so that the merchants of the town could export the Oriental spices to other countries of Western Europe. In 1422 a merchant of Perpignan received a commenda comprising ginger, pepper, cinnamon, and cloves for export to Galicia.[361] But a group of rich and enterprising merchants of Barcelona always had the greatest share in Catalonia's Levant trade. Such a prominent Levant trader was Luis Sirvent, who in 1433 proposed to the Generalitat to establish a state line to Flanders, clearly conceived as completing the network of Catalan shipping and international trade.[362] He was the patron of a galley that went to Alexandria in 1418, 1419, 1422, 1423, 1424, 1425, 1439, 1441, and 1443.[363] Joffre Sirvent, a brother of his, was a great merchant too and engaged extensively in the

[359] ACA Real Patr. 2910/1, f. 6b, 20b.

[360] *Ibid.* f. 7b; Luis de Cavalleria, obviously of the wealthy family of conversos; see Fr. Vendrell, "Aportaciones documentales para el estudio de la familia Caballeria," *Sefarad* III (1943), p. 114 ff.; F. Baer, *A history of the Jews in Christian Spain* (Philadelphia, 1961-1966) II, pp. 30, 58, 72, 372, 464 f.). Perhaps he was a son of Fernando de la Caballeria (son of Vidal); see the genealogical table in the paper of Fr. Vendrell.

[361] *Ibid.* f. 8b; APO, notary Jean Peytavi 859, f. 15a.

[362] Carrère, *Barcelone*, pp. 537, 579 f., 777. He was "consul del mar" in 1435-1436; see *op.cit.*, p. 783, note 1. Certainly this was the same Luis Sirvent who wrote from Alexandria in 1410 the letter published by Ainaud (see above p. 223, n. 138); he should be distinguished from Luis, son of Berenger Sirvent, living in Alexandria in 1434; see Tur V, f. 2a.

[363] See Del Treppo, p. 614 ff.

Levant trade.[364] Another large Levant trader was Miquel Ros, who in 1433 was *consul del mar.*[365]

Because of the continuous acts of aggression, piracy, and raids on the coasts of Egypt and Syria, there was no Catalan consul in Alexandria in the first years of Barsbāy's reign. But from 1429 on, the post was filled. However, Catalan merchants always lived in Alexandria. They hailed from all major towns of the dominions of the crown of Aragon, from Perpignan,[366] Tortosa, Valencia (from this town also Moslems),[367] and others. In the acts of a Venetian notary who exercised his profession in Alexandria in 1448 there appear the names of ten Catalan merchants living there. Some of them even lived a very long time in the Egyptian emporium. Luis Ferrer, who was imprisoned as a guarantor in 1445, was in Alexandria as early as 1435-1436.[368] When peace between the sultan and the king of Aragon had been concluded in 1430, Berenguer Sirvent was the Catalan consul in Alexandria for six years; later from 1438, Pere Muntros; and from 1444, Johan Gavarro, other merchants of Barcelona. In the year 1448 and at the beginning of 1449 the Florentine consul Marioto Squarzalupi represented the Catalan merchants as their vice-consul. So during a certain time they did not have a consul of their own. Then in April 1449 a Catalan, Johan Spaser, was appointed.[369] The commercial activities of the Catalans in Syria, on the other hand, seriously declined in that period. Bertrandon de la Broquière still found Catalan merchants in Damascus in 1432,[370] but apparently there was no longer a Catalan consul there. The Catalan merchants in Egypt and Syria still had close relations with the island of Rhodes at that time. Some of them lived there at first and later transferred their

[364] See Carrère, *op.cit.*, pp. 602, note 5, 613, note 3 and see also pp. 750, 886, note 1, 913, note 2. In 1444 he had been a partner of his brother in the purchase of spices in Alexandria, which resulted in the imprisonment of the guarantors. Another partner was Pere, son of Luis Sirvent. On 1 Febr. 1446 the king gave orders to take measures in this matter; see ACA, Canc. Real 2795, c. 110a/111a. The guarantors who were imprisoned in Alexandria were Luis Ferrer and Francesch Lussa. The merchandise (pepper, ginger, cinnamon, cloves, and clove stalks) had been sold to the Knights of Rhodes for 14,000 ducats; that means at a profit of 55 percent.

[365] Carrère, *op.cit.*, p. 749, and cf. p. 751. He was also a partner in the said transaction in Alexandria.

[366] Crist. del Fiore I, f. 6b ff.

[367] Tur IV, f. 9a ff.; Serv. Pecc. sub 10 Oct. 1448, 6 Febr. 1449; about Ghālib Rufā'īl, see *ibidem* and sub 6 Febr. 1448, 5 Oct. 1449.

[368] Tur II, f. 42b V, f. 66b; ACA, Real Patr. 2910/3, f. 37a.

[369] Capmany, 2.2, no. 23, p. 853a; López de Meneses, "Consulados," p. 115 f., 118 f.; Tur V, f. 1b, 2a f., 4a f., 52a f. Serv. Pecc. sub 10 Febr., 5, 7, 8 and 10 Oct. 1448, 6 Febr. 1449. On the appointment of Johan Spaser in 1449, see Capmany, 2.1, no. 364, p. 527; López de Meneses, p. 119. See also ACA, Cancill. Real 2617, f. 124b ff. (the king confirms the election of Spaser to the post of consul). On other consuls, see above p. 310.

[370] *Voyage*, pp. 30, 32.

activities to Alexandria;[371] others remained in Rhodes and shipped their merchandise from there to Egypt.[372]

The commodities that the Catalans then imported into the Moslem Levant could be classified in two major groups, cloth and agricultural products. Catalan cloth still had a good market in the Levant, and the Catalan merchants shipped many bales of it there. In the documents of the second quarter of the fifteenth century, among the articles sold by the Catalans to Egypt and Syria cloth of Barcelona,[373] Puigcerda,[374] Cerdaña,[375] and Majorca[376] is mentioned. All these fabrics were cheap cloth, amounting to 12 ducats (or a bit more) the piece.[377] But the Catalans also offered taffetas on the markets of Egypt and of Syria,[378] and they even carried English cloth, such as cloth of Bristol, to the Moslem Levant.[379] The agricultural products they offered were mainly honey,[380] olive oil,[381] hazelnuts,[382] almonds,[383] and saffron.[384] All these articles were products of their own country. In addition they offered coral, partly obtained in Sicily,[385] molasses of Sicily,[386] and gossamer.[387]

That Catalan trade in the dominions of the sultan declined greatly from the mid-thirties of the fifteenth century on will be inferred not only from the decrease of Catalan shipping to the ports of Egypt and Syria, but also from the comparison of the investments made by the Catalan merchants in the Levant trade in the 1420's and in the 1430's. There can be no doubt that this retrogression was to a great extent the consequence of the general decline of Catalonia's economy. The textile industry of Catalonia and the volume of her international trade declined. The excellent historian of Spain's economy J. Vicens Vives has concluded that Catalonia's economy flourished until 1410-1412 and that subsequently the decline began. From 1427 on,

371 Tur IV, f. 7a f., 8b f., 9a ff., 10a ff.

372 Tur IV, f. 8a f., 8b f., 9a ff.

373 ACA, Real Patr. 2910/1, f. 2a.

374 Real Patr. 2910/3, f. 1b.

375 *Ibid.* f. 2a.

376 Vat III, f. 4a ff.

377 See Tur II, f. 21a f., 41a ff., 42a f. IV, f. 7a f., 8a, 8b f., 9a ff. V, f. 54a.

378 ACA, Real Patr. 2910/3, f. 3b.

379 *Ibid.* f. 17a (a. 1442, galley of Bartomeu de Lobera, cf. Del Treppo, p. 626) and see Del Treppo, p. 73.

380 Real Patr. 2910/1, f. 7a, 19b; cf. Del Treppo, p. 74.

381 Real Patr. 2910/3, f. f. 38a.

382 Tur IV, f. 9a ff.; Real Patr. 2910/s, f. 2a, 8b, 10a, 10b, 14a, 43b.

383 Real Patr. 2910/1, f. 18b.

384 Real Patr. 2910/3, f. 14b, 35a, 37b, 39b.

385 Real Patr. 2910/1, f. 3b (from Sicily), 11a, 17b; 2910/3, f. 3b, 17b, 38b; vessels (spoons etc.) made of coral f. 5b, paternosters of coral f. 39b.

386 Real Patr. 2910/1, f. 11b, 12a.

387 Real Patr. 2910/3, f. 17a, 43a.

he concluded, the downward trend was rather strong.[388] But, from the registers of the port of Barcelona, it can be seen that in the middle of the fifteenth century the maritime trade was still flourishing.[389] So there must have been other reasons for the decline of the Catalan trade in the Levant. Surely the *circulus vitiosus* of piracy and reprisals was in part responsible. Certainly the enterprising and experienced Catalan merchants were not inclined to give up the profitable branch of trade that the commercial exchanges with the Moslem Levant represented.[390] But not a few of them must have hesitated to invest in the trade with the dominions of the sultan, where confiscation of merchandise and fines, reprisals for the misdeeds of fellow-citizens, were always impending. The onslaughts of the Catalans on the shipping and the coasts of the sultan's dominions were intense in the 1430's; they probably frightened many merchants, or at least induced them to be cautious as to investments in this branch of trade.[391] Heavy expenses for insurance, the necessity of hiring more sailors to protect the ships, and the inclination of the receivers of commendas to claim a greater share of the profit—all these unavoidable corollaries of trade in a region where piracy and raids were rampant must have resulted in the rise of spice prices in Barcelona. The comparison of pepper prices in Barcelona with those in Venice in 1434, 1438, 1449-1450, and 1454 indeed point up this fact.[392]

In the 1420's large investments in the Levant trade amounting to 800-1,000 Barcelona pounds,[393] or even 1,500-1,600,[394] were not rare in Catalonia, although there were many more merchants whose business was of moderate size and who invested 350-400 pounds.[395] In those years, some merchants invested even some thousand pounds in the trade with the dominions of the sultan.[396] But in the 1430's and the 1440's most invest-

[388] "Evolución de la economia catalana durante la primera mitad del siglo XV," in *IV Congreso de historia de la Corona de Aragón* (Palermo, 1950), ponencia 3, pp. 13, 16.

[389] Cl. Carrère, "Le droit d'ancrage et le mouvement du port de Barcelone au milieu du XVe siècle," *EHM* III (1953), p. 146 f.

[390] In order to safeguard themselves, they still apply to the Holy See for licenses for trade with the Moslems in that late period; see Real Patr. 2910/1, f. 3a, 4a (a. 1423), 8b (a. 1426), 10b, 12b, 13a (a. 1425), 14b (a. 1430); 2910/3, f. 7a, 15b.

[391] Another opinion is expressed by Del Treppo, p. 40.

[392] See Del Treppo, p. 70, and cf. F. C. Lane, "Pepper prices before Da Gama," *JEH* 28 (1968), p. 594; my papers "Profits," p. 255; "Spice prices," p. 36. See also, below, Table XLIII.

[393] Real Patr. 2910/1, f. 4a, 4b, 5a, 5b, 7a, 8b, 11b, 12a, 12b, 13a, 14a, 14b, 15a, 16a, 19a, 19b, 20b. The pound of Barcelona was equal to 1 1/3 ducats; see Real Patr. 2910/1, f. 10b 2910/3, f. 2b.

[394] Real Patr. 2910/1, f. 5b, 8a, 9b, 10a.

[395] *Ibid.* f. 4a, 4b, 6a, 6b, 7a, 7b, 8a, 9b, 10a, 10b, 11a, 13a, 15a, 15b, 16a, 16b, 17a, 18b.

[396] Johan Gibert in 1417, 3345 lb; see f. 17b. Nicholau Costo in 1417, 2650 lb; see f. 182a. Francesch Casasagia in 1419 7107 lb; see f. 19b. Joffre Sirvent in 1419, 2500 lb, and in 1430, 2000 lb; see f. 6a, 13a. March Figueret in 1422, 5359 lb, and in 1424, 3800 lb; see f. 20a.

ments were small and many of them amounted to 50-70 or 100-130 pounds, and others to no more than 10-20 ducats. The difference is remarkable. Middling merchants invested 200-300 pounds;[397] investments of 1,500-2,500 were rare.[398]

Consequently, the volume of Catalan trade in the Moslem Levant must have decreased by a great deal from the mid-thirties of the fifteenth century. The five to seven Catalan merchantmen that visited the ports of Egypt and Syria in the 1420's and in the first years of the 1430's certainly carried cash and merchandise worth 200,000-250,000 pounds. Owing to the sharp decline of investments and the decrease of the number of ships sailing from Catalonia to the dominions of the sultan, the total investment in the decade 1435-1445 cannot have been much more than 60,000-80,000 pounds a year. Adding the value of merchandise carried on the ships sailing from Barcelona to Alexandria in 1439, 1440, and 1441, as referred to in the customs registers of the *Real Patrimonio*, one arrives at 5,000-7,000 pounds each. From 1445 on, the volume of Catalonia's Levant trade surely increased again, perhaps reaching 120,000-200,000 pounds. However, in 1446, the two biggest ships of Catalonia departed for the Moslem Levant with cargoes worth no more than 55,000 pounds each.[399] So one must discard the estimate of Luis Sirvent, made in 1433, according to whom a galley returning from Alexandria might carry merchandise worth 160,000 pounds, as much exaggerated.[400]

The Levant trade of France declined considerably in the 1420's, but in the second half of the 1430's and in the 1440's there was a new upswing, although of short duration. The decline in the 1420's was the consequence of the political circumstances. The Hundred Years War had reached a climax; the whole of France suffered from anarchy; and communications between the various provinces were often cut off. So the economy was in disarray. The Provence, under the rule of the House of Anjou, had to sustain the long contest with Alfonso V, and not infrequently the commercial fleet was enlisted to join naval expeditions of the king. In many parts of France the population had substantially decreased. The number of the inhabitants of Montpellier, once a great trading town, and in close contact with the Levant, had dwindled from 4,520 hearths in 1367 to 334

Jacme Casasagia in 1424, 2523 lb; see f. 20b. Miquel Ros in 1429, 2888 lb; see f. 15b. Johan de Palars in 1430, 1945 lb; see f. 14b. Barthomeu de Lobera in 1430, 3500 lb; see f. 12a.

397 Real Patr. 2910/3, f. 3b, 4a, 5a, 9a, 9b, 10b, 11a, 13b, 15a, 15b, 16b, 36a, 40a, 41a.

398 Luis Ferrer in 1439, 1725 lb; see f. 11b. Arnau Porra in 1441, 2,200 duc.; see f. 6a. Luis Schales in 1441, 1,633 lb; see f. 16a. Anthoni Alio in 1442, 2,220 lb; see f. 13a. Barthomeu de Parets in 1443, 2,400 lb; see f. 35b. Johan de Pla in 1447, 1,650 lb; see f. 19a.

399 See Del Treppo, p. 69.

400 Carrère, *Barcelone*, p. 646; Del Treppo, *l.c.* The same is probably true for the claims of Juan de Camos; see above p. 310.

in 1412. Some towns suffered from the devastations wrought by war; Marseilles was conquered in 1423 by the Aragonese and sacked.

So the Italian merchants, both Genoese and Venetians, who had always had a great share in supplying France with Oriental commodities, could fill a vacuum. In addition to the Venetian galleys, which regularly visited Aigues-Mortes, other private ships of Venice plied between the ports of Southern France and the Moslem Levant. A notarial act drawn up in Alexandria refers to a Venetian ship chartered in Venice in 1424 (or 1425) for a trip to Aigues-Mortes and on to Alexandria.[401] In 1430 another Venetian ship sailed from Marseilles to the dominions of the sultan.[402] A ship of Savona departed from Marseilles in 1428 for Alexandria, and some Provençal merchants loaded heavy cargoes of almonds and silver vessels on it. One of them was Jean Forbin, one of the most enterprising traders of Marseilles. Two years later, the same merchant contracted an insurance for his merchandise shipped from Alexandria to Marseilles on the ship of a Florentine, Francesco Ventura.[403] Then a Genoese ship is mentioned in a 1431 notarial act of Marseilles as visiting her port.[404] Catalan ships also visited the ports of Languedoc and the Provence, and Florentine merchants and other Italians, who had their offices in Montpellier and in Avignon, loaded them with agricultural products to be marketed in Egypt.[405]

The striking feature of Southern France's trade with the Levant in that period was its irregularity, but it was by no means extinct. The French diplomat and traveller Lannoy, who visited Alexandria in 1422, recounts that there were no merchants in the small fondaco (*couchier*) of Marseilles.[406] But some acts drawn up in Alexandria in that period by Venetian notaries refer to the activities of merchants from Southern France in the great Egyptian emporium. In 1422 Isarne Pellagulli, a merchant of Montpellier, came from Aigues-Mortes to Alexandria. He had bills of exchange issued in Montpellier amounting to 900 ducats.[407] In 1434 Jean Monier, a merchant of Marseilles, imported olive oil to Egypt. In notarial acts he is called "trader in Alexandria," which means that he stayed there for a long

[401] Crist. del Fiore I, f. 4b ff.

[402] Reynaud, p. 341 f.

[403] *Op.cit. l.c.*; Melis, *Origini*, p. 276.

[404] Ship of family Grimaldi, Reynaud p. 342.

[405] Del Treppo, p. 35.

[406] *Voyages*, p. 77. He says that there are, in addition to the three big fondachi of the Venetians, the Genoese, and the Catalans, "couchiers" of the Anconitans, of the Neapolitans, of the merchants of Marseilles, of the pilgrims and of the merchants of Constantinople, but that there are no merchants staying in them. Even if interpreting this statement as referring to all the fondachi of the minor trading nations, one should beware of drawing conclusions from it, for it may be that the merchants left the town because of an impending Catalan raid, that is, before it actually happened. (Lannoy was apparently in Alexandria in June 1422; see Darrag, *Barsbay*, p. 336.)

[407] Nic. Venier B, 2, f. 44b ff.

time.[408] In 1435 two French merchants, Augustin Sicard of Montpellier and Richard Sahnay of Avignon, signed a document as witnesses.[409] On the other hand, Bertrand de la Broquière mentions the French merchants in Damascus in 1432.[410] Certainly, French trade in the Moslem Levant in the 1420's and at the beginning of the 1430's was at a low ebb, but even in those years there were French consuls in Alexandria. A Venetian chronicler mentions the consul of Provence in Alexandria in 1426.[411] Probably it was Thomas Columbier, who, according to notarial acts, was consul of Marseilles in Alexandria in 1422,[412] and in 1428 "consul of France, Marseilles, and Avignon."[413]

At the end of the 1420's and at the beginning of the 1430's, if not earlier, the "Ste Marie-St. Paul," called "galley of Narbonne" sailed regularly between the coasts of Languedoc, on one hand, and the ports of Egypt and Syria, on the other.[414] On its way to the Levant it also visited several other ports of Southern France. When it anchored in Marseilles in 1429, two merchants of the town, Dominique Sismondelli and Guillaume Nicolai, embarked on it with linen, almonds, and cash, which they had received as commendas from Jean Forbin.[415] In 1431 the galley again visited Marseilles,[416] and in 1432 it called on the ports of Beirut and Alexandria and again anchored in Beirut.[417] But on its return to France, it suffered shipwreck off Corsica.[418]

Shipping from Marseilles to the Levant—that is, the traffic of ships armed and owned by her traders and enterprises in the Levant trade made by them independently—did not come to a standstill after the disaster in 1423. Although it had considerably declined, a group of enterprising merchants began to take up trade with Egypt. Bertrand Forbin armed a galley in 1425 for a journey to the Moslem Levant and, when in 1431 a truce was agreed upon by King René of Anjou and Alfonso V, Jean Forbin, a brother of Bertrand, Dominique Sismondelli, and Jean Boton, sent their galley "Ste Marie" to Alexandria every year. Sismondelli, the son of a Pisan who had settled in Marseilles, went there himself in 1432, 1434, and 1444, and in 1432 Jean Forbin. In the year 1434 the latter also chartered a Genoese ship

[408] Tur V, f. 4a and cf. f. 2a f.
[409] Tur V, f. 53a f., cf. 52a f., 52b.
[410] *Voyage*, p. 32.
[411] *Chron. Morosini*, c. 455.
[412] Nic. Venier, B, 2, f. 45a f.
[413] Tur IV, f. 49b.
[414] Reynaud, p. 341.
[415] Reynaud, p. 341
[416] *Op.cit.*, p. 342.
[417] Broquière, pp. 32, 39.
[418] L. Guiraud, "Recherches et conclusions sur le prétendu rôle de Jacques Coeur," *Mémoires de la Société Archéologique de Montpellier*, 2 série, II, fasc. I (Montpellier, 1900), p. 121 ff.

for the export of olive oil to Alexandria.[419] So the trade of Marseilles with the Moslem Levant began to flourish again.[420] Ships were armed by merchants of Avignon and commuted between the coasts of Southern France and Egypt. In 1433 the ship of Leon Pont of Avignon departed from Marseilles for Alexandria.[421] But meanwhile the truce had come to an end, and the Levant trade of Marseilles and of other towns of Southern France again was drastically reduced. However, it was not suspended altogether as in 1440, for instance, a merchant of Montpellier transported olive oil to Marseilles to have it shipped to Alexandria. When in 1442 Naples finally fell to the king of Aragon and the war between the Anjou and the Aragonese was over, Jean Forbin took up the trade with the dominions of the Mamluks. He sent his agents to Syria in 1443 with merchandise worth 6,000 florins. It was cloth of Wervicq-sur-Lys, linen, and coral.[422]

When the Levant trade of Marseilles had to be discontinued in 1435, a great French merchant, who had his head offices in Montpellier, began to engage in the Levant trade and to usher in a new period in the commercial exchanges between France and the Moslem Levant. Jacques Coeur was one of those men of genius who from time to time appear among thousands of merchants. Although his career came to an end within fifteen years, his achievements for the Levant trade of France were of lasting value.

From 1418 supplier of the royal court and from 1427 mint-master in Bourges, he engaged in many sectors of industry and trade. In 1432 he travelled on the "galley of Narbonne" to Syria, where Bertrandon de la Broquière met him in Damascus. He had come there to purchase spices.[423] Certainly his main intention, however, was to study the conditions of Levant trade on the spot, and when he returned to France he began to make preparations for large-scale commercial exchanges with the dominions of the sultan. It is not unlikely that on his trip in 1432 Jacques Coeur came into contact with the Mamluk government. In the 1440's he had excellent relations with the sultan himself. In 1445 he induced the Knights of Rhodes to conclude peace with the sultan, and thereupon a ship of his brought their envoy to Egypt. Of course this step had not been taken without contacting the sultan beforehand, and obviously he had also the backing of the Holy See, with which he was on excellent terms.[424] In any case, on his trip to

[419] Reynaud, p. 342 f. Sismondelli figures as witness on a notarial act, together with Jean Boton, drawn up in Alexandria on 26 August 1434, Tur V, f. 4a f.

[420] What Reynaud, p. 379 f., says about the acquisition of a ship by Jean Forbin in 1436 in order to employ it in the trade with Egypt is mistaken. Not Egypt is meant, but Chios.

[421] Reynaud, *l.c.* Louis de Pont was also in Alexandria in 1434. He figures as witness on a notarial act of 16 August 1434; see Tur V, f. 2a f., 3a f.

[422] Reynaud, p. 446.

[423] *Voyage*, p. 32.

[424] Pardessus III, introduction p. LXXVIII; P. Clément, *Jacques Coeur et Charles VII* (Paris, 1863) II, p. 275 f.

the Levant in 1432, Coeur had learned how to bring about an upswing in the Levant trade of France. Being mint-master himself, he understood that a great chance for the French Levant traders was the opportunity to benefit from the difference between the gold-silver ratio in Western Europe and that in the Moslem Levant, where silver had a much greater value.[425] Secondly, he understood that the French Levant traders would always lag behind the Venetians as long as they continued to offer the Moslems only cloth, linen, agricultural products, and coral. The Moslems very much needed silver, copper, and other metals, which they partly re-exported to India. From 1444 on Coeur engaged in mining on a large scale, mainly in the mining of silver and lead in the Lyonnais and in the mining of copper in the same province and in the Beaujolais.[426] Exporting silver, copper, and other metals to the Near East in great quantities, Coeur brought about a change in the Levant trade of France.

The head offices of Coeur's enterprises in the Mediterranean trade were in Montpellier, but Marseilles also served him as as a center for his activities, and it was Jean de Village, the husband of one of his nieces and his most faithful and capable collaborator, who was at the head of the latter. By dredging Lattes, the port of Montpellier, and the port of Aigues-Mortes, which had been choked up with sand, Coeur could intensify his Levant trade so much that within a few years he became the main supplier of spices to Southern France. For half a century the spice market of Toulouse, for instance, had been supplied by the Catalans, but after 1436 the Catalans are no longer mentioned as its suppliers.[427]

Later Coeur obtained from King Charles VII an agreement to establish a monopoly in the spice trade, insofar as spices imported into France via a port other than Aigues-Mortes were made liable to an impost of ten percent. This was a blow for the Catalan traders, but since King Alfonso V was a great friend of Coeur, if not his business partner and debtor, the protest of the Town Council of Barcelona, made on behalf of the merchants, and its request for the king to intervene, fell on deaf ears. Coeur even began to import spices into Catalonia.[428] Having begun as a supplier of the Court, Coeur continued to import into France, in addition to spices intended for the general population, costly products, such as Oriental silken stuffs, car-

[425] A. Nagl, "Zum Wertverhältnis zwischen Gold und Silber im 14. Jahrhundert," *Numismatische Zeitschrift* 23 (1891), p. 179; *idem*, "Die Goldwährung und die handelsmässige Geldrechnung im Mittelalter," *Num. Zeitschrift* 26 (1894), pp. 141, 212, 234; A. M. Watson, "Back to gold and silver," *Ec. Hist. Rev.* 2nd. series, 20 (1967), p. 24 f.; my monograph *Les métaux précieux*, p. 49.

[426] H. de Man, *Jacques Coeur* (Bern, 1950) p. 89 ff.

[427] Ph. Wolff, *Commerce et marchands de Toulouse (vers 1350-vers 1450)* (Paris, 1954), p. 146.

[428] Thomas Basin, *Histoire des règnes de Charles VII et de Louis XI*, ed. J. Guicherat (Paris, 1855-1859) I, p. 243; C. Marinescu, "Alfonso le Magnanime," *EHM* III, p. 33 ff.

pets form Persia and Asia Minor, and Chinese porcelain.[429] It may be that he exported to the Moslem Levant, in addition to woolen cloth, honey, olive oil, the commodities the French merchants had formerly offered the Moslems, also paper and Florentine silk stuffs, which he manufactured.[430] In 1444, King Charles VII, who fostered the enterprise of Coeur in any way and probably was his partner, had the galley "Notre Dame" constructed for him, and when it departed for Alexandria in 1445 some traders of Marseilles, such as Dominique Sismondelli, embarked on it.[431] In 1446 Coeur bought another galley, the "Madeleine," in Rhodes. In that year, both galleys went to Beirut and Alexandria. In the same year, Coeur obtained from Pope Nicholas V formal permission to trade with the Moslems, and thereupon Jean de Village, who ranked first among his staff, was sent as ambassador of the king to the sultan. Djaḳmaḳ, whom he brought precious gifts, received him in a very friendly manner and gave him a privilege for the French Levant traders. He promised them freedom of trade and the right to have a consulate as they had had in the past.[432] These promises were contained in a letter of the sultan, which Jean de Village brought the king. The sultan's promise was kept, and a colony of French merchants came into being in Alexandria. The acts of a Venetian notary in Alexandria contain the names of several French merchants who lived in 1448 in the town. Some of them were citizens of Montpellier; others came from the province of Avignon. They imported French cloth and other commodities.[433] At the end of the 1440's Coeur reached the apogee of his career. He added two more galleys to his fleet, and some of them sailed every year between Aigues-Mortes and the Levantine ports. In 1449 again some Marseilles traders embarked on one of Coeur's galleys with their merchandise, cloth of Wervicq-sur-Lys and of Languedoc.[434]

[429] Thomas Basin *l.c.*; cf. Mathieu d'Escouchy, *Chronique*, ed. G. Du Fresne de Beaucourt (Paris, 1863) II, p. 280 f. Jacques Coeur was not the first merchant who imported porcelain into Europe. It had been imported into Catalonia fifty years earlier; see M. Spallanzani, *Ceramiche orientali a Firenze nel rinascimento*, p. 146. Moreover, from a Florentine Merchants' Guide, dating to the beginning of the fourteenth century, one learns that porcelains were already known in Southern Europe and a product that was imported from Damascus, see *op.cit.*, p. 43.

[430] See Thomas Basin *l.c.*; de Man, *op.cit.*, p. 87 f.

[431] Her captain was Philibert de Nau of Montpellier. Arrived in Alexandria, he, together with Johan de Camos, tried to prevent the attack of Gabriel Ortigues on a Moslem ship; see Coll Juliá, "Aspectos del corso catalan," p. 163. About the measures taken by the king on behalf of the enterprise, see Ch. de la Roncière, *Histoire de la marine française* II (Paris, 1900), pp. 277 ff., 281.

[432] Thomas Columbier, see above, was probably the consul of the Provençals (i.e., the consul of Marseilles).

[433] Mathieu d'Escouchy I, p. 121 ff.; Clément, *op.cit.* II, p. 326. For the wide range of Jacques Coeur's activities and his excellent relations with the king of Aragon, another fact is characteristic: one of his galleys which departed in 1446 for the Levant went first to Barcelona; see Del Treppo, p. 628; Serv. Pecc. sub 7 and 10 Oct. 1448.

[434] Reynaud, p. 350.

When the enemies of Coeur brought about his fall in 1451, he was accused of shipping to the Moslem Levant cuirasses, mail-shirts, and weapons, such as guns and crossbows, axes and hoes, which he had given as gifts to the sultan in order to buy pepper without paying customs. He was also denounced as having shipped to the dominions of the sultan a great quantity of copper, ingots of silver, and debased silver coins, against the prohibition of the king. One maintained that his agents shipped great quantities of German money to Rhodes and refunded it, coining debased French money. It was alleged that the amount of silver shipped by him to the Levant reached 200,000 marks. These charges are at least partly confirmed by the acts of a Venetian notary.[435] These are clear indications both as to the character of his activities, e.g., the change he had brought about in the French Levant trade, and to the volume of his trade, for surely the cash (and the silver ingots) were only a part of what he shipped to the Moslem Levant.

The great enterprises of the "galleys of France" did not come to an end when Coeur was sentenced and imprisoned. In 1452 one of his galleys departed again for Beirut, but in 1454 the four galleys were sold to Bernard de Vux, a merchant of Montpellier.[436] However, the traffic of the royal galleys was to be continued later.

Whereas the Genoese, the Catalan, and the French trade in the Moslem Levant declined in the second quarter of the fifteenth century, after a long period of great growth, the attempt of the Florentines to compete with the Venetians in that sector of international trade was a failure from the beginning.

At the same time that Florence sent embassies to the Mamluk sultan and to other rulers in the countries around the Eastern Mediterranean, a great effort was made to organize a service of state galleys, like that of the Venetians. Skilled craftsmen and sailors of Venice and other towns were enticed to come to Florence by offering them better pay.[437] In fact, the Florentine galleys had begun to commute between the coasts of the Tyrrhenian Sea and the Levant some years earlier. In 1419 two Florentine galleys loaded honey for the Levant in Collioure and Barcelona.[438] The journey of the first state galleys which departed from Porto Pisano in July 1422 for Alexandria was not successful. The merchants who embarked on it took with them cloth worth 4,000 florins and 56,000 florins in cash. But,

[435] Jean Chartier, *Chronique de Charles VII*, ed. A. Vallet de Viriville (Paris, 1858) II, p. 327; Ch. de la Roncière, *op.cit.* p. 280; *Les affaires de Jacques Coeur, journal du procureur Dauvet*, ed. M. Mollat (Paris, 1952-1953) I, p. 7; Clément, *Jacques Coeur*, II, p. 148; E. M. Watson, *art. cit.*, p. 20 f.; Serv. Pecc. sub 7 Oct. 1448.

[436] Reynaud, p. 353.

[437] The Venetian Senate took measures against those who accepted these offers; see Misti 54, f. 44a.

[438] Del Treppo, p. 32.

owing to the excitement against the Europeans provoked by the Catalan assault in that year, trade was almost impossible.[439] However, at the beginning of September, of the same year, two other state galleys went to Alexandria. They returned in February 1423 with heavy cargoes. By chance, the accounts of a great Florentine trader who had embarked on the galley have come down to us. Benedetto di Marco Strozzi received commendas of 500-900 florins from relatives and from two merchants of the Tornabuoni family, partly consisting of silk fabrics. In Palermo he received another commenda from Antonio Medici, for Rhodes and Alexandria. It consisted of cloth of Barcelona, Gerona, and Valencia. Finally, in Messina he received commendas consisting of saffron and coral. In Alexandria he bought 149 sportas pepper for 18,096 dinars and some ginger.[440] Altogether the mission of these galleys was a success. From the inventories of the cargoes brought back, it will, however, be concluded that the greatest part was loaded in Rhodes and, secondly, that more than half was unloaded in Sicily. The value of the cargoes brought from the Levant amounted to more than 100,000 ducats.[441] A third journey of the state galleys to Alexandria, made in 1423, was a failure.[442] Then in 1424 two galleys under the command of Benedetto Strozzi were despatched first to Barcelona and from there to Alexandria.[443]

Meanwhile, war broke out between Florence and Milan, and the service of the galley line to Alexandria had to be suspended, but, nevertheless, it was desired to continue the trade with Egypt. In 1426 an effort was made to take up trade with Egypt by the dispatch of state galleys. A Florentine embassy was sent to the sultan in Cairo and obtained from him new promises for the Florentine trade.[444] A year later Roberto Ghetti, envoy to the ruler of Tunis, had instructions to ask him to grant permission for the Florentine galleys to sail from Tunis to Egypt.[445] But this attempt to reestablish the galley line failed. Through the 1430's no other attempt was made. In a letter addressed to the sultan in 1435, the Signoria explained that because of the war in Italy the galley line had to be suspended.[446]

[439] A. Sapori, "I primi viaggi di Levante e di Ponente delle galee florentine," in his *Studi* III, p. 10.

[440] ASF, IIIa serie strozziana, no. 276, f. 2a, 2b, 26b, 33a, 33b, 36b, 37b, 38b, 47b.

[441] Sapori, *art. cit.*, p. 20 ff.; see also *Chron. Morosini*, c. 393, and cf. Mallett, p. 117, who surmises that conditions of trade were still difficult in Alexandria. The value of the cargo was 112,000 ducats, according to Sanuto, *Vite*, c. 942.

[442] Sapori, *art. cit.*, p. 13.

[443] Del Treppo, p. 611, and cf. Mallett, who has doubts about this trip, because he did not know the data in the registers of the customs services of Barcelona.

[444] Pagnini, *Della decima* II, part 2, p. 203 f. This text consists of two documents: (a) a safe conduct for Messer Marzuccho, the Florentine envoy; (b) a letter of the sultan to the Signoria. The text is quoted by Darrag, *Barsbay*, p. 330 (who, however, believed that these documents were connected with an embassy of the sultan to be sent to Florence).

[445] Amari, *I diplomi arabi*, appendix no. 3.

[446] Amari, *op.cit.*, appendix no. 5.

In the 1440's the government of Florence took up the matter time and again. Since the auctions in the 1420's had not been successful, the galleys not finding bidders, it was decided in 1441 that they should be run by the state. But time passed: decisions were taken and not implemented. In 1444 it was decided that henceforth two big galleys should be despatched to Alexandria every year. They were to depart in March or at least before 15 April.[447] A year later Giovenco Stufa was sent as ambassador to the sultan, and the Signoria also sent a letter to the director of the customs services in Alexandria, to prepare the renewal of the galley service. The two galleys, whose captain was Stufa, first visited Tunis, spent two and a half months in Alexandria, and again sailed to Tunis.[448] Once more two years passed before new decisions were taken. In 1447 the lines of the Levant galleys were fixed. The galleys going to Alexandria were to visit Gaeta, Naples, Salerno, Palermo, Messina, Syracuse, and Rhodes on the way to Egypt, and on the return they were to stop at Cyprus, Candia, and Chios.[449] Meanwhile Florence had to fight a new war with the king of Aragon (from 1449 until 1454), and once more decisions taken were not carried out.[450]

The failure was certainly to a large extent related to the character of the Florentine administration, which had no continuity and was devoid of the conservatism of Venice. Further, whereas the success of Venice in the Levant trade was not least the result of the regularity of her galley and cog lines, the Florentines from the beginning did not adhere to a timetable for the sailing of their galleys. Decisions taken were not kept, and the financial difficulties of the Signoria, involved in political conflicts and wars, were another reason for the failure.[451] But the character of Florentine trade was probably the main reason. The freight tariffs that were established for the galleys in 1442 are most instructive insofar as they show what articles the merchants of Florence were interested in. The commodities mentioned as export goods are cloth of Florence, Catalonia, France, Flanders, and England, silken fabrics, olive oil, saffron, coral, copper, tin, paper, and soap.[452] But all other trading nations marketed Florentine cloth and the products of the textile industries of other western countries in the Levant. Every year the Venetians purchased great quantities of Florentine cloth, of which certainly a substantial part was for export to the Levant.[453] The

[447] Sapori, *art. cit.*, p. 6; ASF, Cons. del Mar III, f. 71a f., and cf. Mallett, p. 64. In 1447 it was decided that the galleys should depart on 15 March; see Cons. del Mar IV, fasc. 5, f. 37b.

[448] Amari, *op.cit.*, p. 442, and appendix 6; Mallett, p. 64 f.

[449] Müller, *Documenti*, p. 291; a longer text: ASF, Cons. del Mar IV, fasc. 4, f. 2b.

[450] Cf. Mallett, p. 65.

[451] *Op.cit.*, p. 147 f.

[452] Müller, *Documenti*, p. 357 f. Another freight tariff was fixed in 1460; see *op.cit.*, p. 358.

[453] ASF, Libri di commercio VIII, Nigi di Nerone de' Nigi e compagni, f. 44a, 56b, 57a, 58a

Florentine merchants also used the shipping of other trading nations to export their cloth. In 1429 the Florentines asked the officials of San Giorgio in Genoa to reduce the freight charges on Genoese ships sailing to the Levant with Florentine cloth and silken stuffs. They emphasized in their request that this reduction would influence the Florentine merchants to load other merchandise to be sent to Greece on the Genoese ships in Porto Pisano.[454]

The Florentine merchants had great interest in the spice trade; the customs tariffs established in that period by the Florentine authorities on successive dates testify to this. Further evidence can be found in the Merchants' Guide compiled in Florence.[455] But they could not compete with the Venetians, who almost had a monopoly of the spice supply to Central Europe. This was perhaps less the result of Venetian efficiency than of better communication between Venice and Germany through the Eastern Alps.

Of course, the failure of the galley system did not necessarily entail giving up the development of Florentine trade in the dominions of the sultan. The Florentines had ships of their own which commuted between Alexandria and the ports of the Tyrrhenian sea, those of Italy, and Southern France. In 1430 a ship of the Florentine Francesco Ventura sailed from Alexandria to Marseilles. But they engaged also in the Levant trade, having recourse to the shipping of other nations. In the year 1428 Giovanni Ventura and Galvano de Salviati, two Florentines living in Barcelona, shipped cloth and honey from Aigues-Mortes to Alexandria on a Catalan ship.[456] From various documents that date from the second quarter of the fifteenth century, one learns that the Florentines had a fondaco in Alexandria[457] and that there was always a Florentine consul. The first consul was Ugolino Rendinelli, who died in 1422, and his successor was Antonio Minerbetti.

(cloth sold to Giovanni Portinari in Venice in the late 1440's); cf. Mercanzia 11312 sub 6 Sept. 1413 (purchases of Florentine cloth by the Venetian firm Bertuccio Quirini).

[454] ASF, Mercanzia 11333, letters sub 5 Nov. 1429; cf. Mercanzia 11311, f. 62b f., 89a f., letters to the Council of Barcelona of July 1395, concerning Florentine cloth, which had been loaded in Porto Pisano on a Genoese ship with the destination of Rhodes and had been captured by a Catalan galley.

[455] Tariffe, usi e regole di mercatura, MS. Laurenziana, Acq. e doni 13, of 1422 (containing also dates of the end of the XIVth century), p. 80; Estratto nuovo delle mercatantie e cose che pagano le gabelle, MS. Laurenziana, Antinori 26 (f. 11b: a. 1465); ASF, Miscellanea Repubblicana, Reg. 107, Stracto nuovo delle mercantie et cose che pagano gabelle (of the XVth century). These documents seem to contradict the assertion of Mallett, pp. 121 f., 146, that the Florentines were mainly interested in the import of dyes (for their textile industries). In fact, from the freight inventories of the galleys of 1422-1423 it is seen that the greater part of the dyes purchased in the Levant were unloaded in Sicily.

[456] Melis, *Origini*, p. 276; Del Treppo, in *RSI* 69, p. 521.

[457] Tur IV, f. 2a V, f. 12a f., 25b, 36b.

From 1425 until 1432 Francesco Manelli held the post.[458] He was a veteran of the European merchant colony in Alexandria, where he was already living at the beginning of the century.[459] When the Signoria addressed a letter to the sultan in 1435, he was also requested to do justice to Manelli, who had suffered losses after a Pisan merchant, Giovanni Stefani, fled from Alexandria with merchandise and other goods for which he had not paid. Manelli himself had apparently fled too and the Signoria asked the sultan to allow him to return.[460] In the middle of the fifteenth century Marioto Squarzalupi filled the position of consul for a long time, from 1434 until 1455 at least.[461] The Florentine colony also included several Pisans, such as Rainerio Aiutamicristo, agent of a Palermitan firm,[462] and Filippo Astay, who carried on a lively trade with Rhodes.[463] The Florentines also engaged in trade in Damascus,[464] but there was no Florentine colony in the Syrian capital.

In the middle of the century, the Florentine merchants sold their cloth in Alexandria[465] and also in Damascus, where the Peruzzi had an agent,[466] and they imported molasses and honey.[467] On the other hand, they exported Levantine articles to Italy and to Southern France.[468] In the trade between the big islands of the Mediterranean, on one hand, and Egypt, on the other, they were particularly active. Lorenzo Griffo, for instance, in the late 1420's, engaged in trade between Palermo and Alexandria, where he died (apparently in 1430); his brother Nano too was a merchant in Alexandria.[469] The Florentines were on excellent terms with the Knights of Rhodes, so that Rhodes served as a point of support for their activities in the Eastern Mediterranean. In the middle of the century the Medici invested large sums

[458] *Diario* of Brancacci, pp. 183, 184 (Rendinelli had filled the post before the treaty had been concluded in that year with the sultan); Crist. del Fiore I, f. 13a ff.; Tur IV, f. 2a, 37b f., 47a f., 79a f., 83a f. See, further, Tur V, f. 19b, 36b, 38b.

[459] See Vat. sub 13 and 15 Jan. 1400, 18 Nov. 1404; Leonardo de Valle sub 31 Jan. 1403.

[460] Amari, *I. diplomi*, appendix no. 5 (the quotation of this document by Mallett, p. 64 should be corrected). Giovanni Stefani had fled to Rhodes; see Tur V, f. 36b, 38a f.

[461] Tur II, f. 20a, 21a ff., 42a ff., 44b ff. V, f. 2a f., 3a f., 5b ff., 13a f., 19b, 21a ff., 25b, 51b f., and see above p. 340. About the Florentine consulate in Alexandria, see also G. P., Sent. 54, f. 36a ff. (a. 1426), 107, f. 133b ff. (a. 1443). The chaplain of the consulate is mentioned in G. P., Sent. 33 sub dato 1 March 1424.

[462] Tur IV, f. 37b f., 40a ff.

[463] Tur V, f. 19b, 25b, 30b, 32b, 35a, 45b, 47b f. See, further, Serv. Pecc. sub 5 Febr. 1448 and 9 Sept. 1448 (a Pisan engaged in trade between France and Egypt).

[464] de la Broquière, p. 32; Vat. III, f. 4a f.

[465] See *Diario* of Brancacci, p. 166, 183, about Nano Gucci in 1422. They also marketed French cloth; see Serv. Pecc. sub 7 Oct. 1448.

[466] Crist. del Fiore V, f. 1a.

[467] G. P., Sent. 54, f. 36a ff.; Tur V, f. 49b ff.

[468] See Melis, *Origini*, p. 121, an insurance for merchandise shipped by Luca Capponi in 1451 on the galleys of France from Alexandria to Aigues-Mortes.

[469] Franc. degli Elmi Ba 74/75 sub 2 Oct. 1426; Archivio Comunale Trapani, Lettere Senato I, 1399-1430, f. 298a.

of money in the trade with Rhodes.[470] From Alexandria the Medici shipped spices to Rhodes.[471] The Tuscan merchants in Alexandria were indeed very active in the spice trade,[472] but they also engaged in the export of wheat from Cyprus to Egypt.[473]

At that time, the Levant trade of Naples was very much hampered by the political vicissitudes of the Italian kingdom of the Anjou. During the long contest between Alfonso V of Aragon, on one hand, and Queen Giovanna and King René, on the other, Naples was conquered by the Aragonese forces in 1421 and again in 1423, then lost to the Anjou and their allies in 1424, besieged by the Aragonese in 1438, and finally taken in 1442. The change of rulers was accompanied by fierce fighting, and for a long time both of the fighting parties were represented by armed forces in the town. Under the rule of the House of Anjou, the Genoese had a great share in the international trade of Naples, and when it passed over to the crown of Aragon, the Catalans carried on a lively trade in the town. But the Venetians also took part in the trade, the town being one of the stops of their galley line to Aigues-Mortes.[474] However, even in that difficult period the Levant trade of Naples herself was not discontinued. Not rarely, ships of the Neapolitans sailed to the Moslem Levant. In the year 1435, for example, a Neapolitan galley, whose captain was Leone Chanachi, anchored in Alexandria.[475] The Neapolitans kept their fondaco in Alexandria through this period,[476] and were represented by a consul. From 1427 until 1434 it was Angelo Mazza of Castellamare.[477] Even in that period, the Gaetans also carried on trade in Alexandria, and some of them lived there a long time. Antonio Tarola of Gaeta, who lived some time in Otranto, engaged in trade in Alexandria and stayed there from 1451 until 1455. He was closely connected with a family of Ragusan merchants, the Bunićs.[478] Sometimes Gaetan ships came to Alexandria, carrying olive oil and soap and exporting pepper.[479] The soap of Naples and Gaeta had indeed always a good market

470 ASF, Mercanzia 10831, Accomandite, f. 26b, 27a.

471 Tur V, f. 47a f., 48a.

472 Tur V, f. 36b.

473 Krekić, no. 1258.

474 Misti 56, f. 15b, 81b, 168a.

475 Tur V, f. 66b.

476 Tur V, f. 8b f., 10a f., 10b ff., 12b f., 13a f., 13b f. Piloti p. 182 calls it the "fondaco of the Neapolitans and the Gaetans."

477 Tur IV, f. 7a f., 8a, 8b f., 9a ff., 24b, 47b, 48a V, f. 10a f. 20a, 25b f. In some documents he is called "consul regni Apulie" (see Tur V, f. 1b [a. 1434]) and in others "consul Neapol. regni Sicilie et Apulie" (see Tur V, f. 10b ff. [a. 1434]). He lived in Alexandria a long time and had a tavern there at the beginning of the 1420's; see Nic. Venier B, 2, f. 52a f. (Anzolo da Napoli is undoubtedly the same person.)

478 Tur II, f. 20a; Krekić, no. 1232.

479 Tur V, f. 8b ff. (a. 1434). The ship whose patron was Antonio Faraone (see there, f. 20a) was owned by the duchess of Sessa, who belonged to the highest nobility of the kingdom

in Egypt.[480] Its price in Alexandria was then always higher than that of the soap of Venice,[481] but it was also imported by merchants of various other trading nations. The merchants of Naples and Gaeta engaged in trade between Egypt and Rhodes. For instance, Marchioto Campalona of Gaeta imported Catalan cloth from Rhodes to Alexandria and purchased spices there in 1427.[482] In the mid-thirties of the century Neapolitans and Gaetans shipped spices from Alexandria to Rhodes.[483] They also carried on trade with other Greek territories. Angelo Mazza exported copper to Constantinople.[484]

Even in the second quarter of the fifteenth century, trade and shipping between Sicily and the Moslem Levant was to a great extent in the hands of the Catalans. Catalan ships plied between all major ports of the island and the ports of Egypt and Syria. They sailed from Palermo, Messina, and Syracuse to Alexandria, and vice versa, and Sicilian merchants shipped their merchandise to the Levant on them.[485] The port of Trapani had a lively traffic, and not seldom merchantmen departed from there for the Levant. In the year 1448 the ship of the Catalan Aloysius Bertran sailed from Trapani to Alexandria.[486] Several documents signed by the Jewish merchant Joseph b. Berakot of Trapani, in November 1448, refer perhaps to the journey of another Catalan ship, for one reads there that the ship will sail to Syria.[487] Of course, the Catalans imported spices from the Near East into Sicily. A galley of Perpignan, whose captain was Armengol de Termaldo, imported pepper and ginger from Rhodes to Palermo in 1434. In 1448 Francesc Cervera, a trader of Barcelona who lived in Syracuse, received

---

of Naples and in 1432 had assassinated Gualterio Viola Caristia, the regent of the kingdom. See also Melis, *Origini*, p. 275, an insurance of merchandise sent by a merchant of Nice on the ship of Bartolomeo Priori and Gigo Forti from Gaeta to Alexandria.

[480] *Histoire des prix et des salaires*, p. 353; Tur IV, f. 8b f.

[481] Arch. Lor. Dolfin, price lists of 19 Febr. 1422, 2 May 1422, 13 May 1422, 2 Febr. 1423, 12 Apr. 1423, 31 July 1423, 21 Aug. 1423, 16 March 1424.

[482] Tur IV, f. 7a f.

[483] Tur V, f. 46a ff.

[484] Tur IV, f. 46b f., 47b, 48a.

[485] A Catalan ship sailing from Alexandria to Syracuse and Majorca; see Serv. Pecc. sub 6 Febr. 1448. A merchant of Trapani, Antonio di Lulino, entrusted the Pisan Lorenzo Griffo with the sale of a certain quantity of molasses in Alexandria. Griffo departed on the ship of the Catalan Andrea Spaler from Palermo for Alexandria and died there in 1430. Thereupon the town council of Trapani applied to Francesco Manelli, the Florentine consul, who kept the goods of Griffo, with the request to hand over the sum the molasses had yielded to Nano Griffo, the brother of the deceased, whom the merchant of Trapani had appointed his mandatory; see Arch. Comunale Trapani, Lettere Senato I, 1399-1430, f. 298a. The Senate of Trapani endorsed the power of attorney. Cf. C. Trasselli, "Sicilia, Levante, Tunisia," in his *Mediterraneo e Sicilia*, p. 88. The Florentine consul is called Andrea Franc. Manelli, but probably it was the same Franc. Manelli known from the documents quoted above. The merchandise is called "mel," meaning molasses.

[486] ASTrap, Scanatello sub 26 Sept. 1448.

[487] ASTrap, Miciletto 8594, f. 28a f. He buys coral, ibid. f. 28b. f.

in Alexandria spices from a Moslem of Valencia in order to sell them in Sicily. They were loaded on a Catalan ship.[488] The Catalan merchants also often chartered Sicilian ships for their commercial activities, especially for their trade with the Greek territories.[489]

However, the commercial fleet of Sicily served also the Sicilian merchants themselves for their trade with the Moslem Levant. Many notarial acts of that period refer to the intense traffic between the port of Messina and Syracuse, on one hand, and the ports of Egypt and Syria, on the other. In the months June-July 143 Thucius de Constancio, owner of the ship "Stus Jesus-Sta Maria de la Scala," made various agreements concerning his impending trip to Modon-Crete and Alexandria. He undertook to load merchandise in Syracuse before sailing to the Levant and to return via Rhodes or Candia.[490] A merchantman of Syracuse, whose captain was Degus, son of Johannes, anchored in Alexandria in 1422.[491] In the months February-March 1433 Bartolomeo de Marchiono, owner of the ship "Stus Angelus & Stus Nicolaus," prepared for his departure from Syracuse for Modon-Candia-Alexandria and Rhodes, whence he was to return to Messina. He received commendas to be invested in the purchase of flax and spices.[492] The trade of Palermo was, of course, mainly oriented towards Tuscany, Liguria, Southern France, and Catalonia, but not infrequently ships owned by Sicilians sailed from there to Egypt. In 1427 the ship of Jacobus Formento arrived from Palermo in Alexandria, carrying molasses, Catalan cloth, and saffron. Much of the cargo had been bought in Palermo for Venetian merchants in Alexandria.[493] In the same year the ship of Giovanni Bucello came to Alexandria from Palermo with a cargo of molasses belonging to merchants of Palermo and Florence.[494] The ship of Giovanni Bucello apparently sailed frequently between Palermo and Alexandria. It arrived in the Egyptian port once more in September 1436. That time, too, its cargo consisted to a great extent of molasses.[495]

Certainly the traffic between Sicily and the dominions of the Mamluks was irregular, but its volume cannot have been insignificant. It cannot be accidental that the author of a Merchants' Guide of the middle of the fifteenth century compared the weights of Alexandria first with those of

[488] Comito, Giacomo 844, sub 25 Sept. 1434; Serv. Pecc. sub 6 Febr. 1448.
[489] Andreolo sub 31 Dec. 1427, 2 Jan. and 9 Febr. 1428; Fr. Mallono, f. 121a ff.; travels to Candia, Chios, and Rhodes: see Andreolo, sub 31 Aug. 1429.
[490] Fr. Mallono, 1431-1437, f. 74a f., 80b.
[491] Nic. Venier B; 2, f. 46b f.
[492] Fr. Mallono, f. 324b f. 472b.
[493] Tur IV, v. 23b ff.
[494] Tur IV, f. 40a ff. In February 1428 the ship of Donato Buxello was in Alexandria, perhaps the same, or that of another Sicilian; see Tur IV, f. 46b f.
[495] Tur V, f. 68b., 70a.

Messina.[496] Other sources can be adduced. One finds in the collections of acts that have come down to us from the registers of the notaries of Palermo, Messina, and Syracuse various contracts that are styled in a very general way. They leave it to the discretion of the borrower (receiver of a commenda) to invest the money obtained by the sale of the merchandise with which he was entrusted. He is allowed, under such a contract, to carry the merchandise and to invest its price in "Syria, Barbary, Rhodes, Alexandria, according to his best judgment."[497] But other contracts are explicit. In 1428 a merchant of Barcelona received a loan in Palermo from Battista Agliati of Pisa for a journey to Alexandria.[498] On the other hand, in the acts drawn up by Venetian notaries in Alexandria one finds the names of merchants of Sicily who lived in the Egyptian emporium. One of them was Alessandro Bufardo, a merchant of Gerona, who had lived in Syracuse and was in Alexandria in 1422.[499]

The trading towns of Sicily were great centers for the international cloth trade, and certainly a considerable part of the various textiles sold in Palermo, Messina, and Syracuse was shipped to the Moslem Levant. Catalan cloth still held a foremost place among the woolen stuffs of Western Europe that were exported from Sicily to Egypt. Venetian merchants purchased it through their agents in Palermo and had it shipped to Alexandria.[500] The Catalan cloth included various kinds of cloth of Barcelona,[501] Gerona,[502] Puigcerda,[503] Ampurias,[504] and Perpignan,[505] fabrics of Valencia[506] and Majorca.[507] Also Flemish cloth, mainly that of Wervicq-sur-Lys, was still sold in Palermo, Trapani, and other towns of Sicily.[508] But from the 1420's English cloth was offered everywhere in ever-growing quantities and had

[496] *Libro di mercantantie*, p. 140.

[497] See, for instance, Andreolo sub 6 Oct. 1424.

[498] Comito, Giacomo, 843, f. 846a.

[499] Nic. Venier, B, 2, f. 48a ff.

[500] G. P., Sent. 48, f. 5a f. (a. 1426).

[501] Aprea, Ant., 798, f. 14b (a. 1426) 800 sub 2 Oct. 1443; Andreolo sub 14 Nov. 1426.

[502] Comito, Giac., 845 sub 17 Oct. 1436, 847 sub 24 Nov. 1450.

[503] Comito, Giac. 845 sub 22 Oct. 1436; Aprea, Ant., 799 f. 58a (a. 1442).

[504] Aprea, Ant., 801, f. 223b (a. 1445). Probably the products of Castellon de Ampurias are meant; see M. Gual Camarena, "Para un mapa de la industria textil hispana en la edad media,"*Anuario de estudios medievales* IV (1968), p. 129, and cf. 123.

[505] Comito, Giac., 843, f. 635a, 641b, 642a (a. 1427); Aprea, Ant. 799 f. 58a (a. 1442).

[506] Aprea, Ant., 799, f. 212a (a. 1443) 801, f. 480b (a. 1445); Delampio, Nic., f. 18a (a. 1445).

[507] Andreolo sub 4 Oct. and 29 Oct. 1426, 2 Dec. 1427, 24 Febr. 1429; Comito, Giac., 845 sub 16 Nov. 1436, 1 March 1437; C. Trasselli, "Il mercato dei panni a Palermo nella prima metà del XV secolo," *Economia e storia* IV (1957), pp. 143, 147, 148, 149, 150.

[508] *Art. cit.*, pp. 143, 148, 297 ff., 303, Comito, Giac., 843, sub 20 Febr. 1429, 24 Febr. 1429, 9 Nov. 1429 846, sub 8 July 1444; Aprea, Ant., 800 sub 26 March 1444, 801, f. 273b, 291a, 294b (a. 1445), Andreolo sub 1 Oct. 1426; cloth of Brussels: Aprea, Ant., 799, f. 78b (a. 1442); unspecified Flemish cloth: Comito, Giac., 843, sub 14 June 1429; Aprea, Ant., 801, f. 233b, 285b (a. 1441).

a good market. In 1428 a merchant of Marsala bought cloth of Essex.[509] The inventory of a merchant of Trapani, of 1431-1434, included cloth of London, in addition to Catalan and Florentine cloth.[510] A similar inventory of a shop in Trapani, of 1450, contained a great stock of cloth of London and also cloth of Barcelona, Gerona, and Majorca. The woolen stuffs manufactured in Florence and Genoa are not mentioned at all.[511]

Ancona succeeded in that period in keeping its share of the Levant trade, modest though it was, and to withstand the pressure brought upon her by her powerful neighbor, Venice. In the year 1420 Venice laid an embargo on Anconitan trade with the ports of Segna and Fiume and obtained a verdict of two lawyers that the Adriatic was a Venetian sea. At the end of the 1420's there was again a grave conflict between Ancona and Venice. In 1428 an Anconitan ship had joined the Turks in attacking Venetian cogs off Gallipoli. Ancona sent an embassy to Venice to apologize, maintaining that it had been done by compulsion. The pope, Ancona's protector, intervened on her behalf, but the Serenissima was unmoved. In October 1429 she ordered her warships to capture Anconitan vessels and to sequester their cargoes. Thereupon Florence offered her good offices for a settlement of the conflict. Venice accepted the mediation, but without cancelling the orders given to the war fleet. In 1431 the Serenissima finally yielded to the pressure by the Holy See and revoked the orders on an undertaking by Ancona not to sell weapons to the Turks.[512] The Anconitans were in fact fully aware of the necessity to submit to Venice and to curry favour with her. In 1445 Ancona asked the Serenissima to protect its harbor from foreign warships, and Venice agreed to this request, while Ancona obliged herself not to provide Venice's enemies with victuals.[513] Then, in 1446, Ancona had to apply to Venice for military help to recover territories that had been wrested from her, and once more Venice granted her help.[514] In the middle of the century, the Anconitans behaved rather subserviently to Venice. In fact the small town had become a vassal state of her mighty

[509] Trasselli, *art. cit.*, p. 148 (*panni di sex*); see, further, Comito, Giac., 845, sub 16 Nov. 1436, 12 June 1439; Aprea, Ant., 798, f. 137b (a. 1426) 799, f. 408a (a. 1443).

[510] Trasselli, *art. cit.*, p. 297 ff. Cloth of London also: Comito, Giac., 846 sub 8 Apr. 1444; Randisi, Giac., I, f. 35b (a. 1451). Cloth of Florence: Comito, Giac., 843 sub 12 Nov. 1428, 24 Febr. 1429, 845 sub 23 Oct. 1436, 14 Nov. 1436, 846 sub 8 Apr. 1446; Aprea, Ant., 799, f. 260b, 331a, 418b (a. 1443), 801, f. 278a (a. 1445).

[511] C. Trasselli, "Fromento e panni inglesi nella Sicilia del XV secolo," in his *Mediterraneo e Sicilia*, p. 322. Also, cloth of Languedoc is still marketed (see Aprea, Ant., 799, f. 54a [a. 1442]) and even cloth of Carcassone (see Andreolo sub 12 Nov. 1426).

[512] Misti 53, f. 67b, 162a; *Libr. Com.* IV, lib. 11, no. 127; V. Vitale, "Una contesa tra Ancona e Venezia nel sec. XV," *Atti e memorie della Deputazione di storia patria per le Marche*, N. S. I (1904), p. 57 ff.; my "Il commercio levantino di Ancona," p. 233.

[513] Secreta 16, f. 234b, 235a ff., 239a f.

[514] Secreta 17, f. 32a, 32b, 38a; *Libr. Com.* IV, lib. 13, no. 288, and cf. no. 295, 297.

Table XXXVI - Italian merchants in Alexandria[a] in the second quarter of the XVth century

	Venetians	Genoese	Florentines	Neapolitans[b]	Anconitans
1426	35	12	3	-	1
1427	46	14	2	2	3
1428	49	26	3	1	3
1434	37	5	6	11	9
1435	33	20	7	2	7

a) This table sums up the data found in the registers of the G.P. Sent. and in the acts of Nic. Turiano, of Oct. 1426 until Nov. 1428, and from Aug. 1434 until Oct. 1435.

b) Including Gaetans.

neighbor.[515] So Venice could enjoin that the port of Ancona should serve her forces exclusively and that Ancona should supply victuals only to her.[516] Undoubtedly this relationship made it possible for the Anconitans to maintain their international trade.

Anconitan shipping to the Moslem Levant was regular in the second quarter of the fifteenth century, but did not increase. In most years only one ship sailed from Ancona to the dominions of the sultan. Benvenuto Scottivoli made two trips to Syria in 1440 with his ship, and in 1452 four Anconitan ships sailed to Alexandria,[517] but these were exceptional cases.

[515] See *Libr. Com.* V, lib. 14, nos. 39, 52, 53, 107, 148; M. Natalucci, *Ancona attraverso i secoli* I, p. 465 ff.

[516] Secreta 17, f. 118b.

[517] Ashtor, *art. cit.*, p. 229, and note 78. To the date compiled in this paper, p. 228 f., the following should be added: in 1424 an Anconitan cog sailed to Syria, see *Chron. Morosini*, c. 420; in 1437 the ship of Adoardo di Ancona was in Constantinople, see Badoer c. 22, 47, and that of Antonio Petracha, see Badoer c. 150 (so in the text, but should probably be Antonio Stracha); in 1439 the ship of Grazioso of Ancona carried cotton from Phocea to Ancona, see Badoer c. 320, 327 and the balenier of Benvenuto di Filippo Scottivolo visited Chios and Constantinople, see *op.cit.*, c. 320, 342; in that year the ship of Angelo Joh. Antonii departed for Egypt and Syria, see Chiar. Spampalli III, f. 204b f.; in 1440, a *nave di Ancona* was again in Chios and Constantinople, see Badoer c. 371, 375; in 1444 two Anconitan ships went to Syria, those of Angelo Joh. Ant. Buldoni and Petrello Joh., see Chiar. Spampalli IV, f. 56b f., 79a f., 85a f.; in 1447 Petrello Joh. again visited Syria, see Merc. Benincasa I, f. 74a f., whereas the ship of Paolo Liberii Bonarelli went to Romania, see *ibid.*, f. 99b; in 1448 and in 1449 the "Santa Maria-Sanctus Quiriacus-Sanctus Nicolaus," whose patron was Domenico Martini of Trani, sailed to Romania, see *ibid.*, f. 190b f., 195a f. and II, f. 66b f.; in this latter year Petrello Joh. led his ship to Romania, see there I, f. 248a f. II, f. 14a, and an Anconitan ship came back from Constantinople, see ASV, Senato Mar III, f. 66b; in 1450 the ships of Galeazzo Jacobi Saghini and Angelo Buldoni sailed to the Greek waters, see T. Cinzio, sub 21 and 31 Jan. 1450, and that of Domenico Simonis de Camburano to Syria, see there sub 14 July 1450; in 1451, according to Ragusan documents, a ship of Ancona

The small number of the ships that plied between Ancona and the Levantine coasts should not mislead us, however. The Levant trade of the small Adriatic town was not trifling, because her port served as an outlet for the export of Florentine goods. Florentine merchants lived in Ancona and carried on trade with the Levant.[518] On the other hand, Anconitan ships were often chartered by Ragusans to export great quantities of metals to the Levant.[519] In 1448 an Anconitan ship carrying silver, silken stuffs, precious stones, and coral of Ragusan merchants to Syria suffered shipwreck.[520] Most of the ships sailing from Ancona to the Moslem Levant were privately owned, but also the commune armed merchantmen for the Levant trade.[521]

Anconitan shipping and trade in the Moslem Levant was mainly directed toward Egypt, whereas Syria was less often visited by Anconitan traders. In Alexandria the Anconitan colony had its own fondaco,[522] and consuls through this period. The number of Anconitans in Alexandria was very small, but nevertheless the consul did not always succeed in imposing his authority.[523] Some of the Anconitans in Alexandria were agents of Venetian firms. One of them was Giovanni de Puzo, who lived in Egypt a long time and exported substantial quantities of spices.[524]

The items that the Anconitans exported to the Moslem Levant included agricultural products of the Marches, such as olive oil, nuts, honey, and saffron,[525] and their industrial products, mainly soap and paper of Fabriano, which yielded great profits.[526] They shipped cloth produced in the town itself too.[527] The commodities they imported from the Levant, of course, included spices but also cotton for the markets of Central Italy.[528] The value

anchored in Alexandria, see Krekić, no. 1230, and it may be that it was that of Galeazzo Jacobi Saghini, see Tom. Marchetti VIII, f. 104b f.; Domenico Martini led his ship in that year to Pera, see T. Cinzio sub 5 Nov. 1450. To the ships departing in 1452 for the Moslem Levant should be added that of Nicolò Joh. Petrelli, which sailed to Alexandria and Syria, see Ant. Giov. di Giacomo II, f. 49a f., 50a and to those departing for Romania the ships of Angelo Joh. Antonii, see there f. 165a f., and the "Santa Catarina" of Domenico Simonis Camburano, see there f. 323a. However, according to Tom. Marchetti IX, f. 13a the latter ship was scheduled in the spring to sail to Alexandria.

518 Krekić, no. 914 (a. 1438).

519 *Op.cit.*, no. 1015.

520 *Op.cit.*, no. 1143a.

521 Tur V, f. 21a ff.

522 Tur V, f. 19a, 19b, 20a f., 21a ff. (all of them documents of a. 1434).

523 They were Simone Guidolini from 1424 until 1427, Paolo di Manoli in 1428, Jacobo di Paolo from 1433 until 1436, Simone Guidolini in 1439 (a second time); see my "Il commercio levantino di Ancona," p. 222 f., Antonio Angeli in 1448; see Serv. Pecc. sub 21 May 1448. About disobedience to the consul, see Tur IV, f. 64a f.

524 G. P., Sent. 86, f. 39a ff. 88, f. 12b ff. and cf. "Il commercio levantino di Ancona," p. 245.

525 *Art. cit.*, pp. 228, 229, 240.

526 *Art. cit.*, p. 228, 241.

527 Krekić, no. 1248.

528 *Chron. Morosini*, c. 420.

of the spice shipments was sometimes not unimportant. In 1442 an Anconitan merchant shipped pepper worth 2,800 ducats from Alexandria.[529] The cotton that the Anconitan ships carried to Italy came from Syria and Egypt.[530] The total volume of Ancona's Levant trade was very modest as compared with that of the great trading nations. A Venetian chronicler recounts that the cargo of an Anconitan cog returning from Syria in 1425 was worth 4,000 ducats.[531] But according to a litigation brought before the authorities of Ragusa and referring to the journey of an Anconitan in 1448 to Syria, he took with him, as agent of several merchants, merchandise worth 5,000 ducats. A comparison of the number of Anconitan ships that sailed every year to the Moslem Levant with those of the Venetians, taking into account that the first ones were certainly smaller vessels, leads to the conclusion that the total of the Anconitan investment in the Levant trade in that period could not have been much greater than 20,000-25,000 ducats a year.[532]

The traffic between Ragusa and the Moslem Levant did not increase in that period, either. In some years, one Ragusan ship sailed to the dominions of the Mamluks; in others, two; and in many years, none. The irregularity was a striking feature of the Levant trade of the Dalmatian trading town. But there was a group of enterprising Ragusan shipowners and merchants who were very much interested in the Levant trade. Marin Kisiličić sailed with his ship to Alexandria in 1424, 1434, and 1441, and in 1427 he chartered the ship of another Ragusan for a trip to Egypt.[533] Mihoč Kisiličić, another shipowner of the same family, went with his ship to Egypt in 1443 and in 1450.[534] In the latter year, the ship of Simko Kisiličić also sailed to Alexandria and that of Blasius Petri went first to Ancona and then via Ragusa to Beirut and Acre.[535] Sometimes even ships of other Dalmatian towns visited the ports of the Moslem Levant. In 1451 a ship of Sibenico came to Alexandria.[536] The destination of the Ragusan ships was mostly Alexandria: occasionally the documents referring to their travels mention "Alexandria or Beirut" or "Alexandria or another town."[537] Sometimes the ships sailed to Syracuse or even to Palermo before going on to the Levant.[538]

Among the prominent merchants of Ragusa at this time there were some

[529] Krekić, no. 989.
[530] See "Il commercio levantino di Ancona," p. 243 f.
[531] *Chron. Morosini*, c. 420; Krekić, no. 1143a.
[532] Cf. "Il commercio levantino di Ancona," p. 252 f.
[533] Krekić, nos. 698, 706, 747, 818, 970, and cf. 99a.
[534] *Op.cit.*, nos. 1,000, 1,173; about this family, see Krekić, Introduction, p. 120.
[535] *Op.cit.*, nos. 1,170, 1,187; T. Cinzio sub 9, 11; 16 and 17 Febr. 1450.
[536] *Op.cit.*, no. 1,230.
[537] *Op.cit.*, nos. 818, 1,000.
[538] *Op.cit.*, nos. 970, 1,000.

great spice traders. Michael Lukarević went to Alexandria in 1443 and bought pepper there in company with Marin Bunić, who also engaged in the slave trade.[539] In 1450 Lukarević was again in Alexandria.[540] The Bunićs too were spice traders. Johan Bunić went to Alexandria in 1450 and remained there. In February 1451 he bought cloves and pepper there. His brother Benedict, who also was in Alexandria, stood bail for him.[541] Another family of Levant traders in Ragusa were the Djurdjevićs. Blasius Djurdjević had leased his ship in 1427 to Marin Kisiličić for his trip to Egypt. Mathias Djurdjević sent his agents to Alexandria in 1443, and in 1450, with others, he chartered the ship of Mihoč Kisiličić for a journey to Egypt.[542] Stephan Djurdjević also went to Alexandria in 1450.[543]

These merchants induced the republic of Ragusa to take diplomatic steps to facilitate their activities. So in 1432 Ragusa applied to Sigismund, as king of Hungary and her overlord, to obtain for her from the Council of Basel official permission to carry on trade with the Moslems.[544] Since this intervention apparently was unsuccessful, an envoy of the town, a Dominican, intervened on her behalf at the Council and procured the license she desired.[545] Like Ancona, Ragusa had to contend with the power of the Serenissima, who tried to impede the development of the other trading towns in the Adriatic, and especially to curb their exchanges with the Levant. In 1429 Venice had taken measures against the Ragusan fustian industry, since Ragusan merchants had begun to export these products misrepresenting them as Venetian.[546] In the middle of the century, Venice had apparently once more taken such measures, and Ragusa sent an embassy to Venice, claiming that the export of textiles to the Levant was a necessity for her. But, since the Venetians put a blockade on the maritime trade of Ragusa, the latter was compelled to give up the export of textiles.[547] On the other hand, Ragusa tried to obtain commercial privileges from the rulers of various countries, or at least to smooth away the difficulties the mer-

[539] *Op.cit.*, nos. 1,025, 1,076.

[540] *Op.cit.*, no. 1,262; cf. no. 1,246.

[541] *Op.cit.*, no. 1,262.

[542] *Op.cit.*, nos. 747, 1,045, 1,173. Many documents refer to this trip, because of the conflicts between the merchants and the disobedience of the crew: see *op.cit.*, nos.1,192, 1,201, 1,205, 1,210, 1,230, 1,234, 1,245, 1,258, 1,262, 1,318. The government of Ragusa had to order a second sailing of the ship to carry the merchants back; see *op.cit.*, nos. 1,207, 1,212.

[543] *Op.cit.*, no. 1,210.

[544] *Op.cit.*, nos. 802, 803.

[545] *Op.cit.*, nos. 802, 803, 811, 812, 815. The government of Ragusa maintained that the trade with the dominions of the Mamluks was a necessity for the town since trade in the Balkan countries had become more and more difficult owing to the Turkish expansion. About licenses obtained by single Ragusan traders (at an earlier date), see *op.cit.*, no. 747; Introduction, p. 118 f.

[546] Misti 57, f. 115b.

[547] Krekić, nos. 1,239, 1,248.

chants encountered. Her envoys intervened with the Emperor of Constantinople[548] and negotiated with the Ottoman sultan.[549] Commercial interests ranked first, as was the policy of all other trading nations, so that when Ragusa was requested to take part in a Crusade against the Mamluks in 1444, she flatly refused.[550]

As in earlier periods, the Ragusans exported to the Moslem Levant much olive oil from Apulia and, therefore, their ships often visited some Apulian ports before sailing to the Levant.[551] They marketed their coral there also.[552] A great advantage of the Ragusans was their close contact with Bosnia and Serbia, where great quantities of silver, copper, and lead were hauled from the mines of several districts. In fact, it was the export of the metals of Serbia and Bosnia, where mining had become much more productive in the first half of the fifteenth century, that made the Levant trade of Ragusa possible. The Ragusans offered the silver of Novo Brdo in Southern Serbia and Srebrenica in Bosnia, the lead of Olovo, and copper hauled from several mines. A large portion of the metals of Serbia and Bosnia was purchased by the Venetians (and transported to Venice via Ragusa), and some was marketed by the Ragusans. From 1427 until 1439 the Ragusans had farmed for 200,000 ducats a year from George Brancović, despot of Serbia, the mines of Novo Brdo. He then lost sovereignty over Serbia and recovered it in 1443, and probably the Ragusans again enjoyed the possibility of marketing the silver of Novo Brdo.[553] Obviously, they exported the metals of Serbia and Bosnia to the Moslem Levant.[554] When the countries of the Moslem Levant suffered from a shortage, the Ragusans shipped them wheat, mostly purchased in Apulia.[555] The cargoes that their ships carried from the Levant naturally consisted mostly of spices, but they also bought salt there, which served as ballast.[556]

The survey of the commercial exchanges between the Christian nations, on one hand, and the Moslem Levant, on the other, in the second quarter of the fifteenth century would not be complete without emphasizing the role of the three big islands in the eastern basin of the Mediterranean. Crete, Rhodes, and Cyprus not only served as bases for the trading nations

[548] *Op.cit.*, no. 845, and cf. 887, 900 (a. 1435-1437), 1,197, 1,216, and cf. 1,217, 1,222, (a. 1451).

[549] *Op.cit.*, no. 865 (a. 1436), 895 (a. 1441), 965 (a. 1441).

[550] *Op.cit.*, no. 1076.

[551] *Op.cit.*, nos. 698, 706, 1,176, and cf. 1,173, and see also no. 1,180.

[552] *Op.cit.*, nos. 790, 821, 853.

[553] Broquière, p. 214. And see there the note of Scheferand D. Kovacević, "Dans la Serbie et la Bosnie medievales, les mines d'or et d'argent," *Annales E.S.C.* 15 (1960), pp. 251, 255f., 257.

[554] See Krekić, no. 1,246.

[555] *Op.cit.*, nos. 714, 715, 1,211.

[556] *Op.cit.*, no. 988, 989, 1,046 (and cf. no. 1,045), 1,233.

of Southern and Western Europe: they also exported their own products both to the Western countries and to the Near East. Their commercial exchanges with the dominions of the Mamluks were never cut off.

Crete, the big Venetian colony, exported significant quantities of its famous wines to Egypt, where the Mamluks hailing from Caucasia and Southern Russia were good customers.[557] Further, honey, cheese, figs, and hides were exported from Crete to Egypt.[558] Crete was also a great exchange of slaves, most of them coming from the countries around the Black Sea. Although the slave trade had considerably declined in the middle of the fifteenth century, it was never discontinued, and when the interests of the Serenissima required it, slaves captured by Venetians were sent from Crete to Egypt by order of the local authorities.[559] In the course of time, a colony of Cretan merchants had come into being in Alexandria and in Damietta, just as many Cretan merchants lived in Rhodes and carried on trade there. Not a few of these Cretans who engaged in trade in Alexandria were in fact Venetians.[560] The Cretan merchants were therefore often agents of Venetian firms.[561]

Rhodes was a base not only for the Catalans, Genoese, and French merchants. It served the Venetians as well, who were not on the best of terms

[557] Vat. sub 11 May 1405; Tur IV, f. 33b f., 34b; Serv. Pecc. sub 20 Aug., 27 Sept. 1448, and see my "New data for the history of Levantine Jewries in the fifteenth century," *Bulletin of the Institute of Jewish Studies* III (1975), p. 77 ff. (where several notarial acts are quoted).

[558] Piloti, p. 158 f., and see my "Quelques problèmes que soulève l'histoire des prix dans l'Orient medieval," p. 224 f.; Misti 37, f. 99b ff.; Tur IV, f. 7a; Wansbrough, "Venice and Florence," pp. 493, 519; see further, Fr. Thiriet, "Candie, grande place marchande dans la première moitié du XVe siècle," *Actes du Ier congrès int. des études crétoises* (Hérakleion, 1961) 15, Histoire (1963), pp. 348 ff., 350.

[559] H. Noiret, *Documents inédits pour servir à l'histoire de la domination vénitienne en Crète de 1380 a 1485* (Paris, 1892), p. 416; on the decline of the slave trade of Crete in that period, see Ch. Verlinden, "La Crète, débouche et plaque tournante de la traite des esclaves aux XIVe et XVe siècles," in *Studi A. Fanfani* III, p. 664.

[560] Such merchants were: Jacobus Gradenigo of Candia, who lived in Damietta in 1416, see Crist. Rizzo sub 9 March 1416. Jacobus Gradenigo of Rethymnon, who stayed in 1421 in Alexandria, see Nic. Venier B, 2, f. 29a ff. Joh. Gradenigo of Candia, who lived in Alexandria in 1435, see Tur V, f. 57b. Andrea Loredan, son of Niccolò, who lived in Alexandria in 1421-1422, see Nic. Venier A, f. 13b, 23b. Costantino Quirino of Candia, who was in Alexandria in 1455, see Tur II, f. 8a, 60b f. Niccolò Trevisan of Candia, who, too, was in Alexandria in 1455, see Tur II, f. 49a. At the beginning of the century, Donato Trevisan of Candia sojourned in Alexandria; see Leonardo de Valle sub 21 Febr. 1402, Vat. sub 17 Dec. 1404. Other Cretan merchants in Alexandria were Giorgio di Milano, son of Nicoleto, a great wine trader, who lived there from 1404 until 1435, at least, see Vat. sub 17 Dec. 1404, Tur V, f. 65b ff. For his wine trade see also my paper quoted in note 557 and, further, Tur IV, f. 38b., 43a f., 83b f. In 1418 he carried on trade in Damascus; see Nic. Venier, B, 1, f. 3A. His son Niccolò was in Alexandria from 1420 until 1428; see Nic. Venier, B, 1, f. 10a; Crist. del Fiore I, f. 24a, Tur IV, f. 58b ff. Giorgio di Fiandra of Seteia was a merchant in Alexandria in the 1430's; see Tur V, f. 27b, 57b f. Johan Vassallo of Candia was also a great wine trader in Alexandria; see Tur IV, f. 30a f.

[561] For instance, Giorgio di Milano; see G. P., Sent. 63, f. 41a f.

with the Knights, because the latter sheltered the Catalan pirates.[562] Many European merchants preferred to live in Rhodes, a Christian outpost in the Eastern Mediterranean, and to carry on their activities in Egypt and Syria through agents. Rhodes had the advantage over Cyprus of being nearer to that other great artery of international trade, the Pera-Chios-Flanders line. But Rhodes was also a great spice market. Venetian, Cretan, and Rhodian merchants shipped spices from Alexandria to Rhodes.[563] When relations between the Catalans and the Mamluks were tense, the products of Catalonia changed owners in Rhodes before being shipped to Egypt and Syria. Venetians and others shipped Catalan cloth to Egypt from Rhodes.[564] But Rhodes also exported her own products to the dominions of the sultan. They were honey, hazelnuts, figs, raisins, and cheese.[565] So shipping between Rhodes, on one hand, and Alexandria and Syria, on the other, was intense. Rhodian ships commuted between Rhodes, Beirut, and Chios. The Knights of Rhodes had consulates in Alexandria and Damietta from the beginning of the fifteenth century.[566]

Cyprus too still had a share in the international trade of the Mediterranean. The island exported substantial quantities of her cotton and sugar to European countries, while her camlets had an excellent market in Egypt and Syria; molasses too was exported to Egypt.[567] The hopes of the Genoese to make Cyprus a flourishing base of their own trade had vanished a long time before. The trade of Famagusta, the Genoese point of support, in Cyprus, had declined: the revenues of their colony there had dwindled: and time and again the Genoese government had to cope with the financial difficulties that arose from the decay of the town. In 1447 the colony was ceded to the Bank of San Giorgio.[568] In fact it was the Venetians who were foremost among the Westerners who carried on trade on the island. The king of Cyprus himself was their customer; Venetian merchants in Rhodes

[562] Tension between Venice and the Knights: Misti 56, f. 118a, 119a f. (a. 1427), 57, f. 149a (a. 1429); Venetians in Rhodes: G. P., Sent. 52, f. 83 ff. 55, f. 100a ff.; Tur IV, f. 17a ff.

[563] G. P., Sent. 54, f. 3a ff.; Tur V, f. 55b, 56b, f., 62b f.

[564] G. P., *l.c.*

[565] Piloti, p. 156; Tur IV, f. 9a ff. V, f. 43b f.; Nic. Venier A, 2, f. 16a ff., 50b, 55a; G. P., Sent. 187, f. 75a ff.; see also Vat. sub 16 June 1400, 22 Aug. 1405.

[566] Melis, *Origini*, p. 277; the establishment of the consulates in Egypt had been conceded by the sultan to Philibert de Naillac, Great Master of the Knights, in 1403: see Vertot, *Histoire des Chevaliers* II, p. 308. The consuls in Alexandria were: Georgius Melli from 1400 until 1405 (see Vat. sub 2 March 1400, 10 March 1405); Pietro Delise succeeded him (see Vat. sub 4 Nov. 1405); Johan Lachana was consul in 1421-1422 (see Nic. Venier A, f. 16a B, 2, f. 53b f.) Joh. de Seres held the post in 1448; see Serv. Pecc. sub 21 May 1448. Further, they had consulates in Jerusalem and in Ramla, but these latter should deal with the pilgrims.

[567] Piloti, p. 157 f.

[568] Bănescu, *Le déclin de Famagouste*, pp. 20 f., 34 ff.; de Mas Latrie, *Hist. de Chypre* III, p. 34 f. and cf. Bănescu, *op.cit.*, p. 42 f.

sold him cloth and in the 1420's imported linen of Reims into the island. Venetians in Alexandria sold him soap in 1427 and in 1428 saffron, olive oil, pepper, and other commodities, which had a value of 14,000 ducats.[569] Trade between Venice and Cyprus had become so prosperous that from 1445 until 1461 Venice re-established her galley line to Cyprus,[570] and on the island itself Venetians had acquired so much property (estates) that the king in the 1440's was concerned.[571]

So the commercial exchanges between the great trading nations of Southern Europe and the big islands of the Mediterranean, on one hand, and the Moslem Levant, on the other, were never altogether discontinued, although the volume of the trade of Venice's competitors as a whole had very much declined in the second quarter of the fifteenth century, and the activities of some minor trading nations in the dominions of the Mamluks were often irregular. In addition to the shipping and the trading of all these nations, there were sometimes somewhat sporadic commercial expeditions of other nations. Among these were the Castilians. A notarial act drawn up in Alexandria refers to a Castilian ship that was anchored in the harbor.[572] When English cloth began to conquer the Mediterranean markets, attempts were made by enterprising English merchants to ship it on English ships to the Levant. In 1446 Robert Sturmy, a trader of Bristol, armed the cog "Anne" and loaded it with much English wool, cloth, and tin. The ship was scheduled to sail first to Pisa and then to proceed to Jaffa, the destination of 160 pilgrims who had embarked on it. It arrived there safely, but on the return journey was shipwrecked off Modon.[573]

[569] G. P., Sent. 55, f. 100a ff.; Tur IV, f. 18b, 72a ff.

[570] See A. Tenenti-C. Vivanti, "Les galères marchandes vénitiennes, XIVe-XVIe siècles," *Annales, E.S.C.* 76 (1961), p. 83 ff.

[571] Thiriet, *Rég.* III, nos. 2,613, 2,633, 2,677.

[572] Nic. Venier B, 2, f. 46b f. (a. 1422).

[573] E. M. Carus-Wilson, "The overseas trade of Bristol," in E. Power-M. Postan, *Studies in English trade in the fifteenth century* (London, 1933), p. 225 f.

VI
The Levant Trader at Home and Overseas

In the later Middle Ages the commercial exchanges between the countries of Southern Europe and the Near East also underwent great changes as far as their techniques were concerned too. The commercial techniques employed in the middle of the fifteenth century were imcomparably better developed than those used one hundred and fifty years before. Even the transport facilities had become much better than in the thirteenth century. Finally, there was a considerable change in the stratification of the Levant traders: in the course of time a class of very rich Levant traders had come into being. Great merchants regularly invested substantial sums in the exchanges with the Moslem Levant.

A. At the Head Office

This change was particularly noticeable in Venice, which in the fifteenth century had become the leading trading nation of Southern Europe, as far as the commercial exchanges with the Moslem Levant are concerned. Various documents referring to the trade with the Levant show that the share of the small merchants decreased considerably in Venice by the beginning of the fourteenth century.[1] Genoese documents of the late fourteenth century point to the same phenomenon.[2] In Venice, in the second half of the fifteenth century there was a group of traders who every year invested 10,000 ducats or more in the trade with Egypt and Syria.

The members of the Malipiero family carried on trade with the Moslem Levant both individually and in the form of a family partnership, which

[1] Kedar, *Merchants in crisis*, p. 49 ff.
[2] *Op.cit.*, p. 51 f.

Table XXXVII Trade of the Malipiero family in Syria

a) Anzolo Malipiero and brothers				
	export to Syria (merchandise sold)		purchases in Syria	
1478				
	cloth	2013 duc.	silk and spices	1647 duc.
	tin	257 "		
	total	2270 duc.		
1479				
	export to Aleppo			
	cloth	2182 duc.	silk and spices	9690 duc.
	tin	220 "		
	money	8171 "		
	total	11,573 duc.		
b) Purchases of Lunardo Malipiero				
1475				
	in Damascus: silk, spices, cotton			13,385 duc.[a]
1476				
	spices	7627 duc.		
	silk, cotton, alkali	29,232 "	total	36,859 duc.
1481				
	cotton	763 duc.		
	bocassin	208 "		
			total	972 duc.[b]
c) Tomaso Malipiero				
	export to Syria		purchases in Syria	
1478				
	cloth	2387 duc.	silk	785 duc.[c]
	money	5865 "		
	total	8252 duc.		

bore the name of fraterna, and their investments were sizable.[3] From these accounts one learns that every Malipiero invested 6,000, 8,000, and often much more than 10,000 ducats a year in the trade with Syria. About two-thirds of these investments were in cash.

[3] Arch. Malipiero Ba 161, fasc. 1. If there is no other indication, the data refer to the net price of the purchase. The names Anzolo, Tomaso, and Lunardo were very common in the Malipiero family, so that one cannot easily establish the genealogy of these merchants. It is, however, not unlikely that Tomaso (di Niccolò) was the father of Anzolo and Lunardo, who died in 1520 and 1490 respectively; see the genealogy of the family Zusti, MS. now in possession of the Venetian family Zusti del Giardino, Vol. II, p. 758 f. (I am grateful to Avv. G. Lanfranchi for having copied for me the relevant texts.) About the character of the Venetian (and Florentine) fraterna, see Sieveking, "Aus venet. Handelsbüchern," *Jahrbuch* 26, p. 190 f.

Table XXXVII (continued)

1479					
	(in company with Jac. Guson)				
	money	6644 duc.	spices		4733 duc.
			silk		3930 "
				total	8663 duc.
1482					
	cloth of Bergamo	1452 duc.	silk		8573 duc.[d]
	furs	292 "			
	money	4803 "			
	total	6547 duc.			
1488					
	cloth	3142 duc.	silk		315 duc.
			cotton		1338 duc.
				total	1653 duc.[e]

a) Cf. my paper The Venetian cotton trade, p. 698.

b) This sun includes the expenses in Syria. About his purchase of cotton in 1485, see art. cit., l c.

c) In that year, he also bought a great quantity of spices.

d) Expenses in Syria are included.

It is true that in Venice and other great seaports there were not those rich companies which fulfilled a great role in the inland trade in these times. But family partnerships and casual associations played a great role in the Levant trade.

The firm Niccolò Soranzo & Sons in the year 1488 shipped to Alexandria 427.3 butts (1,708 djarwī ḳinṭārs) olive oil, worth perhaps 10,250 ducats. Andrea & Francesco Bragadin shipped to the same place in the same year 521.7 butts (2,088 ḳinṭārs) which may have yielded 12,530 ducats.[4] Joh. Venier bought pepper in Alexandria for 11,000 ducats in 1491.[5] For companies, such an investment was not at all unusually great by the middle of the fifteenth century. Luca & Andrea Vendramin invested 10,000 ducats, in 1441 in Alexandria, and bought in the same year alkali for 4,095 ducats, in Tripoli.[6] The company of Benedetto Zio, Alvise and Jac. Contarini sent to Aleppo merchandise worth 21,450 ducats in 1479.[7]

[4] G. P., Sent. 188, f. 180b ff.

[5] Same series 191, f. 90b ff.

[6] Same series 88, f. 15a, and see "The Venetian supremacy," p. 45. Then, in 1461, Andrea Vendramin bought 41 bales of spices for 4,100 ducats in Alexandria. In 1462 he shipped cloth to Beirut worth 2,900 ducats which was to be sold in order to buy spices and other Oriental articles; see same series 146, f. 19b ff.

[7] G. P., Sent. 178, f. 35b f.

In addition to these rich merchants, who could invest more than 10,000 ducats in one year in their transactions with the Moslem Levant, there were others who invested up to 10,000 ducats.

The firm Francesco Contarini was one of these. In their accounts, one finds the following data (Table XXXVIII) on its activities in the 1450's.[8]

Table XXXVIII Levant Trade of Franc. Contarini

money shipped to the Moslem Levant			purchases		
1455					
Aleppo	2157 duc.		silk	2010.5 duc.	
Alexandria	300 "		ginger	189 "	
total		2457 duc.	total		2199.5 duc.
1456					
travel of Nic. da Molin to Aleppo	470 duc.		silk	3116 duc.	
			spices	993 "	
travel of Marco Soranzo to Aleppo	413 "		total		4109 duc.
travel of Ant. Grimani to Aleppo	284 "				
total		1167 duc.			
1457					
travel of Piero Contarini to Syria	3367 duc.		pepper	218.5 duc.	
travel of Alvise Erizo to Alex.	376 "				
total		3733 duc.			
1458					
money sent to Piero Contarini in Syria	3400 duc.		silk	1113.5 duc.	
1459					
money sent to the same in Aleppo	4992 "		silk	3945 "	
			spices	1929.3 "	
			raw cotton	1817 "	
			spun	119 "	
			dyes	295 "	
			total		8105 duc.

In 1443 and 1444 the firm Luca Soranzo and Brothers shipped 12,012 ducats to its agent Niccolò Contarini in Tripoli.[9] A merchant who belonged to this class was Marco (son of Andrea) Trevisan, who carried on trade in Aleppo. Of an account concerning his transactions, one finds the data in

[8] Museum Correr, MS. PD C 912/I. Even the data in the following table refer to the net prices, so that the investments were much greater.

[9] G. P., Sent. 104, f. 84b ff.

Table XXXIX Transactions of Marco Trevisan

export to Syria			purchases in Syria		
1471					
textiles	2455 duc.		silk	4844 duc.	
silver[a]	1676 "				
ducats	4813 "				
total		8944 duc.			
			1472		
			silk	306 duc.	
			cotton	8285 "	
			other	241	
			total		8832 duc.

a) Ingots.

Table XXXIX.[10] Many other data referring to investments of 5,000-10,000 ducats a year could be added.[11] Zuan & Michiel Morosini bought 55½ colli spices for 6,945 ducats in 1461 in Alexandria; Luca Pisani acquired pepper for 5,442 ashrafīs and other commodities for 1,932 ashrafīs in 1475 in Aleppo;[12] also in Aleppo in 1476 (or 1477) Piero Donado bought raw cotton for 2,336 ashrafīs, alkali for 1,812, and other articles for 1,287, altogether 5,435 ashrafīs.[13]

These merchants belonged to the merchant aristocracy. The middle class of the Venetian Levant traders consisted of those who could invest 2,000-5,000 ducats a year. In the second half of the fifteenth century, there were many merchants in Venice who belonged to this group. They bought 50 colli spices in Syria,[14] continuing the traditional Levant trade of the Venetians. There are numerous data in various sources referring to their activities.[15]

Even this group of Levantine traders represented a new type of merchant who engaged in international trade. In that period the well-to-do merchant who could invest sizable sums in his transactions and carried on his activities without travelling regularly overseas had indeed become characteristic of the businessman engaged in maritime trade. But it would be a gross ex-

[10] G. P., Ter. IV, f. 10b f.

[11] See same series IX, f. 49a.

[12] Same series IX, f. 13b.

[13] Same series IX, f. 13a.

[14] See G. P., Sent. 119, f. 97a ff. 122, f. 65b ff. 181, f. 89b ff.; see, further, same series 151 bis, f. 8a f.

[15] Crist. del Fiore VI, f. 17b f.

aggeration to maintain that in the later Middle Ages the Levant trade became a matter of trade that was almost wholly in the hands of these merchants. Even in the fifteenth century the Levant traders travelled a great deal in the Near East, and the share of small investors in the Levant trade was still substantial.

This is true for all the South European trading nations. Even in Venice small investments formed a substantial part of the total amount of cash and merchandise shipped every year to the Moslem Levant.[16] In Genoa, people who had small savings invested 22 or 28 ducats or even less in the maritime trade. Others entrusted very small quantities of merchandise to those travelling overseas. Among these small investors there were craftsmen, priests, surgeons and women. The same was true for Barcelona.[17] In small commercial centers, the role that the petty investments fulfilled in their international trade was particularly important. In Ancona, for example, few merchants invested more than 100 ducats a year in the trade with the Moslem Levant. Most investments, given as a sea loan, amounted to 30-40 ducats or even less. The patrons of the ships sailing to the Levantine ports took such loans from many people.[18] In Barcelona, too, frequently 30 ducats would be invested in the trade with Greece or the Moslem Levant. Not a few of the investors were not merchants at all; some were innkeepers, dyers, and cloth manufacturers.[19]

At any rate, the striking feature of late mediaeval Levant trade was the rise of a class of rich sedentary traders who engaged in the commercial exchanges with the Near East and at the same time carried on trade with the Greek countries and Northwestern Europe. These merchants were not capitalists who entrusted great sums of money to agents overseas and awaited their reports and accounts, but were themselves busy through the year. The spices that arrived in Venice at the beginning of the winter were sold in the subsequent months on various markets. Venice supplied Central

[16] Only during a short period, in the fourteenth century, people were not allowed to invest in maritime trade more than they had invested in government bonds; see R. Cessi, "L' 'officium de navigantibus e i sistemi della politica commerciale nel sec. XIV," in his *Politica ed economia di Venezia nel Trecento* (Rome, 1952), p. 23 ff. On the commenda in Venice in the later Middle Ages, see Arcangeli, "La commenda a Venezia specialmente nel secolo XIV," *Rivista italiana per le scienze giuridiche* 33 (1902), p. 158 ff., and especially nos. 6, 9, 10, 13, 14, 15, 18, 20 (comprising commenda contracts of the end of the fourteenth century).

[17] L. Balletto, *Genova, Mediterraneo, Mar Nero*, p. 117, Bernat Nadal II, f. 17a, 19a, 19b f., 20b f., 23a, 27a; A. E. Sayous, "Les méthodes commerciales de Barcelone au XIVe siècle," *Estudis universitaris catalanes* 18 (1933), p. 213.

[18] Angelo di Domenico IX, f. 190a f., 191b, 193b, 195a f., 221a, 229a f., 229b f.; Antonio Giov. di Giacomo VI, f. 432b ff., 29, f. 69b f., 70a f. 30, f. 68b, 160a, Giacomo Alberici VII, f. 106a; see other data in my "Il commercio Levantine di Ancona," p. 248.

[19] Pere Marti VI, sub 4 May 1374, and another act w.d. (apparently of May 1374 too) VIII, 11 Aug.-15 Dec. 1380, f. 38a, 99a.

Italy[20] and Southern France[21] with spices and sold dyes to Majorca.[22] The commercial exchanges between Venice and Germany were increasing almost continuously. The well-being after the Black Death resulted in a greater demand of spices, and Venice had the lion's share in supplying Germany and the other countries of Central Europe with the Oriental commodities. Many Venetian firms were in permanent business contact with German firms.[23] The Genoese were able substantially to increase the export of Oriental spices, aromata, and dyes to Flanders and England as early as the second half of the fourteenth century.[24]

It has been maintained that the rise of a class of sedentary merchants was brought about by the employment of permanent agents overseas over whose activities one could have close control. The investments in partnerships by giving commendas would have been replaced by the association with a *fattore* living in the Levant. There would also have been a strong tendency to shun risks, when after the great plagues of the mid-fourteenth century people had lost confidence in their good luck.[25]

The thousands of documents that have come down to us from the archives of late mediaeval firms do not testify to decreasing interest in the trade with the Levantine countries. The great profits accruing from it appealed to the South European traders no less than in earlier periods. However, there were other changes in the commercial activities that made it possible to carry on trade with the Levant from a desk in the head office. The foremost of these changes was the development of insurance.

The spread of maritime insurance was a great achievement of commercial technique in the fourteenth century. In fact, by the end of the thirteenth century merchants had begun to insure merchandise shipped overseas. In that period, the patrons of the ships insured those who loaded merchandise on their vessels. The insurance was disguised as a loan given to the owner of the merchandise, who did not have to return it in case the merchandise did not arrive. The premium was apparently an addition to the freight charge.[26] Some contracts of this type have come down to us in the collections

[20] Dat 549, accounts of Zanobi di Taddeo Gaddi of 23 January and 9 Oct. 1393, 10 Jan. 1394 for frankincense supplied to the Datini firm of Pisa; his accounts of 19 Oct. 1393, of cloves; of 28 Jan. 1395, of pepper; Dat 550, letter of the Commess. of Zanobi of 10 Jan. 1401.

[21] Dat 550, letter of Commess. of Zanobi of 22 March 1402.

[22] Dat 1082, letter of Francesco Corner and Gabriel Soranzo of 24 July 1396, 19 March 1397.

[23] Ph. Braunstein, "Wirtschaftliche Beziehungen zwischen Nürnberg und Italien," p. 398. See also the list of the German customers of the Soranzo: Sieveking, "Aus ven. Handelsbüchern," *Jahrbuch* 26, p. 215 ff.

[24] See Kedar, p. 14.

[25] *Op.cit.*, pp. 25 ff., 126.

[26] E. Bensa, *Il contratto di assicurazione nel medio evo* (Genoa, 1884), p. 54; Fl. Edler de Roover, "Early examples of marine insurance," *JEH* V (1945), p. 178 f. Of course the loan was not cashed by the borrower unless the merchandise was lost.

of acts drawn up by Palermitan notaries in 1287 and 1299.[27] At the beginning of the fourteenth century, Genoese and Florentines often made insurance contracts.[28] The Venetians, too, began to insure merchandise shipped overseas before the middle of the fourteenth century.[29] In the course of time, new methods which resembled more the true insurance of the modern period began to come into use. By a contract made in the year 1329, a Genoese ship captain insured merchandise loaded on his ship without disguising the transaction as a loan.[30] Then, in the middle of the fourteenth century, the first true insurance contracts appear in the collections of notarial acts drawn up in Palermo: the merchandise loaded on a ship is insured by a third party, without disguising the agreement in any form. The insurers were Genoese (or of Savona).[31] But even in the second half of the fourteenth century, contracts that disguised the insurance agreement were being drawn up. Whereas in an earlier period supposedly a loan had been given, now fictitious sale contracts were made: the insured merchant sold the merchandise to the insurer in case it did not arrive at its destination.[32] This was the kind of insurance commonly made in Genoa in the fourteenth century.[33] The true insurance contract—that is, insurance not dressed as a loan or sale contract—was called "a Florentine contract" in Genoa. This is a clear hint at its Florentine origin.[34] However, the old kinds of insurance contracts were still preferred by many merchants. In 1421, for example, an Anconitan patron insured in Alexandria a merchant of Gaeta who loaded merchandise on the patron's ship.[35]

Despite the inclination to stick to old-fashioned contracts, the insurance of merchandise shipped overseas and of the ships themselves became an integral part of commercial activities at the end of the fourteenth century. The great number of insurance contracts drawn up by some notaries within a short time bears witness to this fact.[36] The necessity for insurance was not equal everywhere. Some regions of the Mediterranean were more dangerous than others, mainly because of the greater number of pirates

[27] R. Zeno, *Documenti*, nos. VIII, IX, 44, 46; cf. Edler, *l.c.*

[28] Bensa, *op.cit.*, pp. 50, 53.

[29] G. Stefani, *Insurance in Venice from the origins to the end of the Serenissima* (Trieste, 1958) I, p. 73.

[30] Bensa, *op.cit.*, p. 190 f.

[31] Zeno, *Documenti*, nos. 190, 191, 194, 202; F. Melis, *Origini*, p. 185 f.; on the role of the Genoese in the development of the insurance, see A. S. Lopez, "Les méthodes commerciales des marchands occidentaux en Asie du XIe au XIVe siècle," in his *Su e giù*, p. 302.

[32] Bensa, *op.cit.*, p. 60.

[33] J. Heers, "Le prix de l'assûrance a la fin du moyen âge," *Revue d'histoire économique et sociale* 37 (1959), p. 11.

[34] Heers, *l.c.* It seems that Florentine merchants introduced insurance to Venice; see Stefani, *op.cit.*, p. 70.

[35] Nic. Venier, A, f. 14a B, 2, f. 30b.

[36] Bensa, *op.cit.*, p. 79.

who infested them. Transport on galleys, whose large crews were a guarantee of stronger resistance to pirates, was considered to be relatively sure. Consequently, in Venice there was often not much inclination to insure merchandise shipped on galleys to the Levant.[37] But, even in Venice, merchants regularly had recourse to insurance in the fifteenth century. In the year 1421 the Serenissima promulgated the first law regulating insurance: it forbade insuring foreign ships.[38] In the great commercial centers of Southern Europe insurance companies came into being, for usually one insurer was not ready to take too great risks. Usually an insurer would sign an obligation for 100 ducats; seldom would he undertake to guarantee more than 200. The insurers even often re-insured themselves. But everywhere there were capitalists who engaged regularly in the insurance business,[39] as one learns from many deeds drawn up in Genoa[40] and Barcelona.[41] As time went on, further progress was made: the opposition to insuring foreigners disappeared, as is shown by the laws successively promulgated by the governments of the trading nations.[42]

The premiums paid for insurance decreased in time. In the middle of the fourteenth century more than 15 percent of the value of the merchandise was paid, but at the end of the century the Datini firm paid only 2.5 percent for the insurance of textile shipped from Porto Pisano to Alexandria.[43] In the fifteenth century in Genoa, merchandise shipped to Alexandria was insured for 5-6 percent and to Chios for 3.6 percent,[44] and in Venice the premium was 6½ percent on the average for merchandise shipped to the Maghreb.[45] In Alexandria the insurance premium of shipments of spices to Chios was 7 percent in 1421.[46] The insurance of merchandise shipped on cogs, whose crews were smaller, always cost more than that of shipments on galleys. For the insurance of merchandise on cogs sailing from Syria to Venice 4-8 percent was paid.[47] But sometimes the premium for such insurance could rise to 15 percent.[48] Insurance of shipments from Venice to

[37] Edler, *art. cit.*, p. 195.
[38] Stefani, *op.cit.*, p. 88.
[39] G. P., Sent. 91, f. 108a, 129a, 143a; Stefani, *op.cit.*, pp. 62, 82, doc. 18; Bensa, *op.cit.*, p. 200. In Barcelona the obligations signed by the insurers were particularly small; see A. E. Sayous, "Les méthodes commerciales de Barcelone au XV siècle," *Rev. hist. de droit français et étranger*, 4e série, XV (1936), p. 268.
[40] Kedar, p. 124.
[41] M. Del Treppo, "Assicurazioni e commercio internazionale a Barcellona nel 1428-1429," *RSI* 69 (1957), p. 520 f.
[42] Bensa, *op.cit.*, p. 121.
[43] Zeno, *Documenti*, no. 190; Melis, *Origini*, p. 74.
[44] Heers, "Le prix de l'assûrance," p. 17; de Luco, p. 196.
[45] G. P., Sent. 93, f. 162a.
[46] Nic. Venier B, 2, f. 40a ff.
[47] *Chron. Morosini*, c. 609.
[48] *Chron. Morosini*, c. 400.

the Tyrrhenian Sea, which was infested by Catalan, Genoese, and Moslem pirates, was particularly expensive; sometimes it cost as much as 19 percent.[49] But the usual rate of the premium in Venice in the second half of the fifteenth century was 6 percent.[50] Merchandise shipped by the Venetian firm A. Baseggio-P. Caroldo in 1479 on the Beirut galleys was insured for a premium of 0.75 percent, whereas Anzolo Malipiero (di Tomaso) paid 2 percent to insure a shipment on the Alexandria galleys in 1492.[51] In Barcelona the range of the rates of premium was mostly 3-5 percent, but often insurance of shipments from Barcelona to Alexandria was much more expensive. In 1440 the premium for such insurance amounted to 7 percent and in 1442 to 11 percent.[52] The same is true for the insurance of shipments on the small Ragusan ships, which could easily be captured by Turkish corsairs. Olive oil shipped from Ragusa to Alexandria in 1424 was insured for a premium of 10 percent.[53]

In addition to the insurance, which diminished the risk of shipping merchandise overseas without accompanying it, another new commercial technique greatly contributed to the development of the Levantine trade by the "sedentary merchant." It was the transfer of money by bill of exchange. Just as the merchants in the South European metropolis were busy through the year, selling the Oriental wares and buying European articles to be shipped to the Levant, so the agents in the Levantine emporia were never idle. Even they had occasion to buy spices and dyes a long time before a convoy of merchantmen arrived and the merchandise could be shipped. So it frequently happened that the agent had no cash and had recourse to a loan which the head office would repay in Europe to whomever the lender wished. This transaction, always connected with a change of currency, as the loan was repaid elsewhere, had come into use in Marseilles and Genoa in the first half of the thirteenth century.[54] In the fifteenth century, 8-12 percent was paid for a loan taken in Alexandria or Damascus against a bill of exchange for Venice.[55] A bill of exchange sent from Chios or Rhodes to Alexandria or from Alexandria to Chios or Rhodes did not cost much less.[56] In a price list drawn up in Damascus in 1386 by a correspondent of the

[49] Stefani, *op.cit.*, p. 61.

[50] *Op.cit.*, p. 84.

[51] Melis, *Origini*, p. 39.

[52] Del Treppo, "Assicurazioni," p. 123, Sayous, "Les méthodes," p. 268.

[53] Krekić, no. 706.

[54] On the origin of the bill of exchange, see my "Banking instruments between the Muslim East and the Christian West," *JEEH* I (1972), p. 553 ff.

[55] See my "Le taux d'intérêt dans l'Orient médiéval," in *Fatti e idee di storia economica. Studi dedicati a Fr. Borlandi* (Bologna, 1977), p. 204 ff. See further *Chron. Morosini*, c. 330 (10 percent for a bill of exchange from Acre to Venice in 1417); Tur V, f. 31a ff. (15 percent for a bill of exchange from Alexandria to Venice).

[56] Tur IV, f. 4b f. (8 percent Alexandria-Rhodes), 26b (9.5 percent Chios-Alexandria), 37a (6 percent Rhodes-Alexandria) (all these documents are of the year 1427).

Datini concern, the difference between the exchange rate of the ducat and that of a bill of exchange, addressed to Venice, amounted to 4 percent[57] (obviously *per mensem*), and since there was surely a three-month delay until payment in the European metropolis, it may be concluded that by the end of the fourteenth century the usual interest paid for a bill of exchange drafted in a Near Eastern trading center for Venice was 12 percent. Apparently the rate of interest paid for such bills of exchange did not rise in the first half of the fifteenth century. But the interest for true loans rose very much, as the liquidity of money in the Near East became an ever-greater problem. At the end of the fifteenth century in the large towns of Egypt and Syria, 2 percent *per mensem* was paid on the average.[58] So the frequent recourse to borrowing money by drafting a bill of exchange made it possible to carry on business almost without a break. Lack of cash did not necessarily entail great losses.

But although the employment of permanent agents in the Levant and the transfer of money by bills of exchange played a great role in the Levant trade in the fifteenth century, the old techniques of investing capital by sea loans and commendas did not go out of use altogether. In the smaller trading centers of Southern Europe, whose connections with the Levantine emporia were on a less frequent and less regular basis and where less capital was available, the old techniques were still commonly used.

In Ancona the old sea loan still held first place among the methods of investing money in the trade with the Levant and the Greek countries. Such a loan, called *cambium* and often given in the form of merchandise (soap or other), was payable two months after the return of the ship. Of course the loan stipulated in the contract included the profit (i.e., the interest) due to the lender.[59] Sometimes it had to be repaid one month,[60] twenty days,[61] or even fifteen days,[62] after the return of the ship. But, on the other hand, there are contracts in which the delay for the repayment is fixed at eight months.[63] Comparing the conditions stipulated in the Anconitan contracts in the first half of the fifteenth century with those in

[57] Dat 1171, price list of 1 Sept. 1386.

[58] See "Le taux d'intérêt," p. 203, and see also Senato Mar XIII, f. 20b ff. (2-3% *per mensem* in Damascus, a. 1490).

[59] Angelo di Domenico II, f. 144a IV, f. 35b f., 39b f., 109b f. VIII, f. 43a f., 49b f., 54b, 59a, 63a f., 102a f., 224b f., 226b f., 232a, 233b; Ant. Giov. di Giacomo III, part I, f. 83a f., 100b f.

[60] Chiar. Spampalli III, f. 204b f.; Tom. Marchetti V, f. 68b f., 113b f. VI, f. 40a, 40b; Ant. Giov. di Giacomo III, part I, f. 99a.

[61] Angelo di Domenico XII, f. 199a f.

[62] Giacomo di Pellegrino, f. 67a; Ang. di Domenico IX, f. 231a f., 232b, 291b; Ant. Giov. di Giacomo III, part I, f. 133b f.; 8 days: Tom. Marchetti VII, f. 171b f.

[63] Ant. Giov. di Giacomo III, part I, f. 327b f. Sometimes the loan was repaid after great delay. From the receipts registered in the notarial acts, one learns that the delay could be 16 months or even two years; see Tom. Marchetti VIII, f. 13b f., 194a. But such cases, probably for exceptional reasons, were rare.

the second half, we can see that in the course of time the delay of the repayment became longer. This change probably points to the fact that more cash was available in the second half of the fifteenth century. Another kind of loan was the true *cambium marittimum*, which was payable abroad, either to the lender or to a person indicated by him. In these contracts the delay allowed to the debtor was usually fifteen days.[64] Since the profit was disguised by including it in the loan, there are few data that indicate the amount of the profit. According to contracts made in 1440 it was 28 percent.[65]

Whereas in Ancona the sea loan was still highly in favor, the commenda was used in other trading towns, as in the past. In 1426 in Ragusa, a Catalan received coral from a compatriot living in the Dalmatian town, to be sold in Syria or in Egypt by a commenda contract. The travelling merchant was to have a quarter of the profit.[66] Even in Messina, in the first half of the fifteenth century, many contracts of this kind were drawn. The merchant departing for the Moslem Levant or the formerly Byzantine territories received money or merchandise, to be shipped at the risk of the creditor, for a quarter of the profit he would realize.[67] In some contracts, the share of the profit due to the partners is not indicated, but it is stipulated that the agreement is made *iuxta usum ripae Mess.*[68] Usually the borrower was a merchant, but sometimes it was the patron of a ship.[69]

In the great South European emporia, like Barcelona, the old commenda contract did not go out of fashion either. Even there many agreements of this kind were still made in the later Middle Ages. One lent a certain amount of money to a merchant departing for the Levant and ordered him to invest it, or provide the profit obtained from the sale of the merchandise he bought with it before leaving, in spices or other commodities. Not rarely the investors themselves handed over a certain quantity of merchandise to the merchant departing for the Levant, with the order to sell it and to invest the price obtained. The profit was to be shared according to the prevailing custom. In Perpignan too the commenda was still the instrument most often used for investment in the trade with the Levant. The travelling merchant usually received the fourth part of the profits. Even in Venice

[64] Tom. Marchetti, V, f. 110b VIII, f. 13b f., 194a; Ang. di Domenico II, f. 86a V, f. 7a, 65b f. VIII, f. 199b; Nic. Cressi V, f. 4a f. (a. 1482) IX, f. 207b, 214b, 22a; Ant. Giov. di Giacomo III, part I, f. 112a 30, f. 50b f. 74, f. 268a f.; Giac. Alberici VII, f. 49a. Sometimes a delay of 20 days is stipulated (see Ang. di Domenico IX, f. 214b), or of 10 days (see same notary VIII, f. 119b f.), or even of eight days (see there, XI, f. 201a).

[65] Tom. Marchetti V, f. 110b. As to the accomanditium (or recomanditium), see *Il commercio levantino di Ancona*, p. 248 and see below.

[66] Krekić, no. 790.

[67] Andreolo, sub 9 Sept., 3 and 6 Oct. 1424.

[68] Andreolo, sub 16 Sept. 1419.

[69] Andreolo, sub 7 Sept. 1419.

the commenda was never out of fashion. Everywhere a quarter of the profit was most often assigned to the travelling merchant.[70]

In Ancona, the commenda contract of the old type was not frequent.[71] But very often merchants gave someone departing for the Levant merchandise to sell for a commission fixed at some percentage of the selling price. Such a contract was called *accomanditium*.[72] The travelling merchant had to hand over the account 15 days after his return and earned 2 percent, according to a contract made in 1442.[73] Sometimes he had instructions, laid down in a *recordatio*, to re-invest the price obtained for the merchandise.[74]

The numerous references to the sea loan, the commenda, and other old established methods of international trade should not mislead us, however. They were customs that had remained from a bygone period. The great international trade had already found new ways of association.

To the development of insurance and the widespread use of the bill of exchange, the perfection of the information service should be added as one of the new techniques. The Levant trader who carried on his activities at his head office in a South European emporium needed current information about the fluctuations in the commercial exchanges. In order to know what to sell and what to keep in his stocks, he needed news of the development of prices of spices in the Near East. Before a trader purchased textiles and metals to be shipped to the Levant, it was desirable to know how great the demand for these articles was there. The letters that have been preserved in the archives of Francesco Datini and of some Venetian firms of the fifteenth century show that their chiefs had organized information networks that supplied them regularly with commercial news. The intervals between the dates at which an agent or a business friend sent letters were very short. The correspondent in the Levantine trading centers waited, of course, until the departure of a ship, but those who transmitted news from one European emporium to another wrote every week or even twice a week. The news which they included in their letters was not only commercial. Since commercial activities depended closely on political circumstances, the

[70] Pere Marti VI, sub 4 May 1374 VIII, 11 Aug. to 15 Dec. 1380, f. 99a; Bernat Nadal I, f. 12a, 67a (a. 1387). Sayous, "Les méthodes commerciales de Barcelone au XIVe siècle," *Estudis univ. cat.* 18, p. 21; *idem*, "Les méthodes commerciales de Barcelone au XVe siècle," *Rev. hist. de droit franc. et étr.* 15, p. 272; APO, F. Bosqueros 731, f. 33a, 34a, 42a f. (a. 1404) 735, f. 1a, 2a, 4b f., 5b, 6a f.; Ant. Guitard 1553, f. 16a 1554, sub 27 Febr. and 1 March 1417. Sieveking, "Aus ven. Handelsbüchern," *Jahrbuch* 26, p. 192 f., Arcangeli, "La commenda a Venezia," p. 132 ff., 153 ff. Madurell-Garcia, no. 123.

[71] Some contracts have come down to us in the notarial acts of the second half of the fifteenth century; see Ant. Giov. di Giacomo III, part I, f. 120b (half of the profit to the creditor, half to the borrower); Mercurio Benincasa I, f. 74a f., 225b f.

[72] Tom. Marchetti I, part 3, f. 188b IV, f. 7b f., 17a f., 18a, 29b f., 34b, 48a VIII, f. 68a; Chiar. Spampalli II, f. 128b f.; Ant. Giov. di Giacomo III, part 1046 l.; f. 178b f.

[73] Tom. Marchetti VI, f. 140a.

[74] Chiar. Spampalli III, f. 156b f.

writers of the letters also supplied political information. Those who supplied current information to the great firms of Venice, Genoa, and Barcelona on commercial fluctuations were agents or business friends. From where did they obtain the news? Reading the exact freight inventories of the convoys of other trading nations, one cannot help but conclude that the writers of the letters had received them from the ships' secretaries, very probably for payment. The political bodies of the trading nations, which protected and directed the activities of the merchants, were also interested in having current and full information. They had other sources of information. The government of Venice, for example, had from the marquess of Ferrara news about an agreement made between the Mamluk sultan and the republic of Florence.[75] The governments of the trading nations also had their own mail service. Small and fast sailing ships, called *grippo*, carried the news in a relatively short time overseas.

The time it took to transmit news from the Levant to the head office of a firm in a South European trading center varied greatly. Sometimes the galleys and cogs that carried the letters would make longer and sometimes shorter stops on their way from Beirut or Alexandria to Venice or Barcelona. Studying the data found in many thousands of letters in the Datini archives, F. Melis has calculated the average time of the transmission of news from Alexandria to Venice, at the end of the fourteenth century and at the beginning of the fifteenth century, as thirty-eight days and that of a letter from Beirut to Venice at thirty-nine on the average. In Genoa one usually received a letter from Alexandria not earlier than about forty-six days, whereas it took fifty-two days to receive a letter from Beirut in Barcelona.[76] These average delays point clearly to the diversity of the ship lines, that is, the speed of the various kinds of vessels and the number of the stops. But it is worthwhile to distinguish between the speed of the transmission of news in the various seasons of the year. The difference between spring and fall, when many ships were commuting between the Levantine ports and the South European emporia, on one hand, and its speed in the winter and mid-summer, on the other, was indeed considerable. In spring and fall, a letter from Alexandria or from Beirut would arrive in Venice within a month.[77]

[75] *Libr. Com.* IV, p. 45.

[76] F. Melis, "Intensità e regolarità nella diffusione dell'informazione economica generale nel Mediterraneo e in Occidente alla fine del medioevo," in *Mélanges F. Braudel* (Toulouse, 1973) I, pp. 405, 410, 411.

[77] A letter written in Beirut on 6 Oct. arrives in Venice on 4 Nov., see Dat 549, letter of Zanobi of 4 Nov. 1389; see further Dat 549, letter of the same of 30 April 1394 (letter from Damascus of 8 April 1395, in Venice on 11 May 1395); Dat 548, letter of the same of 10 Nov. 1384 (letter from Alexandria of 3 Oct. 1384, arrives in Venice on 10 Nov. 1384), Dat 549, his letter of 23 April 1395 (letter from Alexandria of 20 March arrives in Venice on 23 April). On the delay of letters in mid-summer and in winter, see Dat 549, letter of Zanobi

In addition to a well-functioning information service, the great firms that carried on trade in the Moslem Levant by their agents also needed manuals that contained the facts about the conditions of trade in the countries overseas. In order to control the items contained in the accounts and in the letters of the agents, the items had to be checked in the manuals. Because of the bewildering diversity of weights and measures so characteristic of the mediaeval world, the chapters containing such information were the core of these manuals. They also contained chapters on the quality of various commodities and hints on how to recognize the quality of Oriental spices and dyes. In addition they contained data about the currencies of the great trading centers and, last but not least, the customs and various imposts levied in the ports. These manuals were kept up to date, so that the merchant and his staff could always rely on them. They were in fact collective works. Therefore, few of them are known by the names of their compilers; most of them are anonymous. But one can distinguish between some main types, such as the Florentine Merchant Guides called *Libro di mercatura*, and that of the Venetians, called *Tariffa*. The latter contained, mainly, facts about the conditions in the sphere of Venetian trade and statements concerning the rights of the agent overseas, that is, the commission due him and the exact amount of expenses for which he was to be reimbursed.[78] In addition to numerous chapters on weights, currencies, and qualities of various commodities, commercial manuals compiled in Catalonia in the fifteenth century also contain chapters on the features by which merchants should distinguish themselves. These chapters indeed remind one of the Arabic Books of Trade, whereas the Italian Merchant Guides are not influenced by them at all.

It might be thought that the use of the new commercial techniques and especially recourse to all the information by letters and manuals implied a high level of education. But as far as general education is concerned, this was not the case. The letters of the merchants were written in the vernacular Romance language that they spoke;[79] their testimonies before tribunals and consular authorities too were given in these languages. Even the consuls, being veteran merchants, seldom knew Latin. The Catalan consul in Al-

of 29 Oct. 1394 (letter from Damascus of 1 Aug. in Venice on 29 Oct.), his letters of 23 April 1395 (a letter from Damascus of 26 February in Venice on 23 April), of 7 Sept. 1395 (quoting a letter from Damascus of 14 June); Dat 550, of 23 Aug. 1396 (quoting a letter from Damascus of 5 May), 27 Oct. 1395 (quoting a letter from Damascus of 26 April).

[78] U. Tucci, "Tariffe veneziane e libri toscani di mercatura," *Studi Veneziani* X (1968), pp. 84, 90 f.; M. Gual Camarena, "Un manual catalan de mercatura," *Anuario de estudios medievales* I (1964), p. 422; Fr. Sevillano, "Colom. Un manual mallorquin de mercaderia medieval," *An. de est. medievales* IX (1974-1979), p. 520 ff.

[79] The Genoese habit of writing in Latin (cf. Kedar, p. 38) was an exception. Even in Genoa one taught the children Latin mainly for training their minds; see Fr. Borlandi, "La formazione intelettuale del mercante genevese nel medioevo," *ASLSP*, N.S. III, (1963), p. 226.

exandria, for instance, did not accept a Latin document in 1402, because he did not understand it.[80] Obviously the education that the young merchants received was purely vocational.

This professional training, however, made great progress. The methods of bookkeeping employed in the great commercial centers of Southern Europe in the fifteenth century were incomparably better than those used a hundred years before. The account books of the merchants of the thirteenth and fourteenth centuries were rather primitive. Many transactions were registered without indicating their dates, and often the payments made in different currencies were not reduced to the money of account commonly used in the country.[81] The use of such moneys of account, on the other hand, for all calculations was a general custom. The introduction of double-entry bookkeeping was a great step forward. From the time that all transactions were entered twice, with contrary signs but equal amount, the accounts became clear and easy to survey. The new system also had the advantage of making clear which transactions changed the amount of capital. Profits accruing were transferred to the capital account. By the indication where the saldo was entered again it became easy to find all data.[82]

The new method of bookkeeping spread through the major trading centers of Italy at the beginning of the fourteenth century. In Tuscany it had already come into use in the second half of the thirteenth century,[83] and in the first half of the fourteenth century it was used in Genoa[84] as well as in Venice.[85] But it took a long time until the new double-entry bookkeeping was generally accepted and perfected. At the end of the fourteenth century, the Datini company in Avignon did not yet use the new bookkeeping, whereas others did.[86] In the older accounts of the Venetian firm Soranzo & Brothers, which date to the beginning of the fifteenth century, the double-entry bookkeeping is still incomplete. There is no profit or deficit saldo. But the later account books of the firm comprise such saldos and capital accounts too. Profit and loss are used to balance accounts.[87]

B. Shipping the Merchandise

The progress made in shipping in that period was no less remarkable. It underwent various changes, which resulted in the improvement of transport

[80] Leonardo de Valle sub 22 Dec. 1401.
[81] H. Sieveking, "Aus venezianischen Handlungsbüchern," *Jahrbuch* 25, p. 1,498.
[82] *Art. cit.*, pp. 1501, 1505.
[83] F. Melis, *Storia della ragioneria* (Bologna, 1950), pp. 401 f., 435.
[84] F. Besta, *La ragioneria*, 2nd edition, III (Milan, 1916), p. 273.
[85] *Op.cit.*, p. 341 ff., 348; Sieveking, *art. cit.*, p. 1,502; see also V. Alfieri, *La partita doppia* (Turin, 1891), p. 64.
[86] Besta, *op.cit.*, p. 317 f.
[87] Sieveking, *art. cit.*, p. 1,502.

facilities. New types of ships were used in the Mediterranean, and the old ones were perfected.

The introduction of the cog at the beginning of the fourteenth century was a very important step in the development of Mediterranean shipping. In the year 1309 Basque pirates from Bayonne first brought this northern ship into the Mediterranean, and within a short time it was used everywhere. It was a one-masted square-rigged vessel and had two high castles, one on the bow and the other on the stern. This ship, which had no oars at all, was considered a cheap and safe means of transport. It could indeed be managed by few sailors and successfully resisted attacks of pirates.[88] Through the fourteenth century and the first half of the fifteenth century, this vessel was widely used for the transport of bulky and cheap articles, but it was also used for the shipping of spices. Then in the middle of the fifteenth century another type of sailing ship spread in the Mediterranean—the carrack. It had several masts, but the main mast was much higher than the others and carried a very large square sail plus smaller sails. The rigging of this ship made it easy to tack and to sail into the wind.[89]

The galley, which had originally been a warship and was used for the transport of precious merchandise, also changed in that period. Over a period of time, its dimensions increased more and more.

Whereas at the end of the thirteenth century the largest Venetian galleys, those used for the trips to Flanders, could freight 140 tons below deck, in the fifteenth century they carried 200 tons. By the middle of the fifteenth century, the biggest Venetian merchant galleys could even carry 250 tons below deck.[90] The galleys not only became larger; they also changed their character. In fact they became sailing ships, since the oars were used only when entering or leaving a port or in case of emergency, such as the need to approach a coast because of a storm. Consequently, in the middle of the fifteenth century, a third mast was added to the two. So the galley combined the advantages of the round sailing ship—its speed—with that of the warship—its security owing to its numerous crew, which could effectively resist pirates.[91] Therefore at the end of the fourteenth century the galleys were also used by the Catalans for their trade with the Moslem Levant, for they guaranteed the safe transport of the precious Oriental commodities.[92] But, in time, the Catalans began to prefer the Cantabrian big round ships, which

[88] Lane, *Ships and shipbuilders*, p. 37. B. Hagedorn, *Die Entwicklung der wichtigsten Schiffstypen bis ins 19. Jahrhundert* (Berlin, 1914), p. 10 f.

[89] Lane, p. 41 f.

[90] *Op.cit.*, p. 15.

[91] *Op.cit.*, pp. 16, 22, 24. Cf. A. Sacerdote, "Note sulle galere di mercato veneziane nel XV secolo," *Bollettino dell' Istituto di storia della società e della Stato veneziano* IV (1962), p. 80 ff.

[92] Carrère, *Barcelone*, p. 278 f.

they called "Castilian ships" or simply *nau*. They had one or two decks and a great capacity.[93]

The tendency to build bigger vessels was a striking feature of Mediterranean shipping in the fourteenth and the fifteenth centuries. The greater speed of the ships used in the Mediterranean in that period and the increase of capacity made it possible to lower the freight rates. This was indeed a great advantage for the Levant trade.[94]

The Genoese had the biggest ships. According to data collected in the Datini papers, at the end of the fourteenth century, they had 64 ships whose capacity was more than 800 butts, that is, 400 tons.[95] Many of them were used for the traffic with the Levant. The characteristic capacity of the Catalan round ships used for long distance trade was 500-600 butts;[96] the Catalan galleys carried a freight of 270-280 butts.[97] In Venice too big ships were built. The dimensions of the Venetian Alexandria galleys had been fixed in 1352 at 188 tons (400 milliaria). In the year 1440 the Senate decided that henceforth the maximum capacity of the galley should be 188-207 tons (400-440 milliaria). But in 1480 big galleys whose capacity was 235-282 tons (500-600 milliaria) were built, and 211.5 tons (450 mill.) was established as the maximum capacity.[98] The Venetian cotton cogs were much bigger; they had a capacity of 360-480 tons (500-800 butts).[99] These facts show clearly that the size of the ships was fixed mainly because of economic reasons. The Genoese, who specialized in the long-distance trade of bulky and cheap articles like alum, built big vessels. The Venetians, who traded much more with spices, preferred smaller ships with a large crew, which could effectively defend the freight.[100]

The Venetian merchant galleys usually had 180 oarsmen and in addition

[93] *Op.cit.*, p. 280 ff. About this ship, see B. Hagedorn, *op.cit.*, pp. 25, 27.

[94] Cf. Lane, *op.cit.*, p. 46.

[95] F. Melis, "Werner Sombart e i problemi della navigazione nel medio evo," in *L'opera di Werner Sombart nel centenario della nascità* (Milan, 1964), p. 97. About the butt, see Melis, *art. cit.*, p. 95; Carrère, "Le droit d'ancrage," *EHM* III, p. 91; Del Treppo, "Assicurazioni," p. 528; and, on the other hand, G. Luzzatto, "Per la storia delle costruzioni navali a Venezia nei secoli XV e XVI," in his *Studi di storia economica veneziana*, p. 43; Lane, "The merchant marine of the Venetian republic," in his *Venice and history*, p. 144. U. Tucci, "Un problema di metrologia navale: la botta veneziana," *Studi Veneziani* IX (1967), p. 201 ff., especially p. 221. According to these papers two butts should be distinguished, that of the Tyrrhenian Sea of 0,45 t and the Venetian of 0,61 t.

[96] Melis, *art. cit.*, p. 97.

[97] Carrère, "Le droit d'ancrage," p. 95.

[98] Lane, *Venetian ships and shipbuilders*, p. 15.

[99] *Op.cit.*, p. 255 f.; 400 butts were considered to be minimum size; see Misti 34, f. 76b f. 43, f. 65a f.

[100] J. Heers, "Types de navires et spécialisation du trafic en Méditerranée a la fin du Moyen Âge," in *Le navire et l'économie maritime du Moyen Âge au XIIIe siècle, principalment en Méditerranée* (2e colloque internationale d'histoire maritime 1957) (Paris, 1958), p. 110 f.

20 bowmen.[101] Genoese galleys, at the end of the thirteenth century, had 112 oarsmen and in the middle of the fourteenth century 174.[102] The crew of the Catalan galleys was a bit smaller; it numbered about 100 men.[103] The crews of the sailing ships were of course much smaller and in time, owing to the perfection of navigation and greater nautical skill, it was possible to reduce them. Whereas a Venetian cog in the thirteenth century often had a crew of 50 sailors, a cotton cog in the later Middle Ages usually had not much more than 20, 8 apprentices, and some bowmen. In 1433 the Venetian Senate decreed that the Syria cogs should have 8 men for 100 butts. So these cogs had on the average 50 seamen.[104] But there were no fixed rules, since the number of the crews, and especially the number of the bowmen, depended upon the conditions of security prevailing in a particular year. In the first half of the fifteenth century, the Senate sometimes decided that a cotton cog should have 6 bowmen for 100 butts and other times that it should have 8.[105] So a cog of 600 butts would have employed from 36 to 48 bowmen alone. In the year 1426 the Senate decreed that every cotton cog sailing to Syria should have 100 sailors and in addition 4 bowmen for every 100 butts. On the other hand, the Council of the Venetian colony in Alexandria chartered a Venetian cog in 1401 for the transport of merchandise that remained after the loading of the galleys, on condition that it would have a crew of 38 men.[106] From a notarial act drawn up in Alexandria in 1402, it is learned that a Venetian cog anchoring in the port had a crew of 70 men.[107] A Catalan sailing ship, which was chartered in the same year in Alexandria for a trip to Syria and from there to Sicily, had only 35 sailors.[108] But, despite the small crews, the cogs very often proved defendable against the attacks of corsairs and were used for all purposes and on all lines.

The big Genoese ships served mainly on what was the longest artery of European world trade in those days: the line that connected Chios, Rhodes, and the ports of Egypt and Syria with Flanders and England. The Genoese ships sailed directly from the Levantine ports to Northwestern Europe without going first to Genoa and made the same journey in the opposite

[101] Lane, *Venetian ships and shipbuilders*, p. 24; *idem*, "From biremes to triremes," in his *Venice and history*, p. 190; see, further, Misti 49, f. 126b f.

[102] Balletto, *Genova, Mediterraneo, Mar Nero*, pp. 13, 140.

[103] Carrère, *Barcelone*, p. 214.

[104] Lane, *Venetian ships and shipbuilders*, p. 39; Misti 58, f. 212a.

[105] Misti 56, f. 16b f., 23a f., 58, f. 213a.

[106] Misti 55, f. 181a ff. Other times, the crew of 100 men were to include the bowmen; see Misti 47, f. 7a f.

[107] Leonardo de Valle, sub 12 Apr. 1402; Verb. Cons. XII sub 11 Oct. 1401.

[108] Leonardo de Valle sub 1 Sept. 1402.

direction.[109] Another major line of the long-distance trade was that connecting the coasts of Southern France with Egypt and Syria. The French merchantmen, of course, used this line a good deal, visiting some Italian ports, mostly Gaeta and Naples, on the way to the Near East. On the way back, there was usually a stop at Rhodes.[110] Genoese and other Ligurian ships, too, very often sailed from the ports of Languedoc and Provence to Alexandria[111] and from Alexandria via Rhodes to Aigues-Mortes.[112] The Catalans were also very active on this line,[113] and even Venetian merchantmen sometimes used it. They sailed from Venice to Aigues-Mortes and from there to Alexandria.[114] A third major artery of the trade with the Levant was the line connecting Barcelona and the other parts of Catalonia with Alexandria and Beirut. The number of ports the Catalan ships visited in Italy, both on the mainland and in Sicily, and farther in the Eastern Mediterranean on their way to the Moslem Levant, was particularly great, so that their trips often took a very long time. Ships from Venice to Alexandria and Beirut had for a long time sailed along fixed lines, which were rarely modified. Both galleys and cogs visited Corfu, Coron, Modon, and Candia before sailing to the major ports of Syria and Egypt. The Venetian convoys shunned Rhodes because of the rather cool relations between the Serenissima and the Knights.

In addition to these major lines of shipping between the South European emporia and the ports of the Moslem Levant, some short lines fulfilled an important role in the Levant trade. A great part of the European merchandise which was exported to the Moslem Levant was shipped to Chios, Rhodes, and Crete and often changed hands there before being sent to Beirut or Alexandria. Chios, the great Genoese emporium in the Greek archipelago, was also a stopping place on the Alexandria-Constantinople route. The traffic between this Genoese colony and Alexandria was intense through the whole of that period.[115] With the exception of the Venetians, all European trading nations had flourishing colonies in Rhodes and used its port as a point of support for their trade with the Moslem Levant. On the other hand, ships sailing from Rhodes to the Western Mediterranean called in Alexandria.[116] Crete, the backbone of the Venetian colonial empire,

[109] Vat. sub 13 Dec. 1404 and see above.

[110] Vat. sub 10 Dec. 1399; Nic. Venier B, 2; f. 42b ff., and see on travels from Alexandria to Aigues-Mortes Vat. sub 21 Apr. 1400, 11 Aug. 1404; Leonardo de Valle sub 23 Dec. 1401.

[111] Vat. sub 25 Febr. 1400, 1 Sept. 1401.

[112] Vat. sub 1 Oct. 1405; G. P., Sent. 21, f. 19a ff., 21a.

[113] Vat. sub 21 Apr. 1400, 9 Dec. 1405.

[114] G. P., Sent. 10, f. 87a f.; Crist. del Fiore I, f. 4b ff.

[115] Nic. Venier B, 2, f. 38b f.; see, further, there f. 40a ff. See also pp. 133, 228 and below p. 480, about Chios see M. Balard, *La Romanie génoise* (Genoa, 1978), pp. 215 ff., 255 ff.

[116] Nic. Venier B. 2 f. 42b.

chiefly served the empire's own merchants. Venetian and Cretan ships sailed continually between Candia and Alexandria.

Because of the numerous stops made on the trips to the Moslem Levant, the journeys that the merchants of the various trading nations made on these lines took a rather long time. Catalan ships rarely returned from a trip to Syria or Egypt in less than 10 months. For the return from the Levant, one seldom needed less than 100 days.[117] A galley could make the trip in 30 days, but there were only a few ships that did not make several stops. In 1453, on the way from Barcelona to Alexandria, the galley "Santa Maria-Sant Jordi" stopped 2 days in Cagliari, 6 in Naples, 3 in Palermo, 2 in Messina, 2 in Syracuse, and 10 in Rhodes. Then it remained in Alexandria 60 days.[118] The Anconitan ships usually required 8 months for the trip to the Moslem Levant,[119] but sometimes they returned within 5 or 6 months.[120] The Venetian galleys and cogs needed 4 or 5 weeks for the trip to Syria or Egypt.

The diversity of the vessels employed in the shipping is reflected in their prices. At the beginning of the fifteenth century, in Alexandria, a small ship, like a *panfilo* or *spinaccia*, cost 400-600 ducats.[121] A ship of 250 butts was sold in Venice in 1447 for 400 ducats, another in 1433 for 456 ducats.[122] The price of a big round ship in that period was always 4,000-5,000 ducats. Prices on this level are indicated in deeds dated the beginning of the fifteenth century and drawn up in Alexandria.[123] The big Catalan naus fetched very high prices. In the first half of the fifteenth century they cost 6,000-7,000 Barcelona pounds, i.e., 7,800-9,100 ducats.[124] Others were sold for 2000-4000 pounds, i.e., 2,600-3,000 ducats.[125] The prices of the Genoese ships were equal to those of the Catalan ships.[126] The small sailing ships used by the minor trading nations for the traffic to the Levant were much

[117] Del Treppo, "Assicurazioni," p. 336 ff.

[118] Carrère, *Barcelone*, p. 270 ff. Because of the length of the trips which Catalan merchantmen made to the Moslem Levant, commenda loans were repaid with a delay of two to three years or even more; see APO, F. Bosqueros 735, f. 5b, 6a f., 7b, 8a; Ant. Guitard 1554, sub 27 Febr. and 1 March 1417?.

[119] Tom. Marchetti V, f. 110b, 113b f.; Ang. di Domenico V, f. 64a VIII, f. 43a f., 69b f., 261b, 277b IX, f. 222a; Ant. Giov. di Giacomo III, part I, f. 99a, 102a f.

[120] Ang. di Domenico VIII, f. 102a f. IX, f. 193b; Ant. Giov. di Giacomo 27, f. 347'a f. On the other hand, some journeys took 10 months; see Giacomo Alberici VII, f. 106a; Ang. di Domenico IX, f. 190a f.

[121] Leonardo de Valle sub 4 Nov. 1401, 5 Febr. 1403; Vat. sub 1 Oct. 1404, 25 June 1404; Crist. del Fiore I, f. 4a f.

[122] G. P., Sent. 64, f. 25a 128, f. 41b ff.

[123] Vat. sub 13 Dec. 1404, 12 Oct. 1405.

[124] Carrère, *Barcelone*, pp. 211, 282, 283.

[125] *Op.cit.*, p. 296 ff. The ships sailing from Collioure to Italy and the Levant may have been smaller. In 1454 a ship was sold in Perpignan for 1600 ducats; see APO, Ant. Granatge 893, f. 30a.

[126] Vat. sub 29 Dec. 1401; Caito, see note 130.

cheaper. Most ships used by the Anconitans for their maritime trade cost 300-600 ducats:[127] few cost more than 1,000 ducats.[128]

Many of these ships that served on the lines to the Moslem Levant were collective property. In the smaller trading centers of Southern Europe, there were few capitalists who could afford, and were inclined to invest their money in the purchase of whole ships. It was too risky an enterprise, since insurance of ships was not so common as insurance of merchandise, and often the insurers tried to withdraw from their obligation. The possession of a big ship, on the other hand, meant a great investment even for a truly rich merchant. So most ships had several co-owners. In Catalonia one bought *setzenas* (1/16 of a ship), or even a half or a quarter.[129] The Genoese bought *luoghi* (or *loci* in Latin), the Venetians *carati*, i.e., 1/24 of a ship.[130]

In addition to the privately owned ships, those owned by the state, mostly galleys which also served as warships, fulfilled an important role in the Levant trade of all South European trading nations. Both the government of Catalonia and the town of Barcelona had galleys, which they leased to the merchants for their travels to the Levant. However, these galleys were used for the trade with the Moslem Levant only in a certain period. In the 1390's and at the beginning of the fifteenth century, it was the galleys of the town of Barcelona that were chartered and in the 1430's those of the Generalitat.[131] Usually rich and experienced merchants were the patrons who undertook to lease them and to lead the expedition. The patrons indeed needed great experience in the Levant trade and, on the other hand, took the opportunity themselves to engage in trade.[132] But the role of the privately owned ships was incomparably greater in the Levant trade of Catalonia. The role of the state galleys in the Levant trade of Genoa was limited too. Even they sailed on this line only a relatively short time, at the end of the fourteenth century and at the beginning of the fifteenth century. Florence made a great effort to establish state galley lines, which were intended to connect Porto Pisano with the Moslem Levant and with other Mediterranean regions. But the undertaking was not successful.[133] Only Venice succeeded in establishing such lines to the Levant. Contrary to the

[127] Ang. di Domenico X, f. 58b, 144b, 146b XI, f. 102b XII, f. 150a, 164a, 230b; Giacomo Alberici V, f. 125b f. IV, f. 33b VI, f. 18b; see, further, my "Il commercio levantino di Ancona," p. 246 f.

[128] Ang. di Domenico X, f. 237a, 237b f. XII, f. 33b; Ashtor, *l.c.*

[129] Carrère, *op.cit.*, p. 202 f.

[130] ASG, Caito, Andr. V. c. 30a; Nic. Venier B, 2, f. 33a f., 34b f., 37a/b. In Ancona, too, the ships were divided into carats; see Ang. di Domenico X, f. 146b, 237a, 237b f. E. Sayous, "Les transformations des méthodes commerciales dans l'Italie médiévale," *Ann. d'hist. éc. et soc.* I (1929), p. 168.

[131] Carrère, *op.cit.*, p. 264 f.

[132] *Op.cit.*, p. 212n.

[133] See above.

shipping of the other trading nations of Southern Europe, the state galleys of Venice were in the forefront of her Levant trade.

From the year 1329 the Republic chartered her galleys every year to merchants, who took part in an auction.[134] The system of the Venetian state galleys was successful for a variety of reasons. Since the ship patrons were members of profit-seeking partnerships, they had a great personal interest in obtaining full freights. But the registration of the freight and the collecting of the freight charges was entrusted to a body of state officials, the so-called *straordinari*. Consequently, the merchants who loaded merchandise on the galleys were sure that they, as officials, would collect the same rate from all.[135] However, the main reasons for the success of the galley lines were the great security and the regularity. Transport on a ship whose crew numbered 200 men was a better guarantee than the best insurance. The regularity of the service warranted the merchant that he would find merchandise in the Levantine parts, for the agents and the Moslem merchants stocked them for the time of arrival of the galleys, the so-called *mudda*.[136] Every year the Senate fixed the day on which the convoys of the Alexandria and Beirut galleys should depart. At the end of the fourteenth century and at the beginning of the fifteenth century, their departure was usually fixed for a day in the second half of August and, later, upon the request of the merchants, delayed to the beginning of September.[137] Then in the 1430's the departures were postponed to the end of August or to the month of September.[138] In the 1470's the galleys departed from Venice even in October,[139] but in 1481 it was decided that they should again depart at the end of August.[140] The duration of the *mudda*, a true spice fair, was limited by the decisions of the Venetian Senate. At the end of the fourteenth century it would last twenty-eight days in Beirut and in Alexandria, twenty.[141] In addition to Beirut the galleys anchored in Syria and other ports. From 1398 onward one galley was to visit Acre,[142] and from 1400 on another was to visit Tripoli and Latakia.[143] The orders that the Senate gave the captains of the galleys going to Syria changed, however, from year to year, according to the wishes of the merchants. In the year

[134] F. C. Lane, "Merchant galleys 1300-1334, private and communal operation," in his *Venice and history*, p. 194.

[135] *Art. cit.*, p. 223.

[136] The term is apparently an Arabic one, meaning time, duration.

[137] Misti 38, f. 33b, 34b, 70b, 132b, 156a 39, f. 2a, 84b, 114a 40, f. 30a 71b, 85a, 86a, 118b, 128a 41, f. 10a, 15b, 25b, 91a, 96b 42, f. 3a, 3b; 19b, 21a etc.

[138] Misti 58, f. 70a ff. 59, f. 169b ff., 170b ff., 173a, 174b 60, f. 29a f., 35a, 223a ff., 224a f.

[139] Senato Mar XI, f. 48a.

[140] Senato Mar XI, f. 119b XII, f. 17a/b, 56a, 57b, 85a, 117b, 176b.

[141] Misti 42, f. 3a, 3b, 63a, 113b, 114a 43, f. 8b 48, f. 83b f. 54, f. 143a f.

[142] Misti 44, f. 54a.

[143] Misti 45, f. 17a.

1412, for instance, it was decided that two galleys should go to Latakia and Tripoli and in 1413 that all the Syria galleys should go there.[144] Even Jaffa, which served as port of Ramla, was visited by the galleys.[145] The Venetian galley traffic to Egypt and Syria was completed from 1461 by the *trafego* galleys, which first visited the ports of Tunisia and Tripoli and then went to Alexandria and Beirut; they departed in April.[146]

The Venetian galley lines were successfully supplemented by the state lines of cogs to Alexandria and Syria which served as carriers of heavy, cheap commodities, mainly cotton and alkali. They were chosen every year (or more correctly twice a year—for the spring and the fall trip) according to their fitness, from the ships offered, and duly registered by the authorities. The Senate fixed the freight tariffs, just as it did for the galleys, and granted them certain privileges as to customs and other prerogatives.[147] Like the galleys, these cogs were also to depart on dates fixed by the Senate: the Syrian cogs were to depart at the end of January and late in July, so that the cotton *muddas* could be held in March and September;[148] the Alexandria cogs were to depart in July or August.[149] During a certain period, a cotton mudda was also held in Alexandria in March,[150] but later the spring sailing of cotton ships to Egypt was abolished.

Almost countless decisions of the Venetian Senate testify to its firmness in maintaining the timetable of the muddas in Egypt and Syria. Only for exceptional reasons were they prolonged either by the Council of the colonies in Alexandria or in Damascus or by the Senate itself. The numerous decrees that spices or cotton arriving in Venice (or in one of the Venetian colonies in the Levant) after the return of the galleys or the cotton ships should be stored and put under lock and key until the arrival of the next convoy show clearly that the Venetian government had not only the interests of the patrons of the galleys and the cotton cogs in mind. It also wanted to make sure that the German, and other, merchants who came every year after the return of the galleys and the cotton cogs to Venice should find sufficient quantities of merchandise. But it seems that, in addition to the time before Christmas, another fair for spices (without the juridical implication of the former institution) was held in July.[151]

[144] Misti 49, f. 125b f. 50, f. 4b ff.

[145] Misti 47, f. 117b (a. 1407) 48, f. 12b ff., 82a ff.

[146] Senato Mar XIV, f. 33a; J. Sottas, *Les messageries*, p. 11 f.; cf. Ch. VII, note 156.

[147] For the establishment of the system, see the decree of the Senate of 24 July 1366, in Misti 32, f. 3b.

[148] Misti 35, f. 157a. But in the 1360's and early 1370's, they departed later: see Misti 34, f. 76b f., 110a. Sometimes cotton ships sailed to Syria in June or July; see *Chron. Morosini*, c. 353.

[149] Misti 32, f. 131a 34, f. 17b, 108a 35, f. 112a.

[150] Misti 51, f. 88b, 187a, 42, f. 42b.

[151] See F. C. Lane, "Fleets and airs," in his *Venice and history*, p. 134 f.

The strictness of the Venetian authorities in maintaining the fixed time-table of the *muddas* was truly rigid. Rarely was merchandise arriving after the return of the convoys not sequestered.[152] On the other hand, the Venetian government took measures to protect the galleys and cog lines. The primary concern was, of course, their security. Piracy and corsair activities, the latter licensed by certain governments, were never absent entirely in the later Middle Ages. The dangers that arose for the ships sailing to the Moslem Levant from Turkish piracy was not one of the great problems of Venetian shipping, although Turkish privateers sometimes attacked Venetian ships even in the ports of Syria and Egypt or nearby. The Turkish pirates sometimes also infested the Ionian Sea, but mostly they endangered the traffic in the Aegean and attacked the islands held by Venetians in the archipelago.[153] But Genoese pirates, mostly exiles, and Catalan corsairs, who had their bases in Sicily or in Rhodes, for long periods were a great danger to Venetian shipping in the eastern and central basin of the Mediterranean, and they even intruded into the Adriatic. Biscayan pirates were also active in the eastern Mediterranean.[154] The government of Venice sent warships to escort the merchant galleys and the cogs,[155] and in time of special danger decided that the Alexandria and Beirut galleys should sail together as far as Coron and that there or in Modon or Candia a council of patrons should decide whether or not to continue on.[156] In such cases, the cotton ships too were to sail together, as the galleys always did.[157] When the danger of attacks by corsairs was imminent, it was decided by the Senate that the number of the bowmen on the galleys and the cogs should be increased, although a galley bound to the Moslem Levant usually had twenty.[158] It was further agreed that the amount of ordnance that the ships carried should be increased and that those ships that had none should be armed.[159] The Venetian government also protected the economic interests of the galley and cog patrons. Although the decrees enacted by the Senate were different almost every year, two main lines of this legislation are clear. On one hand, the prerogative of the galleys to transport of spices must be guarded against the inclination of the merchants to ship spices on

[152] Misti 39, f. 22a, 56, f. 137a.

[153] A. Tenenti, "Venezia e la pirateria nel Levante 1300 c.-1460 c.," in *Venezia e il Levante fino al secolo XV*, pp. 722, 740. See also the observation of A. M. Lybyer, "The influence of the rise of the Ottoman Turks upon the routes of Oriental trade," in *Annual report of the American Historical Association for 1914* I, p. 125 ff.

[154] *Art. cit.*, p. 740 f.

[155] Misti 29, f. 22b 39, f. 2b 5, f. 48b, 56b f., 58, f. 159a ff.

[156] Misti 44, f. 120a, 48, f. 28a.

[157] Misti 48, f. 98a, 56, f. 57b.

[158] Misti 47, f. 56a, 56b, 117b f., 48, f. 13b f., 27b, 99a, 49, f. 125b f., 50, f. 3b f., 52, f. 22b.

[159] Misti 47, f. 25b, 56, f.141b ff., 154b.

the cogs, whose freight charges were much smaller. Since this principle could not always be enforced, it was permitted to ship on the cogs to Syria precious cloth and on the return certain spices could be shipped, but the same or half of the freight charges were paid as on the galleys, and at least a part of them were assigned to the government or to the galleys, if there remained place in their stacks on the return to Venice. This rule also applied to the supplementary ships (*navi di rata*), which transported the merchandise that remained in Alexandria or Beirut after the departure of the galleys to Venice.[160] Secondly, it was forbidden to ship merchandise to and from the Levant on other ships during a certain time before the departure and return of the galley convoys and cotton cogs.[161]

The freight tariff in international shipping underwent a great change at the end of the fourteenth century and changed again during the fifteenth century. Very often a contract with a shipowner included the obligation to load a certain quantity of various commodities for the payment of a global charge calculated on the basis of what would be paid for the largest part of the shipment. The shipper reserved to himself the right to load an additional (smaller) quantity for which he would pay according to prevailing tariffs or by special agreement. The freight loaded for payment fixed in the contract was called *de firmo*, the other *de rispetto*. Such agreements had been made through the fourteenth century and were also made later, but at the end of the fourteenth century, when larger vessels were beginning to be built for the transport of bulky merchandise, there was a general tendency to differentiate the freight charges for various commodities much more than before. The new freight tariffs made the transport of cheap articles over long distances more profitable, and offered other advantages for the patrons as well, for the latter would otherwise sometimes have sailed in one direction with a very small freight or with none at all.[162] In that period there was a general tendency, owing to the increase of tonnage, to diminish the freight charges. At the end of the fourteenth century they were lower than in the first half. There was also a trend to replace *ad valorem* freight charges by *ad quantitatem* charges.[163]

At the end of the thirteenth century, for the transport of grains in the Black Sea on Genoese ships, 10-20 percent *ad valorem* was paid. A hundred years later, the freight charges for grains were 12-15 percent in the Tyrrhenian Sea.[164] But in the middle of the fifteenth century, the freight charges on Genoese ships for pepper or ginger amounted to 1.8 percent, for cotton

[160] Misti 40, f. 72a, 93b, 41, f. 10a, 47, f. 7a f., 52, f. 101b f., 53, f. 53b, 56, f. 16b f.

[161] Misti 43, f. 130b f., 44, f. 7a f., 48b f., 45, f. 18a f., 46, f. 144b f., 47, f. 25b, 48, f. 158a ff., 49, f. 31b ff., 50, f. 134a, 51, f. 29a f., 136a, 56, f. 60a ff.

[162] F. Melis, "Werner Sombart," pp. 131 f., 137.

[163] *Art. cit.*, pp. 124, 135.

[164] Balletto, *Genova, Mediterraneo, Mar Nero*, p. 132; Melis, *art. cit.*, p. 138.

to 6 percent, and for lead to 13 percent of the value.[165] The freight charges of the state lines of Venice were fixed anew almost every year by the Senate. The shipping of a milliarium (grosso, i.e., 470 kg) of copper on the Alexandria galleys in the second half of the fourteenth century cost 5 ducats or even 5 shillings of grosso, according to these tariffs.[166] These charges probably corresponded to 6 or 3 percent of the value of the merchandise. For a bale of cheap cloth shipped on the Beirut galleys one paid 4¾ ducats and sometimes only 1 ducat. For money and precious stone 1 percent *ad valorem* was paid.[167] The transport of spices from the Levant on galleys was expensive. A charge of 19 *soldi grossorum* or 1 pound 3 gr' for a milliarium (sottile, i.e., 301 kg) probably meant 9 percent of the value.[168] The cogs charged less. In the last third of the fourteenth century and at the beginning of the fifteenth century, 2-3 ducats was the charge to ship a mill' copper or tin on a Venetian cog (of the state lines) sailing to Alexandria,[169] or a ducat less than on the galleys (*sic!*).[170] These charges probably represented 2-4 percent of the value of the shipment. In the 1370's it cost 3 ducats to ship a bale of cloth. Since a bale usually contained 10 pieces, and a piece of cheap Italian cloth cost 13-15 ducats (selling price in Syria), these charges amounted to 2 percent of the value. Shipping of coral, ambergris, and furs cost 1½ percent *ad valorem*.[171] In the 1430's only 1-1½ ducats was charged for a bale of cheap cloth.[172] The charges for the shipping of pepper and ginger from Alexandria to Venice in 1385 were fixed at 4 ducats for a milliarium,[173] less than half of what it cost on a galley. In another tariff, a charge of two ducats was fixed for a collo of Alexandria.[174] These charges corresponded to 2-3½ percent of the value of the spices. The freight charges for spices shipped on the Syria cogs were on the same level. For a Syrian collo of spices (of 90 kg), according to a tariff of the 1420's, only one ducat payment was required;[175] characteristically enough, in an earlier tariff higher charges are found; for a tariff fixed by the Senate in 1411 established 4 ducats for a milliarium.[176] Since

165 Heers, *Gênes*, p. 318.
166 Misti 29, f. 9a, 30, f. 17a.
167 Misti 53, f. 104a, f. 214a ff., 220a, 58, f. 70 ff., 59, f. 57a, 119b. The freight charges for very cheap cloth, however, were more expensive, see Misti 56, f. 32a ff., 57, f. 11b, 13b, 117a.
168 Misti 53, f. 158b ff. (a. 1421), 55, f. 31a, 147a, 149a, 54, f. 116b ff., 57, f. 117a, 58, f. 70a f. (a. 1451).
169 Misti 38, f. 127a, 39, f. 91b, 40, f. 73a, 46, f. 32b f., 144b.
170 Misti 34, f. 76b f., 38, f. 34a.
171 Misti 34, f. 76b f.
172 Misti 57, f. 233a, 58, f. 213a.
173 Misti 39, f. 83b.
174 Misti 57, f. 233a.
175 Misti 55, f. 182a, 56, f. 142b.
176 Misti 48, f. 209a (a. 1411).

this charge probably corresponded to 1.4 percent and 2.5 percent of the value of the spices in Syria, in the 1420's and in 1411, respectively, this was a remarkable decrease of the expenses for transport. But the security of transport by cogs was much less than that on the galleys, so that the merchants were induced to insure spices shipped on cogs and, secondly, they had to pay an additional impost for spices loaded on the cotton ships (see below). The charges in the freight tariffs established by the Venetian Senate for raw and spun cotton and other commodities shipped on the state line of cogs show even more clearly that the costs of transport decreased in the fifteenth century. In the year 1374 the Senate fixed a charge of 10 ducats for a milliarium (301 kg) of raw cotton,[177] and in 1378 it was even 15 ducats.[178] It decreased to 12 ducats in 1405, 7 ducats in 1406, and 6 ducats in the 1420's and the 1430's.[179]

Judicial acts and accounts of some firms show that these tariffs were not always strictly applied. Several judicial acts and other documents refer to the payment of freight charges, which amounted to 9.5 ducats for a milliarium, for spices shipped on the Venetian galleys.[180] This charge corresponded to the official tariff. Domenico di Piero paid 143 ducats in 1474 for 53 colli spices shipped on the Beirut galleys to Venice. If one assumes that a collo was worth 30 ducats, the freight would even in that case have amounted to 9 percent of the value.[181] The firm Franc. Contarini sometimes paid even more, viz. 11.5 ducats for a milliarium.[182] The accounts of the family Malipiero also point to the freight amounting to 9-10 percent of the value of the spices.[183] But from other documents one learns that for the transport of spices on the galleys the payment was *ad valorem* and much less, e.g., 3.2 percent for the shipping of green ginger on the Beirut galleys in 1406, and 6 percent for pepper shipped on the Alexandria galleys in 1444.[184] Domenico di Zorzi paid charges that amounted to perhaps 2.5 percent of their value in 1474 for the transport of various spices on the Beirut galleys.[185] So there must have been special arrangements which entailed reduction of the freight charges.[186]

Transport on ships not supervised by the government—that is, the free

[177] Misti 34, f. 76b.

[178] Misti 36, f. 59b.

[179] Misti 47, f. 7a, 25b, 56, f. 16b f., 142b, 58, f. 22a, 60a ff., but cf. f. 62a. Sometimes the freight charge was even reduced to 5 ducats; see Misti 41, f. 21b.

[180] G. P., Sent. 123, f. 49a ff., 133, f. 40b, 137, f. 6a, 191, f. 24b; Accounts of Franc. Contarini, f. 53a.

[181] G. P., Ter. XI, f. 27b ff.

[182] Accounts Franc. Contarini, f. 55a.

[183] Accounts Malipiero, Ba 161, fasc. VI, VII.

[184] G. P., Sent. 39, f. 3b ff., 98, f. 58a ff.

[185] G. P., Ter XI, f. 28a.

[186] See also the data quoted in my "Profits from trade with the Levant," pp. 265, 266.

lancers engaged in tramping from one port to another—was generally cheaper. When some Anconitans chartered a Catalan vessel in 1402 in Alexandria for a journey to Tripoli and on to Ancona, they stipulated that the charge for a ḳinṭār (of Tripoli) of cotton would be 3 ducats and for a ḳinṭār of alkali, 1.[187] The freight charges for 8570 (Anconitan) pounds of soap from Ancona to Latakia cost 14 ducats in 1460.[188] This was probably 11 percent of their value (in Ancona).[189] But the charter of a whole ship to sail from Beirut to Ancona cost only 350 ducats in 1470.[190]

All these data show how the progress made in the later Middle Ages in shipping, owing to the construction of bigger vessels and the advance in nautical skills, had reduced the freight charges, as compared with what was paid in the period of the Crusades. Some data that have come down to us in Geniza documents that refer to the freight charges paid for olive oil, soap, and wax shipped from Tunis to Sicily or Egypt point to much higher rates.[191]

In addition to the almost progressive reduction in the cost of transport, the great advance of European navigation had another consequence: the Moslems, both the Near Easterners and the Maghrebins, more and more had recourse to European shipping. They used ships of all the European seapowers for their own travels and for the transport of merchandise. The Genoese and Catalans, whose fleets held a dominant position in the Western Mediterranean, of course had the lion's share in the traffic between the Maghreb and the Near East. The Moslems sometimes chartered whole ships of these trading nations on this line.[192] But the Venetians also profitted greatly from the transport of Moslems and from shipping their merchandise from Tunisia to Egypt and vice-versa. Venetian ships carried wheat and olive oil from Tunisia to Alexandria[193] and merchandise of Moslem merchants bought in Egypt to Tunisia.[194] Since the transport of Moslems and their commodities not infrequently resulted in conflicts, the Venetian authorities from time to time forbade it.[195] But these prohibitions were obviously soon forgotten.

[187] Leonardo de Valle sub 19 Aug. 1402 (the shipping of alkali on the Venetian state line of cogs cost 3 ducats for a milliarium of 477 kg in the first decade of the fifteenth century; see Misti 47, f. 7a f. or 2,5, see there f. 25b).

[188] Ant. Giov. of Giacomo 74, f. 1a ff.

[189] See below, Table XL.

[190] Angelo di Domenico IX, f. 44a ff.

[191] S. D. Goitein, *A Mediterranean society* I (Univ. of California Press, 1967), p. 344.

[192] See a contract made in Alexandria in 1447 by a Catalan patron: Tur II, f. 24a and cf. above, Ch. IV, p. 214.

[193] Bibl. Naz. Florence, MS. Gino Capponi, Memorie varie, f. 246b; G. P., Cap. pub. XII, sub 17, and 19 March 1481.

[194] *Chron. Morosini*, c. 559; Misti 54, f. 143a; G. P., Sent. 174, f. 90b ff.

[195] See Verb. Cons. XII sub 12 Febr. 1402; Berchet, *Relazioni*, p. 38.

c. The Merchant Overseas

Whereas the activities of the Levant traders who carried on their business from offices in the European emporia had become much easier because of the great progress of commercial techniques, the agents in the Levant throughout the later Middle Ages encountered the same hardships that had embittered the lives of their predecessors in earlier periods. The enmity of the Moslems toward the "Franks" had not diminished; it had even become greater since the wars of extinction, which the first Mamluk sultans had waged against the Crusader principalities in the second half of the thirteenth century. The officials of the sultan and all those with whom the European merchants came into contact found a thousand ways to extort money from them. Often they were even beaten and imprisoned. But their passion for lucre was so strong that they remained in the trading centers of the Moslem Levant. The colonies of the European trading nations, with their consuls, did not discontinue their activities.

In Egypt, the European merchants carried on trade not only in Alexandria but also in Damietta and Cairo. European ships often anchored in the port of Damietta,[196] and Cretan vessels plied regularly between the ports of the island and the major port of Eastern Egypt.[197] Through the fifteenth century Venice had a vice-consul in the town. At the beginning of the century it was a Greek,[198] and in the middle and the end Venetians held the post.[199] The Greek was probably one of those foreigners who held the post of honorary consul, like the Sicilians who represented the Venetians interests in the trading towns of their island.[200] The Venetians were certainly only vice-consuls, even though they were sometimes called consuls. At the beginning of the fifteenth century there was also a French vice-consul in Damietta.[201] In the capital of Egypt there was no permanent commercial colony of a European trading nation, but the European merchants and other Westerners came there from time to time to conduct their affairs.[202]

At the end of the fourteenth century there were merchant colonies of Genoese and Catalans in Damascus, but in the course of the fifteenth century these colonies disappeared. However, in addition to the Venetians, there were almost always some Genoese or other South European merchants in Damascus,[203] but they formed no permanent organized colonies. When

[196] Ibn Iyās III, p. 182.

[197] Verb. Cons. XII sub 22 May 1402. See also *Voyage de Georges Lengherand, mayeur de Mons en Haynaut, 1485-1486*, ed. M. Godefroy-Menilglaise (Mons, 1961), p. 188.

[198] Nic. Venier A, f. 8b.

[199] G. P., Sent. 119, f. 64a ff.; Malipiero, p. 609.

[200] See Misti 55, f. 157a. But he may also have been a Greek subject of a Venetian colony.

[201] Tur V, f. 30a. Even he was a Greek.

[202] See Nic. Venier A, f. 8b: a Venetian notary in Cairo in 1420.

[203] See infra, Table LV.

Bertrandon de la Broquière visited Damascus in 1432, he met Venetian, Genoese, Florentine, Catalan, and French merchants, but he mentions only a Venetian consul.[204] The Venetians, on the other hand, always had a good-sized colony in the Syrian capital and several colonies in other towns of Syria. In Damascus they even had shops.[205] Venetian colonies existed in Ramla, Acre, Beirut, Tripoli, Ḥamā, Sarmīn, Latakia, and Aleppo. In Acre there was a Venetian vice-consul,[206] and Ḥamā, the center of a large cotton growing region, also had a Venetian vice-consul through the fifteenth century.[207] Apparently some Venetian merchants always lived in Latakia, from which great quantities of cotton were shipped;[208] and from the end of the fourteenth century the town had a Venetian vice-consul.[209] The upswing of the Venetian trade in Aleppo was closely connected with the purchase of Persian silk carried to northern Syria by the caravans from Iraq.[210] Since Aleppo was the terminus of these caravans, a Venetian colony came into being in the town in the second half of the fifteenth century, and in the 1460's it had a vice-consul.[211]

The merchants who remained through the year in Egypt or Syria were always busy. They sold the European commodities that came on the galleys and cogs, and they bought cotton. For throughout the year spice caravans arrived in Alexandria and Damascus. The caravans coming from the Ḥidjāz to Alexandria brought great quantities of spices, 10,000 or 11,000 pondi.[212] Those that came from the Ḥidjāz to Syria carried much smaller quantities, usually 2,000-4,000 (Syrian) colli.[213] But, in addition, spices were brought

[204] *Voyage*, pp. 32, 58.

[205] Lucchetta, "L'affare Zen," p. 161.

[206] See my "Europäischer Handel im spätmittelalterlichen Palästina," p. 114 f.

[207] G. P., Sent. 178, f. 46a.

[208] See Misti 38, f. 32a; G. P., Sent. 27, f. 57a f., 102, f. 73a ff., 107, f. 116b f., 185a ff., 109, f. 225a ff.

[209] Misti 42, f. 5b, 56, f. 41a ff.

[210] I viaggi degli ambasciatori veneti, p. 23, 162 ff., 194.

[211] Cristoforo del Fiore VI, f. 16b f.

[212] Melis, *Origini*, p. 51 (fall 1390): a caravan brought 7,000 pondi spices; Dat 549, letter of Zanobi di Taddeo Gaddi of 11 March 1394: a caravan brought 7,000 pondi pepper and about 2,000 pondi of other spices and aromata; *ibid.*, his letter of 24 April 1394: a caravan came to Alexandria with 11,000 pondi (of which 5,000 was pepper); Dat 550, his letter of 12 May 1396, a caravan carrying 8,000 pondi spices (of which 4.800 is pepper) is expected in Alexandria; Dat 1083, letter of the commessaria of Zanobi of 29 Nov. 1400: another caravan came with 10,000 pondi spices; Ainaud, "Quatre documents," doc. I (written on 13 Febr. 1401) and cf. Dat 550, letter of the commessaria of Zanobi of 19 May 1401: a caravan brought 12,000 pondi.

[213] Dat 548, letter of Zanobi of 21 April 1384: a caravan from Mecca is expected to arrive in Damascus in March and should carry 2,000 ḳinṭārs spices; Dat 549, letter of the same of 20 Sept. 1392: a caravan brought on 22 June to Damascus 11,000 loads of spices; *ibid.*, his letter of 24 Apr. 1394: two caravans came to Damascus at the end of December and brought mostly pepper; Dat 929, letter of the commess. of Zanobi of 27 Nov. 1406: a caravan brought 3,500 loads of spices from Mecca.

to Syria by caravans coming from the Persian Gulf via Iraq.[214] The European merchants who stayed through the year in the Levantine trading towns could always purchase spices, for the spice trade was free. It was neither a monopoly, nor were the prices fixed by the Mamluk officials.[215] However, these were forced purchases, and in a certain period, apparently when the power of the Kārimīs was very great, the Venetians were interested in the collective purchase of spices. In the year 1283 the Maggior Consiglio decreed that the consul in Alexandria should propose that the General Council of the merchants in Alexandria buy pepper collectively.[216]

The purchase of the spices and the sale of the commodities that the Europeans imported into the Moslem Levant was accomplished either by private dealing or by auction. The latter were mostly held in the customs offices.[217] Even private agreements were often made in the customs offices.[218] The striking of bargains in the customs offices, mostly by written deeds, was indeed advantageous for the European merchants, because it made it more difficult for the Moslems to break the contract.[219] The European merchants and the authorities of the trading nations had two major concerns: that the contracts should be kept and that conflicts should be avoided. Therefore the Venetian government decreed time and again that purchases should not be made on credit.[220] The consequences of the flight of a merchant who had bought on credit could be grave. Those who transgressed the Senate's prohibition were therefore liable to severe punishment;[221] but, even so, the prohibition was not kept, because it was a general custom to buy and sell on credit.[222] The Venetian authorities also forbade making purchases in Cairo, obviously because there was no Venetian consul in the capital who could control the activities of the merchants and, secondly, because that would have resulted in dishonest competition since the spices were sold in Cairo at lower prices than in Alexandria.[223] Further, the Senate forbade Venetian subjects to go into partnerships with Moslems.[224]

[214] See above Ch. V, p. 323 and notes 269, 270. See, further, Dat 928, copy of a letter from Damascus, of 22 March 1403.

[215] As supposed by Labib, p. 369, and Cahen, "Douanes et commerce dans les ports méditerranéens de l'Egypte médiévale d'après le Minhādj d'al-Makhzūmī," *JESHO* VII, p. 252; see also Wansbrough, "Venice and Florence," p. 501 (where forced purchases are spoken of and not a monopoly). About the auctions at the beginning of the fairs see above p. 277.

[216] *Deliberazioni del Maggior Consiglio* III, p. 37.

[217] de Mas Latrie, *Traités de paix* II, p. 348. In the Crusader period, the sale of the European commodities by auction was even more common, see Cahen, *art. cit.*, p. 240 f.

[218] *Dipl. Ven.-Lev.* I, no. 4 (p. 7).

[219] Amari, *Diplomi*, p. 352.

[220] Jorga, "Notes et extraits," *ROL* IV, p. 276; Misti 35, f. 113b 51, f. 104a f.; Berchet, *Relazioni*, p. 34, 35, 41.

[221] Senato Mar XIV, f. 18a, 18b.

[222] See G. P., Ter. V, f. 68a: cloth sold in Damascus with delay of payment of two and four months.

[223] Misti 51, f. 104a f.; Senato Mar XIII, f. 91b ff.

[224] Senato Mar XIII, f. 91b ff.

However, despite the numerous decrees and measures of precautions taken by the governments of the European trading nations and the authorities on the spot, the European merchants could not carry on their activities smoothly. They encountered countless difficulties. Those mentioned in the instructions given to the embassies to the sultan were obviously only the crassest excesses and infractions of the agreements laid down in the commercial treaties. Very often merchandise imported by the European merchants was taken away by force, sometimes without payment. The Moslem officials were eager to have the fine European cloth, especially scarlet.[225] Even cheese shipped from Crete to Egypt was taken away.[226] On the other hand, the Europeans were compelled by force to buy various commodities.[227] The spices sold to them were mixed with garbage, although their representatives, ambassadors, and consuls frequently protested against this means of cheating them.[228] The Venetian government, for its part, forbade the merchants to buy pepper and other spices that had not been sieved[229] and, to guarantee efficient sifting of the spices, sent sieves to the Levantine emporia.[230] Many vexations were connected with the payment of customs. Despite the protests of the consuls and the remonstrations of the embassies, the Mamluk officials levied often much more than the amounts corresponding to the rates and the rules fixed in the commercial treaties. The merchandise imported from Europe was sometimes estimated at a higher than true value;[231] the customs were levied before the merchandise arrived[232] or although they were not sold and shipped again by the merchants to their home country,[233] or they were collected twice, against the clauses of the treaties.[234] Reading the texts of the treaties the European trading nations concluded with the sultan, one gets the impression that there was no device that was not used to demand payments from the "Franks," and when they were about to depart they were detained so that new claims could be made.[235] It seems that there was no limit to the vexations and extortions. A Flemish traveller who came to Alexandria in 1470 dwells on the harshness of the customs officers who made a strict perquisition of the travellers' goods.[236] Any pretext was good enough to bring pressure upon the merchants and to extort money. Often they were

[225] G. P., Sent. 54 f. 36a ff. 78, f. 2a ff., 98, f. 185b ff., 99, f. 71b ff., 180b ff.
[226] Same series 56, f. 78b ff. See further 83, f. 204 ff.
[227] Same series 106, f. 66b ff.
[228] Senato Mar VII, f. 192a; Fabri, *Evagatorium* III, p. 33.
[229] Senato Mar XI, f. 166a, XII, f. 191a.
[230] Same series XII, f. 76b f.
[231] Amari, *Diplomi*, pp. 189, 364 f.
[232] *Dipl. Ven.-Lev.* II, pp. 312, 355; Wansbrough, "Venice and Florence," p. 518.
[233] Amari, *op.cit.*, p. 366 f.
[234] Wansbrough, "Venice and Florence," pp. 495, 496.
[235] Wansbrough, "A Mamlūk commercial treaty," nos. XXIV, XXVIII, XXX.
[236] Adorno, p. 171.

imprisoned until they agreed to pay. They were accused of being pirates or of having transgressed the laws of the Moslem state.[237] Notwithstanding all the undertakings not to punish one for another, after the flight or the death of a merchant who had left debts, it happened not rarely that his fellow-citizens and the consul of the merchant's colony were imprisoned.[238]

The European merchants did their best to establish good relations with the Moslems. The merchant colonies and the authorities of the trading nations in the metropolis and in other places ransomed Moslem captives and sent them to the ports of the Mamluk kingdom.[239] One tried to curry favor with the Mamluks by all means. An Arabic chronicler recounts, for instance, that when the sultan came to Damascus once the European merchants threw gold and silver coins upon him.[240] But all these efforts were in vain. It was not only the Moslem merchants and the Mamluk officials who harassed the Europeans. Even the ass and camel drivers who transported the spices bought in Damascus to the port of Beirut found many ways to despoil the merchants of their goods. The registers of the Venetian Senate (Senato Mar) contain many decisions referring to the boycott of these "muccari" (from the Arabic *mukārī*), decreed either by the Council of the Venetian colony in Damascus or by the Senate itself.[241] Some European merchants tried to find individual solutions for the difficulty of living and trading in the Moslem Levant: they applied to the Moslem authorities for the status of permanent residents, but without becoming subjects of the sultan. This status obviously guaranteed them advantages as to customs dues for their merchandise, and probably others too. The governments of the trading nations, of course, took drastic measures against these *fazolati*, whose privileged status rendered unlawful competition with the other European merchants possible.[242]

[237] G. P., Sent. 42 bis, f. 110b ff. 99, f. 31a ff., 106, f. 1a ff. Cristofore del Fiore V, f. [17b f.].

[238] Coll., Not. X, f. 12a.

[239] Cristofore del Fiore I, f. 13a ff. and see p. 221 and below Ch. VII, pp. 452 f., 480, and notes 116-119, 251.

[240] Ibn Iyās III, p. 35. A similar account: Marino Sanuto, *Vite* c. 1066.

[241] Senato Mar IX, f. 156b XI, f. 21a, XII, f. 10a f., 58a f., etc. This boycott is called *abatalatio*, from the Arabic *baṭṭala*. Even against Moslem (and native Christian) merchants and officials it was proclaimed fairly often. About the word *mukārī*, see the sources quoted by Wansbrough, "Venice and Florence," p. 512, note 73.

[242] Nic. Venier B, 2, f. 19b/20a; Misti 53, f. 204b; Jorga, "Notes et extraits," *ROL* V, p. 116, and cf. Heyd II, p. 473, note 7. The word may mean "those who put on Moslem dress," for *fazola* may have been the term by which the Italians called the kerchief (in Arabic *laffa*) put on the turban; see Boerio, *Dizionario del dialetto veneziano* (Venice, 1856), p. 264, and see, further, *Die Pilgerfahrt des Ritters Arnold von Harff von Cöln* (Cologne, 1860), p. 67: the Jewesses of Modon manufacture silk "gurdelen, huven sleuwer ind faciolen." The clauses in the Venetian treaties with the sultan, where it was stipulated that the Venetian should not be obliged to pay the poll tax (the *djizya*, paid by his Christian subjects) may point to the attempts made by the Mamluk officials to impose its payment upon the European merchants

The extortions by the Mamluk authorities (called by the Europeans *mangiarie*) had grave consequences for the merchant colonies. The losses that individual merchants suffered from the confiscation of their merchandise by the Mamluk officials, as well as payments extorted from the colonies as a whole, were defrayed by the common fund, which the Venetians called *cottimo*.[243] The trading nations also imposed the expenses for the embassies sent to the sultan upon the merchants who carried on trade in his dominions.[244] When the Venetian Senate decided to buy a jewel from the sultan, to please him, its price was put on the *cottimo*.[245] The debts of a merchant who had left the Mamluk dominions without paying them[246] and the expenses for the burial of another merchant[247] were covered by the *cottimo*. The difference between the price obtained in the consul's auction of the pepper required to be purchased from the sultan every year and that actually paid to his officials was another reason for the large debts of the merchant colonies. According to Venetian law, all debts of a merchant colony were to be cleared by the end of the year. But in fact only a part was paid, so that, together with the interest, the debt continually increased.[248] But the merchants found ways to evade the payment of the imposts due to the *cottimo*[249] so that the consuls were compelled to take loans at high interest.[250] At the end of the fourteenth century and in the first half of the fifteenth century, the administration of the Venetian merchant colonies in the Moslem Levant and their *cottimo* apparently functioned to the satisfaction of the authorities. But in the second half of the century its administration became a difficult problem, and made drastic measures necessary. It may be that the Mamluks' rapacity had increased toward the end of their rule, and it is also possible that the moral standards of the merchants had deteriorated so that many of them cheated the authorities. The difficulties of the Genoese authorities in managing the administration of their colony in Alexandria were no less. The debts of all the merchant colonies increased steadily. In the year 1490 the debt of the *cottimo* of the Venetian colony

who lived a long time in the sultan's dominions. So these *fazolati* may have made such a payment in order to pay customs according to the rate levied from the non-Moslem subjects of the sultan; see *Dipl. Ven.-Lev.* I, pp. 6, 293.

243 Senato Mar XIII, f. 69a XIV, f. 4a, 41b; G. P., Sent. 90, f. 127b, 97, f. 5a ff., 121, f. 60a ff.

244 Misti 31, f. 53a; plus the price of the presents made to the sultan, Senato Mar XIII, f. 44a f.

245 Senato Mar XIII, f. 26a f.

246 Jorga, "Notes et extraits," *ROL* VII, p. 58.

247 G. P., Sent. 106, f. 1a ff. (in this case, however, one refused to pay through the common fund).

248 Senato Mar VIII, f. 196b.

249 Same series XIV, f. 20a.

250 See above, note 58, and, further, Savi alla mercanzia 947, f. 61.

in Damascus was 20,000 ducats;[251] in 1493 its debts amounted to 90,000 ducats.[252]

The abovementioned amount, however, was only the sum of the debts of the so-called *cottimo general* (or *universal*), for the Venetian authorities distinguished between the debts due to be paid by all those engaged in trade in a certain country and those to be cleared by the merchants in a certain town (*cottimo particular*). The annual purchase of a certain quantity of pepper from the sultan in Alexandria and Damascus was an obligation incumbent upon all the Venetians who traded in Egypt and Syria. So there were good reasons to impose payments for the *cottimo general* upon all of them. The *cottimo general* was therefore sometimes called *danno del piper.* On the other hand, it was maintained that a merchant trading in Damascus should not be obliged to contribute to a fine imposed on Venetians mixed up in a brawl in Tripoli.[253]

The imposts for the *cottimo* of the Venetian colonies varied a good deal. In the first half of the fifteenth century, the rate of the payment was still low, for instance, 1 percent or even less.[254] In 1401 in Alexandria only 1¼ percent was paid, but in the 1450's the rate in Damascus was supposed to be 4 percent, whereas the consul actually levied 6½ percent.[255] In 1465 the levy should have been 6 percent,[256] whereas in the year 1474 2 percent was charged for the *danno del piper* and later it was raised to 4 percent.[257] In 1475 even 7½-8½ percent was paid.[258] An impost of 5 pro mille in Aleppo was levied on the cotton purchases.[259] In the year 1481 an impost of 1/2 percent was imposed upon all Venetian merchants trading in Syria in order to defray the expenses resulting from a conflict in Tripoli.[260] In the 1490's the impost for the cotton purchases in Syria rose considerably; in 1494 in Damascus 6 percent was paid.[261] All these data and others that refer to imposts higher than 10 percent[262] leave no doubt that in the second half of the fifteenth century they were often a heavy burden for the merchants who engaged in trade in Egypt and Syria. In fact, these were payments

[251] Senato Mar XIII, f. 20b f.

[252] Same series XIV, p. 196 f.

[253] See Savi alla mercanzia 949, f. 20; Melis, *Documenti*, p. 186.

[254] Misti 59, f. 126b.

[255] Verb. Cons. XII, sub 17 Oct. 1401; Senato Mar V, f. 99a.

[256] G. P., Sent. 152, f. 98a ff.

[257] Senato Mar X, f. 136a.

[258] G. P., Ter. IX, f. 13a f.

[259] Same series IV, f. 9b.

[260] Same series XI, f. 86a; G. P., Sent. 176, f. 101b.

[261] Berchet, *Relazioni*, p. 39 and see there that once it was raised to 20 percent. Cf. my "Profits," pp. 264, 266.

[262] See also Wilken, "Über die venetianischen Consuln in Alexandrien in 15ten and 16ten Jahrhundert," *Hist.-phil. Abhandl. der Kgl. Akad. der Wiss. zu Berlin* (1831), p. 40; Berchet, *Relazioni*, p. 39; E. Ashtor, "Profits," pp. 264, 266, 267.

extorted by the Moslem authorities but collected by the European consuls. Since it was never known how great these imposts would be in a given year, they undoubtedly seriously hampered the commercial activities of the Levant traders. But they bore all these hardships with a truly impressive tenacity.

The plight of the merchants who carried on trade in the Levantine emporia was not easy, but nevertheless many of them lived there a long time. The supposition that the South European merchants only reluctantly travelled to the Near East and that those who stayed there as agents were mostly young relatives of the Levant traders[263] is not borne out by the documents. Many of the Europeans living in the great trading towns of Egypt and Syria were experienced merchants. Most of them were agents of several firms (*maistri*)[264] for whom they carried on business over a long period of time. In order to be sure that the agents did not cheat their firms in Venice by claiming from one the reimbursement of payments made for the *cottimo*, which in fact had been made for another merchant, the Venetian *fattori* had to register at the consul's office, indicating whom they represented.[265] On the other hand, a firm in Venice or Genoa would make purchases in the Levantine emporia through several *fattori* at the same time.[266] The *fattori* were obliged to keep the orders given them by their employers in the *recordatio*, a written document, and when they did not carry out the orders, they were often sued before a tribunal in the metropolis. Countless acts of such litigations have come down to us in the registers of the Venetian tribunal of the *Giudici di petiziòn*. A *fattore* received from the firm he represented an average commission of 2-3 percent for every transaction. Sometimes the commission would be only 1 percent, and rarely it might amount to 4 percent or more.[267] Some *fattori* had a fixed salary, 80 ducats a year, 111 ducats,[268] or even 300 ducats;[269] others were given a certain sum (in addition to the commission) for their expenses (*spese di bocca*),[270] especially for travel outside the town where they lived.[271] But not infrequently a *fattore* had a *fattore* of his own in another town of the Levantine country in which he engaged in trade.[272] However, the *fattori*

[263] Kedar, *Merchants in crisis*, p. 47.

[264] See, for instance, G. P., Ter. IX, f. 13a ff. how many Venetian firms Niccolò Pisani represented in Aleppo in the 1470's.

[265] G. P., Sent. 100, f. 148b ff.

[266] Same series 52, f. 142b f.

[267] 1 percent: G. P., Sent. 112, f. 85b ff.; 4 percent: G. P., Sent. 107, f. 138a ff.; 5 percent: same series 83, f. 186b ff.

[268] G. P., Sent. 107, f. 19a 125, f. 168a ff.

[269] Same series 99, f. 173b ff.

[270] Same series 104, f. 24b f.

[271] Same series 19, f. 96b f.

[272] Same series 20, f. 83b ff.

did not live only on the revenue they had as representatives of firms in the metropolis. In addition to their activities for these firms, all of them carried on business of their own.[273]

The earnings of the *fattori* must have been very substantial, for otherwise why should so many of them have lived for such a long time in the trading towns of the Moslem Levant, where the conditions of life were quite unpleasant for them? From the judicial and notarial acts one learns that in that period there were European merchants who lived in Egypt or Syria for several years. Some of them stayed there about five years,[274] others from five to ten years.[275] Since these inferences are largely made from the acts drawn up by European notaries in the Levant, of which some collections have been preserved by chance, one can only say how long those merchants lived there at the minimum. They may have lived there a much longer time, but there can be no doubt that not a few of them spent a great part

[273] Same series 19, f. 95a f. 28, f. 26a.

[274] See above Ch. III, p. 134, and notes 172, 178, 182, 184 about some Genoese, and, further: the Genoese Aymon Cattaneo lived in Alexandria (at least) from 1400 until 1404; see Vat. sub 19 Dec. 1400, 5 March 1401, 6 July 1404. Leonardo de Valle sub 21 Febr. 1403, 13 Apr. 1404. The Venetian Marco Soro di Sori lived in Alexandria from 1421 until 1426, see Cristoforo del Fiore I, f. 20b. Nic. Venier B, 1, f. 13a/b, 14b; Tur IV, f. 1a. Another Venetian, Domenico di Piero, stayed in Damascus from 1437 until 1441, see G. P., Sent. 85, f. 135a ff. 86, f. 74a ff.; 87b ff. The Venetian Jacopo Malipiero, fil. Thome, stayed in Alexandria from 1443 until 1448, see G. P., Sent. 107, f. 129a ff., 133b ff., G. P., Straordinario Nodari 18, f. 30b. Lorenzo Contarini was fattore in Beirut in the years 1451-1455 (see G. P., Sent. 117, f. 96a f. 123, f. 70a ff. 87b ff. 125, f. 128a f. 126, f. 118a ff. 129, f. 91a ff. 137, f. 177a ff.), but already in 1437 he had been a merchant in Damascus (see G. P., Sent. 99, f. 14b) and, in 1440, fattore in Beirut (see G. P., Sent. 84, f. 91b ff.).

[275] See above Ch. III, p. 134, and notes 171, 176, about some Genoese and, further: the Genoese Domenico qd. Daniele Salvaygo (or Salvadego) lived in Alexandria from 1400 until 1406 (see Vat sub 17 Jan. 1400, 1 Apr. 1401, 3 Nov. 1405, 22 Jan. 1406) and he was also there in the years 1421-1422 (see Nic. Venier B, 2, f. 28a/b and cf. A, f. 18b, B, 2, f. 31b/32a, 42a, 48b). Another Genoese, Francesco de Negro (or Negrano or Nergano) was merchant in Damascus in 1412-1413, then in 1419 in Beirut and in (about) 1419 again in the latter town (see Giacomo della Torre, nos. 7, 9, 10, 11, 13, 21, 22, 25; Nic. Venier, B, 2, f. 21b/22a; G. P., Sent. 71, f. 65a f.). The Venetian Marco Zorzi (qd Bernardo) lived in Alexandria (at least) from 1410 until 1419 (see G. P., Sent., 42 bis, f. 16a ff., 34a ff., 42a ff., 80a ff., 43, f. 129b ff., 46, f. 18b ff.; Arch. B. Dolfin 181, fasc. 23). The Venetian Pietro Bembo (qd Andrea) lived in Alexandria at least from 1412 until 1422 (see G. P., Sent. 35, f. 6a ff.; Crist. Rizzo sub 20 Nov. 1414, 17 Oct. 1415, 3 Jan. 1416; Nic. Venier A, f. 9b/10a, 10a, 20b f. B, 1, f. 10b, 11b, 14b, B, 2, f. 29a ff., 40a ff.). The Venetian Giorgio Michiel, fil. Franc., lived in Alexandria from 1414 until 1422 (see Crist. Rizzo sub 16 Jan. and 19 Nov. 1414, 3 Jan. and 12 March 1416; Nic. Venier A, f. 8a/b, 11a, 20b f. B, 1, f. 10a, 11a/b, 12b, 13a, 14a, B, 2, f. 29a ff., 40a ff.). The Venetian Leonardo Spiera (qd. Pietro) lived in Alexandria from 1420 until 1428 (see G. P., Sent. 52, f. 142b f., 56, f. 78b ff., 58, f. 72b ff. Nic. Venier A, f. 16a B, 1, f. 12a/b, 12b, B, 2, f. 25b f., 50a; Tur IV f. 6a, 22a, 23b ff., 25a, 27b, 29b, 32a, 33a f., 43b, 52b f., 54a, 60a f., 74b ff., 76a ff., 77b, f., 78a). In 1432 he was already dead (see G. P., Sent. 60, f. 177a ff.). The Venetian Bernardo Donado (qd. Pietro) was in Aleppo in 1471-1472, in 1473 in Tripoli, and in 1480 again in Aleppo (see G. P., Sent. 178, f. 36a ff., 182, f. 149a ff., 185, f. 135a, 162a ff., 186, f. 25b ff., 84b ff.; G. P., Ter III, f. 102a ff. IX, f. 13a).

of their lives in the Moslem Levant. The documents show clearly that some of them lived in the Levant from 11 to 15 years,[276] and others from 15 to 20 years.[277] Some *fattori* even spent more than 20 years in the trading towns of Egypt and Syria. The Venetian Francesco Michiel (qd Joh.) lived in Alexandria at least from 1399 until 1422.[278] Another Venetian, Zuan de Zano (Zanono), son of Andrea, was in Damascus in 1419, and in 1430, together with Giorgio Zanono, he again went to Syria and remained there. He lived in Syria in 1433, 1434, and 1436-1437. In those years he lived in Beirut. Then, in the mid-1450's, he stayed in Damascus.[279] Marco Malipiero (qd Dario) was fattore in Aleppo in 1461, lived in Tripoli from 1464 until 1473, and then in 1480-1482 lived in the latter town and in Aleppo.[280] Naturally, some of these merchants returned for some time to their country during their long sojourn in the Levant: their sojourn in the Levant was not always uninterrupted. Others spent some years in the Levant, returned to their home country for a long time, and again went to the Levant for some years.[281] Some of these merchants were partners of those family

[276] The Venetian Piero Marcello (qd. Niccolò) lived in Latakia in 1424-1425, and in 1435, in Tripoli (see G. P., Sent. 50, f. 63b 70, f. 132a ff. 78, f. 101b ff.). Another Venetian, Nic. da Molin, who was consul in Alexandria in 1424, was a merchant in Tripoli in 1439-1443 (see G. P., Sent. 75, f. 41b ff., 97, f. 91b f., 99, f. 26a ff., 31a ff., 63b ff. 100, f. 84a ff.). Jac. Dolfin, son of Dolfin, was a merchant in Aleppo in 1468-1469, in 1476-1477 in Damascus, and in 1482 in Beirut (see G. P., Sent. 163, f. 115a ff. 175, f. 22a ff.; Senato Mar X, f. 68a XI, f. 150b.).

[277] The Florentine Andrea di Sinibaldo lived more than 16 years in Damascus at the end of the fourteenth century; see above p. 137 f.: the Venetian Lorenzo Soranzo received Bertrandon de la Broquière in Ḥamā in 1432, and was in that town also in 1433, 1446, and 1448, but engaged in trade also in Latakia and in Tripoli (see Bertrandon de la Broquière p. 77; G. P., Sent. 70, f. 26b ff. 107, f. 79b, 149b f. 111, f. 7b ff. 124, f. 36b ff.). Antonio Justignan was in Beirut in 1477 and in Damascus in 1492 (see G. P., Sent. 178, f. 46a ff. 181, f. 94a ff. 188, f. 244b ff. 192, f. 65a ff.; and see also G. P., Ter. XII, f. 98a.).

[278] Verb. Cons. XII, sub 6 Oct. 1401, 22 Oct. 1401, 10 and 18 Apr. 1402; Vat. sub 5 Febr. 1400, 11 Sept. 1401, 14 Aug. 1404, 2 Sept. 1404 and 16, 24 Apr. 1405, 15 and 22 May 1405, 13 Oct. 1405; Leonardo de Valle sub 13 Sept. 1402, 31 Jan. 1403, 28 March 1403, 17 Febr. 1404; G. P., Sent. 32, f. 72a 42 bis, f. 110b ff. 44, f. 120b.

[279] Nic. Venier B, 2, f. 23a/b; G. P., Sent. 70, f. 72a ff. 88, f. 93a ff. 119, f. 97a ff. 121, f. 54a 122, f. 65b f. 123, f. 58a ff. 130, f. 129a ff. 132, f. 233b f. 137, f. 64b ff. 146, f. 19b ff. 181, f. 14a ff.; Misti 60, f. 36a f., 104a; Crist. del Fiore V, f. 11a f., [20a f.].

[280] G. P., Ter. IX, f. 174b f.; G. P., Sent. 153, f. 12a ff. 177, f. 67a ff. 178, f. 144b ff. 182, f. 149a ff. 185, f. 162a ff. 186, f. 84b ff.

[281] Zuan Urso was in Syria in 1428, in the 1430's he lived a long time in Damascus; in 1439 he was in Venice; and in 1440 he was again a merchant in Damascus. In 1444 he lived in Beirut, and in 1460 he was once more a merchant in Damascus; see G. P., Sent. 56, f. 77b ff., 57, f. 95a ff. 84, f. 44a ff., 90, f. 133a, 100, f. 169b ff.; Crist. del Fiore VI, f. 5a f. Marino Contarini (fil. Pietro) was in Alexandria in 1436-1439, then in 1459 (cca), 1462 in Damascus; see G. P., Sent. 91, f. 101b ff., 95, f. 95a ff.; G. P., Cap. pub. VIII, f. 26a ff., Crist. del Fiore VI, f. [12b f.]; Tur V, f. 80a. Niccolò Zane was, together with his brother Lunardo, fattore in Beirut in 1440-1444; later he lived in Tripoli; and from 1458 until 1463 he was again fattore in Beirut; see G. P., Sent. 84, f. 124a 100, f. 169b ff. 109, f. 143a f. 133, f. 87b f. 146, f. 9b ff., 78a f. 147, f. 168a 163, f. 152b ff.; G. P., Ter II, f. 56b f., 57b, 58b; Secreta 21, f. 10b ff.; Crist. del Fiore VI, f. [3a, 4a, 17b f., 18b f.].

enterprises that the Venetians still called *fraterna*. The partners carried on business both in common and on their own. Often one of them lived in the Moslem Levant, while another or several other partners lived in the metropolis.[282] But sometimes two or more brothers engaged in trade in the Levantine emporia, mostly as business partners.[283] Sometimes a merchant took one of his sons with him to the Levant, and together they carried on business in one of the great trading centers of Egypt or Syria.[284] Most of the European merchants who lived in the Moslem Levant a long time were young men or at least came there when they were still young. Many came

[282] G. P., Sent. 32, f. 114b ff., 34, f. 4a ff., 161, f. 126b f.

[283] About two Genoese who were brothers and lived in Alexandria as merchants, see Leonardo de Valle sub 18 Nov. 1402. Two brothers, Domenico and Samuele Salvaygo, of Genoa, lived in Alexandria in 1420; see above note 275 and Nic. Venier B, 2, f. 31a/b. The Genoese Taddeo Vivaldi (qd. Antonio) and his brother Vincenzo were business partners in Alexandria from 1421 until 1428; see Nic. Venier B, 2, f. 32a f., 37b f., 39b, 40a ff.; Tur IV, f. 18a f., 26b, 37a, 38b ff., 76a ff. Two brothers, Agostino and Adoardo Maruffo, of Genoa, were merchants in Alexandria in the 1450's; see Tur II, f. 4a f., 8a, 17b f., 30b, 31a, 48b, 63a f., 71a f. See about the Venetians: Angelo Michiel (qd. Luca), who was a merchant in Alexandria from 1415 until 1428, Arch. B. Dolfin 180, fasc. 13 181, fasc. 23; G. P., Sent. 34, f. 37a ff. 48 f. 5a f. 56 f. 78b ff.; Crist. Rizzo sub 14 Jan. 1414, 8 June 1415, 17 Oct. 1415, 31 Aug. 1416; Crist. del Fiore I, f. 1b f., 5b f., 13a ff., 22a f.; Nic. Venier A, f. 8a, 8b, 8b/9a B, 1, f. 8a (cf. A, f. 7a), 10a, 13b, 14a, 14b 17a f. B, 2, f. 30b, 40a ff.; Tur IV, f. 1b, 2b, 3a, 6b, 15b f., 19b ff., 34b f., 43a, 44b, 73b f., 82a f. His brother Pietro was in Alexandria in 1422; see Nic. Venier B, 1, f. 14a and another brother, Toma, in 1418, 1420, 1422, and 1426; see Arch. B. Dolfin 180, fasc. 13; Nic. Venier B, 1, f. 8a (cf. A, f. 7a), 14a; G. P., Sent. 48, f. 5a f.

Niccolò Bernardo (son of Francesco) was in Alexandria in 1421-1424; see Nic. Venier B, 1, f. 12a; Arch. Lor. Dolfin, his letters of 8 and 19 Febr. 1422, 2 May 1422; Melis, *Documenti*, p. 190, and see also G. P., Sent. 34, f. 37a ff. 65, f. 105a ff. A brother of his, Pietro, was from 1416 until 1422 in Alexandria; see Misti 53, f. 25b f.; Crist. Rizzo sub 6 Aug. 1416; Arch. B. Dolfin 180, fasc. 13 181, fasc. 23; Nic. Venier A, f. 8a/b B, 1, f. 10a, 13b f. B, 2, 40a ff. Three brothers, sons of Donato Correr, were in Alexandria in the years 1420-1422; see Nic. Venier A, f. 7a, 20b B, 1, f. 8a, 13b, 17a/b B, 2, f. 55a f. The brothers Zuan and Andrea Contarini, sons of Alvise, were fattori in Beirut in the 1420's and the 1430's: about Zuan, who was at first a merchant in Latakia; see G. P., Sent. 38, f. 66a ff. 52, f. 85b f. 56, f. 77b f. 68, f. 27a ff. 70, f. 40a ff., 72a ff. 79, f. 115a ff. 84, f. 39a ff. 87, f. 40b f. 88, f. 52b ff.; Tur IV, f. 86a f., 87a f.; about Andrea, see G. P., Sent. 52, f. 85b f. 70, f. 40a ff., 72a ff. 77, f. 56a ff.; Tur IV, f. 86a f., 87a f.

Three sons of the Venetian Francesco Uberti, namely Antonio, Farinato, and Giovan-Francesco, ran a company in Damascus from 1460 until 1469; see Crist. del Fiore VI, f. [6a f., 8a, 8b, 10a ff., 11a ff.]; G. P., Sent. 151 bis, f. 70b ff. 174, f. 4a f.; G. P., Ter. II, f. 57b. Marco Antonio Contarini, son of Michiel, was in the years 1478-1481 a merchant in Damascus, then in company with his brother Tomado a merchant in Beirut; see G. P., Sent. 181, f. 89a ff., 91a ff. 182, f. 11a ff., 87b ff. 188, f. 45a ff.; G. P., Ter. XI, f. 76b f., 80b f.; G. P., Cap. pub. XII, sub 30 March 1481; Senato Mar XI, f. 121b.

[284] The Venetian Bartolomeo de la Porta was a merchant in Alexandria from 1421 until 1427; see Nic. Venier B, 1, f. 10b B, 2, f. 2a, 21a f., 40a ff., 48a f.; Tur IV, f. 1b, 31a f.; Crist. del Fiore I, f. 13a f.; Francesco degli Elmi Ba 74/75, an undated act of a. 1426. His son Angeleto was there in 1422 and 1426; see Nic. Venier A, f. 20a B, 1, f. 13a B, 2, f. 50a; Crist. del Fiore I, f. 16a, ff. Marco Zeno (qd. Pietro) was in Alexandria in 1432-1435, and at the same time his son Pietro was there; see Misti 58, f. 58b; about a father and his son engaging in trade in Damascus, see G. P., Ter. IV, f. 180a.

to the Levant as apprentices (*zoveni* in Venetian), and, at the beginning, they or their fathers paid the veteran merchants under whose guidance they worked and with whom they lived, for their maintenance.[285] But later the young man had his board free[286] and also engaged in trade on his own in addition to working for his chief.[287] However, since so many merchants lived many years in the Levant, there were also elderly ones among them.[288]

Sojourning a long time in the Levant, one had of course to adapt oneself to circumstances and to establish oneself as well as possible. Some of the merchants lived in the fondaco of their nation. In Alexandria the Venetians had two fondachi, and during a certain period the Genoese also had two.[289] But even in Alexandria some Venetians rented private houses and lived there.[290] In the towns where the merchants had no fondachi, all of them rented private houses or apartments. In Damascus there were apparently no fondachi of European merchants at all. Most of them lived in the commercial quarter called the Bazar of the Franks in the Italian sources. According to an Arabic chronicler at the end of the fourteenth century, the majority of them lived in the market-hall (*ḳaysarīya*) of Ibn al-Bābī.[291] Some documents of the middle of the fifteenth century refer to the houses that the Venetian merchants rented in Damascus.[292] The latter may have been elsewhere, in a true residential quarter. Living in a Levantine town and travelling the countryside where strangers were sometimes in danger, one put on Oriental dress.[293] The European merchants were also allowed to ride on horseback, a right strictly denied to the non-Moslem subjects of the sultan and even to the pilgrims going to Jerusalem.[294]

The *fattori* in the Levantine trading towns never had their wives with them. Even the consuls lived there without their spouses.[295] The household of a merchant was taken care of by servants, who hailed from many European countries. Of course many of them were Italians, but not a few were Germans. There were servants from Nürnberg,[296] Salzburg,[297] Vi-

[285] G. P., Sent. 43, f. 129b f.; see, further, in my "Quelques problèmes," p. 230 ff.

[286] G. P., Sent. 106, f. 15b ff.

[287] See *ibidem* and same series 96, f. 152b f.; see also Nic. Venier, B, 1, f. 2a ff. (a Genoese).

[288] A European merchant more than seventy years old who had throughout his life carried on trade in Damascus; see G. P., Sent. 188, f. 206a ff.

[289] Nic. Venier B, 2, f. 30a.

[290] G. P., Sent. 97, f. 151a.

[291] Muḥ. Ibn Ṣaṣrā, *A Chronicle of Damascus 1389-1397*, ed. and transl. W. M. Brinner (Univ. of California Press, 1963) II, p. 173 (transl. I, p. 229) (a *ḳaysarīya* was a compound of shops about which there were apartments).

[292] Misti 60, f. 212b; Crist. del Fiore VI, f. [4a].

[293] G. P., Sent. 97, f. 25a ff., and see above Ch. V, p. 305.

[294] G. P., Sent. 107, f. 116b f. 124, f. 18a ff.

[295] Misti 45, f. 88b.

[296] Vat sub 28 July and 11 Aug. 1404.

[297] Vat sub 21 Apr. 1405.

enna,[298] and other towns of Germany and Austria.[299] The Venetians also had servants from Dalmatia, young men from Zara,[300] Ragusa, [301] and Cattaro.[302] Others were Hungarians.[303] The French merchants had servants from their own country.[304] In addition to these servants, the merchants also had slaves,[305] more often, slave-girls. The latter were mostly young girls from the Oriental countries. Some of them were Greek[306] or Circassian;[307] others were Russian[308] or Bulgarian.[309] But there were also Hungarian slave girls among them,[310] as well as Ethiopian[311] and Negroes.[312] Since a free European woman is very seldom mentioned in the notarial acts,[313] there can be little doubt that these slave girls served their masters as concubines. Those few free European women who were to be found in the Levantine towns were mostly widows of innkeepers and old women.[314]

Some of the male servants of the merchants were also craftsmen, tailors, barbers, or goldsmiths.[315] But there were also artisans who exercised their professions as full-time jobs in the European merchant colonies in the Levant. There were tailors,[316] often even two at the same time in a big Levantine trading center.[317] There were also shoemakers,[318] goldsmiths,[319]

[298] Nic. Venier B, 2, f. 50a.

[299] Vat sub 11 Jan. 1401, 17 Aug. 1401, 13 Sept. 1401, 29 Aug. 1404, 13 Sept. 1404; Leonardo de Valle sub 12 Apr. 1402, 21 Febr. 1403 (Theotonicus de Transilvania); Crist. Rizzo sub 18 Nov. 1414, 12 Febr. 1415, 8 June 1415, 6 Aug. 1416; Tur II, f. 33a f. (German servant of the Florentine consul in Alexandria); Crist. del Fiore I, f. 16a; G. P., Sent. 107, f. 42b ff.; *I viaggi degli ambasciatori veneti*, p. 96.

[300] Crist. del Fiore VI, f. [8b].

[301] Crist. del Fiore V, f. 15b f.

[302] G. P., Sent. 191, f. 23b ff.

[303] Vat sub 30 Sept. 1404; *I viaggi degli ambasciatori veneti*, pp. 177, 215.

[304] Leonardo de Valle sub 5 Sept. 1403 (but not always; see Nic. Venier B, 2, f. 44b f.).

[305] Crist. Rizzo sub 12 Nov. 1414, 8 Sept. 1415; Tur IV, f. 2b.

[306] Vat sub 19 Aug. 1401.

[307] Leonardo de Valle sub 18 July 1403.

[308] Vat sub 12 Oct. 1400; Crist. del Fiore V, f. 4a.

[309] Vat sub 14 Aug. 1404, Leonardo de Valle sub 3 July 1403; Crist. Rizzo sub 8 Nov. 1414, 6 June 1416.

[310] Vat sub 10 March 1401.

[311] Francesco degli Elmi 74/75, sub 23 Sept. 1426.

[312] Vat sub 4 Febr. 1401, 10 March 1401; Tur II, f. 3a, 33a f. (slave girl of the Florentine consul in Alexandria).

[313] Greek women, Leonardo de Valle sub 4 Nov. 1402; a Sicilian woman, Vat sub 20 Jan. 1401.

[314] Vat sub 11 May 1405, 28 July 1406. See, further, Crist. Rizzo sub 22 Dec. 1415: a free woman from Bulgaria is the concubine of a Cretan merchant.

[315] See Tur II, f. 67a f.; Verb. Cons. XII sub 2 May 1402, 4 Aug. 1402.

[316] See Tur II, f., 33a f.: a tailor who has his workshop in the big Venetian fondaco in Alexandria; at the same time there is another Venetian tailor in Alexandria; see Tur II, f. 55b f. (a. 1455). About European tailors, see also Vat sub 23 Febr. 1400.

[317] See about Pietro Fontano of Milan and Bartolomeo Stefani of Pavia, tailors in Damascus in 1456; Crist. del Fiore V, f. 15b f.

[318] Crist. del Fiore VI, f. [8b].

[319] G. P., Sent. VIII, f. 35a f.; Crist. del Fiore V, f. 11b f.; Tur V, f. 23b f. (a Venetian).

furriers,[320] and Italian pharmacists.[321] Of course, there were always European barbers in the merchant colonies, because they fulfilled the role of surgeons as well.[322] Since these barbers were not always occupied, they often served as witnesses of notarial deeds. From these documents one learns that sometimes there were two European barbers in a single Levantine emporium.[323] The Venetian merchant colonies in Alexandria and Damascus always had a barber in their employ.[324] They also employed medical doctors, although apparently not always. In the year 1415 the Jew Moses Caravido was the doctor of the Venetians in Alexandria, and in 1427 the doctor was another Jew whose name was Juda.[325] In 1460 the Senate decided that an Italian doctor should be employed by the Venetian colony in Alexandria and he should have a salary of 200 ducats a year.[326] Even European musicians lived in the Levantine emporia. In the 1450's two Italian *ioculatores* lived in Alexandria at the same time.[327] All these artisans, doctors, and entertainers came from different European countries. Many of them were Italian, others Dalmatians[328] or Catalans.[329] The colonies of the Europeans indeed attracted people from various countries, that is, people not belonging to the trading nations.[330]

The same could be said of the clergymen, both secular and regular, who were to be found in Alexandria, Damascus, and elsewhere. Among them were Franciscans from Majorca and Apulia, Dominicans from Genoa, and, of course, priests from Venice.[331] Some of these clergymen were obviously travellers, such as pilgrims, returning from the Holy Land. Others had been chaplains of a consul and remained for some time in the Levant.[332] The chaplains of the consuls who served as notaries for the merchant colonies had plenty of work, so that there was a place for other clergymen who could fulfill this task. Since they received a fee for every deed, they

320 Gherardo of Piacenza in 1456 in Damascus; see Crist. del Fiore V, f. [17a f.].

321 Crist. del Fiore V, f. 15b f.

322 Antonio Barbitonsor from Cremona is in Alexandria in 1422; see Nic. Venier A, f. 18a/b.

323 Crist. del Fiore V, f. 15b f., 16b [17a f.].

324 Crist. del Fiore V, f. 7a f., 11b f., 12a VI, f. [4a f., 8b, 13a f., 14a]; Tur II, f. 77b; Francesco degli Elmi 74/75, fasc. IV, f. 162a/b.

325 Crist. Rizzo sub 14 June 1415, and see my "New data for the history of Levantine Jewries," *Bulletin of the Institute of Jewish Studies* III, p. 76, and see there note 4, that at the same time there was a barber from Florence in Alexandria.

326 Senato Mar VI, f. 173b.

327 Crist. del Fiore V, f. 1b f., [18a f.].

328 Crist. del Fiore V, f. 15b f.

329 Vat sub 1 Dec. 1400.

330 M. Balard has made the same observation dealing with the Genoese colony in Caffa; see his remarks in "Sociétés et compagnies," p. 349.

331 Vat sub 16 Febr. 1400, 28 July 1400, 10 Aug. 1400, 4 Febr. 1401; Leonardo de Valle sub 22 Dec. 1401, 7 Jan. 1402; Crist. Rizzo sub 9 March 1416; Nic. Venier B, 2, f. 5b; Crist. del Fiore VI, f. [3b, 4a f.].

332 Tur V, f. 1a.

were probably well off and could afford to buy slaves. Giovanni Marin, a former chaplain of the Venetian consul in Alexandria, bought a slave girl and a slave there in 1414.[333]

These colonies also had their taverns maintained by professional innkeepers. In a notarial act drawn up in Alexandria in 1421 not less than five innkeepers are mentioned, one of them an Anconitan, one a man from Rhodes, one from Cyprus, one a native Christian, and one a Greek or Cretan.[334] But Venetians also kept inns in Alexandria.[335] Probably all of them offered their guests wine imported from Crete.[336]

Almost all of the Europeans who lived in the Levantine emporia or visited them engaged in trade, not only the professional merchants. The sailors on the ships sailing to the Levantine ports carried some merchandise with them, sold it, and bought some Oriental commodities.[337] Of course, the secretary of a ship could do the same.[338] The artisans who lived in the trading towns of the Moslem Levant, too, carried on trade, though on a modest scale.[339] Everyone was a trader.

From time to time the governments of the trading nations tried to impose a ruling on their subjects to the effect that they should carry on their activities without associating with people belonging to the colonies of other nations. Genoese laws forbade her subjects to form partnerships with non-Genoese[340] or to accept them as fellows of Genoese caravans.[341] But these decrees soon fell into abeyance. In fact, Genoese were *fattori* of Venetians;[342] and Florentines and Anconitans, too, were the agents of Venetian firms.[343] Notarial acts refer to companies established by Genoese and Venetians.[344] Surely the governments of the trading nations had good reasons to enact decrees against commercial association with the subjects of other states. They wanted to avoid responsibility for the activities of people of other nations. A conflict resulting from the raid of corsairs of another trading nation could cause losses to merchants who were partners with people belonging to the latter. The authorities of the trading nations had even more reason to forbid such associations with the subjects of the sultan.

[333] Cr. Rizzo sub 8 and 12 Nov. 1414.

[334] Nic. Venier B, 2, f. 55a f. and cf. A, f. 17a/b.

[335] Nic. Venier A, f. 13b, and see there B, 2, f. 49a, about another, Anconitan, innkeeper.

[336] Nic. Venier A, f. 11a; Tur II, f. 60b f. cf. my paper "New data," p. 76 ff.

[337] This was an old established custom; see Goitein, *Letters of mediaeval Jewish traders*, p. 86.

[338] Coll. Not. VIII, f. 12a.

[339] Crist. del Fiore V, f. [17a].

[340] Mon. Hist. Patr., Leges municipales (Turin, 1838), col. 349.

[341] *Op.cit.*, col. 346 ff.

[342] Crist. del Fiore V, f. 12b ff.; G. P., Sent. 162, f. 25a ff.

[343] Crist. del Fiore V, f. 1a ff.; G. P., Sent. 86, f. 39a ff. 88, f. 12b ff.

[344] Nic. Venier B, 2, f. 40a ff.

In 1346 the Senate of Venice forbade subjects of the republic to be in company with a Moslem courtier or to receive deposits from Moslems. In addition, it was decided that Venetians should not have banks in Alexandria.[345] However, even these decrees were not kept. The right to keep a money changing table in Alexandria was farmed out by the Venetian consul,[346] and the money changers not rarely fulfilled the task of bankers.

However, despite the commercial relations, the colonies of the various European trading nations kept apart. Each was an entity to itself, to which belonged merchants of the nation's metropolis, merchants of smaller towns in its neighborhood and their servants. Not all trading nations recognized the merchants of the smaller towns who joined their colonies overseas as full members. The Florentines, for instance, distinguished between the citizens of the metropolis and those of the towns subject to her.[347]

Even in other respects the colonies of the European merchants in the Levant were organized in different ways. Generally speaking, one may say that the Genoese colonies were much more independent of their metropolis than the colonies of other trading nations. The Venetian colonies were closely watched, and their local authorities strictly supervised by the government of the Serenissima.[348] The heads of the colonies of the major trading nations were councils; the Venetian Councils of XII and the Genoese Councils of VI. At the end of the fifteenth century, when Venice's Levant trade had reached its apogee, both the colonies in Beirut and in Aleppo had Councils of XII. The Councils of XII of the Venetians were appointed by the consul.[349] When it was necessary a General Council of the colony was convened. Both councils took decisions by the majority of the merchants present.[350] The Councils of XII of the Venetian colonies were supposed to consist of nobili only, as far as possible.[351] The General Council of the Venetian colonies (called *Maggior Consiglio*) deliberated and took decisions concerning the *cottimo*, the common purchase of pepper, and other matters that were not purely administrative.[352] The Council of XII appointed administrators of bequests of merchants who had died in the Levantine em-

[345] *Dipl. Ven.-Lev.* I, no. 164.

[346] Misti 30, f. 68b.

[347] Mollat-Johansen-Postan-Verlinden, "L'économie européenne etc.," in *Relazioni del X Congresso di scienze storiche* III, p. 750.

[348] P. S. Leicht, "Le colonie veneziane," *Rivista di storia del diritto italiano* 25 (1952), p. 53.

[349] G. P., Sent. 186, f. 127b ff. As to the origin of the Venetian Councils of XII, Berchet, *Relazioni*, p. 31, quotes a decision of the Maggior Consiglio of the year 1331, but it refers to the Venetian colonies in Apulia and to a general rule, then already established a long time. See further *op.cit.*, p. 33; Misti 59, f. 128b. For the Genoese Councils of VI, see Vat sub 2 Dec. 1399, 8 July 1404, 3 Aug. 1405, and see above.

[350] Misti 26, f. 56b 27, f. 96b 35, f. 113a, and see above p. 126.

[351] Misti 59, f. 128b.

[352] Verb. Cons. XII sub 21 Oct. 1402.

poria; it decided if the consul should go to Cairo to appear before the sultan, at the expense of the merchants, and it chose the supplementary ship for the transport of the *rata*.[353] It also appointed assessors (called *camerarii*) who, together with the consul, administered the financial activities of the colony.[354]

The consuls represented the merchant colonies to the sultan and his officials, maintained discipline within the group—that is, enforced the laws enacted by the government of the metropolis and the local council—and fulfilled the role of judges. The consuls' right to judge in matters of civil law between members of their colony was recognized in the privileges granted to the trading nations by the sultan. In fact, the Moslem rulers had given them these rights from the beginning of the thirteenth century.[355] In the countries of Northern Africa, the consuls could also judge in litigations between one of their fellow-citizens and a Moslem, if the former were the defendant.[356] For, according to a principle generally accepted in the Middle Ages, litigation between two men belonging to different nations was brought before a tribunal of the defendant's nation. In the Levantine countries, the European trading nations did not succeed in obtaining such concessions. In a treaty concluded between Venice and the first Mamluk sultan of Egypt, al-Malik al-Muʿizz Aybak, in 1254 the Serenissima did obtain such a concession.[357] But, according to the treaties with his successors, litigations between Moslems and Venetians were brought before Moslem judges. All the privileges granted by the Mamluks to the European trading nations contain only the concession that such cases should be judged by secular judges and not by the cadi.

In the countries of the Maghreb, the European trading nations had also obtained the right of jurisdiction in criminal cases.[358] In the Levantine countries it was granted only exceptionally. The Venetians obtained this right from the prince of Aleppo by a treaty of 1229.[359] The treaties between the Mamluk sultans and the European trading nations, on the other hand, usually contain a clause concerning the exclusive right of the Moslem judges

[353] G. P., Sent. 99, f. 147b ff. 127, f. 13b ff.; Verb. Cons. XII sub 11 Oct. 1401, 4 Aug. 1402, 12 Aug. 1402.

[354] Leicht, "Le colonie veneziane," p. 51; Crist. del Fiore I, f. 11a f. (they were also called *datiarius* and had of course a salary).

[355] See the treaties of Venice with the sultan concluded in 1302 and 1355, *Dipl. Ven.-Lev.* I, p. 7, 295. Cf. W. Heffening, *Das islamische Fremdenrecht* (Hanover, 1925), p. 125 ff.

[356] de Mas Latrie, *Traités* II, pp. 74 f., 197, 202, 343.

[357] Tafel-Thomas II, p. 487.

[358] de Mas Latrie I, p. 87. In fact, the right is given only to the Catalans *expressis verbis* in a treaty concluded with the prince of Tunis in 1323; see *op.cit.* II, p. 322. But several other treaties apparently imply the right.

[359] Tafel-Thomas II, p. 276.

to intervene in criminal cases in which Europeans were involved.[360] Litigations between European merchants belonging to different trading nations were of course much more frequent. According to the general principle of personal law prevailing in the Middle Ages, claims of a European against the members of another European merchant colony were to be brought before the defendant's consul; e.g., a Venetian could sue a Genoese before the latter's consul.[361]

The Venetian consuls were appointed by the Maggior Consiglio in Venice,[362] whereas the consulates of the Genoese colonies were sometimes filled by appointments by the authorities in the metropolis and sometimes farmed out.[363] For a long time the term of a Venetian consulate was fixed at two years,[364] but in the middle of the fifteenth century the Senate decided that a consul should hold his post six additional months without a salary.[365] Then, in 1472, the tenure of the consuls in Alexandria and Damascus was again reduced to two years.[366] The consuls of the European trading nations received not only a salary from their governments, but also an honorarium from the sultan, the so-called *djāmakīya*. This honorarium was simply a restitution of part of the customs paid by the Europeans. It should have amounted to 200 dinars a year,[367] but it seems that only the Venetian consul in Alexandria received it regularly, whereas the other consuls, the Venetian consul in Damascus and the consuls of the other trading nations, sometimes received it and at other times claimed it in vain.[368] The salary of the Venetian consul in Alexandria changed from time to time. At the end of the fourteenth century, he received 350 ducats a year and in addition the consular dues levied from the merchants. But he had to pay the salaries of his staff. At the beginning of the fifteenth century, the salary was reduced to 200 ducats.[369] In 1375 the Venetian consul in Damascus received 500

[360] *Dipl. Ven.-Lev.* I, p. 7, 295.

[361] Verb. Cons. XII sub 22 Dec. 1401; Nic. Venier B, 2, f. 40a ff.

[362] Misti 41, f. 92b.

[363] Musso, "I Genovesi e il Levante," p. 94.

[364] Misti 38, f. 135a.

[365] Coll., Not. IX, f. 105a (the decree was of a. 1451).

[366] Coll., Not. IX, f. 125a.

[367] Misti 35, f. 9b ff. 37, f. 99b ff. 41, f. 92b 47, f. 40a; Piloti, p. 166; see also Misti 39, f. 25b: Venice claims a salary from the sultan for the consul in Latakia.

[368] Misti 51, f. 141b ff.

[369] In the middle of the fourteenth century, he had 300 dinars a year; see Misti 22, f. 90b, but had to pay the salaries of the chaplain, four servants, and a cook. In 1359, 100 dinars was added to the consul's salary, but he was forbidden to engage in the trade of wine; see Misti 29, f. 20a. Then, in 1370, his salary was again increased, this time by 100 ducats; see Misti 33, f. 53b. The fines imposed on merchants guilty of some transgression and the *consolazium* (consular dues for import and export) were an additional part of his revenue; see Misti 41, f. 92b. Before 1403, the consul's salary consisted of a fixed payment of 350 ducats, the consular dues, and in addition 200 ducats from the fines and the rent of the Venetian inn. But in that year the latter payment was abolished and, on the other hand, one

ducats a year from his government, in addition to the consular dues. Then, in 1386, the Senate decided that in addition to his salary of 500 ducats, he should receive only half of the fines that he might impose.[370] Even the Venetian consul in the small town of Sarmīn had a very high salary. In the year 1388 the Senate decided that he should have no more than 600 dinars a year from all his revenues.[371]

The Venetian consuls were forbidden to engage in trade. This was a law that had been enacted in 1272 and had been strictly enforced ever since.[372] Even the adult sons who lived with the consuls were not to engage in trade.[373] This prohibition, however, was not absolute. For the Venetian consul could engage in the trade of pearls and precious stones, and invest in the enterprises of others.[374] So it came about that the prohibition was often evaded.[375] The other trading nations did not forbid their consuls to carry on business at all, and all of them engaged in trade.[376]

The consuls of the European trading nations were highly respected dignitaries; in fact, they also fulfilled the task of resident ambassadors of their governments. Consequently, they enjoyed some of the privileges conceded to diplomats. The Venetian consul in Alexandria, in virtue of a treaty of the year 1361, had the right to import into Egypt and to export (apparently every year) goods worth 2,000 dinars (sc. without paying customs).[377] But the consuls were also very busy and had always to be on the scene. Sometimes they were assisted by two "councillors," chosen among the prominent merchants of the colony.[378] When the consul had to depart, the council of the colony elected a vice-consul, who fulfilled his tasks but had no salary and could pursue his ordinary activities. In order to indemnify him for the loss of time, the Venetians granted him at least a part of the consul's salary, or the revenue from the consular dues.[379] Some of the Venetian vice-consuls

decreed that some articles which had been exempted from the *consolazium* should henceforth be liable to it; see Misti 46, f. 94a. This decision was confirmed in 1400 (see Misti 47, f. 40) and again in 1474 (see Misti 50, f. 106b.).

[370] Misti 34, f. 153a 40, f. 24a.

[371] Same series 40, f. 117b.

[372] D. Jacoby, "L'expansion occidentale dans le Levant: les Vénitiens a Acre dans la seconde moitié du treizième siècle," *Journal of Mediaeval History* III (1977), p. 232 and note 26.

[373] Wilken, *art. cit.* p. 52; Berchet, *La republica di Venezia e la Persia*, p. 81; Misti 24 f. 90b 34, f. 158a 41, f. 92b; Senato Mar XII, f. 168a f. 168b.

[374] See Misti 22, f. 90b.

[375] See G. P., Sent. 20, f. 12b ff. 76, f. 51b ff. 107, f. 42a ff. 181, f. 122a ff.

[376] Vat sub 15 March 1400 (consul of Ancona in Alexandria), 10 Aug. 1400 (Catalan consul), 9 March 1401 (Genoese consul).

[377] *Dipl. Ven.-Lev.* I, p. 294; II, pp. 21, 80. The privileges of 1344 and 1355 granted him the right only for goods worth 1000 dinars (the interpretation given by Heyd II, p. 48, should be corrected).

[378] Leonardo de Valle sub 5 Nov. 1403 (acts of Venetians).

[379] Misti 41, f. 105a 60, f. 34a (this is a decision which was to become a permanent law). Sometimes he had the full salary (but if he was not a noble, only half of it); see Misti 45, f.

in the Syrian and Palestinian towns probably had the same status; others, like those of Tripoli and Sarmīn, were, for a certain time, true consuls.

In addition to the negotiations with the Moslem authorities and his judicial activities, a consul had two other major tasks, which were not at all easy: he had to maintain discipline within his merchant colony and to represent it before the consuls of other trading nations.

Obviously, among the merchants who came from various countries of Southern Europe to the Levant and who always took many risks, hoping to make great profits, there were not a few who behaved dishonestly toward others and to the consular authorities. Time and again, the consuls had to take measures against merchants who avoided their obligations toward the common fund of the colony. A merchant could make his purchases through Oriental Christians from whom he received the commodities in Cyprus, or he could cheat the authorities of the colony in another way.[380] He could conceal the property left by deceased merchants,[381] or disclose the decisions of the colony's council to the Moslems;[382] he might buy spices which were not sieved, contrary to the decisions of the consular authorities,[383] etc. Sometimes a consul had recourse to the Moslem authorities in order to compel a merchant to pay what he ought to pay to the authorities of the colony,[384] but more frequently the merchants applied to the Moslems instead of submitting their claims to their consul. In litigation between people of different trading nations, this was almost usual, although it was a generally accepted moral principle that the claimant should apply to the defendant's consul.[385] Sometimes one even sued a compatriot before the Moslem authorities.[386] In the case of conflicts between the consuls of various trading nations, one had no scruples to do this.[387]

However, the deeds drawn up by the notaries should not blur the portrait, for of course they usually refer to the conflicts between merchants, shipowners, and other Europeans coming to the Levantine emporia. Other sources reveal that the same merchants were also faithful to their religion and sought and found ways to express their devotion. Some of them on

85b. See, further, about his appointment Misti 32, f. 66b 45, f. 85b. Sometimes he was appointed by the General Council of the colony; see Senato Mar XIV, f. 75b.

380 Savi alla mercanzia Ba 947, f. 58; Senato Mar VII, f. 101b.

381 Misti 32, f. 127b.

382 Senato Mar XIII, f. 92b.

383 Same series VIII, f. 126a.

384 G. P., Straordinario Nodari 18, sub 9 Sept. 1449.

385 Nic. Venier B, 2, f. 46b ff.; Tur II, f. 54b, 64a ff.; Leonardo de Valle sub 5 March 1403; Vat III, f. 5b f. (a. 1437) and see especially Vat sub 8 Dec. 1405: the Genoese consul in Alexandria threatens a merchant of Montpellier with denunciation to the *ḥādjib*, if he does not pay his debt to a Genoese. The Frenchman declares that a European should not do this to another, but should apply to the latter's consul.

386 Crist. del Fiore VI, f. [3a].

387 Vat sub 1 Dec. 1400, 9 Dec. 1405.

the occasion of a commercial journey made a pilgrimage to Jerusalem,[388] and the consuls also asked their governments for permission to leave their posts and to go to Jerusalem.[389] Christian captives were ransomed or other Christians stood surety for them, when they were released on condition, e.g., that they would obtain the liberation of Moslem captives.[390] Gifts were also made to the Friars in Jerusalem.[391] Some merchants even felt remorseful for carrying on trade with the Moslems and applied to the Holy See to grant them absolution or to allow them to engage in this trade.[392]

D. The Profits

Profits from the export of European commodities to the Levant and from the import of Oriental articles into the European countries varied greatly. They depended upon the political and economic circumstances. A political crisis would compel the merchants to sell their stocks in the Moslem Levant at very cheap prices; a war between European states could induce them to lower the prices of the spices they had imported. A dearth in Syria would result in a great increase of cotton prices and diminish the profits of the merchants who marketed it in Southern Europe. But even so, the large amount of data in various sources renders it possible to make some guesses as to the average level of profits.

The prices of the most important commodities in the Leventine trade found in price lists and in other documents of the European and Levantine emporia point to the range of gross profits. References to the expenses make more accurate suppositions feasible. The accounts that have come down to us in the archives of some firms and the judicial acts of litigations between employers and agents, and merchants and shipowners, contain precious information.

Data on the prices of copper, one of the important export goods of the Levant traders, are especially numerous.[393] They show a decrease at the beginning of the fifteenth century, a rise in the second decade, and a new downward trend from the middle of the century. The profits on the export of copper to the Moslem Levant cannot have been great at the end of the

[388] G. P., Sent. 97, f. 75a ff.

[389] Misti 44, f. 52b 51, f. 52a 52, f. 190a.

[390] Crist. del Fiore I, f. 13a ff.

[391] ASV, Cancell. Inferiore, Notai, Ba 132, Giov. Negro sub 13 Febr. 1421 (will of Zuan Nadal, made in Damascus).

[392] L. Balletto, *Genova, Mediterraneo, Mar Nero,* p. 33 ff. See also Crist. del Fiore I, f. 8b ff.: Andrea Cazal gives a procurra for obtaining revocation of excommunication because of the export of forbidden merchandise to the Moslem countries.

[393] Copper prices in Venice, see *Les métaux précieux,* p. 116 ff.; infra Appendix C 1; prices in the Levant, *Les métaux précieux,* pp. 62, 117f.; Appendix C 2.

fourteenth century,[394] and even in the first half of the fifteenth century the gross profits cannot have been more than 25 percent of the cost price. In the second half of the century, when the output of the copper mines in Germany and Slovakia increased substantially, the profits accruing from its export to the Levant began to increase.

Because of the great diversity of the numerous kinds of cloth, it is difficult to establish characteristic price differences between the European and the Levantine trading centers.[395] It is much more feasible to draw a comparison between the various prices of soap, another industrial product of which great quantities were shipped to the Moslem Levant. This data contained in Table XL leave no doubt: the difference between the prices of soap in the Levant and in the major trading centers of Europe, which were also centers of the soap industry, were commonly 50 percent, and that between the prices in Ancona and the Levant, 100 percent.

The prices of the Indian spices imported into the South European emporia are given in many price lists and can be checked in judicial and other documents. By comparing their prices with those in the Moslem Levant, we can draw some very firm conclusions.[396] The data in Tables XLI and XLII point clearly to an average price difference of 50 percent. As far as pepper is concerned, this was the case, for instance, in 1386, 1393, 1394, 1395, and 1399.[397] Among the prices of beledi ginger in the Levantine emporia and in Venice, those of the years 1392, 1394, 1396, and 1399 are the most characteristic.

The following tables comprise the prices of pepper and ginger in Alexandria and Damascus, on one hand, and in Venice, the greatest spice market in Southern Europe, on the other. But the prices of spices (and other Levantine commodities) were not equal in Venice and in the other South European markets. Table XLIII contains data, which have been culled from the Datini records, about the prices of these articles in the three major emporia of Southern Europe at the end of the fourteenth century. According to these data, there was a difference of 10 percent between the price of pepper in Genoa and in Venice. In Barcelona, too, pepper was apparently more expensive than in Venice, but the price difference was smaller. The

394 See above, p. 160.
395 But see below.
396 Cf. Table 3 in my "Profits." Whereas in that table the prices of pepper in the Levant and in Venice in the same year have been compared, in the following table the prices in the Levantine emporia at a certain date are confronted with those that pepper fetched some months later in Venice, that is, at the time the merchandise bought at that price was sold there. In the same way, the following tables of ginger and cotton prices have been arranged. Other comparative data see in my "Il volume del commercio levantino," p. 428.
397 See, further, my "Profits," p. 256. Sieveking, "Aus venet. Handelsbüchern," *Jahrbuch* 26, p. 194, overestimates the usual profits of the spice traders, maintaining that often their profits amounted to 100 percent.

Table XL Soap prices

Venice migl. of 301 kg	Genoa cant. of 47.5 kg	Ancona migl. of 346 kg	Alexandria[a] kinṭār of 96 kg	source
1393 white 21 duc. black 13 "				Melis, Doc., p. 302
	1396 hard 5 duc.		26 Feb. 1396 soap of Gaeta 7.5 din. " pf Ragusa 7 din.	Op. cit., p. 304; price lists Dat 1171
			19 Oct. 1396 white 6 din.	
			22 Feb. 1418 of Venice 6.24 " Naples 6.5 din.	price lists Lor. Dolfin
			1418 of Gaeta 6.5 din.	Arch. B. Dolfin 180, fasc. 15
			19 Feb. 1422 of Venice 7 din. " Naples 7.5 "	price lists Lor Dolfin
			2 Feb. 1423 of Venice 2.75 " Naples 7.5 din.	price lists Lor. Dolfin
			12 April 1423 of Venice 7.5 " Naples 8125 din.	Arch. Lor. Dolfin, letter of Nic. Bernardo
			17 July 1423 of Venice 8 din.	letter of the same
			31 July 1423 of Venice 7.5 " " Naples 8 "	letter of the same
			21 Aug. 1423 of Venice 7.25 " " Naples 8.5 "	price lists Lor. Dolfin

Table XL (continued)

Venice migl. of 301 kg	Genoa cant. of 47.5 kg	Ancona migl. of 346 kg	Alexandria[a] kinṭār of 96 kg	source
			16 March 1424 of Venice 6.75 " " Naples 7.25 "	Melis, Doc., p. 190
1426 16 duc.			1426 6.25 duc.[b]	G.P., Sent. 48 f. 132a f.
			May 1427 8 duc.	Tur IV, f. 18b
			before 1440 of Venice 6 din. " Genoa 7 " " Pisa 7 " " Gaeta 7 " " Tripoli 7 "	Uzzano, p. 112
		1459 14 duc., of Gaeta 9 duc.		Ang. di Domenico II, f. 143a, f. 180a ASF Conv. Soppress. 78, Vol. 322, c. 45[c]
		1461 13.33 duc.		Ang. di Dom. IV, f. 102b f.
		1470 14 duc.		Ang. di Dom. IX, f. 208a
		1473 14 duc.		Ang. di Dom. XII,
		1484 13.9 duc.		Ant. Giov. di Giac. 32, f. 185a
		1486 12.5 duc.		Nic. Cressi VI, f. 82a
		1489 6.2 duc.		Giac. Alberici VI, f. 56b
		1492 11 duc.		Giac. Alberici VIII, f. 116b
		9 "		Giac. Alberici VIII, f. 118a
		12 "		l.c.
		10.5 "		Giac. Alberici VIII, 59a f.

Table XL (continued)

Venice migl. of 301 kg	Genoa cant. of 47.5 kg	Ancona migl. of 346 kg	Alexandria[a] kinṭār of 96 kg	source
		1493		
		12 duc.		Giac. Alberici VIII IX, f. 52a
		1494		
		13 duc.		Giac. Alberici VIII X, f. 55b
		12 "		Giac. Alberici VIII X, f. 85b

a) This table contains only data on the prices of soap imported from Europe.

b) The origin of the article is not indicated; it was probably Venetian soap.

c) In the same year a kintar (i.e. of 180 kg.) of non-specified soap coast 12 ashrafis in Damascus, see G.P., Sent. 152, f. 98a f. Probably even this soap was Venetian.

prices of beledi ginger appear to show the same pattern.[398] The high spice prices in Genoa may have been due in part to the fact that a large part of the merchandise was not directly imported from the Moslem Levant, but was purchased in Chios. Another more important reason for the high prices of spices in Genoa was the high customs levied there. But, during a certain period, at least at the end of the fourteenth century, the profits of the Genoese Levant traders must have been greater than those of the Venetians. The difference between the cotton prices in the Levant and in the South European emporia were much greater than the differences of the spice prices.[399] The data contained in Table XLIV apparently confirm the conclusions drawn elsewhere, namely, that cotton cost about 80 percent more on the markets of Southern Europe than in the Moslem Levant.[400]

So the range of the gross profits of the Levant trade is very clear.[401] But what were his expenses? The major items of expenses were the customs paid in the European and Levantine ports and the freight charges. The data

[398] See also in my "Il volume del commercio levantino," p. 428.

[399] Other data are to be found in my "Profits," Table 7. Even in the following table, prices of cotton in the Levant are compared with its prices a short time later on the South European markets.

[400] See my "Profits," pp. 258, 268. Sieveking, *art. cit.*, p. 193, concluded that the usual price difference was 36-37 percent. This is an underestimate.

[401] The data on the cotton prices in Ancona in the 1490's are not sufficient to conclude that the profits of the Anconitan cotton traders were smaller than those of the Venetian, since we do not know cotton prices in Syria in those years.

Table XLI Price of a carica (120 kg) pepper (in ducats) in the Levant and in Venice

date	Alexandria	Damascus	Venice
Aug. 1384	42		55.8
Jan.-May 1385			
spring 1386	40.6	66.6	61.1
Sept. 1386		40.5	
Feb. 1387			53.5
Sept. 1392	86	75	
Nov.-Dec. 1392			94.2
spring 1393	60		
July 1393			83.5
Sept. 1393	56		
Nov.-Dec. 1393			67.3
Feb.-April 1394	51.6	48.4	
Nov.-Dec. 1394			63.5
spring 1395	44.3	43.3	
Aug.-Sept. 1395			60.8
Feb.-April 1396	54	66.6	
July-Aug. 1396			70.8
Sept.-Oct. 1396	61.2		
Dec. 1396			68.5
Feb. 1397	50		
May 1397			66.1
Feb.-April 1397	47		
Dec. 1397			56.5
spring 1398	46.6		
May-July 1398			56.9
Sept. 1398	48.4		
Nov. 1398			59.6
Feb. 1399	41.6		
April-Sept. 1399			60.4

on freight charges in the sources are clearer than those referring to customs and other expenses.

In Venice 2-1/2 percent *ad valorem* was paid for the export of foreign cloth at the beginning of the fourteenth century; and from 1400, in addition to other customs, 1 percent was paid to the office called *tabula*.[402] The dues for the export of Venetian cloth were lower. In 1417 they were liable to 1 percent, but were exempted from other *dazii* (amounting to 0.25 percent

[402] ASV, Compilazione leggi, Ba 162, f. 35a, 142a f.

Table XLII Prices of 100 light Ven. pounds beledi ginger (in ducats) in the Levant and in Venice

date	Alexandria	Damascus	Venice	source
June-July 1392		24.16		
Aug.-Nov. 1392			40	Dat 549, letters of Zanobi of 27 Aug., 22 Nov. 1392.
Feb.		30.4		
May-July 1393			40	Dat 549, letter of the same of 31 May, 28 June, 15 and 26 July 1393
Jan.-March 1394		30		
April 1394			53	Dat 549, letter of the same of 2 April 1394
Sept.-Oct. 1394		35.4		
Jan.-Feb. 1395		45 - 60		Dat 549, letters of the same of 14 Jan., 16 Feb. 1395.
March-April 1395	31	35.4		
Sept. 1395		40	60	Dat 549, letter of the same of 1 Sept. 1395
Dec. 1395			54	Dat 549, letter of the same of 23 Dec. 1395
March 1396	33.3	43.3		
July-Aug. 1396			50-52	Dat 926, letters of the same of 29 July, 17 and 28 Aug. 1396
Oct. 1396	37.5			
Dec. 1396			52	Dat 926, letter of the same of 10 Dec. 1396
Feb. 1399		11.1		
Sept. 1399			22	Dat 927, letter of Piero di Giov. Dini of 6 Sept. 1399.

and similar rates).[403] For metals, in the first half of the fourteenth century, the payment was 5 percent.[404] For the shipping of money on Venetian ships 1 percent freight was paid, and when it arrived in the Mamluk kingdom, there was a duty of 1 percent. In the fourteenth century, this duty had amounted to 2 percent.[405] The customs to be paid to the ports of Egypt and

[403] Coll., Not. V, f. 82b.

[404] There f. 32a, 33b.

[405] *Dipl. Ven.-Lev.* I, p. 292, II, p. 20; Uzzano, p. 113; G. P., Sent. 155, f. 42b (a. 1468). Marino Sanuto the Elder reports that one paid for the import of gold and silver handed over to the Sultanian Mints for coining as dinars and dirhams 6-2/3 percent or 3-1/2-4-1/2 percent; see *Secreta fidelium crucis,* p. 24. In the privilege that the sultan granted the Venetians in 1345, he emphasized indeed that the reduction of the import due to 2 percent was a great favor; see *Dipl. Ven.-Lev.* I, p. 292.

Table XLIII Spice prices in Venice, Genoa and Barcelona (in ducats)

a) Price of pepper (a carica of Venice)

date	Venice	Genoa	Barcelona	source
		20 Aug. 1382 65.5	3 Oct. 1382 48	Heers, Il commercio, p. 203
		13 March 1383 63.6	30 March 1383 61.2	Ibidem
1384[a]	58.4		1384 60	Dat 548, letters of Inghilese d'inghilese
July 1384	59.6	June 1384 61.4		Dat 548, letters of Donato Dini; day, Douanes, p. XXXVIII
June 1385	57.3	June 1385 59.1		Dat 548, letter of Zanobi; Day l.c.
4 July 1387	53.8	4 July 1387 54.6		Dat 548, letter of Zanobi; Heers, Il commercio, p. 203
2 Dec. 1392	96.1	26 Dec. 1392 101.5	4 Dec. 1392 75.6	Dat 549, letter of Zanobi; Heers l.c.
20 Jan. 1394	67.6		20 Jan. 1394 81.6	Dat 549, letter of Zanobi; Heers l.c.
31 March 1395	58.8	7 Mar. 1395 64.2		Dat 549, letter of Zanobi; Heers l.c.
12 Feb. 1296	66.5	6 Feb. 1396 74.2		Dat 549, letters of Zanobi; Heers l.c.
20 Jan. 1397	68.8	12 Jan. 1397 59.7		Dat 550, letter of Zanobi, Heers l.c.
6 July 1398	56.9	6 July 1398 62.4		Dat 926, letter of Zanobi Dat 660, letter of Francesco di Marco & Andrea di Bernardo
22 Oct. 1398	58	2 Oct. 1398 181.8		Dat 926, letter of Zanobi; Dat 660, letter of Franc. di Marco & Andrea di Bonnano
6 Nov. 1400	58.5	26 Nov. 1400 74.2	4 Dec. 1400 62.7	Dat 927, letter of Com; of Zanobi
11 Feb. 1402	55.7	6 & 16 Feb. 1402 72.7		Dat 927, letter of Com. of Zanobi; Dat 662, letter of Maffio di Giov. & Cie
9 May 1403	59.6	7 May 1403 68.2		Dat 928, letter of Com. of Zanobi; Dat 663, letter of Boninsegna di Marco
11 Oct. 1404	58.5	8 Oct. 1404 66.7		Dat 929, letter of Perluccio del Maestro Paolo; Heers l.c.

Syria for the import of European commodities in principle amounted to 10 percent,[406] and the Florentines even paid 14 percent.[407] But, from several documents, one learns that the import dues actually levied in Egypt in the

[406] Misti 53, f. 25b f., and see also Misti 37, f. 100a: 10 percent for import of cheese from Crete into Egypt, Pasi, f. 48a. At the end of the thirteenth century, a much higher custom was levied for metals. Marino Sanuto the Elder says that the custom due for the import of copper was 25 percent and that for tin 20 percent; see *Secreta l.c.*

[407] Wansbrough, "A Mamlūk commercial treaty," p. 64.

Table XLIII (continued)

b) Price of beledi of ginger (100 light Venet. pounds)

date	Venice	Genoa	Barcelona	source
		20 Aug. 1382 30.4	3 Oct. 1382 29.7	Heers p. 203
		13 March 1383 28.8	30 March 1383 27	Ibidem
1384	24.5[b]			Dat 548, letters of Inghilese d'Inghilese
2 Dec. 1392	37.5	26 Dec. 1392 37.9	4 Dec. 1392 33	Dat 549, letter of Zanobi; Heers l.c.
15 March 1395	55.5	7 March 1395 50		Dat 549, letter of Alessandro Borromeo & Domenico di Andrea Heers l.c.
29 Feb. 1396	51.5	6 Feb. 1396 60.6		Dat 549, letter of Zanobi; Heers l.c.
27 Jan. 1397	51	12 Jan. 1397 41.7		Dat 550, letter of Zanobi; Heers l.c.
22 Oct. 1398	26	2 Oct. 1398 75.7		Dat 926, letter of Zanobi; Dat 660, letter of Franc. di Marco & Andrea di Ronnano
6 Nov. 1400	17	26 Oct. 1400 21.2	4 Dec. 1400 17.1	Dat 927, letter of Com. of Zanobi, Heers l.c.
28 Jan. 1402	24	29 Jan. 1402 28		Dat 927, letter of Com. of Zanobi; Dat 662, letter of Maffio di Giov. & Cie.
9 May 1403	22	7 May 1403 26.5		Dat 928, letter of Com. of Zanobi; Dat 663, letter of Boninsegna di Marco
12 Oct. 1404	21.5	8 Oct. 1404 24.2		Dat 929, letter of Perluccio de Maestro Paolo; Heers l.c.

a) This is an average: the letters of this merchant show that from May to December 1384, there were fluctuations between 56.1 and 60.7 ducats.

b) See the preceding note. The prices of beledi ginger vary from 20 to 29 ducats.

fifteenth century usually amounted to a lower rate.[408] In Syria the customs in the fifteenth century were lower. Only 2-3 percent was paid for the import of European commodities.[409] Although one paid for merchandise imported to inland towns twice, first in the port and then in the town where it was sold, the customs seldom amounted to 6-7 percent.[410]

[408] See my "Profits," p. 267; MS. Egerton 73, f. 62b (2-1/2 percent and 10 percent for various kinds of cloth).

[409] *Dipl. Ven.-Lev.* II, p. 314 (but see there that one had levied much more); Jorga, "Notes et extraits," *ROL* VIII, p. 56 ff.; Uzzano, p. 113; Wansbrough, "Venice and Florence," p. 491; *Libro de conexenses* f. 62b; MS. Egerton 73, f. 62b; Pasi, f. 48a; G. P., Sent. 151 bis, f. 86a, 90a 163, f. 44a 176, f. 101b.

[410] G. P., Sent. 151 bis, f. 82a ff.

Table XLIV Cotton prices in the Levant and in Italy[a]
(prices of 1000 light Ven. pounds in ducats)

date	Syria	Venice	Ancona	source	price diff.
May 1394		April 1394			
	(average) 25.9[b]	73.3			
fall fair 1394		Nov. 1394			
	of Hamath 51.8	75			
	of Sarmin 27.6	61			
Aug. 1395		Nov.-Dec. 1395			
	(average) 38	50-75			
March 1396		Dec. 1396			
	(average) 42.85	70			
March 1408		Juen 1408			
	(average) 71.9	of Hamath 100-110			
		of Sarmin 85-90		Dat 930, letter of Com. of Zanobi of 18 May 1408	48.7%
			May 1408		
			(average) 106.6	Dat 1044, letter of Jacopo & Francesco & Cie (of Ancona), of 2 May 1408	
		(average) 99		G.P. Sent. Int. VIII , f. 64b f.	37.5%[c]
1410		June 1410		Dat 930, letter of Bindo di Gherardo Piaciti of 31 May 1410	
	in Latakia 46.6	(average) 57.5			
		" 90		G.P., Sent. Int. VIII, F. 80a f.	58%
1429			1433	Chiar. Spampalli II, f. 98a ff.	
	in Latakia 32.2		56.5		76%
			47.8		48%
1443		1443		G.P., Sent. 160, f. 96a	
	in Damascus 25.55[d]	43.7			72.8%
1453-55			1459	Ang. di Dom. II, f. 55a, 89a	
	in Tripoli 30.5		46.9		54%
			43.3		42.6%
1481-88					
	of Hamath 31.2				
		1493		Giac. Alberici IX, f. 189a	
		34.5			
		1494		Giac. Alberici X, f. 6a	
		33.4			
		34.8		there f. 9a	
		17.9		" f. 136a	

a) For the prices in Syria see Table XXIV and the prices in Venice until 1402 Table XII.

b) There is no specification as to the kind of cotton.

c) The comparison refers only to the latter item.

d) This price is calculated on the assumption that the indication as to price of cotton in Damascus refers to a Tiberias ḳinṭār of 270 kg.

Even the customs for the export of spices from the Levantine ports were supposed to be 10 percent, and from some accounts one learns that this rule was kept. A Florentine merchant paid in 1422 customs according to this rate. But very often as a matter of fact only 8-9 percent or even less was paid.[411] Some judicial acts referring to the purchase of spices and dyes in Egypt and Syria in the fifteenth century point to 2.5-3 percent actually being paid. The Venetian firm Antonio Zane paid 2 percent for spices and dyes bought in Damascus in 1411 and 1416.[412] The same rate applied to the export of Brazil-wood from Syria in 1466, and for gum-lac in the 1470's.[413] The customs for the export of cotton were lower than those paid for spices. To judge from Merchant Guides and judicial acts, they varied from 2 to 7 percent.[414] But there were also other fees, e.g., the brokerage, which, according to some commercial treaties and the accounts that have come down to us from some firms, amounted to 2 percent on the average.[415]

The customs due in Venice for the import of spices depended upon the ships upon which they were transported, and, in addition there were frequent changes. In the first half of the fourteenth century, spices and other commodities imported on galleys were exempted from customs, whereas those shipped on other vessels were liable to the payment of 5 percent.[416] But, at the end of the fourteenth century and in the fifteenth century, there was an impost of 3 percent for spices shipped to Venice on the galleys.[417] For other merchandise transported on the galleys, the duty paid was 2 percent.[418] The impost of 3 percent, however, was not the only payment required for spices coming on galleys. There were other customs (*dazii*), so that altogether 3-1/5 percent was paid.[419] Spices shipped on the cogs were liable to 5 percent, the impost of 3 percent and the customs (*dazii*) amounting to 2 percent. But sometimes the total was reduced to 3 percent,

[411] See the data quoted in "Profits," p. 264, and further accounts Benedetto Strozzi, f. 37a.

[412] Arch. Ant. Zane, accounts of purchases of cloves, gum-lac, and other commodities in Damascus, a. 1411; pepper bought in Damascus, a. 1413; cinnamon bought there in 1416; pepper bought in Alexandria, a. 1414.

[413] G. P., Sent. 152, f. 98a ff. 170, f. 32a ff.

[414] *Anonymous Merchant Guide*, Marciana, f. 77b (54 dirh. dreto del chazandar in Acre, that is, 1 ducat for a sack worth perhaps 30); MS Egerton 73 has f. 62a sub Tarifa di Alexandria among the expenses for the export of cotton *p' portar a marina p' sacco* 115 dirh. and *p' 10 chadi de la porta* the same sum. Since in the time in which the treatise was compiled, a ducat was exchanged for 230 dirh., see *ibidem*, the custom for the export of 1 sack was 1 ducat. See, further, G. P., Sent. 51, f. 17b f. 107, f. 138a 137, f. 21a ff.

[415] See my "Profits," p. 264.

[416] Pegolotti, p. 142. The impost of 5 percent was already levied at the beginning of the fourteenth century: see Mag. Cons., Magnus et Capricornus, f. 41a; *Misti*, ed. Cessi I, p. 93.

[417] Misti 53, f. 92a 55, f. 98b 56, f. 83a 57, f. 54b, 58, f. 159a ff., 181a 59, f. 51b 60, f. 6a, 100b; Coll., Not. V, f. 110a; Senato Mar VI, f. 80a. About the office of the straordinario, see Lane, "Merchant galleys, 1300-1334," p. 221.

[418] Coll., Not. XII, f. 117a.

[419] Senato Mar XI, f. 156b XII, f. 195a; Wansbrough in *BSOAS* 26, p. 526, note 6, *BSOAS* 28, p. 516. Accounts Soranzo, f. 41b; Accounts Franc. Contarini, f. 62a.

for example, when merchandise was transported on the supplementary ships (*navi di rata*) or when an exception was made and spices were allowed to be shipped on cotton cogs.[420] According to a law passed by the Maggior Consiglio in 1301, the payment of the impost of 5 percent even exempted the merchandise from the liability to other duties.[421] The customs for the import of cotton in Venice was 3 percent, and in addition it was liable to some minor dazi.[422]

In Florence, according to various tariffs of the fifteenth century, 3 percent or 5 percent was paid for the import of spices,[423] that is, according to the same rates as in Venice; whereas customs in Genoa were much higher, amounting to as much as 20 percent.[424]

Finally, the consular dues must be taken into consideration. The Genoese often, or more correctly, almost regularly, imposed special dues for trade with the Moslem Levant. In the 1370's 1/2 percent was levied, and at the beginning of the fifteenth century it usually amounted to 1 percent; in the 1470's, in Alexandria, 1 1/3 percent was levied both for import and export.[425] The consolatium levied by the Venetian consuls was very low; it did not amount to more than 0.2 percent for spices.[426]

Because of the great variety of commodities that the European merchants imported into the Levant, it is almost impossible to talk about average profits. The freight charges, e.g., for some goods, like cloth, were rather small, and for others very high. The freight of copper could amount to as much as 15 percent, and that for olive oil, another bulky and relatively cheap product, was no smaller.[427] In the year 1405 two Genoese merchants imported 2,740 jars olive oil from Andalusia to Alexandria of which 2,266 were sold for 6,382 dinars. The freight charges for the whole shipment amounted to 1,400 dinars.[428] The expenses for the export of cloth to the Levant, both the freight charges and the customs in the Levant, were much smaller. In 1474 the Venetian firm Lunardo Sanudo sold cloth of Bergamo in Tripoli for 505 ducats (selling price) and had to defray expenses in Syria amounting to 25 (5.2 percent). For the sale of Brescia cloth, which yielded 970 ducats and 40 dirhams, expenses in Syria were 72, i.e., 8 percent.[429] The Venetian firm Pietro Bono in 1465 (cca) exported 93 pieces of Brescia cloth to Aleppo, and it was sold for 1,272 ducats. All the expenses in Syria

420 Misti 38, f. 34a 40, f. 73b, 119a 41, f. 21b. See also Misti 50, f. 49a.
421 Mag. Cons., Magnus et Capricornus, f. 18a.
422 Misti 40, f. 115a f.; Thiriet, *Rég.* III, p. 120; Accounts Soranzo, f. 46a.
423 See the sources quoted in my "Profits," p. 268.
424 Heers, *Gênes*, p. 127 f.
425 See above, Ch. IV, p. 228; ASG 2774 C, f. 7b and cf. 17b, 21b. Musso, *Navigazione*, p. 134.
426 Misti 41, f. 92b 46, f. 94a.
427 G. P., Sent. 191, f. 40b, ff.
428 Vat. sub 3 Jan. 1405, 2 Dec. 1405, 22 Dec. 1405.
429 ASV, Avog. di comun Ba 109, fasc. IV.

amounted to 163.74 ducats, i.e., 12.8 percent of the selling price.[430] In the year, 1468, the same firm sold 149 pieces of this cloth for 1,201.4 ducats through an agent in Aleppo, and had (in Syria) expenses of 69.9 ducats, i.e., 6 percent. However, this account did not cover all expenses.[431] So all expenses, including the freight, for the export of cloth to the Levant must have amounted to 10-20 percent,[432] and since the difference between the prices of cloth in Southern Europe and in the Levant were 20-40 percent, apparently the net profit was 15-30 percent and sometimes even more.[433]

Expenses for the import of spices from the Moslem Levant to Venice, for those shipped on galleys, may be summed up as follows:

Duties in the Levant	9%
Commission to the *fattore*	3%
Freight	10%
Customs in Venice	3%
Total	25%

Since the price difference between pepper and ginger in the Moslem Levant and in Venice was 50 percent, the net profit would have been 20-25 percent. In fact it was greater. When the price of pepper rose above 100 ducats a sporta, the freight charges amounted to only 8 percent. But often the spices were shipped on cogs, in which case the transport was much cheaper, usually less than half of the shipping charges on the galleys. Even transport on the galleys was often much cheaper, owing to special agreements; and the same is true for the customs levied in the Levant. The impost of 5 percent due for shipping spices on cogs in many years was reduced by the Venetian Senate to the 3 percent to be paid to the *straordinari*. Accordingly, often all expenses of the trader amounted to 15 percent or even less, so that the net profit was 35 percent of the cost price. The profits of the Genoese Levant traders were certainly not smaller. For profits of 60 percent were apparently not rare.[434]

The expenses of the cotton trader were much greater. The data in our sources would suggest the following model of expenses for the export of Syrian cotton on the cogs of the State line to Venice:

Customs in Syria	5%
Commission to the *fattore*	3%
Freight[435]	23%
Customs in Venice	3%
Total	34%

[430] G. P., Sent. 151 bis, f. 82a ff.
[431] Same accounts, 90a.
[432] See "Profits," p. 267.
[433] See *art. cit.*, p. 269; Kedar, *Merchants in crisis*, p. 64.
[434] See above p. 394 and, further, Liagre-De Sturler, no. 360.
[435] 7 duc. for a mill. worth 30 duc.

The price difference being 80 percent or more, the net profits still amounted to 45-50 percent.

However, in some merchant letters of the end of the fourteenth century, much smaller profits are spoken of. According to these letters the profit from the import of pepper and ginger to Venice was 5-10 percent.[436] A report of the Venetian chronicler Morosini, referring to the year 1401, deals with the net profit of 20 percent from the import of gum-lac.[437] It may be that the profits of the spice traders were smaller at the end of the fourteenth century, perhaps because of the greater competition. Venice had not yet monopolized the spice trade, and one had to content himself with lower profits.

From the middle of the fifteenth century, on the other hand, the payments to the *cottimo*, the general fund of the Venetian colonies, increased very much. These imposts must have had a great impact upon the Venetian Levant trade. But even in that period one did not always pay so much for the *cottimo*. The payments to the *cottimo* due for the import into the Levant were always much lower.[438]

Some data found in judicial acts from later periods show that our conclusions are not exaggerated. These data referring to the import of spices from the Levant to Venice show that 45-60 percent was earned.[439] Our conclusions are also borne out by the accounts of some firms.

The comparison of the profits yielded by the export of European commodities to the Moslem Levant and by the import of Oriental articles into Southern Europe in the later Middle Ages with the profits of Levant traders in the period of the Crusades shows a remarkable decline. The Judaeo-Arabic letters which were found in the Cairo Geniza and date to the eleventh century point to profits of 100 percent and more, realized by the export of dyes, purple cloth, pearls, and other articles from Egypt to Tunisia and farther on to Spain.[440] On the other hand, the profits of the late mediaeval Levant traders were much greater than those the great commercial companies of Central Europe had from their international trade in the same period. The Ravensburg Company earned 10 percent a year on the average in the middle of the fifteenth century, and the Vöhlin-Welser earned 9 percent at the beginning of the sixteenth century.[441] The Nürnberg firms

[436] Dat 549, letters of Zanobi di Taddeo Gaddi of 4 Jan. and 7 Nov. 1394; Dat 797, letter of the same of 12 Nov. 1394.

[437] *Chron. Morosini* c. 205.

[438] See the tables in my "Profits," p. 264 ff.; "Le monopole de Barsbay d'après les sources vénitiennes," p. 566, and see above.

[439] G. P., Sent. 76, f. 49b 79, f. 115a ff. 84, f. 44b ff.

[440] Goitein, *Letters*, pp. 31, 33; *id.*, *Mediterranean Society* I, p. 202.

[441] Schulte, pp. 635, 642.

Table XLV Accounts of Venetian Levant traders[a]

A Spice traders			
a) Accounts of Michele Boldu			
purchase of pepper in Alexandria in 1355			
	net price	346.93 din.	
	expenses[b]	35.4	(16%)
	other expenses[c]	20.37	
b) Accounts of Ant. Zane			
purchase of gum-lac in Damascus in 1411			
	net price	24,885 dirh.	
	all expenses in Syria	1,852	(7.4%)[d]
purchase of cloves			
	net price	5,711 dirh.	
	all expenses in Syria	355 "	(6.2%)
purchase of pepper in Damascus in 1413			
	net price	318 duc.	
	all expenses in Syria	18 "	(5.66%)
purchase of cinnamon in Damascus in 1416			
	net price	88 duc.	
	all expenses in Syria	17 "	(19%)
purchase of pepper			
	net price	81 duc.	
	all expenses in Syria	9 "	(11%)
purchase of beledi ginger in Damascus in 1423			
	net price	136 duc.	
	all expenses in Syria	10 "	(7.35%)

had no greater profits either in that period.[442] The profits from international trade in Central Europe were certainly low, because of the much higher expenses of land trade.[443] In the Near East, one earned much more even by land trade. According to the accounts of a merchant of Shiraz who exported spices to Herat and Saray in the year 1438, his net profits were 50 percent.[444]

[442] Braunstein, "Wirtschaftl. Beziehungen zwischen Nürnberg u. Italien," p. 401.

[443] See *art. cit.*, p. 386.

[444] W. Hinz, "Ein mittelalterlische Handelsunternehmen im 15. Jahrhundert," in *Welt des Orients* I (1947-1952), p. 330.

Table XLV (continued)

c) Accounts of Lorenzo Dolfin

purchase of pepper in Alexandria in 1420

net price	140 din.	
all expenses in Alex.	4.66 duc.	(3.3%)

purchase of gum-lac in Damascus in 1421

net price	90 din.	
all expenses in Syria	9 "	(10%)

purchase of pepper in Alexandria in 1423

net price	117.5 din.	
all expenses in Alex.	7 "	(6%)

purchase of pepper in Acre in 1423

net price	236 duc.	
all expenses in Syria	56 "	(23.7%)

purchase of pepper in Damascus in 1424

net price	282 duc.	
all expenses in Syria	25 "	(8.9%)

purchase of pepper in Acre in 1426

net price	226 duc.	
all expenses in Syria	52 "	(23%)

d) Accounts of Marco Morosini

purchase of pepper in Alexandria in 1458

net price	135 duc.	
all expenses	24 "	(18%)[e]

e) Accounts of Ieronimo Bernardo

purchases in Alexandria in 1461 of Brazil-wood

net price	156 duc.	
expenses in Alex.	26 "	(16.7%)
freight charges	10 "	(6.4%)

B Cotton traders

a) Accounts of the fraterna Soranzo[f]

purchases of cotton in Ramla in 1412

gross price	214.5 duc.	
expenses in Venice	77 "	(35%)
	profit 99 duc.	(39%)

purchases in Sarmin in 1414

gross price in Syria	707 duc.	
expenses in Venice	72.5 "	(10.35%)
	profit 212 duc.	(27%)

b) Accounts of Lorenzo Dolfin

purchase of cotton in Latakia in 1426

net price	59 duc.	
all expenses in Syria	10 "	(17%)

Table XLV (continued)

purchase of cotton in Acre in 1426			
net price	226 duc.		
all expenses in Syria	52 "		(23%)
c) Accounts of the firm A. Baseggio - P. Caroldo			
purchase of cotton in Acre in 1481			
201 sacks			
	gross price	4423 duc.	
	freight	424.5 "	(9.6%)
	insurance	63	(1.5%)
	customs in Venice	184.5	(4.1%)
	other expenses	133.5	
		5528.5 duc.	
		all expenses 18%	
		profit 1150 duc. (26%)	

a) Sources: ASV, Proc. S. Marco, Ba 153, Com. Michele Boldu; Arch. A. Zane; Arch. Lor. Dolfin; G. P., Sent. 133, f. 39b f. 155, f. 40b ff.; Accounts Soranzo c. 33b; Melis, Origini, p. 78 f.

b) This item does not include the customs in Alexandria, but 9 din. for "spese" Neither is the freight included.

c) These are the expenses for the shipment of 800 duc. to Alexandria.

d) These expenses comprise the main duty amounting to 2% and consular dues amounting to 1%.

e) Comprising freight charges on the galleys and the impost of 3% in Venice.

f) These accounts should be added to those quoted above Ch. IV, p. 258.

VII
Mediaeval Levant Trade at Its Height (1453-1498)

A. New Economic and Political Tides

Some time after the middle of the fifteenth century the economies of the Near East and of the European countries began to show sharply contrasting trends. The general decay of the Levantine countries increased more rapidly, and its various phenomena were the striking features of several sectors of economic and social life. At the same time, most European countries began to recover economically after the long period of contraction subsequent to the famines of the first half of the fourteenth century and the Black Death. This contrast of economic development on the northern and southeastern shores of the Mediterranean is obviously at variance with geographical determinism, supposing parallel trends in all the regions around the Mediterranean.

In the Levantine countries depopulation continued and apparently at a faster pace. They were haunted by successive major epidemics, called *ṭaʿūn* by the Arabic chroniclers, although one cannot be sure that it was always the plague. There were such epidemics in Egypt, Syria, and Palestine in 1459-1460, 1468, 1469, 1476-1477, 1492, and 1497-1498. In addition to the epidemics, there were endemic diseases that caused great losses to populations already considerably diminished.[1] Both villages and towns were afflicted. In some sources one finds data concerning the number of villages in Egypt. They shed a strong light on the downward trend of the Levantine populations.[2] Despite the temporary fluctuations, due to periods of drought and epidemics of pestilence, these data (discarding the obviously mistaken account of 1460) clearly point to the downward trend of Egypt's agrarian population. From the beginning of the fourteenth century the number of

[1] See my *Social and econ. history*, p. 302.

[2] See *op.cit.*, p. 303, and my lecture "Le Proche-Orient au bas moyen âge—une région sous-développée," ch. VI, *Istituto Fr. Datini, Settimane di studio* X (1978), p. 384 ff.

Table XLVI Number of villages in Egypt

	956	2395
reign of al-Ḥākim	(996-1020)	2390
" " al-Mustanṣir	(1035-94)	2186
	1210	2071
	1315	2454
	1375	2163
	1434	2170
	1460	2365
	1477	2121

villages declined continuously. Even the population of the towns decreased. A French scholar has concluded that Cairo had 430,000 inhabitants in the middle of the sixteenth century against 600,000 at the beginning of the fourteenth century.[3] Depopulation and abandonment of the villages was probably even more tangible in Syria. When the Turkish officials took a census in 1519-1520, they found that in the province of Tripoli the population of several villages had decreased from 3,000 to 800.[4] After a careful study of the Turkish *tapu* registers, Ö. L. Barkan arrived at the conclusion that the total of Syria's population (including Palestine and the province of Adana) amounted to 571,600 in the 1520's.[5] The demographer R. Bachi, using the most modern methods of his disipline, calculated the population of Palestine on the eve of the Ottoman conquest at no more than 140,000-150,000.[6] So there must have been a great decline of the Levantine populations in the second half of the fifteenth century, when European populations were again beginning to increase. The supposition of F. Braudel that demographic trends in the Mediterranean countries were mostly the

[3] M. Clerget, *Le Caire* (Cairo, 1934) I, p. 240. J. L. Abu-Lughod, *Cairo* (Princeton, 1971), p. 37, believes that the population of the town in the first half of the fourteenth century did not exceed half a million. On the other hand, this author supposes, see p. 44, that the size of the town did not change from the end of the fifteenth century until the time of the French expedition, when it had 250,000 inhabitants. This is also the conclusion of M. W. Dols, *The Black death in the Middle East* (Princeton, 1977), pp. 196, 198. All the estimates of the total population of Egypt before and after the great plague are purely hypothetical. But whether it numbered 3 or 4 millions before the plague, it certainly diminished by a third then and decreased in the period subsequent to it; see Dols, p. 230.

[4] R. Mantran-J. Sauvaget, *Règlements fiscaux ottamans. Les provinces syriennes* (Paris, 1951), p. 80.

[5] "Essai sur les données statistiques des registres de recensement dans l'empire ottoman aux XVe et XVIe siècles," *JESHO* I (1958), p. 20.

[6] R. Bachi, *The population of Israel* (Jerusalem, 1977), p. 23.

Table XLVII Average wheat prices in Egypt

	price of 100 kg
end of XIIIth century	1.07 canonical dinars
1320-1330	0.86
middle of XIVth century	0.89
beginning of XVth century	0.94
middle of XVth century	0.74
end of XVth century	0.56

same does not hold,[7] just as it is contradicted by accounts of the High Middle Ages and of the sixteenth century. From 970 Egypt enjoyed a demographic boom for about a hundred years, whereas Syria's population apparently decreased greatly.[8] After the conquest by the Ottomans, there was a demographic upsurge of the towns of Palestine, but their populations began to decline from the 1560's. This is the conclusion of two scholars who have made a thorough study of *tapu* registers of that period.[9] Rightly, the authors contrast their results with the sweeping statements of Braudel.[10]

How weighty a factor depopulation was in the late mediaeval Levant is emphasized by data on the development of grain prices. Although Egypt's fertile soil still yielded harvests that made it possible in many years to export considerable quantities of wheat and barley, prices went down because of the diminishing demand. From data in the Arabic chronicles of the Mamluk period it is possible to calculate average price levels.[11] On the other hand, Egypt no longer produced quantities of grains that could supply stocks for the years in which harvests were bad. Consequently, the country suffered in the fifteenth century from cycles of dearth.[12]

Another striking phenomenon of the economic life of the Near East in the second half of the fifteenth century was impoverishment. Not only did the totals of the national income decrease, but also the great majority of the population had to live on a lower level than that of a hundred years before. The downward trend was the consequence of the decline of production, both in agriculture and in industry; the prevailing deflationary

[7] *La Méditerranée et le mond méditerranéen a l'époque de Philippe II*, 2nd edition (Paris, 1966) I, p. 368.

[8] *Social and econ. history*, pp. 202 f., 217 f.

[9] A. Cohen-B. Lewis, *Population and revenues in the towns of Palestine in the sixteenth century* (Princeton, 1978), pp. 20 f., 26.

[10] *Op.cit.*, p. 22.

[11] See my "Quelques problèmes que soulève l'histoire des prix dans l'Orient médiéval," p. 212.

[12] *Art. cit.*, p. 208.

development of the monetary system; and the expenses for the costly military expeditions of the Mamluks, a great part of which were made outside the frontiers of the kingdom. The once powerful class of great capitalists, the Kārimīs, had been brought down in the second quarter of the century by Sultan Barsbāy, and the lower bourgeoisie, consisting of shopkeepers and small merchants, was oppressed by the arbitrary taxation and by the compulsory purchases of government-owned goods.[13] It is true that there came into being a new class of wealthy merchant bourgeoisie, mostly consisting of wholesale merchants or industrialists. But the wealth of this class could not be compared with that of the Kārimīs, and its majority suffered from the progressive decline of the industries. Of course, the industries were not wholly extinct. Egypt still exported powdered sugar,[14] and Syria offered her *bocasin*. But, on the other hand, articles for which Egypt and Syria had once been renowned had to be imported in the second half of the fifteenth century. Costly silken stuffs were imported from Southern Europe, other textiles from India.[15] In 1466 the sultan himself requested the government of Venice to send him silken stuffs and glass for windows.[16] The eagerness of the sultan to have Venetian velvets and crystal was so well known that when there were deliberations in Venice about an embassy to be sent to Cairo it was proposed, in the same year, to let him have some quantities of these articles as presents.[17] A letter written in 1459 by the Florentine consul in Alexandria is explicit on the market trends in Egypt. The author of the letter emphasizes that the kinds of cloth requested are the cheaper Catalan, whereas the precious cloth can be offered only to the sultan's court.[18] Consequently, the Florentines and other South European merchants imported into the Moslem Levant either the very high priced, or very cheap cloth.[19] The cleavage between the great majority of the population and the military aristocracy became greater than in any previous time. Only this class could afford the costly silken stuffs, brocades, and velvets offered by the Florentines, Venetians, and other Italian merchants.[20] Certainly, in the towns of Egypt and Syria there was also a class of skilled craftsmen and unskilled workers, who could increase their income considerably after the great loss of working hands through the Black Death and the subsequent epidemics. But these classes were apparently not nu-

[13] *Social and econ. history*, p. 320.
[14] ASF, Miscell. Repubbl., Reg. 107, f. 16b (customs tariff of fifteenth century) and see in the letter quoted in note 18 (sugar of al-Fuwwa is listed as an export of Egypt).
[15] ʿAbdalbāsiṭ 812, f. 371b f.
[16] Senato Mar VII, f. 97b.
[17] Secreta 22, f. 130b.
[18] ASF, letter of Marioto Squarzalupi.
[19] See my "Observations on Venetian trade in the Levant," p. 571 ff.
[20] See Mallett, *Florentine galleys*, p. 122.

merous. They also lived under the impact of the continuously decreasing wealth of the military aristocracy. Many deeds of the fifteenth century point to the decline of the salaries of the administrative staff of schools, mosques, and various waḳf foundations. Accountants, cashiers, and librarians were much worse off than in the fourteenth century.[21] The lower echelons of the clergy also had salaries that were smaller than in preceding periods, and the same was the case for the teachers at the *madrasas* and elementary schools.[22] The worsening of their economic situation, however, was also the consequence of the greater demand for posts, a phenomenon resulting from the growth of a new class of intellectuals, educated at the numerous madrasas and always looking for employment.

But, whatever the causes, these classes and other strata of the Near Eastern society had to lower their standard of living. A striking feature of the new economic situation was the change in the composition of the food basket. Formerly the populations of the Near East ate white bread. But, at the end of the fifteenth century, people in Cairo began to eat millet and *dhura* bread. Similar changes probably took place in Syria and Palestine for, according to the Turkish *tapu* registers, in several districts of these countries the barley crops were equal to or greater than the wheat crops,[23] and there were many who could not afford even this poor food. In the towns of Egypt and Syria there were many proletarians who lived on the fringes of society, people without regular occupation or income, poor who were always ready to hire themselves to rebels and to indulge in plundering.

At a time when the Moslem Levant sank to the nadir of its economic development, a new upswing began in most European countries. The new upward trend expressed itself in all sectors of economic and social life.

A basic phenomenon was a new swing in population trends. From 1450 to 1460, populations began to increase everywhere. True, population figures in the middle of the fifteenth century were still lower than they had been a hundred years before, and even in the second half of the century many European countries were struck by the plague, and their populations diminished or remained stationary for this or another reason.[24] But, as far as one can judge from the scattered data, the long tide of depopulation had come to its end. In some provinces of France the new trend must have been spectacular, especially in Burgundy and in Normandy. In Provence, the demographic upsurge that began in the last third of the fifteenth century

[21] See my "I salari nel medio Oriente durante l'epoca medioevale," *RSI* 78 (1966), p. 333.

[22] See my "I salari," p. 335 f.; "Prix et salaires dans l'Orient médiéval à la basse époque," *Revue des études islamiques* 39 (1971), p. 111.

[23] *Social and econ. history*, p. 319.

[24] J. C. Russell in *The Fontana economic history of Europe, the Middle Ages* (London, 1976), p. 36; K. F. Helleiner, "The population of Europe from the Black Death to the eve of the vital revolution," *CEHE* IV (1967), pp.12, 18.

was very swift. The population increased by 200-300 percent from 1471 to 1540.[25] In some provinces of Spain and in England the upswing had already begun in the fourth decade of the century.[26] Even in several provinces of Italy populations increased, though slowly. Venice had perhaps 84,000 inhabitants in 1424; it had 105,000 in 1509.[27] The population of the industrial town of Brescia numbered 15,000 in 1440 and, in 1493, 48,650 (including the suburbs 56,000).[28] The population of Padua increased from 16,730 in 1430 to 27,000 at the beginning of the sixteenth century.[29] At the turn of the century, Palermo had 55,000 inhabitants, Bologna 55,000, Verona 37,570, and Cremona 40,000.[30] According to the overall estimate of J. C. Russell, the population of the whole of Europe rose from 42.4 million in 1400 to 56.8 in 1500; another scholar believes that it increased from 45 million to 69 million.[31]

When the population again began to increase, the contraction so characteristic for the late mediaeval economy of Europe had not yet been overcome. Reduced demand for grains, owing to depopulation since the middle of the fourteenth century, had resulted in lower grain prices, in the falling of land prices, in decreasing rents and, consequently, in a considerable deterioration of the economic situation of landlords. All these trends were perceptible in Central Europe and in many other regions. Everywhere the value of estates diminished;[32] grain prices remained low in some regions even in the second half of the fifteenth century, probably because land that had been abandoned was again brought under the plough, when populations began once more to increase.[33] Consequently, the prices of industrial products manufactured in the towns were high because of the shortage of labor; the peasants found themselves in a very bad position; many villages were abandoned altogether in that period. In all periods of history agricultural settlements that did not prove profitable were given up, but it seems that

[25] J. C. Russell, *Late ancient and mediaeval populations* (Philadelphia, 1958), pp. 118, 119; E. Baratier, *La démographie provençale du XIIIe au XVIe siècle* (Paris, 1961), p. 94.

[26] J. C. Russell, *British mediaeval population* (Albuquerque, 1948), p. 272; Helleiner, *art. cit.*, p. 12.

[27] K. J. Beloch, *Bevölkerungsgeschichte Italiens* III (Berlin, 1961), pp. 5, 17.

[28] *Op.cit.*, p. 121 f.

[29] *Op.cit.*, p. 69.

[30] *Op.cit.*, p. 357.

[31] Russell, *Late ancient and mediaeval populations*, p. 148, and cf. pp. 117, 119, 121, 123, 126, 129; M. K. Bennett, *The world's food* (New York, 1954), p. 9.

[32] M. A. Postan, "The fifteenth century," *Ec. Hist. Rev.* IX (1938/9), p. 162; id., *The mediaeval economy and society* (London 1972), p. 176 f.; W. Abel, *Agrarkrisen und Agrarkonjunktur*, 2nd edition (Hamburg 1966), p. 76 f.; H. Bjørkvik, "Villages désertés, bilan de la recherche en Norvège et en Suède," in *Villages desertés et histoire économique, XIe-XVIIIe siècles* (Paris 1965), p. 589 f., 591.

[33] Abel, *Agrarkrisen*, pp. 56, 69, 286; J. Pelc, *Ceny w Krakowie w latach 1369-1600* (Lwów, 1935), p. 127; H. Miskimin, *The economy of late renaissance Europe, 1460-1600* (Cambridge, 1977), p. 49 f.

in some countries of Europe the number of such instances was particularly great in the time subsequent to the Black Death. In several provinces of Germany and Austria, 45-70 percent of the villages were abandoned.[34] Another aspect of the agrarian crisis was the recession of wheat growing and the increase of cattle rearing.[35] Against this very dim view that has been conceived of agricultural conditions in Europe at the waning of the Middle Ages, other facts could be adduced, however. It seems that in several regions of Central Europe grain prices began to rise from 1450 and especially from 1470 on,[36] and there can be doubt that the retrogression of wheat growing was accompanied by a great increase in other sectors of agriculture, especially in the growing of industrial plants, e.g., of woad[37] and the wine culture.[38] The abandonment of villages was not a general phenomenon. It was hardly perceptible in northern and northeastern Germany; it happened only in a few provinces of France;[39] and in other countries it was not the effect of the depopulation and of lower grain prices.[40]

Contradictory arguments could also be adduced concerning another question, namely, the growth or the fall of the per capita income in the latter half of the fifteenth century, as compared with earlier periods. The contraction of grain growing, the most important sector of mediaeval economy, apparently tips the balance toward the assumption of decreasing per capita income.[41] But what is much more significant is certainly the actual distribution of the national income and, in fact, there can be not the slightest doubt that at the end of the Middle Ages much broader segments of Western society enjoyed well-being. The shortage of labor resulted everywhere in the rise of wages, as is borne out by the fixing of maximum wages in various countries.[42] According to the data, there is no doubt that there was

[34] W. Abel, *Die Wüstungen des ausgehenden Mittelalters*, 2nd ed. (Stuttgart, 1955), pp. 5 ff., 27.

[35] Abel, *Agrarkrisen*, p. 70 ff.

[36] M. J. Elsas, *Umriss einer Geschichte der Preise und Löhne in Deutschland* (Leiden, 1936-1949) I, p. 80 f. II, part b, p. 67.

[37] Fr. Borlandı, "Note per la storia della produzione a del commercio di una materia prima, il guado nel medioevo," in *Studi in onore di Gino Luzzatto* (Milan, 1950) I, pp. 302 f., 303 f., 314.

[38] M. Mollat-P. Johansen-M. Postan-Ch. Verlinden, "L'économie européenne aux deux derniers siècles du moyen âge," in *Relazioni del X Congresso int. di scienze storiche* III (Florence, 1955), p. 687.

[39] J.-M. Pesez-E. Le Roy Ladurie, "Le cas français," in *Villages désertés*, p. 153, and cf. p. 177f.

[40] Ch. Klapisch-Zuber-J. Day, "Villages désertés en Italie," in *op.cit.*, pp. 438 f., 456.

[41] R. Romano-A. Tenenti, *Die Grundlegung der modernen Welt* (Frankfort o/M, 1967), p. 26.

[42] Th. Rogers, *Six centuries of work and wages*, 16 ed. (London, 1949), pp. 226 ff., 233, 236 f.; W. Beveridge, "Wages in the *Winchester Manors*," *Ec. Hist. Rev.* VII (1936-1937), pp. 40, 41, 51; M. Postan, "Some economic evidence of declining populations in the later Middle Ages," *Ec. Hist. Rev.* 2nd series II (1949-1950), pp. 226, 233.

greater consumption of meat and a general improvement of nourishment and dress, and countless data show that there was a higher standard of living than before, even greater expenses for luxury and public buildings. The fifteenth century was the golden age of craftsmen and of townspeople in general.[43] So it may be concluded that the number of those who could afford the Oriental spices probably increased in that period. Even scholars who hold a rather pessimistic view of economic conditions of that period state that the number of well-being craftsmen in the town was not insignificant.[44]

There was another phenomenon of late mediaeval economic life that was favorable to the development of the Levant trade. This was the increase of mining and the production of metal work, for the Levantine countries suffered a great shortage of silver, copper, tin, and lead, and greater output of these metals enabled the European merchants to make greater purchases of spices on the Levantine markets.

In the twelfth and thirteenth centuries methods of mining in Europe had been rather primitive. Most of the work was restricted to quarrying and digging caves, whose bases were not deep; deep shafts were dug only infrequently. The water was drained from the shafts by simple methods, using leather baskets wound up by hand-turned windlasses or passed along a chain of men. Even the smelting of the ores was done in a very primitive way. The washing, breaking, and crushing was done by hand labor and the smelting in open air hearths or in tiny forges, operated by hand or by foot-driven bellows. But in the middle of the fifteenth century there were some important innovations which brought about great changes. Workers began to dig deep shafts and learned how to drain the water by more sophisticated methods. In Saxony and Slovakia pumps that were activated by the rotation of horse-driven wheels began to come into use.[45] The use of blast furnaces made it possible to produce great quantities of cast iron. The ore was kept in contact with carbon at high temperatures on large fires for a long time so that cast iron was produced by the absorption of the carbon. The fluid unforged iron was melted again in refinery furnaces. Consequently, production increased. For, by the method called the "indirect" melting (because it had to be done twice), the loss of iron in the drops was much smaller.[46] Everywhere water power came into use for the operation of the bellows and iron works. This great innovation occurred in France, in Upper Italy,

[43] F. Lütge, "Das 14/15. Jahrhundert in der Sozial-u. Wirtschaftsgeschichte," *Jahrbücher für Nationalökonomie u. Statistik* 162 (1950), p. 190; C. M. Cipolla, *Storia economica dell'Europa pre-industriale* (Bologna, 1974), p. 260.

[44] Abel, *Agrarkrisen*, p. 62; Miskimin, *op.cit.*, pp. 21, 62, 63.

[45] J. U. Nef, "Mining and metallurgy in mediaeval civilization," *CEHE* II (1952), p. 463.

[46] Nef, *art. cit.*, p. 464; R. Sprandel, *Das Eisengewerbe im Mittelalter* (Stuttgart, 1968), p. 226.

in the Upper Palatinate, and in the mining centers of Austria.[47] Another important innovation was made in the separation of silver from argentiferous copper ore and in its refining by liquidation and the use of lead. This method, the so-called *saigern,* introduced in 1451 in Saxony by Johannsen Funcke, meant great progress in silver production.[48] Capitalists of Nürnberg built such refining sheds (*Saigerhütten*) in Thuringia in 1472 and in 1479.[49] In addition, new and rich seams of ore were discovered in several regions.

So there was a great increase in the production of various metals. In the last quarter of the fifteenth century, the production of copper increased greatly in the mines of Mansfeld,[50] and from 1460 in those of the Rammelsberg, where it had been discontinued after a long period of decline.[51] Also in other provinces of central Germany, copper mining flourished in the second half of the fifteenth century.[52] The new increase was, however, especially spectacular in Bohemia and in Saxony[53] and the Harz (in addition to the Rammelsberg).[54] In Austria too such greater quantities of copper were obtained from the ores that at the beginning of the sixteenth century this country was first among the copper-mining regions of Central Europe.[55] In order to evaluate the importance of this phenomenon for the activities of the Italian trading towns, it is worthwhile to point to the role that the Venetians had in the production and marketing of the copper of Austria. The Venetian Antonio Cavallo obtained a monopoly of copper mining in Tyrol in 1477. In 1491, however, he was bankrupt. Thereupon the Paumgartner Company of Kufstein monopolized the marketing of the Tyrolese copper, whereas the Fuggers engaged in copper mining in Slovakia from 1491. In the same year they built a refining shed in Arnoldstein (Carinthia), and from 1494 they were also in control of the copper production of Tyrol. A very great part of the copper of Tyrol was sold by them in Venice and from there shipped to the Moslem Levant.[56]

[47] Sprandel, *op.cit.,* p. 223.

[48] Nef, *art. cit.,* pp. 463, 479.

[49] W. Möllenberg, *Die Eroberung des Weltmarktes durch das Mansfeldische Kupfer* (Gotha, 1911), pp. 5, 6 ff.; cf. R. Dietrich, "Untersuchungen zum Frühkapitalismus im mittelhochdeutschen Erzbergbau und Metallhandel," *Jahrbuch für die Geschichte Mittel-und Ostdeutschlands* IX/X (1961), p.130 f.

[50] Möllenberg, *op.cit.,* p. 14.

[51] W. Borchardt, *Geschichte des Rammelsberger Bergbaues von seiner Aufnahme bis zur Neuzeit,* p. 90 ff.

[52] J. Kohl, *Zur Geschichte des Bergbaues im vormaligen Fürstentume Kulmbach-Bayreuth* (Hof, 1913), pp. 22 f., 29 f.; W. G. Neukam, "Ein Gewerkenbuch von Goldkronach aus den Jahren 1481/83," *Mitteilungen des Vereines f. Geschichte der Stadt Nürnberg* 44 (1953), p. 47.

[53] Nef, *art. cit.,* p. 578.

[54] P. Fleck, *Zur Geschichte des Kupfers* (Marburg, 1908), p. 17 f.

[55] R. Hildebrandt, "Augsburger u. Nürnberger Kupferhandel 1500-1619," *Zeitschrift f. Wirtschafts-u. Sozialwissenschaften* 92 (1972), part 1, p. 3.

[56] O. Pickl, "Kupfererzeugung u. Kupferhandel in den Ostalpen," in *Schwerpunkte der*

As in copper mining, there was a great upswing in the production of silver and iron. In some mines of Schwaz in Tyrol, as in those of the Falkenstein, the production of silver had already begun in 1409,[57] but the great growth of silver mining began there at the end of the 1420's.[58] In the 1460's the production increased considerably.[59] At the same time there was a great increase in iron production in Germany, Sweden, Upper Italy, and some provinces of Spain.[60] In the 1440's iron was beginning to be taken from seams recently discovered in some districts of Austria.[61] The development of iron mining in central and southern Sweden was particularly fast.[62] The total iron production of Europe may have increased from 25,000-30,000 tons a year at the beginning of the fifteenth century to 40,000 at the end of the century.[63]

The growth in the production and working of metals in Central Europe had a great impact on the trade with the Mediterranean world, not least because of the great role capitalists of Nürnberg played in this sector. They were indeed also the most active of the German merchants who engaged in trade with the Italian emporia.

There were also some trends in the industrial life of fifteenth-century Europe that were particularly stimulating as far as the trade with the Levant was concerned. The contraction subsequent to the Black Death did not diminish industrial production, but brought about changes of its structures and a shift in the relative importance of various sectors. In some regions of Western Europe and in Poland a new peasant (home) industry developed.[64] It is true that the flourishing of the cloth industries of England, Flanders, and Florence was followed by a long period of unchanged or even decreasing production. The stagnation of the English cloth industry over a long period was certainly connected with political circumstances.[65] But after the end of the Hundred Years War, a new phase in the expansion of the English cloth industry in the Mediterranean world began. Characteristically, the English began to export their cloth themselves to southern

---

Kupferproduktion u. des Kupferhandels in Europa 1500-1650, ed. H. Kellenbenz (Cologne, 1977), p. 136 ff.; cf. E. Egg, "Schwaz ist aller Bergwerke Mutter," *Der Anschnitt* 16 (1964), p. 12; E. Ashtor, *Les métaux précieux*, p. 58 f.

[57] M. v. Isser-Gaudenthurm, "Schwazer Bergwerksgeschichte," *Berg-u. Hüttenmännisches Jahrbuch der montanistischen Hochschulen von Leoben und Příbram* 52 (1904), p.412 f.

[58] *Op.cit.* 53, p. 42 ff.; St. Worms, *Schwazer Bergbau im fünfzehnten Jahrhundert* (Vienna, 1904), p. 12 f., 17; cf. Egg, *art. cit.*, p. 10; Pickl, *art. cit.*, p. 118 f.

[59] J. U. Nef, "Silver production in Central Europe 1450-1618," *Journal of Political Economy* 49 (1941), p. 585.

[60] R. Sprandel, *Das Eisengewerbe*, p. 270 f.

[61] *Op.cit.*, p. 148.

[62] *Op.cit.*, p. 210 f.

[63] *Op.cit.*, p. 277.

[64] Romano-Tenenti, *op.cit.*, p. 34 f.

[65] See Ph. Wolff, "English cloth in Toulouse (1380-1450)," *Ec. Hist. Rev.*, 2nd series I, (1949-1950), p. 291.

France and Italy in that period.[66] The export of the cloth of Flanders to Poland and Prussia increased in the period of the great contraction; in other words, it had been shifted in other directions.[67] The production of high-class cloth also flourished in Florence in the second half of the fifteenth century, as is convincingly shown by the great import of English wool and the data on sales of cloth at the fair of Salerno in 1478 and on export to Turkey.[68] New centers of cloth manufacturing sprang up, such as that of Fribourg in Switzerland, whose products were probably marketed in the Near East as "cloth of Geneva" (where it had been bought by the Italians).[69] The great development of the silk industry in some towns of Italy was very important for the trade with the Levant, where the silk industry had decayed a long time before. It enabled the Levant traders to supply the aristocracy of the Near East with those brocades and velvets and other silken stuffs which they so readily bought. Lucca, the cradle of the Italian silk industry, was famous for its heavy samite and satin, whereas the new centers, Bologna, Florence, Genoa, and Venice, produced light-weight silken stuffs, such as carsenet, zendal, taffeta, and damask.[70] In Florence the silk industry reached a considerable size, since in 1474 not less than 84 workshops produced silken stuffs. In the middle of the fifteenth century, silken stuffs were beginning to be produced in Siena and Milan and later also in France.[71] Other textile industries whose products were exported into the Moslem Levant and bartered against spices flourished again in that period in Europe. In the second half of the fifteenth century new centers of the linen industry came into being in Brabant and in Hainaut.[72]

[66] See A. Silvestri, *Il commercio a Salerno nella seconda metà del Quattrocento* (Salerno, 1952), p. 141 ff. (appointment of a consul of the French, German, and English merchants in Naples, a. 1461), ASMess, Pagliarino, Matteo VI a, f. 17b; an English merchant in Messina, a. 1468; Borlandi in Studi Luzzatto I, p. 302; Giacomo Comito 851, f. 92a f.; a Londoner in Palermo; W. Cunningham, *The growth of English industry and commerce 5th ed. I: during the early and Middle Ages* (Cambridge, 1910), p. 417: in 1485 the Florentine Lorenzo Strocci is appointed English consul in Pisa, the first instance of an official appointment of an English consul in the Mediterranean countries.

[67] Mollat-Johansen-Postan-Sapori-Verlinden, p. 707.

[68] *Op.cit.* p. 700 ff.; A. Sapori, "Una fiera in Italia alla fine del Quattrocento," in *Studi I*, pp. 455, 456; Mallett, *Florentine galleys*, p. 122; P. Earle, "The commercial development of Ancona, 1479-1551," *Ec. Hist. Rev.*, 2nd series 22 (1969), p. 34. H. Hoshino, *L'arte della lana in Firenze* (Florence, 1980), p. 238 ff.

[69] See H. Ammann, "Die Zurzacher Messen im Mittelalter," in *Taschenbuch der Historischen Gesellschaft des Kantons Aargau* (Aarau, 1923), p. 56; *idem*, "Neue Beiträge zur Geschichte der Zurzacher Messen," in *Taschenbuch*, etc., 1929, p. 19 ff.

[70] Fl. Edler de Roover, "Lucchese silk," *Ciba Review* 80 (1950), pp. 2,913, 2,923. See, further, R. di Tucci, "Lineamenti storici dell'industria serica genovese," *ASLSP* 71 (1948), pp. 23, 53 ff.; P. Massa, "L'arte genovese della seta nella normativa del XV e del XVI secolo," *ASLSP* N. S. X (1970), p. 21 f.; U. Dorini, *L'arte della seta in Toscana* (Florence, 1928), p. 37 f.

[71] A. Doren, *Italienische Wirtschaftsgeschichte* I (Jena, 1934), p. 495 f.; Mollat-Johansen-Postan-Sapori-Verlinden, p. 726.

[72] Mollat-Johansen, etc. p. 719 ff.

The development of new industries resulted in the growth of various sectors of international trade. The intense activities carried on at several fairs which developed in that period bear witness to this upswing. Merchants from all over Europe met at the fairs of Geneva, Lyon, and Frankfort-on-the-Main and considerable quantities of cloth were sold, of which a not insignificant part was later shipped to the Near East. The German fairs were attended by merchants of Cracow and other towns of Eastern Europe, a region where urban life was developing and where the standard of living was rising. So they served as outlet and bridge to new markets for Oriental commodities. But Polish merchants also came to Venice.[73] The importance of the increased production of metals for international trade was another remarkable fact, particularly as far as the trade with the Mediterranean world was concerned. It is indeed a matter of fact that the great trading companies of southern Germany of the end of the Middle Ages were much engaged in the trade of metals. This was true for the Herwart, Rehlinger, Fugger, and other companies.[74]

Despite the development of fairs, which had a truly international character, the commercial powers kept a sharp eye to keep others from intruding into regions where they monopolized trade. The failure of a great English merchant who tried to market the cloth and other products of his country himself in the Near East illustrated this attitude. Robert Sturmy of Bristol, who had already made an attempt to send a ship into the Mediterranean, embarked on a ship of his in 1457, accompanied by two caravels, for a trip to the Eastern Mediterranean. He loaded upon them 6,000 pieces of cloth as well as tin, lead, and wool. He did reach the Moslem Levant and exchanged his goods for spices, but on the return trip the Genoese ruler of Mytilene, Giuliano Gattiluso, lay in wait for him near Malta and captured two of his ships. Sturmy himself apparently perished on this occasion.[75] This act of piracy had disastrous consequences for Genoese trade in England. The Genoese merchants were imprisoned and their goods sequestered, and for some years Italian trade in England was in full crisis.[76]

Certainly there were other years of crisis in international trade, when

[73] See H. Ammann, "Die deutschen und schweizerischen Messen des Mittelalters," in *La Foire, recueils de la Société J. Bodin* V (1953), pp. 155 ff., 159 f.; *idem, Die wirtschaftliche Stellung der Reichstadt Nürnberg im Spätmittelalter* (Nürnberg, 1970), p. 91; *idem*, "Genfer Handelsbücher des 15. Jahrhunderts," in *Anzeiger für Schweizerische Geschichte* 51 (1920), p. 21; *idem*, "Die Zurzacher Messen," p. 67; Fr. Borel, *Les foires de Genève au quinzième siècle* (Geneva, 1892), p. 156 ff.; Miskimin, *op.cit.*, p. 57; M. Malowist, "Les routes du commerce et les marchandises du Levant dans la vie de la Pologne au bas moyen âge et au début de l'époque moderne," in *Mediterraneo e Oceano Indiano*, pp. 163, 167.

[74] H. Kellenbenz, *Deutsche Wirtschaftsgeschichte I* (Munich, 1977), p. 185 ff.

[75] E. H. Carus Wilson, "The overseas trade of Bristol," in E. Power-M. Postan, *Studies in English trade in the fifteenth century*, p. 227 f.

[76] J. Heers, "Les Génois en Angleterre, la crise de 1458-1466," in *Studi in onore di A. Sapori* (Milan, 1957) I, p. 810 ff.

the most enterprising Italian merchants had to limit their activities, could not market their stocks, and suffered losses. Obviously this was mostly due to political circumstances. As far as the Levant traders were concerned, it was sometimes the effect of economic conditions overseas.

In 1457 the Venetian Senate had decided that seven ships should sail to the cotton spring fair in Syria, but only six registered. In that year no one made a bid for the Aigues-Mortes galleys, so that the two galleys had to be leased for the symbolical payment of one ducat each. Even the Barbary galleys found no bidder.[77] In the year 1475 the patrons who leased the galleys had to be given loans and, on the other hand, great quantities of merchandise came back from Aigues-Mortes, Barbary, and Alexandria.[78] In 1480 much of the merchandise, especially cloth, shipped to Alexandria and Beirut on the Venetian galleys was not sold, so that it was allowed to be shipped again without paying customs.[79]

However, these years of crisis were quite exceptional. As a whole, the second half of the fifteenth century was a period of economic prosperity all over Europe, and the conditions for a profitable marketing of the Oriental spices were favorable. But in contradistinction to the economic conditions, the political circumstances were inauspicious. The sky of the Eastern Mediterranean and the Greek waters was clouded and looked more and more threatening. The expansion of the Ottoman Turks endangered the positions of the South European trading nations and their lines of communication, and this had far-reaching consequences for the Levant trade. In the 1450's the three great commercial powers of Southern Europe still held strong positions in all regions of the Mediterranean. The Catalan expansion had been crowned by the conquest of Sicily and Naples, while Rhodes, always closely linked to the Catalans, served them as a base in the Eastern Mediterranean. Genoa, it is true, was no longer an independent power. In 1458 it came under French rule; in 1461 it was again independent; but then in 1463 it was occupied by the Duke of Milan. However, the three most important bases of Genoese trade in the Levant and the formerly Byzantine territories were still held by the Genoese; their control of Caffa, Pera, and Chios was not yet challenged. Venice reached the apogee of her political grandeur in the 1450's. The long wars in Lombardy were concluded in 1454 by the peace of Lodi, a treaty which left the Venetians the rule over Brescia, Bergamo, and Crema. So Venice had become a land power too, and not by chance she began to call herself "a second Rome" in official documents.[80]

That fateful day in May 1453 on which Constantinople fell to the Turks

[77] Senato Mar V, f. 179a, 190a, 191b.
[78] Senato Mar X, f. 35a.
[79] Senato Mar XI, f. 67a, 78a, 98b.
[80] Thiriet, *Rég.* III, p. 242.

announced that a heavy storm was brewing. One did not have to be an especially farseeing observer to become aware of the great dangers ahead. Although the fall of Constantinople could have been foreseen, and it would have been a matter of their own interests to save the town, the attitude of the Christian powers toward the tottering remnant of the Byzantine empire had been lukewarm. When King Wladislaw set out for his campaign against the Turks in 1444, the help that Venice granted him was reserved, although her positions were in the first line of Ottoman expansion. Then, in 1446, the Serenissima, always having in mind the priority of her commercial interests, concluded a treaty with the Ottomans and in 1451, just before the final onslaught on Constantinople, she concluded another treaty with them. The appeals of the Byzantine emperor who, in 1451 and in 1452, desperately applied to Venice and all other Christian powers fell on deaf ears. Even a patriotic historian of Venice must confess that the Serenissima played a double game in those days.[81] When Venice decided to support Constantinople effectively, it was too late. The policy of Venice, whose attitude was so important because of her naval power, did not change after the fall of Constantinople. The Serenissima gave priority to her interest in trade with Turkey over the projects of a Crusade against the powerful enemy of Christianity. Tirelessly her diplomats pleaded with the pope and others that she had done more than other powers for Constantinople and could not be blamed for her policy. As a matter of fact, the other Christian powers did not show real enthusiasm for a great military expedition either.[82] In fact, Venice was also interested in appropriating some of the remnants of the Byzantine territories and mainly in enjoying freedom of trade in the dominions of the Ottomans. And, by a treaty with the sultan concluded a year after the fall of Constantinople, that is what she obtained. In addition, Venice was able to add some islands in the Aegean to her possessions.[83]

The conquest of Constantinople by the Ottomans was followed by other successes; their expansion seemed to be irresistible. In 1455 they took Phocea, where the Genoese exploited the rich alum deposits; then they

[81] J. Romanin, *Storia* IV, p. 190. See also D. A. Zakythinos, "L'attitude de Venise face au déclin et à la chute de Constantinople," in *Venezia, centro di mediazione* I, p. 61 ff., who distinguishes between the various phases in the attitude of Venice toward the question of Constantinople's survival. See, on the other hand, the opinions of Kretschmayr, Cessi, Fr. Babinger, and E. Schilbach, who emphasize the weakness of Venice, which did not have an army comparable to the Ottoman and knew well the self-interested and ambiguous policy of the other Christian powers: Kretschmayr, *Geschichte von Venedig* II, p. 363; R. Cessi, *Storia della repubblica di Venezia* (Milan, 1968) I, p. 396; Fr. Babinger, "Le vicende veneziane nella lotta contro i Turchi durante di secolo XV," in his *Aufsätze zur Geschichte Südosteuropas u. der Levante* (Munich, 1962) I, pp. 240 ff., 242; E. Schilbach, "Venedigs widersprüchliche Haltung zur türkisch-osmanischen Expansion," in *Venezia, centro di mediazione* I, p. 77 ff.

[82] Thiriet, *Rég.* III, pp. 189 f., 192, 197, 205, 221, 223 f., 227.

[83] *Op.cit.*, p. 195, 214, 225.

conquered the island of Samothrake, and in 1462, the big island of Lesbos. In the year 1458 Athens came under their control. These conquests of the Ottomans were hard blows for the Genoese, but the danger to the Venetian possessions in the Aegean was also imminent; the Venetians engaged in almost feverish efforts to build up their defenses. Every year the Senate appropriated great sums for the strengthening of the fortifications of Negrepont and Candia, Modon and Coron; supplied these places and others with weapons; and reinforced their garrisons. New galleys were built, and old ones were repaired. The expansion of the Ottomans in the Aegean and the Balkans and the closing of the Black Sea induced the Venetians and the other commercial powers of Southern Europe to intensify their activities in the dominions of the Mamluks. With the fall of Constantinople, the trade with Egypt and Syria was even more than before the vital artery of the Levant trade. Only there could the Italian merchants of that period obtain spices and other Indian articles. But Turkish corsairs began to threaten the Italian merchantmen, and the security of the ships sailing to Syria and Egypt became a major problem. Time and again special measures of precaution had to be taken,[84] and at the same time Venice embarked on a policy of alliances aimed at the encircling of the Ottomans. In 1454 the Serenissima concluded a political and commercial treaty with the prince of Caraman, one of the successor states of the Seldjukids in southern Asia Minor. Thereupon a new galley line was established to replace, to some extent at least, the Romania line that was no longer functioning.[85] But when the fears of the Venetians materialized and in 1463 the war broke out between Venice and the Turks, the prince of Caraman proved to be no match for the Ottomans. The long war put a heavy strain on the resources of Venice, for expenses amounted to 1.2 million ducats a year, and in the first battle she lost one of her dominions to the Turks. In 1470 Negrepont fell, despite the great efforts made to defend the island. In 1460 the Ottomans invaded Dalmatia and appeared in the Friuli; in the year 1472 they again invaded this province so near to Venice.

Waging war through many years with the mighty military power that the Ottomans were, and looking desperately for allies, Venice tried to enlist the help of Uzun Ḥasan, the Turcoman ruler of Iraq and Western Persia. First Lazzaro Quirino, then Caterino Zeno, was despatched as ambassador to the Turcoman prince, and then in 1473 Giosafa Barbaro was sent. In fact, Uzun Ḥasan was eager to ally himself with the Venetians and other Christian powers and in 1464, 1465, and 1471 sent ambassadors to the

[84] Senato Mar V, f. 104a and cf. 107b (a. 1455), 105a, 170b (a. 1456); VI f. 46a, 53b (a. 1458), 145b (a. 1460) (quoted, but with errors by Thiriet, *Rég.* III, p. 230), 202 f. (a. 1460); Thiriet, *Rég.* III, p. 210 f. (a. 1456).

[85] *Libri Com.* V. lib. 14, no. 282; Thiriet, *Rég.* III, p. 197 f.

European powers. Then in 1472 Ḥādjdjī Muḥammad and the physician Isaac (a Spanish Jew) came to Venice, the pope, and the king of Hungary as his ambassadors.[86] According to his instructions Barbaro was to propose an alliance, including mutual obligations in war and peace. Venice sent firearms to the Turcoman prince and obliged herself to demand the whole of Anatolia for Uzun Ḥasan in case of victory.[87] Then in 1474 another ambassador, Ambrogio Contarini, was sent to Uzun Ḥasan.[88] These diplomatic missions inevitably embroiled the Venetians with the Mamluk sultan of Cairo, with whom they had the greatest interest to be at peace, in that they did what they could to invite Uzun Ḥasan to attack the Ottomans, no matter from what direction. So they had to reckon with the possibility that he might invade Syria in order to attack the Ottomans from the south (and not from the Armenian highlands). This possibility is already mentioned in the secret instructions given to Barbaro in February 1473, and there is the statement there that it is difficult to say if this (the invasion of Syria by the Turcomans) would be good or bad for the Venetian merchants.[89] Naturally this double game of Venice with the Mamluks resulted in the sultan of Cairo's taking measures against the Venetian merchants, but the Serenissima stuck to her policy. In February 1474 the Senate gave orders to Ambrogio Contarini that in case it should prove impossible to convince Uzun Ḥasan to invade Anatolia, he should try to influence Uzun Ḥasan to invade Syria.[90] But the hopes of Venice to hit the Ottomans through the aid of Uzun Ḥasan were in vain. He suffered a crushing defeat by the Turks in August 1473, and died in 1477, without having succeeded in launching another attack on the Ottomans. In 1479 peace was finally concluded between Venice and the Ottomans. The Serenissima lost several towns in Albania. Already in 1475 the latter had occupied Caffa, the great

[86] Secreta 25, f. 175b; E. Cornet, *Le guerre de' Veneti nell'Asia (1470-74)* (Vienna, 1856), pp. 23, 25, 30 ff.; G. Berchet, *La republica di Venezia e la Persia*, pp. 3, 5, 8; see also the list of all documents referring to the relations between Venice and Uzan Ḥasan and the latter's embassies and despatches: G. Berchet, *La republica di Venezia e la Persia, nuovi documenti e regesti* (Venice, 1866), p. 36 ff. Lazzaro Quirino had visited him twice, in 1464, see Domenico Malipiero, p. 25, and in 1469, see *I viaggi degli ambasciatori veneti*, p. 12. About Uzun Ḥasan's envoys, see Caterino Zeno, *Storia curiosa delle sue avventure in Persia*, ed. V. Formaleone (Venice, 1783), p. 88, and see also pp. 95, 97 (Caterino Zeno fulfills a mission of Uzun Ḥasan to the king of Poland), and see also *I viaggi* etc., p. 163. About Uzun Ḥasan, see J. E. Woods, *The Aqqoyunlu* (Minneapolis, 1976), p. 90 ff., and about the shadow which the alliance with him cast upon Venice's relations with the European powers see B. V. Palombini, *Bündniswerben abendländischer Mächte um Persien 1453-1600* (Wiesbaden, 1968), p. 15.

[87] Berchet, *La republica di Venezia e la Persia*, doc. X.

[88] The reports of these ambassadors have recently been published by L. Lockhart a.o., *I viaggi degli ambasciatori veneti*, etc.

[89] Berchet, *op.cit.*, docs. X, XV.

[90] Secreta 26, f. 68a ff., published by Cornet, *op.cit.*, p. 123 f.

Genoese emporium on the shores of the Black Sea. Even before the great war with the Turks, the Venetians had the greatest difficulty in maintaining their position in Tana.[91]

After the conclusion of peace between Venice and the Ottomans there was still always imminent danger of attacks on the Venetian (and other Italian) ships. Frequently measures of precaution were taken,[92] but sometimes the danger materialised. In 1493 Turkish corsairs captured the ship of Zuan Boza, a Venetian, sailing to Alexandria.[93]

The expansion of the Ottomans stimulated the intensification of the relations between the South European trading nations, on the one hand, and the sultan of Cairo, on the other hand. Venice especially, the leading commercial power in the Eastern Mediterranean, had the greatest interest in fostering friendly relations with the sultan of Cairo, since the trade with his dominions was the most important sector of her world trade. The alliance with Uzun Ḥasan was no more than an interlude. After the end of the war with the Turks, Venice took up her traditional policy of keeping peace with the Mamluks. The king of Hungary also sought the friendship of the sultan, a natural ally against the Turks. In 1488 a Hungarian embassy came to Cairo.[94] The sultan too had to adapt his attitude to the new political situation.

He was aware of the danger that before long the Ottomans would attack him, so he began to make diplomatic efforts to win the support of the Christian powers. This policy was in conformity with that pursued by other Oriental rulers who applied to the Christian kings for help against the Ottomans.[95] In 1479 he sent an embassy to the king of Naples and to the king of Aragon. Then in 1484 and in 1485 embassies of the sultan came again to Naples.[96] In those years the contest between the Mamluks and the Ottomans over the control of the border lands of Asia Minor and Syria were actually fought by the princes of the Turcoman dynasty of Dhu 'l-ḳadr who were supported by the two rivalling powers. Then, in 1485, open war broke out and lasted until 1491.[97] During this war Sultan Ḳā'itbāy took new steps in the European capitals. In 1489 an envoy of the pope visited Cairo, and, when he returned, an ambassador of the sultan went with him to Rome. The pope even allowed an envoy of the sultan, who

[91] ASV, Mag. Cons., Regina, f. 27b.
[92] Senato Mar XIII, f. 13a.
[93] Secreta 34, f. 169a f.
[94] Ibn Iyās III, p. 248.
[95] Vallet de Viriville, *Histoire de Charles VII* (Paris, 1862-1865) III, p. 442.
[96] Ibn Iyās III, p. 145; cf., below, note 148, 381.
[97] See *Enc. of Islam*² IV, p. 462 f. s.v. Ḳā'itbāy (M. Sobernheim-E. Ashtor), and EI² II, p. 239 f. s.v. Dhu 'l-Ḳadr (J. H. Mordtmann-V. L. Ménage).

returned some time before from another capital where he had fulfilled a mission, to buy weapons.[98]

However, although the new political circumstances induced the sultan and the European trading nations to draw together, there remained the old problems which from time to time aroused conflicts. The Mamluk government tried to increase its revenue from the pepper the trading nations ought to buy from its stocks. These obligatory purchases were imposed upon all European trading nations, and frequently there were conflicts as to the quantity and the price of the pepper to be bought.[99] Secondly, there was the problem of piracy and aggression on the coasts of the Mamluk dominions. The Mamluks reacted violently to the attacks and took measures of reprisal against all European traders, who were found in Egypt and in Syria. In May 1464 a Mamluk officer was captured by corsairs when he was on an official mission to Cyprus.[100] In May 1472 a squadron of five corsair ships attacked the Moslem merchantmen off Rosetta, and some months later the Christian corsairs captured a big Moslem ship not far from Damietta.[101] In 1473 European corsairs again committed acts of agression on the Egyptian coast, and the Mamluks counterattacked every time.[102] Despite the measures of precaution taken by the Mamluks, such as the construction of fortifications on the coast, there were other much more portentous acts of aggression and the diplomatic representatives of the trading nations had to employ all their skills in order to smooth over the difficulties.

B. The Golden Period of Venice's Trade

This was primarily the task of the Venetian diplomats, upon whose patience and tenacity the continuation of normal trade depended fairly often. The Venetian government time and again demonstrated its good will and its interest in friendly relations with the sultan. Mamluks who had been captured by Venetian ships were set free and sent to Egypt,[103] and the same was done after a captain had taken some Turks prisoner; they had apparently embarked on his ship in a port of Egypt or Syria. The captain was punished, and there was even an order that Turks should not be accepted as passengers, so that conflicts should be avoided. The captain himself was imprisoned.

[98] J. Wansbrough, "A Mamlūk commercial treaty," p. 45 and cf. p. 44.

[99] G. Musso, "Nuovi documenti," pp. 492, 493 (Genoese); Crist. del Fiore VI, no. 13 [6b f.] (Florentines, Anconitans), no. 14 [7a f.] (Catalans), and see below.

[100] *Ḥawādith*, p. 467; Ibn Iyās² II, p. 425.

[101] al-Djawharī, *Inbā-al-haṣr*, pp. 441 f., 481.

[102] Ibn Iyās III, 76, 85 f.

[103] Senato Mar VII, f. 33b and cf. Noiret, *Doc.*, p. 463 f. (These Mamluks were not captured by a pilgrim galley, as Thiriet has it, *Rég.* III, p. 239. It was the captain of this galley who brought the news to Venice.)

At the same time the Venetian government sent a letter to the sultan, asking him not to take reprisals in similar cases (as he had done in this one).[104] Similar measures were taken when the Venetian war fleet captured a Genoese ship with Moslem passengers; orders were given to liberate them.[105]

Notwithstanding the leniency and readiness to make concessions, the Venetians could not avoid conflicts. The Mamluk authorities tried to require the Venetians to purchase greater quantities of pepper than those agreed upon, and demanded exorbitant prices.[106] It was only after a long series of negotiations that the price of 80 ducats for a sporta pepper to be bought from the sultan by the Venetians was fixed.[107] Sometimes Venetian merchants were also compelled to buy other spices, e.g., cinnamon, from the stocks of the sultan.[108] In addition, there was the question of how much pepper they were to buy from him in Syria. In 1467 they had to buy 229 sportas in Damascus; in 1468, 308.[109] The greediness and violence of the Mamluk officials, especially in Syria, brought about many conflicts. Sometimes the consuls were maltreated,[110] sometimes there were incidents caused by others, who had nothing to do with the commercial activities. Occasionally, slaves tried to embark on Venetian ships in order to escape from their lords. Thereupon a brawl would ensue, and the Venetian merchants, the consul, and the sailors would be imprisoned.[111] In the year 1456 the Mamluk authorities of Tripoli took by force a Venetian ship for the transport of timber from Lajazzo to Damietta. They imposed the purchase of a certain quantity of alkali upon the Venetians, and they were imprisoned when they tried to resist. The Venetian consul in Alexandria, who represented the Venetian interests at the court of Cairo, received orders to lodge a protest with the sultan, but he died before he set out for Cairo.[112] In addition to the continuous endeavors to increase the quantity of pepper that the Venetians were to buy from the sultan, the Mamluk officials, against the clauses of the commercial treaties, also compelled them to pay the debts of others.[113]

In 1460 the Venetian government sent Maffio Michiel as ambassador to the sultan, to deal with the difficulties that the merchants encountered in his dominions. Michiel was to protest against the high prices charged for

[104] Senato Mar VII, f. 190b f., 191b.
[105] Secreta 27, f. 102a f.
[106] Senato Mar VI, f. 5b.
[107] Marino Sanuto, *Diarii* II, cols. 165, 175, 1198.
[108] Senato Mar VII, f. 29b, 33a.
[109] Senato Mar VIII, f. 192a. See, further, Secreta 26, f. 139a.
[110] Senato Mar IX, f. 113b.
[111] Senato Mar XI, f. 150b.
[112] Senato Mar V, f. 172a, 186a VI, f. 17a.
[113] Senato Mar VI, f. 184a.

the pepper that the Venetians had been compelled to buy from the sultan in Syria. As a matter of principle, the Venetian government did not recognize at all the obligation to buy pepper from the sultan. But it was ready to agree that for every purchase of spices and other commodities amounting to 1,000 ducats one sporta pepper should be bought from the sultan and at 10-20 ducats more than its commercial price. The sultan was also requested to forbid the Moslem merchants to sell to the Venetians on credit, so that there should not be conflicts and some Venetians would be compelled to pay the debts of others. Further, the ambassador should protest against the levying of new fees upon the cotton export from Tripoli and Latakia. He should also protest the fact that the Moslem merchants took merchandise by force from the Venetians in Alexandria and paid them in pepper instead of in money.[114] Sultan Īnāl apparently agreed to most of Maffio Michiel's requests. After his death, his son and successor Abu'l-Fatḥ Aḥmad addressed a letter to the government of Venice in June 1461, in which he stated that he was reducing the price of the pepper to be bought from the sultan's stocks to 85 ducats. The *Libri Commemoriali*, where the sultan's letter is copied, contain an addition stating that he kept his promise.[115] But this was probably true for only a very short time, for in 1463 (or 1464) the price was increased.

In the year 1464 an act of aggression committed by the Knights of Rhodes brought about a grave conflict between the European trading nations and the sultan. When a Venetian galley, which had many Moslem merchants from the Maghreb with their merchandise on board, had come to Rhodes because of a storm, the Knights captured these Moslems and their goods. Thereupon the sultan had all European merchants to be found in Egypt and Syria imprisoned and their goods seized. The government of Venice reacted to the aggression of the Knights vigorously. In September 1464 the commander of the war fleet was sent to Rhodes and ordered to present an ultimatum to be effected in three hours. If the Knights did not immediately set free the Moslems and give back their merchandise, the Venetian forces would attack and put the island to fire and sword.[116] It was also proposed to send Maffio Michiel to Cairo again, as he had proved his diplomatic talents. But when he declined because of his old age, the consul in Alexandria was ordered to appear before the sultan as soon as possible and to explain that Venice had no guilt. The Serenissima had sent 45 galleys and other ships against the Knights, and the commander had orders not to depart before the merchants had been liberated and their goods been given

[114] Senato Mar VI, f. 180a, 191a; Secreta 31, f. 10b ff.

[115] ASV, Libri Com. 15, f. 69a (ed. Predelli, no. 75); Marino Sanuto *Vite de' duchi*, col. 1169.

[116] Secreta 22, f. 37b f.

back.[117] The Venetian government, which had always had difficulties in its relations with the Knights of Rhodes, also addressed letters to the king of France and the Duke of Burgundy, blaming the Knights for what they had done, and claiming that they were allied to the Turks.[118] In fact, the Knights surrendered and set the Moslem prisoners free, whereupon the sultan liberated the merchants who had been imprisoned, although apparently not all of them.[119] On the other hand, he sent an ambassador to Venice to claim the payment of indemnity. In the spring of 1465 a Mamluk official, whose name was Djānī Beg, came to Venice and demanded the payment of 15,000 ducats.[120] Thereupon the Venetian Senate decided to suspend the galley services to Egypt and Syria that year and to send an ambassador to Cairo.[121] The Mamluk envoy was to depart for Egypt, together with the ambassador Filippo Corner.[122] The Venetian ambassador was to plead that the Serenissima had done her best to obtain the liberation of the Maghrebins and had had great expenses for the naval expedition. If the sultan did not agree to give back the 30,000 ducats that he had taken from the Venetians, supposedly as a deposit, the ambassador was to threaten that the Venetians would depart from his dominions. But if the sultan agreed to the restitution of the money (i.e., the deposit), the ambassador was to complain that the merchants and the consul in Damascus had been beaten. He was also to raise the question of the obligatory purchase of pepper. Once again, he should emphasize that Venice opposed the obligation of buying pepper from the sultan, but if a certain quantity had to be bought the commercial price should be paid. In Alexandria the Venetians were compelled to pay 100 ducats, whereas the commercial price was 90. The ambassador was also to insist on the principle that the pepper bought by the Venetian merchants from the sultan in Damascus should be all that the Venetians had to buy from him in Syria. Further, he should claim the restitution of copper and

[117] *Ibid.*, f. 39a f.

[118] *Ibid.*, f. 72b, 73a f.

[119] *Ḥawādith*, p. 488 f.; ʿAbdalbāsiṭ 812, f. 163b. Sultan Khūshḳadam (1461-1467) was one of those Mamluk rulers who curried favor with the zealots by a show of orthodoxy. He re-enacted the old repressive laws concerning the status of the non-Moslems; see E. Ashtor, *History of the Jews under the Mamlūks* II, p. 75 f.

[120] He was in Venice in June 1465; see Senato Mar VIII, f. 25b, 27b; Secreta 22, f. 91b, 92b. His name is mentioned there f. 49b, 66b. He was apparently Djāni Beg at-tardjumān, who had fulfilled a diplomatic mission in Cyprus in February 1464; see *Ḥawādith*, p. 455. Interpreters were entrusted by the sultan with diplomatic missions on other occasions too; see J. Wansbrough, "A Mamlūk ambassador to Venice in 913/1507," *BSOAS* 26 (1963), p. 503 ff.

[121] Senato Mar VIII, f. 25b. But of course this does not mean that the spice trade of the Venetians was discontinued. Spices were shipped to Candia; see Senato Mar VIII, f. 52b, and therefrom they were later transported to Venice.

[122] Senato Mar VIII, f. 27b.

paper, which had been taken from the Venetian merchants.[123] The sultan obviously seized the opportunity to squeeze a certain amount of money from the Venetians and did not liberate all the merchants who had been imprisoned. Once more Djānī Beg came to Venice.[124] Then, in March 1466, the government of Venice addressed a letter to the sultan, thanking him for the liberation of the merchants who finally had been set free and again rejecting his claim for indemnity.[125]

Then for some years the Venetians carried on their activities in Egypt and Syria without major conflicts. But in 1471 they were again seriously injured and the consul in Damascus was beaten, imprisoned, and sent to Cairo. So again it was decided to send an ambassador to the sultan. The first appointee to the mission declined, and only six months after the decision had been taken was the mission entrusted to Zuan Emo.[126] He was instructed to protest against the injuries and also against the cheating of the Venetian merchants by the Mamluk officials, who compelled them to buy pepper (from the sultan's stocks) mixed with stones. Further, he was to protest against the Mamluk governors in Syria who allowed the Turkish corsairs to attack the Venetian ships in the ports. According to the text of his *commissio* (the instructions) this was the main purpose of his mission. The interplay between the new political tide in the Eastern Mediterranean and the Levant trade emerges, however, from another passage in these instructions. The Venetian government obviously feared that the sultan had knowledge of its contacts with Uzun Ḥasan. So the ambassador was ordered to tell the sultan, if he should raise the matter, that the despatch of Venetian envoys to the Turcoman ruler was by no means an unfriendly act toward him. It was done only because Uzun Ḥasan had sent an embassy to Venice.[127] Zuan Emo carried on his negotiations for a rather long time until he was instructed in October 1472 to return to Venice. He arrived

[123] Secreta 22, f. 93a f.

[124] He was in Venice in November-December 1465, and in January 1466; see Senato Mar VIII, f. 49a, 50a, 52a.

[125] Senato Mar VIII, f. 66b.

[126] Senato Mar IX, f. 113b, 131a. He was one of the most experienced diplomats of Venice and in the 1470's was ambassador to the courts of Naples, Sicily and Hungary, to the Diet of Ratisbon and to Florence; see Secreta 24, f. 19a, 22a f., 25, f. 26a, 27b 26, f. 44a, cf. 60a, 55a, 78b, 72b, 83a, 84a, 85a, 87a, 89a, 100b, 103b, 105b; 107b, 112b, 116b, 124a, 134b 28, f. 93b; *Lib. Com.* V. lib. 16, no. 66.

[127] Secreta 25, f. 142a ff. The Mamluks were not on good terms with the Ottomans nor with Uzun Ḥasan, but their fear of the latter was greater, and in 1465 they had sent an embassy to Mehmed the Conqueror to propose to him an alliance against the common enemy; see Ibn Iyās^2 II, p. 427. In the year 1472 even the relations between the Mamluks and the European trading nations had worsened. ʿAbdalbāsiṭ 812, f. 236a f., 239b, recounts that in May 1472 Europeans who engaged in trade in the dominions of the sultan were imprisoned, and brought to Cairo, where some of them embraced Islam. A year later European corsairs committed acts of aggression on the Egyptian coast; see *op.cit.* f. 245b.

there in December.[128] His mission must have been successful, but we do not know if the sultan accused the Venetians of having incited Uzun Ḥasan to invade Syria. It seems that even the Venetian merchants in northern Syria did not know of the double game of their government, so that they fled panic-stricken from Aleppo, when the avanguard of Uzun Ḥasan approached the Syrian frontier. A letter of the Venetian merchant Bernardo Donado states that he fled from Aleppo to Beirut and left about 700 pieces of cloth in some storage rooms, most of it English, and the rest in Bergamo and Florence. Its value amounted to 6,000 ducats (approximately).[129]

In January 1473 the sultan addressed a letter to the doge in which he mentioned that he had complied with the requests of Zuan Emo and given orders accordingly to the governors of the provinces. On the other hand, he drew attention to the fact that the gold and silver coins (and ingots) that the Venetians brought to his dominions were debased and the pieces of cloth shorter than their usual measures.[130] The Venetian government answered by letter in May 1473, claiming that the promises made to Zuan Emo had not been kept. The merchants and the consul who had been imprisoned in Damascus had not been liberated, and the sultan was requested to set them free.[131] But less than two months later the Venetian government again had to write to the sultan and complain about the imprisonment of the Venetian merchants. This letter explicitly refers to the suspicion of collaboration with Uzun Ḥasan. From this and other documents (see below), it emerges that the merchants had been imprisoned because of conflicts arising from their commercial activities and that later Venice's collaboration with Uzun Ḥasan was also brought to bear against them. In fact, the Mamluks caught a Venetian, Piero Malipiero, who went from Cyprus as an envoy to Uzun Ḥasan and, on the other hand, an ambassador of the Ottoman sultan had captured an envoy of the Turcoman ruler with letters to the European powers and brought them to Cairo in April 1473.

[128] Senato Mar IX, f. 147a, 150b. According to ʿAbdalbāsiṭ 812, f. 239a, he had arrived in September.

[129] G. P., Ter. III, f. 102a ff. The Venetians certainly fled in the winter 1472-1473; see Ibn Iyās III, pp. 78, 82, and cf. Weil V, p. 240; J. E. Evrard, *Zur Geschichte Aleppos und Nordsyriens im letzten halben Jahrhundert der Mamlukenherrschaft (872-921 AH)* (Munich, 1974), p. 25 f. See also Wood, *The Aqqoyunlu*, p. 129 f.

[130] The Arabic original and a Venetian version have been published by J. Wansbrough, "A Mamlūk letter of 877/1473," *BSOAS* 24 (1961), p. 200 ff. The supposition of Wansbrough (made in this paper) that the imprisonment of the consul of Damascus was a reprisal against the alliance of the Venetians and Uzun Ḥasan is not likely. One reads in the instructions of Zuan Emo: *Si de Usuno Cassano tibi allique faret mentio* etc. If the main purpose of Emo's mission was to deal with reprisals against the merchants because of the said alliance, the Senate could not doubt that the sultan would raise this question and would not have added at the end of the instructions an answer to be given to a possible claim. But see below.

[131] Secreta 26, f. 13a. *Lettere al Senato Veneto di Giosafatto Barbaro*, ed. E. Cornet (Vienna, 1852), p. 57.

The Venetian government again stressed in the same letter that its alliance with Uzun Ḥasan was directed only against the Ottomans, enemy of both Venice and the Mamluks.[132] In the middle of 1473 the relations of Venice with the sultan had deteriorated into a full crisis. The merchants who travelled in the galleys to Alexandria and to Beirut were forbidden to go ashore,[133] and it was decided to send a secretary as envoy to the sultan (an ambassador of lower rank); Zuan Dario, one of the outstanding Venetian diplomats, was appointed to this mission.[134] He was instructed to plead that the arrest of the merchants and the consul in Damascus was in contradiction to the agreements between Venice and the sultan. The Venetian merchants in Damascus had been forced to buy 1,000 sportas pepper from the sultan's stocks, whereas the Venetians had undertaken to buy only one sporta for every 1,000 ducats invested in spices or other merchandise in Syria. Venice was no longer ready to acquiesce in the extortion from her merchants in Damascus or Aleppo, where their goods had also been sequestered. The Venetian envoy was ordered to demand that the sultan liberate the merchants and also that he should allow the Venetians to depart from his dominions (*sc.* with their goods). The Venetians would henceforth carry on trade with his subjects on board their ships only. If the sultan would agree to the requests and set free the merchants, the envoy should remain in Cairo until the implementation of this promise. Further, he was to tell the sultan that in the future the Venetians would not buy pepper from him at all. He was to explain again that Venice had not incited Uzun Ḥasan against the Mamluks, but in the same instructions Dario was told that if on his way to Egypt he should hear that Uzan Ḥasan had meanwhile invaded Syria and the Venetian war fleet had joined action, he should come back.[135] The usual double game!

The mission of Zuan Dario was obviously successful. The merchants were set free, and once more it was agreed that the Venetians should buy one sporta for every 1,000 ducats invested in Syria. But conditions in Syria had become so difficult for the Venetians that both the consul and the merchants left Damascus. In 1475 the galleys visited Beirut, but a proposition in the Senate to appoint a new consul for Damascus was turned down. On the other hand, a letter was addressed to the governor of Da-

[132] *Ibid.*, f. 22a; Ibn Iyās III, p. 84; Evrard, *op.cit.*, p. 26 f.

[133] Senato Mar IX, f. 185a.

[134] Senato Mar IX, f. 178b. The secretaries were not nobili; that means they were second-class citizens. It was Zuan Dario who concluded the peace with the Ottomans in 1479, see Romanin, *Storia* IV, f. p. 278. About Dario, see Fr. Babinger, *Johannes Darius (1414-1494), Sachwalter Venedigs im Morgenland und sein griechischer Umkreis* (Sitzber. der Bayer. Akademie der Wiss., Phil.-hist. Kl., 1961, Heft 5). (Babinger does not mention this mission of Dario.)

[135] Secreta 26, f. 31b ff. The instructions are dated September 1473. The mission was obviously fulfilled in the winter 1473-1474. In December 1474 the Senate decided to send Dario to Constantinople; see Babinger, p. 80.

mascus, requesting that the merchants coming with the galleys should be treated kindly.[136] Then it was decided to send another secretary, Zuan Dedo, to the sultan, in order to come to an agreement concerning the quantity of pepper that the Venetians must buy from him.[137] Dedo was instructed in February 1476 to tell the sultan that, despite the suggestions of the Mamluk authorities, no new consul would be appointed in Damascus until an agreement could be reached concerning the pepper purchases. In return for the undertakings of the sultan, the Venetians had again accepted the imposition that for every investment of 1,000 ducats two sportas pepper would be purchased. The envoy was instructed to threaten discontinuation of Venetian trade with the Mamluk dominions if the sultan did not promise that his undertakings would be kept. Dedo was also to protest against the Mamluk authorities in Damascus, who had required the Venetians to supply the Mint every year with a certain quantity of silver. He was also instructed to ask for special orders that the Venetian consuls in Syria should not be beaten and that certain custom officials should be removed from their posts. He was to protest, especially, against the sultan's merchant ʿAbdalḳādir Ibn ʿUlayba, who had imprisoned a Venetian in his own house. He was also to demand that the Venetians should not be made responsible for the misdeeds of Rhodian, Catalan, or other corsairs.[138] As so often in the past, the sultan gave the Venetian diplomat a friendly and satisfactory answer, promised that the merchants would be well treated, and a short time later it was learned in Venice that Venetian merchants in Damascus had been imprisoned.[139]

Actually, when the instructions had been given to Zuan Dedo it was not yet known in Venice that a new act of aggression by some Provençals had brought about another conflict between the sultan and the trading nations.

In January 1476 some Provençal merchants had captured a group of prominent Moslem traders, among them the sultan's merchant Ibn ʿUlayba, in Alexandria, and had brought them to Rhodes. Thereupon the sultan had ordered that all the European merchants and their consuls in his dominions should be imprisoned, and it had been for this reason that the Venetians in Syria were in prison. The Venetians had also been compelled to give a deposit of 10,000 ducats until the Moslem captives were liberated. The Mamluk authorities also sequestered a great quantity of merchandise that the Venetians had bought in Damascus.[140] Then the sultan sent an ambassador to Venice. He was a Maghrebin merchant, Muḥammad Ibn Maḥ-

[136] Secreta 27, f. 23b f., 24a, 24b.
[137] Senato Mar X, f. 62b.
[138] Secreta 27, f. 55b ff.
[139] *Ibid.*, f. 98a f.
[140] Ibn Iyās III, p. 110; ʿAbdalbāsiṭ 812, f. 269a. According to as-Sakhāwī, *Continuation of adh-Dhahabī*, MS. Bodl. 853, f. 60b, these Europeans were Catalans, but this is obviously a mistake. See, further, Senato Mar XI, f. 28b, 86a.

fūẓ, who fulfilled several diplomatic missions on behalf of the Mamluk government. He informed the Venetian government that the arrest of the merchants in Damascus had been ordered when Ieronimo Contarini had gone to Rhodes upon the request of the sultan and, having failed to obtain the liberation of the Moslem captives, had used insolent language before the sultan. The sultan asked the Venetian government to use its influence in Rhodes for the liberation of the said Moslem merchants. Since the Venetians were on bad terms with the Knights, they, of course, could not intervene and wrote to the sultan, claiming the release of the consul and the merchants who had been imprisoned in Damascus.[141] Meanwhile orders were given to the captains of the galley convoys to Alexandria and Beirut to take special measures of precaution.[142] In order to settle the new conflict, the experienced Zuan Dario was again sent to Cairo.[143] At that time the war with Turkey overshadowed other problems, and the attitude toward the Mamluks could not be too firm. According to his instructions of August 1477, Dario should of course claim first of all the liberation of the merchants and also the restitution of the "deposit."[144] He was not fully successful. Although the captives had returned from Rhodes, the deposit had not yet been given back in the 1480's.[145]

While these negotiations were dragging on, the problem of Cyprus and its relations with the sultan had for some years become the major item of the Venetian-Mamluk contacts, and any failure of Venice's endeavors to satisfy the sultan could have grave consequences for the trade with his dominions. The Venetian protectorate over Cyprus established in 1474, when Caterina Corner, a Venetian noblewoman and widow of the king, had become actual ruler of the island, and later the direct rule upon her abdication in 1489, meant, on one hand, a great success for Venice and, on the other, strained her relations with the sultan. The acquisition of Cyprus not only compensated for the loss of Negrepont, but also enabled Venice to exploit the great agricultural resources of the island—sugar and cotton—without being impeded by an unpredictable administration. But Cyprus was a state tributary to the sultan, who could oppose the change of its status. When Caterina was still queen of Cyprus, the Venetian government

[141] Secreta 27, f. 94a ff., 95a ff., 96a. (Obviously, meanwhile a new consul of Damascus had been appointed.) ʿAbdalbāsiṭ 812, f. 271a f. recounts that in May 1476 an envoy of the Franks (more exactly "from the land of the Franks") came to Cairo for negotiations concerning the release of the captives. There is no hint as to his identity. See also Senato Terra VII, f. 130a.

[142] Senato Mar X, f. 94a.

[143] *Ibid.*, f. 138a.

[144] Secreta 28, f. 42b f.; cf. Babinger, p. 82 f.

[145] Senato Mar XI, f. 83a, 86a, and see below. The résumé which Labib p. 372 has made of the Arabic account is mistaken. The merchants were not released because of the pressure brought upon the Knights by the trading nations, but ransomed themselves; see Ibn Iyās III, p. 115.

urged her to pay the tribute regularly.[146] She was even asked to write subservient letters to the sultan, calling herself *io tua schiava* (I your slave girl).[147] Reading these documents, one is perplexed, but it must be confessed that the goal was reached. Despite the intrigues of the enemies of Caterina Corner, the Venetians succeeded in keeping control of Cyprus, so important for the defense of their possessions against the Ottomans, and in remaining on good terms with the sultan. Even an attempt by the king of Naples to intervene failed. The sultan of Egypt too made efforts to prevent Cyprus from coming under Venetian rule. He sent an embassy to Naples to negotiate with King Ferrante. The marriage of a son of the latter with the queen of Cyprus was suggested.[148]

When Venice took over actual rule of Cyprus and feared intervention by the sultan, an ambassador was again sent to him. It was Piero Diedo, who went to Cairo in 1489. He was asked to explain to the sultan that under Venetian rule Cyprus would be a strong base against the Ottomans (with whom the sultan was then at war). The ambassador was again to deal with the obligatory purchase of pepper in Syria and insist that the Venetians not be required to buy more than a sporta from the sultan for every 1,000 ducats invested in Syria. He was also to demand the restitution of the deposit taken from the Venetians in 1476.[149] Piero Diedo did reach an agreement with the sultan, but died in Egypt before signing it. Thereupon another secretary, Zuan Borghi, was sent to Cairo and, in February 1490, signed the agreement which settled the question of the tribute to be paid henceforth by Venice for the possession of Cyprus.[150] In April 1490 new instructions were sent to Borghi, and a letter was written to the sultan

[146] Secreta 26, f. 138b f. 28, f. 139b 29, f. 46a f.

[147] Secreta 34, f. 32b.

[148] G. Magnanite, "L'acquisto dell'isola di Cipro da parte della republica di Venezia," *Archivio Veneto*, Va serie, 9-10 (1929), p. 78 ff. 11-12 (1929), p. 1 ff.; J. Richard, "Chypre du protectorat a la domination venitienne," in *Venezia e il Levante fino al secolo XV*, I, part I, pp. 656 f., 672. About the negotiations between the king of Naples and the sultan see F. Forcellini, *Strane peripezie d'un bastardo di casa d'Aragona* (Naples, 1915), p. 88 ff. The embassy was obviously that headed by Ibn Maḥfūẓ; see above and see below p. 497. Forcellini quotes a document referring to the presents given to the Mamluk embassy. Apparently the embassy of the sultan came first to Naples, proceeded to Catalonia, and returned to Naples; see Forcellini, pp. 74 f., 88 f., that it was in Naples at the end of 1479, went then to Catalonia, and was again in Naples at the end of 1480. See also *Travelogue* of Meshullam of Volterra p. 48, and cf. about the project of the marriage Romanin IV, p. 316; de Mas Latrie, *Histoire* III, pp. 404 f., 436 f.

[149] Secreta 34, f. 33a ff., 36a f., 37a; Senato Mar XII, f. 184a, 184b. The ambassador was instructed to make presents to the sultan's chief interpreter Taghrībirdī, whose influence could be helpful. About this personality, apparently a Spanish converso, see my *History of the Jews in Egypt and in Syria under the Mamluks* II, p. 530 f; J. Wansbrough, "A Mamlūk ambassador to Venice in 913/1507," *BSOAS* 26 (1963), p. 503 ff. Cf. de Mas Latrie, *Histoire* III, p. 425, about a preceding mission to the sultan from Cyprus (which perhaps was not executed or was not considered as sufficient).

[150] *Libr. Com.* V, lib. 16, no. 171 (where one reads that Taghrībirdī was present).

protesting against the maltreatment of the Venetian merchants in Alexandria and Damascus.[151]

These untiring endeavors on behalf of the normal course of commercial activities were continued until the end of the fifteenth century. Time and again the consul of Alexandria appeared before the sultan, or special envoys were despatched to Cairo to lodge protests. In February 1492 Zuan Borghi was again sent to the sultan. The instructions he was given shed light on the claims and counterclaims of the Venetians and the Mamluk officials. He was to demand punishment of the officials who had maltreated the Venetians in Alexandria and raise the question of the payment of a great sum demanded of them. They had been asked to pay 28,000 ducats for pepper bought over a fourteen-year period from the sultan, in addition to the price already paid. When later it became known that 18,000 ducats had been extorted in 1491 from the Venetians in Alexandria, it was proposed to the Senate to suspend the galley service to Egypt.[152] In August 1492 the government of Venice again addressed the sultan, protesting against extortions.[153] On the other hand, the Mamluks had a great interest in increasing their trade with the South European nations. In February 1496 the governor of Alexandria wrote to the government of Venice, promising a friendly attitude to the merchants and recalling the old privileges of the Venetians. He also mentioned the death of ʿAlī Bāy, the former governor of Alexandria, who had maltreated the European merchants without the sultan's knowledge.[154]

The numerous and lengthy documents referring to the wearying negotiations between the Venetian embassies and the sultan should not mislead us. In fact, in the second half of the fifteenth century there were no more violent clashes or grave conflicts as there had been in the preceding period. The sultan had renounced the establishment of a pepper monopoly. At the end of the fifteenth century, an agreement had been reached between

[151] Secreta 34, f. 62b f.

[152] *Ibid.*, f. 110b ff. According to Malipiero, p. 625, 30,000 ducats were demanded of the Venetians, since it was maintained that they had paid 80 ducats for a sporta (of the sultan's pepper), although they had obliged themselves to pay 100. See, further, Secreta 34, f. 121a, 122b.

[153] *Ibid.*, f. 128a f.

[154] Marino Sanuto, *Diarii* I, col. 133 ff. The letter quoted by the Venetian chronicler in extenso, among other letters received in April 1496, has the date 19 Feb. 900, which should be corrected to 901 (H.). ʿAlī Bāy, governor of Alexandria, is indeed well known from Arabic sources. He had been appointed to the post in 1482 (see Ibn Iyās III, p. 188) and was dismissed in 1491, because of his misbehavior (see *op.cit.* p. 274, and cf. p. 262). But he succeeded in changing the mind of the sultan and was apparently reinstated; see *aḍ-Ḍaw al-lāmiʿ* V, p. 151. In November 1495 he was appointed emir of 1000, and in the report about his promotion he is called governor of Alexandria; see Ibn Iyās III, p. 309. So he must have died shortly after this date. (Even before coming to Alexandria he had maltreated the Venetians in Syria, so that in 1482 the Venetian government ordered the consul in Damascus to send an envoy to Cairo and to lodge a protest before the sultan; see Senato Mar XI, f. 149b).

the Venetians and the sultan as to the quantity of pepper that was obligatory to buy from him: they obliged themselves to buy from him 210 sportas every year in Egypt and 530 in Syria.[155] On the other hand, the sultan, being aware of the danger of an attack by the Ottomans, considered the European powers as potential allies. In the long period from Djaḳmaḳ's accession to the throne to the death of Ḳā'itbāy in 1496, Venetian trade with the Mamluk dominions was seldom discontinued. The new tide in the economic life of the European countries, on the other hand, stimulated the activities of the Levant traders, among whom the Venetians held uncontested supremacy in that period. So it was a period in which the Venetian trade in the Moslem Levant increased, despite all the difficulties inherent in exchanges with the Levant countries. But it was not a rapid or spectacular growth; it was rather slow and modest.

In 1461, a new galley line was established, that of the so-called *galee de trafego*. These galleys visited Syracuse, Tunis, and Tripoli and went from there to Alexandria. They could then make another trip to Tripoli and Tunis and return to Alexandria. In Alexandria they loaded spices which had remained there because the galleys of the Alexandria line had no more room, and for the same purpose one of these two galleys could go to Beirut. The return voyage to Venice was to be made together with the Alexandria and Beirut convoys. The *galee de trafego* were to anchor in Tunis and Tripoli fifteen days each and in Alexandria twenty-five.[156]

The Venetians carried on intense trade not only in Alexandria and in Damascus, but in other towns as well. In Egypt they engaged in trade in Damietta, where a vice-consul resided and where Venetian ships anchored.[157] In Syria there were vice-consulates in Beirut,[158] Tripoli,[159] Latakia,[160] Ḥamā,[161] and Aleppo.[162] The latter town became a great center of Venetian trade in the second half of the fifteenth century. Since the caravans from Persia carrying silk arrived first in Aleppo, large purchases of this commodity were made there,[163] but spices were also bought there.[164] On the other hand, the Venetians sold great quantities of cloth in Aleppo which

155 Tucher, p. 692; Marino Sanuto, *Diarii* II, col. 172 III, col. 1198 VI col. 1199; ASV, Libr. Com. 19, f. 26a, 30a and cf. *Libr. Com.* VI, lib. 19, nos. 47, 57.

156 Senato Mar VI, f. 206b VII, f. 41a. Later, in 1464, it was decreed that they should also visit Djerba, see *ibid.*, f. 147. Cf. A. Tenenti-C. Vivanti, "Les galères marchandes vénitiennes, XIVᵉ-XVIᵉ siècles," *Annales E.S.C.* 16 (1961), p. 83 ff.

157 Romanin, *Storia* IV, p. 316; Secreta 21, f. 10b ff. See Pasi, f. 47a, about the export of almonds and olive oil from Apulia to Damietta.

158 Senato Mar VI, f. 209b (a. 1460), VII, f. 1b, XIV, f. 4a.

159 G. P., Sent. 136, f. 106a ff. (a. 1461).

160 Senato Mar VII, f. 43a (a. 1462).

161 *L.c.*

162 *L.c.* and VIII, f. 87b f.; Crist. del Fiore VI, no. 31.

163 G. P., Sent. 156, f. 86b f., 88a ff., 89a ff., 178, f. 36a f. 186, f. 25b ff.; G. P. Ter. IV, f. 11b (a. 1471).

164 G. P., Sent. 186, f. 25b ff.; G. P., Ter. IV, f. 13a.

was probably marketed by Syrian and Iraqi merchants in the neighboring countries.[165] The Venetians offered cloth of Brescia,[166] of Bergamo and Padua,[167] and garbo of Florence,[168] as well as costly scarlets.[169] In the late fifteenth century the largest Venetian firms traded in Aleppo. In the registers of the Venetian custom services and the judicial acts of the *Giudici di petiziòn* there are accounts and documents referring to business conducted in Aleppo by Marco Malipiero and brothers,[170] Michiel Priuli,[171] and Marco and Andrea Trevisan.[172] Excerpts from the accounts of the Venetian consulate in Aleppo of the years 1474 and 1477 refer to purchases of great quantities of cotton by the brothers Luca and Niccolò Pisani, agents of Cristoforo Priuli and others, and of the sizable purchases made by Hermolao Gritti and Donà Contarini.[173] Also Piero Pisani carried on business in Aleppo.[174] In the year 1466, the Venetian authorities decided that the merchants should leave Aleppo because of the intolerable extortions by the Mamluk officials, but this decision was either revoked or not implemented. At the end of the fifteenth century not less than 40 Venetian firms had their agent in Aleppo.[175] In Palestine too the Venetian merchants were very active in that period. They traded in Nablus[176] and Ramla, and in Acre, where the cotton of the Galilee and the valley of Esdraelon was shipped out, there was a Venetian vice-consul.[177]

As in preceding periods, the Venetians imported great quantities of cloth into Egypt and Syria. Owing to the progressive impoverishment of the Moslem Levant, cheap cloth was the major textile product sold there. Among the cheap woolen stuffs the Venetians imported, mainly into Syria, the cloth of Brescia was the most important. Brescia, which was under Venetian rule form 1426, produced various kinds of cloth in different colors. The average price of a piece in the middle of the fifteenth century was 12-15 ducats (sale price in the Levant). In the last quarter of the century, however, it became more expensive. The Venetian merchant Antonio Polani marketed Brescia cloth for 1,650 ducats in Damascus, in 1459.[178] The Venetians also sold cloth of Bergamo, which was even cheaper than the Brescia cloth. A

[165] G. P., Ter. XI, f. 29a f.; Senato Mar VIII, f. 87b f., 151 b.
[166] G. P., Ter. III, f. 10b f. (a. 1458) IV, f. 11a (a. 1471).
[167] G. P., Ter. IV, f. 11a.
[168] G. P., Ter. IV, f. 9b, 10b, 11a (a. 1471).
[169] G. P., Ter. IV, f. 9b.
[170] G. P., Sent. 177, f. 67a ff. See also above p. 368 f. about the trade of the Malipieros.
[171] G. P., Sent. 178, f. 36a f.
[172] G. P., Ter. IV, f. 8b ff. (a. 1472).
[173] G. P., Ter. IX, f. 13a f.
[174] *Ibid.*, f. 10a.
[175] Senato Mar VIII, f. 91b; Berchet, *Relazioni*, p. 20.
[176] Secreta 27, f. 55b ff.
[177] Roberto da Sanseverino, *Viaggio in Terra Santa* (Bologna, 1969), p. 178 (a. 1451).
[178] Ashtor, "Exportation de textiles," p. 321 ff.

Table XLVIII Price of pepper in Alexandria, second half of the XVth century

date		price of a sporta	source
1455		60 duc.	Tur II, f. 57a ff., 59b f.
1458		93 "	G.P., Sent. 133, f. 39b ff.
fair 1458		85 - 86 "	ASF, letter M. Squarzalupi[a]
" 1460 (?)		93 "	G.P., Sent. 140, f. 25b ff.
1461		90 "	G.P., Ter. IV, f. 49a
fair 1461		85.4 "	G.P., Sent. 134, f. 46a ff. cf. 135, f. 116b ff. 137 f. 2b ff.
1463 (?)		77 "	same series 144, f. 117a f.[b]
1466		100 "	" " 150, f. 77b
1470	1 collo	150 "	" " 154, f. 137a f.
		70 "	" " 171, f. 182a
1471		70 "	" " 190, f. 66b ff. 80b ff.[c]
17 April 1472		70 "	ASG, 2774 C, F. 14b, 19a[d]
		71.5 "	Ibid. f. 14b[e]
5 Nov. 1472		71.5 "	Ibid. f. 20a f.[f]
	from the sultan	77 "	Ibid. f. 19b
20 April 1473		70 "	Ibid. f. 27b[g]
10 Dec. 1473		66 "	Ibid. f. 28a[h]
15 Feb. 1474		62 "	Ibid. f. 31a, cf. 29b[i]
3 March 1474		63 "	l.c.[j]
15 Dec. 1474	from the sultan	75 "	Ibid. f. 30b
22 Dec. 1474		58 "	Ibid. f. 29b[k]
		75 "	Ibid. f. 35b, 36a[l]
1475		50 "	G.P., Sent. 161, f. 126b ff. 129b
1476		69.5 "	same series 166, f. 46b ff.
1478		75 "	same series 176, f. 1a ff.[m]
1478 (?)	by barter	80 "	same series 182, f. 54b ff.
summer 1479		50 "	Joh. Tucher, p. 692[o]
1487	1 collo	100 "	G.P., Sent. 186, f. 157a[p]
1488		66 " (?)	same series 188, f. 180b ff.[r]
1491	by barter and delivered on the ship	74 duc.	same series 191, f. 40b ff.[s]
1491-97	1 quintal	75 cruzados	Roteiro, p. 115[t]
fall 1496		66-68 duc.	Priuli, Diarii I, p. 60
" 1497		74-75 "	Op. cit., p. 73
Sept. 1498	70 duc., then	78 "	Marino Sanuto, Diarii II, col. 87, 165
		81-85 "	Priuli I, p. 109

a - t See my paper Spice prices, notes 55 - 73

piece of it cost 6-12 ducats.[179] Other woolen stuffs of Northern Italy that the Venetians imported into the Mamluk dominions were cloth of Padua,[180] Vicenza,[181] and Feltre.[182] The Florentine cloth they offered in that period was mostly cheap garbo, like *panni di fontego*, whose price declined very greatly. A piece of it sold for 3-5 ducats.[183] But *panni bastardi*, whose average price amounted to 20-22 ducats in the Levant were also sold.[184] The falling prices of all these articles point clearly to the adaptation of the importers to the economic conditions of the declining Oriental countries. Everywhere the Venetians offered very cheap cloth.[185] The English cloth they imported into the Moslem Levant was also mostly the cheap product, such as cloth of Essex, worth 3-5 ducats a piece,[186] or kerseys, worsted fabrics, which sometimes were dyed in Venice,[187] but the Venetians also marketed cloth of Southampton, a better kind.[188] A Venetian Merchants Guide of the fifteenth century indicates that cloth of Southampton and *bastardi* were exported to Syria and Egypt.[189] From this manual it may also be inferred that the kerseys were chief among the English cloth then exported to the Moslem Levant, and this conclusion is borne out by other documents.[190] The cloth of Venice herself was mostly of the expensive variety, such as scarlets, which were sold to the Mamluk aristocracy.[191] Even in that period the Venetians imported Flemish cloth into the Moslem Levant,[192] and further, they offered French[193] and Swiss cloth, called *panni di Ginevra*.[194]

179 See above, note 167, and *art. cit.*, p. 324 f.; see, further, G. P., Sent. 160, f. 82b ff., 166, f. 6b; Senato Mar XII, f. 10a f.

180 "Exportation de textiles," p. 318 f.

181 *Art. cit.*, p. 319 f.

182 Pasi, f. 53a.

183 "Exportation de textiles," p. 315.

184 *Art. cit.*, p. 346 f.; see, further, G. P., Sent. 162, f. 32b ff. (Aleppo, about 1470), 163, f. 157b (Beirut, a. 1458).

185 See Senato Mar VIII, f. 151b; the Venetian agent Andrea Bono sent from Tripoli to Aleppo 104 pieces of cloth worth 350 ducats and 75 pieces worth 250 ducats (a litigation of a. 1468).

186 "Exportation de textiles," p. 343 f.; see also G. P., Sent. 163, f. 44a (Aleppo a. 1475).

187 *Art. cit.*, p. 344 ff.; Pasi, f. 29a f., compares the measures of the kersey with the pics of the major towns of Syria and Egypt.

188 Senato Mar V; f. 152b. About the cloth of Southampton and its prices, see L'export de textiles, p. 341 f.

189 Pasi, f. 53a.

190 *Op.cit.*, f. 29a f.; G. P., Sent. 188, f. 238a ff.

191 Senato Mar VII, f. 1b; see, further, *ibid.* f. 58a f. XIII, f. 94a f., XIV, f. 4a. About the sale prices, see "Exportation de textiles," p. 361.

192 Senato Mar V, f. 151a (a. 1456).

193 G. P., Ter. VIII, f. 30a.

194 Pasi, f. 53a; cf. "Exportation de textiles," p. 336, where the suppositions of Ammann about its origin are quoted. But probably a great part of it was cloth of Fribourg, which produced a substantial volume in that period; see H.-C. Peyer, "Wollverarbeitung und Handel

Woolen cloth ranked first among the textiles that the Venetians marketed in the Moslem Levant, but they also sold silken stuffs there. Being a precious commodity, silk could be shipped only on galleys.[195] Another product they imported into Egypt and Syria was linen of St. Gallen, which had replaced that of Constance.[196]

The volume of the Venetian copper imported into the dominions of the Mamluks certainly increased in the second half of the fifteenth century, when copper production again began to flourish in several regions of Central Europe. They sold in Egypt and in Syria copper of Central Germany that of the Rammelsberg and Mansfeld (called "of Goslar" and "Eisleben" respectively), that of Schwaz in Tyrol, and that of Slovakia.[197] In 1492 King Maximilian alone sold the Venetians 24,000 quintals (of Bozen), and in 1496 Jakob Fugger, in company with the Gossenbrot and Herwart (all of these firms of Augsburg), sold a similar quantity to the Venetians. In that year 10,000 ḳinṭār (*djarwī*), which had not been sold, remained in Alexandria, where a great part of the European copper arrived.[198] According to Sultan Ḳānṣūh al-Ghawrī, at the end of the fifteenth century the Venetians imported 3,000-4,000 ḳinṭārs of copper every year (in pani, probably representing a value of 70,000 ducats). Indeed, so much copper was offered in the Levant that the price went down.[199] In addition to copper, the Venetians also shipped a not insignificant quantity of tin to Egypt and Syria.[200]

As in earlier periods, they imported olive oil,[201] honey,[202] almonds, and hazelnuts, both of Apulia and the Campania.[203] When Egypt and Syria suffered from a scarcity, they imported wheat, barley, and flour too. Several judicial acts refer to the sizable import of wheat into Syria by Venetian merchants in 1470-1471;[204] it had been bought in Sicily, Naples, and else-

---

von Wollprodukten in der Schweiz vom 14. bis 17. Jahrhundert," *IIa Settimana di studio, Istituto Datini* (Florence, 1976), p. 65 ff.

[195] Senato Mar V, f. 166b VI, f. 89a.

[196] "Exportation de textiles," p. 357.

[197] See Ph. Braunstein, "Le marché du cuivre à Venise à la fin du Moyen Age," in *Schwerpunkte der Kupferproduktion u. des Kupferhandels in Europa 1500-1650*, pp. 83, 86, 87.

[198] M. Janssen, *Jakob Fugger, der Reiche* (Leipzig, 1910), pp. 22, 52; Marino Sanuto, *Diarii* I, col. 380; on the volume of the copper export from Venice to Egypt, see Braunstein, *art. cit.* p. 91 ff.; about the export of copper wire, see G. P., Sent. 133, f. 56a ff.

[199] Reinaud, "Traités de commerce entre la république de Venise et les derniers sultans mamlouks d'Egypte," *JA* 1829, II, p. 31 f.; Ashtor, *Les métaux précieux*, pp. 61 ff., 64.

[200] G. P., Sent. 160, f. 111a ff., 167, f. 177b f., 172, f. 1a f., 178, f. 35b ff.

[201] Pasi, f. 47a, 80a. See also Reinaud, "Traités de commerce," *JA* 1829, II, p. 32.

[202] Pasi, f. 51b.

[203] Pasi, f. 11a, 42b, 47a, 50b. About the import of hazelnuts and chestnuts, see also *The travels of Martin Baumgartner*, in A. and J. Churchill, *A collection of voyages and travels* (London, 1732), p. 437 f.

[204] G. P., Sent. 155, f. 82b, 156, f. 164a ff., 159, f. 6b ff., 128a ff., 152a ff., 163, f. 117b, 167, f. 3a ff., 169, f. 60a ff., 190, f. 66b ff. (sold to the sultan!); G. P., Ter. IV, f. 97b; Senato Mar IX, f. 16b.

where. In 1478 the Venetians again imported grains from Cyprus into Egypt and Syria.[205] Other acts refer to the import of grains into Egypt in 1482.[206]

Among the industrial products that the Venetians imported into the Moslem Levant in that period, there were sizable quantities of soap.[207] In order to foster the Venetian soap industry, whose products were exported to the Levant, in 1489 Venetians were forbidden to invest capital in the soap industries of Gaeta and Gallipoli, to buy their products, or to ship them to the Levant.[208] The export of Murano glass to Syria and Egypt became a profitable trade in that period, and the Venetians marketed enamelled glass, crystal, and other kinds of glass there.[209]

All these articles had been exported by the Venetians to the Near East a long time before. But when they took the lead in the Levant trade, their share of articles that had earlier been sold chiefly by the Genoese and the Catalans became the largest. Coral was such an article. The Venetians themselves did not always buy it from middlemen who obtained it from the coral fishers, as they had done in earlier periods. Often they themselves farmed the coral fisheries. In 1470 (approximately), a Venetian firm leased the rights to a coral fishery on the North African coast from Genoese who had rights there.[210] In 1493 a Venetian firm farmed the coral fisheries of Marsa al-Kharaz for five years.[211] Such enterprises must have been not exceptional, since in 1485 coral farmers are also mentioned.[212] Sometimes the coral was transported to Candia, stocked there, and then shipped to Syria by the Beirut galleys. Since the import of coral into Syria and Egypt had become an important branch of the Venetian Levant trade, special galleys were assigned to transport it, the so-called *galea di corallo* (*galea coralorum, galea ad corallos*). Such a galley service is mentioned as early as 1474.[213] This galley first went to Marsa al-Kharaz and Tunis and then to Beirut. It anchored in Marsa al-Kharaz eight days, sometimes served as *galea di rata* in Beirut, and also collected sugar in Cyprus.[214] The coral trade flourished since the Mamluks were eager to have it. In 1465 Filippo

205 G. P., Sent. 168, f. 52a ff., 182, f. 54b ff.

206 G. P., Ter. IX, f. 165b.

207 Senato Mar XIII, f. 90b; G. P., Sent. 152, f. 72b ff.

208 Senato Terra X, f. 170a f. In 1496, after the departure of the galleys in Alexandria, according to Marino Sanuto, *Diarii* I, col. 380, there remained 200,000 mier of soap. But this account is obviously mistaken and probably should be 200 mier (i.e., 90 t).

209 G. P., Sent. 130, f. 45b ff., 169, f. 19a; G. P., Ter. IV, f. 70b.

210 Senato Mar IX, f. 104b.

211 *Ibid.* XIV, f. 46b f.

212 Secreta 32, f. 158b.

213 Senato Mar X, f. 29a.

214 *Ibid.* f. 89b; Incanti I, f. 37a (a. 1475), 42b (a. 1476), 49b (a. 1477), 64b (a. 1479), 80b (a. 1481). In earlier periods before the Venetians became the first commercial power in the Levant, they shipped coral to the Mamluk dominions from Venice; see Misti 34, f. 47b, 76b.

Table XLIX Price of ginger in Damascus[a], XVth century

date	beledi	Meccan	colombino	source
21 Sept. 1403	80 duc. (2000 dir.)			Dat 928, letter of Comm. of Zanobi di Taddeo Gaddi of 24 Nov. 1403
mid. Oct. 1403	72-80 duc. (1800-2000)[b]			Dat 714, letter of Paris Soranzo of 24 Nov. 1403
6 Nov. 1406	Beirut 128 duc.	68 duc.		Dat 1171, price lists
1408	1 collo 53 duc.			G.P., Sent. 28, f. 47a f.
begin. Oct. 1409	83.3 " Beirut 85			same series 35, f. 23a ff.[c]
Nov. 1409	106.6 " Beirut 102 "			Ibid.
26 March 1411	95 duc. (4000)			price lists Arch Zane
	85-90 "			Arch. Zane, letter of B. Dandolo
30 April 1411	90 duc. (3900)	51 duc. (2200)		price lists A. Zane
27 July 1411	95 "	60 "	90 duc.	Ibid.
	90-92	76 "	125-140 duc.	Arch. Zane, letter of B. Dandolo
8 Oct. 1411	100 duc.	62 "	90 duc.	price lists A. Zane
5 Nov. 1411	75 "			Arch. Zane, letter of B. Dandolo
14 April 1412	65 "	50 "	60 "	price lists A. Zane
24 April 1412	53-60 duc.			Arch. Zane, letter of B. Dandolo
10 May 1412	65 duc.	40 "	60 "	price lists Zane
1412	Ramla 95 " [d]			Accounts Soranzo c. 36b
1413	1 pondo 25 duc. 10 dir.[e]			accounts Piero Morosini[f]
23 March 1413	65-80 duc.	45-48 "		Arch. Zane, letter of L. Foscarini
14 April 1413	110 "	55 "		price lists Zane
22 May, 1413	85 "	48 "		Ibid.
8 June, 1413	110 "	55 "	95 "	Ibid.
16 Aug. 1413	100 "	50 "		Ibid.
14 Sept. 1413	106 - 110 duc. by barter 115	51 duc.		Arch. Zane, letter of L. Foscarini
19 Oct. 1413	110 duc.	50 "	100 duc.	price lists A. Zane
	105-108 duc.	50 "	97 "	Arch. Zane, letter of L. Foscarini
24 March 1414	86-87 duc. then 80, then 70			Ibidem, letter of the same
1414	Beirut 1 pondo 83 duc.			G.P., Sent. 28, f. 12b

Table XLIX (continued)

date	beledi	Meccan	colombino	source
30 Sept. 1416	225-230 duc.	58 "		Arch. Zane, letter of N. Contarini
14 April, 1417	165 "	52 "		price lists A. Zane
	158-165 "	48-50"		Arch. Zane, letter of N. Contarini
end 1417	120 "	55 "		Nic. Venier B, 2, f. 2a ff.[g]
1418	96-98 "	53-55"		Arch. B. Dolfin, Ba 180, fasc. 15
1423	102-105 "			accounts, A. Zane, Ba 128a fasc. V
1424	96 "	54 "		Melis, Doc., p. 318
1 pondo	70.9 "			Accounts Soranzo c. 118
1425(?)	Beirut 1 collo 85 duc.			G.P., Sent. 45, f. 61a ff.[h]
1428	115-125 "			same series 52, f. 62a[i]
	of bad quality	80		
before 1440	100 duc.	50 "		Uzzano, p. 114
1429	Beirut 1 pondo 90 duc.			G.P., Sent. 54, f. 63b
1429(?)	" 1 collo 60 "			Ibid. f. 62b f.[j]
1429(?)	1 collo 80 "			G.P., Sent. 52, f. 6a[k]
1433	by barter 80 duc.			Vat. III, f. 4a f.
1437	1 pondo 25 "			G.P., Sent. 84, f. 49a ff.[l]
	" 22.5 "			same series 99, f. 14b
1440(?)	1 collo 39 "			same series 100, f. 196a
1471	42 "			G.P., Ter V, f. 68a
	40 "			Ibid. f. 207a
30 Jan. 1478	56 duc.			ASV, PSM. Com. m. Ba 161, fasc. IX, accounts
1483	1 collo 27 duc., 48 dir.			G.P., Sent. 182, f. 146a[m]
21 Aug. 1484	30 ashr.			Melis, Doc., p. 186
22 April 1489	30 duc.			ASV, Misc. Gregolin, Ba 6, letter A. del Negro
summer 1496	54-55 duc.			Priuli I, p. 59
summer 1497	by barter 85 duc.			Op. cit., p. 73

a) The prices listed in this table are those of Damascus, if no other place is indicated; if the price is given in dirhams, it has been calculated according to the exchange rates compiled in my paper Etudes sur le systeme monétaire, p. 277.

b) The kind of ginger is not specified.

c-d) See my paper Spice prices p. 33 and the notes.

e) The kintar of Ramla was equal to 240 kg., see Pasi (Venice 1512) f. 106.
f-m) See my paper Spice prices and the notes.

Corner, Venetian ambassador to the sultan, had to protest against an order of the sultan to sequester coral that had been imported by the Venetians into Syria, as long as the same quantity was not to be imported into Egypt.[215] Some of the coral imported into the Mamluk dominions was re-exported to India and other countries, and some was worked in Egypt and Syria. In Alexandria there was a "street of the coral workers."[216] In Venice, too, coral was worked and made into paternosters,[217] which were shipped to the Levant.[218] That the import of worked and raw coral into the Moslem Levant had become an important sector of Venetian trade in the second half of the fifteenth century is borne out by a judicial act referring to a transaction of Niccolò Malipiero and Brothers. In the year 1489 (approximately), together with other Venetians they had bought coral from Genoese for 18,300 ducats to be delivered to them in Tunis and shipped from there to Alexandria.[219]

The growth of the Venetian Levant trade in the second half of the fifteenth century was brought about by various factors. The decline of the Levantine industries, and the new tide in the economic life of Western and Central Europe certainly had a great impact upon it. The upsurge of the silk industry in some European countries had as a consequence that the Venetians acquired in Syria great quantities of silk coming from Persia. But the flourishing of Venetian trade in the Levant was also made possible by the low prices of the spices purchased in the Moslem Levant. The progressive impoverishment of the Moslem Levant, the low domestic prices and undoubtedly low cost prices in India, resulted in a relatively low level of spice prices on the Near Eastern markets.

The price of pepper, which had been very low in the 1440's, rose at the end of the 1450's to 90 ducats; then in the seventh decade of the century it was generally 80 ducats,[220] going down in the 1470's to 70 ducats a sporta and sometimes even less. In the 1480's and in the first quinquennium of the 1490's it amounted to 66-68 ducats.

Altogether pepper was cheaper in that period than it had been a hundred years before.

The curve of the ginger prices was different from that of the pepper price. In the middle of the fifteenth century, it went down less than the pepper price. In the 1470's, it was cheaper than it had been 20-30 years before, whereas the price of pepper had risen. In the ninth decade of the

215 Secreta 22, f. 94b.

216 See *JA* 1920 II, p. 18; P. Kahle, "Die Katastrophe des mittelalterlichen Alexandrien," in *Mélanges Maspéro* III (Cairo, 1935-1940), p. 149.

217 See the inventory of a bequest left in Venice (about 1494), G. P., Sent. 192, f. 115b.

218 G. P., Sent. 123, f. 80b ff.

219 G. P., Sent. 187, f. 152a.

220 Secreta 22, f. 93a ff. (instructions for Filippo Corner, where one reads that this was the price in Damascus and in Alexandria; that means both the price of a sporta and of a ḳinṭār).

fifteenth century, its price was half of what it cost in the middle of the century. So the downward trend of the ginger price was sharper than that of the pepper price. This phenomenon was certainly the effect of conditions in India. The Arabic chroniclers of this period dwell on this interdependence.[221] The great increase of the export of pepper to Europe at the end of the fifteenth century was certainly connected with the fall of its prices on the Levantine markets. Other spices, aromata, and dyes were also very cheap at the end of the fifteenth century, e.g., cloves, frankincense, and Brazilwood.[222]

The volume of the Venetian spice trade in Egypt and Syria increased very greatly in the second half of the fifteenth century. Whereas in the last decade of the fourteenth century and in the first years of the fifteenth century Venetians bought on the average 1,500-2,000 sportas pepper in the Moslem Levant, they bought 2,500 in the 1490's. The increase of the ginger purchases was spectacular; they rose from 2,000 spice ḳinṭārs to 6,000-7,000.[223]

Even in that period the Venetians exported great quantities of cotton from Syria. A Venetian Merchants Guide of 1493 contains data about the expenses for cotton purchases in Syria and their shipment from Latakia, Tripoli, Beirut, and Acre.[224] The accounts of some Venetian firms of the second half of the fifteenth century refer to sizable purchases in Syria. Lunardo Malipiero bought cotton for 2,515 ducats in 1475, for 5,188 ducats in 1476, and for 4,240 ducats in 1485. Tomaso Malipiero bought cotton for 1,338 ducats in 1488. The Venetian firm Alvise Baseggio-Polo Caroldo

[221] ʿAbdalbāsiṭ 812, f. 371b f.

[222] *Histoire des prix et des salaires*, pp. 342, 418, 419. But the prices of other spices were high, e.g., that of nutmeg, see *op.cit.*, p. 336. Even the difference was undoubtedly due to conditions in India.

[223] See my "The Volume of Levantine Trade," p. 608. The calculations of C.H.H. Wake are based on the assumption that the Egyptian pondo of the second half of the fifteenth century contained 500 kg and the Syrian collo 120 kg; see his paper "The changing pattern of Europe's pepper and spice imports, ca 1400-1700," *JEEH* VIII (1979), p. 366 ff. If that were correct, the increase of the Venetian spice trade in that period would have been even greater. But in fact in the second half of the fifteenth century the pondo of Alexandria contained 360 kg; see G. P., Straordin. Nodari 19, f. 11b, 12b, 13b (a. 1454); G. P., Sent. 150, f. 49a ff. (a. 1461); G. P., Ter. VIII, f. 50b (a. 1483) and sometimes 450 kg, see G. P., Ter. IV, f. 49a (a. 1462); G. P., Sent. 161, f. 126b ff. (a. 1475). But the Venetian authorities always reckoned 1 Alexandrian bale at 1¼ Syrian bales; see Senato Mar VIII, f. 144b (a. 1467) XII, f. 106a (a. 1487). The Syrian collo was equal to 50 Damascene raṭls (or 300 light Venetian pounds) until the end of the fifteenth century, see G. P., Straordin. Nodari 19, f. 15b, 17a, 18a, 19b (a. 1454); G. P., Ter. II, f. 26b, 34b (a. 1466) XIV, 30a (a. 1493). However, Wake reckons the Egyptian bale at the end of the fourteenth century at 750 light Venetian pounds, making it equal to the sporta, although it contained only 180 kg; see my paper in *JEEH* IV, p. 577. About the calculations of Wake, see my "The Volume of mediaeval Spice Trade," *JEEH* IX (1980), p. 753 ff.

[224] MS. Marciana It. VII 384, f. 76a, 77a, 77b, 79b, 87b f. Cotton purchased in Sarmīn was shipped from Tripoli; see G. P., Straordin. Nodari 23, f. 63a (a. 1460).

purchased cotton for 4,782 ducats in 1480 and in 1481 for 2,698 ducats.[225] But it seems that at that time the Venetians began to increase their cotton purchases in Turkey and in the principality of Caraman (*golfo di Ghiaccia*). In 1482 it was decided that the same rules (as to the fairs) should be valid for the export of cotton from these regions as for the cotton coming from Syria. At the same time, the Venetians began to export cotton from Naples.[226] So it seems that the volume of the Venetian cotton trade in Syria decreased slightly in that period. The data in Table L would point to spring convoys of 6-7 ships and to fall convoys of 2-3. So the average total of cotton ships that went to Syria every year would have been about 9 in the second half of the fifteenth century, a bit less than in the preceding period.

Cotton prices were very low in the second half of the fifteenth century, just as were the pepper prices. In the 1440's they were lower than at the end of the fourteenth century. But where the price of pepper rose again in the second half of the century by 50 percent, cotton remained cheap. Its price at the end of the fifteenth century was the same as it had been in the middle of the century or even lower. The great decline of the cotton prices, as compared with the pepper price, probably points to a lesser demand.

Whereas the cotton purchases of the Venetians in Syria may have decreased in the second half of the fifteenth century, the spice trade flourished more than in any time before.

The two galley lines of Alexandria and Beirut functioned regularly and the number of the galleys that visited these ports increased.[227] In the 1480's, the number of the galleys reached a record, it surpassed their number in the years of the great boom at the end of the fourteenth century. The total of the galleys that sailed on the Alexandria and Beirut lines from 1451 to 1498 was 340 galleys against 313 in the first half of the century. In addition to the Alexandria and Beirut galleys, the *galee de trafego*, two or three a year, transported spices from Egypt and Syria to Venice.

The data about the auctions of the Levant galleys show clearly the upswing of Venice's Levant trade in that period. The data in Table LIII show that from 1458 to 1464 the auctions of the Alexandria and Beirut galleys yielded 1,500-1,800 l (*di grossi*) a year and from 1467 more than 2,000 l. The sums obtained for the Beirut galleys in the 1450's and 1460's surpassed those paid for the Alexandria galleys. Altogether the auctions yielded much more than in preceding periods.

[225] See my "The Venetian cotton trade," p. 698, 699.

[226] Senato Mar IX. f. 177b XI, f. 133a.

[227] See the data compiled in my "The Venetian supremacy," p. 19 ff. The following corrections should be made: in 1475 and in 1461 there was a nave di rata (see Senato Mar VI, f. 68a VII, f. 42a) and in 1469 four galleys went to Alexandria and four to Beirut (see Senato Mar VIII, f. 202b, 203a). For the galleys in 1497 and 1498, see Marino Sanuto, *Diarii* I, col. 734, 1032.

Table L Venetian cotton cogs,
1453 - 1498

year		Syria cogs	Alexandria cogs[a]	source
1455	fall	2		Senato Mar V, f. 105a
1456	fall	4	2	Coll., Not. IX, f. 81a, cf. Senato Mar V, f. 154b f., 164b
1457	spring	7	1	Coll., Not. IX, f. 93b f.; Senato Mar V, f. 179a VI, f. 2b f.
1458			1	Senato Mar VI, f. 77b
1459	spring	6		Senato Mar VI, f. 113b
1464	fall	3		Senato Mar VII, f. 181b
1470	spring	4 galleys		Senato Mar IX, f. 32b
1471			2[b]	Ibid. f. 78a
1477	spring	4		Coll., Not. XI, f. 111b
1480	fall	2		Secreta 29, f. 123a
1484	fall	2		Senato Mar XII, f. 17b
1486	fall	3	2	Secreta 33, f. 28a f.; Senato Mar XIII, f. 8ab[c]
1487			1	Senato Mar XII, f. 117a
1488			1	Ibid. f. 146a
1490			1	Senato Mar XIII, f. 20a
1493			2	Senato Mar XIV, f. 18a

a) In our source it is not said that these cogs sailed to Egypt to load cotton, but they sailed there in the late summer.

b) These two ships sailed both to Syria and to Egypt.

c) In the text it is not said that the ships sailed to the cotton fair, but that they would depart at the end of July or at the beginning of August.

From these data one can also draw some conclusions as to the importance of the Egyptian-Syrian trade for Venice. In 1466 the sums yielded by each of the Alexandria and Beirut galleys were double and more than that obtained for the Barbary galley, and the sum obtained for both Levant lines four times as much as the sum paid for the Flanders and Aigues-Mortes galleys. In 1468 the Alexandria and Beirut galleys were leased for a sum ten times as much as that paid for the three other galley lines together. In 1469 the auctions of the Alexandria galleys yielded about eight times as much as the auctions of the other three lines together, and the auction of

Table LI Cotton prices in Syria, from 1422 to the end of the XVth century

date	place	price of a kinṭār	source
Sept. 1422	Acre	33 - 37 duc.	Arch. L. Dolfin, letter of Z. Franco
Oct. 1422	"	39 - 40 "	Ibid., letter of Z. Loredan
March 1423	Lattakia	of Djabala 42 duc., 8 dir.	Arch. L. Dolfin, accounts
	Acre	43 duc.	
	Lattakia	43 "	
	Hamath	39 - 41 "	
Oct. 1423	Acre	35 - 44 duc., hopes that it will go down to 33	Ibid., letter of Z. Franco
1423[a]	"	42 duc., 28 dir.	Ibid., accounts
1425	Hamath	29 duc., 11 dir. - 30 duc., 15 dir.	G.P., Sent. 65, f. 129a ff.
Nov. 1425	Acre	30 - 31.5 duc.	Arch. L. Dolfin, letter of Greg. Hurso
1426		30 duc., 8 dir.	Ibid., accounts
1427	Hamath	29 duc.	
	Tripoli	22 "	
June 1428	Lattakia	by barter 25 duc.	same series 50, f. 23a ff.
1429	"	" " 22.5 "	" " 52, f. 135b f.
1434		of Hamath, with expenses 40 duc. of Acre 31.66 duc.	Sassi, p. 222 ff. l. c.
1435	Damascus	a Tiberias kinṭār 34 duc.	Vat III, f. 3a f.[a]
1441	"	of Tiberias, a Tiberias kinṭār 23 duc.	G.P., Sent. 95, f. 108b f.
1441/2	Tripoli	of Hamath 24. 2 duc.	same series 92, f. 136b f.
1443	Damascus	23 duc.	" " 123, f. 53b ff.
1443(?)	"	19.7 "	" " 100, f. 127a ff.
1444	Tripoli	of Hamath 19 duc.	" " 106, f. 66b ff.
1444(?)	Damascus	by barter 18.75 "[b]	" " 102, f. 80b
1444(?)	Tripoli	16.25 "	" " 102, f. 61a ff.
1445(?)	"	16. "[c]	" " 107, f. 42b ff.
Noc. 1445	Acre	18.75 "[d]	Arch. L. Dolfin, letter of Alv. Gabriel
1446	"	22.6 "[e]	G.P., Sent. 117, f. 33b f.
1446(?)	Tripoli	according to plaintiff 17.5 duc., " " defendant 21.5 "	l.c.
1447	Acre	a Tiberias kinṭār 47.2 duc. of bad quality 5 "	same series 107, f. 185a ff.
1453	Tripoli	21.7 duc.	" " 155, f. 19b
1435(?)	Tripoli	23 "	" " 107, f. 27b f.
1458	Beirut(?)	15.2 " (?)	" " 163, f. 157b[f]
1473	Tripoli	16 - 17.4 duc.	" " 161, f. 185a
		17.4 "	" " 163, f. 90a ff.

Table LI (continued)

date	place	price of a kinṭār		source
1476	Beirut	5	"	Arch. Baseggio-Caroldo
1480	"	26 - 28	"	Ibid.
1481	Hamath	21	"	Accounts Malipiero
		24	"	Accounts Baseggio-Caroldo
	Tripoli	26	"	Ibidem
Sept. 1481	Acre	28 ashr.		ASV, PSM Com. m. Ba 116, fasc. 14, letter to Al. Baseggio
Nov. 1481	"	17 duc.		Ibid.
1482	Tripoli	10.5 "		ASV, PSM Com. m. Ba 161, fasc. VIII, accounts Tomaso Malipiero
1488	Aleppo	of Hamath 21-21.25 duc.		Ibid.

a) About this kinṭār see my paper The Venetian cotton trade, note 701.

b-e) See art. cit. notes 207 - 210.

f) 760 dirhams, calculated at 50 dirhams the ducat, cf. my paper Etudes sur le système monétaire, p. 279.

Table LII Decennial totals of Venetian Levant galleys, second half of the XVth century

	Alexandria	Beirut	total
1451 - 1460	33	36	69
1461 - 1470	30	35	65
1471 - 1480	39	32	71
1481 - 1490	46	33	79
1491 - 1498	32	24	56

the Beirut galleys about ten times as much.[228] The trade with Egypt and Syria was indeed considered to be the main artery of Venice's trade, as explicitly stated in several resolutions of the Senate.[229]

The sources of this period contain few data about the total investment of the Venetian merchants in the Levant trade, but several documents refer to the exceptionally rich cargoes of the ships sailing to the Moslem Levant. Sometimes these ships were escorted by warships, or other precautionary

[228] See Senato Mar VIII, f. 61a, 62b, 73b, 154a, 156a, 159b, 201a, 201b, 202a.

[229] Senato Mar X, f. 62b XI, f. 174a. Cf. F. C. Lane, "Venetian shipping during the commercial revolution," in his *Venice and history*, p. 15.

Table LIII Auctions of the Venetian Levant galleys[a]
1453 - 1498

date	Alexandria	Beirut	line to Romania	Cyprus	source
1453	515^{11} duc.	546^{13} duc.	-	143^{5} duc.	Senato Mar II, f. 188b f. 190b; Thiriet *Rég. III*, p. 186
1454	257^{10} "	595^{9} "	166 duc.	40^{3}	Senato Mar V, f. 36a, 37a, 37b, f. 43b; Thiriet III, p. 198
1455	495^{5} "	716^{7} "	100^{1} "[b]	90^{1} "	Thiriet III, p. 205
1456	661^{2} "	605^{1} "		131^{3} "	Senato Mar V. f. 160a, 162a; Thiriet III, p. 213
1457	137^{2}	258^{1} "		50^{2} "	Senato Mar VI, f. 22b, 24b; Thiriet III, p. 217
1458	695^{9} "	772^{2} "		114^{3} "	Senato Mar VI, F. 70b, 72b, 74b; cf. Thiriet III, p. 220
1459	644^{1} "	998^{5} "	63	143	Senato Mar VI, f. 123b, 126a, 128b; cf. Thiriet III, p. 226
1460	697^{3} "	855^{1}	210^{1} duc.	164^{1} "	Thiriet III, p. 230, 232
1461	819^{9} "	872	73^{3} "	29^{3} "	Senato Mar VII, f. 17a; Thiriet III, p. 236
1462	965^{3} "	983^{6} "	160^{2} "		Senato Mar VII, f. 65a; Thiriet III, p. 241
1463	903^{2} "	975^{4} "			Senato Mar VII, f. 119a, 121a; Thiriet III, p. 249
1464	678^{2} "	1003			Senato Mar VII, f. 173a, 175a
1465	-	-			
1466	454	509^{8} "			Senato Mar VIII, f. 78b, 80b
1467	1098^{6} sol.	1152^{14} sol.			Senato Mar. VIII, f. 129a, 131a
1468	894	1226^{8} duc.			Senato Mar VIII, f. 173b
1469	1007	1154			Senato Mar VIII, f. 202b, 203a
1470	922^{6} duc.	979^{7} duc.			Incanti I, f. 11b 13b
1471	966	805			" f. 16b, 17b
1472	778^{2} duc	737^{13} duc.			" f. 19b, 24b
1473	623^{2} duc.	220^{6} duc.			Incanti I, f. 24a
1474	847^{2} "	1012 "			" f. 29b, 30b
1475	551^{10} "	365^{2} "			" f. 36b, 37b
1476	982^{11} "	571^{6} "			" f. 43a, 44a
1477	1042^{10} "	798^{14} "			" f. 50a, 51a
1478	21^{9} duc.	431^{12} duc.			Incanti I, f. 56b, 58a
1479	1084^{11} "	834^{2} "	159^{5} duc.		" f. 63b, 65a, 66a
1480	503^{1} "	739^{5} "	80^{5} "		" f. 70b, 72a, 75b
1481	1040^{4} "	888 "			" f. 81a, 81b
1482	804^{2} "	785	410 "		" f. 87a, 87b, 88b
1483	410^{2} "	389^{3} duc.			f. 94b; 95a
1484	405^{6} "	194^{3} "	11 "		" f. 100b, 101a, 105b
1485	12880 "	7310 "			" f. 107b
1486	830 "	245^{3} duc.			" f. 117a, 118a

Table LIII (continued)

date	Alexandria	Beirut	line to Romania	Cyprus	source
1487	1139^{10} duc.	651^{19} "	240^{4} sol.		" f. 122b, 124a
1488	1046^{4} "	636	483^{3} duc.		" f. 124b, 129b
1489	802^{4} "	350^{1} duc.			Incanti II, f. 5b
1490	637^{14} "	326^{6}	138^{8} "		" f. 14a, 17b, 18b
1491	758 "	440^{8} duc.	20^{2} "		" f. 25a, 28a
1492	817^{3} duc.	543^{13} "			" f. 28b, 29b
1493	1107 "	609			" f. 36a, 36b
1494	984^{7} duc.	611^{1} duc.			" f. 44a, 44b
1495	908^{7} "	887^{2} "			" f. 51b
1496	984^{10} "	836^{4} "			" f. 56b, 57a
1497	818^{3} "	22^{4} "			Incanti II, part 4, f. 6a, 8a
1498	200^{3} "	2 duc.			" f. 10a, 11a

a) The amounts are given in lire di grossi and the fractions in ducats or soldi.

b) Galley to Caramania.

measures were taken.[230] Two cogs sailing to Egypt in August 1493 had cargoes worth more than 50,000 ducats each.[231] Sometimes such great quantities of spices had been stocked by the Venetian merchants in Alexandria that measures had to be taken to ship them to Venice or to Venetian territories.[232] In September 1470 it wa• decided to send four additional galleys, in addition to the eight regular galleys, to Alexandria and Beirut, to collect the large quantities of spices the merchants had bought.[233]

The data concerning the total investments and the cargoes of the galley convoys returning from the Levant refer almost exclusively to the last years of the century.

The accounts of the Venetian chroniclers compiled in Table LIV point to a yearly investment of 300,000-360,000 ducats in cash. Together with the merchandise carried by the galleys to Alexandria and Beirut it must have reached 450,000-550,000 ducats. The investment in the purchase of Syrian cotton probably decreased in that period. It may have amounted, on the average, to 130,000-180,000 ducats a year, including the price of other commodities shipped to Venice on the cogs. So one would conclude that the total investment of the Venetians in the Levant trade amounted to

230 Senato Mar VI f. 136a, VII, f. 47b; see, further, XI, f. 52a, 56a f.; 56b, 71a, 82a, 82b, 150a, 177b, 183a; Secreta 29, f. 123a 30, f. 31a f.

231 Senato Mar XIV, f. 18a.

232 Senato Mar XII, f. 64a and cf. 66a.

233 Senato Mar IX, f. 57a f.

Table LIV Volume of Venice's Levant trade, in the second half of the fifteenth century

a) Cash and cargoes shipped to the Levant (or total investment)

year	Alexandria galleys	Beirut galleys	cotton cogs to Syria	source
1480	282,000 duc.			Tucher, p. 692[a]
1494			spring fair 200,000 duc.	Senato Mar XIV, f. 28a f.
1495	190,000 " merchandise 80,000 duc.[b]			Priuli I, p. 30
1496	220,000 duc. merchandise 150,000 duc.[c]	120,000 duc.	spring fair 50,000 duc. merchandise 20,000 duc.[f]	Sanuto Diarii 1, col. 270, 380; Priuli I, 48; Malipiero p. 629
1497	300,000 duc.	60,000 duc.		Sanuto Diarii 1, col. 734; Malipiero, p. 646
1498	200,000 duc.	60,000 duc.		Malipiero, p. 646
	240,000 " merchandise 40,000 duc.[d]	70,000 " merchandise 80,000 duc.[e]		Priuli I, p. 94

a) The German traveller says that an impost for the cottimo amounting to 2.66% yielded 7-8000 ducats.

b) This is an estimate.

c) This is the value of the merchandise that remained in Alexandria that year after the return of the galleys.

d-e) Same as b.

b) Value of cargoes of the galleys returning from the Levant[a]

date	Alexandria galleys	Beirut galleys	source
1472	200,000 duc.[b]		Senato Mar IX, f. 185b
1496	250,000 "	150,000 duc.[c]	Priuli I, p. 59f.
1497	295,000 " d	100,000 " e	Op. cit. I, p. 73
1498	270,000 "	150,000 "	Op. cit. I, p. 109

a) These are our estimates which, owing to the incomplete data of Priuli and the careless edition of the text, should be considered as approximate.

b) Total of the purchases made in Alexandria that year.

c) Adding the number of the bales of spices listed by Priuli one obtains 4152 and together with the 300 bales of silk 4452, but the author says that the total was 4300.

d) The total of the bales listed is 2424, but the chronicler gives a total of 4320.

e) The author lists 2157 colli and says that the total was 2639. So we have added another 20,000 to the estimated value of 80,000 ducats (of 500 colli at 40 duc. each).

f) In that year, a supplementary ship carried spices from Alexandria to Venice, see Sanuto, Diarii II, col. 172.

580,000-730,000 ducats a year at the end of the fifteenth century. A statement made by Sultan Ḳānṣūh al-Ghawrī in his negotiations with a Venetian ambassador in 1512 can be considered as pointing to this order of magnitude. He maintained that at the end of the fifteenth century the Venetians invested 300,000 ducats in cash and 300,000 ducats in merchandise every year in the trade with Egypt alone. This statement was undoubtedly exaggerated, but it cannot be discarded altogether as a testimony to the great volume of Venetian trade in the Levant. Another hint as to the great volume of Venice's trade in the last third of the fifteenth century is to be found in a letter written by the Venetian Paolo Morosini to the German Gregor von Hainburg (who died in 1472). He said that the volume of the German-Venetian trade amounted to a million ducats a year.[234]

From the estimates of the cargoes of the galleys returning to Venice, it may be inferred that in the 1490's the Venetians bought spices and other Indian articles in Alexandria every year whose value was almost 300,000 ducats. This is the result of the estimates of their purchases in 1497 and 1498. In the year 1496 a great quantity of merchandise which the Venetians had imported remained in Alexandria; that is, it had not been bartered.[235] Together with the purchase of spices and other commodities in Syria, the galleys appear to have carried to Venice merchandise worth 400,000-450,000 ducats every year. The other commodities bought in the Moslem Levant were shipped on the cotton cogs or other private merchantmen.[236]

Consequently, the conclusion is that at the end of the fifteenth century the Venetian investment in the trade with the Moslem Levant was slightly greater than in the middle of the century, although cotton prices had fallen very greatly.

Finally, these data show that at the end of the fifteenth century the investment in Egypt was much greater than in Syria. That this had been very different in the middle of the century is shown by the comparison of the amounts yielded by the galley auctions. Another change that had apparently occurred was the considerable increase of the merchandise shipped

[234] C. A. Marin, *Storia civile e politica del commercio di Venezia* VII (Venice, 1800), p. 295; F. Reinaud, "Traités de commerce," *JA* 1829 II, pp.29, 32 f.; see also my monograph *Les métaux précieux*, p. 67. Wholly unfounded is the supposition of Labib, p. 473, of a decline of Venice's Levant trade in the 1490's as a consequence of the bankruptcy of Venetian banks and the great purchases of spices by the French. Really large banks were not bankrupt before 1499, when their failure was an effect of the war; see F. C. Lane, "Venetian bankers (1496-1533)," in *Venice and history*, p. 78 f., and cf. Romano-Tenenti-Tucci, "Venise et la route du Cap 1499-1517," in *Méditerranée e Oceano Indiano*, p. 124; G. Valentinelli; *Bibliotheca manuscript. ad S. Marci*, Cod. Lat. III (Venice, 1870), p. 257; cf. W. Heyd, "Das Haus der deutschen Kaufleute in Venedig," *HZ* 32 (1874), p. 217.

[235] Marino Sanuto, *Diarii* I, col. 380, but cf. *Les métaux précieux*, p. 83.

[236] The value of cargo of the galleys returning from Alexandria in 1508 was estimated at 400,000 ducats; see Marino Sanuto, *Diarii* VII, col. 597, but in that year the spice prices had soared, cf. *ibid.*, col. 204.

to the dominions of the Mamluks. At the end of the fifteenth century it made up to 40 percent of the total investment. This conclusion is based on data concerning the investments of single firms. According to some judicial acts, half of the investment made by a firm in the trade with the Moslem Levant consisted of cash, the other of merchandise;[237] in the accounts of a great merchant, it is found that in 1482 he shipped cloth to the Moslem Levant amounting to 1,444 ducats and silver valued at 3,428 ducats, in one year. So the cloth amounted to 35 percent of the investment (reckoning the silver as cash).[238]

c. The Other Trading Nations

In the second half of the fifteenth century, the supremacy of Venice in the Levant trade was almost crushing; the share that the other trading nations had in the commercial exchanges with the Moslem Levant was altogether much smaller. The further decline of their Levant trade was the outcome of conditions—political and economic—in their own countries. Their activities in the Moslem Levant were irregular and had ups and downs, whereas the well-functioning galley and cog lines of the Venetians assured them of the faithfulness of their suppliers and customers. In the Near Eastern countries themselves the Venetian money replaced other currencies. At the end of the fifteenth century, only Venetian silver money (the *marcello*) was legal tender (in addition to the local *mu'ayyadī* and Syrian *dirham*), so that Genoese had to buy the means of exchange from the Venetians to make their purchases.[239] Another evidence of the Venetian supremacy is the fact that the Venetian privileges served as models for the commercial treaties that other trading nations concluded with the sultan of Cairo.

Despite her political decline and the interests in other sectors of international trade, Genoa still tried to keep a prominent position in the Levant trade. In the year 1462 Genoa reinstated the old privileges for the German merchants,[240] and Milan, always closely connected with Genoese trade, also confirmed their privileges several times.[241] In fact, the commercial exchanges between Milan and Constance and Milan and Cologne were an important axis of international trade and in Genoa itself the Ravensburg Company bought considerable quantities of spices.[242] Merchants of Nürn-

[237] G. P., Sent. 123, f. 49a ff.
[238] ASV, PSM Com. m. 161, fasc. 1, accounts of Tomaso Malipiero.
[239] Loggia, Girolamo, filza II, c. 306.
[240] Schulte I, p. 536.
[241] *Op.cit.*, p. 558.
[242] *Op.cit.*, pp. 543, 554, 618.

berg also purchased spices in Genoa.[243] On the other hand, the Genoese obtained copper, which they could offer in the Moslem Levant, from the German traders.[244]

Nor were the diplomatic contacts between Genoa and the court of the sultan of Cairo suspended. Genoa tried from time to time to enhance her position in the Levant by interventions with the sultan. Of course the Genoese had to deal with the same difficulties as the Venetians. They too had to buy certain quantities of pepper from the sultan's stocks, both in Egypt and Syria,[245] and the corsair activities of Genoese, who were in fact no longer subjects of the republic, from time to time poisoned the relations with the sultan. From Arabic chronicles one learns that in 1459 a squadron of the Mamluk war fleet coming back from an expedition to the coasts of Asia Minor (where it had escorted ships collecting timber) caught the crew of a European ship. The sultan imprisoned the crew and the Genoese consul. Then he demanded a ransom from him of 100,000 ducats, but was satisfied with a smaller sum.[246] So obviously there must have been serious tension between the sultan and Genoa. Genoese sources state that an embassy visited the sultan in 1472 to conclude peace.[247] Probably the incident in 1459 had been one of many. In 1476 a Mamluk ambassador came to Genoa.[248] Then, in 1477, Genoa contacted the Holy See as to the papal attitude to sending another embassy to Cairo.[249] In 1496 again there was a Genoese embassy in Cairo.[250] The Genoese also took other steps to please the sultan, such as ransoming Moslem captives.[251]

But the Genoese concentrated their activities in the Eastern Mediterranean in Chios. Genoese ships sailing to the Moslem Levant first went to Chios, and spices bought in Alexandria or in Beirut were transported there.[252] Even after the conquest of Phocea by the Turks and when Chios was already tributary to the latter and, on the other hand, the rich alum deposits of Tolfa had been discovered in 1461, a lively alum trade was conducted on the Aegean island. The Genoese of Chios still exported alum of Phocea;[253] Caffa remained another point of support for the Genoese trade even after

[243] *Op.cit.*, pp. 660 ff., 710.

[244] *Op.cit.*, p. 543.

[245] Loggia, Girolamo, filza II, c. 235; 2774 C, f. 27b, 28a, 32a, 35b.

[246] See *an-Nudjūm az-zāhira* VII, p. 522, note aa; *Ḥawādith*, p. 329 f; Ibn Iyās² II, p. 356, where one reads that the number of the Genoese captives was 150.

[247] Musso, "Nuovi doc.," p. 460.

[248] *Art. cit.*, p. 453.

[249] *Art. cit.*, p. 448.

[250] Primi Cancellieri Ba 88, 2, pp. 312, 314-18, 322, 324-26; see also p. 309: deliberations in 1494 concerning an embassy to the sultan.

[251] ASG, Arch. Segr., Lit. 1810, f. 69a (a. 1491).

[252] Musso, *art. cit.*, p. 491; ASG, Car. Vet. 1553, f. 23a-49a, 68a ff., 197b ff.

[253] See G. Pistarino, "Chio dei Genovesi," *Studi Medievali* X (1969), part I, p. 62; Musso, "Nuovi doc.," p. 445.

the conquest by the Ottomans in 1475, and Genoese merchants remained there.[254]

Genoese activities in Egypt and Syria were, however, never discontinued. Incomplete though our sources are, they leave no doubt that every year two to three Genoese ships anchored in the ports of Egypt and Syria.[255] Not all Genoese ships sailed first to Chios. Some, like that of Oberto and Ilario Squarzafico, chartered in 1464 by Bernardo Lercaro and Benedetto Italiano for a voyage to Egypt and Rhodes, went directly to Alexandria.[256] There was also intense Genoese shipping along the coast of Northern Africa, and not a few of the ships sailing on this line went to Egypt. These ships carried cloth of Flanders and other commodities and transported Moslem merchants from the Maghreb countries. A piece joined to the award concerning the profits from the journey of the ship of Giuliano Grimaldi, which had apparently sailed in 1479 or in 1480 from the Maghreb to Alexandria, contains the names of 208 Moslem merchants who had used it for the shipping of their merchandise to Alexandria. Some of them were traders of Alexandria; others were Tunisians or were simply called Maghrebins. In the year 1479 a Genoese ship sailing to Alexandria had 300 Moslem passengers on board.[257]

[254] Musso, *art. cit.*, p. 491.

[255] In 1455 the ship of Battista Salvaygo visited Syrian ports; see Crist. del Fiore V, f. 12b, 14a f., 14b f. In 1458 the ship of Oberto Squarzafico visited Beirut (see Car. Vet. 1553, f. 23a ff.) and in 1467 it was again in Beirut (see Musso, I Genovesi e il Levante, p. 84); in 1459 the ship of Maurizio Cattaneo sailed from Barbary to Alexandria and Chios (see Heers in *Le Moyen Age* 63, p. 104) and the ship of Demetrios Spinola came from Beirut to Chios (see ASG, S. Giorgio, Sala 38/54, f. 4b [I did not find the text in J. Heers, *Le livre des comptes de Giovanni Piccamiglio, homme d'affaires génois 1456-1459*, p. 249, where it should appear]). About Genoese ships which went from the Maghreb in 1469 and 1470 to Alexandria, see R. Brunschvig, *Deux récits de voyage inédits en Afrique du Nord au XVe siècle* (Paris, 1936), pp. 95, 220. Anselme Adorno embarked in 1470 in Tunis on the ship of Cosma de Negrono for Alexandria; see his travelogue, p. 141. In the year 1472, the ships of Iofredo Spinola and Barnaba Iustiniano were in Alexandria; see ASG, 2774 C, f. 7b; Bat. de Luco, p. 20. In 1474 the ship of Lodixio Iustiniano anchored in Alexandria (see ASG, 2774 C, f. 62b) and in 1476 those of Gentile Pallavicini and Paolo Gentile (see Musso, "Nuovi doc.," p. 490 and Costa, Lor. 10, no. 97). In 1480 (approximately) the ship of Giuliano Grimaldi went from Tunis to Alexandria, in 1481 that of Costantino Doria anchored in the Egyptian port (see Musso, "I Genovesi," pp. 85, 88, and see also the travelogue of Meshullam of Volterra, p. 39); that he came from Chios to Alexandria on a Genoese ship in 1481. Three Genoese ships went to Alexandria in 1482, namely, those of Iuliano Grimaldi, Domenico Fieschi, and Ieronimo de Negro; see M. L. Balletto, *Navi e navigazione a Genova nel Quattrocento, La gabella marinariorum (1482-1491)* (Genoa, 1973), pp. 46, 53, 56. (And two others went to *partes orientales*; see *op.cit.* p. 31.) Apparently in 1485 the ship of Giovanbattista Spinola came to Beirut (see Musso, "I Genovesi," p. 86 f.) and another Genoese ship visited Alexandria (see Musso, "Nuovi doc.," p. 490). In 1487 the ship of Giorgio Doria anchored in Alexandria (see ASG, Arch. Segr. 745, c. 75a/b; in 1493); the "Pallavicina" was in Beirut (see Musso, "Nuovi doc.," p. 490).

[256] Foglietta, Oberto 9, no. 30 (Heers, *Gênes*, p. 374, has erroneously the date a. 1449). Cf. Heers in *Le Moyen Age* 63, p. 105.

[257] Costa, Lor. 10, c. 185; Marino Sanuto, *Diarii* I, col. 768.

The commodities that the Genoese sold in the second half of the fifteenth century on the Levantine markets cover a wide range. They marketed Florentine cloth;[258] much more English cloth, such as woolen stuffs of London, both cheap and expensive;[259] French;[260] and Catalan cloth.[261] They also sold costly scarlets[262] and silken stuffs,[263] velvets and others.[264] They marketed textile products as coverings.[265] In addition, they offered paper certainly that they produced in Sampierdarena and Voltri,[266] and, as in earlier periods, they imported into Egypt and Syria a great deal of coral, which sold for many thousands of ducats.[267] In the middle of the fifteenth century Genoese held the coral fisheries of Marsa al-Kharaz (formerly farmed to Catalans), and later they also obtained coral in the area around Alghero.[268] Coral exported from Rhodes (where it had probably been worked) was exchanged by Genoese agents in Syria for pearls.[269] But at the end of the fifteenth century this sector of Genoese trade with the Moslem Levant was obviously in crisis. In the year 1496 it was necessary to take measures to increase the export of coral to the Moslem Levant. The export dues were reduced to half. Further, it was forbidden to ship coral obtained in Corsica to the Levant on non-Genoese ships.[270] The import of mastic of Chios into the Mamluk dominions was another typically Genoese business, and it was continued in that period.[271] The Genoese also sold ambergris,[272] ostrich feathers, and wax[273] in Egypt and Syria. Finally, they imported, as always, various victuals, such as olive oil,[274] raisins,[275] hazelnuts,[276] and, in times of scarcities, grains.[277]

[258] Musso, "I Genovesi," p. 88.

[259] ASG, 2774 C, f. 23b, 28b, 33b, 35b; see, further, Musso, "Nuovi doc.," p. 491; "I Genovesi," p. 90 f.

[260] ASG, 2774 C, f. 22b, 35b; Tur II, f. 17b f.

[261] ASG, 2774 C, f. 33b (cloth of Majorca); G. P., Sent. 162, f. 25b f.; Musso, "Nuovi doc.," p. 483 (cloth of Perpignan sold in Tyre).

[262] ASG, 2774 C, f. 12b.

[263] Primi Cancellieri Ba 88a, pp. 314-18; Musso, "Nuovi doc.," p. 491; "I Genovesi," p. 88.

[264] ASG, 2774 C, f. 28b.

[265] Senato Mar VI, f. 84a.

[266] Musso, "I Genovesi," p. 89; Loggia, Girolamo, filza II, c. 235.

[267] Cristofore del Fiore V, f. 12b f., 14a f., 14b f., 15b, 21b f. ASG, 2774 C, f. 32b (great quantities sold for 6100 duc. and 11,000 duc. respectively); Heers, *Gênes*, p. 374, and see also Musso, "Nuovi doc.," pp. 453, 490; "I Genovesi," p. 90.

[268] Heers, *Gênes*, pp. 378, 426 f.

[269] Fazio, Ant., Senior 16, no. 406.

[270] Primi Cancellieri, Ba 88, c. 319, 321, 330 f.

[271] ASG, 2774 C, f. 32b (where a great quantity is spoken of; it was sold for 9450 duc.); see, further, Musso, "I Genovesi," pp. 86, 87, 95.

[272] Musso, "Nuovi doc.," p. 491.

[273] Batt. de Luco, p. 38.

[274] ASG, 2774 C, f. 14b, 19B.

[275] *Ibid.*, f. 32b (a great quantity, sold for 11,920 duc.), 33b, 36b.

[276] Heers, *Gênes*, p. 374; id., *Giovanni Piccamiglio*, p. 232; Musso, "I Genovesi," p. 89.

[277] Musso, *art. cit.*, p. 91.

The commodities that the Genoese exported in that period from Egypt and Syria also covered a wide range. They bought much pepper, ginger, frankincense, gum-lac, indigo, and rhubarb, both in Egypt and in Syria.[278] They exported these spices and aromata not only to Genoa but also to Sicily. A notarial act refers to the export by Genoese of galingale from the Levant to Messina.[279] They also engaged quite extensively in the trade of jewels. Various data in the archives of the Genoese consulate in Alexandria testify to the purchase of precious stones for thousands of ducats.[280] In Syria, they bought cotton, bocasin,[281] and alkali;[282] in Egypt, flax.[283]

Alexandria was, of course, the center of the Genoese activities in Egypt, but they also carried on trade in Damietta[284] and in Cairo. In the capital of Egypt they marketed European cloth in the 1450's.[285] In Syria they engaged in trade in Beirut, as Lanzalotto Cigala in 1454,[286] but mainly in Damascus.[287]

In addition to the true Genoese, other Ligurian merchants engaged in the Levant trade then. One of them was Gabriele Rusca of Savona, who apparently lived in Beirut a long time and died there in 1477. In some documents he is called "consul of the Lombardians and others."[288] The merchants of Savona certainly exported to the Levant the paper manufactured in Quiliano and also perhaps cloth from their workshops.[289]

However, the number of the Genoese and other Ligurian merchants who carried on trade in Egypt and Syria at that time must have declined greatly, as compared with the Genoese colonies in Egypt and Syria in earlier periods. This conclusion is drawn from the numbers of the Genoese merchants mentioned in the acts of Italian notaries working in Alexandria and Damascus and also from those who appear in the accounts of the Genoese consulate in Alexandria in the 1470's. These data will lead us to assume that the Venetian colony in Alexandria then numbered about 35-50 merchants and the Genoese only 10-15. Probably 20-25 Venetian merchants and less than 5 Genoese lived in Damascus. A list of the debtors to the

278 ASG, 2774 C, f. 14b, 18b, 19a, 25b, 34b, 35b, 36a; Car. Vet. 1553, f. 23a f., 49b, 68a ff., 197b ff.

279 Loggia, Girolamo, filza II, c. 235.

280 ASG, 2774 C, f. 21b, 27b (for 7,900 duc.), 29b (for 6,000 duc.), 34b (for 1,800 duc.), 36b. See, further, Musso, "I Genovesi," p. 89; "Nuovi doc.," p. 491.

281 Car. Vet. 1553, f. 23a, 23b, 28a.

282 Airolo, Batt., no. 13; Musso, "I Genovesi," pp. 88, 90.

283 Costa, Lor. 10, nos. 97, 383.

284 Musso, "I Genovesi," p. 85.

285 Tur II, f. 11a, 11b; see also Marino Sanuto, *Diarii* II, cols. 634, 637.

286 Fazio, Ant. Senior 16, no. 406.

287 Musso, "I Genovesi," pp. 85, 87, 96.

288 F. Noberasco, "I commerci savonesi del sec. XV," *Atti della Società Savonese di storia patria* VII (1924), p. 120; I. Scovazzi-F. Noberasco, *Storia di Savona* III, p. 172; see also Noberasco, *art. cit.*, p. 120 f. about trade with *partes orientales*.

289 Noberasco, *art. cit.*, pp. 83, 120; Scovazzi-Noberasco, *op.cit.* III, p. 173.

Table LV Venetian and Genoese merchants in the Levant[a], (second half of the fifteenth century)

a) Venetians and Genoese in Alexandria in the 1450's

	Venetians	Genoese
1455	37	9
1456[b]	24	10

b) Genoese in Alexandria in the 1470's

1472	4
1473	13
1474	15
1475	12

c) Venetians and Genoese in Damascus in the 1450's and the 1460's

	Venetians	Genoese
1455	24	4
1456	14	2
1457	34	1
1461	17	-
1462	18	1
1463	23	-

a) These data are culled from the notarial acts of Nic. Turiano, drawn up in Alexandria in 1455 and in 1456, those of Cristofore del Fiore, Damascus, in 1455-1456 and 1461-63, the accounts of the Genoese consulate in Alexandria of 1472-1475 and the Sentenze and Terminazioni of the Giudici di petizion.

b) Few notarial acts have come down to us from the registers of Nic. Turiano for this year.

Genoese consulate in Alexandria compiled in 1502 comprised 86 names,[290] but the list certainly refers to debts contracted during a period of several years.

In the third quarter of the fifteenth century and also in the 1480's, the

[290] Primi Cancellieri Ba 88, 2, c. 275-277; another copy has 95 names. As to the number of the Venetians, a passage in the travelogue of Adorno and a statement of Sultan Ḳānṣūh al-Ghawrī should be quoted. The Flemish traveller who came to Alexandria in 1470 says, p. 166, that the number of the Venetians who live in the town sometimes reaches 60. The sultan, on the other hand, mentioned in negotiations with a Venetian ambassador in 1512 that at the end of the fifteenth century there were always at least 15 prominent Venetian merchants in Alexandria; see *JA* 1829 II, p. 30. But the statements of Ḳānṣūh al-Ghawrī should be considered *cum grano salis*; see above p. 478.

Genoese consulate in Alexandria still functioned fully.[291] Several travellers, who visited Alexandria in the 1470's and 1480's, mention in their travelogues the beautiful Genoese fondaco,[292] and the accounts of the consulate of the 1470's refer to its chaplain, its physician, and its interpreters.[293] But in the 1490's the administration of the consulate was thrown into disorder. Often farmers of the imposts did not pay the rates.[294] In 1494 the consulate had large debts.[295] Then in 1497 the consul had fled, and Genoese trade in Egypt and Syria had been suspended. Thereupon the Bank of S. Giorgio had to grant a credit of 5,000 ducats to the consulate.[296]

The volume of Genoese trade in the Moslem Levant seriously declined in the last third of the fifteenth century. In 1494, there were deliberations in Genoa about the reasons for its decay, and two years later again there were deliberations and efforts were made to find a remedy for the problems of the Genoese colony in Alexandria, which was considered to be of great importance. The authorities of S. Giorgio authorized a committee of four officials, which dealt with the problems of the Levant trade, to appoint the consul in Alexandria.[297] The totals in Table LVI are calculated from the accounts of the consulate concerning the imposts levied on import and export in Alexandria in the years 1472-1475.

If the presumed import and export transactions in Syria are added to these totals, the sum comes to 130,000-150,000 ducats a year. Comparing this amount with the total of Genoa's trade in 1470 and 1480, one sees that it still represented 23 percent and 28 percent, respectively, of its international trade.[298] That means that the importance of the Genoese trade with the Moslem Levant, compared with the world trade of Genoa, had

[291] The Genoese consuls mentioned in notarial acts and in other documents are the following: Nic. de Castiglione, before 1452, see Tur II, f. 30b, 31a, ff.; Bartol. Marini, a. 1455, see Tur II, f. 4a f., 9a f. 48a ff.; Donato de Via, a. 1456, see Tur II, f. 69b ff.; Agostino de Via, a. 1463, see Musso, "Genovesi," p. 93, f. Pietro de Persisa a. 1470, see Adorno, p. 473; Giorgio Benigassio, a. 1471-1475, see registers of the consulate ASG, 2774 C from 15 Dec. 1471 until 18 Apr. 1475; Jeronimo Carmelino, a. 1486, see ASG, Arch. Segr. 745, c. 75a/b; Paolo Centurione, in the 1490's, see Musso, "Genovesi," p. 96; finally, Giov. de Prato, who was appointed in 1478 and could not take over, should be mentioned. He obtained the right to send a substitute to Alexandria; see ASG, Arch. Segr. 1801, c. 162b ff. (of 1 Jan. 1479). On the chaplains in the 1450's, see Tur II, f. 11a, 12b, 17a, 31a ff., 69b ff.

[292] Adorno, p. 166; Breydenbach, in *Reyssbuch*, p. 205; F. Fabri, *Evagatorium* III, p. 163; *idem*, *Eigentlich Beschreibung der hin und widerfahrt zu dem Heyligen Landt gen Jerusalem* (Bautzen, 1557), f. 189b f.

[293] ASG, 2774 C, f. 1b, 4b, 6b, 9a, 22b.

[294] ASG, S. Giorgio, Div. Off., no. 26 (2252), f. 197a.

[295] Primi Cancellieri, Ba 88, 2, c. 309.

[296] ASG, 2774 C, Instruc. sub 24 May 1497.

[297] Primi Cancellieri, Ba 88, p. 322; Ba 88, 2, c. 309. One reads there that Genoese trade (negociatio) had already decayed a long time before *(nec dum plurimum diminuta sed in toto extincta . . . cum magna et intolerabile iactura totius rei publicae Janue)*.

[298] Cf. Sieveking, "Aus Genueser Rechnungs-u. Steuerbüchern," p. 52.

Table LVI Volume of Genoese trade with Egypt[a], 1472 - April 1475

date	import	export	all transactions	presumed total of import	presumed total of export
1472		1350 duc.	33,775 duc.	16,887 duc.	18,237 duc.
1473	20,789 duc.	21,585 "	37,660 "	39,616 "	40,415 "
1474	42,695 "	31,590 "	31,590 "	58,490 "	47,385 "
Jan.-April 1475	5,010 "	4,680 "	28,378 "	19,199 "	18,769 "

a) The amounts of the payments of dues "for import and export" have been divided here into two halves and added to the volume of the import and export transactions as declared by the merchants. The results are summed up in the column "presumed totals". About the source, ASG 2774 C, see G. Musso, Nuovi doc., p. 460.

not declined.[299] It had even increased. In fact, it was the value of world trade of Genoa that had decreased and, on the other hand, the spices bought in the Moslem Levant were expensive articles. In 1496 an impost (*drictus*) of 3 percent on trade with the Moslem Levant was farmed out for 5,000 ducats.[300] This amount would point to a total (of import and export) of 200,000 ducats at least. But one cannot be sure that the sum had been paid for one year only. However, it does seem that Genoa intensified her commercial activities in Egypt and Syria at the turn of the century. In 1500 a Genoese ship carrying merchandise worth 100,000 ducats and 50,000 ducats in cash arrived in Alexandria, and there was another Genoese ship in the port.[301] However that may have been, all these data show that the average investment of the Genoese in the trade with the Moslem Levant in the last quarter of the fifteenth century amounted to no more than 70,000-80,000 ducats a year.

Even the Levant trade of the Catalans was very irregular and decreased considerably in that period. This was certainly the consequence of the decline of the Catalan economy, itself closely connected with the political circumstances of the country.

[299] Cf. my "Il volume del commercio levantino," p. 420. It is true that in that paper the prices of the spices are calculated on the FOB basis, whereas those taken into consideration for the imposts in Genoa were CIF prices. Further, both in 1470 and in 1480, Genoa's international trade was at an ebb, and, comparing our data with those referring to the imposts levied in Genoa in 1490, one will conclude that the volume of Genoese trade in Egypt and in Syria in the last quarter of the fifteenth century was much smaller, compared with the whole of her international trade. But it seems that in the 1490's Genoese trade in the Mamluk dominions had again increased.

[300] Primi Cancellieri, Ba 88, p. 327.

[301] Marino Sanuto, *Diarii* III, col. 941 f.

The policy of the king of Aragon and his attitude toward the trade with the Mamluk dominions in the 1450's were more favorable to its development. In 1452 Alfonso V promulgated a decree about freedom of trade with Egypt and Syria.[302] A year later, the Council of Barcelona requested that the king make peace with the sultan and that he forbid the loading in Catalan ports of merchandise on foreign ships that were to sail to the Levant. The king agreed at least to the second request, which was intended to foster Catalan trade with the Mamluk dominions. But the king still organized squadrons of corsair ships which should attack the ships of the Moslems and those of the Genoese who transported Moslems from Egypt to Tunisia and vice versa.[303] After the death of Alfonso V in 1458, his successor took steps to conclude peace with the sultan. In 1460 his envoy, who was authorized to come to an agreement with the sultan, was in Rhodes.[304] But two years later the Catalonian civil war, which lasted until 1478 and brought about an economic crisis, began. Catalonia's international trade almost came to a standstill. The impact of the political conditions upon Catalonia's trade with the Levant is clearly shown by the data on Catalan shipping to the Eastern Mediterranean in that period (Table LVII).

From Table LVII we see that until 1459 almost every year two to three Catalan ships sailed to the ports of Egypt and Syria. Some of them were particularly big ones, of 1,000 or 1,400 butts. But in the 1460's Catalan shipping to the Moslem Levant decreased considerably. In some years only one ship visited Alexandria, in others none. From 1467 until 1477 Catalan shipping to the dominions of the Mamluks was apparently suspended altogether. Then it was taken up again but was very irregular. In some years one Catalan galley visited Alexandria or Beirut, in others none. Only in the year 1485 five ships sailed to the Mamluk dominions. But in the 1490's there was an upswing. In 1491 three Catalan ships sailed to the Moslem Levant; in 1492, four.[305] However, the commercial exchanges between Catalonia and the Moslem Levant were never broken off altogether. Sometimes foreign ships sailed between the Catalan ports and the Levant, and sometimes Catalan merchants embarked on French ships sailing from the coasts of southern France to the Near East.[306]

The number of Catalan merchants who sojourned for long periods in Alexandria declined considerably at that time. To judge from the acts of an Italian notary who practiced in Alexandria in 1455 and in 1456, there

[302] López de Meneses, "Los consulados," p. 119.

[303] Capmany, 2.1, no. 370, pp. 535-40; C. Marinescu, "Notes sur les corsaires au service d'Alfonse V d'Aragon, roi de Naples," in *Mélanges d'histoire générale, Université de Cluj* (Cluj, 1927), p. 157 ff.

[304] Coll. Julia, *art. cit.*, p. 166.

[305] Cf. Del Treppo, p. 45 ff.

[306] Tur II, f. 34b.

Table LVII Catalan shipping to the Levant[a], 1453 - 1498

date	Alexandria	Beirut	Alex. and Beirut	Rhodes or Levant	"Levant"
1453	2	-	-	1[b]	-
1454	1	-	2[c]	4	1
1455	1	-	-	5	1[d]
1456	3	-	-	1[e]	-
1457	1	-	-	2[f]	-
1458	3	-	-	3	-
1459	2	-	-	2	-
1460	-	-	1[g]	5	-
1461	1	-	-	1	-
1462	1	-	-	1	-
1463	-	-	-	2	-
1464	-	-	-	5	-
1465	-	-	-	-	-
1466	1	-	-	1[h]	-
1467	-	-	-	-[i]	-
	1468-1476	—			
1477	-	1	-	-	-
1478	-	1	-	-	-
	1479-1481	—			
1482	1	-		-	-
1483	-	1		-	-
1484	1	-		-	-
1485	2	3		-	-
	1486-1489	—			
1490	-	1		-	-
1491	-	3		-	-
1492	-	4		-	-
1493	1	1		-	-
1494	-	-		-	-
1495	1	-		-	-
	1496-1498	—			

a) This table contains only data about Catalan ships. The data are compiled from Carrère, p. 866 ff.; Del Treppo, p. 630 ff.; Capmany, Memorias I, part 2, p. 60, 61 f. II, no. 193, 210, and some other sources.

b) Carrère, p. 866 has another ship (a galley) sailing from Majorca to Rhodes and Alexandria.

c) According to Carrère l.c., in that year the ship of Ramon Dez Pla would have made the journey twice to Alexandria. On the other hand, the galley of Majorca would have visited Rhodes only. Instead of the ships of Jacme Carbo and Franci Setanti sailing to Rhodes, this author has the ship of Johan Comcs (which departed only in 1455!).

Table LVII (continued)

d) In the table of Mlle Carrère the galley of Majorca going to Alexandria is missing. Further she has four other ships (those of Rafael Sollers, Antoni de Villatorta, Miquel Prats, Thomas Pujades) sailing to Rhodes and three sailing to the "Levant". Three ships listed by Del Treppo are missing in her table.

e) Mlle Carrère has in addition a caravel of Berenguer Sayol going to Rhodes.

f) According to the data found by Mlle Carrère the ship of Francesc Rebater sailed at the beginning of the year to Alexandria and at its end to Rhodes, but the latter trip probably took place in the spring of 1458. Instead of the caravel of Bernat de Alicant sailing to Alexandria, Carrère has that of Francesc de Busquets going to Alexandria and Beirut and instead of that of Johan de Muntbar sailing to Rhodes, that of Pere Puyol.

g) Mlle Carrère has in addition two ships sailing to Alexandria, those of Melchior Mathes and of Johan Bertran, but the latter probably departed in the spring of 1461. The ship of Nic. Oms sailing to Rhodes is missing.

h) Giac. Comito 853 sub 25 May 1466 (an insurance act).

i) In this year perhaps six foreign ships commuted between the Catalan ports and the Moslem Levant, but it is not certain, see Del Treppo, p. 49.

---

may have been 11-15 Catalan merchants in the great Egyptian emporium in those years.[307] Some of them were of Majorca,[308] others of Gerona[309] or of Palamos.[310] In the 1460's the Catalan colony in Alexandria dwindled. Some pilgrims who returned via Alexandria to Germany in 1483 said that in the Catalan fondaco there were few merchants and that therefore the pilgrims were lodged there.[311] Before the civil war in Catalonia and the great decline of Catalan trade in the Levant, some Catalan merchants engaged in trade in Syria also. Pere de Baiarono of Barcelona imported coral and cloth of Barcelona into Syria in 1456.[312] Another merchant of Barcelona, Gabriel Olias, imported antimony-sulphide in 1461-1462.[313]

In the 1450's and at the beginning of the 1460's the Catalan merchants still imported into the Moslem Levant much cloth, both the products of

[307] In fact, we find in the acts of Nic. Turiano dating of 1456 the names of not less than 24 Catalan merchants, but some of them came to Alexandria on the same ship and probably departed on it.

[308] Tur II, f. 51a, 73b ff.

[309] Tur II, f. 72a ff.

[310] Tur II, f. 51a. Four of the Catalan merchants who were in Alexandria in 1455 belonged to the family de la Caballeria: Martin, see Tur II, f. 35a; Francesc, see there f. 34a, 34b, 35a, 37a, 39a; Johan, see there f. 34a, 37a, 39a, and Alfonso, see there f. 21a ff., 23a, 35a, 41a f., 42a f. (the last named had been in Alexandria already in 1441). These four merchants established a company; see there f. 35a, 39a. Martin and Alfonso were perhaps sons of Bonafos; see Vendrell, "Aportaciones para el estudio de la familia Caballeria," *Sefarad* III, genealogical table opposite to p. 142, and cf. Ch. V, note 360.

[311] Breydenbach, pp. 203, 205; F. Fabri, *Evagatorium* III, pp. 149, 163.

[312] Cristofore del Fiore V, f. [17b f.].

[313] G. P., Sent. 162, f. 25b ff. See also Crist. del Fiore VI, no. 14 f. [7a f.] about Barangarius de San Clement of Castellon, who was a merchant in Damascus in 1461.

their own industry and French cloth.[314] Further, they marketed in Egypt and in Syria great quantities of coral, a part of which came from Sardinia and was loaded on the Catalan ships in Alghero.[315] But from 1463 for a long time they were replaced as importers of these commodities by other Levant traders.

From time to time the king took measures to renew the trade with the Moslem Levant. In 1472 he issued special passports to all those (even foreigners) who would depart from his land for the Moslem Levant.[316] These steps, however, had no success.

The decline of Catalan trade in the Mamluk dominions is mirrored by the conditions of the Catalan consulate in Alexandria. In the mid-1450's the Catalans once more had no consul in the town. So the merchants again chose Marioto Squarzalupi, the Florentine consul, to represent their interests and he applied in 1455 to the king of Aragon for letters of appointment.[317] For some time the Florentine consul fulfilled the hopes of the Catalans. When in 1458 the ship of Francesc Ça-Closa came from Rhodes to Alexandria and was captured there by a Genoese pirate, Squarzalupi tried to make a deal with the Mamluk authorities to recover the cargo.[318] However, a year later, in 1459, he was dismissed by the king.[319] In 1485 the Council of Barcelona appointed Juan de Viastrosa consul in Alexandria, but it took some months until he left for Egypt. The letters of recommendation issued by the Council bear the date of 10 May 1486.[320] The Catalan consul who is mentioned in an order of King Fernando el Catolico of the year 1488 was probably the same Juan de Viastrosa.[321] Five years later, in 1492, he died and his son Jacme succeeded him.[322] Both he and the next consul, Jacme Fontelles, held the post only a very short time, for already in November 1493 a new consul, Miguel Marques, was appointed.[323] But Marques encountered opposition in the small Catalan colony and could not impose his authority. When in 1495 the Catalan government armed a ship to take up trade with Egypt, the council of Barcelona wrote not to the consul but to Luis Soler, then acting as consul of Naples in Alexandria,

[314] Tur II, f. 34a, 35a, 37a; Giacomo Comito, 849, sub 10 March 1454; Ant. Vılanova, lib. III, f. 121b; *idem*, Man. com., f. 75a; Esteban Mir, f. 41b. Madurell-Garcia, nos. 243-245.

[315] Tur II, f. 50b, 51a f. Ant' Vilanova, lıb. com., f. 12b, 13a, 75a, 85b, 86a, 116b; Esteban Mir, f. 30a, 43a. Madurell-Garcia, nos. 236, 237, 246.

[316] Capmany, 1, pp. 252-53.

[317] Tur II, f. 5a f.

[318] Capmany, *l.c.* and 2.1, no. 376, p. 546.

[319] *Op.cit.* 1, p. 746, cf. pp. 813-14; 2.1, nos. 381-82, pp. 558-60.

[320] López de Meneses, "Les consulados," p. 120 f.

[321] Antonio de la Torre y del Cerro, *Documentos sobre relaciones internacionales de los Reyes Católicos* (Barcelona, 1949-1966) III, p. 145 f.

[322] Capmany, 1, p. 369; 2.1, no. 419, pp. 607-09.

[323] López de Meneses, *art. cit.*, p. 122.

and asked him to be helpful.[324] Three years later the council applied to the sultan, and to his interpreter Taghrībirdī, himself a Catalan, in the matter of the discord within the Catalan colony in Alexandria.[325] Further, a letter was written to Philip de Parets, consul of Naples and France, recommending the Catalan consul to him.[326]

The volume of the Levant trade of most other South European commercial powers in the late fifteenth century was smaller than before. Its striking feature was its irregularity. In some years its volume was probably sizable; in others it must have been insignificant. Characteristically, some European travellers who visited Alexandria in 1483 mention only the fondachi of the Venetians, the Genoese, and the Catalans, and the consuls of these trading nations.[327] The Jewish traveller Meshullam of Volterra, who came to Alexandria in 1481, and the German traveller Arnold von Harff, who was there in 1497, mention only these fondachi and consuls.[328] Even the Venetian consul in Alexandria in a letter written in 1498 describing conditions in the Egyptian port refers to these trading nations only.[329]

The commercial exchanges of southern France with the dominions of the Mamluks were particularly irregular in that period. The enterprise of Jacques Coeur came to a sudden standstill after his downfall, but it was not a complete failure. At least it came about that the role of the other trading nations as suppliers of France with the Oriental spices was redimensioned to a great extent. This was especially true for the Catalans.

In the 1450's the international trade of Montpellier began to develop once more. Bernard de Vux, the rich merchant of this town who had bought the galleys of Jacques Coeur, established their service on the line to the Levant. King Charles VII granted his support to the merchants who took up the trade with the Moslem Levant. He gave them letters of recommendation to the sultan of Cairo and to other Moslem rulers, and tried to smooth away conflicts applying to the sultan.[330] Another merchant of Montpellier, Lazarin d'Andrea, who had been patron of one of the galleys of Jacques Coeur, took a very active part in the renewal of the French trade with the Levant. According to a notarial act drawn up in Alexandria, he was patron of a French ship anchoring in 1455 in the Egyptian port.[331] But also merchants of Marseilles and Perpignan embarked on the galleys that

[324] Capmany, 2.1, no. 423, pp. 616-17.
[325] *Op.cit.*, 2.1, no. 427, p. 623.
[326] *Op.cit.* 2.1, no. 428, p. 624.
[327] Breydenbach, p. 203; F. Fabri, *Evagatorium* III, p. 163.
[328] *Travelogue*, p. 49; *Die Pilgerfahrt des Ritters Arnold von Harff*, p. 79.
[329] Marino Sanuto, *Diarii* II, col. 171.
[330] Reynaud, p. 354 f. Vallet de Viriville, *Histoire de Charles VII*, III, p. 440. When some merchants were detained in Alexandria, steps were made for their release; see *Ordonnances des rois de France* XIV, p. 395.
[331] Tur II, f. 21a ff. Cf. about him Del Treppo, p. 242 and Pigeonneau, *op.cit.*, p. 379.

went to the Moslem Levant and exported cloth and other articles.[332] Then political events caused a new setback. The renewal of direct trade between France and the Moslem Levant was of short duration. After the death of Alfonso V, a new war between the dynasties of Aragon and Anjou began, and French shipping to the Levant was again discontinued. However, during the war, which lasted until 1463, the commercial exchanges between Southern France and the Levant were not interrupted altogether. Venetian and Florentine ships regularly visited Marseilles, Bouc, and Aigues-Mortes and imported the Oriental commodities.

After the end of the war, a new era began in the Levant trade of France. King Louis XI pursued a very clearsighted economic policy. One of his aims was to exclude the foreign traders from the commercial exchanges between France and the Levant. In 1463 he forbade the import of spices into France other than through the ports of Languedoc and Roussillon and via Lyon, or by foreigners who were not residents of his kingdom, for sale at the fair of Lyon.[333] This decree must have been a hard blow for the Venetians and other foreign Levant traders, if the director of the company of the galleys could maintain in 1464 that their revenues from this import trade had been 200,000-300,000 gold coins a year.[334] The merchants of Marseilles were also hurt, and the king had to contend with strong opposition. There were vigorous protests, and the king had to soften the rigidity of the decree. However, he did not revoke it altogether and took other measures to foster French trade with the Levant. Upon his order two big galleys, the "Notre Dame-Saint Martin" and "Notre Dame-Saint Nicolas," were built, and from 1465 they began to call between southern France and the Moslem Levant. They departed from Aigues-Mortes, visited Marseilles, Nice, Savona, Pisa, Gaeta, Naples, Palermo, Messina, and Rhodes before going to the dominions of the Mamluks. One of them was to visit Alexandria, the other Beirut. In 1466 two other galleys were built.[335]

The services of "the galleys of France" at first functioned rather efficiently. In 1467 three of them visited Barcelona before going to the Levant.[336] They loaded merchandise in Marseilles in 1468,[337] and in 1469 the French asked the Venetian government for safe conducts (because of the

[332] Reynaud, p. 355 f., APO, Ant. Granatge 893, f. 34a. In the second half of the fifteenth century Collioure no more served as a port for trips to the Levant. According to the findings of Br. Lainé, in her unpublished thesis (submitted to the Ecole des chartes) *La vie économique et sociale à Collioure (1360-1490)*, p. 77, there were no more departures of ships from Collioure for the Levant after 1459.

[333] Gandilhon, *Politique économique de Louis XI* (Paris, 1941), p. 245.

[334] *Op.cit.*, p. 251.

[335] *Op.cit.*, p. 246 ff.

[336] Del Treppo, p. 634. Madurell-Garcia, no. 246.

[337] Reynaud, p. 359.

war with the Turks).[338] Notarial acts drawn up in Naples testify to their visit there in 1472 and the travelogue of German pilgrims to their trip to the Levant in the same year.[339] Then, in 1474, the galleys were requisitioned by King Louis XI for his campaign in the Roussillon, and the travels to the Levant were again suspended.[340] The service was re-established in 1476, and on this occasion the headquarters were transferred to Marseilles. Once more the king of France addressed a letter to the sultan of Cairo, asking him to receive the merchants coming to his dominions well. The galleys commuted regularly in the late 1470's between Marseilles and Alexandria. The king also took another step to increase the commercial exchanges of France with the Moslem Levant. He again softened his orders concerning the ports through which the import of spices would be allowed.[341] By a treaty with Venice in 1478, Louis XI made further concessions.[342]

His successor, Charles VIII, upon his accession to the throne in 1484, changed the economic policy altogether. Abolishing protectionism, he proclaimed liberty of trade; that is, he allowed everyone to import spices and foreign cloth. But a year later he had to renounce the unlimited freedom of trade and decreed that spices should be imported only via Aigues-Mortes.[343] In 1496 he again changed his policy and forbade the import of cloth and silken stuffs from Italy other than from Florence, and he laid an embargo on imports from Venice.[344] These changes of the French economic policy of course had their effect upon the commercial exchanges of the country with the Moslem Levant. In the 1480's and the 1490's the "galleys of France" functioned as before. The Jewish traveller Obadiah of Bertinoro embarked on one of them in 1488 in Palermo to travel to Egypt. A notarial act drawn up in Marseilles refers to their visit there in 1491.[345] But the limitation that spices could be imported only through certain ports induced the merchants of other towns to curb their activities in the Levant trade. This was probably true for the merchants of Marseilles, although they certainly never discontinued their exchanges with the Levant altogether. Some of them embarked on the "galleys of France" or had recourse to the services of Venetian galleys. Some enterprising traders of Marseilles, among them the Forbin family, even invested substantial sums in the trade with

[338] Senato Mar IX, f. 25a.

[339] Nic. della Morte 1471/2, sub 12 Aug. 1472. L. Conrady, *Vier rheinische Pilgerschriften des XIV, XV und XVI. Jahrhunderts* (Wiesbaden, 1882), p. 108.

[340] Gandilhon, *op.cit.*, p. 253.

[341] *Op.cit.*, p. 368 f.; Collier, p. 89 ff.

[342] Reynaud, p. 369 f.

[343] Collier, p. 90.

[344] Marino Sanuto, *Diarii* I, col. 139 f.

[345] *Travelogue*, p. 107; see also *Calendar of state papers and manuscripts relating to English affairs existing in Venice* I, ed. by Rawdon Brown (London, 1864), p. 156 f.: decision of the Venetian Senate of November 1485 to seize a galley of France in Alexandria; Collier, p. 91.

the Moslem Levant in this period. From 1475 the "Sainte Marie-La Blanche," a privately owned ship, sailed between Marseilles and the Mamluk dominions. In the last quarter of the fifteenth century even the merchants of provinces of France which were far from the coasts of the Tyrrhenian Sea showed great interest in the trade with the Levant, and French princes intervened on their behalf. In 1379 the duke of Bretagne applied to the Holy See with the request to grant his subjects the permission to carry on trade with the Moslems.[346]

The number of the French merchants spending long periods in the Levantine emporia in that period was very small. One can hardly speak of French colonies. The acts of an Italian notary, who worked in the mid-1450's in Alexandria, mention the names of a merchant of Marseilles, Zannono Aycard, and that of François Seza of Nice.[347] The merchants of Montpellier were more numerous than the Provençals. In the same acts, the names of Albert Savignac of Montpellier,[348] of Pierre Columbier,[349] and of Etienne Belon are mentioned.[350] Merchants of Montpellier carried on trade in Syria too. One of them was Jean Praduel, who went from Venice to Damascus in 1462.[351]

From the notarial acts drawn up in the middle of the fifteenth century one must conclude that there was neither a French (or Provençal) fondaco nor a French consul in Alexandria.[352] But in the 1470's the French again had a consul there,[353] and at the end of the century Philip de Parets was consul of Naples and France.[354]

The commodities the French then imported into the Moslem Levant were cloth,[355] including English fabrics,[356] and, as in earlier periods, olive oil, honey, almonds, and coral.[357] The volume of the trade carried on by means of the "galleys of France" cannot have been small. They were very big ships, and an account that has come down to us of the trip of the galley "Notre Dame-Saint Louis" in 1470 points to a very precious cargo.[358]

[346] Reynaud, p. 363 f., 365 f., 369. G. A. Lobineau, *Histoire de Bretagne* (Paris, 1707) I, p. 733; cf. Pardessus, *Collection* III, p. CXVI.

[347] Tur II, f. 31a ff., 32a, 35b. See also there f. 11a, 11b about other Frenchmen.

[348] Tur II, f. 33a f.

[349] Tur II, f. 24b f., 34a, 37a, 38b f., 39b ff. He was already in 1435 in Alexandria; see Tur V, f. 51a f., 52b.

[350] Tur II, f. 24b f.

[351] G. P., Sent. 138, f. 164 f.

[352] See especially Tur V, f. 52b. The supposition of Labib, p. 368, that the merchants of Marseilles had a fondaco in Alexandria until the end of the fifteenth century is not supported by any source.

[353] ASG, 2774 C, f. sub 1 Aug. 1476. Musso, "Nuovi doc.," p. 491, quotes a document referring to a French consul in Beirut in 1473.

[354] See above, note 326.

[355] Reynaud, p. 362; Collier, p. 91.

[356] Reynaud, p. 366.

[357] See *ibidem*.

[358] Pigeonneau, *op.cit.*, app. V.

The commercial activities of the Florentines in the Mamluk dominions were of the same stamp as those of the French—they were very irregular. The Florentines did not succeed in establishing a ship line to the Moslem Levant which would function regularly, although they made many efforts to this effect.

In the year 1456 two galleys went from Porto Pisano to Alexandria and returned in the same year.[359] Two years later, it was decided that the galleys visiting Tunis should be authorized to continue their trips to Alexandria. To foster trade with Egypt it was decided in 1460 that a conductor of a galley to Tunis could make a second trip to Tunis-Alexandria-Rhodes and back to Porto Pisano via Tunis, paying half the rent of the first trip.[360] In 1461 it was decided that every year two state galleys should be rented for the trade with Tunis and should be allowed to make a second trip on the same condition.[361] Four years later, in 1465, three galleys were sent to Syria. The captain of this convoy, Bernardo Corsi, was also authorized to visit Alexandria. It seems that this expedition had no sequel; that is, a galley line to the Mamluk dominions was not established. But in the year 1471 two galleys of the Medici were making preparations in Chios for the journey to Alexandria. Another galley, which was apparently leased by the Medici from King Ferrante of Naples and sailed between the ports of various Mediterranean countries, was the Ferrandina. In 1472 it visited Alexandria.[362]

The account of this sporadic shipping shows clearly that the major commercial interests of Florence lay elsewhere. In fact, the Florentines at that time were busy developing their trade with Turkey. They exported to Turkey both the products of their own woolen industry and English cloth[363] and purchased great quantities of silk there.[364] The Capponi[365] and the Medici themselves and other great Florentine firms invested considerable amounts in the trade with the formerly Byzantine territories.[366] Constantinople attracted the Florentines much more than did Alexandria, and, as long as the service of the state galleys was maintained, this capital was their favorite target.[367]

However, in the 1450's the Florentines carried on trade in Alexandria also. In the mid-1450's there were about half a dozen Florentines in the

[359] Mallet, p. 65.
[360] Amari, *Dipl. arabi*, app. no. 32.
[361] ASF, Provv. 151, f. 335a; cf. Mallet, p. 66.
[362] Mallet, pp. 70, 101, 102.
[363] ASF, 3a serie Strozziana, no. 1750, f. 17a.
[364] *Ibidem* no. 1746, f. 132a, 138a, 148b (a. 1461); 152a (a. 1462).
[365] ASF, Mercanzia 10831, Accommandite f. 27a (a. 1452).
[366] Same series 26b; see, further, 40b (a. 1459), 49a (a. 1462).
[367] See Mallet, p. 68 f.

Egyptian emporium.[368] In the 1450's and in the 1460's they were not absent from Syria either. In 1454, Cosma Moletti, who was an agent of some Florentine firms in Damascus, imported cloth.[369] On the other hand, the Florentines exported spices from Syria, e.g., Peruzzo Peruzzi and Bondazio Bernardo in 1461.[370] But at the end of the 1450's Florentine trade in the Mamluk dominions declined very much. A letter written in 1459 to Florence by Marioto Squarzalupi, Florentine consul in Alexandria, is outspoken. He says that Florentine trade in the Egyptian emporium is almost extinct. Florentine cloth had always had a great market in Egypt, but at the time he wrote his letter Catalan cloth, that of Majorca and Gerona, was preferred, and the *garbo* cloth was much less in demand. Consequently, he believed that it would be better to ship the cheaper kinds of Florentine cloth to Turkey. The fine Florentine cloth was still requested by the sultan's court and fetched higher prices than Venetian cloth. One could sell it for 40-50 ducats the piece or even 6-12 ducats the pic.[371] The documents of the 1470's and the 1480's seldom mention the names of Florentines who engaged in trade in Egypt or Syria. In the accounts of the Genoese consulate in Alexandria of the year 1475, one Florentine called Guglielmo Gruhi appears.[372] From the 1480's there have come down to us some letters of Alessandro Frescobaldi, a Florentine merchant, who stayed a long time in Alexandria.[373] But whereas the number of Florentine merchants in Egypt and Syria was insignificant, enterprising traders in Florence and Florentines living elsewhere still engaged in commercial exchanges with the Mamluk dominions. In 1475 Rainaldo Altoviti sent an agent of his, Louis Aymé of Marseilles, to Alexandria, where the latter died. Thereupon Altoviti sent Zanobi Carnesecchi to Egypt to recover his goods. The Florentine government gave him letters to the governor of Alexandria and to Marioto Squarzalupi, the Florentine consul in 1476.[374]

Although the Florentine colony in Alexandria was very small, it had its own fondaco in the middle of the fifteenth century. It is mentioned in several notarial acts of the 1450's.[375] But later the Florentines lost it and

[368] Tur II, f. 8a f., 14a, 14b f., 19b, 35b, 51a f., 52a f., 66a f.

[369] Crist. del Fiore V, f. 1a.

[370] *Ibid.* VI, f. [6b f.].

[371] ASF, Conv. soppressi, no. 78, vol. 322, c. 45. About the pic see Ashtor, "Exportation de textiles," p. 361.

[372] ASG, 2774 C, f. 34b.

[373] ASF, Conv. soppressi, no. 78, Badie familie 319, no. 137 (139), of 1 Nov. 1482; 133 (135) of 9 Febr. 1484; 138 (140) of 2 Febr. 1485; cf Heers. *Gênes*, p. 400 f. (where the date should be corrected).

[374] Amari, *Dipl. arabi*, app. no. 28. Altoviti lived in Marseilles, see Reynaud, p. 365 and see *op.cit.*, p. 366 f., about his endeavors to recover his goods.

[375] Tur II, f. 4a f., 5a f., 11a.

at the end of the 1480's had to apply to the sultan to grant them another.[376] The Florentine consulate in Alexandria was filled many years by Marioto Squarzalupi. He held the post at least from 1434 through the 1450's. In the year 1465 he was reinstated in his post,[377] but in the 1480's the Florentines no longer had a consulate in Alexandria, and their commercial activities must have been at a very low ebb.

The government of Florence did not acquiesce in the failure to develop the trade with the Mamluk dominions and time and again took diplomatic steps to obtain privileges from the sultan and to encourage the activities of the merchants. Bernardo de Corsi, who went as captain of a galley convoy to Syria and Egypt in 1465, was also appointed ambassador to the sultan. His task was to get the sultan to agree that the Florentine merchants should pay customs only for merchandise that remained in his dominions.[378] Then twenty years passed in which the diplomatic relations between Florence and the sultan were altogether suspended. But in the 1480's a new effort was made to conclude a commercial treaty to foster Florentine trade in Egypt and Syria.

Actually, it was the Mamluk sultan who took the initiative. Being very much interested in the intensification of commercial exchanges with the European trading nations and also in political relations in that period, he wrote a letter in 1484 to the Signoria, inviting her again to send her merchants to Egypt and to appoint a consul in Alexandria.[379] However, from the letter of the sultan it appears that the Florentines had contacted Ibn Maḥfūẓ when he visited the king of Naples in 1480 and in 1484. In 1485 there were again contacts between them and an envoy of the sultan in Naples, himself an Italian. A year later, the Florentine merchant Paolo de Colle was in Cairo, fulfilling a diplomatic mission.[380] But he died in Egypt before he succeeded in coming to a full agreement with the Mamluk government. The sultan, then at war with the Ottomans, and hoping to enlist help from the Christian powers, once more took the initiative. In November 1487 he sent his experienced diplomat, Muḥammad Ibn Maḥfūẓ, as ambassador to Florence. Ibn Maḥfūẓ brought to Lorenzo il Magnifico the draft of a treaty which had been elaborated in Cairo as a result of the negotiations of Paolo de Colle.[381] The Florentine government began to

[376] Wansbrough, "A Mamlūk commercial treaty," pp. 60, 69 (no. XXIX) (the doubts of W. as to whether the Florentines ever had a fondaco, see there, p. 73, are unfounded).

[377] Tur V, f. 2a f., 3a f., 5b ff., 13a f., 21a ff.; Tur II, f. 4a f., 14a, 49b, 51a ff. and see also above his letter of 1459; Amari, *Diplomi arabi*, app. no. 22.

[378] Amari, *Dipl. arabi*, app. no. 23.

[379] *Op.cit.*, p. 46.

[380] See Wansbrough, "A Mamlūk commercial treaty," p. 42; Fr. Babinger, *Spätmittelalterliche fränkische Briefschafter aus dem grossherrlichen Sera zu Stambul* (Munich, 1963), p. 42 ff.

[381] Wansbrough, *art. cit.*, pp. 42, 50; Amari, *Dipl. arabi*, ser II, no. 45.

examine the draft, and a committee of commercial experts drafted propositions for additions and corrections to the proposed treaty,[382] while the Florentine consul in Pera was ordered to allay the suspicion of the Ottoman sultan that the diplomatic contacts with the Mamluks were aimed against him.[383]

In the summer of 1488 a Florentine embassy departed for Cairo. The ambassador, Luigi della Stufa, with whom Ibn Maḥfūẓ returned to Cairo, took the proposed additions with him.[384] In October 1489 a treaty was finally concluded.[385] In addition to many clauses found in similar treaties, it contained the promise that the Mamluk officials would not cause delay of Florentine activities by postponing the levying of customs, and there was the undertaking that the Moslem authorities would assist the Florentines if they should be attacked by other Europeans; that is, upon coming to a Mamluk port, they could apply to the Mamluk authorities for reprisals against European trading nations. On the other hand, under the new treaty the Florentines had to sell molasses, which they imported into Egypt, exclusively to the sultan, without paying customs. This clause sheds light on the industrial decay of Egypt. Even the sultan's court had to be supplied with molasses of South European sugar factories! For all other goods imported the Florentines had to pay a 14 percent custom under the treaty, much more than the Venetians. Many requests contained in the draft of propositions and corrections were rejected altogether. The Florentines had claimed the right to make their transactions on board their ships and to carry on spice trade before the auctions of the pepper. In the Florentine draft there were various clauses that had been copied from the treaties between Venice and the sultan. Even they were dropped. The Florentines had asked that they should not be made responsible for the misdeeds of corsairs and that Moslem corsairs who attacked Florentine ships should be punished by the Mamluks. Finally, they had wished to have a consul in Damascus.

Before that treaty was concluded, the Florentine trade in Egypt must have had a very small volume. For in November 1489 Luigi della Stufa wrote to Lorenzo il Magnifico, lamenting his situation in Cairo. He said that he remained without money and that there was no one to whom he

[382] Amari, *Dipl. arabi*, ser. II, no. 44.

[383] Müller, *Documenti*, no. 203.

[384] His instructions Amari, *op.cit.*, ser. II, no. 46; the draft proposed by him to the sultan no. 47; the credentials *Epist. Bart. Scalae*, in A. M. Bandini, *Collectio veterum aliquot monumentorum* (Arezzo, 1752), p. 12 f.

[385] An Italian text of the treaty has been published by Pagnini, *Della decima* II, p. 213 ff. and Amari, *op.cit.*, serie II, no. 48; the Arabic original by Wansbrough, *art. cit.*, p. 52 ff. with English translation and notes). See, further, the sultan's letter to Lorenzo il Magnifico informing him of the conclusion of the treaty Amari, *op.cit.*, ser. I, no. 39.

could apply. So it seems that there were no Florentines in Egypt. Even the treaty apparently did not bring about an increase in the trade between Florence and the Mamluk dominions. It seems that the Florentine consulate in Alexandria was not filled. In 1496 the Mamluk sultan again took the initiative in relations with Florence, sending Ibn Maḥfūẓ to Florence with a letter to the Signoria, inviting her to appoint a consul in Alexandria.[386] The negotiations resulted in the conclusion of a new treaty in the same year, 1496. This treaty was in fact an old one; it was almost a copy of that concluded between Venice and the sultan in 1442.[387] Among the clauses not taken away from that treaty, there is one promising the Florentines a fondaco in Alexandria, if a consul were appointed. Another clause refers to the right of the Florentines to sell their merchandise outside Alexandria. A year later, in 1497, another treaty was concluded.[388] Even this one is copied from the treaty between Venice and the Mamluk sultan. The difference between it and that concluded a year before is the addition of some clauses concerning the trade in Syria. Most of these clauses, e.g., that concerning the right to appoint a consul in Jerusalem, were rather anachronistic in a Florentine-Mamluk treaty of 1497. But these clauses did not have to be tested by their application by the Mamluk officials, because Florentine trade in Syria did not develop. The new treaty also contained the concession that Florentines would not be made responsible for the misdeeds of corsairs. Since this clause is styled in a very general way, it would have applied to Florentine corsairs too.

That all these embassies and treaties had so little success, insofar as the trade between Florence and the Mamluk dominions did not increase in volume, was undoubtedly the effect of the needs of the Florentine economy. The Florentines exported great quantities of fine and cheap cloth and silken stuffs in Turkey, much of it bartered against silk.[389] They could not offer great quantities of copper in the Near East, as did the Venetians, but exported, in addition to cloth and silken stuffs, olive oil, hazelnuts, and soap purchased in various regions. It would be exaggerated to say that in fact they were not interested in the purchase of spices. The data concerning the relatively small shipments of spices imported via Pisa probably do not refer to all that arrived in Florence from the Near East. Anyhow, the volume of direct trade between Florence and the Mamluk dominions remained small. The cargoes of the galleys that came back from Syria and Egypt in 1466 may have been worth as little as 18,000-20,000 ducats.[390]

[386] Amari, *op.cit.*, ser. I, no. 41; ASF, MaP, f. 41, no. 384.

[387] Amari, *op.cit.*, ser. I, no. 40.

[388] The text has been published by Wansbrough, "Venice and Florence in the Mamlūk commercial treaties," p. 497 ff. (with an English translation and notes).

[389] See above and cf. Mallet, p. 122.

[390] See Wansbrough, "A commercial treaty," p. 62; and see the inventory Mallet, p. 118.

Naples was one of the great centers of international trade in the Mediterranean in the second half of the fifteenth century, and there were manifold exchanges between the kingdom of Naples and the Moslem countries. But, since the king of Naples pursued a free trade policy, a great share of these exchanges was in the hands of foreigners. King Ferrante encouraged the activities of other trading nations in his kingdom. The Venetians were exempted from customs altogether.[391] In 1465 King Ferrante granted liberty of trade to the Ragusans,[392] and in 1481 he granted them customs exemptions like those enjoyed by the Venetians.[393] In fact the king had already abolished all export customs in 1471.[394] Although this policy was not always consistent and all the decrees concerning the abolishment of customs were not implemented, they had far-reaching consequences for the foreign trade of the kingdom.

The capital of the kingdom, where merchants of many countries engaged in trade, became a great center for exchange of cloth. Notarial acts drawn up in Naples in the 1460's and the 1470's mirror the lively trade of cloth manufactured in various countries. Much Florentine cloth, both fine cloth[395] and *panni di garbo*,[396] was sold. A notarial act refers to the sale by a Florentine merchant of cloth worth 5,000 ducats to the Court.[397] Flemish cloth,[398] Catalan cloth of Majorca,[399] Perpignan,[400] and Valencia[401] were sold. There was a great supply of cheap French cloth, mainly fabrics of Languedoc, which apparently had a good market,[402] as well as fabrics of Montivilliers.[403] English cloth was also marketed in Naples. Genoese merchants sold cheap kersey.[404] The Florentines also sold their silk fabrics[405] and velvets.[406] They engaged in banking too, especially the Strozzi and Medici.[407] In addition to Naples, the town of Salerno, where every year a

[391] *Il Codice Chigi*, ed. Jole Mazzoleni (Naples, 1965), no. 161.

[392] *Regesta della Cancelleria aragonese di Napoli*, ed. J. Mazzoleni (Naples, 1951), no. 175.

[393] *Op.cit.*, no. 183.

[394] L. Bianchini, *Storia delle finanze del Regno delle due Sicilie*, ed. L. de Rosa (Naples, 1971), p. 178f.

[395] Nic. della Morte 1471/2 sub 5 Oct. 1471, 29 March 1472.

[396] Petr. Pisani IV, f. 45a f., 129a f., 134b; Nic. della Morte 1471/2 sub 12 Nov. 1471.

[397] Nic. della Morte *ibid.* sub 21 Oct. 1473 and see there another sizable transaction sub 4 Nov. 1473.

[398] *Ibid.* sub 16 Dec. 1474.

[399] Petr. Pisani IV, f. 172b; Nic. della Morte 1471/2 sub 6 Oct. 1471.

[400] Petr. Pisani IV, f. 81b; Nic. della Morte 1471/2 sub 22 Apr. 1474.

[401] Nic. della Morte *ibid.* sub 1 Oct. 1471.

[402] Petr. Pisani IV, f. 27a, 27b f., 29a, 33b, 43a, 43b, 44b, f., 46a, 55a, 77b, 81a, 89b, 96a f., 98a, 102b, 115b, 135b, 136b, 146.

[403] Petr. Pisani IV, f. 84a.

[404] *Ibid.*, f. 116b, 174a.

[405] *Ibid.*, f. 11a f., 44a f.

[406] Nic. della Morte 1471/2 sub 25 Oct. 1473.

[407] Petr. Pisani IV, f. 17a, Nic. della Morte 1471/2 sub 7 Oct. 1472, 24 Jan. 1474.

fair was held, served as a great cloth market.[408] Much of the cloth sold in Naples and Salerno was certainly shipped to the eastern Mediterranean.

Foreign merchants had the greatest share in the trade between Naples and the Levant, and the policy of King Ferrante especially fostered their activities. In the middle of the fifteenth century the Catalans were chief among the foreign traders of Naples, but the Genoese were the main suppliers of spices.[409] The "galleys of France" also played a great role in the commercial exchanges between Naples and the dominions of the Mamluks. Neapolitans and other merchants shipped their goods to Egypt and Syria on them. From a notarial act, one learns that a merchant of Montpellier sold English and Flemish cloth in Naples in 1472 to another merchant who departed on the "galleys of France."[410] But the subjects of the king of Naples themselves also engaged in trade with the Moslem Levant and in shipping to its major ports.

Neapolitan ships carried heavy cargoes of hazelnuts to Alexandria. A German traveller who visited Alexandria in 1483 mentions a ship coming from Naples with a cargo of hazelnuts worth 10,000 ducats.[411] A document of 1484 refers to the return to Naples of a ship of Jacme Calataiud, a counsellor of the king. It came from Alexandria, and Genoese merchants had loaded spices and alkali on it to be sent to Genoa.[412] The king himself carried on trade with the Levant and exported various articles there on his own ships. In the year 1454 the big galley of Pere Pujades, a royal ship, went to Alexandria. Then in the 1470's another ship of the king, San Michele, commuted between Naples and the Levant. In 1477 it carried a shipment of cloth to Egypt and two years later suffered shipwreck in the port of Alexandria.[413] Also, private merchants engaged in the import of spices from the Levant. According to a Merchants' Guide of the end of the fifteenth century, great quantities of pepper, cinnamon, ginger, and other spices, bought in Egypt, were offered at the fairs held twice a year in Lanciano in the Abruzzi.[414]

In the 1470's and the 1480's a great merchant of Naples, who had major

[408] The acts drawn up by the Neapolitan notary Petruccio Pisani at the fair of Salerno in 1478 have been published by A. Silvestri, *Il commercio di Salerno nella seconda metà del Quattrocento* (Salerno, 1952), p. 141 ff., and cf. the analysis by A. Sapori, "Una fiera in Italia alla fine del Quattrocento," in his *Studi* I, p. 443 ff. (the analysis in the review of Silvestri's book by H. Ammann in *VSWG* 42 (1955), p. 266 ff., should accordingly be corrected).

[409] Del Treppo, p. 236, 241 f.

[410] Nic. della Morte 1471/2 sub 12 May 1472.

[411] Breydenbach, p. 204; cf. F. Fabri, *Evagatorium* III, p. 153.

[412] Silvestri, *op.cit.*, p. 93.

[413] Melis, *Origini*, p. 18 f.; I. Schiappoli, "La marina degli Aragonesi di Napoli," *Arch. Stor. Prov. Nap.*, N. S. 27 (1941), p. 30.

[414] Pasi, f. 43b; see also f. 47a about the trade between Apulia and Damietta. See, further, Uzzano, p. 97, comparison of the weights used in Naples and in Damietta for lead.

enterprises in several sectors of industry and trade, carried on trade with Egypt, using his own numerous ships. The rather meteoric appearance of Francesco Coppola, Conte di Sarno, can only be compared to that of Jacques Coeur, and like the great French merchant he was a true financial genius.

From 1470 Coppola was farmer of the customs in Naples, then farmer of the taxes of a province. He was also a great industrialist and owned cloth and silk factories and a paper mill, plus, together with his father, a soap plant. He engaged in the mining of silver and lead, he exploited alum deposits and had coral fisheries in Tunisia.[415] But first of all he was a great merchant. At first he had, together with his father, supplied the king with wheat, but the Coppolas also exported wheat in company with the king to Catalonia.[416] Later Coppola, in company with the king, established a monopoly of the kingdom's foreign trade: it was forbidden to import or to export any merchandise without offering it first to him.[417] Later the king withdrew from the company, and Coppola enjoyed the rights alone. He also bought many ships.[418] During the War of Ferrara in 1482-1483 he could offer the king the loan of 20 galleys, 15 big round ships, and 11 others.[419]

The trade with the Levant was one of the many activities of this great merchant. A contemporary poet could write:[420]

> Equora . . . tuis sulcant iam navibus omnes
> Mercibus atque tuis totius se sublimet orbis
> Europam atque Africam Asiamque tue petiere triremes

His galleys visited Alexandria[421] and carried heavy loads of spices from there. So he could sell spices like pepper to the Genoese, and after his downfall and execution in 1487 a shipment of cinnamon and cloves belonging to his brother, obviously one of his partners, was confiscated in Naples.[422]

Among the commodities exported from the kingdom of Naples, foods held the first place. King Ferrante himself shipped olive oil to Egypt.[423]

[415] I. Schiappoli, "Il conte di Sarno," *Arch. Stor. Prov. Nap.*, N. S. 22 (1936), p. 24, 27 ff., 35f., 36 f., 74, 75, 84 ff.

[416] *Art. cit.*, p. 31 ff.

[417] C. Porzio, *La congiura dei baroni del regno di Napoli contro il re Ferdinando Primo e gli altri scritti*, ed. E. Pontieri (Naples, 1958), p. 21 (the first edition is of 1565).

[418] Tristano Caracciolo, *Opuscula historica: De varietate fortunae*, R. I. S. XXII (Milan, 1725), col. 87.

[419] *Cronaca di Napoli di Notar Giacomo* (Naples, 1845), p. 150.

[420] G. de Blasiis, "Un Poema inedito in lode del Conte di Sarno," *Arch. Stor. Prov. Nap.* VIII (1885), p. 756.

[421] Silvestri, *Il commercio di Salerno*, p. 29; about his trade in Alexandria see also *Regis Ferdinandi Primi instructionum liber*, ed. L. Volpicella (Naples, 1916), p. 57.

[422] Schiappoli, "Il conte di Sarno," pp. 112, 113.

[423] Schiappoli, "La marina degli Aragonesi di Napoli," p. 30.

Hazelnuts too were an important article of export,[424] and Venetian merchants were granted permission to export grains from Bari to Alexandria.[425] The soap of Gaeta always had a good market in Egypt, as shown by price lists and other documents.[426]

Despite the manifold commercial exchanges between the kingdom of Naples and the Moslem Levant in the second half of the fifteenth century, the colony of the merchants of Naples in Egypt was very small. Of course some merchants of Naples and Gaeta always lived in Alexandria. The names of two men of Gaeta appear as those of witnesses on a notarial act drawn up in Alexandria in 1455.[427] From another act, one learns that the Gaetan Antonio Tarola, who had carried on trade in Alexandria in 1451, was there again in 1455.[428] Some Neapolitans engaged also in trade in Syria. The firm Benedetto Salutati & Cie, for instance, conducted business in Tripoli in the 1470's.[429]

But, for a long time, the Neapolitans had neither a fondaco nor a consul in Alexandria. In the year 1455 a man of Castellamare complained in Alexandria that he had no consul to protect him.[430]

However, there were diplomatic contacts between the court of Naples and the sultan, and the Aragonese kings did intervene on behalf of her subjects who traded with the Mamluk dominions. The letter the Mamluk sultan addressed in 1484 to Lorenzo il Magnifico refers to a visit of his ambassador Ibn Maḥfūẓ to Naples.[431] It is however very probable that he was referring to a mission fulfilled some years before.[432] In the 1480's and the 1490's, there was again a Neapolitan consul in Alexandria. In 1480, a notary of Gaeta, Francesco Gaietano was appointed Neapolitan consul in Alexandria. But when Bartomeu de Parets, a veteran Levant trader and subject of the king, died in Alexandria, the consul did not succeed in obtaining his bequest. So the king of Naples sent an embassy on a special galley to Egypt to collect the bequest, and surely the king used the occasion to enhance the position of the Neapolitans in the Mamluk dominions. To be sure, Bartomeu de Parets, who had carried on business in the 1450's in

[424] See the letter of Marioto Squarzalupi quoted above, note 371.

[425] *Fonti aragonesi, a cura degli archivisti napolitani* VI (Naples, 1968), p. 70 f. In that year there was indeed a great scarcity in Egypt, see my "Quelques problèmes," p. 210; *Histoire des prix et des salaires*, p. 292.

[426] See "Quelques problèmes," p. 229, and the letter of Marioto Squarzalupi.

[427] Tur II, f. 34a, 34b.

[428] *Ibid.*, f. 20a.

[429] G. P., Ter. XI, f. 29b.

[430] Tur II, f. 54b.

[431] See above, note 379.

[432] See above note 148. When the Mamluk embassy visited Naples in 1479-1480, it was Francesco Coppola who negotiated with it.

Alexandria and Rhodes[433] and in the late 1470's again in Rhodes,[434] was apparently a very rich man, and a son of his was a counsellor of the king. So the desire to recover his goods was sincere, but an epidemic broke out on the ship carrying the embassy to Egypt, one of the ambassadors died, and the ship turned back. Then King Ferrante sent Luis Soler as ambassador to Egypt in 1492, and he instructed him to claim the bequest in virtue of agreements that had been made in the past between the king of Naples and the sultan.[435] Luis Soler apparently remained in Alexandria as consul, for in 1495 the Council of Barcelona asked him to recommend a Catalan ship.[436] Then, in 1498, Philip de Parets was consul of Naples in Alexandria.[437]

As in earlier periods, Sicily served the South European trading nations as a great exchange and supplied them with its own products. Since its major ports were regularly visited by their merchants, the Sicilian commercial fleet played a relatively small role in the trade with the Levant.

In preceding periods, the Catalans held the first place in these exchanges, but in the 1460's, during the civil war in Catalonia, their share in Sicily's Levant trade decreased. Just at that time Venice had established the *trafego* line, and her galleys visited Syracuse regularly before going to Tunis and Alexandria. Sicilian merchants embarked on them and travelled to Alexandria, where they bought spices.[438] Others shipped their merchandise on the Venetian galleys to the Moslem ports. In 1486 some Jewish traders of Syracuse founded a company for the export of coral (also worked coral, such as paternosters), raw silk, cheese, tinsel, verdigris, and other products, to be shipped on the Venetian *trafego* galleys.[439] Palermo and Messina were stops of the "galleys of France," and merchants of Palermo and other towns of Sicily embarked on them to travel to the Levant. But of course Venetian and Genoese ships also visited Palermo and Messina on their way to Alexandria and loaded merchandise of Sicilian merchants. A notarial act drawn up in Palermo in 1458 refers to the charter of a Venetian ship for the

[433] Forcellini, *Strane peripezie*, p. 88 f. Tur II, f. 20b, 30a, 34a, 38b f., 39a, 41a, 46a f.; Del Treppo, p. 80 note 166.

[434] Reynaud, p. 375.

[435] Fr. Trinchera, *Codice aragonese* II, part 1 (Naples, 1868), no. 77 (p. 68 f.), 123 (p. 103 f.).

[436] Capmany 2.1, no. 423, pp. 616-17; cf. above.

[437] Capmany 2.1, no. 428, p. 627, where one reads that he was himself a native of Barcelona. Later, in 1510-1512, he was also consul of the Catalans and even of the French in Alexandria. See Fr. Lucchetta "L'affare Zen," *Studi Veneziani*, p. 163; Jean Thenaud, *Le voyage d'Outremer*, p. XLV, 4, 57 (where one reads that he spoke Arabic), and cf. Heyd II, p. 539. Capmany, no. 430; Pedro Martyr d'Anghiera, *Legatio Babylonica* (printed with his *De rebus oceanicis & orbis novo decades*) (Basle, 1533), f. 80b, 81b; G. Salles, "Les origines des premiers consulats de la nation française a l'étranger," *Revue d'histoire diplomatique* IX (1895), p. 551 ff.

[438] Vallone, Nic. 10229, f. 300a f. (a. 1482).

[439] Piduni, Ant. 10245, f. 92a ff. Another product exported by them was *cuculum*, an Italian game resembling bowls; see Sella, *Gloss. Lat. -ital., Stato della Chiesa-Veneto* (Città del Vaticano, 1944), p. 192. See also Vallone 10228, f. 170a f.; the patron of a Venetian galley acknowledges the payment of freight charges by a Jew of Syracuse.

transport of a great quantity of molasses to Alexandria, and another, of 1460, apparently to a Genoese ship, which had sailed from Palermo and Messina to the Egyptian port with merchandise loaded in Sicily. Venetian and Genoese merchants who travelled on these ships received commendas for trade with the Moslem Levant, for instance a Genoese in Messina in 1466.[440] But Sicilian ships also sailed between the island and the Levantine coasts; they visited Alexandria in the 1470's,[441] and connected some ports of the Italian mainland with the Moslem Levant. In the year 1470, a Sicilian ship, "Santa Maria-Santo Cristoforo-San Niccolò," sailed from Venice to Ancona and on to Syria, carrying grains.[442]

The commercial exchanges between Sicily and Egypt were manifold, with Sicily exporting much more to the dominions of the Mamluks than it imported from them. A notarial act of 1453 refers to the payment made by the agent of a merchant of Alexandria to Benedictus Ayem, a Jew of Palermo.[443] In addition to the molasses and other Sicilian products marketed in the Levant, cloth of various countries was shipped to the Near East. Many notarial acts drawn up in the second half of the fifteenth century in the major towns of Sicily leave no doubt of the fact that Catalan cloth lost ground and was replaced by French and English fabrics.[444] Also, Flemish cloth was still marketed in the towns of Sicily.[445] The documents that have come down to us from the Sicilian notaries of that period testify to a flourishing iron trade, and it is not unlikely that a considerable part of it was shipped to the Moslem Levant, where this metal was altogether lacking.[446]

Ancona's trade with the Levant was still encumbered by the frequent conflicts with the Serenissima. Time and again the mighty republic granted her citizens the right of reprisal against the Anconitans, and orders were given to sequester Anconitan goods wherever possible. Sometimes these orders were the sequel of conflicts in the Adriatic or the Ionian Sea; sometimes, as in 1461, they resulted from conflicts in Egypt. The intervention of the pope, the protector of Ancona, was not always successful.[447] The

[440] *Travelogue of Obadiah of Bertinoro*, p. 108. Giacomo Comito 850 sub 5 Sept. 1458, 18 Febr. 1460 854 sub 9 Oct. 1466.

[441] Musso, "Nuovi doc.," p. 461.

[442] Ang. Domenico VIII, f. 294b ff.

[443] Aprea, Ant. 811, f. 174b.

[444] French cloth: ASPal, Secrezia, Atti 553, f. 75a (a. 1471), 72a (imported by a merchant of Montpellier); English cloth: Giacomo Comito 849, sub 23 May 1454: Matteo Fallera 1749, f. 152b ff. (a. 1480); ASPal, Secrezia, Atti 555, sub 7 Febr. 1477; ASMess, Pagliarino, Matteo VIa, f. 66b, 79b, 93b (a. 1468).

[445] Randisi, Giac., 1152, f. 35b (a. 1460); cloth of Wervicq: Giacomo Comito 849, sub 27 Nov. 1454; ASMess Pagliarino, Matteo VIa, f. 80a, 81b (a. 1468).

[446] Iron of Genoa: Giacomo Comito 849, sub 12 June 1454; Randisi, Giac., 1150, fasc. II, f. 81b (a. 1453), III, f. 10a, 11b (a. 1453); of Venice, *ibid.*, III, f. 8a 1152, f. 64b (a. 1460); of Pisa (that means Elba!) *ibid.*, 1150, II, f. 23b (a. 1452), 81b IV, f. 95b (1453); of Spain *ibid.*, 1150, fasc. II, f. 88b (a. 1452).

[447] Secreta 20, f. 75a (a. 1455), 157a f. (a. 1458); Senato Mar VII, f. 42a.

Anconitans, on the other hand, were often compelled to ask help from Venice, even against the pope.[448] Although these requests were not always granted, Venice considered the small republic as a vassal state and behaved toward it accordingly.[449] During the long war between Venice and the Ottomans in 1463-1479, relations between the Serenissima and Ancona were particularly strained. The Venetians of course suspected the Anconitans of supplying provisions and war material to the Turks. In 1467 the government of Venice gave orders to the war fleet to capture Anconitan ships sailing to the Straits or therein, and some Anconitan ships were indeed taken and brought to Venice. Among them there were the ships of Pietro Dionisio and Andrea d'Agli which were returning from Constantinople. When in 1468 an Anconitan embassy asked that the sequestered goods be returned and that the Serenissima allow Anconitan shipping in the Greek waters, the request was turned down.[450] The sequestered goods were obviously timber, iron foundry goods, weapons, and copper, which the Anconitans had bought in Segna and Fiume. In 1471 the same requests were again turned down. The Anconitans turned to the pope, but it was only in 1472 that the Serenissima agreed to the restitution of part of the sequestered goods, declaring once more that Anconitan shipping to Turkey would not be permitted. The intervention of the papal legate, who claimed that the Venetians made the sea-borne trade of Ancona altogether impossible, did not influence the attitude of the Serenissima.[451] In 1473 and in 1483 there were new conflicts.[452] Actually, the rigidity of the Venetians was not unfounded; in fact, the Anconitans engaged in the supply of iron and weapons to the Turks, and even Venetians used the port of Ancona for this purpose.[453]

Anconitan trade with Turkey increased in the second half of the fifteenth century. In addition to the trade of war material, the role of Ancona as a major port for the export of Florentine cloth to Turkey was an important reason for this upswing. Florentine merchants lived in Ancona and engaged in many businesses there. They exported to Albania, Greece, and Turkey their own cloth and that of Bergamo, l'Aquila, Perpignan, and others.[454]

[448] Secreta 21, f. 26b f.

[449] *Libr. Com.* V, lib. 15, nos. 142, 151 (a. 1468), lib. 16, no. 157 (a. 1480).

[450] Secreta 23, f. 33a, 88b, 92a, 130a; see also *ibid.* f. 84b; Senato Mar VIII, f. 139b.

[451] Secreta 25, f. 58a ff., 65a ff., 136a ff., 137b ff., 138b f. 26, f. 26a, 26b f.; the Venetian government repeated the statement of its policy concerning shipping to the Straits in 1475; see Secreta 27, f. 34a.

[452] Secreta 26, f. 45a ff., 171a.

[453] See Ph. Braunstein, "Le marché de fer a Venise au XVe siècle," *Studi Veneziani* VIII (1966), pp. 275, 289.

[454] Ang. di Domenico I, f. 27a (a. 1458) II, f. 200a, 235b f. Ciriaco Thome III, 1475, f. 4b f.; Giac. Alberici IV, f. 102a f. (a. 1487). About the Florentines who engaged in Anconitan

The Genoese and Catalans too carried on trade in Ancona, and the latter had a consulate there.[455]

Whereas Ancona's trade with Turkey increased in the second half of the fifteenth century, the volume of its commercial exchanges with the Mamluk dominions was the same as in the first half. In the 1450's and the 1460's Anconitan shipping to Egypt and Syria declined. From 1469 it increased again. In that year, and in 1470, it could even be called intense, as, owing to the dearth of grains in these countries, great shipments of grain could be marketed there. In the years 1481-1495 (for which we have copious information) more than one ship rarely went from Ancona to Egypt or Syria, whereas often two or three or even more sailed to Turkey. However, ships of various other trading nations sailed on the lines connecting Ancona with the coasts of the Moslem Levant.[456] Genoese ships often anchored in Ancona,[457] and Ragusan ships frequently visited Ancona before sailing to the Levant or to Turkey, just as Anconitan ships visited Ragusa on their trips to the Near East.[458] The Anconitan ships going to Syria visited not only Beirut, but also Tripoli and Latakia,[459] obviously to load cotton and alkali there. In Ancona there was a lively trade of these two commodities, which were the raw materials for the fustian and soap industries.[460]

The articles that the Anconitans exported in that period into the dominions of the Mamluks were the same as in the preceding period. They shipped soap,[461] paper of Fabriano,[462] and various textiles such as fustian,[463] Florentine garbo cloth,[464] and brocades.[465] Since a cloth industry began to develop in Ancona in that period, it may be that its products too were exported

maritime trade, see also Ant. Giov. Giac. 16, f. 111a f., 112a f., 30, f. 60a f., 64a, 74b f., 31, f. 142a f. see also about the activities of the agents of the Medici and Strozzi in Ancona Ant. Giov. Giac. I (73), f. 36a f. (a. 1461). P. Earle, "The commercial development of Ancona (1479-1551)," *Ec. Hist. Rev.*, 2 series, 22 (1969), p. 34.

455 See Melchior Bernabe V, f. 116b (a. 1484); A. Polverari, "Il consolato dei Catalani in Ancona verso la fine del Quattrocento," *Quaderni storici delle Marche* IV (1967), p. 131 ff.

456 See Ant. Giov. Giac. 15, f. 92a (a. 1466): a Venetian ship sails from Ancona to Beirut.

457 Ang. di Domenico I, f. 2a 2b f. II, f. 235b f. X, f. 46b f. Ant. Giov. Giac. III, part 1, f. 277b f.; Giac. Alberici V, f. 125b f. VI, f. 18b; a Catalan ship: Melchior Bernabe V, f. 116b.

458 See Ant. Giov. Giac. 74 (1960), f. 1a ff. 30, f. 360a, 360b (a. 1483).

459 Ang. di Damenico VIII, f. 226b f.; Ant. Giov. Giac. 74 (1460), f. 1a.

460 Cotton trade: Ang. di Domenico I, f. 154a f. (a. 1458) XII, f. 29b; Ant. Giov. Giac. 74, f. 83a 15, f. 192b (a. 1466); Nic. Cressi VII, f. 149b, 150a; a part of this cotton came from Turkey, see Ang. di Domenico VIII, f. 162a; IX, f. 57a X, f. 83b f.; cf. my "Il commercio levantino di Ancona," p. 245.

461 Ant. Giov. Giac. 74, f. 1a f. (a. 1460, a great quantity); on the export of soap to Greece and Turkey, see Ang. di Domenico X, f. 67b XII, f. 132a f.

462 Ang. di Domenico VIII, f. 54b.

463 Melchior Bernabe VI, f. 129a.

464 Ant. Giov. Giac. 28, f. 134a f., and see there f. 122a f., 133a about the export of other cloth.

465 Ant. Giov. Giac. III, part 1, f. 178b f.

Table LVIII Anconitan shipping to the Levant[a], 1453 - 1493

a)

date	Alexandria	Syria	Alexandria and Syria	Romania	Syria/Romania	"Levant"
1453	1	-	1	1	-	-
1454	-	-	-	-	-	-
1455	-	-	-	-	1	-
1456	-	-	-	-	-	-
1457	1	-	-	1	-	-
1458	-	-	-	-	-	-
1459	-	1	-	1	-	-
1460	-	-	-	-	-	-
1461	-	-	-	2	-	-
1462	-	-	-	1	-	-
1463	-	-	-	-	-	-
1464	-	-	-	-	1	-
1465	-	-	-	3	-	-
1466	1	1	-	2	-	-
1467	-	-	-	4	-	-
1468	-	-	-	2	-	-
1469	-	1	2	5	3	-
1470	1	5	-	2	-	-
1471	-	1	-	2	-	-
1472	-	1	-	1	-	-
1473	-	-	-	3	-	-
1474	-	-	-	4	-	-
1475	-	-	-	2	-	-
	1476 - 1477	—				
1478	-	-	-	2	-	-
1479	2	-	-	1	-	-
1480	1	-	-	-	-	-
1481	1	1	-	-	-	-
1482	1	-	-	3	-	-
1483	-	1	-	2	-	-

to the Levant.[466] Even wine was shipped there.[467] The cargo of the Anconitan ships returning from Egypt consisted of pepper[468] and other spices, whereas those coming from Syria carried cotton[469] and alkali.[470]

According to notarial acts and other documents, there were always some

[466] Ang. di Domenico X, f. 78a f. (a. 1471). But probably the cheap cloth which the Anconitans offered in the Levant was that produced in the small towns of its hinterland.

[467] Melchior Bernabe II, f. 124b.

[468] ASG, 2774 C, f. 29b, 31a.

[469] Ang. di Domenico XI, f. 209a.

[470] *Ibidem* and cf. my "Il commercio levantino di Ancona," p. 245.

Table LVIII (continued)

date	Alexandria	Syria	Alexandria and Syria	Romania	Syria/Romania	"Levant"
1484	-	-	-	1	-	-
1485	-	1	-	2	-	-
1486	-	-	-	3	-	-
1487	-	-	-	5	-	1
1488	-	-	-	3	-	-
1489	-	2	-	6	-	-
1490	1	-	-	-	-	-
1491	-	1	-	3	-	-
1492	-	-	-	3	-	-
1493	-	-	-	2	-	-
1497	-	-	-	1	-	-

a) This table contains data about Anconitan ships only.

b) Decennial total of Anconitan Levant shipping:

	Egypt	Syria	both	Romania	Levant	total
1453 - 1460	2	1	1	3	-	7
1461 - 1470	2	7	2	21	4	36
1471 - 1480	3	2	-	15	-	20
1481 - 1490	3	5	-	26	1	35
1491 - 1498	1	1	-	9	-	11

Anconitan merchants in Alexandria. In a Merchants' Guide of the late fifteenth century, one finds an account of the trade carried on by the Anconitans in Damietta. According to this account, the Anconitans exported spices and sugar from Damietta and imported soap and olive oil.[471] Some Anconitans carried on trade in Syria, and a notarial act drawn up in Damascus in 1461 refers indeed to the activities of the Anconitan merchant Agapiro Pagliaresi.[472] But the point of support of Anconitan trade in the Levant was Alexandria. German pilgrims, who returned from Palestine in 1483 via Alexandria and who have left us detailed descriptions of the European merchant colonies, do not mention the Anconitans at all. However, a Flemish traveller who came to Alexandria in 1470 says that they had a

[471] See *art. cit.*, p. 239; Pasi, f. 47a.

[472] Crist. del Fiore VI, f. [6b f.]. The family name *di Aleppo*, which appears in the acts of Anconitan notaries of that period, obviously points to travels to this Syrian emporium; see Ang. di Domenico X, f. 206b.

fondaco there, and the Jewish traveller Obadiah of Bertinoro, who visited the town in 1488, refers in his letters to the consul of Ancona.[473]

The capital invested in Ancona's trade with the Levant was rather small. There were in the little town a few rich merchants who invested 150-175 ducats a year in the trade with Egypt or Syria,[474] whereas investments of 500 ducats are rarely mentioned in the notarial acts.[475] If one adds the loans known to us from notarial acts given to merchants and seamen departing for the Levant on one ship, one seldom finds sums greater than 1,000 ducats. Of course, the data known to us refer only to a part of the transactions, but there is no reason to believe that the volume of Anconitan trade with the Moslem Levant increased in that period. The total of the investments cannot have surpassed 25,000 ducats a year, except in truly exceptional years such as 1469-1470.

The volume of Ragusan trade with the Moslem Levant was then also very modest. In the years immediately subsequent to the fall of Constantinople, the Ragusans were mainly interested in the trade with Albania, Greece, and Turkey. Their ships frequently visited Valona, Arta, Patras, Rhodes, Chios, and Constantinople. In 1458 the small republic made some diplomatic moves at the court of the Ottoman sultan in order to obtain favorable conditions for her trade in all his dominions.[476] But Ragusan shipping to Egypt and Syria was not discontinued. Some acts of Anconitan notaries refer to the travels of Ragusan ships that first visited Ancona and then sailed to Egypt or Syria. In 1460 the ship of Luca Stefani sailed from Ancona to Latakia; in 1483 that of Paolo Andrea went from Ancona to Ragusa and on to Alexandria; and in 1484 that of Michael Johan Blacus sailed form Ancona to Valona, Beirut, and Tripoli.[477] From time to time Ragusan merchants went to Syria and engaged in business there. In the early 1450's some of them were captured on the way to Damascus, with about 5,000 ducats in their possession.[478]

Estimates of investments that the various trading nations made at the end of the fifteenth century in the Moslem Levant come to a grand total that perhaps slightly surpasses their investments at the end of the fourteenth century. In the last two decades of the fourteenth century it had been a million ducats. It had probably increased until the end of the fifteenth

[473] Obadiah de Bertinoro, p. 116; Adorno, p. 166.

[474] Ang. di Domenico IX, f. 207b f., 231a f.; Ant. Giov. Giac. 30, f. 84b f.

[475] Ant. Giov. Giac. III, part 1, f. 227b f.; an investment of 818 ducats in the trade with "Romania"; see Ant. Giov. Giac. 32, f. 181a f. On the other hand, some notarial acts refer to very small investments in the Levant trade, such as 5, 7 or 9 ducats; see Ant. Giov. di Giac. II, f. 48b., 130b; Giov. Massi, f. 15 a f.; Tom. Marchetti IX, f. 7a.

[476] Krekić, no. 1364.

[477] Ant. Giov. Giac. 74 (1460), f. 1a ff. 30, f. 360a, 360b; Giacomo Alberici II, f. 175b.

[478] Heers, *Gênes*, p. 378.

century to 1.1 million ducats, to which the Venetians alone contributed 650,000. But the investments of the Genoese and the Catalans had decreased considerably. These two trading nations invested no more than 200,000 ducats a year in purchases in the Moslem Levant at the end of the fifteenth century. On the other hand, the Levant trade of the French had increased substantially, and the same was true for the activities of the Neapolitans.

The estimates cannot be wholly mistaken, for a French traveller who was in Egypt in 1512 heard that the customs offices in Alexandria were leased for 250,000 ashrafis a year.[479] If one supposes that the customs amounted to 10 percent on the average and adds the profits of the lessee, the total of imports or exports must have amounted to 1.4-1.5 million ducats. This total, however, included the trade with the Maghreb and Turkey. On the other hand, one must add the volume of the European trade of Syria. Although it had declined at the end of the fifteenth century, it undoubtedly compensated the sum to be attributed to the commercial exchanges of Egypt with the Maghreb and Turkey. Further, one should take into consideration the capital invested by the European Levant traders by way of indirect transfer, for often the agents in the Levant had recourse to loans by drafting bills of exchange. The total (unknown to us) should be added to the amounts carried on the galleys and cogs.

However that may be, all these data and estimates show that theories of a decline of trade between Europe and the Mamluk dominions at the end of the fifteenth century are baseless.[480]

But certainly one must distinguish between the favorable balance of payments characteristic of the trade of Egypt and Syria with the European trading nations in the fifteenth century[481] and the balance of trade as a whole.

The commercial exchanges of these countries with the South European trading nations were undoubtedly very profitable. The profits from the transit trade of the Indian spices and the customs levied upon it must have amounted to some 100,000 ducats a year. In addition, they sold to the Europeans their own products: cotton and others. Consequently, the surplus of exports to Europe amounted perhaps to 350,000 ducats, even taking into consideration the great expenses for services offered by European shipping.[482] On the other hand, the Near Eastern countries also purchased

[479] Jean Thenaud, *Le voyage d'Outremer*, p. 27.

[480] Cl. Cahen, "Quelques mots sur le déclin commerciel du monde musulman a la fin du Moyen Age," in *Studies in the Economic History of the Middle East*, ed. M. A. Cook (London, 1970), p. 31 ff.; Labib, *Handelsgeschichte*, p. 369.

[481] R. S. Lopez, "Il problema della bilancia dei pagamenti nel commercio di Levante," in *Venezia e il Levante fino al XV sec.*, p. 449.

[482] See above p. 213 and see Musso, "Nuovi doc.," p. 461 (a Turk charters a Genoese ship): Tucher, p. 691: Andrea Contarini leases his ship to Turkish merchants.

a great quantity of spices for domestic consumption, imported slaves from various countries, and olive oil from the Maghreb. The total of these imports must have amounted to a surplus of 500,000 ducats or more over exports to India, Turkey, and the Maghreb.[483] So the commercial balance of the Mamluk dominions would have been negative, if they had not compensated by the import of gold from Western Sudan. This was exchanged against commodities of little value, salt and the like. Although this import trade had probably decreased when the Portuguese reached the coasts of Senegal, it was never discontinued.

The volume of the Levant trade and its impact on the balance of trade of the Near Eastern countries is only one aspect of these exchanges, however. Another, no less important, is the fact that a large part of the spices and the other Oriental commodities was bartered against industrial products of various European countries. In fact, the commercial exchanges between Southern Europe and the Moslem Levant had the character of relations between a developed region and an underdeveloped one. It was not a pre-imperialist form of colonialism. The Western powers had not yet established their domination; but their economic superiority, which dates from that period, paved the way to imperialism.

[483] However, one should not exaggerate, as does A. Udovitch. He supposes that in that period Egypt spent 100,000-280,000 ducats a year for the purchase of mamluks and also great sums for the purchase of furs; see R. Lopez-H. Miskimin-A. Udovitch, "England to Egypt, Long-Term Trends and Long-Distance Trade," in *Studies in the Economic History of the Middle East*, ed. M. A. Cook, p. 126 f. and cf. my *Les métaux précieux*, p. 88 ff. It is also unlikely that there was no export trade of Syria and Egypt with Turkey, see Udovitch p. 127. The accounts of Giac. Badoer, see above, p. 282 n. 87, and that of Bertrandon de la Broquière, about the spice caravan going from Syria to Turkey, contradict this supposition.

Appendices

A 1

Venetian cog lines to the Moslem Levant, 1370 - 1402

date		to Syria	Alexandria	source
1371			1	Misti 33, f. 110b; Libri com. III, lib. 7, no. 351
1372			1	Misti 34, f. 7b f.; Libri com. l. c.
1373	fall	1	4	Misti 34, f. 47a ff., 50b, 57a; Libri com. III, lib. 7, no. 267
1374	spring	2		Misti 34, f. 76b f.; Libri com. III, lib. 7, no. 669
	fall	4		
1375			1	Misti 35, f. 112a; Libri com. l. c.
1376			1	Misti l. c. ; Libri com. l. c.
1377			1	Misti 35, f. 157a
1378 - 1381		-	-	
1382			2	Misti 37, f. 48a
1383			-	
1384			2	Misti 38, f. 127a; Coll., Not. II, f. 27a; Dat 548, letter of Zanobi of 29 Nov. 1384
1385	spring	9	3	Misti 39, f. 83b, 91b; Coll., Not. II, f. 47a, Dat 548, letter of Zanobi of 22 May 1385
1386			1	Misti 40, f. 31a ff.; Coll. Not. II, f. 69a
1387			1	Misti 40, f. 73a
1388			1	Misti 40, f. 120a f.
1389	spring	4[a]	1	Misti 41, f. 11a, 21b; Dat 549, letter of Zanobi of 6 May 1389
	fall	2		
		1 suppl.		
1390			1[b]	Coll., Not. II, f. 167a
1391			1	Misti 42, f. 4a f.
1392	fall	3	1	Misti 42, f. 42b; Braunstein, Rel., p. 268
1395	spring	8	1	Misti 43, f. 65a f.; Dat 926, letter of Zanobi of 26 May 1395
1396	spring	7	1	Misti 43, f. 130b f.; Dat 926, letter of Zanobi of 1 Apr. 1396
1397			1	Misti 44, f. 7a f.
1398	fall	3	1	Misti 44, f. 48b f.; 53a
1399	fall	7[c]	1	Misti 44, f. 110a; Dat 712; letter of Manuele Davanzati & Cie of 31 July 1399[c]
1400	spring	10	1	Misti 45, f. 18a f.; Dat 550, letter of Zanobi of 15 May 1400, letter of Com. of Zanobi of 18 and 19 Dec. 1400; Dat 713, letter of Simone di Lappacino of 23 Nov. 1400
	fall	6		

A 1 (continued)

date		to Syria	Alexandria	source
1401	spring	3	2	Dat 713, letter of Bindo di Gherardo Piaciti of 26 May 1401
		additional cog		
1402			1	Misti 46, f. 32b f.; Verb. Cons. XII, sub 11 Oct. 1401

a) According to Misti only two, but Zanobi di Taddeo Gaddi reports that there were four.

b) It was decided to dispatch two cogs, but only one of those which had been proposed was found fit.

c) According to two letters of Zanobi di Taddeo Gaddi, Dat 927 dated 22 Nov. 1399,there were only six cogs.

For the cogs from 1403 onwards see Table XXIV.

A 2

Ligurian shipping to the Levant[a],
1370 - 1410

	departures		arrivals	
year	ship (patron)	line	ship (patron)	line
1370				
	galley of Domenico Doria[1]	Syria		
1371			galley of Nic. Struppa[2] arriv. 19 Jan.	Alexandria
			Lanzarotto Cattaneo[3] arriv. 18 March	"
			galley of Lodisio Bellaveo[4] arriv. 13 March	"
			Matteo Maruffo[5] arriv. 19 June	Alex.-Tunis-Porto Pisano-Genoa
1372	Vicenzo di St Orio- Ant. St Cir[6]	Valencia-Alexandria		
1374				
	Giovanni Antozo[7]	Marseilles-Naples-Rhodes-Beirut		
1376				
	Lodisio Joannisbono[8]	Alexandria	John Dentuto[18]	Alexandria
	Ant. di Vignolo[9]	"	Ant. di Vignolo[19]	"
	Oberto Squarzafico[10]	"	Pietro Dentuto[20]	"
	Bart. Pendola[11]	"		
	Cassano Rechana[12]	"		
	Lorenzo Raynaldi[13]	Apulia-Alex.		
	Borelo di Negro[14]	Gaeta-Alex.		
	Manuele de Verdereto[15]	Naples-Alex.		
	Ant. Grasso[16]	Spain-Alex.		
	Basilio Lomellino[17]	" "		
1377				
	Oberto Grimaldi[21]	Alexandria	Joh. Grillo[39]	Alexandria
	Oberto Vivaldi[22]	"	Rafaele de Moronecio[40]	"
	Lodisio Joannisbono[23]	"	Manuele de Verdereto[41]	"
	Franc. Casali[24]	"	Pietro Dentuto[42]	"
	Giorgio Lomellino[25]	"	Ant. di Vignolo[43]	"
	Nic. Recanelis[26]	"	Simone Lecavello[44]	"
	galley of Cassano Cigalla[27]	Syria	Covello Vespera[45]	"
	Andaro de Moneglia[28]	"	Oberto Squarzafico[46]	"
	Covello Vespera[29]	Gaeta-Naples-Alexandria	Lodisio Joannisbono[47]	"
	Ant. di Vignolo[30]	Naples-Alexandria	Luchetto Busenga[48]	"
	Filippo Grillo[31]	" "	Ioffredo Panzano[49]	Beirut
	Oberto Squarzafico[32]	" "	Basilio Lomellino[50]	Alexandria

A 2 (continued)

year	departures ship (patron)	line	arrivals ship (patron)	line
	(continued)			
	Lanfranco Marini[34]	Porto Pisano-Alex.		Sluys
	Marco Gentile[35]	Spain-Alex.		
	Ant. Drago[36]	" "		
	Ant. Grasso[37]	" "		
	Manuele Lomellino[38]	" "		
1379			Rafaele de Castello[51] arriv. 2 Nov.	Alex.
1387	Joh. de Flisco[52]	Egypt (?)		
	Rafaele Vatacio[53]	Barcelona-Alex.		
1388			Oberto Vivaldi[54]	Turkey-Alex. -Sluys- Middlebourg
1390			3 unknown ships[55]	
1391			Buto Squarzafico[56] arriv. 27 March	Alexandria
			Pietro Camilla[57]	Alex.-London
1393	Sta Maria-St Johann patron: Domenico de Roncagliolo[58]	Genoa-Sevilla-Alex.-Syria	Oberto de Rossano[63]	Alex.-Rhodes-Malaga-Sluys/Genoa-Southampton
	Paolo Centurione[59]	" "		
	Leonello de Nigro[60]	Syria-Egypt		
	Triadino Lomellino[61]	Sevilla-Alex.		
	Lodisio Camilla[62]	" "		
1394	Niccolò Marchetti[64]	" "	Giorgio Riccio[65] arriv. 14 Nov.	Alex.
			Cristofano Lomellino[66] arriv. 14 Nov.	"
			Pietro Dentuto[67]	"
			Ottaviano Lercaro[68]	Alex.-Flanders
1395	galley of Lodisio Camilla[69]	Syria	2 galleys[71] arriv. 1 Dec.	Syria
	Joh. Centurione[70]	"	Ottaviano Lercaro arriv. 6 May	Alex.
			N... Grillo[73] arriv. 17 July	Beirut
			unknown cog[74] arriv. 17 July	"
			Barnaba Dentuto[75]	Alex.
			2 unknown ships[76]	Alex.-Bruges
			...Maruffo[77] (dep. 22 Nov.)	Alex.-Flanders

A 2 (continued)

	departures		arrivals	
year	ship (patron)	line	ship (patron)	line
1396	galley of Lodisio Camilla[78]	Beirut	2 galleys[79] arriv. 10 April	Alex.
			Rafaele Squarzafico[80] arriv. 18 March	"
			2 ships[81]	Alex.-Flanders
1397	galleys of Genoa[82]	Gaeta-Syria	Cristofano Lomellino[83]	Alex.-Sluys
			Paolo Lercaro[84] arriv. 6 Jan.	Alexandria
			"Lomellina"[85] arriv. 6 Jan.	"
1398	Sta Maria-St Jacobus patron: Novello Lercaro[86]	Aigues-Mortes-Alex.	Ottaviano Lercaro[87]	Alex.-Sluys
			Paolo Centurione[88]	Alexandria
			Nic. de Moneglia[89]	Alex.-Genoa-Savona
1399	Cosma Grimaldi[90]	Damietta	2 galleys[92]	Beirut
	Novello Lercaro[91]	Valencia-Alex.		
1400	Cosma Grimaldi	Syria	Teramo Moneglia[93]	Syria-Gaeta-Genoa
	Sta Maria patron: Gabriele Grillo	Savona- Alex.	7 ships to Flanders[94]	
1401			Nic. Andrea Lomellino[95]	Alex.-Modon-Flanders
			Sta Maria-St Antonio patron: Rafaele Lercaro[96]	Alex.-Flanders
			St Johann Battista-St Nicolò patrons: Julian Marini[97]	Chios-Modon-Flanders
1402	Cosma Grimaldi[98]	Alexandria		
	2 galleys	Cyprus-Alex.		
1403	3 " [99]	" "		
1405			Guglielmo Marini[100] arriv. 12 Feb.	Syria
1406			unknown ship[101]	Beirut-Portofino
1407			Alberto Cicogna[102]	Alex.-Sevilla

A 2 (continued)

	departures		arrivals	
year	ship (patron)	line	ship (patron)	line
1409				
	Sta Maria-St Nic.-St Teramo patron: Stefano Colombetto[103]	Savona-Gaeta-Naples-Salerno-Rhodes-Alex.		
1410				
			Gregorio Cigalla[104]	Beirut

1) Liagre-De Sturler, no. 326.
2) - 5) Drictus Alexandriae.
6) Liagre-De Sturler, no. 105.
7) Baratier, p. 226.
8) - 49) J. Day, Douanes.
50) Liagre-De Sturler, no. 355.
51) Heers, Il commercio, p. 171.
52) Foglietta, Oberto, Sen. III, c. 2. The destination of the travel is not indicated exactly. The contract refers only to the dominions of the sultan of Cairo.
53) Musso, Navigazione, p. 117.
54) Liagre-de Sturler, no. 521.
55) Melis, Origini, p. 50 f. One of these ships should depart on 15 Nov., the other on 20 Nov., the date of the departure of the third ship is not indicated.
56) Dat 1171, cargo inventory. cf. Les métaux précieux, p. 120 f. According to Melis l. c., the ship "Squarzafica" bound to depart on 1 Dec. 1390 from Alexandria was that of Luciano Squarzafico, but perhaps it was indeed that of Buto.
57) Musso, op. cit., p. 138 f.
58) Op. cit., p. 135, 137, 178.
59) Op. cit., p. 178; see further Caito, Andreolo IV, c. 211a/b V, c. 87a/b.
60) Musso, op. cit., p. 136.
61) Op. cit., p. 177.
62) Op. cit., p. 178; see also Maggiolo, Teramo I, c. 184b.
63) Liagre - De Sturler, no. 542, 543.
64) Musso, op. cit., p. 178.
65) - 66) Dat 1171, cargo inventories; cf. Les métaux précieux, p. 121.
67) - 68) Dat 1171, cargo inventories.
69) - 70) Musso, op. cit., p. 74.
71) Dat 1171, cargo inventory.
72) Dat 1171; cf. Heers, Il commercio, p. 170 f. The ship ought to continue its travel to Flanders.
73) - 74) Dat 1171, cargo inventories (the two ships came together).
75) Liagre - De Sturler, no. 591. The ship should go on to Sluys.
76) Dat 549, letters of Zanobi di Taddeo Gaddi of 4 March, 17 April 1395.

A 2 (continued)

77) Dat 1171, cargo inventory.

78) Melis, Origini, p. 72.

79) - 80) Dat 1171, cargo inventories.

81) Dat 797, letter of Zanobi of 10 May 1396.

82) Dat 649, letter of Ant. and Doffo degli Spini of 26 Oct. 1397 (the number of the galleys is not given).

83) Liagre - De Sturler, no. 593; Melis, Origini, p. 67.

84) Melis l. c.; Dat 1171, cargo inventory.

85) Dat 1171, cargo inventory.

86) Vat sub 2 Dec. 1399. The owner of the ship was Angelo Cibo, a Genoese living in Montpellier.

87) Liagre - De Sturler, no. 618.

88) Op. cit., no. 611.

89) Op. cit., no. 617.

90) Vat sub 17 Jan. 1400. The ship was wrecked off Damietta.

91) Dat 777, letter of Agnolo di Ser Pino & Giuliano di Giovanni of 16 July 1399.

92) Dat 550, letter of Donato di Bonifazio of 4 Dec. 1399.

93) Musso, op. cit., p. 78, 136, 179.

94) Bautier, Relations, p. 297.

95) Vat sub 9 March, 16 Dec. 1400.

96) Vat sub 25 Feb. 1401.

97) Vat sub 16 and 29 Dec. 1400.

98) Musso, op. cit., p. 77.

99) Ant. Com. 26, c. 33, 36.

100) Musso, op. cit., p. 138.

101) Op. cit., p. 136 f.

102) Op. cit., p. 170.

103) Op. cit., p. 170 f. The ship should go on to Rhodes, Chios, Metelino, Modon, Chios (a second time), Majorca, Southampton, Sluys. The contract of the charter was made on 26 Nov. 1408.

104) Musso, op. cit., p. 139.

---

a) If the name of the ship and that of the patron are indicated in the source, both of them are quoted. Otherwise the name of the patron only is given. The same method has been followed in the subsequent tables. If the ship sailed from Genoa or returned there, the name of the town is not quoted here. In the case the kind of the ship is not specified here, it is a round ship. Many of the freight inventories of the ships listed here have been printed in my paper Il volume del commercio levantino di Genova.

A 3

Catalan shipping to the Moslem Levant[a],
1370 - 1401

year	departures: ship (patron)	departures: line	arrivals: ship (patron)	arrivals: line
1371				
	Sta Maria patron: Franc. Ca-Closa[1]	Alexandria	unknown ship[2] arriv. 7 Nov.	Alex.-Barcelona
1373				
	Sta Tecla patron: Franc. Ca-Closa[3]	Alexandria		
	Franc. Casasagia[4]	Cyprus-Syria		
1374				
	Bernat Sala[5]	Alex. - Beirut		
1377				
	Jacme Sorell & Arnau Guerau of Majorca[6]	Beirut		
1378				
	Sta Eulalia patron: Jacme Carbon[7]	Genoa-Pisa-Syria		
1379				
	Sta Eulalia patron: Franc. Casasagia[8]	Beirut	Franc. Casasagia[9] arrov- 2n March	Beirut
1380				
	Jacme Carbon[10]	Alexandria		
1381				
	Franc. Casasagia[11] June	Beirut		
1383				
	Arnau Guerau[12] Sept.	Alexandria	Joh. Carbo[13] arriv. 7 Sept.	Beirut
1384				
	Pere Oliver[14]	Beirut (?)	Capo de Bon[15] arriv. 4 April	Beirut
1385				
	Mateu Elats (?)[16]	Alexandria		
1386				
			Joh. Manresa[17] arriv. 7 Nov.	Beirut
1387				
	Franc. Casasagia[18]	Cyprus-Beirut		
	St Johan patron: P. Terasa[19]	Collioure-Cyprus- Beirut		
1389				
	Franc. Casasagia[20]	Beirut	Pere Salom[21] arriv. 1 March	Beirut

A 3 (continued)

	departures		arrivals	
year	ship (patron)	line	ship (patron)	line
1390				
	... Casasagia[22]	Alexandria		
	Guillermo Morey[23]	"		
	... Sola[24]			
	Martin Vicent[25]	Alexandria	Martin Vicent[27] arriv. 24 Oct.	Alexandria
	Barthomeu Vidal[26] 19 Nov.			
1391				
	Martin Vicent[28] 28 Feb.	Alexandria	Franc. Casasagia[33] arr. 30 May	Alex.-Beirut
	galley of Jacme Sellares[29] 13 May	"	... Morey[34]	Alex.
	Esteva Borel[30] 17 Sept.	"	ship of the town[35] arriv. 30 May	"
	... Pascual[31] 17 Sept.		ship of deputacion[36] arriv. 30 May	"
	Nicolau Careras[32] 30 July		galley of the town[37] arriv. 4 Aug.	"
			... Vidal[38]	"
			Joh. Morella[39] arriv. 30 May	Beirut
			Pere Dertazo[40] arriv. Nov.	"
1392				
	Bernat Ca-Closa[41] 22 Jan.	Alex.-Beirut		
	Guillem Pujades[42] 18 Oct.	" "		
	... Vinals[43] 20 Nov.	Alexandria		
1393				
	Ramon Ferrer-Joh. Pellicer	Beirut	... Ca-Closa[45] arriv. 12 June	Alexandria
			... Pujades[46] arriv. 18 Sept.	"
1394				
	... Pujades[47] 28 May	Rhodes-Cyprus-Alexandria	Ramon de Pons[50]	Beirut
	Martin Vicent[48]	Rhodes-Cyprus-Alexandria	... Pascal[51] arriv. 23 March	Beirut-Collioure
	Franc. Fugassot[49]	Alexandria	ship of Perpignan[52]	Beirut
1395				
	3 galleys of the town[53]	Alex.-Beirut	3 galleys[54] departed from Beirut 12 Aug.	Beirut
	Sta Eulalia patron: Bart. Vidal			
	St. Gabriel patron: Pere Quintaner		4 ships in Rhodes (on return to Catalonia)[55]	Alex.(?)
	St. Francesco patron: Miquel Gualbes		2 ships[56] departed from Beirut 17 June	Beirut

A 3 (continued)

year	departures ship (patron)	line	arrivals ship (patron)	line
1396				
	5 galleys[57]	Syria	5 galleys[59] arriv. 2 Aug.	Beirut
	Joh. Manresa[58]	Collioure-Beirut		
1397				
	4 galleys[60]	Syria	4 galleys[62] arr. 3 Oct.	Beirut
	ship of Honoré of Perpignan[61]		1 galley[63]	Beirut-Valencia
			Joh. Manresa[64]	Beirut-Collioure
			Guillem Pons[65]	Beirut
1398				
	3 galleys of the town[66]	Beirut		
	3 other galleys[67]	"		
	Pere Bruniquer[68] July			
	Pere Muntros[69] July			
	Honoré of Perpignan[70]	Collioure-Beirut		
1399				
	Nicolau Pujades[71] 23 July	Alexandria	Pere Bruniquer[73]	
	Miquel Gualbes[72] Nov.	Beirut	galliot[75] arriv. 6 Oct.	Beirut
1400				
	Bernat Roger[76] Jan.	Syria	... Pujades[77] departed from Alex. 25 Oct. 1399	Alexandria
			Pere Bruniquer[78]	Syria
			Pere Muntros[79]	Beirut
			Pere Bastier[80]	Beirut-Marseilles-Aigues-Mortes-Collioure
1401				
	Guillem Lot[81]	Modon-Alex.	Ramon Forner[86]	Alex.-Provence-Mallorca-Barcelona
	Miquel Biurq[82]	Rhodes-Cyprus-Beirut		
	Pere Aleu[83]	" "	Joh. Bastier[87] departed from Alex. 18 March	Alex.
	Bernant Savall[84]	" "		
	Barthomeu Sacot[85]		unknown ship[88]	Beirut

1) López Meneses, *Los consulados*, p. 101; Sáez Pomés, p. 375.

2) Dat 1171, cargo inventory.

3) Sáez Pomés, l. c.

4) Sáez Pomés, p. 366 f.

A 3 (continued)

5) Pere Marti VI, sub 4 May 1374.
6) López Meneses, p. 126; appendix VII.
7) Rubió i Lluch, Diplomatari, no. 388.
8) López Meneses, p. 127; the ship received the Royal license to depart on 15 June. Consequently the patron applied for it after his return from Beirut in March.
9) Dat 1171, cargo inventory; cf. Heers, Il commercio, p. 174.
10) Pere Marti VIII, 11 Aug. - 15 Dec. 1380, f. 99a.
11) - 12) Carrère, Barcelone, p. 263.
13) Dat 1171, cargo inventory.
14) Rubió i Lluch, op. cit., no. 622.
15) Dat 1171, cargo inventory, published by Spallanzani, Ceramiche orientali, p. 145 f.
16) Pere Marti VIII, 15 April - 13 Aug. 1385, f. 102a f.
17) Dat 1171, cargo inventory. The Italians pronounced (and wrote) Merasa etc.
18) Bernat Nadal I, f. 37a, 67a f.
19) APO, P. de Ornos, f. 79b f.
20) Carrère, p. 282.
21) Dat 1171, cargo inventory published by Spallanzani, op. cit., p. 146 f. cf. Heers, Il commercio, p. 174.
22) - 25) Del Treppo, p. 698 ff.
26) Del Treppo, l.c.; Capmany, Memorias II, appendix XXI (where one finds Buenaventura Vidal).
27) Capmany l. c.
28) - 39) Del Treppo l. c.; Capmany l. c.
31) - 38) Capmany l. c.; cargo inventory of the ship of Franc Casasagia, Dat 1171.
39) Dat 1171, cargo inventory; cf. Heers, l. c. who reads Maiella. The inventory has been published by Spallanzani, op. cit., p. 147 f.
40) Dat 1171, cargo inventory.
41) López Meneses, p. 112; Capmany l. c.
42) - 43) Del Treppo l. c.; Capmany l. c.
44) Carrère, p. 282.
45) - 46) Capmany l. c.
47) Capmany l. c.; Del Treppo l. c.
48) Del Treppo l. c.
49) Carrère, p. 235.
50) Dat 797, letter of Zanobi di Taddeo Gaddi of 31 Oct. 1394; the writer of the letter surmises that this Catalan ship is that of Ramon de Pons.
51) Dat 1171, cargo inventory.
52) Dat 549, letter of Zanobi of 4 Nov. 1394.
53) Capmany III, p. 180; Carrère, p. 265, 278; Lopez Meneses, p. 134; Del Treppo l. c.
54) Dat 1171, cargo inventory.
55) Dat 710, letter of Zanobi of 17 April 1395. The writer of the letter does not say wherefrom the ships came, but speaking about their cargoes he sums up the quantity of pepper in sportas.
56) Dat 1171, cargo inventory.
57) Carrère, p. 278.

A 3 (continued)

58) See contract of 13 Oct. 1395 in APO, B. 250, liasse 24.

59) Dat 1171, cargo inventory; another copy of it, ibidem, had the date ... Sept. 1396.

60) Carrère, p. 278.

61) Dat 1160, contract of insurance of 20 Oct. 1397.

62) - 63) Carrère, p. 644.

64) Dat 1171, cargo inventory; Carrère, p. 270.

65) Carrère, p. 644.

66) - 69) Op. cit., p. 279, 644.

70) Dat 1160, contract of 20 Oct. 1397.

71) Dat 637, letter of Simone d'Andrea Bellandi from Barcelona, of 24 July 1399.

72) Carrère, p. 265.

73) - 74) Dat 1159, no. 143.

75) Carrère, p. 270.

76) Op. cit., p. 278.

77) Dat 1083, letter of Com. of Zanobi of 29 Nov. 1400.

78) Dat 550, letter of Com. of Zanobi of 1 Jan. 1401.

79) Dat 1158, no. 126. In Dat 550, letter of Com. of Zanobi of 1 Jan. 1401 one reads that a Catalan ship returning from Syria perhaps suffered shipwreck.

80) Dat 1171, cargo inventory. The ship departed from Beirut on 28 January and arrived in Marseilles on 3 April. Cf. Table XVII ("ship of Collioure").

81) Vat sub 18 July 1401.

82) - 85) Carrère, p. 644.

86) Vat sub 25 Jan. 1401.

87) Dat 1171, cargo inventory. This was the ship of Pere Tequin, see above Ch. III, p.

88) Dat 713, letter of Simone de Lappacino of 8 Feb. 1401.

---

a) If there is no other indication, the ship departed from Barcelona or arrived in that town.

A 4

French shipping to the Moslem Levant[a], 1381 - 1410

year	departures ship (patron)	departures line	arrivals ship (patron)	arrivals line
1374	Royal Galley[a]	Alexandria		
	Bernat Ca Clascania[b]	Rhodes-Cyprus-Beirut		
	Jacme Oliverii[c]	Alexandria-Beirut		
1375	Bernat Januarii-Ramon Fontanies[d]	Cyprus-Beirut		
1376	Pere Blanes[e]	Rhodes-Cyprus-Beirut		
1381	St Antoine[1]	Marseilles-Alexandria-Rhodes		
1382	St Antoine[2]	" "		
1383	St Antoine[3]	Marseilles-Alexandria		
1387	Sta Maria[4]	Leucate-Rhodes-Alex.-Beirut		
1388	P. Terasa of Collioure[5]	Rhodes-Beirut		
1389	Sta Maria[6]	Collioure-Marseilles-Rhodes-Alexandria		
1394			Paolo de Montesimoli[7]	Alex.-Gaeta-Aigues-Mortes
			unknown ship[8]	Alex-Pisa-Aigues-Mortes
			unknown ship[9]	Beirut-Aigues-Mortes
1395			unknown ship[10]	" "
1396			Jac. Ibalvi[11]	Beirut-Famagusta-Aigues-Mortes
1397			... Luciano[12] arriv. 28 July	Alex.-Marseilles
1399	Sta Maria-St Nicolò patron: Novello Lercaro[13]	Aigues-Mortes-Alexandria	Catalan galley[14]	Beirut-Aigues-Mortes

A 4 (continued)

year	departures: ship (patron)	line	arrivals: ship (patron)	line
1400				
	Sta Maria-St Antonio patron: Rafaele Lercaro[15]	Aigues-Mortes-Naples	Novello Lercaro[16] arriv. 5 Jan.	Alex.-Aigues-Mortes
			"ship of Collioure[17]	Beirut-Marseilles
			St Antonio patron: Bernat Roger[18]	Alex.-Syracuse-Aigues-Mortes
			Alvise Giuffrida[19]	Alex.-Provence
			unknown ship[20]	Beirut-Aigues-Mortes
			Pere Bastier[21] depart. from Beirut 28 Jan.	" "
			Nic. Riccione[22]	Syria-Pisa-Provence
1401	Gerard Doni[f]	Cyprus-Beirut-Alexandria		
1401				
	Julian Centurione[23]	Aigues-Mortes-Alexandria	unknown Genoese ship[24]	Alex-Provence
1403				
	Ramon Ferrer[25]	" "	Pierre Miquel[26]	Alex.-Nice-Aigues-Mortes
			"ship of Tortosa"[27]	Alex.-Aigues-Mortes
1406				
			"ship of Collioure" patron: Joh.Bastier[28] arriv. in Aigues-Mortes 30 Aug.	Beirut-Aigues-Mortes-Collioure
1410				
	Sta Maria-St Johann patron: Ant. Noziglia[29]	Aigues-Mortes-Gaeta-Palermo-Chios-Alex.-Pera	... Pons[30]	Beirut-Collioure

a) Madurell-Garcia, no. 133.

b) Op. cit., no. 135.

c) Op. cit., nos. 136, 138.

d) Op. cit., no. 140.

e) Op. cit., no. 141.

f) Op. cit., no. 167. The document which we quote is a commenda contract made on 23 Nov. 1400. So it is probable that the ship departed in 1401.

1) - 3) Baratier, p. 236. The ship was chartered by the Italian merchants of Avignon.

4) See Livre des comptes de Jacme Olivier, ed. A. Blanc, p. 128 ff.

5) Op. cit., p. 168 ff. It is not stated in the source if the ship departed from Leucate or from Collioure.

A 4 (continued)

6) Baratier, table of shipping.

7) Dat 1171, cargo inventory.

8) Dat 549, letter of Zanobi of 21 May 1394. The ship continued its trip to Barcelona and Flanders.

9) Dat 549, letter of the same of 4 Nov. 1394.

10) Dat 549, letter of the same of 4 March 1395.

11) - 12) Dat 1171, cargo inventory.

13) Vat sub 2 Dec., 9 Dec. 1399, 2 Feb. 1400. The owner of the ship was the same Angelo Cibo, a Genoese living in Montpellier, who owned the Sta Maria--St. Jacobus, see above A 2 sub a. 1398. But this ship had apparently as co-proprietor Triadino Lomellino.

14) Heers, Il commercio, p. 175.

15) Vat sub 25 Feb. 1401.

16) Dat 1171, cargo inventory; cf. Les métaux précieux, p. 122. The inventory has no date, but as one learns from the acts of Ant. de Vataciis quoted above note 13 that Lercaro was at the end of the year 1399 no more in Alexandria, it refers very probably to the return cargo brought by him from Egypt.

17) Heers, art. cit., p. 175.

18) Vat sub 21 April 1400. This is a Catalan ship.

19) Dat 1083, letter of Commess. of Zanobi di Taddeo Gaddi of 29 Nov. 1400. The ship is a spinazza.

20) Dat 713, letter of Bindo di Gherardo Piaciti of 3 April 1400. This is a Catalan ship (see above A 3 s. a. 1400).

21) Dat 1171, cargo inventory.

22) Dat 550, letter of Com. of Zanobi of 10 Jan. 1401. The ship was wrecked in the archipelago.

23) Vat sub 1 Sept. 1401.

24) Ainaud, Quatre documents, doc. I. The ship ought to depart in March.

25) Dat 844, letter of Andrea di Giov. Brandi of 7 May 1403; about this Catalan ship see A 3, sub a. 1403.

26) Dat 907, letter of Jean Fabre of 20 Nov. 1403.

27) Dat 844, letter of Andrea di Giov. Brandi of 7 May 1403.

28) Dat 929, letter of Com. of Zanobi of 27 Nov. 1406; Dat 1171, cargo inventory (where one reads Giov. Botto).

29) Musso, Navig., p. 171 (it is a Genoese ship).

30) Dat 907, letter of Tomaso Tequin of 30 April 1410.

a) This list comprises both French and foreign ships which served the merchants of Southern France. Very often the whole or a great part of the freight of the Catalan and Genoese ships sailing from the ports of Southern France belonged to French merchants or to foreign merchants living there, so that one should classify these ships as French ones. But of course it is very difficult to draw a line of distinction between "French shipping" to the Levant and, on the other hand, Catalan and Genoese shipping, and especially as a part of what is now France belonged in that period to the kingdom of Catalonia.

A 5

Anconitan shipping to the Levant in the period after the conquest of Constantinople[a]

year	ship (patron)	line	cargo	source
1453	St Jacobus-St Quiriacus-St Nicola patron: Domenico Martini of Trani	Alexandria	brocarts	Ant. Giov. Giac. III, part 1, f. 83a f., 99a, 110a f., 112a, 133b ff., 138b f., 178b f.
	St Antonius patron: Anton Fazioli	Tripoli (Libya) -Alex.-Syria		Ibid. f. 327b f.
	Angelo Joh. Buldoni	Romania		Albertini X, part 1, f. 201 ff.
1455	Domenico Martini of Trani	Ragusa-Alexandria		Tom. Marchetti X, f. 6b
1457	Sta Crux	Chios	olive oil	Ant. Giov. Giac. VI, f. 253b f.
	Sta Maria-St Jacobus - St Nicholaus	Alexandria		Ibid., f. 432b f.
	Ragusan ship patron: Tomas Luce	Chios		Ibid., f. 514b f.
1459	Ragusan ship patron: Tomas Luce	Chios	grains	Ang. di Dom. II, f. 117a f.
	Domenico Martini	Romania	soap	Ibid., f. 78a ff., 86a, 88a
	Andrea degli Agli	Ragusa-Rhodes-Beirut-Tripoli		Ibid., f. 144a
1461	Oddo degli Agli	Romania	soap cloth	Ang. di Dom. IV, f. 102b ff., 109b ff.
	Clemente Gaspari	"	soap	Ibid., f. 33b ff., 39b ff.
1462	Ant. Jacobus Bartolomei	Chios-Pera		Ant. Giov. Giac. 11, f. 366b f.
1464	Florentine ship	captured near Tenedos		Müller, Doc., p. 200
	Joh. Dionisii	Ragusa-Chios-Acre-Beirut-Tripoli	grains olive oil honey	Ang. di Domenico V, f. 7a, 54b ff., 64a, 65b ff., 66a ff.; Ant. Giov. Giac. 13, f. 162b
1465	Andrea degli Agli	Pera	weapons iron goods	Braunstein, Studi Ven. VIII, p. 289
	Domenico Martini of Trani	Ragusa-Chios-Acre		Ant. Giov. Giac. 14, f. 85b f.
	Angelo Joh. Buldoni	Ragusa-Chios		Ibid., f. 119b f., 140a f., 170a f.
1466	Andrea degli Agli			Braunstein l. c.
	Felice Lelugello of Venice	Rhodes-Beirut		Ant. Giov. Giac. 15, f. 92a
	Angelo Joh. Buldoni	Romania		Ibid., f. 268a f.
	Bartolomeus Marini	Alexandria		Ant. Giov. Giac. 16, f. 31b
1467	Bartolomeus Marini	Pera		Ibid., f. 89b
	Angelo Joh. Buldoni	Ragusa-Chios-Pera		Ibid., f. 90b f., 100a f., 111a f., 112a f., 123b f., 126a ff.

A 5 (continued)

year	ship (patron)	line	cargo	source
	Andrea degli Agli	Pera	iron goods	Braunstein l. c.
	Pietro Dionisii	"	weapons, iron goods	Ibidem
1468	Anton Petri Matarozi	Chios		Ang. di Dom. VIII, f. 79a
	Leonardo de Ferretri	Pera	soap	Ibid.
1469	Cristoforo de Joh.	Chios	grains	ASV, Secreta 25, f. 136b f.
	Cursino Cursini	Romania	cloth	Ang. di Dom. VIII, f. 197a ff., 205a ff., 207b, 240b
	Angelo Joh. Buldoni	Ragusa-Chios-Pera	wine, soap, leather, fustian, pepper, paper, ship-biscuits	Ibid., f. 139b, 192a, 219a ff., 241b 257a 261a 264a, 264b, 281a
	Bart. Marini	Cyprus-Tripoli-Alexandria		Ibid., f. 43a ff., 54b, 59a
	"ship of Otranto", Sta Maria-St Niccolò patron: Jac. Gatti	Ragusa-Rhodes-Alexandria	wheat	Ibid., f. 65b ff., 66a ff.
	Bart. Marini	Candia-Romania Syria	"	Ibid., f. 261b, ff., 269b
	Joh. Dionisii	Candia-Beirut-Tripoli/Romania	"	Ibid., f. 221a, 224b f., 226b ff., 232a, 233a ff.
	Pasqualino Antonii	Cyprus-Alex.-Syria	"	Ibid., f. 102a ff.
	Sicilian ship, Sta Maria-St Cristoforo-St Nicolò patron: Joh. Petri Trento	Syria-Lajazzo	"	Ibid., f. 294 b f.
	Ant. Petri Matarozi	Romania		Ibid., f. 316b
1470	Piermatteo Simonis	Syria/Romania	wheat	Ibidem, f. 238b, 275a, 277b; Ant. Giov. Giac. 18, f. 163b f.
	Aquila de Dio	Beirut-Tripoli		Ang. di Dom. IX, f. 44a ff.
	Ant. Petri Matarozi	Chios-Pera		Ibid., f. 40a, 68a, 92a f., 94b f., 95b
	Anton Rubei	Calabria-Tripoli		Ibid., f. 190a, 202b f.
	Ant. Cursini	Alexandria		Ibid., f. 195a f., 221b
	Piergentile Bonarelli	Ragusa-Beirut-Tripoli		Ibid., f. 214b, 231a
	Bart. Marini	Beirut-Tripoli		Ibid., f. 222a
	Ant. Petri de Curzola	Cotrone-Beirut		Ibid., f. 139b
	Angelo Joh. Buldoni	Romania		ASV, Secreta 25, f. 136 b f.
1471	caravel of Ant. Petri of Curzola	Beirut	import: potash	Ang. di Dom. X, f. 83b f.
	Franc. Ant. Ferretti	Chios-Constantinople	grains, soap, cloth	Ang. di Dom. X, f. 45b, 49a, 50b f., 51a f. 56b, 67b f., 68a f.
	Paolo Doria (Genoese)	Chios-Pera	soap	Ibid., f. 46b, 66a f. 67b
	Ant. Petri Matarozi	Chios-Pera	soap, cloth	Ibid., f. 57a, 59b, 69b, 71a, 74a f.

A 5 (*continued*)

year	ship (patron)	line	cargo	source
1472	Cinzio Antonjacobi Stracha	Valona-Chios-Pera		Ang. di Dom. 11, f. 128a, 139a f.
	Ant. Petri Matarozi	Beirut		Ibid., f. 183 a
1473	Ant. Cursini	Pera	soap, cloth	Ang. di Dom. 12, f. 132a f., 181a; Ant. Giov. Giac. 21, f. 189 b f.
	Jacob Ant. di Baruto	Apulia-Chios-Pera	soap, cloth, paper	Ang. di Dom. 12, f. 159b, 160a, 175 a f., 197a, 199a; Ant. Giov. Giac. 21, f. 200a
	Jacob. Sgamba	Candia		Ang. di Dom. 12, f. 199a f.
1474	Bart. Marini	Chios-Constantinople		Ant. Giov. Giac. 22, f. 29b, 92b
	Jacob Ant. di Baruto	Ragusa-Chios-Constantinople		Ibid., f. 257b f.
	Ant. Petri Matarozi	Ragusa-Chios-Constantinople		Ibid., f. 270b f., 282a f.
	Ant. Marini	Ragusa-Chios-Constantinople		Ibid., f. 283b f.
1475	Jacob Ant. di Baruto	Chios-Constantinople		Ant. Giov. Giac. 23, f 184b, 192b, f.: Corrado di Nic. II, f. 250a
	Ant. Cursini	Constantinople	cloth	Ciriaco Tome 1475, f. 4b[b]
1478	Bart. Marini	Constantinople-Black Sea		Ant. Giov. Giac. 26, f. 128b f.; Nic. Cressi III, f. 70a
	Jacob Ant. di Baruto	Apulia-Chios-Pera		Giorgio di Pietro, f. 77b, 78a; Ant. Giov. Giac. 26, f. 13b, 34a, 35b f., 38a
1479	Bart. Marini	Segna-Alex.-Danietta	wine, tow	Melch. Bernabe II, f. 124b
	Jacob Ant. di Baruto	Alexandria		Ant. Giov. Giac. 27, f. 345b, 347a f.
1480	Jacob Ant. di Baruto	Alexandria		Ant. Giov. Giac. 28, f. 122a f., 133a, 133a, 134a; Melch. Bernabe III, f.
1481	Joh. Monoli	Alexandria		Ant. Giov. Giac. 29, f. 211b f.; Corrado di Nic. III, f. 578a f.
	Jacob Ant. di Baruto	Beirut-Tripoli		Ant. Giov. Giac. 29, f. 69b f., 70a f., 72b f., 83b f., 86b f., 95b f., 97b f., 104b f., 106b, 107b
	Michael Joh. de Blaneis	Ragusa-Chios-Constantinople		Ibid., f. 30b f.
1482	Franc. Nic. Ferrantini	Constantinople	fustian	Ant. Giov. Giac. 30, f. 64a; Nic. Cressi V, 4a f.
	Sta Maria patron: Joh. de Blaneis	Chios-Constantinople		Ant. Giov. Giac. 30, f. 47b f., 74b f.
	Jacob Ant. di Baruto	Canea-Rhodes-Alex.		Ibid., f. 50b ff., 84a
	Michael Joh. Allis of Ragusa	Ragusa-Pera-Constantinople		Ibid., f. 86a ff.

A 5 (continued)

year	ship (patron)	line	cargo	source
	Pietro Joh. of Pesaro	Ragusa-Pera-Constantinople		Ibid., f. 60a f.
	Quiriacus Pasqualini	Chios-Pera-Constantinople		Ibid., f. 60a f.
1483	Bart. Bricius	Romania	soap	Nic. Cressi V, f. 78a f.
	Bart. Jacobi of Ragusa[c]	Constantinople	soap	Ibid., f. 94a f., 95a f. 96a; Ant. Giov. Giac. 31, f. 118b, 121a f., 142 a
	Bartolino Bonarelli	Ragusa-Para-Constantinople		Ant. Giov. Giac. 31, f. 60a ff.
	Faziolus Fazioli	Beirut		Ibid., f. 246b
1484	Ieronimo degli agli	Romania	cloth	Giac. Alberici II, f. 200a
	Blasius de Avina	Ragusa-Chios-Pera		Ant. Giov. Giac. 32, f. 167a f., 181a f., 185b f.
1485	St Cristoforo patron: Ieronimo degli Agli	Pera-Constantinople		Nic. Cressi V, f. 306a, Melch. Bernabe VI f. 63b, 71a, 71b
	Marcello Jacobi Pizori	Romania		Ant. Giov. Giacomo 33, f. 78a f., 79a
	Bart. Quiriaci	Beirut-Tripoli	fustian	Melch. Bernabe VI, f. 126a, 129a.
1486	St Cristoforo patron: Ieronimo degli Agli	Pera-Constantinople	soap imp.: wool, carpets	Nic. Cressi VI, f. 43a; Melch. Bernabe VII f. 101a, 106b, 108a, f., 124a, 133a, 110a, 110b; Giac. Alberici IV(48), f. 64a f., 74a f., 76b f., 77a 82a
	Sta Maria patron: Piergentile Bonarelli	Chios-Pera-Constantinople		Nic. Cressi VI, f. 60 ff., 96a 95b; Melch. Bernabe VII. f. 11a, 133a, 137a, 140a; Giac. Alberici III, f. 62a.
1487	Bart. Nassini	Levante	paper	Giac. Alberici IV, 1487, f. 21a f.
	Bartolino Quiriaci	Ragusa-Chios-Constantinople		Ant. Giov. Giac. 35, f. 16b, 17b, 21b f.
	Tiburzio de Florencia	Constantinople		Melch. Bernabe VIII, f. 36a
	Franc. Nic. Ferrantini	Ragusa-Chios-Constantinople	soap	Ant. Giov. Giac. 35, f. 56a; Melch. Bernabe VIII, f. 77b f., 80b f., 81b f.
	Nic. Petrucci	Ragusa-Chios Pera	soap	Ant. Giov. Giac. 35, f. 60b f., 61b; Melch. Bernabe VIII, f. 85a f., 93a f.
	Nic. Georgii di Baruto	Ragusa-Chios-Gallipoli		Ant. Giov. Giac. 35, f. 62a
1488	S. Cristoforo patron: Antonjacob Bompiani	Constantinople	soap, olive oil	Giac. Alberici IV, 1488, f. 35a f.
	Sta Maria patron: Joh. Dionisii	Pera		Ibid., f. 37a
	Ant. Jacobi Fanelli	Constantinople	soap, paper	Melchior Benrabe IX, f. 78a f.

A 5 (continued)

year	ship (patron)	line	cargo	source
1489	Franc. Nic. Ferrantini	Constantinople		Giac. Alberici VI, f. 49a
	Sta Maria patron: Bart. Nassini	Pera	soap	Giac. Alberici VI, f. 56b
	Joh. de Redulfis-Tiburzio de Flor.	Chios-Pera		Ant. Giov. Giac. 36, f. 22b
	Bart. Quiriaci	Ragusa-Valona-Chios-Pera		Ant. Giov. Giac. 35, f. 158a 36, f. 25a
	Franc. Nicolai Fazioli	Ragusa-Chios-Gallipoli	soap	Ant. Giov. Giac. 36, f. 26b, 32a, 35a
	Joh. Basti	Chios-Gallipoli-Pera		Ibid., f. 94b f., 100a
	Joh. Pauli Monoli	Beirut-Tripoli		Ibid., f. 96b, cf. 97a
	Nic. Petrucci	Beirut-Tripoli		Ibid., f. 97b f., 100a f.
1490	Nic. Petrucci	Alexandria		Melch. Bernabe 10, f. 135b, 136b
	Sta Maria-Stella patron: Jeronimo degli Agli	Romania		Melch. Bernabe IX. f. 214a, 222a f.
1491	Sta Maria patron: Franc. Nic. Ferrantini	Pera	leather imp.: cotton	Nic. Cressi VII, 1491, f. 70b
	Sta Maria[d] patron: Marcellino Pizori	Pera-Constantinople		Giac. Alberici VII, f. 49a
	Carolus Monoli[e]	Romania		Melch. Bernabe X, f. 192b, 213 b f.
	Sta Maria patron: Carolus Monoli	Beirut-(Tripoli)		Ibid., f. 106a
1492	St Cristoforo patron: Johan Battista Iustinian	Constantinople		Giac. Alberici VIII, f. 65a
	Sta Maria patron: Calvutius de Fermo	Pera-Constantinople		Ibid., f. 27b f. 35b f.
	Joh. Poligeorgii	Ragusa-Chios-Pera		Ant. Giov. Giac. 38, f. 51b
1493	Sta Maria patron: Marioto Franc. Puti	Constantinople-Pera		Giac. Alberici IX, f. 51b f.
	Joh. de Napoli	Pera		Ant. Giov. Giac. 39, f. 32a, 33b
1497	Sta Maria patron: Redulfo Anello	Constantinople		Giac. Alberici 13, a. 1497, f. 118a

a) This table is a supplement and a continuation to the list of Anconitan ships sailing to the Levant in Il commercio levantino di Ancona, p. 235 ff. New data have been added here to that list which comprised the years 1453-1469, but the notes have been omitted here. If the contract between the ship patron and the

A 5 (continued)

merchants who charter the ships leaves to the latter the choice of the final destination, the various parts have been marked by diagonal lines. The names of the patrons are quoted as they are to be found in the original documents. The table comprises not only Anconitan ships, but also foreign ships which were chartered to Anconitans for trips to the Moslem Levant. If there is no other indication, the cargo is the export freight. To the ships listed here there should be added some Ragusan ships which visited Ancona before sailing to the Levant, see above p.

b) According to Melis, Origini, p. 119: Nic. Cursini.

c) The patron of this ship was, according to other documents, Blaxius de Ragusa or Blaxius de Avina, the son or the father of Bartolomeo. They are also called "de Avina," see the documents quoted and in addition Ant. Giov. di Giac. 31, f. 164 b f.

d) According to Melch. Bernabe X, f. 253 b f. the name of the ship was Santo Cristoforo.

e) This trip was made in the first half of the year, that to Syria (see next item) in its second half.

f) Ant. Giov. Giac. 38, f. 51b, 54a has Joh. Nic. Giustinian.

A 6

European ships in Alexandria, according to the acts of Alexandrian notaries[a]
1400 - 1405, 1427, 1435

a. 1400

Venetian:	
Bart. Trevisan	Vat act without date
Genoese:	
Viscomes Grimaldi	Vat sub 14 Jan.
Sta Maria-St Nicola	
patron: Novello Lercaro	Vat sub 1 Feb.
Manuele Doris	Vat sub 16 June
St Jacobus[b]	Vat sub 9 Aug.
Andrea Lomellino	Vat sub 16 Dec.
St Joh. Battista-St Nicola	Vat sub 16 and 29 Dec.
patron: Julian Marini	
Catalan:	
St Anton	
patron: Bernat Roger	Vat sub 21 April
Ant. Sori, of Barcelona	Vat sub 10 Aug.
Florentine:	
Jacobus de Bartol.	Vat sub 14 Oct.
Napolitan:	
Antoniello de Letere de Scala[c]	Vat sub 22 and 25 May
Anconitan:	
Masello di Grasso	Vat sub 29 March 1401[d]
Rhodian:	
Domenico Grimani	Vat sub 16 June

a. 1401

Venetian	
Marco de Cloderiis	Vat sub 16 May
Micaletto Zorzi	Verb. Cons. XII, sub 11 Oct.
Nic. Barbo	Ibidem
Genoese:	
Sta Maria-St Antonio	
patron: Rafaele Lercaro	Vat sub 25 Feb., 9 March
Nic. Andrea Lomellino	Vat sub 9 March
two cogs of Joh. Lomellino	Vat sub ... March
Germanus de Tholon	Vat sub 16 May

A 6 (continued)

Julian Centurione	Vat sub 1 Sept.
spinazza Sta Caterina	Leonardo de Valle
patron: Ant. de Monte Nigro	sub 4 Nov.
St Joh. Battista-St Nicola	
patron: Julian Marin	Vat sub 16 May
Catalan:	
Guillem Lot	Vat sub 18 and 26 July
Ramon Forner	Vat sub 11 April
Guillem Passador	Leonardo de Valle sub 22 Dec.
Jacob Fugasot	Ibidem
Joh. Bastier	Ibidem[e]
Gerardo de Doni	Vat sub 7 June
French:	
Joh. Miquel	Leonardo de Valle
Ant. Miquel de Manella[f]	Vat sub 26 Feb. and 1 April
Sicilian:	
Bartolomeo Amati	Leonardo de Valle sub 17 Nov.
Blasio Malipetro	Vat, sub 23 Aug.
Cretan:	
Stamati Roseis, of Candia	Vat sub 10 March

a. 1402

Venetian:	
Marco de Benedetti	Leonardo de Valle sub 12 April
Ant. Blanco	Verb. Cons. XII, sub 12 Feb., 30 July
Nic. Barbo	Ibid., sub 30 July
Victor Fiolo	Ibid., sub 20 March
Catalan:	
Miquel Pauldaga-Francesc Sanagla of Barcelona	Leonardo de Valle sub 18 Aug.
Sta Clara-St Felix	
patron: Guillem Marullo, of St Felix	Leonardo de Valle sub 1 Sept.
Cypriot:	
Zorzi de Cipro	Leonardo de Valle sub 25 Oct.
Cretan:	
Teodoro Zucheto	Verb. Cons. XII, sub 12 Aug.; Leonardo de Valle sub 29 Sept.

A 6 (continued)

(continued)

Greek:	
Jani Chazamati	Verb. Cons. XII, sub 9 and 16 March; Leonardo de Valle sub 16 March
Sicilian:	
Bart. Amati	Leonardo de Valle sub 14 April, 1 May
a. 1403	
Venetian:	
Nic. Barbo	Leonardo de Valle sub 16 Sept.
Marco de Cloderiis	Ibid., sub 5 Nov.
Bart. de Benedetto	Ibid., sub 18 July
Catalan:	
Ant. Sori, of Barcelona	Ibid., sub 24 March
Joh. Bonino	Ibid., sub 4 July
French:	
Ant. Michael	Ibid., sub 24 March
unknown ship of Provence	Ibid., sub 9 March
Cretan:	
Manoli Maidazo of Candia	Ibid., sub 5 Nov.
Rhodian:	
galliot of Rhodes	Ibid., sub 5 Feb.[g]
Unknown:	
Jacobello de la Seta	Ibid., sub 12 April
a. 1404	
Venetian:	
Marco de Cloderiis	Vat sub 2 Sept. 1404
Pietro Michiel	Ibid., sub 29 Aug. 1404
Genoese:	
Joh. Bolexio de Reveia[h]	Ibid., sub 2 July 1404
Paolo Lercaro	Ibid., sub 2 Sept. 1404
Pietro di Sestri of Pera	Ibid., sub 26 July 1404
Catalan:	
Sta Trinitas	
patron: Berenguer Vidal	Ibid., without date (fall 1404)[i]

A 6 (continued)

French:	
Michael de Bera of Marseilles[j]	Ibid., sub 11 Aug. 1404
Sta Eulalia - St Olivus	
patron: Rafael Ferandus[k]	Ibid., sub 27 Sept. 1404
Sta Maria	
patron: Joh. Ignis de Tasia of Biscaya[l]	Ibid., sub 1 Oct. 1404
Florentine:	
St Salvator	
patron: Guglielmo di Pietro of Pisa	Ibid., sub 2 July 1404
Sicilian:	
Sta Maria de la Scala	
patron: Pasqual Pauli of Messina[m]	Ibid., sub 28 July 1404
Cypriot:	
St Niccolò	
patron: Bartol. de Ponco, of Cerini[n]	Ibid., sub 3 Dec. 1404
Ragusan:	
Michael de Alegueti[o]	Ibid., sub 8 Aug. 1404
a. 1405	
Venetian:	
Giacomo Sabadini	Vat sub 24 Dec. 1405
Genoese:	
Urbano de Final	Ibid., sub 2 Sept.
Joh. Spinola	
arriv. 13 July	Ibid., sub 7 Sept.
St Nicolò	
patron: Pietro Cattaneo	Ibid., sub 28 Sept., 1 Oct. 1405
Sta Maria	
patron: Andello Imperiale[p]	Ibid., sub 3 Nov. 1405
Bart. Pinello	Ibid., sub 3 Nov. 1405
Oberto Cicogna	Ibid., sub ... Dec. 1405
Catalan:	
Bernat Prat	Ibid., sub 27 Jan. 1405
Bernat Oliva	Ibid., sub 22 June 1405
Bernat Pellicer of Barcelona	Ibid., sub 5 May 1405
Jacme Todera	Ibidem, sub 23 July 1405
Bernat Fustier	
arriv. 30 Oct.	Ibidem, sub 6 Nov.

A 6 (continued)

a. 1405 (continued)

Francesch Rispal	Ibidem, sub 13 Nov. 1405
St Nicolo e Sta Maria	Ibidem, sub 5 May, 22 June 1405
patron: Arnau Sorel	
Nicholau Puyad[r]	Ibidem, sub 13 Nov. 1405
Sicilian:	
Sta Maria de la Scala	
patron: Pasqual Pauli of Messina	Ibid., sub 9 April 1405
Sta Maria de la Scala	
patron: Ant. Porzello of Messina[s]	Ibid., sub 12 Oct. 1405
Ant. Calafat of Messina	Ibid., sub 1 and 18 July 1405
Porello de Luzeri[t]	Ibid., sub 18 July 1405
Maltese:	
St Salvator	
patron: Nic. de Bonfio[u]	Ibid., sub ... Feb. 13 and 21 April 1405
Rhodian:	
Emmanue Sagudini	Ibid., sub 14 May 1405 5 June
Andrea Canavazuol	Ibid., sub 7 Oct. 1405

a. 1427

Venetian:	
Alvise Zotarello	Tur IV, f. 5b f.
Bart. Benedetto	Ibid., f. 6b
Jacobus de Frederico	Ibid., f. 13b f.
Genoese:	
Augusto Gropello	Ibid., f. 40a ff.
Jacobus de Fornari	l. c.
Alberto Fodrano	l. c.
Catalan:	
Ant. Roig	Ibid., f. 11b
Sicilian:	
Joh. Bucello	
arriv. 7 Sept. 1427	Ibid., f. 40a ff.
Jac. de Fornieto	Ibid., f. 23b ff.
Cretan:	
Joh. Jalina	Ibid., f. 3b f., 22b, 63b
Georgio Andrinopoliti	Ibid., f. 32a f.
Greek:	
Demetrius Focada of Negroponte	Ibid., f. 41b

A 6 (continued)

a. 1435

Venetian

Anzolo di Ca di Pesaro	Tur V, f. 26a
Ricardo Andree	Ibid., f. 41a f.
Jacobus Contarini	Ibid., f. 58a, 58b
Micaleto Zimalarcha	Ibid., f. 62a f;
Silvestro Pauli	Ibid., f. 63a f.
Genoese:	
Joh Oliva	Ibid., f. 37a f., 45b, 48a, 51b f.[v]
Pietro Fallamonegra[w]	Ibid., f. 44a ff., 45a, 46a
Gregorio Daliego	Ibid., f. 57a f.
Catalan:	
Esteban Torres[x]	Ibid., f. 48b f., 49b f., 52b
Cretan:	
Micaleto Thiliaca[y]	Ibid., f. 62b f.
Joh Langadoti	Ibid., f. 53a f., 55a
Ant. Trevisan	Ibid., f. 59b
Rhodian:	
Joh. Vixino	Ibid., f. 46a ff., 48a, 48b f.

NOTES

a) In addition some references to ships in the registers of the Council of the Venetian colony in Alexandria are quoted.

b) This ship is characterised in the contract of sale, which is quoted here,as "griparia de portata cantar' 600 subtil." Probably the Alexandrian spice kintar (of 45 kg) is meant, so that the capacity of the ship was 27 t only. It was indeed sold for 85 ducats.

c) He was an Amalfitan, see above p.

d) The ship ought to depart in October from Ancona.

e) This was the ship of Pere Tequin of Perpignan.

f) The ship is characterised as spinazza.

g) This is a contract of sale.

h) This is apparently the same patron called in another act, of 12 Sept., Ballosius de porto Moresii.

i) Contract of sale. It is a very small ship, of 150 butts.

j) This ship was a spinazza.

k) It is a ship of Bayonne.

l) Even this ship is a spinazza.

m) This is a panfilo.

n) This ship is a gripparia.

o) The ship is a spinazza.

A 6 (continued)

p) This is a big ship, for according to this act, a sale contract, 1/8 of it was sold for 380 ducats. So the ship was estimated at 3040 ducats.

r) Cf. Del Treppo, p. 610: Nic. Poigalt.

s) This is another ship having 400 butts and called by the same name (Sta Maria della Scala mentioned in the first place had only 130 butts, see above). It was sold for 3500 ducats.

t) This was a small ship, as it is characterised in the act as cochina.

u) This is a gripparia.

v) In this act the patron is called Zuliano Oliva.

w) This ship came from Rhodes to Alexandria and went on to the Maghreb.

x) The ship sailed from Alexandria to Rhodes.

y) As x.

B

The Levant trade of Jacme Olivier of Narbonne.
Data about his export shipments to
Egypt and Syria[a]

a. 1381			
	to Alexandria:		
	24 pieces of cloth, each worth 12.5 fl.,		300 fl.
	other cloth		203.75
		total	503.75 fl.[b]
a. 1382			
	to Alexandria and Beirut:		
	cloth, the piece 11.75 fl.,		
	and linen		928.75 fl.
a. 1383			
	to Damascus:		
	honey		161 fl.
	other commodities		464
		total	625 fl.
a. 1384			
	to Alexandria:		
	19 pieces cloth of Narbonne, 12.83 fl. each		244 fl.
	79 quintals honey		186
	ambergris		137.5
	other commodities		672.5
	a bill of exchange		125
		total	1365 fl.
a. 1385			
	To Alexandria:		
	honey		41.2 fl.
	cash		208.75
	to Damascus:		
	cloth 46 pieces, each worth 9.5 fl.		722
		total	971.95 fl.
a. 1386			
	to Alexandria:		
	46.5 quintals honey		117.5 fl.
	a bill of exchange		132.5
		total	250 fl.

Jacme Olivier [2]

a. 1387		
to Rhodes, Alexandria, Beirut:		
88.5 pieces cloth, each worth 10 fl.		885 fl.
20 pieces linen, each worth 3 fl.		60
47.5 quintals honey, each worth 2.5 fl.		117.5
	total	1062.5 fl.
a. 1388		
to Rhodes, Beirut:		
50 pieces cloth, each worth 10 fl.		500 fl.
4 " " " " 15 "		60
to Alexandria:		
25 quintals honey		46.25
	total	606.25 fl.
a. 1390		
to Alexandria and Beirut		
a commenda		1022.5 fl.
another commenda		500
	total	1522.5 fl.

a) This merchant carried on trade with the Greek territories too. About the sources of these accounts see above p.

b) For the price of the commodities shipped to the Levant pepper, ginger and cinnamon were bought.

Appendix C

Prices of export and import goods

1. Copper prices in Venice[a]

date	kind of copper	price	source
26 May 1395	rame di bolla[b]	L 8 s f [c]	Dat 926, letter of Zanobi di Taddeo Gaddi
10 June "	" " "	82.5 duc.	Ibidem, letter of the same
20 Aug. "	copper[d]	81 "	Ibidem, letter of the same
3 Oct. 1396	rame di bolla	85 "	Ibidem, letter of the same
19 March 1398	" "	L 6	Ibidem, letter of Piero di Giovanni Dini
	stazato[e]	L 7 s 5	ibidem
22 Jan. 1400	rame di bolla	L 8 s 16	Dat 927, letter of Bernardo degli Alberti
20 Nov. "	" "	87 duc.	Dat 712, letter of Com. of Zanobi di Taddeo Gaddi
	scacciato[f]	74 "	ibidem
1445	refined copper[g]	92 "	G.P., Sent. 99, f. 42a f.

a) This list of prices is a supplement to that in Les métaux précieux, p. 116 ff. The prices are those of a migliaio grosso of 477 kg.

b) Small tablets, see Pegolotti, p. 380 f.

c) These are lire di grossi, one of them being equal to 10 ducats.

d) "fine", perhaps thin plates.

e) About the difference between the kind of copper which bears the bolla of San Marco and the other kinds of small tablets see Pegolotti l.c.

f) Another kind of small tablets.

g) covado.

2. Copper prices in the Levant[a]

date	place	kind of copper	price	source
1396	Damascus	non-specified[b]	32 dinars (800 dirh.)	Misti 44, f. 55a, cf. Melis, Aspetti, p. 384
1397	"	rame di bolla	16.5 din.	Dat 797, letter of Zanobi of 12 Dec. 1397
1399	Alexandria	" "	16 din.	Dat 844, letter of Scolaio di Giov. Spini from Ancona of 29 May 1399
1401	Alexandria	non-specified	17.5 din.	Ainaud, Quatre doc., doc. I
22 March 1403	Damascus	rame di bolla	40 " (1200 dirh.)	Dat 928, copy of a letter from Damascus of that date
1405	Alexandria	" "	11.5 din.	G.P., Sent. 18, f. 15a ff.
1410	"	plates[c]	15 "	Ainaud, art. cit., doc. II
March 1424	"	"	14 "	Melis, Doc. , p. 190
1434	"	copper wire	28 duc.	G.P., Sent. 104, f. 9b f.[d]
1438	"	non-specified	15 "	Badoer c. 299

Appendix C (continued)

1440	Damascus	non-specified	35 " (1400 dirh.)[e]	G.P., Sent. 165, f. 93b ff.
1441	Alexandria	" " [f]	26 duc	same series 96, f. 81a ff.
1459	"	" "	20 "	ASF, Conv. opp., vol. 322, c. 45
1481	Acre	bars	36 ashrafis	Archives Baseggio

a) *The prices of copper in Alexandria are those of a djarwi kintar of 96.7 kg and* those of Damascus refer to the kintar of 185 kg. Other prices of copper in the Moslem Levant, see in Lee metaux precieux p. 61 ff.

b) If the kind of copper is not specified, it was probably most often also rame di bolla or another kind of small tablets whose price was more or less the same.

c) Tole (here in Catalan: taulles).

d) Cf. G.P., Sent. 104, f. 128b f.: 100 (heavy) Ven. pounds - 15.7 duc.

e) The ducat is calculated at 40 dirh., see my paper Etudes sur le système monétaire, p. 278.

f) First one reads in this document about barile di rame and then about zerti lavori de rame (i.e. copper vessels).

3. Prices of pepper in Syria[a]

date	price of a ḳinṭār		source
end 1379	44 din.	(1100 dirh.)	Dat 1171
April 1386	80 "	(2000)	Ibidem
1 Sept. 1386	48.6 "	(1215)	Melis, Doc., p. 318
2 April 1388	52 "	(1300)	Dat 709, letter of Zanobi di Taddeo Gaddi of 12 May 1388
10 July 1392	76-80 "	(1990-2000)	Dat 549, letter of the same of 9 Oct. 1392.
Sept. 1392	90 "	(2100)	Braunstein, Relations d'affaires, Mélanges d'archéol. et d'hist. (Rome) 76 (1964), p. 269
1394	44-60 "	(1100-1500)[b]	Dat 710, letter of Agostino Binozzi & fratelli of 22 Nov. 1394
29 Aug. 1394	60 "	(1500)	Ibid., letter of Zanobi di Taddeo Gaddi of 4 Nov. 1394
20 Sept. "	60 "	(1500)	Ibid., letter of the same of 7 Nov. 1394
23 Oct. "	56 "	(1400)	Melis, Doc., p. 384
6 Jan. 1395	52 "	(1300)	Dat 710, letter of Zanobi of 30 March 1395
28 Feb. 1395	56 "	(1400)	Ibid., letter of the same of 17 April 1395
24 March "	52 "	(1500)	Ibid., letter of the same of 6 May 1395
14 June "	53 "	(1525)	Dat 710, letter of the same of 7 Sept. 1395
2 Aug. "	57.2 "	(1430)	Melis, Doc., p. 184
12 Aug. "	58 "	(1450)	Dat 927, letter of Zanobi of 5 Oct. 1395
begin. 1396	82 "	(2050)	Dat 926, letter of the same of 1 April 1396
" " "[d]	80 "	(2000)[e]	Ibid., letter of the same of 6 May 1396

Appendix C (continued)

date	price of a ḳinṭār	source
15 March "	78-80 " (1950-2000)	Melis, Doc., p. 154
8 April "	80 " (2000)	Heers, Il commercio, p. 205
5 Aug. "	82 " (2050)	Dat 926, letter of Zanobi of 23 Aug. 1396
15 Aug. 1398	60 " (1500)	Heers l. c.
15 Sept. "	58 " (1450)	Ibidem
14 Feb. 1300	50 " (1500)	Dat 1171, price list
end 1400	"in Syria", dearth 141, then 170 din.	Dat 713, letter of Simone di Lappacino of 8 Jan. 1401
1402	Jerusalem 69.3 din. (2080)[f]	G.P., Sent. IX, f. 17a ff., 18b ff.
21 Sept. 1403	43.3 din.(1300)	Dat 928, letter of commess. of Zanobi
Oct. "	55 " (1650)	Ibid., letter of the same
middle Oct."	43.3 " (1300)	Dat 714, letter of Paris Soranzo of 24 Nov. 1403
1403	Ramla 100 duc.[g]	
1412	Ramla 160 duc.	Accounts Soranzo, f. 36b
1413	120 "	ASV, Miscell. di carte non appartenenti a nessun archivio Ba 8, fasc. 1
1413	with expenses in Syria: 162.5 duc.	Accounts Soranzo, f. 40b
	" " " " 159 duc.	Ibidem f. 43b
1423	113 duc.	Accounts Giustinian, part 2, f. 4b
1424	i pondo 81.6 duc.	Accounts Soranzo c. 118a
1425	128 duc.	Accounts Giustinian part 22 , f. 10b
1428 (?)	71.3 "	G.P., Sent. 77a f. 140b
1437	Acre with all expenses 60.6 duc.	G.P., Sent. 86, f. 20b ff
1437	fall fair the sultan sells to the Ven. for 100 duc.	Zancaruola II, c. 568b; Chron. Dolfin, f. 379a
April-May 1438	the sultan demands from the Ven. 103 duc.	Jorga, ROL VI, p. 406
1471	60 "	G.P., Ter V, f. 68a
7 Dec. 1471	53 "	Ibid. f. 207a
1472	i collo 35 "	Senato Mar X, f. 133b f.
1473 (cca)	Tripoli 1 collo 45 or 46.3 or 47.2 duc.	G.P., Sent. 158, f. 43a ff.
1473 (cca)	1 collo 33 duc.	Senato Mar X, f. 25a
before 1479	" 30 "	Ibid. XI, f. 40a
1479	45-3/4 ashr.	G.P., Ter IX, f. 148a
1482	1 collo 30.5 duc.	Senato Mar XI, f. 149a

a) The following data should be added to those listed in Histoire des prix et des salaires, p. 410. If no other place is mentioned, the prices listed in this table are those of Damascus. The price of 1400 is reported as that of "Syria", which probably means also Damascus.

Appendix C (continued)

b) This is the price at which the Venetians bought pepper through the year until the arrival of the galleys. In another letter the prices mentioned are for the same period 1188 - 1288 dirh., see Dat. 549, letter of Zanobi di Taddeo Gaddi of 29 Oct. 1394. In a third letter Zanobi reports that they were 1188 - 1300, see ibid., letter of 4 Nov. 1394.

c) The writer of the letter quotes another written in Damascus, but does not mention its date.

d) As c.

e) 200 d., should be 2000 d. (dirhams).

f) This is the price fixed by the tribunal. Both the plaintiff and the defendant indicated higher prices. The price is calculated at 30 dirh. the dinar. But the tribunal calculated at 28 dirh. So the price would have been 74.3 dinar. The kintar is probably the Damascene and not the heavier kintar of Ramla which was equal to 800 light Venetian pounds, i.e. 241 kg, see Pasi, c. 5a.

g) This price was claimed by the Venetian government from the Genoese for pepper which had been robbed. It was demanded 180 duc. for 1.8 kintar of Ramla. The Genoese offered two thirds of the price claimed.

4. Price of ginger in Alexandria
(price of 1 kinṭār fulfuli)

date	beledi	Meccan	colombino	sources
2nd. quarter of XIVth cent.	12 din.			Tarifa p. 61
Aug. 1347	22 din.	20-21 din.		Pignol Zucchello no. 44
Sept. "		20 "		Op. cit. no. 45
Nov. "		19-20 "		Op. cit. no. 56
Dec. "		18-19 "		Op. cit. no. 57
23 Dec."		18-20 "		Op. cit. no. 58
Feb. 1348	18.5 din.			Op. cit. no. 61
1393[a]	30 "		28 "	Dat 710, letter of Zanobi di Taddeo Gaddi of 25 Oct. 1393
29 Jan. 1395	45 "	16-18 "		Ibid., letter of the same of 30 March 1395
26 March "	46 "	23 "		Ibid., letter of the same of 17 April 1395
spring "[b]	47 "	22 "		Dat 926, letter of the same 13 July 1395
9 July "	44 "	22 "[c]		Dat 710, letter of the same of 7 Sept. 1395
12 Aug. "	44 "	22.5 "		Dat 527, letter of the same of 5 Oct. 1395
26 Feb. 1396	42 "	16 "	40 "	Dat 1171
March "[d]	40 "	24 "		Dat 526, letter of Zanobi of 13 May 1396
12 March "	30 "	12 "		Ibid., letter of Piero di Giovanni Dini

Appendix C (continued)

date	beledi	Meccan	colombino	sources
May-June " [e]		24 "		Ibid., letter of Zanobi of 23 Aug. 1396
July "	15 "	8 "	16 "	Dat 1171
Oct. "	45 "	23 "	43 "	Ibidem
end of XIV cent.	8-10 "			Reinaud, JA 1829, II, p. 30
1401	14 "	11 "		Dat 927, letter of Comm. of Zanobi of 20 and 22 May 1401
18 Jan. 1402	18 "	13-14 "		Dat 928, letter of the same of 17 April 1402
April 1403		14 din.		Dat 928, letter of Com. of Zanobi of 9 May 1403
29 Sept. 1403[f]	20-22 din.	16 "		Ibid., letter of the same of 17 Nov. 1403
8 Oct. 1403		15 "		Ibid., letter of the same of 24 Nov. 1403
mid-Nov. "		16 "		Dat 714, anonymous letter of 9 Feb. 1404
March 1410	22-23 "	11 "	20 din.	Ainaud, Quatre docs., doc. III.
Nov. "	24 "	11 "		Art. cit., doc. III
1413	22 "			Accounts Soranzo, f. 42b
25 Nov. 1422	133 duc.[g]			Accounts Ben. Strozzi, f. 2b
Sept. 1439	10 "			Jorga, ROL VI, p. 422
1441	12 "			G.P., Sent. 86, f. 76a ff.
1447	18 "[h]			Tur II, f. 24a
1453	16 "			Tur II, f. 59b f.
March 1459	14-15			Letter Squarzalupi
1461	14 duc.	7.8 duc.		G.P., Tur IV, f. 49a, 49b
"	1 collo 100 duc.[i]			G.P., Sent. 166, f. 129a ff.
1469[j]	11.8 duc. 1 collo 120 duc.			G.P., Sent. 153, f. 54b ff.
before 1470	" 120 duc.			Ibid. f. 84a ff.
1477	21 duc.			G.P., Sent. 169, f. 58b

a) The writer of the letter quotes news from Alexandria without indicating their date.

b) As a.

c) The writer of the letter says that the Catalans bought for 50 and 25 dinars respectively.

d) As a.

e) As a.

f) *It is not said in this letter that this was the price of ginger in Alexandria, but* there can be no doubt about it.

g) It is not said that beledi ginger was bought at this price. But certainly it was this kind of ginger.

Appendix C (continued)

h) As g.

i) The claimant demanded 133 duc.

j) There is no date in the act, but one reads there that the merchandise was shipped to Venice on the galley of Joh. Vallaresso and according to Senato Mar VIII, f. 203a he was indeed in that year patron of an Alexandria galley. On the other hand one reads in the same act that Ant. Contarini was captain of that convoy, whereas according to Coll., Not. XI, f. 46a in 1469 Jacob. Zorzi held this post. Probably the latter was replaced by Contarini.

Appendix D

Venetian Consuls in Egypt and in Syria

In the Venetian sources several lists of consuls have come down to us. A list of the consuls in Alexandria from the year 1443 is contained in the Segretario alle voci, V, f. 38b and VI, f. 93b. Between these two lists, which are in fact two copies of the same list, there are some minor differences. The consuls of Venice in Damascus from 1452 are listed in Segretario alle voci V, f. 39a and VI, f. 94a. Even these two lists are copies of the same document and comprise some variations. Similar lists are to be found in MS. Marciana Cl. VII, no. CXCVIII, Reggimenti. That of the consuls in Alexandria begins in the year 1344 and that of the consuls in Damascus in 1384. The list of the consuls in Tripoli in the same MS. is a fragmentary one (about the MS. see de Mas Latrie, Traites II, p. 258).

From the Marciana MS. the list of the consuls in Alexandria, Damascus and Tripoli has been printed by C. Poma, "Il consolato veneto. in Egitto," Bollettino del Ministero degli Affari esteri 1897, p. 469 ff., and that of the consuls in Damascus by Berchet, Relazioni, p. 55 ff.

All these lists are incomplete and comprise mistakes. Here they have been completed and corrected according to the data in the registers of the Senate and the Collegio, notarial and judicial acts. But of course the following lists are not complete either. They are tentative ones.

1. Consuls in Alexandria

		sources
Francesco de Canal	1302-1303	See Heyd II, p. 38
Pancrazio Venier	1304-	Op. cit., p. 39
Gabriele Marcello	1308	Giomo, Lettere di collegio, no. 36
Pietro Giustinian	1344-	Poma, p. 469 ff.
Soranzo Soranzo	before 1349	Misti 25, f. 13b
Andrea Zane	1349-1350	Poma, p. l.c.
Marino Michiel	1350-1353	Poma l. c. Cf. Misti 30, f. 68b. G.P., Sent. Int. V, f. 44a, 45b
Pietro Iustiniano	1355-1356	Misti 27, f. 21a, 96b 30, f. 68b
Marco Iustinian	1359-1361	Misti 30, f. 5a, 68b,; Poma l.c.
Andrea delle Grazie	1361	Libri Comm. III, lib. 7, no. 268
Nicolo Contarini	1361	Poma l.c.

Andrea Venier	1363-1365	Misti 31, f. 38b 33, f. 77a; Heyd II, p. 52; Bibl. Ec. des chartes 1873, p. 78 ff.
Johan Badoer	1365-1367	Misti 32, f. 71a; M.C. Novella, f. f. 263a; Misti 32, f. 127b
Marino Vener	1367	Misti 32, f. 87a
Johan Barbarigo	1372-75	M.C. Novella, f. 362a f.; Coll., Secreta 1366-72, f. 26b
Domenico Bono	before 1382	Misti 37, f. 49a
Egidio Morosini	1384-1386	Misti 39, f. 25b; Poma l.c.
Alvise Morosini	1386-	Poma l.c.
Pietro Quirini	1390	Misti 41, f. 92b; cf. Wilken p. 32
Johan da Canal	1392-	Misti 42, f. 75a
Francesco Malipiero	1396-1397 (?)	Misti 44, f. 55a
Peracio Malipiero	139801399	Misti 44, f. 52b, 122b
Antonio de Mula	1399-1401	Misti 44, f. 131b 45, f. 85b, 88b; Vat f. 5a, sub 25 May 1400, 20 Oct., 29 Dec. 1400
Vettore Marvello	1401-1403	G.P., Sent. 41, f. 76a ff., Leonardo de Valle sub 20 Nov. 1401, 16 March, 12 April and 5 Nov. 1403; cf. Misti 47, f. 113a
Andrea Iustinian	1403-1406	Vat sub 13 Nov. 1404, 8 July 1405, 10 Jan. 1406; Poma l.c.
Bartolomeo Storlado	1406-1408	Misti 47, f. 113a 48, f. 29b Poma l.c.
Biegio Dolfin	1408-1410	Misti 48, f. 29b, 157a; Poma l.c.
Lorenzo Capello	1410-1412	Misti 48, f. 157a, 170b f.; Poma l.c.
Piero Trevisan	1412-1414	G.P., Sent. 54, f. 144a and cf. 71, f. 80b 68, f. 75a ff.; Crist. Rizzo sub 8 Nov. 1414a; Poma l.c.
Bartolomeo Storlado	1414-1416	G.P., Sent. 65, f. 103a ff.; Crist. Rizzo sub 30 Oct. 1414, 5 Jan. and 9 March 1416; Morosini c. 295; Poma l.c.
Fantin Viaro	1416-1418	Misti 52, f. 76a, 152a; Poma l.c.
Biegio Dolfin ("the Elder")	1418-1420	Misti 53, f. 72a; G.P., Sent. 34, f. 37a b ff.; Nic. Venier A, f. 8b; Poma l.c.
Francesco Michiel ("the Elder")	1420-1422	Misti 53, f. 72a; G.P., Sent. 42 bis, g f. 110b F. Sent Int. IX, f. 15b, 18b Nic. Venier B, 2, f. 25b, 40a ff.; B, 1.f. 11a Poma l.c.
Lunardo de Priuli	1422-1424	Misti 55, f. 96b; Nic. Venier B, 2, f. 40a ff.; Poma l.c.
Marco Morosini	1424-1426	Misti 55, f. 59b; 56, f. 70a, 71a ff.; Cristoforo del Fiore I, f. 12a ff., 22a f.; degli Elmi 74/75 sub 2 Oct. 1426; Tur IV, f. 1a, 5b; Morosini c. 428; Jorga, "Notes et extraits," ROL V, p. 176 f., 345; Poma l.c.

Luca Trun ("the Elder")	1426-1428	G.P., Sent. 54, f. 36a ff.; Tur IV, f. 63b; Poma l.c.
Benedetto Dandolo	1428-1431	G.P., Sent. 63, f. 94b ff. 69, f. 66a ff. 83, f. 2a ff.; Jorga in ROL VI, p. 71, 103 f.; cf. Tur V, f. 61b; Marino Sanuto, Vite, c. 1018 Poma l.c. Misti 58, f. 44a, 45a
Marco Geno ("the Elder")	1431-1433	Misti 58, f. 115a; Tur V, f. 1a, 23b f.; Poma l.c.
Nicolo da Molin	1434-1435	Misti 59, f. 71a 60, f. 32b, 39b; G.P., Sent. 74, f. 130b; Tur V, f. 1b, 13a f., 15a f., 16a ff., 18a f., 18b, 19a, 20a, 20'b, 23b f., 24b, 44a ff.;
Lunardo Venier	1436	G.P., Sent. 76, f. 51b ff.
Giovanni Pisani	1437-1439	M.C. Ursa, f. 121b
Zorzi Soranzo	1439-1441	Poma l.c.
Andrea Gabriel	1441-1443	Poma l.c.
Polo Valaresso ("the Elder")	1443-1444	Segretario alle voci V, f. 38b VI, f. 93b; Jorga in ROL VII, p. 380 f.[c] Poma l.c.
Dardo Foscarini ("the Elder")	1444-1447	Poma l.c.
Marino de Priuli	1447-1449	Jorga in ROL VIII, p. 56 ff.; Poma l.c.
Marco Quirini ("the Elder")	1449-1452	Poma l.c.[e]
Francesco Donato	1454-1457	Segretario alle voci l.c.; Coll., Not. IX, f. 27a; Senato Mar VI, f. 18a; Tur II, f. 17a 43b, 56b f., 64a f., 76b; Poma l.c.[f]
Bernardo Contarini	1457-1459	Coll., Not. IX, f. 105a; Senato Mar VI, f. 18a; Poma l.c.[g]
Joh. Maffio Contarini	1460-1463	Coll., Not. IX, f. 179a X, f. 5a; Poma l.c.[h]
Andrea Duodo	1463-1466	Segretario alle voci l.c.; Secreta 22, f. 39a f.; Poma l.c.[i]
Ludovico Gabriel	1466-1469	Segretario alle voci l.c.; Senato Mar VIII, f. 126a; Wilken p. 32 Poma l.c.[j]
Johan Maffio Contarini	1469-1471	Segretario alle voci l.c.; Senato Mar IX, f. 113b; Poma l.c.[k]
Giacomo Querini	1473-1474	Poma l.c.
Francesco Bembo	1474-1477	Segretario alle voci l.c.; Senato Mar X, f. 135b; Secreta 26, f. 138a f. 27, f. 96a; Poma l.c.[l]
Andrea Trevisan	1477-1480	Segretario alle voci l.c.; Poma l.c.[m]
Antonio Contrarini	1480-1483	Senato Mar XI, f. 83a; Poma l.c.
Andrea Gabriel	1483-1486	Segretario alle voci l.c.; Senato Mar XII, f. 66a; Poma l.c.
Lunardo Longo	1486-1489	Segretario alle voci l.c.; Senato Mar XII, f. 75b, 82a; Poma l.c.[n]
Polo da Canal	1489	Segretario alle voci l.c.; Poma l.c.[o]

Ambrosio Contarini	1490-1492	Segretario alle voci l.c.; Senato Mar XIV, f. 18a; G.P., Sent 37, f. 21b;[p]
Giosafa Barbara		p. 27, 62 Poma l.c. [q]
Nicolo Malipiero	1492-1493	Segretario alle voci l.c.; Senato Mar IXV, f. 4b f.; Poma l.c.[r]
Alvise Arimondo	1493-1495	Segretario alle voci l.c.; Senato Mar XIV, f. 75b; Poma l.c.[t]
Bartolomeo Contarini	1495-1496	Poma l.c.
Francesco Bernardo	1496-1498	Coll., Not. XIV, f. 139a; Senato Mar XIV, f. 75b[u]

a) In this act he is mentioned as a former consul.

b) In the decision of the Senate of August 30, 1420 contained in Misti l.c. one reads that Biegio Dolfin died in the preceding year. So he was deceased either at the end of 1419 or at the beginning of 1420. But since this decision comprises orders to the new consul who will go to Alexandria (iturus), B. Dolfin must have died at the beginning of 1420.

c) He was appointed in September 1443, see Jorga l.c., and took over on November 3, 1443, see Segr. alle voci l.c.

d) Zaccaria Contarini, who is mentioned in Tur II, f. 42a of January 14, 1444 as Venetian consul in Alexandria, was probably vice-consul.

e) In a Ragusan act Francesco Malipiero is mentioned as Venetian consul in Alexandria in the year 1450, see Krekic, no. 1258. Even he was probably the acting vice-consul.

f) According to Segr. alle voci he took over on Dec. 15, 1454. Probably he died at the beginning of 1457, for his decease is spoken of in a session of the Senate in May 1457, see Senato Mar l.c., and see the following note.

g) He held his post probably until the end of 1459, for it was decided by the Collegio on April 19, 1457, see Not. l.c., that he should serve two years and a half.

h) Poma has 1459-1462, but he was in February and in July 1460 still in Venice, see Coll., Not. l.c.

i) The exact dates of his tenure of the office were August 2, 1463 to Oct. 9, 1466 (Segr. alle voci VI l.c. has 38 Oct. 1466): Poma has 1462-1466.

j) Poma has Alessandro Gabriel (Alessandro in place of Alvise!); the exact dates of his tenure of office are Oct. 19, 1466 to Nov. 3, 1469.

k) He took over on Nov. 3, 1469.

l) He entered office according to Segr. alle voci V l.c. in Oct. 1474 and according to Segr. alle voci VI in Nov. 1474.

m) The exact dates of his tenure of office are Oct. 1477 (Segr. alle voci VI has Nov. 1477) to Oct. 1480. No days are given.

n) The exact dates of his office holding are Sept. 1486 to July 7, 1489.

o) He died on the way (obiit in itinere), on 7 July, see Segr. alle voci V, l.c. or on 4 July, see Segr. alle voci VI l.c., obviously on his way to Egypt

p) The act quoted here is contained in a sheet attached to a volume of the Senteneze of the 1420's.

q) He entered office on 30 June 1490 and held it until 16 Oct. 1492.

r) According to Segr. alle voci he entered office on 16 Oct. 1492 and died in May 1493. But this is mistaken as one reads in the registers of Senato Mar l.c. that on 11 March 1495 one knew in Venice about his decease.

s) He took over, according to Segr. alle voci, on 7 Oct. 1493, and on the other hand there was a vice-consul in Alexandria in October 1495.

t) He was elected in August 1495, see Senato Mar l.c., but did not depart before 14 May 1496, see Coll., Not., l.c.

---

2. Consuls (or Vice-Consuls) in Damietta

Michaleto Papadopolo	1420	Nic. Venier A, f. 8b
Antonio Amirando	1444	G.P., Sent. 119, f. 64a ff.
Piero di Piero	1488	Malipiero, p. 609; Mas Latrie, Hist. III, p. 438

3. Consuls in Damascus

Marco Brici	1370-	Misti 33, f. 54a 34, f. 156a[a]
Johan Barbarigo	1375-1376	Misti 35, f. 9b ff., 152a
Domenico Bono	before 1382	Misti 37, f. 48 ff.
Francesco Bragadin	1381	Misti 37, f. 101a 42, f. 15bf
Johan Barbarigo	1382-1384	Misti 37, f. 97b 38, f. 135a
Francesco Foscolo	1384-1386	Berchet, Relazioni, p. 55 ff.
Giovanni Mocenigo	1386-	Berchet l.c.
Luca Bragadin	1390-1391	Misti 41, f. 105a 42, f. 15b
Johan Barbarigo	1392	Misti 42, f. 72a
Polo Zane	1400-1401	Misti 45, f. 50a, 94a

Francesco Foscarini	1405-1407	Berchet l.c.
Giovanni Zorzi	1407-1409	Berchet l.c.
Battista Emo	1409-1411	Berchet l.c.
Pietro Mudazio	1411-1413	Misti 49, f. 127b; Giacomo della Torre no. 2, 12, 19; Berchet l.c.[b]
Giovanni Dolfin	1413-1415	Coll. Not. IV, f. 157a; Morosini c. 281; Berchet l.c.
Jacobo Pesaro	1415-1417	Misti 51, f. 52a; Berchet l.c.
Luca Trun	1417-1419	Misti 52, f. 41a 53, f. 25a 57, f. 184a; Nic. Venier B, 2, f. 1a, 9b f. Berchet l.c.
Troilo Malipiero	1419-1421	Misti 52, f. 100a 53, f. 130a; G.P., Sent. 36, f. 89b f.; Sent. Int. IX, f. 7a; Franc. Negro Ba 132 sub 13 Febr. 1421; Jorga in ROL V, p. 115 f.: Berchet l.c.
Lorenzo Malipiero	1421-1423	Misti 54, f. 40b; Berchet l.c.
Bartolomeo Storlado	1423-1425	Misti 54, f. 141b f., 142b 55, f. 35a, 160b; Morosini c. 410; Jorga in ROL V, f. 173; Berchet l.c.
Zaccaria Trevisan	1425-1427	Misti 55, f. 160b, 163b; Berchet l.c.
Andrea Corner	1427-1429	Misti 57, f. 184a; Berchet l.c.
Stefano Quirini	1429-1431	Berchet l.c.
Giovanni Dolfin	1431-1433	Misti 58, f. 80a, 95b; Berchet l.c.
Lorenzo Mudazio	1434-1436	Misti 59, f. 68a, 71a 60, f. 6a, 32b; Vat III, f. (1a ff.); Berchet l.c.
Marino Zane	1439-1440	Misti 60, f. 212b; Senato Mar I, f. 143b f.; G.P., Sent 86, f. 87b ff. Jorga in ROL VII, p. 93; Berchet l.c.
Nicolo Soranzo	1442-	Senato Mar I, f. 98a f. cf. Jorga in G.P., Sent. 92, f. ROL VII, p. 62 f. 127a ff.; Berchet l.c.
Pietro Quirini	1442-1444	Berchet l.c.
Bartolomeo Lombardo	1444	Ibidem
Luca de Lege	1444-1446	Coll., Not. VIII, f. 52b; G.P., Sent. 106, f. 1a ff.; Berchet l.c.
Antonio de Mezo	1446	Berchet l.c.
Leon Molin	1446-	Ibidem
Maffio Michiel	1452-1454	Segretario alle voci V, f. 39a VI, f. 14a[e]
Marino Molin	1454-1456	Segretario alle voci l.c. Coll., Not. IX, f. 104b; Crist. del Fiore V, f. 4a (23a ff.): Berchet l.c.[f]
Stefano Malipiero	1457-1460	Segretario alle voci l.c. Coll., Not. IX, f. 34a, 150a; Roberto da Sanseverino, p. 180; Berchet l.c.[g]

Michele Cappello	1460-1463	Segretario alle voci l.c. Senato Mar VII, f. 25b G.P., Cap. pub. VIII, f. 26a; Crist. del Fiore VI, f. 1b, 7a f.; Berchet l.c.[h]
Jeronimo Bembo	1463-1466	Segretario alle voci l.c. Coll., Not. X, f. 79b, 91b; G.P., Sent. 140, f. 83a; G.P., Ter II, II, f. 57b; Crist. del Fiore VI, f. 20a ff. Berchet l.c.[i]
Marco Priuli	1466-1469	Segretario alle voci l.c. Senato Mar VIII, f. 17a; Berchet l.c.[j]
Giovanni Priuli	1469-1472	Segretario alle voci l.c. Senato Mar IX, f. 144a; Berchet l.c.[k]
Toma Malipiero	1472-1473	Coll., Not. XI, f. 125a; Berchet l.c.
Hermolao Minio	1473-1474	Senato Mar XI, f. 176b f.; G.P., Sent. 181, f. 122a ff.; Berchet l.c.[l]
Giovanni Priuli	1474-	Berchet l.c.
Alvise Mimo	1479-	G.P., Ter IX, f. 148a
Francesco Bembo	1480-1482	Segretario alle voci l.c.; Berchet l.c.[m]
Francesco Marcello	1482-1485	Segretario alle voci l.c. Senato Mar XI, f. 149b XIII, f. 20b ff., 24b ff.; Berchet l.c.[n]
Giovanni Mocenigo	1485-1487	Segretario alle voci l.c.; Senato Mar XII, f. 52a XIII, f. 20b ff., 24b ff.; Berchet l.c.[o]
Tomaso Falier	1487-1489	Segretario alle voci l.c.; Senato Mar XII, f. 117a; G.P., Sent. 188, f. 206a ff.; Berchet l.c.[p]
Antonio Moro	1489-1492	Segretario alle voci l.c. Berchet l.c.[r]
Ieronimo Bembo	1492-1493	Segretario alle voci l.c.; Berchet l.c.[s]
Luigi Arimondo	1493-1494	Berchet l.c.[t]
Giovanni Vallaresso	1494-1496	Segretario alle voci l.c.; Berchet l.c.[u]
Benedetto Sanuto	1496-1500	Segretario alle voci l.c. Berchet l.c.[v]

---

a) From the act quoted in last place one could conclude that Brici held the post until 1375, but this conclusion would be contradicted by the instructions given to Joh' Barbarigo, ambassador to the sultan in 1375.

b) Berchet has Muazzo.

c) In the decision of the Senate of August 4, 1434 it is said that he is about to depart for Damascus (iturus). So Berchet, who has 1433-1436 as the dates of his tenure of office is mistaken. See Misti 59, f. 68a.

d) According to Berchet, he entered his office in 1441, but he was in June 1442 still in Venice, see Senato Mar l.c.

e) The exact dates of his tenure of office were May 14, 1452 to September 22, 1454.

f) According to Berchet, he took over in 1453, but in Coll. Not. l.c., one reads that he entered his office on Sept. 22, 1454. Segretario alle voci which has for his tenure of office the dates Sept. 22, 1454 to Sept. 16, 1457.

g) Berchet quotes from his sources the year 1456 as beginning of his tenure of office, but from Coll., Not. and Senato Mar l.c. one learns that he was appointed on Nov. 25, 1456 and was on Aug. 7, 1457 still in Venice. Segr. alle voci has for his tenure of office the dates Sept. 16, 1457 to Aug. 1, 1460.

h) Since Stefano Malipiero was in 1460 still consul, see Senato Mar VI, f. 150a, he cannot have taken over in 1459, as Berchet says. The exact dates of his tenure of office were August 1, 1460 to August 28, 1463.

i) Berchet has Girolamo Bembo and gives as date for the beginning of his tenure 1462. But from Coll., Not. X, f. 79b one learns that he prepared himself for the departure in May 1463. The exact dates of his tenure of office were according to Segr. alle voci Aug. 29, 1463 to Oct. 22, 1466.

j) He entered office on Oct. 22, 1466 and died on Sept. 19, 1469.

k) The date on which he entered office was Oct. 27, 1469. As to the duration of his tenure of office Segr. alle voci has erroneous dates. For one reads there that he returned to Venice in 1474 and on the other hand no other consul in Alexandria is listed in this source before Ermolao Minio, who supposedly took over in Oct. 1477 (see Segr. alle voci V l.c., where no date is given; Segr. alle voci V l.c. has Nov. 1478). But all this is mistaken. According to Coll., Not. XI, f. 125a Toma Malipiero was already elected in May 1472.

l) Senato Mar and Berchet have Almoro Minio.

m) According to Segr. alle voci V l.c. he entered office on Oct. 26, 1480 and according to Segr. alle voci VI l.c. in Nov. 1480. He remained in office until Aug. 1482.

n) For the beginning of his tenure of office Berchet has 1481, but Segr. alle voci gives the date Aug. 1482 (without indicating the day). About the end of his tenure see infra.

o) In Senato Mar XII l.c. one reads that he will depart with the following cotton cogs in fall 1485, so that the date which Berchet gives for the beginning of his tenure of office viz. 1484, must be corrected.

p) He entered office in August 1487 and died in April 1489.

r) *Segr. alle voci* gives for his tenure of office the dates: Aug. 1489-Oct. 8, 1492.

s) He entered office on Oct. 8, 1492.

t) The name of this consul is missing in *Segr. alle voci*.

u) The exact dates of his tenure of office are Oct. 8, 1494 to Oct. 1496.

v) According to *Segr. alle voci* he took over in Oct. 1496 and his successor Pietro Balbo on April 7, 1500. This is confirmed by Marino Sanuto, Diarii I, col; 866. Berchet has for the beginning of Balbo's tenure of office the date 1498.

---

4. *Venetian Vice-Consuls in Acre*

Zorzi Franco	1428	Tur IV, f. 85b
Zuan Amadi	1441	G.P., Sent. 99, f. 2a ff.
Jeronimo Gabriel	1458	Roberto da Sanseverino, p. 178

5. *Venetian Vice-Consuls in Beirut*

Nicolo Mudazio	1412	G.P., Sent. 71, f. 55a ff.
Polo Barbarigo	1428	Tur IV, f. 85b f., 86a f., 86b f.

6. *Venetian Consuls in Tripoli*

Antonio de Priuli	1438	G.P., Sent. 79, f. 118a ff.
Costantino de Priuli	before Oct. 1443	Reggimenti p. 249; G.P., Sent. 102, f. 59b ff., 61a ff., 66a ff., 104, f. 86b ff.; Jorga, "Notes et extraits," *ROL* VII, p. 77[a]
Bartolomeo Lombardo	1444-1446	Reggimenti l.c.
Antonio de Mozo	1446-1447	Reggimenti l.c.; G.P., Sent. 107, f. 42b ff. and cf. 154b ff., 64a ff. 109, f. 143a f.; G.P., Straordi nario Nodari 18, sine pagina (sub Sept. 9, 1449)
Marco Donado	1450 (cca)	G.P., Sent. 118, f. 31a f.

---

a) He was obviously the first true consul, since the consulate was established in 1441. His predecessors were vice-consuls. He received his instructions from the Senate on Sept. 22, 1442.

---

7. *Venetian Vice-Consuls in Aleppo*

Agostino Soranzo	1463	Crist. del Fiore VI, f. 16b f.

Bibliography

A List of Sources and Basic Learned Works Which Are Often Quoted and Their Abbreviations

A. Sources

1. Arabic sources

(A) MSS.

ʿAbdalbāsiṭ ʿAbdalbāsiṭ b. Khalīl: *Nayl al-amal,* Bodl. 803, 812.

ʿAbdalbāsiṭ, MS. Vat. ʿAbdalbāsiṭ b. Khalīl: *ar-Rauḍ al-bāsim fī ḥawādith al-ʿumr wa 't-tarādjim* MS. Vat. 728, 729.

Cont. of Baybars al-Manṣūrī *Continuation of Baybars al-Manṣūrī,* Bodl. 704.

Ibn Ḥadjar Ibn Ḥadjar al-ʿAskalānī: *Inbā al-ghumr bi-anbā al-ʿumr,* Yeni Cami 814.

Ibn Ḳāḍī Shuhba Ibn Ḳāḍī Shuhba: *al-Iʿlām bi-ta'rīkh al-islām,* Bodl. 721, Paris 1598, 1599.

al-Manhal aṣ-ṣāfī Ibn Taghrībirdī: *al-Manhal aṣ-ṣāfī,* Paris 2068-2072.

(B) PRINTED WORKS

aḍ-Ḍaw al-lāmiʿ as-Sakhāwī, Muḥammad: *aḍ-Ḍaw al-lāmiʿ fī aʿyān al-ḳarn at-tāsiʿ,* I-XII, Cairo 1353-1355 h.

ad-Durar al-kāmina Ibn Ḥadjar al-ʿAskalānī: *ad-Durar al-kāmina,* I-IV, Cairo 1966-1967.

ad-Dhahabī, *Duwal al-islām* adh-Dhahabī, Muḥammad: *Duwal al-islām* I-II, Hydarabad 1337 h.

al-Djawharī, *Inbā al-haṣr* al-Djauharī, ʿAlī b. Dā'ūd: *Inbā al-haṣr bi-abnā al-ʿaṣr,* Cairo 1970.

al-Djawharī, *Nuzha* al-Djauharī, ʿAlī b. Dā'ūd: *Nuzhat an-nufūs wa'l-abdān fī tawārīkh az-zamān,* Cairo 1970.

Ḥawādith Ibn Taghrīdirdī: *Muntakhabāt min Ḥawādith ad-duhūr fī mada 'l-ayyām wa 'sh-shuhūr,* ed. Popper, Berkeley 1930-1942.

Ibn Baṭṭūṭa Ibn Baṭṭūṭa, Muḥammad b. ʿAbdallāh: *Voyages d'Ibn Batoutah,* texte arabe accompagné d'une traduction par C. Defrémery et B. R. Sanguinetti, I-IV, Paris 1854.

Ibn Dukmāḳ Ibn Duḳmāḳ, Ibrāhīm b. Muḥammad: *Kitāb al-Intiṣār li-wāsiṭāt ʿiḳd al-amṣār*, Cairo 1893.

Ibn al-Furāt Ibn al-Furāt, Nāṣir ad-dīn Muḥammad: *Ta'rīkh ad-duwal wa 'l-mulūk*, ed. C. K. Zurayk, VII-IX, Beirut 1936-1942.

Ibn Ḥadjar Ibn Ḥadjar al-ʿAsḳalānī: *Inbā al-ghumr bi-anbā al-'umr*, I-III, ed. Ḥ. Ḥabashī, Cairo 1969-1972.[1]

Ibn Iyās Ibn Iyās, Zain ad-dīn Muḥammad: *Badā'iʿ az-zuhūr fī waḳā'iʿ ad-duhūr*, Būlāḳ 1311 h. Second edition: Vol. I, part 2, by M. Mostafa, Wiesbaden 1974.—Ibn Iyās^2 I, part 2. Vol. II, by M. Mostafa, Wiesbaden 1972.—Ibn Iyās^2 II. Vol. III-V, by P. Kahle—M. Mostafa, Constantinople 1936-1945.—Ibn Iyās^2 III-V.

Ibn Kathīr Ibn Kathīr, ʿImād ad-dīn Ismāʿīl: *al-Bidāya wa 'n-nihāya*, I-XIV, Cairo 1351-1358 h.

Ibn Ṭūlūn Ibn Ṭūlūn, Shams ad-dīn Muḥammad: *Mufākahat al-khillān fī ḥawādith az-zamān*, I-II, Cairo 1962-1964.

Khiṭaṭ al-Maḳrīzī, Taḳi 'd-dīn Aḥmad: *al-Mawāʿiẓ wa 'l-iʿtibār fī dhikr al-khiṭaṭ wa 'l-āthār*, I-II, Būlāḳ 1270 h.

an-Nudjūm az-zāhira Ibn Taghrībirdī: *an-Nudjūm az-zāhira fī mulūk Miṣr wa 'l-Ḳāhira*, ed. W. Popper, V-VII, Berkeley 1915-1936.

Ṣāliḥ b. Yaḥyā Ṣāliḥ b. Yaḥyā: *Ta'rīkh Bairūt*, Beirut 1927.

as-Sallāmī as-Sallāmī: *Ḥaulīyāt dimishḳīya* 834-839 h., ed. Ḥ. Ḥabashī, Cairo 1968.

Ṣubḥ al-aʿshā al-Ḳalḳashandī, Aḥmad b. ʿAlī: *Kitāb Ṣubḥ al-aʿshā*, I-XIV, Cairo 1913-1919.

Sulūk al-Maḳrīzī, Taḳi 'd-dīn Aḥmad: *as-Sulūk li-maʿrifat duwal al-mulūk*, ed. M. M. Ziyāda, I-IV, Cairo 1931-1973. French translation: Histoire des sultans mamlouks de l'Egypte . . . par E. Quatremère, I-II, Paris 1844-1845.—Quatremère, Hist. des sultans mamlouks.

2. European sources

(A) VENICE, ARCHIVIO DI STATO (ASV)

Official documents

Maggior Consiglio, Deliberazioni

8 Magnus et Capricornus, 1299-1308.—Mag. cons., Magnus et Capricornus.

10 Presbiter, 1308-1310.—Mag. Cons., Presbiter.

12 Clericus Civicus, 1315-1318.—Mag. Cons., Clericus Civicus.

15 Fronesis, 1318-1325.—Mag. Cons., Fronesis.

[1] The fourth volume of this edition is neither in possession of the University Library of Jerusalem, nor is it to be found in the libraries of London and Oxford. So the MS., see above, is quoted instead of it.

18 Spiritus, 1325-1349.—Mag. Cons., Spiritus.
20 Novella, 1350-1384.—Mag. Cons., Novella.
21 Leona, 1384-1415.—Mag. Cons., Leona.
22 Ursa, 1415-1454.—Mag. Cons., Ursa.
23 Regina, 1455-1479.—Mag. Cons., Regina.

Senato
Deliberazioni miste, reg. 17-60.—Misti.
Mar, reg. 1-14.—Senato Mar.
Secreta, reg. 1-36.—Secreta.
Incanti, reg. I-II.—Incanti.

Collegio, Notatorio, reg. 2-14.—Coll., Not.
Liber secretorum, 1354-1363.
" " 1363-1366.
" " 1366-1372.

Segretario alle voci, V; VI.—Segr. alle voci.

Cinque savi alla mercanzia, Busta 944, 947.—Savi alla mercanzia.

Consoli di mercanti, Capitolari, Ba 1.—Consoli di mercanti, Cap.

Giudici di petiziòn.
Sentenze a giustizia, reg. 2-192.—G. P., Sent.[2]
Terminazioni, reg. 1-17.—G. P., Ter.
Sentenze e interdetti, reg. 5-9, 11.—G. P., Sent. Int.
Lettere, reg. 1-2.—G. P., Lett.
Capitoli pubblicati, giuramenti et altre, reg. 1, 3-13.—G. P., Cap.
Extraordinario Nodari, reg. 15-20, 22.—G. P., Straordinario Nodari.

Consiglio dei mercanti veneziani in Alessandria, Verbali, Oct. 1401-Oct. 1403, Cancelleria Inferiore, Ba 229, fasc. V.—Verbali Cons. XII.

Notaries
Cancelleria Inferiore
Ba 36, fasc. I Campiono, Giovanni.—Giov. Campiono.
Ba 74-76 degli Elmi, Francesco.—Fr. degli Elmi.
Ba 83 del Fiore, Cristoforo.—Crist. del Fiore.
Ba 174 Rizzo, Cristoforo.—Crist. Rizzo.
Ba 211 Turiano, Niccolò.—Tur.
Ba 229 de Valle, Leonardo.—Leonardo de Valle.
Ba 222 de Vataciis, Antonello.—Vat.
Ba 230 Venier, Niccolo.—Nic. Venier.
Notarile
215 Peccator-Servadio.-Serv. Pecc.
14832 della Torre, Giacomo.—Giac. della Torre.

[2] Several registers of the various series of this tribunal have been lost or are mislaid and could not be studied.

Archives of firms
Procuratori di S. Marco (PSM)
Commissarie miste
Ba 116, 117 Alvise Baseggio-Polo Caroldo.—Arch. Baseggio-Caroldo.
Ba 128a, fasc. V Antonio Zane.—Arch. Zane.
Ba 161, fasc. I, VI, VIII Family Malipiero.—Arch. Malipiero.
Ba 180, 181 Biegio Dolfin.—Arch. B. Dolfin.
Commissarie di Citra
Ba 91a, fasc. VII Fraterna Giustinian.—Frat. Giustinian.
Ba 282, tomo III, fasc. II Lorenzo Dolfin.—Arch. Lor. Dolfin.
Miscellanea Gregolin
Ba 14 Conti Soranzo.—Arch. Soranzo.
Miscellanea di carte non appartenenti a nessun archivio
Ba 8, fasc. I Papers of Donado Soranzo.—Miscell. di carte non appartenenti a ness. archivio, Ba 8.
Ba 29 Liber tegnudo . . . de la compagnia di Ser Andrea Zorzi-Fraterna Sanudo.—Arch. Zorzi-Sanudo.

(B) VENICE, MUSEO CORRER

PD C 911/I 912/I Archives of Francesco Contarini.—Arch. Fr. Contarini.

(C) VENICE, BIBLIOTECA MARCIANA

Cronaca Dolfina Ital. VII DCCXCIV.—*Chron. Dolfin.*
Copy of Cronaca of Antonio Morosini, MS. Vienna, Ital. VII MMIXL (1831/32).—*Chron. Morosini.*[3]
Cronaca di Girolamo Savina, Ital. VII CXXXIV (7735).—*Chron. Savina.*
Cronaca Zancaruola, Ital. VII XLIX-L.—*Zancaruola.*
Tarifa di pexi e spesse achade a metter e trare merchadantia de la terra di Allesandria e altri lochi,[4] It. VII CCCLXXXIV (7530).—*Anonymous Merchant Guide.*

(D) GENOA, ARCHIVIO DI STATO (ASG)

Official documents
Antico Commune, reg. 17, 18, 26.—Ant. Com.
Archivio Segreto 2774 C.—ASG 2774 C.
Caratorum Veterum 1552 (a. 1445), 1553 (a. 1458).—Carat. Vet.
Drictus Alexandriae 1367.—Drictus Alexandriae.
Primi Cancellieri di S. Giorgio, Ba 88, 88a.—Primi Cancellieri.

Notaries
142 Airolo, Battista.—Airolo.
657 Bagnara, Branco.—Bagnara Branco.

[3] The work is quoted here according to the original pagination (of the Vienna MS.).

312, 313 Caito, Andreolo.—Caito, Andr.
44, 46 Fazio, Antonio, Senior.—Fazio, Ant.
469 Foglietta, Oberto, Senior.—Foglietta, Oberto, Senior.
405 Gatto, Bartolomeo, IX, X.—Gatto, Bart.
114 Loggia, Girolamo.—Loggia, Gir.
12 Oddone, Domenico.—Oddone.
409 Parisola, Ghirardo.—Parisola.

(E) FLORENCE, ARCHIVIO DI STATO (ASF)

IIIa serie Strozziana, no. 276.—Accounts of Benedetto Strozzi.
Conventi soppressi, no. 78, vol. 322, c. 45, letter of Marioto Squarzalupi to Francesco di Nerone, of 2 March 1459.—Letter Squarzalupi.

(F) FLORENCE, BIBLIOTECA NAZIONALE

Memorie varie di Venezia, MS. Gino Capponi CXLVI, tomo II.—Memorie varie di Venezia.
Anonymous Merchant Guide, MS. Tordi 139.—MS. Tordi 139.

(G) PRATO, ARCHIVIO DI STATO

Fondo Francesco Datini (Dat)

Ba 548-550	Letters	from	Venice	to	Pisa
709-715	"	"	"	"	Florence
797	"	"	"	"	Genoa
926-930	"	"	"	"	Barcelona
1082-1083	"	"	"	"	Majorca
660, 662-663	"	"	Genoa to Florence		
637	"	"	Barcelona to Florence		
705	"	"	Valencia to Florence		
906, 907	"	"	Perpignan to Barcelona		
1158, 1159	Insurance acts				
1171	Quaderni de prezzi e di carichi di navi				

(H) ANCONA, ARCHIVIO DE STATO (ASAn)

Notaries
Giacomo Alberici, 1-13.—Giac. Alberici.
Mercurio Benincasa, I-II.—Merc. Benincasa.
Melchior Bernabe, 1-11.—Melch. Bernabe.
Tomaso Cinzio.—T. Cinzio.
Niccolò Cressi, I-VII.—Nic. Cressi.
Angelo di Domenico, 1-12.—Ang. di Domenico.

Antonio Giovanni di Giacomo, 1-42.—Ant. Giov. de Giac.
Tomaso Marchetti, I-X.—Tom. Marchetti.
Giovanni Massi.—G. Massi.
Giacomo di Pellegrino.—Giac. Pellegrino.
Corrado di Niccolò, I-V.—Corr. di Nic.
Chiarozzo Spampalli, I-IV.—Chiar. Spampalli.
Ciriaco Tome di Sant'Angelo 1465-1474, 1485-1494.—Ciriaco Tome.

(I) NAPLES, ARCHIVIO DE STATO (ASNap)

Notaries
7 Nicola della Morte.[4]—Nic. della Morte.
4-5 Pisano, Petruccio.—Petruccio Pisano.

(J) PALERMO, ARCHIVIO DE STATO (ASPal)

Secrezia
Atti, 553-555.—Secrezia, Atti.

Notaries
Aprea, Antonino, 798-801, 808, 811, 814.—Aprea, Ant.
Comito, Giacomo, 843-854.—Giac. Comito.
Delampio, Niccolò 1149.—Delampio, Nic.
Fallera, Matteo, 1749-1751.—Fallera, Matteo.
Randisi, Giacomo, 1150-1152.—Giac. Randisi.

(K) MESSINA, ARCHIVIO DI STATO (ASMess)

Notaries
Andreolo, Tomaso.—Andreolo.
Mallono, Francesco, 1431-1437.—Mallono.
Pagliarino, Matteo, II, IIIa.—Pagliarino.

(L) SYRACUSE, ARCHIVIO DI STATO (ASSir)

Notaries
10244 Piduni, Antonio.—Piduni.
10227 Vallone, Niccolò.—Vallone.

(M) TRAPANI, ARCHIVIO DI STATO (ASTrap)

Notaries
154-156 Miciletto, Giacomo.—Miciletto.
194 Scanatello, Giovanni.—Scanatello.

[4] The volume has the title 1471/2, but it contains also acts of the years 1473, 1474 and 1475.

(N) BARCELONA, ARCHIVO DE LA CORONA DE ARAGÓN (ACA)

Cancilleria Real, reg. 2647, 2648, 2692, 2694, 2696-2699,—ACA.
Real Patrimonio 2910/1; 2910/2, 2910/3.—Real Patrimonio.

(O) BARCELONA, ARCHIVO HISTORICO DE PROTOCOLOS (AHPB)

Notaries
Tomas de Bellmunt, Quartus liber manualis commendarum, 18.1.1414-21.1.1417.—Tomas de Bellmunt.
Berenguer Ermengol, Manual 2.1.1378-30.12.1378.—Berenguer Ermengol.
Pere Marti, Manual V, 20.6.1373-17.8.1373
" VI, 28.3.1374-6.6.1374
" VIII, 11.8.138L-15.12.1380
" 21.6.1381-3.10.1381
" 15.4.1385-13.8.1385.—Pere Marti.
Esteban Mir, Manualis securitatum.—Esteban Mir.
Bernat, Nadal, Liber primus commendarum, 1385-1387
" secundus " 1395-1406.—Bernat, Nadal.
Pere de Torre V, part 2.—Pere de Torre.
Pere Triter, Tercius liber securitatum, 1490-1491.—Pere Triter.
Anton Vilanova, Liber commendarum.—Anton Vilanova.

(P) BARCELONA, BIBLIOTECA DE LA UNIVERSIDAD (BUB)

MS. 4 Liber de conexenses de spicies e de drogues e de avissaments de pesas canes e massures de divers ses terres, a. 1455.—Liber de conexenses.

(Q) PERPIGNAN, ARCHIVES DÉPARTEMENTALES DES PYRENÉES ORIENTALES (APO)

Official documents
Procuracio Real, reg. IV, IX.—Proc. Real.

Notaries
B. 196, 198, Raymond Ferrer, Notule.—R. Ferrer.
Ferriol Bosqueros 731, 734, 735, 771.—F. Bosqueros.
Ant. Guitard, 1552-1560.—Ant. Guitard.
B. 184, Pierre d'Ornos, Manual.—P. Ornos.

(R) LONDON, BRITISH LIBRARY
Anonymous Merchant's Guide, MS. Egerton 73.—MS. Egerton 73.

Printed Works

Adorno, Anselme: *Itinéraire d'Anselme Adorno en Terre Sainte (1470-1471)*, ed. and transl. J. Heers and G. de Groer, Paris 1978.—Adorno.

Ainaud; J.: "Quatre documents sobre el comerç catala amb Siria i Alexandria (1401-1410)," in *Homenaje a Jaime Vicens Vives*, Barcelona 1965, p. 327-331.—Ainaud, "Quatre doc."

Alarcón y Santón, M. A.-Garcia de Linares, R.: *Los documentos arabes diplomáticos del Archivo de la Corona de Aragón*, ed. . . . and transl., Madrid 1940.—Alarcón.

Amari, M.: *I diplomi arabi del R. Archivio fiorentino*, Florence 1863.—Amari, *Diplomi.*

Angelini, C. ed.: *Viaggi in Terrasanta*, Florence 1944.—Angelini, *Viaggi.*

d'Anglure, Ogier: *Le Saint voyage de Jhérusalem du seigneur d'Anglure*, ed. Fr. Bonnardot-A. Longnon, Paris 1878.—d'Anglure.

Il libro dei conti di Giacomo Badoer (Costantinopoli 1436-1440), . . . ed. U. Dorini-T. Bertelè, Rome 1956.—Badoer.

Benvenuto de Brixano, notaio in Candia 1301-1302, ed. R. Morozzo della Rocca, Venice 1950.—Benvenuto de Brixano.

Berchet, G.: *Relazioni dei consoli veneti nella Siria*, Turin 1866.—Berchet, *Relazioni.*

Brancacci, Felice: *Diario di Felice Brancacci, ambasciatore con Carlo Federighi al Cairo*, ed. D. Catelacci, in *ASI*, ser. IV, tomo VIII (1881), p. 160-188, 326-334.—Brancacci, *Diario.*

de la Broquière, Bertrandon: *Le voyage d'Outremer*, ed. Ch. Schefer, Paris 1892.—de la Broquière.

Day, J. (ed.): *Les douanes de Gênes 1376-1377*, I-II, Paris 1963.—Day, *Douanes.*

Le deliberazioni del Consiglio dei rogati (Senato), serie "Mixtorum," ed. R. Cessi-P. Sambin, I-II, Venice 1960-1961—*Misti*, ed. Cessi.

Deliberazioni del Maggior Consiglio di Venezia, ed. R. Cessi, I-III, Bologna 1931-1950.—*Deliberazioni del Maggior Consiglio.*

Desimoni, C.: "Actes passés à Famagouste, de 1299 à 1301, par devant le notaire Lamberto de Sambuceto," *ROL* I (1893), p. 58-139, 275-312, 321-353.—Desimoni.

Diplomatarium Veneto-Levantinum sive acta et diplomata res venetas graecas atque Levantis illustrantia a. 1300-1350, ed. G. M. Thomas-R. Predelli, I-II, Venice 1880-1899.—*Dipl. Ven.-Lev.*

Doehaerd, R.: *Les relations commerciales entre Gênes, la Belgique et l'Ou-*

tremont d'après les archives notariales génoises aux XIIIe et XIVe siècles, I-III, Brussels 1941.—Doehaerd, *Relations.*

Doehaerd, R.-Kerremans, Ch.: *Les relations commerciales entre Gênes, la Belgique et l'Outremont d'après les archives notariales génoises,* 1400-1440, Brussels 1952.—Doehaerd-Kerremans.

Fabri, Felix: *Evagatorium in Terram Sanctam, Arabiae et Aegypti peregrinationes,* ed. C. D. Hassler, I-III, Stuttgart 1843-1849.—Fabri, *Evagatorium.*

Finke, H.: *Acta Aragonensia, Quellen zur deutschen, italienischen, französ., span., zur Kirchen- u. Kulturgeschichte aus der diplomatischen Korrespondenz Jaymes II (1291-1327),* I-III, Berlin 1908-1922. Finke, *Acta Aragonensia.*

Giomo, G. (ed.): *Lettere di Collegio rectius Minor Consiglio 1308-1310,* Venice 1910.—Giomo, *Lettere di collegio.*

Jorga, N.: "Notes et extraits pur servir à l'histoire des croisades au XVe siècle," *ROL* IV (1896), pp. 226-320, 503-622 V (1897), pp. 108-212, 311-388 VI (1898), pp. 50-143, 370-434 VII (1899), pp. 38-107, 375-429. VIII (1900/1901), pp. 1-115.—Jorga.

Krekić, B.: *Dubrovnik (Raguse) et le Levant au moyen âge,* Paris 1961.—Krekić.

Lannoy, Ghillebert; *Voyages et ambassades de messire Guillebert de Lannoy, 1399-1450,* Mons 1840.—Lannoy, *Voyages.*

Lettere di mercanti a Pignol Zucchello (1336-1350), ed. R. Morozzo della Rocca, Venice 1957.—*Lettere a Pignol Zucchello.*

Liagre-De Sturler, L.: *Les relations commerciales entre Gênes, la Belgique et l'Outremont, d'après les archives notariales génoises, 1320-1400,* I-II, Brussels 1969.—Liagre-De Sturler.

I libri commemoriali della Republica di Venezia regeste . . . ed. R. Predelli, I-VI, Venice 1880-1903.—*Libri com.*

El libro di mercatantie et usanze de' paesi, ed. Fr. Borlandi, Turin 1936.—*El libro di mercatantie.*

de Luco, Battista: *Battista de Luco, mercante genovese del secolo XV, e il suo cartulario,* ed. L. Balletto, Genoa 1979.—*Bat. de Luco.*

Madurell Marimon, J. M. Garcia Sanz, A.: Comendas barcelonesas de la baja edad media, Barcelona, 1973.—Mardurell-Garcia.

Malipiero, Domenico: "Annali Veneti dall'anno 1457-1500," *ASI* VII (1843-44), part I, p. 3-586, part 2, p. 589-720.—Malipiero.

Masiá de Ros, A.: *La corona de Aragón y los estados del norte de Africa,* Barcelona 1951.—Masiá de Ros.

Melis, F.: *Documenti per la storia economica dei secoli XIII-XVI,* Florence 1972.—Melis, *Doc.*

Meshullam di Volterra, *Travelogue* (in Hebrew), ed. A. Yaari, Jerusalem 1979.—Meshullam di Volterra, *Travelogue.*

Monumenta Historiae Patriae II, Leges municipales, Turin 1838.—Mon. Hist. Patr. II.

Morosini, Antonio: *Chronique d'Antonio Morosini, extraits relatifs à l'histoire de France,* publ. par G. Lefèvre-Pontalis, I-IV, Paris 1898-1902.—Morosini, *Chronique.*

Müller, G.: *Documenti sylle relazioni delle città toscane coll'Oriente cristiano e coi Turchi fino all'anno MDXXXI,* Florence 1879.—Müller, *Documenti.*

Nicola de Boateriis, notaio in Famagosta e Venezia (1355-1365), ed. A. Lombardo, Venice 1973.—Nicola de Boateriis.

Noiret, H.: *Documents inédits pour servir à l'histoire de la domination vénitienne en Crète de 1380 à 1485,* Rome 1892 (Bibl. des écoles franç . . . d'Athènes et de Rome, 61).—Noiret, *Documents.*

Obadiah of Bertinoro: *Travelogue* (in Hebrew), ed. A. Yaari, *Iggrōth Ereș Yisrael,* Tel Aviv 1943, p. 98-144.—Obadiah of Bertinoro, *Travelogue.*

Pagnini del Ventura, G. Fr.: *Della decima e di varie altre gravezze imposte dal comune di Firenze, della moneta e della mercatura de' Fiorentini fino al secolo XVI,* I-IV, Lisbon 1765-1766.—Pagnini, *Della decima.*

de Paxi, Bartholomeo: *Tariffa de pexi et mesure,* Venice 1503.—Pasi.

Pegolotti, Francesco Balducci: *La pratica della mercatura,* ed. A. Evans, Cambridge Mass. 1936.—Pegolotti.

Piloti, Emmanuel: *Traité d'Emmanuel Piloti sur le Passage en Terre Sainte (1420),* ed. P.-H. Dopp, Louvain 1958.—Piloti.

Pizolo, Pietro, *rotais in Candia,* ed. S. Carbone, I, Venice 1978, II (in press).—Pizolo.

Priuli, Girolamo: *I diarii,* I-II, Bologna 1912-1936.—Priuli.

Reyssbuch dess heyligen Landes, Frankfort o/M 1609.—*Reyssbuch.*

Rubió i Lluch, A.: *Diplomatari de l'Oriente catalá, 1305-1409,* Barcelona 1947.—Rubio i Lluch, *Diplomatari.*

Saminiato de' Ricci; *Il manuale di mercatura di Saminiato de' Ricci,* ed. A. Borlandi, Genoa 1963.—Saminiato de' Ricci.

Sanuto, Marino (the Elder): *Liber secretorum fidelium crucis,* in *Gesta Dei per Francos,* ed. J. Bongars, Hanau 1611.—Marino Sanuto, *Secreta fidelium crucis.*

Sanuto, Marino (the Younger): *I diarii,* I-LVIII, Venice 1879-1903.—Marino Sanuto, *Diarii.*

Vite de' duchi di Venezia, (in) Muratori, *Rerum Ital. Script.* XXII (Milan 1783), col. 405-1252.—Marino Sanuto, *Vite.*

Sassi, S.: *Sulle vicende di due aziende mercantili veneziane del Quattrocento,* Naples s.d.—Sassi.

Tafel, L. Fr.-Thomas, G. M.: *Urkunden zur älteren Handels-und Staatsgeschichte der Republik Venedig, mit besonderer Beziehung auf Byzanz und die Levante vom 9. bis zum Ausgang des 15. Jahrhunderts*, I-III, Vienna 1856-1857.—Tafel-Thomas.

Tarifa zoè noticia dy pexi e mexure di luogi e tere che s'adovra marchadantia per el mondo, Venice 1925.—*Tarifa*.

Thiriet, Fr.: *Délibérations des assemblées vénitiennes concernant la Romanie*, I-II, Paris 1966-1971.—Thiriet.

Assemblées Régestes des délibérations du Sénat de Venise concernant la Romanie, I-III, Paris 1955-1961.—Thiriet, *Rég*.

Tucher, Johan: *Travelogue* (in German), (in) *Reyssbuch*, Frankfort o/M 1609, I, p. 652-698.—Tucher.

Uzzano, Giovanni da: *La pratica della mercatura*, (in) Pagnini, *Della decima* IV, p. 1-196.—Uzzano.

I viaggi in Persia degli ambasciatori veneti Barbaro e Contarini, ed. L. Lockhart, R. Morozzo della Rocca, M. Fr. Tiepolo, Rome 1973.—*I viaggi degli ambasciatori veneti*.

Visit to the Holy Places of Egypt, Sinai, Palestine and Syria in 1384, by Frescobaldi, Gucci & Sigoli, transl. . . . by Th. Bellorini and E. Hoade, Jerusalem 1948.—*A visit to the Holy Places*.

Zaccaria de Fredo, notaio in Candia (1352-1357), ed. A. Lombardo, Venice 1968.—*Zaccaria de Fredo*.

Zeno, R.: *Documenti per la storia del diritto marittimo nei secol XIII e XIV*, Turin 1936.—Zeno, *Documenti*.

Zibaldone da Canal, ed. A. Stussi, Venice 1967.—*Zibaldone da Canal*.

c. Learned Books and Papers

Albertini, C.: *Storia d'Ancona*, MS. in the Bibl. Comunale, Ancona.—Albertini.

Ashtor, E.: Aspetti della espansione italiana nel basso medioevo," *RSI* 90 (1978), p. 4-29.—Ashtor, "Aspetti."

"Il commercio levantino di Ancona nel basso medioevo," *RSI* 88 (1976), p. 213-253.—"Il commercio levantino di Ancona."[x]

"Etudes sur le système monétaire des Mamlouks circassiens," *Isr. Oriental Studies* VI (1976), p. 264-287.—"Etudes sur le système monétaire."

"L'exportation de textiles occidentaux dans le Proche Orient musulman au bas Moyen Age (1370-1517)," *Studi in memoria di F. Melis* (Naples 1978) III, p. 303-377.—"L'exportation de textiles."

Histoire des prix et des salaires dans l'Orient médiéval, Paris 1969.—*Histoire des prix et salaires.*

"The Kārimī merchants," *JRAS* 1956, p. 45-56.—"The Kārimī merchants."[x]

"Les lainages dans l'Orient médiéval," in *Atti della 2a settimana di studio, Istituto Fr. Datini*, Florence 1976, p. 657-687.—"Les lainages."[a]

"Levantine sugar industry in the later Middle Ages—an example of technological decline," *Isr. Oriental Studies* VII (1977), p. 226-276.—"Levantine sugar industry."

Les métaux précieux et la balance des payements du Proche-Orient à la basse-époque, Paris 1971.—*Les métaux précieux.*

"Observations on Venetian Trade in the Levant in the XIVth century," *JEEH* V (1976), p. 533-586.—"Observations on Venetian trade."

"Profits from trade with the Levant in the fifteenth century," *BSOAS* 38 (1975), p. 250-275.—"Profits."

"Quelques problèmes que soulève l'histoire des prix dans l'Orient médiéval," in *Studies in memory of Gaston Wiet*, Jerusalem 1977, p. 203-234.—"Quelques problèmes."

A social and economic history of the Near East in the Middle Ages, London 1976.—*Social and economic history.*

"Spice prices in the Near East in the 15th century," *JRAS* 1976, p. 26-41.—"Spice prices."[x]

Studies in the Levantine trade in the Middle Ages, London 1978.—*Studies in the Levantine trade.*

"The Venetian cotton trade in Syria in the later Middle Ages," *Studi Medievali* 17 (1976), p. 675-715.—"The Venetian cotton trade."[x]

"The Venetian supremacy in Levantine trade: monopoly or pre-colonialism?"; *JEEH* III (1974), p. 5-53.—"The Venetian supremacy."

"The Volume of Levantine trade in the later Middle Ages (1370-1498)," *JEEH* III (1975), p. 573-612.—"The Volume of Levantine Trade."[x]

Atiya, A. S.: *Egypt and Aragon, embassies and diplomatic correspondence between 1300 and 1330 A.D.*, Leipzig 1938 (Abhdl. für die Kunde des Morgenlandes 23, no. 7).—Atiya, *Egypt and Aragon.*

Balletto, L.: *Genova, Mediterraneo, Mar Nero (secc. XIII-XV)*, Genoa 1976. Balletto, *Genova, Mediterraneo, Mar Nero.*

Bănescu, N.: *Le déclin de Famagouste—fin du royaume de Chypre, notes et documents*, Bucarest 1946.—Bănescu, *Le déclin de Famagouste.*

Bautier, R.-H.: "Les relations économiques des occidentaux avec les pays d'Orient, au moyen âge, points de vue et documents," in *Sociétés et compagnies*, p. 263-331.—Bautier, "Les relations."

Brătianu, G. I.: *Recherches sur le commerce génois dans la Mer Noire au XIIIe siècle*, Paris 1929.—Brătianu, *Recherches*.

Berchet, G.: *La republica di Venezia e la Persia*, Turin 1865.—Berchet, *La republica di Venezia e la Persia*.

Braunstein, Ph.: "Wirtschaftliche Beziehungen zwischen Nürnberg und Italien im Spätmittelalter," in *Beiträge zur Wirtschaftsgeschichte Nürnbergs* I (1967), p. 377-406.—Braunstein, "Wirtschaftl. Beziehungen zwischen Nürnberg u. Italien.

Capmany y de Montpalau, A. de: *Memorias históricas sobre la marina, comercio y artes de la antigua ciudad de Barcelona* I-II, Barcelona, 1961-1963. Capmany, *Memorias*.

Carabellese, Fr.: *Carlo d'Angiò nei rapporti politici e commerciali con Venezia e l'Oriente*, Bari 1911.—Carabellese, *Carlo d'Angiò*.

Carrère, Cl.: *Barcelone, centre économique à l'époque des difficultés 1380-1462*, Paris 1967.—Carrère, *Barcelone*.

Coll Juliá, N.: "Aspectos del corso catalán y del comercio internacional en el siglo XV," *EHM* IV (1954), p. 157-187.—Coll Juliá, "Aspectos del corso catalán."

Darrag, A.: *L'Egypte sous le règne de Barsbay 825-841/1422-1438*; Damascus 1961.—Darrag, *Barsbay*.

Davidsohn, R.: *Geschichte von Florenz* I-IV, Berlin 1896-1927.—Davidsohn, *Geschichte von Florenz*.

Delaville Le Roulx, J.M.A.: *La France en Orient au XIVe siècle; expéditions du maréchal Boucicaut*, I-II, Paris 1886.—Delaville Le Roulx.

Del Treppo, M.: *I mercanti catalani e l'espansione della corona d'Aragona nel secolo XV*, Naples 1972.—Del Treppo.

Fernandez de Navarrete, M.: *Disertacion histórica sobre la parte que tuvieron los Españoles en las guerras de ultramar o de las Cruzadas*, Madrid 1817 (Real Acad. de la historia, *Memorias* V).—Fernandez de Navarrete.

Giunta, Fr.: *Aragonesi e catalani nel mediterraneo*, I-II, Palermo 1953-1959.—Giunta, *Aragonesi*.

Heers, J.: "Il commercio nel Mediterraneo alla fine del sec. XIV e nei primi anni del XV," *ASI* 113 (1955), p. 157-209.—Heers, "Il commercio." Gênes au XVe siècle, Paris 1961.—Heers, *Gênes*.

Heyd, W.: *Histoire du commerce du Levant au moyen-âge*, French transl. by F. Raynaud. I-II, Leipzig 1885-1886.—Heyd.

Histoire du commerce de Marseille, publiée par la Chambre de commerce de Marseille, vol. II: *de 1291 à 1423* by E. Baratier, *de 1423 à 1480*, by F. Reynaud, Paris 1951.—Baratier, Reynaud, vol. III, *de 1480 à 1515*, by R. Collier, *de 1515 à 1599*, by J. Billioud, Paris 1951.—Collier.

Kedar, B. Z.: *Merchants in crisis, Genoese and Venetian men of affairs and the fourteenth-century depression*, Yale Univ. Press 1976.—Kedar.

Kretschmayr, H.: *Geschichte von Venedig*, I-III, Aalen 1920-1964.—Kretschmayr.

Labib, S. Y.: *Handelsgeschichte Ägyptens im Spätmittelalter (1171-1517)*, Wiesbaden 1965.—Labib, *Handelsgeschichte*.

Lane, F. C.: *Andrea Barbarigo, merchant of Venice 1418-1449*, Baltimore 1944.—Lane, *Andrea Barbarigo*.

Venetian ships and shipbuilders of the renaissance, 1934.—Lane, *Ships and shipbuilders*.

Venice, a maritime republic, Johns Hopkins Univ. Press 1973.—Lane, *Venice*.

Venice and history, the collected papers of Frederic C. Lane, Johns Hopkins Univ. Press, 1966.—Lane, *Venice and history*.

Lopez, R. S.: *Storia delle colonie genovesi nel Mediterraneo*, Bologna 1938.—Lopez, *Storia delle colonie genovesi*.

Su e giù per la storia di Genova, Genoa 1975.—Lopez, *Su e giù*.

López de Meneses, A.: "Los consulados catalanes de Alejandria y Damasco en el reinado de Pedro el Ceremonioso," *EEMCA* VI (1956), p. 83-183.—López de Meneses, "Los consulados."

Lucchetta, Fr.: "L' 'affare Zen' in Levante nel primo Cinquecento," *Studi Veneziani* X (1968), p. 109-219.—Lucchetta, "L'affare Zen."

Luzzatto, G.: *Studi di storia economica veneziana*, Padua 1954.—Luzzatto, *Studi di storia economica*.

Mallett, M. M.: *The Florentine galleys in the fifteenth century*, Oxford 1967.—Mallett.

de Mas Latrie, L.: *Histoire de l'île de Chypre sous le règne des princes de la maison de Lusignan*, I-III, Paris 1852-1882.—de Mas Latrie, *Histoire*.

———. *Traités de paix et de commerce et documents divers contenant les relations des chrétiens avec les Arabes de l'Afrique septentrionale au Moyen Age*, Paris 1866-1867.—de Mas Latrie, *Traités*.

Mediterraneo e Oceano Indiano, Atti del VI colloquio int. di storia marittima, 1962, Florence 1970.—*Mediterraneo e Oceano Indiano*.

Melis, F.: *Aspetti della vita economica medievale, studi dell'archivio Datini de Prato*, Siena 1962.—Melis, *Aspetti*.

Origini e sviluppi della assicurazione in Italia (secolo XIV-XVI), vol. I: Le fonti, Rome 1975.—Melis, *Origini*.

Musso, G. G.: "Armamento e navigazione a Genova tra il Tre e il Quatrrocento (appunti e documenti)," in *Genova e commercio nell'evoluzione della marina genovese tra XV e XVII secolo*, I-II, Genoa 1970-1973, II, p. 5-77.—Musso, "Armamento."

———. "I Genovesi e il Levante tra medioevo ed età moderna, ricerche d'archivio," reprint from *Genova, la Liguria e l'Oltremare tra medioevo ed età moderna, studi e ricerche d'archivio*, ed. R. Belvedere, Genoa 1976.—Musso," I Genovesi e il Levante."

———. *Navigazione e commercio genovese con il Levante nei documenti dell'archivio di Stato di Genova (secc. XIV-XV)*, Rome 1975.—Musso, *Navigazione.*

———. "Nuovi documenti dell'Archivio di Stato di Genova sui Genovesi e il Levante nel secondo Quattrocento," *Rassegna degli Archivi di Stato* 27 (1967), p. 4443-496.—Musso, "Nuovi documenti."

Natalucci, M.: *Ancona attraverso i secoli, ricostruzione delle vicende storiche della città*, I-III, Città del Castello 1961.—Natalucci, *Ancona attraverso i secoli.*

Pardessus, J. M.: *Collection de lois maritimes antérieures au XVIIIe siècle*, I-VI, Paris 1828-1848.—Pardessus.

Pigeonneau, H.: *Histoire du commerce de la France*, I-II, Paris 1885-1889.—Pigeonneau.

Romanin, S.: *Storia documentata di Venezia*, 2a ed., I-X, Venice 1972-1975.—Romanin.

Sáez Pomés, M.: "Los Aragoneses en la conquista y saqueo de Alejandria por Pedro I de Chipro," *EEMCA* V (1952), p. 361-405.—Sáez Pomés.

Sapori, A.: *Studi di storia economica*, I-III, Florence 1955-1967.—Sapori, *Studi.*

Schulte, A.: *Geschichte dès mittelalterlichen Handels und Verkehrs zwischen Westdeutschland und Italien mit Ausschluss von Venedig*, I-II, Carlsruhe 1900.—Schulte.

Scovazzi, I.—Noberasco, F.: *Storia di Savona*, I-III, Savona 1926.—Scovazzi-Noberasco, *Storia di Savona.*

Setton K. M.: *The Papacy and the Levant (1204-1571)*, I-II, Philadelphia 1976-1978.—Setton, *Papacy and Levant.*

Sieveking, H.: "Aus venetianischen Handelsbüchern," *Jahrbuch für Gesetzgebung, Verwaltung und Volkswirtschaft im Deutschen Reich* 25 (1901), p. 1489 ff. 26 (1902), p. 189 ff.

Silberschmidt, M.: *Das orientalische Problem zur Zeit der Entstehung des türkischen Reiches, nach venezianischen Quellen*, Leipzig 1923.—Silberschmidt, *Das orientalische Problem.*

Simonsfeld, H.: *Der Fondaco dei Tedeschi in Venedig und die deutsch-venetianischen Handelsbeziehungen*, I-II, Stuttgart 1887.—Simonsfeld, *Der Fondaco dei Tedeschi.*

Sociétés et compagnies de commerce en Orient et dans l'Océan indien, Actes du huitième colloque international d'histoire maritime, Beyrouth 1960, Paris 1970.—*Sociétés et compagnies.*

Sottas, J.: *Les messageries maritimes de Venise aux IXVe et XVe siècles*, Paris 1938.—Sottas.

Thiriet, Fr.: "Quelques observations sur le trafic des galées vénitiennes d'après les chiffres des incanti (XIVe-XVe siècles)," in *Studi in onore di A. Fanfani*, Milano 1962, III, p. 494-522.—Thiriet, "Quelques observations."

Trasselli, C.: *Mediterraneo e Sicilia all'inizio dell'epoca moderna*, Cosenza 1977.—Trasselli, *Mediterraneo e Sicilia.*

Venezia, centro di mediazione tra Oriente e Occidente, Atti del II Convegno int. di storia della civiltà veneziana, 1973, Florence 1977.—*Venezia, centro di mediazione.*

Venezia e il Levante fino al secolo XV, Atti del I Convegno int. di storia della civiltà veneziana, 1968, Florence 1973.—*Venezia e il Levante fino al sec. XV.*

de Vertot, R. A.: *Histoire des chevaliers Hospitaliers de S. Jean de Jérusalem*, 4e éd., II, Paris 1755.—Vertot.

Wansbrough, J.: "A Mamluk commercial treaty concluded with the Republic of Florence 894/1489," in *Documents from Islamic chanceries*, ed. S. M. Stern, Oxford 1965, p. 39-79.—Wansbrough, "A commercial treaty."

"Venice and Florence in the Mamluk commercial privileges," *BSOAS* 28 (1965), p. 483-523.—Wansbrough, "Venice and Florence."

Weil, G.: *Geschichte der Chalifen*, I-V, Mannheim-Stuttgart 1846-1862.—Weil.

D. Periodicals and Collective Works

AOL	*Archives de l'Orient Latin*
Arch. Stor. Prov. Nap.	*Archivio Storico per le provincie napoletane*
ASI	*Archivio Storico Italiano*
ASLSP	*Atti della Società Ligure di Storia Patria*
BAH	*Boletin de la Academia de historia* (Madrid)
BEO	*Bulletin d'études orientales*
BSOAS	*Bulletin of the School of Oriental and African Studies* (London)
CEHE	*Cambridge Economic History of Europe*
Ec. Hist. Rev.	*Economic History Review*
EEMCA	*Estudios de edad media de la Corona de Aragon*
EHM	*Estudios de historia moderna*
HZ	*Historische Zeitschrift*
JA	*Journal Asiatique*

JAOS	*Journal of the American Oriental Society*
JEEH	*Journal of European Economic History*
JEH	*Journal of Economic History*
JESHO	*Journal of the Economic and Social History of the Orient*
JRAS	*Journal of the Royal Asiatic Society* (London)
ROC	*Revue de l'Orient chrétien*
ROL	*Revue de l'Orient Latin*
RSI	*Rivista Storica Italiana*
VSWG	*Vierteljahrschrift für Sozial- und Wirtschaftsgeschichte*

Index

1. Names of Persons, Nations, etc.
2. Geographical Names
3. Subjects

The indexes also comprise some data quoted in the notes. On the other hand, the names of the ship patrons and the consuls listed in Appendix A and D are excluded.

1. Names of Persons, Nations, etc.

2. Geographical Names

3. Subjects

Library of Congress Cataloging in Publication Data

Ashtor, Eliyahu, 1914-
Levant trade in the later Middle Ages.

Includes bibliographical references and index.
1. Near East—Commerce—Europe—History. 2. Europe—Commerce—Near East—History. I. Title.
HF3756.A83 1983 382'.094'056 83-42545
ISBN 0-691-05386-3

www.ingramcontent.com/pod-product-compliance
Ingram Content Group UK Ltd.
Pitfield, Milton Keynes, MK11 3LW, UK
UKHW010438210225
455383UK00003B/64

9 780691 612928